Ford C-MAX
Owners Workshop Manual

M R Storey

Models covered

(4900 - 400)

C-MAX MPV models
Petrol: 1.6 litre (1596cc), 1.8 litre (1798cc) & 2.0 litre (1998cc)
Turbo-Diesel: 1.6 litre (1560cc), 1.8 litre (1753cc) & 2.0 litre (1997cc/1998cc)

Does NOT cover 1.8 litre 'flex fuel' models, or CVT or 'Powershift' transmissions
Does NOT cover new C-MAX range introduced October 2010

© Haynes Publishing 2011

ABCDE
FGHIJ
KLMNO
PQRST

A book in the **Haynes Owners Workshop Manual Series**

ISBN **978 1 84425 900 7**

British Library Cataloguing in Publication Data
A catalogue record for this book is available from the British Library.

Printed in the USA

Haynes Publishing
Sparkford, Yeovil, Somerset BA22 7JJ, England

Haynes North America, Inc
861 Lawrence Drive, Newbury Park, California 91320, USA

Haynes Publishing Nordiska AB
Box 1504, 751 45 UPPSALA, Sverige

Contents

LIVING WITH YOUR FORD C-MAX

| Introduction | Page | 0•4 |
| Safety first! | Page | 0•5 |

Roadside repairs

If your car won't start	Page	0•6
Jump starting	Page	0•7
Wheel changing	Page	0•8
Identifying leaks	Page	0•9
Towing	Page	0•9

Weekly checks

Introduction	Page	0•10
Underbonnet check points	Page	0•10
Engine oil level	Page	0•11
Coolant level	Page	0•11
Brake and clutch fluid level	Page	0•12
Power steering fluid level	Page	0•12
Tyre condition and pressure	Page	0•13
Washer fluid level	Page	0•14
Wiper blades	Page	0•14
Battery	Page	0•15
Bulbs and fuses	Page	0•16

Lubricants and fluids

| | Page | 0•16 |

Tyre pressures

| | Page | 0•16 |

MAINTENANCE

Routine maintenance and servicing

Petrol models	Page	1A•1
Servicing specifications	Page	1A•2
Maintenance schedule	Page	1A•3
Maintenance procedures	Page	1A•5
Diesel models	Page	1B•1
Servicing specifications	Page	1B•2
Maintenance schedule	Page	1B•3
Maintenance procedures	Page	1B•5

Contents

REPAIRS & OVERHAUL

Engine and associated systems
1.6 litre petrol engine in-car repair procedures   Page   **2A•1**
1.8 & 2.0 litre petrol engines in-car repair procedures   Page   **2B•1**
1.6 litre diesel engine in-car repair procedures   Page   **2C•1**
1.8 litre diesel engine in-car repair procedures   Page   **2D•1**
2.0 litre diesel engine in-car repair procedures   Page   **2E•1**
Engine removal and overhaul procedures   Page   **2F•1**
Cooling, heating and air conditioning systems   Page   **3•1**
Fuel and exhaust systems – petrol models   Page   **4A•1**
Fuel and exhaust systems – diesel models   Page   **4B•1**
Emission control systems – petrol models   Page   **4C•1**
Emission control systems – diesel models   Page   **4D•1**
Starting and charging systems   Page   **5A•1**
Ignition system – petrol engines   Page   **5B•1**
Pre/post-heating system – diesel engines   Page   **5C•1**

Transmission
Clutch   Page   **6•1**
Manual transmission   Page   **7A•1**
Automatic transmission   Page   **7B•1**
Driveshafts   Page   **8•1**

Brakes and suspension
Braking system   Page   **9•1**
Suspension and steering   Page   **10•1**

Body equipment
Bodywork and fittings   Page   **11•1**
Body electrical systems   Page   **12•1**

Wiring diagrams
  Page   **12•23**

REFERENCE
Dimensions and weights   Page   **REF•1**
Fuel economy   Page   **REF•2**
Conversion factors   Page   **REF•6**
Buying spare parts   Page   **REF•7**
Vehicle identification numbers   Page   **REF•7**
General repair procedures   Page   **REF•8**
Jacking and vehicle support   Page   **REF•9**
Tools and working facilities   Page   **REF•10**
MOT test checks   Page   **REF•12**
Fault finding   Page   **REF•16**

Index
  Page   **REF•24**

Based on the Mk 2 Ford Focus, the Focus C-MAX was first introduced 2003. A minor face lift in 2006 saw slight changes to the interior and an updated exterior that introduced elements of Ford's 'kinetic' design concept to the range. All models are 5-door and all feature removable, independent rear seats. At launch three trim levels were originally available – LX, Zetec and Ghia. These were later refined to Style, Zetec and Titanium.

Safety features include door side impact bars, airbags for the driver and front seat passenger, side airbags, head airbags, whiplash protection system (front seats), and an advanced seat belt system with pretensioners and load limiters. Vehicle security is enhanced, with an engine immobiliser, shielded locks, and security-coded audio equipment being fitted as standard, as well as double-locking doors on most models.

The 16-valve DOHC (double overhead camshaft) four-cylinder petrol engines are available in 1.6, 1.8 and 2.0 litre capacities, and are based on the familiar Ford range of engines. The engines are controlled by a sophisticated engine management system, which combines multipoint sequential fuel injection and distributorless ignition systems with evaporative emissions control, exhaust gas recirculation, variable intake geometry and a three-way regulated catalytic converter to ensure compliance with increasingly stringent emissions control standards, while providing the expected levels of performance and fuel economy. The 1.6 litre engine is also available

with variable valve timing for the intake and exhaust camshafts, further improving the engine's output, driveability and emissions.

Three sizes of diesel engine are available, with the 1.6 and 2.0 litre models being shared by Citroën and Peugeot – a result of joint projects between Ford and PSA (Citroën/Peugeot's parent company), whilst the 1.8 litre unit is of Ford's own design. All of the engines are four-cylinder turbo diesel units, and the 1.6 and 2.0 litre units are a 16-valve DOHC design. They incorporate the latest design of direct injection common rail fuel system, with a variable geometry turbocharger, intercooler, catalytic converter and exhaust particulate filter (certain markets only).

The transversely-mounted engines drive the front roadwheels through either a five- or six-speed manual transmission with a hydraulically-operated clutch, or through an electronically-controlled four-speed automatic transmission.

The fully-independent suspension is by MacPherson struts and transverse lower arms at the front, with multilink independent suspension at the rear; anti-roll bars are fitted at front and rear.

The vacuum servo-assisted brakes are disc at the front and either disc or drum at the rear. An electronically-controlled Anti-lock Braking System (ABS) is fitted on all models, with Dynamic Stability and Traction Control System (DSTC) also available. Some higher specification models also feature a motorised handbrake, often referred to as an 'electronic parking brake' (EPB).

Power-assisted steering is standard on all models. Air conditioning is available, and all models have an ergonomically-designed passenger cabin with high levels of safety and comfort for all passengers.

Provided that regular servicing is carried out in accordance with the manufacturer's recommendations, the C-MAX should prove a reliable and economical car. The engine compartment is well-designed, and most of the items needing frequent attention are easily accessible.

Your Ford C-MAX manual

The aim of this manual is to help you get the best value from your vehicle. It can do so in several ways. It can help you decide what work must be done (even should you choose to get it done by a garage). It will also provide information on routine maintenance and servicing, and give a logical course of action and diagnosis when random faults occur. However, it is hoped that you will use the manual by tackling the work yourself. On simpler jobs it may even be quicker than booking the car into a garage and going there twice, to leave and collect it. Perhaps most important, a lot of money can be saved by avoiding the costs a garage must charge to cover its labour and overheads.

The manual has drawings and descriptions to show the function of the various components so that their layout can be understood. Tasks are described and photographed in a clear step-by-step sequence. The illustrations are numbered by the Section number and paragraph number to which they relate – if there is more than one illustration per paragraph, the sequence is denoted alphabetically.

References to the 'left' or 'right' of the vehicle are in the sense of a person in the driver's seat, facing forwards.

Acknowledgements

Thanks are due to Draper Tools Limited, who provided some of the workshop tools, and to all those people at Sparkford who helped in the production of this manual.

We take great pride in the accuracy of information given in this manual, but vehicle manufacturers make alterations and design changes during the production run of a particular vehicle of which they do not inform us. No liability can be accepted by the authors or publishers for loss, damage or injury caused by any errors in, or omissions from, the information given.

Working on your car can be dangerous. This page shows just some of the potential risks and hazards, with the aim of creating a safety-conscious attitude.

General hazards

Scalding

• Don't remove the radiator or expansion tank cap while the engine is hot.
• Engine oil, transmission fluid or power steering fluid may also be dangerously hot if the engine has recently been running.

Burning

• Beware of burns from the exhaust system and from any part of the engine. Brake discs and drums can also be extremely hot immediately after use.

Crushing

• When working under or near a raised vehicle, always supplement the jack with axle stands, or use drive-on ramps. *Never venture under a car which is only supported by a jack*.
• Take care if loosening or tightening high-torque nuts when the vehicle is on stands. Initial loosening and final tightening should be done with the wheels on the ground.

Fire

• Fuel is highly flammable; fuel vapour is explosive.
• Don't let fuel spill onto a hot engine.
• Do not smoke or allow naked lights (including pilot lights) anywhere near a vehicle being worked on. Also beware of creating sparks (electrically or by use of tools).
• Fuel vapour is heavier than air, so don't work on the fuel system with the vehicle over an inspection pit.
• Another cause of fire is an electrical overload or short-circuit. Take care when repairing or modifying the vehicle wiring.
• Keep a fire extinguisher handy, of a type suitable for use on fuel and electrical fires.

Electric shock

• Ignition HT and Xenon headlight voltages can be dangerous, especially to people with heart problems or a pacemaker. Don't work on or near these systems with the engine running or the ignition switched on.

• Mains voltage is also dangerous. Make sure that any mains-operated equipment is correctly earthed. Mains power points should be protected by a residual current device (RCD) circuit breaker.

Fume or gas intoxication

• Exhaust fumes are poisonous; they can contain carbon monoxide, which is rapidly fatal if inhaled. Never run the engine in a confined space such as a garage with the doors shut.

• Fuel vapour is also poisonous, as are the vapours from some cleaning solvents and paint thinners.

Poisonous or irritant substances

• Avoid skin contact with battery acid and with any fuel, fluid or lubricant, especially antifreeze, brake hydraulic fluid and Diesel fuel. Don't syphon them by mouth. If such a substance is swallowed or gets into the eyes, seek medical advice.
• Prolonged contact with used engine oil can cause skin cancer. Wear gloves or use a barrier cream if necessary. Change out of oil-soaked clothes and do not keep oily rags in your pocket.
• Air conditioning refrigerant forms a poisonous gas if exposed to a naked flame (including a cigarette). It can also cause skin burns on contact.

Asbestos

• Asbestos dust can cause cancer if inhaled or swallowed. Asbestos may be found in gaskets and in brake and clutch linings. When dealing with such components it is safest to assume that they contain asbestos.

Special hazards

Hydrofluoric acid

• This extremely corrosive acid is formed when certain types of synthetic rubber, found in some O-rings, oil seals, fuel hoses etc, are exposed to temperatures above 4000C. The rubber changes into a charred or sticky substance containing the acid. *Once formed, the acid remains dangerous for years. If it gets onto the skin, it may be necessary to amputate the limb concerned*.
• When dealing with a vehicle which has suffered a fire, or with components salvaged from such a vehicle, wear protective gloves and discard them after use.

The battery

• Batteries contain sulphuric acid, which attacks clothing, eyes and skin. Take care when topping-up or carrying the battery.
• The hydrogen gas given off by the battery is highly explosive. Never cause a spark or allow a naked light nearby. Be careful when connecting and disconnecting battery chargers or jump leads.

Air bags

• Air bags can cause injury if they go off accidentally. Take care when removing the steering wheel and trim panels. Special storage instructions may apply.

Diesel injection equipment

• Diesel injection pumps supply fuel at very high pressure. Take care when working on the fuel injectors and fuel pipes.

⚠️ *Warning: Never expose the hands, face or any other part of the body to injector spray; the fuel can penetrate the skin with potentially fatal results.*

Remember...

DO

• Do use eye protection when using power tools, and when working under the vehicle.

• Do wear gloves or use barrier cream to protect your hands when necessary.

• Do get someone to check periodically that all is well when working alone on the vehicle.

• Do keep loose clothing and long hair well out of the way of moving mechanical parts.

• Do remove rings, wristwatch etc, before working on the vehicle – especially the electrical system.

• Do ensure that any lifting or jacking equipment has a safe working load rating adequate for the job.

DON'T

• Don't attempt to lift a heavy component which may be beyond your capability – get assistance.

• Don't rush to finish a job, or take unverified short cuts.

• Don't use ill-fitting tools which may slip and cause injury.

• Don't leave tools or parts lying around where someone can trip over them. Mop up oil and fuel spills at once.

• Don't allow children or pets to play in or near a vehicle being worked on.

The following pages are intended to help in dealing with common roadside emergencies and breakdowns. You will find more detailed fault finding information at the back of the manual, and repair information in the main chapters.

If your car won't start and the starter motor doesn't turn

☐ If it's a model with automatic transmission, make sure the selector is in P or N.
☐ Open the bonnet and make sure that the battery terminals are clean and tight (unclip the battery cover for access).
☐ Switch on the headlights and try to start the engine. If the headlights go very dim when you're trying to start, the battery is probably flat. Get out of trouble by jump starting (see next page) using a friend's car.

If your car won't start even though the starter motor turns as normal

☐ Is there fuel in the tank?
☐ Has the engine immobiliser been deactivated? This should happen automatically, on inserting the ignition key. However, if a replacement key has been obtained (other than from a Ford dealer), it may not contain the transponder chip necessary to deactivate the system. Even 'proper' replacement keys have to be coded to work properly – a procedure for this is outlined in the vehicle handbook.
☐ Is there moisture on electrical components under the bonnet? Switch off the ignition, then wipe off any obvious dampness with a dry cloth. Remove the plastic cover on the top of the engine (where applicable). Spray a water-repellent aerosol product (WD-40 or equivalent) on ignition and fuel system electrical connectors like those shown in the photos. Pay special attention to the ignition coil wiring connector and HT leads (where applicable).

A Remove the cover and check the condition and security of the battery connections.

B Remove the engine cover and check that the wiring connectors are securely connected to the four ignition coils (petrol models only).

C Check the plugs and wiring of all the critical engine connectors. Work around the engine bay methodically.

Check that electrical connections are secure (with the ignition switched off) and spray them with a water-dispersant spray like WD-40 if you suspect a problem due to damp.

D With the ignition off, check the fuses in the fusebox behind the passenger side glovebox and the main fusebox adjacent to the battery.

HAYNES HiNT
Jump starting will get you out of trouble, but you must correct whatever made the battery go flat in the first place. There are three possibilities:

1 *The battery has been drained by repeated attempts to start, or by leaving the lights on.*

2 *The charging system is not working properly (alternator drivebelt slack or broken, alternator wiring fault or alternator itself faulty).*

3 *The battery itself is at fault (electrolyte low, or battery worn out).*

When jump-starting a car using a booster battery, observe the following precautions:

✔ Before connecting the booster battery, make sure that the ignition is switched off.

Caution: Remove the key in case the central locking engages when the jump leads are connected

✔ Ensure that all electrical equipment (lights, heater, wipers, etc) is switched off.

✔ Take note of any special precautions printed on the battery case.

✔ Make sure that the booster battery is the same voltage as the discharged one in the vehicle.

✔ If the battery is being jump-started from the battery in another vehicle, the two vehicles MUST NOT TOUCH each other.

✔ Make sure that the transmission is in neutral (or PARK, in the case of automatic transmission).

1 Connect one end of the red jump lead to the positive (+) terminal of the flat battery

2 Connect the other end of the red lead to the positive (+) terminal of the booster battery.

3 Connect one end of the black jump lead to the negative (-) terminal of the booster battery

4 Connect the other end of the black jump lead to a bolt or bracket on the engine block, well away from the battery, on the vehicle to be started.

5 Make sure that the jump leads will not come into contact with the fan, drive-belts or other moving parts of the engine.

6 Start the engine using the booster battery and run it at idle speed. Switch on the lights, rear window demister and heater blower motor, then disconnect the jump leads in the reverse order of connection. Turn off the lights etc.

Wheel changing

⚠️ *Warning: Do not change a wheel in a situation where you risk being hit by other traffic. On busy roads, try to stop in a lay-by or a gateway. Be wary of passing traffic while changing the wheel – it is easy to become distracted by the job in hand.*

Preparation

☐ When a puncture occurs, stop as soon as it is safe to do so.
☐ Park on firm level ground, if possible, and well out of the way of other traffic.
☐ Use hazard warning lights if necessary.

☐ If you have one, use a warning triangle to alert other drivers of your presence.
☐ Apply the handbrake and engage first or reverse gear (or P on models with automatic transmission).

☐ Chock the wheel diagonally opposite the one being removed – a couple of large stones will do for this.
☐ If the ground is soft, use a flat piece of wood to spread the load under the jack.

Changing the wheel

1 The spare wheel and tools are stored under the floor in the luggage compartment. Lift up the cover panel. Unscrew the retaining bolt, and lift the spare wheel out. The jack and wheel brace are located beneath the spare wheel. The screw-in towing eye is located alongside the spare wheel.

2 Where applicable, using the flat end of the wheel brace, prise off the wheel trim or centre cover for access to the wheel nuts. Models with alloy wheels may have special locking nuts – these are removed with a special tool, which should be provided with the wheel brace (or it may be in the glovebox).

3 Slacken each wheel nut by a half turn, using the wheel brace. If the nuts are too tight, DON'T stand on the wheel brace to undo them – call for assistance from one of the motoring organisations.

4 Two jacking points are provided on each side – use the one nearest the punctured wheel. Locate the jack head in the groove at the jacking point in the lower sill flange (don't jack the vehicle at any other point of the sill, nor on a plastic panel).

5 Turn the jack handle clockwise until the wheel is raised clear of the ground. Unscrew the wheel nuts, noting which way round they fit (tapered side inwards), and remove the wheel.

6 Fit the spare wheel, and screw on the nuts. Lightly tighten the nuts with the wheel brace, then lower the vehicle to the ground. Securely tighten the wheel nuts, then refit the wheel trim or centre cover, as applicable.

Using tyre sealant

1 Later models maybe supplied with a compressor and sealant instead of a spare wheel. Follow the graphic instructions printed on the lid.

2 Install the sealant bottle, following the instructions and inflate the tyre. It should be noted that the sealant is only suitable for repairs in the tyre tread up to a diameter of 6 mm. It is not suitable for repairs to the tyre sidewall.

Finally . . .

☐ Remove the wheel chocks. Stow the punctured wheel and tools, and secure them in position.
☐ Check the tyre pressure on the tyre just fitted. If it is low, drive slowly to the next garage and inflate the tyre to the correct pressure. In the case of the narrow 'space-saver' spare wheel this pressure is much higher than for a normal tyre.
☐ The wheel nuts should be slackened and retightened to the correct torque at the earliest possible opportunity.

Note: *Some models are supplied with a 'space-saver' spare wheel. This is intended only for temporary use, and must be replaced with a standard wheel as soon as possible. Drive with particular care with this wheel fitted, especially through corners and when braking; do not exceed 50 mph.*

Identifying leaks

Puddles on the garage floor or drive, or obvious wetness under the bonnet or underneath the car, suggest a leak that needs investigating. It can sometimes be difficult to decide where the leak is coming from, especially if an engine undershield is fitted. Leaking oil or fluid can also be blown rearwards by the passage of air under the car, giving a false impression of where the problem lies.

 Warning: Most automotive oils and fluids are poisonous. Wash them off skin, and change out of contaminated clothing, without delay.

 The smell of a fluid leaking from the car may provide a clue to what's leaking. Some fluids are distinctively coloured. It may help to remove the engine undershield, clean the car carefully and to park it over some clean paper overnight as an aid to locating the source of the leak.
Remember that some leaks may only occur while the engine is running.

Sump oil

Engine oil may leak from the drain plug...

Oil from filter

...or from the base of the oil filter.

Gearbox oil

Gearbox oil can leak from the seals at the inboard ends of the driveshafts.

Antifreeze

Leaking antifreeze often leaves a crystalline deposit like this.

Brake fluid

A leak occurring at a wheel is almost certainly brake fluid.

Power steering fluid

Power steering fluid may leak from the pipe connectors on the steering rack.

Towing

When all else fails, you may find yourself having to get a tow home – or of course you may be helping somebody else. Long-distance recovery should only be done by a garage or breakdown service. For shorter distances, DIY towing using another car is easy enough, but observe the following points:

☐ Use a proper tow-rope – they are not expensive. The vehicle being towed must display an ON TOW sign in its rear window.

☐ Always turn the ignition key to the 'On' position when the vehicle is being towed, so that the steering lock is released, and the direction indicator and brake lights work.

☐ The towing eye is of the screw-in type, and is found in the spare wheel well. The towing eye screws into a threaded hole, accessible after prising out a cover on the right-hand side of the front or rear bumper. **Note:** *The towing eye has a left-hand thread – rotate it anti-clockwise to install it.*

☐ Before being towed, release the handbrake and make sure the transmission is in neutral. On models with automatic transmission, special precautions apply – do not exceed 30 mph or travel further than 30 miles, and the wheels must always roll forwards.

☐ Note that greater-than-usual pedal pressure will be required to operate the brakes, since the vacuum servo unit is only operational with the engine running.

☐ The driver of the car being towed must keep the tow-rope taut at all times to avoid snatching.

☐ Make sure that both drivers know the route before setting off.

☐ Only drive at moderate speeds and keep the distance towed to a minimum. Drive smoothly and allow plenty of time for slowing down at junctions.

Introduction

There are some very simple checks which need only take a few minutes to carry out, but which could save you a lot of inconvenience and expense.

These *Weekly checks* require no great skill or special tools, and the small amount of time they take to perform could prove to be very well spent, for example:

☐ Keeping an eye on tyre condition and pressures, will not only help to stop them wearing out prematurely, but could also save your life.

☐ Many breakdowns are caused by electrical problems. Battery-related faults are particularly common, and a quick check on a regular basis will often prevent the majority of these.

☐ If your car develops a brake fluid leak, the first time you might know about it is when your brakes don't work properly. Checking the level regularly will give advance warning of this kind of problem.

☐ If the oil or coolant levels run low, the cost of repairing any engine damage will be far greater than fixing the leak, for example.

Underbonnet check points

◀ 1.8 litre petrol engine

A *Engine oil level dipstick*

B *Engine oil filler cap*

C *Coolant expansion tank*

D *Brake and clutch fluid reservoir (hidden below cowl)*

E *Screen washer fluid reservoir*

F *Battery*

◀ 1.8 litre diesel engine

A *Engine oil level dipstick*

B *Engine oil filler cap*

C *Coolant expansion tank*

D *Brake and clutch fluid reservoir (hidden below cowl)*

E *Screen washer fluid reservoir*

F *Battery*

Engine oil level

Before you start
✔ Make sure that the car is on level ground.
✔ Check the oil level before the car is driven, or at least 5 minutes after the engine has been switched off.

 HAYNES HiNT *If the oil is checked immediately after driving the vehicle, some of the oil will remain in the upper engine components, resulting in an inaccurate reading on the dipstick.*

The correct oil
Modern engines place great demands on their oil. It is very important that the correct oil for your car is used (see *Lubricants and fluids*).

Car care
● If you have to add oil frequently, you should check whether you have any oil leaks. Place some clean paper under the car overnight, and check for stains in the morning. If there are no leaks, then the engine may be burning oil.
● Always maintain the level between the upper and lower dipstick marks (see photo 2). If the level is too low, severe engine damage may occur. Oil seal failure may result if the engine is overfilled by adding too much oil.

1 The dipstick is located at the front of the engine (see *Underbonnet check points* for exact location). Withdraw the dipstick. Using a clean rag or paper towel, remove all oil from the dipstick.

2 Insert the clean dipstick into the tube as far as it will go, then withdraw it again. Note the oil level on the end of the dipstick, which should be between the MAX and MIN marks. If the oil level is only just above, or below, the MIN mark, topping-up is required.

3 Oil is added through the filler cap. Unscrew the filler cap and top up the level; a funnel may be useful in reducing spillage.

4 Add the oil slowly, checking the level on the dipstick often, and allowing time for the oil to run to the sump. Add oil until the level is just up to the MAX mark on the dipstick – don't overfill (see *Car care*)

Coolant level

⚠ *Warning: Do not attempt to remove the expansion tank pressure cap when the engine is hot, as there is a very great risk of scalding. Do not leave open containers of coolant about, as it is poisonous.*

Car care
● With a sealed-type cooling system, adding coolant should not be necessary on a regular basis. If frequent topping-up is required, it is likely there is a leak. Check the radiator, all hoses and joint faces for signs of staining or wetness, and rectify as necessary.

● It is important that antifreeze is used in the cooling system all year round, not just during the winter months. Don't top-up with water alone, as the antifreeze will become diluted.

1 The coolant level varies with the temperature of the engine, and is visible through the expansion tank. When the engine is cold, the coolant level should be between the MAX and MIN marks on the front of the reservoir. When the engine is hot, the level may rise slightly above the MAX mark.

2 If topping-up is necessary, wait until the engine is **cold**. Slowly unscrew the expansion tank cap, to release any pressure present in the cooling system, and remove it.

3 Add a mixture of water and antifreeze to the expansion tank until the coolant level is halfway between the level marks. Use only the specified antifreeze – if using Ford antifreeze, make sure it is the same type and colour as that already in the system (see *Lubricants and fluids*). Refit the cap and tighten it securely.

Brake and clutch fluid level

Note: *All manual transmission models have a hydraulically-operated clutch, which uses the same fluid as the braking system.*

Warning:
- **Brake fluid can harm your eyes and damage painted surfaces, so use extreme caution when handling and pouring it.**
- **Do not use fluid that has been standing open for some time, as it absorbs moisture from the air, which can cause a dangerous loss of braking effectiveness.**

 HAYNES HINT
- *Make sure that your car is on level ground.*
- *The fluid level in the reservoir will drop slightly as the brake pads wear down, but the fluid level must never be allowed to drop below the MIN mark.*

Safety first!

● If the reservoir requires repeated topping-up this is an indication of a fluid leak somewhere in the system, which should be investigated immediately.

● If a leak is suspected, the car should not be driven until the braking system has been checked. Never take any risks where brakes are concerned

1 The brake fluid reservoir is located on the right-hand side of the engine compartment.

2 The MAX and MIN marks are indicated on the front of the reservoir. The fluid level must be kept between the marks at all times.

3 If topping-up is necessary, first wipe clean the area around the filler cap to prevent dirt entering the hydraulic system. Unscrew the reservoir cap and carefully lift it out of position, holding the wiring connector plug and taking care not to damage the level sender float. Inspect the reservoir; if the fluid is dirty, the hydraulic system should be drained and refilled (see Chapter 1).

4 Carefully add fluid, taking care not to spill it onto the surrounding components. Use only the specified fluid; mixing different types can cause damage to the system. Access is very difficult, so we used a clean syringe and a length of screen washer tube. After topping-up to the correct level, securely refit the cap and wipe off any spilt fluid.

Power steering fluid level

Note: *Only the 1.6 petrol models have an accessible power steering fluid reservoir. All other models are quipped with Electro-Hydraulic power steering (EHPS). According to Ford, there is no requirement to check the fluid level on EHPS systems. However, it may be prudent to check the level every few months or so.*

Before you start

✔ Park the vehicle on level ground.
✔ Set the steering wheel straight-ahead.
✔ The engine should be turned off.

Safety first!

● The need for frequent topping-up indicates a leak, which should be investigated immediately.

1 On 1.6 petrol engines the reservoir is mounted at the front right-hand side of the engine compartment. The fluid level can be viewed through the reservoir body, and should be between the MIN and MAX marks when the engine is cold. If the level is checked when the engine is running or hot, the level may rise slightly above the MAX mark.

2 On all other models, remove the headlight to gain access to the reservoir as described in Chapter 12.

3 If topping-up is necessary, use the specified type of fluid – do not overfill the reservoir. Undo the reservoir cap. Take care not to introduce dirt into the system when topping-up. When the level is correct, securely refit the cap.

Tyre condition and pressure

It is very important that tyres are in good condition, and at the correct pressure - having a tyre failure at any speed is highly dangerous. Tyre wear is influenced by driving style - harsh braking and acceleration, or fast cornering, will all produce more rapid tyre wear. As a general rule, the front tyres wear out faster than the rears. Interchanging the tyres from front to rear ("rotating" the tyres) may result in more even wear. However, if this is completely effective, you may have the expense of replacing all four tyres at once! Remove any nails or stones embedded in the tread before they penetrate the tyre to cause deflation. If removal of a nail does reveal that the tyre has been punctured, refit the nail so that its point of penetration is marked. Then immediately change the wheel, and have the tyre repaired by a tyre dealer.

Regularly check the tyres for damage in the form of cuts or bulges, especially in the sidewalls. Periodically remove the wheels, and clean any dirt or mud from the inside and outside surfaces. Examine the wheel rims for signs of rusting, corrosion or other damage. Light alloy wheels are easily damaged by "kerbing" whilst parking; steel wheels may also become dented or buckled. A new wheel is very often the only way to overcome severe damage.

New tyres should be balanced when they are fitted, but it may become necessary to re-balance them as they wear, or if the balance weights fitted to the wheel rim should fall off. Unbalanced tyres will wear more quickly, as will the steering and suspension components. Wheel imbalance is normally signified by vibration, particularly at a certain speed (typically around 50 mph). If this vibration is felt only through the steering, then it is likely that just the front wheels need balancing. If, however, the vibration is felt through the whole car, the rear wheels could be out of balance. Wheel balancing should be carried out by a tyre dealer or garage.

1 Tread Depth - visual check
The original tyres have tread wear safety bands (B), which will appear when the tread depth reaches approximately 1.6 mm. The band positions are indicated by a triangular mark on the tyre sidewall (A).

2 Tread Depth - manual check
Alternatively, tread wear can be monitored with a simple, inexpensive device known as a tread depth indicator gauge.

3 Tyre Pressure Check
Check the tyre pressures regularly with the tyres cold. Do not adjust the tyre pressures immediately after the vehicle has been used, or an inaccurate setting will result.

Tyre tread wear patterns

Shoulder Wear

Underinflation (wear on both sides)
Under-inflation will cause overheating of the tyre, because the tyre will flex too much, and the tread will not sit correctly on the road surface. This will cause a loss of grip and excessive wear, not to mention the danger of sudden tyre failure due to heat build-up.
Check and adjust pressures
Incorrect wheel camber (wear on one side)
Repair or renew suspension parts
Hard cornering
Reduce speed!

Centre Wear

Overinflation
Over-inflation will cause rapid wear of the centre part of the tyre tread, coupled with reduced grip, harsher ride, and the danger of shock damage occurring in the tyre casing.
Check and adjust pressures

If you sometimes have to inflate your car's tyres to the higher pressures specified for maximum load or sustained high speed, don't forget to reduce the pressures to normal afterwards.

Uneven Wear

Front tyres may wear unevenly as a result of wheel misalignment. Most tyre dealers and garages can check and adjust the wheel alignment (or "tracking") for a modest charge.
Incorrect camber or castor
Repair or renew suspension parts
Malfunctioning suspension
Repair or renew suspension parts
Unbalanced wheel
Balance tyres
Incorrect toe setting
Adjust front wheel alignment
Note: *The feathered edge of the tread which typifies toe wear is best checked by feel.*

Washer fluid level

● The windscreen washer reservoir also supplies the tailgate washer jet, where applicable. On models so equipped, the same reservoir also serves the headlight washers.

● Screen wash additives not only keep the windscreen clean during bad weather, they also prevent the washer system freezing in cold weather – which is when you are likely to need it most. Don't top-up using plain water, as the screen wash will become diluted, and will freeze in cold weather.

Caution: On no account use engine coolant antifreeze in the screen washer system – this may damage the paintwork.

1 The washer fluid reservoir filler neck is located above the coolant header tank on the right-hand side of the engine compartment. The washer level cannot easily be seen. Remove the filler cap, and look down the filler neck – if fluid is not visible, topping-up may be required.

2 When topping-up the reservoir, add a screen wash additive in the quantities recommended on the additive bottle.

Wiper blades

● Only fit good-quality wiper blades.

● When removing an old wiper blade, note how it is fitted. Fitting new blades can be a tricky exercise, and noting how the old blade came off can save time.

● While the wiper blade is removed, take care not to knock the wiper arm from its locked position, or it could strike the glass.

● Offer the new blade into position the same way round as the old one. Ensure that it clicks home securely, otherwise it may come off in use, damaging the glass.

Note: *Fitting details for wiper blades vary according to model, and according to whether genuine Ford wiper blades have been fitted. Use the procedures and illustrations shown as a guide for your car.*

HAYNES HiNT *If smearing is still a problem despite fitting new wiper blades, try cleaning the glass with neat screenwash additive or methylated spirit.*

1 Check the condition of the wiper blades; if they are cracked or show any signs of deterioration, or if the glass swept area is smeared, renew them. Wiper blades should be renewed annually, regardless of their apparent condition.

2 To remove a windscreen wiper blade, pull the arm fully away from the glass until it locks. Position the blade at 90° to the arm and lift it from place.

3 To remove the tailgate blade, lift the arm, position the blade at 90° to the arm, and pull the blade from the arm.

Battery

Caution: Before carrying out any work on the vehicle battery, read the precautions given in 'Safety first!' at the start of this manual.

✔ Make sure that the battery tray is in good condition, and that the clamp is tight. Any 'white' corrosion on the terminals or surrounding area can be removed with a solution of water and baking soda; thoroughly rinse all cleaned areas with water. Any metal parts damaged by corrosion should be covered with a zinc-based primer, then painted.

✔ Periodically check the charge condition of the battery. On the original-equipment battery, the state of charge is shown by an indicator 'eye' in the top of the battery, which should be green – if the indicator is clear, or red, the battery may need charging or even renewal (see Chapter 5A).

✔ If the battery is flat, and you need to jump start your vehicle, see *Roadside Repairs*.

Battery corrosion can be kept to a minimum by applying a layer of petroleum jelly to the clamps and terminals after they are reconnected.

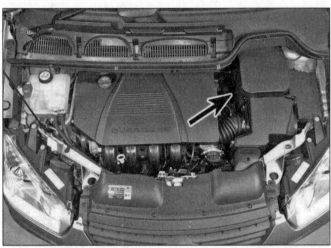

1 The battery is located in the left-hand rear corner of the engine compartment.

2 Unclip and remove the battery cover to gain access. The exterior of the battery should be inspected periodically for damage such as a cracked case or cover.

3 Check the tightness of battery clamps to ensure good electrical connections. You should not be able to move them. Also check each cable for cracks and frayed conductors.

4 If corrosion (white, fluffy deposits) is evident, remove the cables from the battery terminals, clean them with a small wire brush, then refit them. Automotive stores sell a tool for cleaning the battery post . . .

5 . . . as well as the battery cable clamps

Bulbs and fuses

✔ Check all external lights and the horn. Refer to the appropriate Sections of Chapter 12 for details if any of the circuits are found to be inoperative.

✔ Visually check all accessible wiring connectors, harnesses and retaining clips for security, and for signs of chafing or damage.

If you need to check your brake lights and indicators unaided, back up to a wall or garage door and operate the lights. The reflected light should show if they are working properly.

1 If a single indicator light, stop-light or headlight has failed, it is likely that a bulb has blown and will need to be renewed. Refer to Chapter 12 for details. If both stop-lights have failed, it is possible that the switch has failed (see Chapter 9).

2 If more than one indicator light or tail light has failed, it is likely that either a fuse has blown or that there is a fault in the circuit (see Chapter 12). The main fusebox is located below the glovebox on the passenger's side. To access the main fusebox, undo the 2 bolts and pull the trim panel downwards, then undo the two bolts and lower the fusebox from position. Pull the fusebox rearwards and lower it completely. The auxiliary fuse/relay box is located on the left-hand side of the engine compartment – unclip and remove the cover for access.

3 To renew a blown fuse, simply pull it out and fit a new fuse of the correct rating (see Chapter 12). Spare fuses, and a fuse removal tool, are provided on the inside of the auxiliary fusebox lid. If the fuse blows again, it is important that you find out why – a complete checking procedure is given in Chapter 12.

Lubricants and fluids

Engine	Multigrade engine oil, viscosity SAE 5W/30 to Ford specification WSS-M2C913-B
Cooling system	Motorcraft SuperPlus pink/red antifreeze to Ford specification WSS-M97B44-D
Manual transmission	SAE 75W/90 gear oil to Ford specification WSD-M2C200-C
Automatic transmission	Automatic transmission fluid to Ford specification WSS-M2C938-A
Brake and clutch hydraulic system	Hydraulic fluid to Ford specification ESD-M6C57-A, Super DOT 4, paraffin-free
Power steering	Ford or Motorcraft power steering fluid to Ford specification WSS-M2C204-A2

Tyre pressures (cold)

Details of the tyre pressures applicable to your vehicle are given on a sticker attached to the driver's side door pillar.

Chapter 1 Part A:
Routine maintenance & servicing – petrol models

Contents

	Section number		Section number
Air filter element renewal	18	Hinge and lock lubrication	12
Automatic transmission fluid level check	22	Lights and horn operation check	5
Auxiliary drivebelt check	4	Manual transmission oil level check	23
Auxiliary drivebelt renewal	21	Pollen filter renewal	15
Brake fluid renewal	24	Regular maintenance	2
Brake pads, shoes and discs check	7	Remote control battery renewal	25
Coolant strength check	17	Road test	14
Coolant renewal	26	Roadwheel nut tightness check	13
Driveshaft rubber gaiter and joint check	10	Seat belt check	16
Engine compartment wiring check	6	Spark plug renewal	19
Engine oil and filter renewal	3	Steering, suspension and roadwheel check	9
Exhaust system check	8	Timing belt renewal	20
General information	1	Underbody and hose/pipe check	11

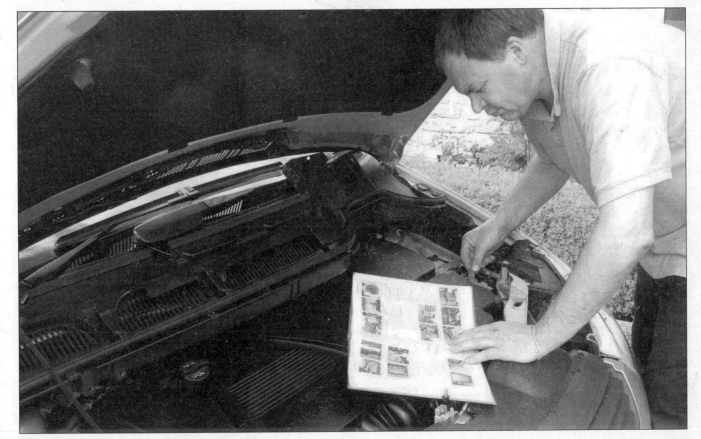

Degrees of difficulty

Easy, suitable for novice with little experience	**Fairly easy,** suitable for beginner with some experience	**Fairly difficult,** suitable for competent DIY mechanic	**Difficult,** suitable for experienced DIY mechanic	**Very difficult,** suitable for expert DIY or professional

Lubricants and fluids . . . .   Refer to end of *Weekly checks* on page 0•16

Capacities

Engine oil (including filter)

1.6 litre engines	4.1 litres
1.8 litre engines	4.3 litres
2.0 litre engines	4.3 litres

Cooling system (approximate)

1.6 litre engines:
  Non-Ti-VCT engines:
    With air conditioning . . . . 5.8 litres
    Without air conditioning . . . . 5.5 litres
  Ti-VCT engines . . . . 6.0 litres
1.8 litre engines . . . . 6.5 litres
2.0 litre engines . . . . 6.3 litres

Transmission

Manual transmission:
  1.6 and 1.8 litre models . . . . 2.3 litres
  2.0 litre models . . . . 1.9 litres
Automatic transmission (total capacity) . . . . 6.7 litres

Washer fluid reservoir

Without headlamp washers . . . . 3.3 litres
With headlamp washers . . . . 4.5 litres

Fuel tank

All models . . . . 55.0 litres

Cooling system

Antifreeze mixture:
  50% antifreeze . . . . Protection down to –37°C
  55% antifreeze . . . . Protection down to –45°C
Note: *Refer to antifreeze manufacturer for latest recommendations.*

Ignition system

Spark plugs type . . . . Refer to Ford dealer or parts specialist

Brakes

Friction material minimum thickness:
  Front or rear brake pads . . . . 1.5 mm
  Rear brake shoes . . . . 1.0 mm

Remote control battery

Type CR2032, 3V

Torque wrench settings

	Nm	lbf ft
Auxiliary drivebelt idler pulley mounting bolts/nut	25	18
Engine oil drain plug	28	21
Ignition coil retaining bolts	10	7
Manual transmission oil level/filler plug	35	26
Roadwheel nuts	130	96
Spark plugs:		
1.6 litre models	15	11
1.8 and 2.0 litre models	12	9

The maintenance intervals in this manual are provided with the assumption that you, not the dealer, will be carrying out the work. These are the minimum maintenance intervals recommended by us for vehicles driven daily. If you wish to keep your vehicle in peak condition at all times, you may wish to perform some of these procedures more often. We encourage frequent maintenance, because it enhances the efficiency, performance and resale value of your vehicle.

If the vehicle is driven in dusty areas, used to tow a trailer, or driven frequently at slow speeds (idling in traffic) or on short journeys, more frequent maintenance intervals are recommended.

When the vehicle is new, it should be serviced by a dealer service department (or other workshop recognised by the vehicle manufacturer as providing the same standard of service) in order to preserve the warranty. The vehicle manufacturer may reject warranty claims if you are unable to prove that servicing has been carried out as and when specified, using only original equipment parts or parts certified to be of equivalent quality.

Every 250 miles or weekly
☐ Refer to Weekly checks

Every 6000 miles or 6 months, whichever comes first
☐ Renew the engine oil and filter (Section 3)
Note: *Ford recommend that the engine oil and filter are changed every 12 500 miles or 12 months. However, oil and filter changes are good for the engine and we recommend that the oil and filter are renewed more frequently, especially if the vehicle is used on a lot of short journeys.*

Every 12 500 miles or 12 months, whichever comes first
In addition to the items listed above, carry out the following:
☐ Check the condition of the auxiliary drivebelt (Section 4)
☐ Check the operation of the lights and the horn (Section 5)
☐ Check the condition of the engine compartment wiring (Section 6)
☐ Check the condition of the brake pads, shoes and discs (Section 7)
☐ Check the exhaust system (Section 8)
☐ Check the steering and suspension components for condition and security (Section 9)
☐ Check the condition of the driveshaft joints and gaiters (Section 10)
☐ Check the underbody and all hoses/pipes (Section 11)
☐ Lubricate all hinges and locks (Section 12)
☐ Roadwheel nuts tightness check (Section 13)
☐ Carry out a road test (Section 14)
☐ Renew the pollen filter (Section 15)
Note: *If the vehicle is used in dusty conditions, the pollen filter should be renewed more frequently.*
☐ Check the condition of the seat belts (Section 16)
☐ Check the antifreeze/inhibitor strength (Section 17)

Every 37 500 miles or 3 years, whichever comes first
In addition to the items listed above, carry out the following:
☐ Renew the air filter (Section 18)
Note: *If the vehicle is used in dusty conditions, the air filter should be renewed more frequently.*
☐ Renew the spark plugs (Section 19)

Every 50 000 miles or 4 years, whichever comes first
☐ Renew the timing belt and tensioner – and 1.6 litre engines only (Section 20)
Note: *The Ford interval for belt renewal is 100 000 miles or 8 years. It is strongly recommended, however, that the interval is reduced, particularly on vehicles which are subjected to intensive use, ie, mainly short journeys or a lot of stop-start driving. The actual belt renewal interval is therefore very much up to the individual owner, but bear in mind that severe engine damage will result if the belt breaks.*

Every 100 000 miles or 8 years, whichever comes first
☐ Renew the auxiliary drivebelt (Section 21)

Every 2 years, regardless of mileage
☐ Check the automatic transmission fluid level (Section 22)
☐ Check the manual transmission oil level (Section 23)
☐ Renew the brake fluid (Section 24)
☐ Renew the remote control battery (Section 25)
☐ Renew the coolant (Section 26)
Note: *If Ford pink/red antifreeze is used, the coolant can then be left indefinitely, providing the strength of the mixture is checked every year. If any antifreeze other than Ford's is to be used, the coolant must be renewed at regular intervals to provide an equivalent degree of protection; the conventional recommendation is to renew the coolant every two years.*

Underbonnet view of a 1.8 litre model

1   Engine oil level dipstick
2   Oil filler cap
3   Coolant expansion tank cap
4   Power steering fluid reservoir (below headlight)
5   Air filter element cover
6   Battery cover
7   Brake/clutch fluid reservoir (hidden below windscreen cowl)
8   Washer fluid reservoir cap
9   Fuse/relay box

Front underbody view

1   Oil filter cartridge
2   Engine oil drain plug
3   Suspension control arm
4   Track rod end
5   Right-hand driveshaft
6   Catalytic converter
7   Underfloor brace
8   Brake caliper

Rear underbody view

1 Anti-roll bar
2 Carbon canister
3 Fuel tank
4 Silencer
5 Shock absorber
6 Lateral link
7 Lower control arm
8 Tie rod

Maintenance procedures

1 General information

1 This Chapter is designed to help the home mechanic maintain his/her vehicle for safety, economy, long life and peak performance.
2 The Chapter contains a master maintenance schedule, followed by Sections dealing specifically with each task in the schedule. Visual checks, adjustments, component renewal and other helpful items are included. Refer to the accompanying illustrations of the engine compartment and the underside of the vehicle for the locations of the various components.
3 Servicing your vehicle in accordance with the mileage/time maintenance schedule and the following Sections will provide a planned maintenance programme, which should result in a long and reliable service life. This is a comprehensive plan, so maintaining some items but not others at the specified service intervals will not produce the same results.
4 As you service your vehicle, you will discover that many of the procedures can – and should – be grouped together, because of the particular procedure being performed, or because of the proximity of two otherwise-unrelated components to one another. For example, if the vehicle is raised for any reason, the exhaust can be inspected at the same time as the suspension and steering components.
5 The first step in this maintenance

programme is to prepare yourself before the actual work begins. Read through all the Sections relevant to the work to be carried out, then make a list and gather all the parts and tools required. If a problem is encountered, seek advice from a parts specialist, or a dealer service department.

2 Regular maintenance

1 If, from the time the vehicle is new, the routine maintenance schedule is followed closely, and frequent checks are made of fluid levels and high-wear items, as suggested throughout this manual, the engine will be kept in relatively good running condition, and the need for additional work will be minimised.
2 It is possible that there will be times when the engine is running poorly due to the lack of regular maintenance. This is even more likely if a used vehicle, which has not received regular and frequent maintenance checks, is purchased. In such cases, additional work may need to be carried out, outside of the regular maintenance intervals.
3 If engine wear is suspected, a compression test (refer to Chapter 2) will provide valuable information regarding the overall performance of the main internal components. Such a test can be used as a basis to decide on the extent of the work to be carried out. If, for example,

a compression test indicates serious internal engine wear, conventional maintenance as described in this Chapter will not greatly improve the performance of the engine, and may prove a waste of time and money, unless extensive overhaul work is carried out first.
4 The following series of operations are those most often required to improve the performance of a generally poor-running engine:

Primary operations

a) Clean, inspect and test the battery (refer to 'Weekly checks').
b) Check all the engine-related fluids (refer to 'Weekly checks').
c) Check the condition and tension of the auxiliary drivebelt (Section 4).
d) Renew the spark plugs (Section 19).
e) Check the condition of the air filter, and renew if necessary (Section 18).
f) Check the condition of all hoses, and check for fluid leaks (Section 11).
5 If the above operations do not prove fully effective, carry out the following secondary operations:

Secondary operations

All items listed under Primary operations, plus the following:
a) Check the charging system (refer to Chapter 5).
b) Check the ignition system (refer to Chapter 5).
c) Check the fuel system (refer to Chapter 4).

3.4 Undo the fasteners (arrowed) and remove the engine undershield

3.6a Engine oil sump drain plug (arrowed) – 1.8 litre engine

Every 6000 miles or 6 months

3 Engine oil and filter renewal

1 Frequent oil and filter changes are the most important preventative maintenance procedures which can be undertaken by the DIY owner. As engine oil ages, it becomes diluted and contaminated, which leads to premature engine wear.

2 Before starting this procedure, gather together all the necessary tools and materials. Also make sure that you have plenty of clean rags and newspapers handy, to mop-up any spills. Ideally, the engine oil should be warm, as it will drain more easily, and more built-up sludge will be removed with it.

3 Take care not to touch the exhaust (especially the catalytic converter) or any other hot parts of the engine when working under the vehicle. To avoid any possibility of scalding, and to protect yourself from possible skin irritants and other harmful contaminants in used engine oils, it is advisable to wear gloves when carrying out this work.

4 Firmly apply the handbrake, then jack up the front of the vehicle and support it on axle stands (see *Jacking and vehicle support*). Where fitted, release the fasteners and remove the engine undershield **(see illustration)**.

5 Remove the oil filler cap.

6 Using a spanner, or preferably a socket and bar, slacken the sump drain plug about half a turn **(see illustrations)**. Position the draining container under the drain plug, then remove the plug completely.

7 Allow some time for the oil to drain, noting that it may be necessary to reposition the container as the oil flow slows to a trickle.

8 After all the oil has drained, wipe the drain plug with a clean rag. Examine the condition of the drain plug sealing ring, and renew it if it shows signs of flattening or other damage which may prevent an oil-tight seal (it is generally considered good practice to fit a new seal every time. Note that on some models the seal is integral with the drain plug **(see illustration)**. Clean the area around the drain plug opening, and refit the plug complete with the seal and tighten it to the specified torque.

9 Move the container into position under the oil filter, which is located on the front of the cylinder block **(see illustrations)**.

10 Use an oil filter removal tool if necessary to slacken the filter initially, then unscrew it by hand the rest of the way **(see illustration)**. Empty the oil from the old filter into the container, then puncture the top of the filter, and allow the remaining oil to drain from the filter into the container.

11 Use a clean rag to remove all oil, dirt and sludge from the filter sealing area on the engine.

12 Apply a light coating of clean engine oil to the sealing ring on the new filter, then screw the filter into position on the engine **(see**

3.6b Loosen the drain plug a half turn

3.8 On some drain plugs, the seal is integral with the plug

3.9a Oil filter cartridge (arrowed) – 1.6 litre engines ...

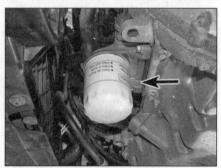

3.9b ... 1.8 and 2.0 litre engines

3.10 Using a strap wrench to slacken the filter cartridge

3.12a Apply a light coating of clean engine oil to the sealing ring . . .

3.12b . . . and screw the cartridge into place by hand

illustrations). Tighten the filter firmly by hand only – **do not** use any tools.

13 Remove the old oil and all tools from under the car, refit the engine undershield (where applicable), then lower the car to the ground.

14 Fill the engine, using the correct grade and type of oil (refer to *Weekly checks* for details of topping-up). An oil can spout or funnel may help to reduce spillage. Pour in half the specified quantity of oil first, then wait a few minutes for the oil to run to the sump.

15 Continue adding oil a small quantity at a time until the level is up to the MIN mark on the dipstick. Adding around 0.5 litre of oil will now bring the level up to the MAX on the dipstick – do not worry if a little too much goes in, as some of the excess will be taken up in filling the oil filter. Refit the dipstick and the filler cap.

16 Start the engine and run it for a few minutes; check for leaks around the oil filter and the sump drain plug. Note that there may be a few seconds delay before the oil pressure warning light goes out when the engine is started, as the oil circulates through the engine oil galleries and the new oil filter before the pressure builds-up.

17 Switch off the engine, and wait a few minutes for the oil to settle in the sump once more. With the new oil circulated and the filter completely full, recheck the level on the dipstick, and add more oil as necessary.

18 Dispose of the used engine oil and the old oil filter safely, with reference to *General repair procedures* in the *Reference* section of this manual. Many local recycling points have containers for waste oil, with oil filter disposal receptacles alongside.

Every 12 500 miles or 12 months

4 Auxiliary drivebelt check

1 Two auxiliary drivebelts maybe fitted – one from the crankshaft pulley to the alternator, power steering pump and coolant pump, and one from the crankshaft pulley to the air conditioning compressor (where applicable). On 1.8 and 2.0 litre engines, an automatic adjuster is fitted to the main auxiliary drivebelt, so checking the drivebelt tension is unnecessary. On 1.6 litre engines, no provision is made to adjust the main auxiliary drivebelt tension. On all models, no provision is made to adjust the air conditioning drivebelt tension.

2 Due to their function and material make-up, drivebelts are prone to failure after a long period of time, and should therefore be inspected regularly.

3 Since the drivebelt is located very close to the right-hand side of the engine compartment, it is possible to gain better access by raising the front of the vehicle and removing the right-hand wheel, then undoing the fasteners and removing the engine undershield (where fitted) **(see illustration 3.4)**.

4 With the engine stopped, inspect the full length of the drivebelt for cracks and separation of the belt plies. It will be necessary to turn the engine (using a spanner or socket and bar on the crankshaft pulley bolt) in order to move the belt from the pulleys so that the belt can be inspected thoroughly. Twist the belt between the pulleys so that both sides can be viewed. Also check for fraying, and glazing which gives the belt a shiny appearance. Check the pulleys for nicks, cracks, distortion and corrosion.

5 Note that it is not unusual for a ribbed belt to exhibit small cracks in the edges of the belt ribs, and unless these are extensive or very deep, belt renewal is not essential.

5 Lights and horn operation check

1 With the ignition switched on where necessary, check the operation of all exterior lights.

2 Check the brake lights with the help of an assistant, or by reversing up close to a reflective door. Make sure that all the rear lights are capable of operating independently, without affecting any of the other lights – for example, switch on as many rear lights as possible, then try the brake lights. If any unusual results are found, this is usually due to an earth fault or other poor connection at that rear light unit.

3 Again with the help of an assistant or using a reflective surface, check as far as possible that the headlights work on both main and dipped beam.

4 Renew any defective bulbs with reference to Chapter 12.

5 Check the operation of all interior lights, including the glovebox and luggage area illumination lights. Switch on the ignition, and check that all relevant warning lights come on as expected – the vehicle handbook should give details of these. Now start the engine, and check that the appropriate lights go out. When you are next driving at night, check that all the instrument panel and facia lighting works correctly. If any problems are found, refer to Chapter 12.

6 Finally, choose an appropriate time of day to test the operation of the horn.

6 Engine compartment wiring check

1 With the vehicle parked on level ground, apply the handbrake firmly and open the bonnet. Using an inspection light or a small electric torch, check all visible wiring within and beneath the engine compartment.

2 What you are looking for is wiring that is obviously damaged by chafing against sharp edges, or against moving suspension/ transmission components and/or the auxiliary drivebelt, by being trapped or crushed between carelessly-refitted components, or melted by being forced into contact with the hot engine castings, coolant pipes, etc. In almost all cases, damage of this sort is caused in the first instance by incorrect routing on reassembly after previous work has been carried out.

3 Depending on the extent of the problem,

6.5 Ensure all electrical connectors are securely clipped together

damaged wiring may be repaired by rejoining the break or splicing-in a new length of wire, using solder to ensure a good connection, and remaking the insulation with adhesive insulating tape or heat-shrink tubing, as appropriate. If the damage is extensive, given the implications for the vehicle's future reliability, the best long-term answer may well be to renew that entire section of the loom, however expensive this may appear.

4 When the damage has been repaired, ensure that the wiring loom is re-routed correctly, so that it is clear of other components, and not stretched or kinked, and is secured out of harm's way using the plastic clips, guides and ties provided.

5 Check all electrical connectors, ensuring that they are clean, securely fastened, and that each is locked by its plastic tabs or wire clip, as appropriate **(see illustration)**. If any connector shows external signs of corrosion (accumulations of white or green deposits, or streaks of 'rust'), or if any is thought to be dirty, it must be unplugged and cleaned using electrical contact cleaner. If the connector pins are severely corroded, the connector must be renewed; note that this may mean the renewal of that entire section of the loom – see your local Ford dealer for details.

6 If the cleaner completely removes the corrosion to leave the connector in a satisfactory condition, it would be wise to pack the connector with a suitable material which will exclude dirt and moisture, preventing the corrosion from occurring again; a Ford dealer may be able to recommend a suitable product.

7.4 Measure the thickness of the brake pad friction material (arrowed)

7 Check the condition of the battery connections – remake the connections or renew the leads if a fault is found (see Chapter 5). Use the same techniques to ensure that all earth points in the engine compartment provide good electrical contact through clean, metal-to-metal joints, and that all are securely fastened.

8 On diesel engine models, check the wiring to the glow plugs, referring to Chapter 5 if necessary.

7 Brake pads, shoes and discs check

1 The work described in this Section should be carried out at the specified intervals, or whenever a defect is suspected in the braking system. Any of the following symptoms could indicate a potential brake system defect:
   a) The vehicle pulls to one side when the brake pedal is depressed.
   b) The brakes make squealing, scraping or dragging noises when applied.
   c) Brake pedal travel is excessive, or pedal feel is poor.
   d) The brake fluid requires repeated topping-up. Note that, because the hydraulic clutch shares the same fluid as the braking system (see Chapter 6), this problem could be due to a leak in the clutch system.

Front disc brakes

2 Apply the handbrake, then loosen the front wheel nuts. Jack up the front of the vehicle, and support it on axle stands (see *Jacking and vehicle support*).

3 For better access to the brake calipers, remove the wheels.

4 Look through the inspection window in the caliper, and check that the thickness of the friction lining material on each of the pads is not less than the recommended minimum thickness given in the Specifications **(see illustration)**.

5 If it is difficult to determine the exact thickness of the pad linings, or if you are at all concerned about the condition of the pads, then remove them from the calipers for further inspection (refer to Chapter 9).

6 Check the other caliper in the same way.

7 If any one of the brake pads has worn down to, or below, the specified limit, *all four* pads at that end of the car must be renewed as a set. If the pads on one side are significantly more worn than the other, this may indicate that the caliper pistons have partially seized – refer to the brake pad renewal procedure in Chapter 9, and push the pistons back into the caliper to free them.

8 Measure the thickness of the discs with a micrometer, if available, to make sure that they still have service life remaining. Do not be fooled by the lip of rust which often forms on the outer edge of the disc, which may make the disc appear thicker than it really is – scrape off the loose rust if necessary, without scoring the disc friction (shiny) surface.

9 If any disc is thinner than the specified minimum thickness, renew it (refer to Chapter 9).

10 Check the general condition of the discs. Look for excessive scoring and discolouration caused by overheating. If these conditions exist, remove the relevant disc and have it resurfaced or renewed (refer to Chapter 9).

11 Make sure that the handbrake is firmly applied, then check that the transmission is in neutral. Spin the wheel, and check that the brake is not binding. Some drag is normal with a disc brake, but it should not require any great effort to turn the wheel – also, do not confuse brake drag with resistance from the transmission.

12 Before refitting the wheels, check all brake lines and hoses (refer to Chapter 9). In particular, check the flexible hoses in the vicinity of the calipers, where they are subjected to most movement **(see illustration)**. Bend them between the fingers (but do not actually bend them double, or the casing may be damaged) and check that this does not reveal previously-hidden cracks, cuts or splits.

13 On completion, refit the wheels and lower the car to the ground. Tighten the wheel nuts to the specified torque.

Rear disc brakes

14 Loosen the rear wheel nuts, then chock the front wheels. Jack up the rear of the car, and support it on axle stands. Release the handbrake and remove the rear wheels.

15 The procedure for checking the rear brakes is much the same as described in paragraphs 2 to 13 above. Check that the rear brakes are not binding, noting that transmission resistance is not a factor on the rear wheels. Abnormal effort may indicate that the handbrake needs adjusting – see Chapter 9.

Rear drum brakes

16 Loosen the rear wheel nuts, then chock the front wheels. Jack up the rear of the car, and support on axle stands (see *Jacking and vehicle support*). Release the handbrake and remove the rear wheels.

17 Spin the wheel to check that the brake is not binding. A small amount of resistance

7.12 Check the condition of the rubber brake hoses by bending them slightly and looking for cracks

from the brake is acceptable, but no great effort should be required to turn the wheel hub. Abnormal effort may indicate that the handbrake needs adjusting – see Chapter 9.

18 To check the brake shoe lining thickness without removing the brake drums, prise the rubber plugs from the backplates, and use an electric torch to inspect the linings of the leading brake shoes. Check that the thickness of the lining material on the brake shoes is not less than the recommendation given in the Specifications.

19 If it is difficult to determine the exact thickness of the brake shoe linings, or if you are at all concerned about the condition of the shoes, then remove the rear drums for a more comprehensive inspection (refer to Chapter 9).

20 With the drum removed, check the shoe return and hold-down springs for correct installation, and check the wheel cylinders for leakage of brake fluid. Apart from fluid being visible, a leaking wheel cylinder may be characterised by an excessive build-up of brake dust (stuck to the fluid which has leaked) at the cylinder seals.

21 Check the friction surface of the brake drums for scoring and discoloration. If excessive, the drum should be resurfaced or renewed.

22 Before refitting the wheels, check all brake lines and hoses (refer to Chapter 9). On completion, apply the handbrake and check that the rear wheels are locked. The handbrake can be adjusted as described in Chapter 9.

23 On completion, refit the wheels and lower the car to the ground. Tighten the wheel nuts to the specified torque.

8 Exhaust system check

1 With the engine cold (at least three hours after the vehicle has been driven), check the complete exhaust system, from its starting point at the engine to the end of the tailpipe. Ideally, this should be done on a hoist, where unrestricted access is available; if a hoist is not available, raise and support the vehicle on axle stands (see *Jacking and vehicle support*).

2 Make sure that all brackets and rubber mountings are in good condition, and tight; if any of the mountings are to be renewed, ensure that the new ones are of the correct type – in the case of the rubber mountings, their colour is a good guide. Those nearest to the catalytic converter are more heat-resistant than the others **(see illustration)**.

3 Check the pipes and connections for evidence of leaks, severe corrosion, or damage. One of the most common points for a leak to develop is around the welded joints between the pipes and silencers. Leakage at any of the joints or in other parts of the system will usually show up as a black sooty stain in the vicinity of the leak. **Note:** *Exhaust sealants should not be used on any part of the exhaust*

8.2 Check the condition of the exhaust rubber mountings

system upstream of the catalytic converter (between the converter and engine) – even if the sealant does not contain additives harmful to the converter, pieces of it may break off and foul the element, causing local overheating.

4 At the same time, inspect the underside of the body for holes, corrosion, open seams, etc, which may allow exhaust gases to enter the passenger compartment. Seal all body openings with silicone or body putty.

5 Rattles and other noises can often be traced to the exhaust system, especially the rubber mountings. Try to move the system, silencer(s), heat shields and catalytic converter. If any components can touch the body or suspension parts, secure the exhaust system with new mountings.

6 On petrol models, check the running condition of the engine by inspecting inside the end of the tailpipe; the exhaust deposits here are an indication of the engine's state of tune. The inside of the tailpipe should be dry, and should vary in colour from dark grey to light grey/brown; if it is black and sooty, or coated with white deposits, this may indicate the need for a full fuel system inspection.

9 Steering, suspension and roadwheel check

Front suspension and steering

1 Apply the handbrake, then raise the front of the vehicle and support it on axle stands (see *Jacking and vehicle support*).

9.2 Check the condition of the steering rack gaiters

2 Visually inspect the balljoint dust covers and the steering rack gaiters for splits, chafing or deterioration **(see illustration)**. Any wear of these components will cause loss of lubricant, together with dirt and water entry, resulting in rapid deterioration of the balljoints or steering gear.

3 Check the power-assisted steering fluid hoses for chafing or deterioration, and the pipe and hose unions for fluid leaks. Also check for signs of fluid leakage under pressure from the steering gear rubber gaiters, which would indicate failed fluid seals within the steering gear.

4 Grasp the roadwheel at the 12 o'clock and 6 o'clock positions, and try to rock it **(see illustration)**. Very slight free play may be felt, but if the movement is appreciable, further investigation is necessary to determine the source. Continue rocking the wheel while an assistant depresses the footbrake. If the movement is now eliminated or significantly reduced, it is likely that the hub bearings are at fault. If the free play is still evident with the footbrake depressed, then there is wear in the suspension joints or mountings.

5 Now grasp the wheel at the 9 o'clock and 3 o'clock positions, and try to rock it as before. Any movement felt now may again be caused by wear in the hub bearings or the steering track rod balljoints. If the outer track rod balljoint is worn, the visual movement will be obvious. If the inner joint is suspect, it can be felt by placing a hand over the rack-and-pinion rubber gaiter, and gripping the track rod. If the wheel is now rocked, movement will be felt at the inner joint if wear has taken place.

6 Using a large screwdriver or flat bar, check for wear in the suspension mounting and subframe bushes by levering between the relevant suspension component and its attachment point. Some movement is to be expected as the mountings are made of rubber, but excessive wear should be obvious. Also check the condition of any visible rubber bushes, looking for splits, cracks or contamination of the rubber.

7 With the vehicle standing on its wheels, have an assistant turn the steering wheel back-and-forth, about an eighth of a turn each way. There should be very little, if any, lost movement between the steering wheel

9.4 Check for wear in the wheel bearing by grasping the wheel and trying to rock it

10.2 Squeeze the driveshaft gaiters and check for cracks

and roadwheels. If this is not the case, closely observe the joints and mountings previously described, but in addition, check the steering column joints for wear, and also check the rack-and-pinion steering gear itself.

Rear suspension

8 Chock the front wheels, then raise the rear of the vehicle and support it on axle stands (see *Jacking and vehicle support*).

9 Check the rear hub bearings for wear, using the method described for the front hub bearings (paragraph 4).

10 Using a large screwdriver or flat bar, check for wear in the suspension mounting bushes by levering between the relevant suspension component and its attachment point. Some movement is to be expected as the mountings are made of rubber, but excessive wear should be obvious.

Roadwheel check and balancing

11 Periodically remove the roadwheels, and clean any dirt or mud from the inside and outside surfaces. Examine the wheel rims for signs of rusting, corrosion or other damage. Light alloy wheels are easily damaged by 'kerbing' whilst parking, and similarly, steel wheels may become dented or buckled. Renewal of the wheel is very often the only course of remedial action possible.

12 The balance of each wheel and tyre assembly should be maintained, not only to avoid excessive tyre wear, but also to avoid wear in the steering and suspension components. Wheel imbalance is normally signified by vibration through the vehicle's

11.5 Check the security of the air intake pipes

bodyshell, although in many cases it is particularly noticeable through the steering wheel. Conversely, it should be noted that wear or damage in suspension or steering components may cause excessive tyre wear. Out-of-round or out-of-true tyres, damaged wheels and wheel bearing wear/maladjustment also fall into this category. Balancing will not usually cure vibration caused by such wear.

13 Wheel balancing may be carried out with the wheel either on or off the vehicle. If balanced on the vehicle, ensure that the wheel-to-hub relationship is marked in some way prior to subsequent wheel removal, so that it may be refitted in its original position.

10 Driveshaft rubber gaiter and joint check

1 The driveshaft rubber gaiters are very important, because they prevent dirt, water and foreign material from entering and damaging the joints. External contamination can cause the gaiter material to deteriorate prematurely, so it's a good idea to wash the gaiters with soap and water occasionally.

2 With the vehicle raised and securely supported on axle stands (see *Jacking and vehicle support*), turn the steering onto full-lock, then slowly rotate each front wheel in turn. Inspect the condition of the outer constant velocity (CV) joint rubber gaiters, squeezing the gaiters to open out the folds. Check for signs of cracking, splits, or deterioration of the rubber, which may allow the escape of grease, and lead to the ingress of water and grit into the joint. Also check the security and condition of the retaining clips. Repeat these checks on the inner tripod joints **(see illustration)**. If any damage or deterioration is found, the gaiters should be renewed as described in Chapter 8.

3 At the same time, check the general condition of the outer CV joints themselves, by first holding the driveshaft and attempting to rotate the wheels. Repeat this check on the inner joints, by holding the inner joint yoke and attempting to rotate the driveshaft.

4 Any appreciable movement in the joint indicates wear in the joint, wear in the driveshaft splines, or a loose driveshaft retaining bolt.

11 Underbody and hose/pipe check

⚠ *Warning: Renewal of air conditioning hoses must be left to a dealer service department or air conditioning specialist who has the equipment to depressurise the system safely. Never remove air conditioning components or hoses until the system has been depressurised.*

General

1 Visually inspect the engine joint faces, gaskets and seals for any signs of water or oil leaks. Pay particular attention to the areas around the cylinder head cover, cylinder head, oil filter and sump joint faces. Bear in mind that, over a period of time, some very slight seepage from these areas is to be expected – what you are really looking for is any indication of a serious leak. Should a leak be found, renew the offending gasket or oil seal by referring to the appropriate Chapters in this manual.

2 High temperatures in the engine compartment can cause the deterioration of the rubber and plastic hoses used for engine, accessory and emission systems operation. Periodic inspection should be made for cracks, loose clamps, material hardening and leaks.

3 When checking the hoses, ensure that all the cable-ties or clips used to retain the hoses are in place, and in good condition. Clips which are broken or missing can lead to chafing of the hoses, pipes or wiring, which could cause more serious problems in the future.

4 Carefully check the large top and bottom radiator hoses, along with the other smaller-diameter cooling system hoses and metal pipes; do not forget the heater hoses/pipes which run from the engine to the bulkhead. Inspect each hose along its entire length, renewing any that is cracked, swollen or shows signs of deterioration. Cracks may become more apparent if the hose is squeezed, and may often be apparent at the hose ends.

5 Make sure that all hose connections are tight. If the large-diameter air hoses from the air cleaner are loose, they will leak air, and upset the engine idle quality **(see illustration)**. If the spring clamps that are used to secure some of the hoses appear to be slackening, they should be updated with worm-drive clips to prevent the possibility of leaks.

6 Some other hoses are secured to their fittings with clamps. Where clamps are used, check to be sure they haven't lost their tension, allowing the hose to leak. If clamps aren't used, make sure the hose has not expanded and/or hardened where it slips over the fitting, allowing it to leak.

7 Check all fluid reservoirs, filler caps, drain plugs and fittings, etc, looking for any signs of leakage of oil, transmission and/or brake hydraulic fluid, coolant and power steering fluid. Also check the clutch hydraulic fluid lines which lead from the fluid reservoir and slave cylinder (on the transmission).

8 If the vehicle is regularly parked in the same place, close inspection of the ground underneath it will soon show any leaks; ignore the puddle of water which will be left if the air conditioning system is in use. Place a clean piece of cardboard below the engine, and examine it for signs of contamination after the vehicle has been parked over it overnight – be aware, however, of the fire risk inherent in placing combustible material below the catalytic converter.

9 Remember that some leaks will only occur with the engine running, or when the engine is hot or cold. With the handbrake firmly applied, start the engine from cold, and let the engine idle while you examine the underside of the engine compartment for signs of leakage.

10 If an unusual smell is noticed inside or around the car, especially when the engine is thoroughly hot, this may point to the presence of a leak.

11 As soon as a leak is detected, its source must be traced and rectified. Where oil has been leaking for some time, it is usually necessary to use a steam cleaner, pressure washer or similar, to clean away the accumulated dirt, so that the exact source of the leak can be identified.

Vacuum hoses

12 It is quite common for vacuum hoses, especially those in the emissions system, to be colour-coded, or to be identified by coloured stripes moulded into them. Various systems require hoses with different wall thicknesses, collapse resistance and temperature resistance. When renewing hoses, be sure the new ones are made of the same material.

13 Often the only effective way to check a hose is to remove it completely from the vehicle. If more than one hose is removed, be sure to label the hoses and fittings to ensure correct installation.

14 When checking vacuum hoses, be sure to include any plastic T-fittings in the check. Inspect the fittings for cracks, and check the hose where it fits over the fitting for distortion, which could cause leakage.

15 A small piece of vacuum hose (quarter-inch inside diameter) can be used as a stethoscope to detect vacuum leaks. Hold one end of the hose to your ear, and probe around vacuum hoses and fittings, listening for the 'hissing' sound characteristic of a vacuum leak.

⚠ **Warning: When probing with the vacuum hose stethoscope, be very careful not to come into contact with moving engine components such as the auxiliary drivebelt, radiator electric cooling fan, etc.**

Fuel hoses

⚠ **Warning: There are certain precautions which must be taken when inspecting or servicing fuel system components. Work in a well-ventilated area, and do not allow open flames (cigarettes, appliance pilot lights, etc) or bare light bulbs near the work area. Mop-up any spills immediately, and do not store fuel-soaked rags where they could ignite.**

16 Check all fuel hoses for deterioration and chafing. Check especially for cracks in areas where the hose bends, and also just before fittings, such as where a hose attaches to the fuel rail or filter **(see illustration)**.

17 High-quality fuel line, usually identified by the word 'Fluoroelastomer' printed on the hose, should be used for fuel line renewal. Never, under any circumstances, use non-reinforced vacuum line, clear plastic tubing or water hose as a substitute for fuel lines.

18 Spring type clamps may be used on fuel lines. These clamps often lose their tension over a period of time, and can be 'sprung' during removal. Renew all spring type clamps with proper petrol pipe clips whenever a hose is renewed.

Metal pipes

19 Sections of metal piping are often used for fuel line between the fuel filter and the engine, and for some brake, power steering and air conditioning applications. Check carefully to be sure the piping has not been bent or crimped, and that cracks have not started in the line; also check for signs of excessive corrosion. Also make sure that they are correctly supported in their clips **(see illustration)**. Where applicable, check the PVC coating on the lines for damage.

20 If a section of metal fuel line must be renewed, only seamless steel piping should be used, since copper and aluminium piping don't have the strength necessary to withstand normal engine vibration.

21 Check the metal lines where they enter the brake master cylinder, ABS hydraulic unit or clutch master/slave cylinders (as applicable) for cracks in the lines or loose fittings. Any sign of brake fluid leakage calls for an immediate and thorough inspection.

Underbody

22 With the vehicle raised and supported on axle stands or over an inspection pit, thoroughly inspect the underbody and wheel arches for signs of damage and corrosion. In particular, examine the bottom of the side sills, and any concealed areas where mud can collect.

23 Where corrosion and rust is evident, press and tap firmly on the panel with a screwdriver, and check for any serious corrosion which would necessitate repairs.

24 If the panel is not seriously corroded, clean away the rust, and apply a new coating of underseal. Refer to Chapter 11 for more details of body repairs.

25 At the same time, inspect the lower body panels for stone damage and general condition.

12 Hinge and lock lubrication

1 Work around the vehicle and lubricate the hinges of the bonnet, doors and tailgate with a light machine oil.

2 Check carefully the security and operation of all hinges, latches and locks, adjusting them where required. Check the operation of the central locking system (if fitted).

11.16 Check the security of the fuel pipe where it joins the fuel rail (arrowed)

3 Where applicable, check the condition and operation of the tailgate struts, renewing them if either is leaking or no longer able to support the tailgate securely when raised.

13 Roadwheel nut tightness check

1 Checking the tightness of the wheel nuts is more relevant than you might think. Apart from the obvious safety aspect of ensuring they are sufficiently tight, this check will reveal whether they have been overtightened, as may have happened the last time new tyres were fitted, for example. If the car suffers a puncture, you may find that the wheel nuts cannot be loosened with the wheel brace.

2 Apply the handbrake, chock the wheels, and engage 1st gear (or P).

3 Remove the wheel cover (or wheel centre cover), using the flat end of the wheel brace supplied in the tool kit.

4 Loosen the first wheel nut, using the wheel brace if possible. If the nut proves stubborn, use a close-fitting socket and a long extension bar.

⚠ **Warning: Do not use makeshift means to loosen the wheel nuts if the proper tools are not available. If extra force is required, make sure that the tools fit properly, and are of good quality. Even so, consider the consequences of the tool slipping or breaking, and take precautions – wearing stout gloves is advisable to protect your**

11.19 Check the fuel and brake pipes under the vehicle body

15.1 Squeeze together the sides and remove the two fasteners (arrowed)

15.3 Rotate the fasteners (arrowed) anti-clockwise and lift the fuse/junction box from the bracket

hands. Do not be tempted to stand on the tools used – they are not designed for this, and there is a high risk of personal injury if the tool slips or breaks. If the wheel nuts are simply too tight, take the car to a garage equipped with suitable power tools.

5 Once the nut has been loosened, remove it and check that the wheel stud threads are clean. Use a small wire brush to clean any rust or dirt from the threads, if necessary.

6 Refit the nut, with the tapered side facing inwards. Tighten it fully, using the wheel brace alone – no other tools. This will ensure that the wheel nuts can be loosened using the wheel brace if a puncture occurs. However, if a torque wrench is available, tighten the nut to the specified torque wrench setting.

7 Repeat the procedure for the remaining nuts, then refit the wheel cover or centre cover, as applicable.

8 Work around the car, checking and retightening the nuts for all four wheels.

14 Road test

Braking system

1 Make sure that the vehicle does not pull to one side when braking, and that the wheels do not lock when braking hard.

2 Check that there is no vibration through the steering when braking. As all models are

15.4 Undo the 2 nuts (arrowed) securing the bracket

equipped with ABS brakes, if vibration is felt through the pedal under heavy braking, this is a normal characteristic of the system operation, and is not a cause for concern.

3 Check that the handbrake operates correctly, without excessive movement of the lever, and that it holds the vehicle stationary on a slope, in both directions (facing up and down a slope). In service, the handbrake should be fully applied within 3 to 5 clicks of the handbrake lever ratchet. Should adjustment be necessary, refer to Chapter 9, Section 22, for the full procedure description.

4 With the engine switched off, test the operation of the brake servo unit as follows. Depress the footbrake four or five times to exhaust the vacuum, then start the engine. As the engine starts, there should be a noticeable 'give' in the brake pedal as vacuum builds-up. Allow the engine to run for at least two minutes, and then switch it off. If the brake pedal is now depressed again, it should be possible to detect a hiss from the servo as the pedal is depressed. After about four or five applications, no further hissing should be heard, and the pedal should feel considerably harder.

Steering and suspension

5 Check for any abnormalities in the steering, suspension, handling or road 'feel'.

6 Drive the vehicle, and check that there are no unusual vibrations or noises.

7 Check that the steering feels positive, with no excessive sloppiness or roughness, and check for any suspension noises when cornering and driving over bumps.

Drivetrain

8 Check the performance of the engine, transmission and driveshafts.

9 Check that the engine starts correctly, both when cold and when hot. On diesel models, observe the glow plug warning light, and cjeck that it comes on and goes off correctly.

10 Listen for any unusual noises from the engine and transmission.

11 Make sure that the engine runs smoothly when idling, and that there is no hesitation when accelerating.

12 On manual transmission models, check

that all gears can be engaged smoothly without noise, and that the gear lever action is smooth and not abnormally vague or 'notchy'.

13 On automatic transmission models, make sure that all gearchanges occur smoothly without snatching, and without an increase in engine speed between changes. Check that all the gear positions can be selected with the vehicle at rest. If any problems are found, they should be referred to a Ford dealer.

14 Listen for a metallic clicking sound from the front of the vehicle as the vehicle is driven slowly in a circle with the steering on full-lock. Carry out this check in both directions. If a clicking noise is heard, this indicates wear in a driveshaft joint, in which case renew the joint if necessary.

Clutch

15 Check that the clutch pedal moves smoothly and easily through its full travel, and that the clutch itself functions correctly, with no trace of slip or drag.

16 If the clutch is slow to release, it is possible that the system requires bleeding (see Chapter 6). Also check the fluid pipes under the bonnet for signs of leakage.

17 Check the clutch as described in Chapter 6.

Instruments and electrical equipment

18 Check the operation of all instruments and electrical equipment.

19 Make sure that all instruments read correctly, and switch on all electrical equipment in turn, to check that it functions properly.

15 Pollen filter renewal

1 Release the 2 fasteners and remove the trim panel above the passenger's side footwell **(see illustration)**.

2 Whilst not strictly necessary, access to the filter is considerable easier with the glovebox removed as described in Chapter 11.

3 Undo the 2 fasteners securing the fusebox/central junction box and then lift it from the mounting bracket on the bulkhead **(see illustration)**. Move the fusebox/module to one side; there is no need to disconnect the wiring plugs.

4 Release the clips securing the wiring harness to the fusebox/module mounting bracket, then undo the 2 nuts and remove the bracket **(see illustration)**.

5 On models with air conditioning, undo the retaining bolt and remove the cool air pipe from the heater housing to the side of the glovebox **(see illustration)**.

6 Disconnect the wiring plugs from the recirculation flap motor and heater blower motor resistor.

15.5 Undo the bolt (arrowed) securing the glovebox cooling pipe

15.7a Undo the 3 bolts (arrowed), remove the cover . . .

15.7b . . . and pull the pollen filter from the housing

7 Undo the 3 bolts, remove the cover and pull the filter from the housing **(see illustrations)**.
8 Fit the new filter using a reversal of the removal procedure, ensuring that the filter is fitted with the airflow arrows pointing straight back into the cabin.

16 Seat belt check

1 Check the seat belts for satisfactory operation and condition. Inspect the webbing for fraying and cuts. Check that they retract smoothly and without binding into their reels.
2 Check the seat belt mountings, ensuring that all the bolts are securely tightened.

17 Coolant strength check

⚠ *Warning: Do not allow antifreeze to come in contact with your skin or painted surfaces of the vehicle. Flush contaminated areas immediately with plenty of water. Don't store new coolant, or leave old coolant lying around, where it's accessible to children or pets – they're attracted by its sweet smell. Ingestion of even a small amount of coolant can be fatal. Wipe up garage-floor and drip-pan spills immediately. Keep antifreeze containers covered, and repair cooling system leaks as soon as they're noticed.*

⚠ *Warning: Never remove the expansion tank filler cap when the engine is running, or has just been switched off, as the cooling system will be hot, and the consequent escaping steam and scalding coolant could cause serious injury.*

⚠ *Warning: Wait until the engine is cold before starting these procedures.*

1 Use a hydrometer to check the strength of the antifreeze. Follow the instructions provided with your hydrometer. The antifreeze strength should be approximately 50%. If it is significantly less than this, drain a little coolant from the radiator (see Section 26), add antifreeze to the coolant expansion tank, then recheck the strength.

Every 37 500 miles or 3 years

18 Air filter element renewal

Caution: Never drive the vehicle with the air cleaner filter element removed. Excessive engine wear could result, and backfiring could even cause a fire under the bonnet.

1.6 litre models

1 The air filter element is located in the air cleaner assembly on the left-hand side of the engine compartment.
2 Remove the four bolts securing the cover to the air cleaner housing **(see illustration)**.
3 The cover can now be lifted, and the filter element removed **(see illustrations)**.
4 If carrying out a routine service, the element must be renewed regardless of its apparent condition.
5 If you are checking the element for any other reason, inspect its lower surface; if it is oily or very dirty, renew the element. If it is only moderately dusty, it can be re-used by blowing it clean from the upper to the lower surface with compressed air. Because it is a pleated-paper type filter, it cannot be washed or re-oiled. If it cannot be cleaned satisfactorily with compressed air, discard and renew it.

⚠ *Warning: Wear eye protection when using compressed air.*

1.8 and 2.0 litre models

6 The air filter element is located in the air

18.2 Undo the air filter cover bolts (arrowed) . . .

18.3a . . . lift up the cover . . .

18.3b . . . and remove the filter element

18.8 Undo the filter cover bolts (arrowed)

18.9 Lift the cover and pull out the filter element

cleaner assembly on the left-hand side of the engine compartment.

7 Pull the plastic cover upwards from the top of the engine.

8 Undo the 6 Torx bolts securing the cover to the air cleaner housing **(see illustration)**.

9 The left-hand end of the cover can now be lifted, and the filter element removed **(see illustration)**. If preferred, the cover can be removed completely – this will allow a more thorough cleaning of the filter housing.

10 Loosen the clip and disconnect the air intake duct from the air cleaner.

11 Withdraw the cover and remove the filter element, noting its direction of fitting.

12 If carrying out a routine service, the element must be renewed regardless of its apparent condition.

13 If you are checking the element for any other reason, inspect its lower surface; if it is oily or very dirty, renew the element. If it is only moderately dusty, it can be re-used by blowing it clean from the upper to the lower surface with compressed air. Because it is a pleated-paper type filter, it cannot be washed or re-oiled. If it cannot be cleaned satisfactorily with compressed air, discard and renew it.

 Warning: Wear eye protection when using compressed air.

All models

14 Where the air cleaner cover was removed, wipe out the inside of the housing. Check that no foreign matter is visible, either in the air intake or in the air mass meter.

19.6 Pull the HT lead (arrowed) from the top of the spark plug

15 Refitting is the reverse of the removal procedure, noting the following points:
a) *Make sure that the filter is fitted the correct way up (observe any direction-of-fitting markings).*
b) *Ensure that the element and cover are securely seated, so that unfiltered air cannot enter the engine.*
c) *Where removed, secure the cover with the bolts, and ensure that the air intake duct securing clip is fully tightened.*

19 Spark plug renewal

1 The correct functioning of the spark plugs is vital for the correct running and efficiency of the engine. It is essential that the plugs fitted are appropriate for the engine.

2 If the correct type is used and the engine is in good condition, the spark plugs should not need attention between scheduled intervals. Spark plug cleaning is rarely necessary, and should not be attempted unless specialised equipment is available, as damage can easily be caused to the firing ends.

3 Spark plug removal and refitting requires a spark plug socket, with an extension which can be turned by a ratchet handle or similar. This socket is lined with a rubber sleeve, to protect the porcelain insulator of the spark plug, and to hold the plug while you insert it into the spark plug hole. You will also need feeler blades, to check and adjust the spark plug electrode gap, and (ideally) a torque wrench to tighten the new plugs to the specified torque.

1.6 litre models

4 To remove the spark plugs, first open the bonnet; the plugs are easily reached at the top of the engine.

5 Note how the spark plug (HT) leads are routed and secured by the clips on the cylinder head cover; unclip the leads as necessary, to provide enough slack in the lead. To prevent the possibility of mixing up spark plug (HT) leads, it is a good idea to try to work on one spark plug at a time.

6 If the marks on the original-equipment spark plug (HT) leads cannot be seen, mark the leads

1 to 4, to correspond to the cylinder the lead serves (No 1 cylinder is at the timing belt end of the engine). Pull the leads from the plugs by gripping the rubber boot sealing the cylinder head cover opening, not the lead, otherwise the lead connection may be fractured **(see illustration)**.

7 It is advisable to soak up any water in the spark plug recesses with a rag, and to remove any dirt from them using a clean brush, vacuum cleaner or compressed air before removing the plugs, to prevent any dirt or water from dropping into the cylinders.

 Warning: Wear eye protection when using compressed air.

8 Unscrew the spark plugs, ensuring that the socket is kept in alignment with each plug – if the socket is forcibly moved to either side, the porcelain top of the plug may be broken off. Remove the plug from the engine.

9 If any undue difficulty is encountered when unscrewing any of the spark plugs, carefully check the cylinder head threads and sealing surfaces for signs of wear, excessive corrosion or damage; if any of these conditions is found, seek the advice of a Ford dealer as to the best method of repair.

10 As each plug is removed, examine it as follows – this will give a good indication of the condition of the engine:
a) *If the insulator nose of the spark plug is clean and white, with no deposits, this is indicative of a weak mixture.*
b) *If the tip and insulator nose are covered with hard black-looking deposits, then this is indicative that the mixture is too rich.*
c) *Should the plug be black and oily, then it is likely that the engine is fairly worn, as well as the mixture being too rich.*
d) *If the insulator nose is covered with light tan to greyish-brown deposits, then the mixture is correct, and it is likely that the engine is in good condition.*

11 If you are renewing the spark plugs, purchase the new plugs, then check each of them first for faults such as cracked insulators or damaged threads.

12 The spark plug electrode gap is of considerable importance as, if it is too large or too small, the size of the spark and its efficiency will be seriously impaired. However, several models covered by this manual use spark plugs with multiple earth electrodes – *unless there is clear information to the contrary, no attempt should be made to adjust the plug gap on a spark plug with more than one earth electrode.*

13 To set the electrode gap on plugs with one earth electrode, measure the gap with a feeler gauge, and then bend open, or closed, the outer plug electrode until the correct gap is achieved **(see illustrations)**. The centre electrode should never be bent, as this may crack the insulation and cause plug failure, if nothing worse. If the outer electrode is not exactly over the centre electrode, bend it gently to align them.

19.13a Check the electrode gap with a set of feeler gauges

19.13b Adjust the electrode gap

19.18 Pull the engine cover upwards

14 Before fitting the spark plugs, check that the threaded connector sleeves at the top of the plugs are tight (where fitted), and that the plug exterior surfaces and threads are clean. Brown staining on the porcelain, immediately above the metal body, is quite normal, and does not necessarily indicate a leak between the body and insulator.

15 On installing the spark plugs, first check that the cylinder head thread and sealing surface are as clean as possible; use a clean rag wrapped around a paintbrush to wipe clean the sealing surface. Apply a smear of copper-based grease or anti-seize compound to the threads of each plug, and screw them in by hand where possible. Take extra care to enter the plug threads correctly, as the cylinder head is made of aluminium alloy – it's often difficult to insert spark plugs into their holes without cross-threading them.

16 When each spark plug is started correctly on its threads, screw it down until it just seats lightly, then tighten it to the specified torque wrench setting. If a torque wrench is not available – and this is one case where the use of a torque wrench is strongly recommended – tighten each spark plug through *no more than* 1/16th of a turn. *Do not* exceed the specified

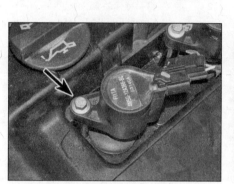

19.19a Undo the coil retaining bolt (arrowed) . . .

torque setting, and *NEVER* overtighten spark plugs.

17 Reconnect the spark plug (HT) leads in their correct order, using a twisting motion on the boot until it is firmly seated on the end of the spark plug and on the cylinder head cover.

1.8 and 2.0 litre models

18 To remove the spark plugs, first open the bonnet; the plugs are easily reached at the top of the engine. Pull the plastic cover on the top of the engine straight up to release its mountings **(see illustration)**.

19 The ignition coils are fitted one per plug,

19.19b . . . and lift it from place

on the top of each spark plug. To aid refitment, use paint (or similar) to identify the ignition coils so they are refitted to their original positions. Disconnect the wiring plug, undo the retaining bolt and lift each coil from place **(see illustrations)**.

20 Continue as described in paragraphs 7 to 16.

21 Align the coil with the mounting bolt hole, then push it down firmly onto the spark plug. Tighten the retaining bolt to the specified torque and reconnect the wiring plug.

22 The remainder of refitting is a reversal of removal.

Every 50 000 miles or 4 years

| **20 Timing belt renewal** | The procedure (applicable only to the 1.6 litre engines) is described in Chapter 2A. |

Every 100 000 miles or 8 years

21 Auxiliary drivebelt renewal

1.6 litre engines

1 Slacken the right-hand front roadwheel nuts,

raise the front of the vehicle and support on axle stands (see *Jacking and vehicle support*). Where fitted – undo the fasteners and remove the engine undershield **(see illustration 3.4)**. Remove the roadwheel.

2 Undo the fasteners, then remove the wheel arch liner and splash shield under the belt(s).

3 Using a sharp knife, cut through the air

conditioning compressor drivebelt (where fitted) and the main auxiliary drivebelt, then remove them **(see illustration)**.

4 Ensure the pulley grooves are clean.

5 New auxiliary belts are supplied by Ford with fitting tools included. Fit the main auxiliary drivebelt fitting tool to the crankshaft pulley, with the centre of the tool in the 12 o'clock

21.3 Cut through the drivebelt

21.5a Fit the tool to the crankshaft pulley in the 12 o'clock position . . .

21.5b . . . with the curved side (arrowed) of the tool towards the engine

position, and the curved side towards the engine **(see illustrations)**.

6 Refit the roadwheel, lower the vehicle to the ground and select 1st gear or Park.

7 Position the new auxiliary belt around the crankshaft pulley, power steering pump pulley and coolant pump pulley. Ensure the belt is correctly located in the pulley grooves.

8 Fit the installation tool supplied in the kit to the coolant pump pulley as shown **(see illustration)**. An audible click will be heard when the tool is correctly located on the pulley. If the coolant pump pulley bolts have been previously slackened, take the opportunity to tighten the bolts whilst the tool is fitted.

9 Rotate the coolant pump pulley and installation tool 90° anti-clockwise.

10 Slide the belt from the coolant pump pulley, and fit it around the alternator pulley. Ensure the belt is correctly located in the pulley grooves.

11 Rotate the installation tool and pulley clockwise by hand until the tension on the belt increases, then use a spanner to rotate the tool/pulley clockwise and install the belt on the underside of the pulley **(see illustrations)**. This procedure should be carried out in front of the engine mounting. Use a second spanner to fully rotate the tool/pulley.

12 Release the tool from the coolant pump pulley, then select neutral gear and raise the front of the vehicle again.

13 Rotate the crankshaft pulley approximately 90° using a spanner on the pulley bolt/nut. Remove the installation tool from the crankshaft pulley.

14 Continue to rotate the crankshaft pulley through 2 complete revolutions, and check that the belt is correctly located in the pulley grooves.

15 On models with air conditioning, the new compressor drivebelt is supplied by Ford in a kit with the necessary installation tool.

Begin by fitting the installation tool to the crankshaft pulley in the 7 o'clock position **(see illustration)**.

16 Fit the new belt around the compressor pulley, ensuring the belt correctly locates in the pulley grooves, then fit the belt under the crankshaft pulley and around the installation tool **(see illustration)**.

17 Rotate the installation tool clockwise until the tension increases, holding the belt into the grooves on the underside of the crankshaft pulley, then use a socket on the crankshaft pulley, and rotate the pulley clockwise until the tool is in the 3 o'clock position **(see illustration)**.

18 Remove the installation tool, then rotate the crankshaft pulley 1 complete revolution clockwise and check the belt is correctly located in the pulley grooves.

19 The remainder of refitting is a reversal of removal. Note that when refitting the wheel arch liner, the longest bolt is the rearmost.

21.8 Fit the installation tool (arrowed) to the coolant pump pulley

21.11a Rotate the coolant pump pulley/tool by hand until it catches the belt . . .

21.11b . . . then use a spanner to fully rotate the pulley/tool

21.15 Fit the compressor drivebelt installation tool in the 7 o'clock position

21.16 Fit the belt around the tool . . .

21.17 . . . then rotate the crankshaft pulley clockwise

1.8 & 2.0 litre engines

20 Slacken the right-hand front roadwheel nuts, raise the front of the vehicle and support on axle stands (see *Jacking and vehicle support*). Where fitted – undo the fasteners and remove the engine undershield **(see illustration 3.4)**. Remove the roadwheel. Undo the fasteners, then remove the wheel arch liner and splash shield under the belt(s).

21 Using a sharp knife, cut through the air conditioning compressor drivebelt (where fitted), and remove it. Unclip the power steering pipe where applicable. Remove the plastic cover from the top of the engine.

Models up to 02/2008

22 Using a spanner on the centre bolt, rotate the main auxiliary drivebelt tensioner anti-clockwise to relieve the tension, and remove the belt **(see illustration)**.

23 Ensure the pulley grooves are clean.

24 Fit the new drivebelt onto the crankshaft, alternator, and coolant pump, then turn the tensioner anti-clockwise and locate the drivebelt on the pulley. Make sure that the drivebelt is correctly seated in all of the pulley grooves, then release the tensioner **(see illustration)**.

Models from 02/2008

25 Undo the 2 bolts and 1 nut securing the auxiliary drivebelt idler pulley to the cylinder head **(see illustration)**.

26 Insert a long bar/rod of suitable diameter into the hole in the top of the idler mounting assembly. Using moderate force only, lever the assembly towards the left-hand side of the vehicle, then pull the assembly forwards

21.22 Rotate the tensioner anti-clockwise

a little, and allow the rod/bar to move to the right-hand side until the belt can be removed from the pulley **(see illustration)**. Remove the belt from the remaining pulleys.

27 Ensure the pulley grooves are clean.

28 Fit the new drivebelt onto the crankshaft, alternator, and coolant pump, then loop the belt over the idler pulley. At this point the idler pulley mounting assembly should be unbolted, free to pivot on the lower mounting stud with the bar/rod inserted into the top hole.

29 Using moderate force only, pull the rod/bar across the left-hand side of the vehicle, and re-align the idler assembly mounting holes. Insert the bolts, then tighten the nut/bolts to the specified torque. Remove the bar/rod, then make sure that the drivebelt is correctly seated in all of the pulley grooves **(see illustration)**.

All engines

30 On models with air conditioning, the new

21.24 Auxiliary drivebelt routing – 1.8 and 2.0 litre engines

1 *Crankshaft pulley*
2 *Tensioner pulley*
3 *Coolant pump pulley*
4 *Alternator pulley*

compressor drivebelt is supplied by Ford in a kit with the necessary installation tool. Begin by fitting the installation tool to the crankshaft pulley in the 9 o'clock position **(see illustration)**.

31 Fit the new belt around the compressor pulley, ensuring the belt correctly locates in the pulley grooves, then fit the belt around the installation tool **(see illustration)**.

32 Fit the belt guide tool to the compressor. The curved end of the tool fits around the belt, and the flat end fits between the compressor and the sump **(see illustration)**.

21.25 Undo the auxiliary belt tensioner bolts/nut (arrowed)

21.26 Lever the tensioner to the left, then forwards, then to the right and remove the belt

21.29 Auxiliary drivebelt routing – post-02/2008

J46815

21.30 Fit the installation tool (arrowed) to the crankshaft in the 9 o'clock position

21.31 Fit the belt around the tool

33 Using a spanner on the crankshaft pulley, rotate the pulley clockwise until the installation tool on the pulley is in the 6 o'clock position. Guide the belt onto the pulleys as the crankshaft is rotated **(see illustration)**.

34 Remove the installation tool, then rotate the crankshaft pulley 1 complete revolution clockwise and check the belt is correctly located in the pulley grooves.

35 Remove the belt guide tool from the compressor.

36 The remainder of refitting is a reversal of removal.

21.32 Insert the guide tool between the compressor and the sump – note how the tool fits around the compressor bolt (arrowed)

21.33 Rotate the crankshaft clockwise until the installation tool is in the 6 o'clock position

Every 2 years, regardless of mileage

22 Automatic transmission fluid level check

1 The fluid level **must** be checked with the engine/transmission at operating temperature. This can be achieved by checking the level after a journey of at least 10 miles. If the level is checked when cold, follow this up with a level check when the fluid is hot.

2 Park the car on level ground, and apply the handbrake very firmly. As an added precaution, chock the front and rear wheels, so that the car cannot move.

3 With the engine idling, apply the footbrake, then move the selector lever gently from position P to position 1 and back to P.

4 The fluid level dipstick is located on the rear of the transmission. Before removing the dipstick, thoroughly clean the area around it – no dirt or debris must be allowed to enter the transmission.

5 Extract the dipstick, and wipe it clean using a clean piece of rag or tissue. Re-insert the dipstick completely, then pull it out once more. The fluid level should be between the reference marks on the side of the dipstick **(see illustrations)**. **Note:** *If the level is checked when cold, the reading obtained will*

appear to be low – recheck the level when hot before topping-up, as the transmission must not be overfilled.

6 If topping-up is required, this is done via the dipstick tube. It is most important that no dirt or debris enters the transmission as this is done – use a clean funnel (preferably with a filter) and fresh fluid from a clean container.

7 Pour the fresh fluid a little at a time down the dipstick tube, checking the level frequently. The difference between the MIN and MAX marks is 0.4 litres.

8 When the level is correct, refit the dipstick and switch off the engine.

9 The need for regular topping-up of the transmission fluid indicates a leak, which should be found and rectified without delay.

23 Manual transmission oil level check

1 The manual transmission does not have a dipstick. To check the oil level, raise the vehicle and support it securely on axle stands (see *Jacking and vehicle support*), making sure that the vehicle is level. Undo the fasteners and remove the engine undershield (where fitted).

2 On 1.6 and 1.8 litre models, to gain access

22.5a Pull the automatic transmission fluid level dipstick from place

22.5b Dipstick fluid level upper and lower markings (arrowed)

to the filler/level plug, it is first necessary to unclip the plastic cover from the gear selector cables at the front of the transmission.

3 On the lower front side of the transmission housing, you will see the filler/level plug, which has a large Allen key fitting **(see illustration)**. Note it is the plug furthest from the engine; where applicable, do not confuse it with the blanking plug near the bellhousing.

4 Remove all traces of dirt, then unscrew the filler/level plug from the front face of the transmission. Access to the plug is not that easy; use a suitable Allen key or socket, and take care, as the plug will probably be very tight.

5 If the lubricant level is correct, the oil should be up to the lower edge of the hole.

6 If the transmission needs more lubricant (if the level is not up to the hole), use a syringe, or a plastic bottle and tube, to add more.

7 Stop filling the transmission when the oil begins to run out of the hole, then wait until the flow of oil ceases – do not refit the plug immediately, or the transmission may end up being overfilled.

8 When the level is correct, clean and refit the filler level plug. Tighten it to the specified torque.

9 Drive the vehicle a short distance, then check for leaks.

10 A need for regular topping-up can only be due to a leak, which should be found and rectified without delay.

23.3 Filler/level plug (arrowed)

24 Brake fluid renewal

 Warning: Brake hydraulic fluid can harm your eyes and damage painted surfaces, so use extreme caution when handling and pouring it. Do not use fluid that has been standing open for some time, as it absorbs moisture from the air. Excess moisture can cause a dangerous loss of braking effectiveness. Brake fluid is also highly flammable – treat it with the same respect as petrol.

1 The procedure is similar to that for the bleeding of the hydraulic system as described in Chapter 9.

2 Reduce the fluid level in the reservoir (by siphoning or using a poultry baster), but do not allow the fluid level to drop far enough to allow air into the system.

⚠️ **Warning: Do not siphon the fluid by mouth; it is poisonous.**

3 Working as described in Chapter 9, open the first bleed screw in the sequence, and pump the brake pedal gently until nearly all the old fluid has been emptied from the master cylinder reservoir. Top-up to the MAX level with new fluid, and continue pumping until only the new fluid remains in the reservoir, and new fluid can be seen emerging from the bleed screw. Tighten the screw, and top the reservoir level

up to the MAX level line. Old hydraulic fluid is invariably much darker in colour than the new, making it easy to distinguish the two.

4 Work through all the remaining bleed screws in the sequence until new fluid can be seen at all of them. Be careful to keep the master cylinder reservoir topped-up to above the MIN level at all times, or air may enter the system and greatly increase the length of the task.

5 When the operation is complete, check that all bleed screws are securely tightened, and that their dust caps are refitted. Wash off all traces of spilt fluid, and recheck the master cylinder reservoir fluid level.

6 Check the operation of the brakes before taking the car on the road.

7 Finally, check the operation of the clutch. Since the clutch shares the same fluid reservoir as the braking system, it may also be necessary to bleed the clutch as described in Chapter 6.

25 Remote control battery renewal

1 Although not in the Ford maintenance schedule, we recommend that the battery is changed every 2 years, regardless of the vehicle's mileage. However, if the door locks repeatedly fail to respond to signals from the remote control at the normal distance, change the battery in the remote control before attempting to troubleshoot any of the vehicle's other systems.

Type 1

2 Press the button to release the key blade. On passive type controls, remove the spare key.

3 On non-passive type controls, insert a small flat-bladed screwdriver into the slot provided, push the screwdriver towards the key blade, and carefully prise the 2 halves of the control apart **(see illustrations)**.

4 On both types of control, insert a screwdriver as shown and separate the two halves **(see illustration)**.

5 Note the fitted position of the battery (positive side down), then prise the battery from place, and insert the new one **(see illustration)**. Avoid touching the battery or the terminals with bare fingers.

6 Snap the 2 halves of the control together.

7 Refit the key blade, and check for correct operation.

25.3a Insert a screwdriver into the slot . . .

25.3b . . . and prise apart the 2 halves

25.4 Separate the 2 halves

25.5 The battery fits positive side down

25.8 Insert a screwdriver into the slot

25.9 Release the clip each side (arrowed)

25.10 The battery fits positive side up

Type 2

8 Insert a small flat-bladed screwdriver into the slot provided and slide the transmitter unit from the key **(see illustration)**.

9 Use the screwdriver to release the clip each side and open the transmitter unit **(see illustration)**.

10 Note the fitted position of the battery (positive side up), then prise the battery from place, and insert the new one **(see illustration)**. Avoid touching the battery or the terminals with bare fingers.

11 Snap the 2 halves of the transmitter together, and re-attach it to the key.

26 Coolant renewal

⚠️ **Warning: Do not allow antifreeze to come in contact with your skin or painted surfaces of the vehicle. Flush contaminated areas immediately with plenty of water. Don't store new coolant, or leave old coolant lying around, where it's accessible to children or pets – they're attracted by its sweet smell. Ingestion of even a small amount of coolant can be fatal. Wipe up garage-floor and drip-pan spills immediately. Keep antifreeze containers covered, and repair cooling system leaks as soon as they're noticed.**

⚠️ **Warning: Never remove the expansion tank filler cap when the engine is running, or has just been switched off, as the cooling**

26.4 Slacken the radiator drain plug

system will be hot, and the consequent escaping steam and scalding coolant could cause serious injury.

⚠️ **Warning: Wait until the engine is cold before starting these procedures.**

Note: *If the pink/red Ford antifreeze is used, the coolant can then be left indefinitely, providing the strength of the mixture is checked every year. If any antifreeze other than Ford's is to be used, the coolant must be renewed at regular intervals to provide an equivalent degree of protection; the conventional recommendation is to renew the coolant every two years.*

Coolant draining

1 To drain the system, first remove the expansion tank filler cap.

2 If the additional working clearance is required, raise the front of the vehicle and support it securely on axle stands (see *Jacking and vehicle support*).

3 Where fitted, undo the fasteners and remove the engine undershield **(see illustration 3.4)**.

4 Place a large drain tray underneath, and unscrew the radiator drain plug **(see illustration)**; direct as much of the escaping coolant as possible into the tray.

5 Once the coolant has stopped draining from the radiator, close the drain plug.

System flushing

6 With time, the cooling system may gradually lose its efficiency, as the radiator core becomes choked with rust, scale deposits from the water, and other sediment. To minimise this, as well as using only good-quality antifreeze and clean soft water, the system should be flushed as follows whenever any part of it is disturbed, and/or when the coolant is renewed.

7 With the coolant drained, refit the drain plug and refill the system with fresh water. Refit the expansion tank filler cap, start the engine and warm it up to normal operating temperature, then stop it and (after allowing it to cool down completely) drain the system again. Repeat as necessary until only clean water can be seen to emerge, then refill finally with the specified coolant mixture.

8 If only clean, soft water and good-quality antifreeze (even if not to Ford's specification) has been used, and the coolant has been renewed at the suggested intervals, the above procedure

will be sufficient to keep the system clean for a considerable length of time. If, however, the system has been neglected, a more thorough operation will be required, as follows.

9 First drain the coolant, then disconnect the radiator top and bottom hoses. Insert a garden hose into the radiator top hose connection, and allow water to circulate through the radiator until it runs clean from the bottom outlet.

10 To flush the engine, insert the garden hose into the radiator bottom hose, wrap a piece of rag around the garden hose to seal the connection, and allow water to circulate until it runs clear.

11 Try the effect of repeating this procedure in the top hose, although this may not be effective, since the thermostat will probably close and prevent the flow of water.

12 In severe cases of contamination, reverse-flushing of the radiator may be necessary. This may be achieved by inserting the garden hose into the bottom outlet, wrapping a piece of rag around the hose to seal the connection, then flushing the radiator until clear water emerges from the top hose outlet.

13 If the radiator is suspected of being severely choked, remove the radiator (Chapter 3), turn it upside-down, and repeat the procedure described in paragraph 12.

14 Flushing the heater matrix can be achieved using a similar procedure to that described in paragraph 12, once the heater intake and outlet hoses have been identified. These two hoses will be of the same diameter, and pass through the engine compartment bulkhead (refer to the heater matrix removal procedure in Chapter 3 for more details).

15 The use of chemical cleaners is not recommended, and should be necessary only as a last resort; the scouring action of some chemical cleaners may lead to other cooling system problems. Normally, regular renewal of the coolant will prevent excessive contamination of the system.

Coolant filling

16 With the cooling system drained and flushed, ensure that all disturbed hose unions are correctly secured, and that the radiator/engine drain plug(s) is securely tightened. Refit the engine undershield (where applicable). If it was raised, lower the vehicle to the ground.

17 Set the heater temperature control to maximum heat, but ensure the blower is turned off.

18 Prepare a sufficient quantity of the specified coolant mixture (see below); allow for a surplus, so as to have a reserve supply for topping-up.

19 Slowly fill the system through the expansion tank. Since the tank is the highest point in the system, all the air in the system should be displaced into the tank by the rising liquid. Slow pouring reduces the possibility of air being trapped and forming airlocks.

20 Continue filling until the coolant level reaches the expansion tank MAX level line (see *Weekly checks*), then cover the filler opening to prevent coolant splashing out.

21 Start the engine and run it at 2500 rpm for 2 minutes. If the level in the expansion tank drops significantly, top-up to the MAX level line, to minimise the amount of air circulating in the system.

22 Fill the expansion tank to the MAX level line, refit the expansion tank cap, and run the engine at 2500 rpm until the thermostat opens and the engine is at normal operating temperature. Check this by feeling the radiator bottom hose – if it's hot, then the thermostat has opened.

23 Briefly run the engine at 4000 rpm, then run it at 2500 rpm for approximately 3 minutes.

24 Stop the engine, wash off any spilt coolant from the engine compartment and bodywork, then leave the car to cool down *completely* (overnight, if possible).

25 With the system cool, open the expansion tank, and top-up the tank to the MAX level line. Refit the filler cap, tightening it securely, and clean up any further spillage.

26 After refilling, always check carefully all components of the system (but especially any unions disturbed during draining and flushing) for signs of coolant leaks. Fresh antifreeze has a searching action, which will rapidly expose any weak points in the system.

Antifreeze type and mixture

Note: *Do not use engine antifreeze in the windscreen/tailgate washer system, as it will damage the vehicle's paintwork. A screenwash additive should be added to the washer system in its maker's recommended quantities.*

27 If the vehicle's history (and therefore the quality of the antifreeze in it) is unknown, owners are advised to drain and thoroughly reverse-flush the system, before refilling with fresh coolant mixture.

28 If the antifreeze used is to Ford's specification, the levels of protection it affords are indicated in the coolant packaging.

29 To give the recommended *standard* mixture ratio for antifreeze, 50% (by volume) of antifreeze must be mixed with 50% of clean, soft water; if you are using any other type of antifreeze, follow its manufacturer's instructions to achieve the correct ratio.

30 You are unlikely to fully drain the system at any one time (unless the engine is being completely stripped), and the capacities quoted in Specifications are therefore slightly academic for routine coolant renewal. As a guide, only two-thirds of the system's total capacity is likely to be needed for coolant renewal.

31 As the drained system will be partially filled with flushing water, in order to establish the recommended mixture ratio, measure out 50% of the system capacity in antifreeze and pour it into the hose/expansion tank as described above, then top-up with water. Any topping-up while refilling the system should be done with water – for *Weekly checks* use a suitable mixture.

32 Before adding antifreeze, the cooling system should be drained, preferably flushed, and all hoses checked for condition and security. As noted earlier, fresh antifreeze will rapidly find any weaknesses in the system.

33 After filling with antifreeze, a label should be attached to the expansion tank, stating the type and concentration of antifreeze used, and the date installed. Any subsequent topping-up should be made with the same type and concentration of antifreeze.

General cooling system checks

34 The engine should be cold for the cooling system checks, so perform the following procedure before driving the vehicle, or after it has been shut off for at least three hours.

35 Remove the expansion tank filler cap, and clean it thoroughly inside and out with a rag. Also clean the filler neck on the expansion tank. The presence of rust or corrosion in the filler neck indicates that the coolant should be changed. The coolant inside the expansion tank should be relatively clean and transparent. If it is rust-coloured, drain and flush the system, and refill with a fresh coolant mixture.

36 Carefully check the radiator hoses and heater hoses along their entire length; renew any hose which is cracked, swollen or deteriorated.

37 Inspect all other cooling system components (joint faces, etc) for leaks. A leak in the cooling system will usually show up as white- or antifreeze-coloured deposits on the area adjoining the leak. Where any problems of this nature are found on system components, renew the component or gasket with reference to Chapter 3.

38 Clean the front of the radiator with a soft brush to remove all insects, leaves, etc, embedded in the radiator fins. Be careful not to damage the radiator fins, or cut your fingers on them. To do a more thorough job, remove the radiator grille as described in Chapter 11.

Airlocks

39 If, after draining and refilling the system, symptoms of overheating are found which did not occur previously, then the fault is almost certainly due to trapped air at some point in the system, causing an airlock and restricting the flow of coolant; usually, the air is trapped because the system was refilled too quickly.

40 If an airlock is suspected, first try gently squeezing all visible coolant hoses. A coolant hose which is full of air feels quite different to one full of coolant when squeezed. After refilling the system, most airlocks will clear once the system has cooled, and been topped-up.

41 While the engine is running at operating temperature, switch on the heater and heater fan, and check for heat output. Provided there is sufficient coolant in the system, lack of heat output could be due to an airlock in the system.

42 Airlocks can have more serious effects than simply reducing heater output – a severe airlock could reduce coolant flow around the engine. Check that the radiator top hose is hot when the engine is at operating temperature – a top hose which stays cold could be the result of an airlock (or a non-opening thermostat).

43 If the problem persists, stop the engine and allow it to cool down **completely**, before unscrewing the expansion tank filler cap or loosening the hose clips and squeezing the hoses to bleed out the trapped air. In the worst case, the system will have to be at least partially drained (this time, the coolant can be saved for re-use) and flushed to clear the problem. If all else fails, have the system evacuated and vacuum-filled by a suitably-equipped garage.

Expansion tank pressure cap check

44 Wait until the engine is completely cold – perform this check before the engine is started for the first time in the day.

45 Place a wad of cloth over the expansion tank cap, then unscrew it slowly and remove it.

46 Examine the condition of the rubber seal on the underside of the cap. If the rubber appears to have hardened, or cracks are visible in the seal edges, a new cap should be fitted.

47 If the car is several years old, or has covered a large mileage, consider renewing the cap regardless of its apparent condition – they are not expensive. If the pressure relief valve built into the cap fails, excess pressure in the system will lead to puzzling failures of hoses and other cooling system components.

Notes

Chapter 1 Part B
Routine maintenance & servicing – diesel models

Contents

	Section number		Section number
Air filter element renewal	19	General information	1
Auxiliary drivebelt check	4	Handbrake check and adjustment	17
Auxiliary drivebelt renewal	23	Hinge and lock lubrication	13
Brake fluid renewal	24	Lights and horn operation check	4
Brake pads, shoes and discs check	8	Manual transmission oil level check	27
Coolant renewal	26	Pollen filter renewal	16
Coolant strength check	17	Regular maintenance	2
Driveshaft rubber gaiter and joint check	11	Remote control battery renewal	25
Engine compartment wiring check	6	Road test	15
Engine oil and filter renewal	3	Roadwheel nut tightness check	14
Exhaust particulate filter additive tank refilling	20	Seat belt check	7
Exhaust particulate filter renewal	22	Steering, suspension and roadwheel check	10
Exhaust system check	9	Timing belt renewal	21
Fuel filter water draining and renewal	18	Underbody and hose/pipe check	12

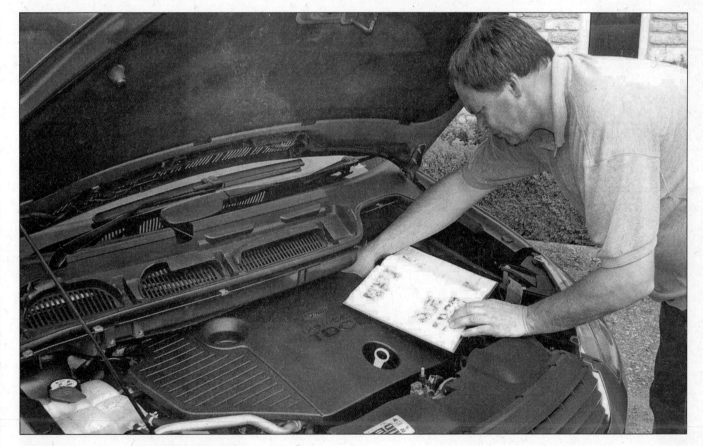

Degrees of difficulty

| **Easy,** suitable for novice with little experience | | **Fairly easy,** suitable for beginner with some experience | | **Fairly difficult,** suitable for competent DIY mechanic | | **Difficult,** suitable for experienced DIY mechanic | | **Very difficult,** suitable for expert DIY or professional | 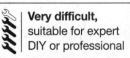 |

Lubricants and fluids . . . . Refer to end of *Weekly checks* on page 0•16

Capacities

Engine oil (including filter)
1.6 litre engines . . . . 3.8 litres
1.8 litre engines . . . . 5.6 litres
2.0 litre engines . . . . 5.5 litres

Cooling system (approximate)
1.6 litre engines . . . . 7.3 litres
1.8 litre engines . . . . 8.1 litres
2.0 litre engines . . . . 8.4 litres

Washer fluid reservoir
All models . . . . 3.3 litres

Fuel tank
All models . . . . 53.0 litres

Cooling system

Antifreeze mixture:
50% antifreeze . . . . Protection down to –37°C
55% antifreeze . . . . Protection down to –45°C
Note: *Refer to antifreeze manufacturer for latest recommendations.*

Brakes

Friction material minimum thickness:
Brake pads . . . . 1.5 mm
Brake shoes . . . . 1.0 mm

Torque wrench settings

	Nm	lbf ft
Engine oil drain plug:		
1.6 litre engines	34	25
1.8 litre engines	36	27
2.0 litre engines	34	25
Engine oil filter housing cap:		
1.6 and 2.0 litre engines	24	18
1.8 litre engines	Not applicable	
Roadwheel nuts	130	96

The maintenance intervals in this manual are provided with the assumption that you, not the dealer, will be carrying out the work. These are the minimum maintenance intervals recommended by us for vehicles driven daily. If you wish to keep your vehicle in peak condition at all times, you may wish to perform some of these procedures more often. We encourage frequent maintenance, because it enhances the efficiency, performance and resale value of your vehicle.

If the vehicle is driven in dusty areas, used to tow a trailer, or driven frequently at slow speeds (idling in traffic) or on short journeys, more frequent maintenance intervals are recommended.

When the vehicle is new, it should be serviced by a dealer service department (or other workshop recognised by the vehicle manufacturer as providing the same standard of service) in order to preserve the warranty. The vehicle manufacturer may reject warranty claims if you are unable to prove that servicing has been carried out as and when specified, using only original equipment parts or parts certified to be of equivalent quality.

Every 250 miles or weekly

☐ Refer to *Weekly checks*

Every 6000 miles or 6 months, whichever comes first

☐ Renew the engine oil and filter (Section 3)

Note: *Ford recommend that the engine oil and filter are changed every 12 500 miles or 12 months. However, oil and filter changes are good for the engine and we recommend that the oil and filter are renewed more frequently, especially if the vehicle is used on a lot of short journeys.*

Every 12 500 miles or 12 months, whichever comes first

In addition to the items listed above, carry out the following:
☐ Check the condition of the auxiliary drivebelt (Section 4)
☐ Check the operation of the lights and the horn (Section 5)
☐ Check under the bonnet for fluid leaks and hose condition (Section 5)
☐ Check the condition of the engine compartment wiring (Section 6)
☐ Check the condition of the seat belts (Section 7)
☐ Check the condition of the brake pads, shoes and discs (Section 8)
☐ Check the exhaust system (Section 9)
☐ Check the steering and suspension components for condition and security (Section 10)
☐ Check the condition of the driveshaft joints and gaiters (Section 11)
☐ Check the underbody and all pipes/hoses (Section 12)
☐ Lubricate all hinges and locks (Section 13)
☐ Check roadwheel nut tightness (Section 14)
☐ Carry out a road test (Section 15)
☐ Renew the pollen filter (Section 16)

Note: *If the vehicle is used in dusty conditions, the pollen filter should be renewed more frequently.*
☐ Check the antifreeze/inhibitor strength (Section 17)

Every 37 500 miles or 3 years, whichever comes first

In addition to the items listed above, carry out the following:
☐ Renew the fuel filter (Section 18)
☐ Renew the air filter (Section 19)

Note: *If the vehicle is used in dusty conditions, the air filter should be renewed more frequently.*
☐ Refill the exhaust particulate filter additive tank (Section 20)

Every 62 500 miles or 5 years, whichever comes first

☐ Renew the timing belt and tensioner (Section 21)

Note: *The Ford interval for belt renewal is actually at a much higher mileage than this (consult your dealer for the intervals). It is strongly recommended, however, that the interval is reduced, particularly on vehicles which are subjected to intensive use, ie, mainly short journeys or a lot of stop-start driving. The actual belt renewal interval is therefore very much up to the individual owner, but bear in mind that severe engine damage will result if the belt breaks.*

Every 75 000 miles

☐ Renew the exhaust particulate filter (Section 22)

Every 100 000 miles or 8 years, whichever comes first

☐ Renew the auxiliary belt (Section 23)

Every 2 years, regardless of mileage

☐ Renew the brake fluid (Section 24)
☐ Renew the remote control battery (Section 25)
☐ Renew the coolant (Section 26)

Note: *If Ford pink/red antifreeze is used, the coolant can then be left indefinitely, providing the strength of the mixture is checked every year. If any antifreeze other than Ford's is to be used, the coolant must be renewed at regular intervals to provide an equivalent degree of protection; the conventional recommendation is to renew the coolant every two years.*
☐ Check the manual transmission oil level (Section 27)

Underbonnet view of a 1.8 litre model

1 Engine oil level dipstick
2 Oil filler cap
3 Coolant expansion tank cap
4 Washer fluid reservoir cap
5 Brake/clutch fluid reservoir cap (hidden below windscreen cowl)
6 Air filter element cover
7 Fuel filter
8 Battery cover
9 Fuse/relay box cover

Front underbody view of a 1.8 litre model

1 Engine oil sump drain plug
2 Air conditioning compressor
3 Right-hand driveshaft intermediate bearing
4 Lower control arm
5 Track rod end
6 Front subframe
7 Front brake caliper
8 Starter motor

1 Anti-roll bar
2 Shock absorber
3 Handbrake cable
4 Hub carrier/lateral link
5 Lower control arm
6 Tie rod
7 Fuel tank

Maintenance procedures

1 General information

1 This Chapter is designed to help the home mechanic maintain his/her vehicle for safety, economy, long life and peak performance.
2 The Chapter contains a master maintenance schedule, followed by Sections dealing specifically with each task in the schedule. Visual checks, adjustments, component renewal and other helpful items are included. Refer to the accompanying illustrations of the engine compartment and the underside of the vehicle for the locations of the various components.
3 Servicing your vehicle in accordance with the mileage/time maintenance schedule and the following Sections will provide a planned maintenance programme, which should result in a long and reliable service life. This is a comprehensive plan, so maintaining some items but not others at the specified service intervals will not produce the same results.
4 As you service your vehicle, you will discover that many of the procedures can – and should – be grouped together, because of the particular procedure being performed, or because of the proximity of two otherwise-unrelated components to one another. For example, if the vehicle is raised for any reason, the exhaust can be inspected at the same time as the suspension and steering components.
5 The first step in this maintenance

programme is to prepare yourself before the actual work begins. Read through all the Sections relevant to the work to be carried out, then make a list and gather all the parts and tools required. If a problem is encountered, seek advice from a parts specialist, or a dealer service department.

2 Regular maintenance

1 If, from the time the vehicle is new, the routine maintenance schedule is followed closely, and frequent checks are made of fluid levels and high-wear items, as suggested throughout this manual, the engine will be kept in relatively good running condition, and the need for additional work will be minimised.
2 It is possible that there will be times when the engine is running poorly due to the lack of regular maintenance. This is even more likely if a used vehicle, which has not received regular and frequent maintenance checks, is purchased. In such cases, additional work may need to be carried out, outside of the regular maintenance intervals.
3 If engine wear is suspected, a compression test or leakdown test (refer to the relevant part of Chapter 2) will provide valuable information regarding the overall performance of the main internal components. Such a test can be used as a basis to decide on the extent of the work to be carried out. If, for example,

a compression or leakdown test indicates serious internal engine wear, conventional maintenance as described in this Chapter will not greatly improve the performance of the engine, and may prove a waste of time and money, unless extensive overhaul work is carried out first.
4 The following series of operations are those most often required to improve the performance of a generally poor-running engine:

Primary operations

a) Clean, inspect and test the battery (refer to 'Weekly checks').
b) Check all the engine-related fluids (refer to 'Weekly checks').
c) Check the condition and tension of the auxiliary drivebelt (Section 4).
d) Check the condition of the air filter, and renew if necessary (Section 19).
e) Renew the fuel filter (Section 18).
f) Check the condition of all hoses, and check for fluid leaks (Section 12).

5 If the above operations do not prove fully effective, carry out the following secondary operations:

Secondary operations

All items listed under *Primary operations*, plus the following:
a) Check the charging system (refer to Chapter 5).
b) Check the preheating system (refer to Chapter 5).
c) Check the fuel system (refer to Chapter 4).

3.3 Remove the plastic cover by pulling it upwards starting at the front edge

3.5a The engine oil filter (arrowed) is located at the front, left-hand corner of the cylinder block

3.5b Unscrew the cap and remove it complete with filter element

Every 6000 miles or 6 months

3 Engine oil and filter renewal

1 Frequent oil and filter changes are the most important preventative maintenance procedures which can be undertaken by the DIY owner. As engine oil ages, it becomes diluted and contaminated, which leads to premature engine wear.

2 Before starting this procedure, gather together all the necessary tools and materials. Also make sure that you have plenty of clean rags and newspapers handy, to mop-up any spills. Ideally, the engine oil should be warm, as it will drain more easily, and more built-up sludge will be removed with it. Take care not to touch the exhaust or any other hot parts of the engine when working under the vehicle. To avoid any possibility of scalding, and to protect yourself from possible skin irritants and other harmful contaminants in used engine oils, it is advisable to wear gloves when carrying out this work.

3 Remove the plastic cover on the top of the engine. Pull up the right-hand rear corner and the front edges, then pull the cover forwards to release it **(see illustration)**.

1.6 litre engines

4 Remove the air cleaner assembly as described in Chapter 4.

3.7 The engine oil filter (arrowed) is located on the rear of the cylinder block, above the right-hand driveshaft

3.10b . . . and Torx bolt on the side (arrowed) . . .

3.10a Disconnect the wiring plug, unclip the fuel pipe, then undo the 4 bolts (arrowed) . . .

3.10c Lift up the fuel filter and move it to one side

5 Using a socket on an extension bar undo the oil filter housing cap. Lift the cap up, with the filter element inside it. Discard the filter and the O-ring seal around the circumference of the cap **(see illustrations)**.

1.8 litre engines

6 The canister-type oil filter is located on the rear of the engine block. Firmly apply the handbrake, then jack up the front of the vehicle and support it on axle stands (see *Jacking and vehicle support*). Undo the fasteners and remove the engine undershield (where fitted).

7 Move a container into position under the oil filter, then use an oil filter removal tool if necessary to slacken the filter cartridge initially, then unscrew it by hand the rest of the way **(see illustration)**. Empty the oil from the old filter into the container.

8 Use a clean rag to remove all oil, dirt and sludge from the filter sealing area on the engine.

9 Apply a light coating of clean engine oil to the sealing ring on the new filter, then screw the filter into position on the engine. Tighten the filter firmly by hand only – do not use any tools.

2.0 litre engines

10 Release the wiring harnesses from the cable ties on the fuel filter bracket, then disconnect the filter wiring plug, release the fuel pipe from the clip, undo the 4 bolts and 1 Torx bolt on the side, then lift up the filter with the bracket, and place it to one side **(see illustrations)**.

11 Using a 27 mm socket on an extension bar, undo the oil filter housing cap. Lift the cap up, with the oil filter inside it. Discard the filter and the O-ring around the circumference of the cap **(see illustrations)**.

All engines

12 If not already done so, firmly apply the handbrake, then jack up the front of the vehicle and support it on axle stands (see *Jacking and vehicle support*). Unscrew the fasteners and remove the plastic undershield below the engine **(see illustration)**.

3.11a Undo the oil filter cap (arrowed) . . .

3.11b . . . then lift up the cap with the filter element . . .

3.11c . . . pull the element from the cap . . .

3.11d . . . and discard the O-ring seal

3.12 Undo the fasteners (arrowed) and remove the engine undershield

3.13a Engine oil sump drain plug (arrowed) – 1.6 litre engine . . .

13 Using a spanner, socket or Allen key as applicable, slacken the drain plug about half a turn **(see illustrations)**. Position the draining container under the drain plug, then remove the plug completely **(see Haynes Hint)**.

14 Allow some time for the oil to drain, noting that it may be necessary to reposition the container as the oil flow slows to a trickle.

15 After all the oil has drained, wipe the drain plug and the sealing washer (where fitted) with a clean rag. Examine the condition of the sealing washer, and renew it if it shows signs of scoring or other damage which may prevent an oil-tight seal (it is generally considered good practice to fit a new washer every time). Clean the area around the drain plug opening, and refit the plug complete with the washer and tighten it to the specified torque **(see illustration)**.

16 Remove the old oil and all tools from under the vehicle, refit the undershield, then lower the vehicle to the ground.

1.6 litre engines

17 Ensure the oil filter housing and cap are clean, then fit a new O-ring seal to the cap.

18 Fit the new filter element into the cap, then fit the cap to the housing and tighten it to the specified torque.

2.0 litre engines

19 Ensure the oil filter housing and cap are clean, then fit a new O-ring seal to the cap.

20 Fit the new filter element into the cap, then fit the cap to the housing and tighten it to the specified torque.

21 Position the fuel filter and bracket, then refit the retaining bolts and tighten them securely. Refit the pipe into the clip, reconnect the wiring plug and secure the wiring harnesses to the bracket.

3.13b . . . 1.8 litre engine (arrowed) . . .

All engines

22 With the car on level ground, fill the engine, using the correct grade and type of oil (refer to *Weekly checks* for details of topping-up). An oil can spout or funnel may help to reduce

3.13c . . . and 2.0 litre engine (arrowed)

HAYNES HINT

As the drain plug releases from the threads, move it away sharply so the stream of oil issuing from the sump runs into the container, not up your sleeve.

3.15 Renew the sump plug sealing washer

spillage. Pour in half the specified quantity of oil first, then wait a few minutes for the oil to run to the sump.

23 Continue adding oil a small quantity at a time until the level is up to the MIN mark on the dipstick. Adding around 1.0 litre of oil will now bring the level up to the MAX on the dipstick – do not worry if a little too much goes in, as some of the excess will be taken up in filling the oil filter. Refit the dipstick and the filler cap.

24 Start the engine and run it for a few minutes, while checking for leaks around the oil filter seal and the sump drain plug. Note that there may be a delay of a few seconds before the low oil pressure warning light goes out when the engine is first started, as the oil circulates through the new oil filter and the engine oil galleries before the pressure builds-up.

25 Stop the engine, and wait a few minutes for the oil to settle in the sump once more.

With the new oil circulated and the filter now completely full, recheck the level on the dipstick, and add more oil as necessary.

26 Dispose of the used engine oil and the old oil filter safely, with reference to *General repair procedures* in the *Reference* section of this manual. Many local recycling points have containers for waste oil with oil filter disposal receptacles alongside.

Every 12 500 miles or 12 months

4 Auxiliary drivebelt check

1 A single auxiliary drivebelt is fitted at the right-hand side of the engine. An automatic adjuster is fitted, so checking the drivebelt tension is unnecessary.

2 Due to their function and material make-up, drivebelts are prone to failure after a long period of time, and should therefore be inspected regularly.

3 Since the drivebelt is located very close to the right-hand side of the engine compartment, it is possible to gain better access by raising the front of the vehicle, undoing the fasteners and removing the engine undershield **(see illustration 3.12)**.

4 With the engine stopped, inspect the full length of the drivebelt for cracks and separation of the belt plies. It will be necessary to turn the engine (using a spanner or socket and bar on the crankshaft pulley bolt) in order to move the belt from the pulleys so that the belt can be inspected thoroughly. Twist the belt between the pulleys so that both sides can be viewed. Also check for fraying, and glazing which gives the belt a shiny appearance. Check the pulleys for nicks, cracks, distortion and corrosion.

5 Note that it is not unusual for a ribbed belt to exhibit small cracks in the edges of the belt ribs, and unless these are extensive or very deep, belt renewal is not essential.

5 Lights and horn operation check

1 Refer to Chapter 1A, Section 5.

6 Engine compartment wiring check

1 Refer to Chapter 1A, Section 6.

7 Seat belt check

1 Refer to Chapter 1A, Section 16.

8 Brake pads, shoes and discs check

1 Refer to Chapter 1A, Section 7.

9 Exhaust system check

1 Refer to Chapter 1A, Section 8.

10 Steering, suspension and roadwheel check

1 Refer to Chapter 1A, Section 9.

11 Driveshaft rubber gaiter and joint check

1 Refer to Chapter 1A, Section 10.

12 Underbody and hose/pipe check

1 Refer to Chapter 1A, Section 11.

2 In addition, it is not unusual for a high-mileage diesel engine to exhibit a 'film'

of diesel fuel around the injectors, resulting in an oily appearance. Unless there is clear evidence of a significant fuel leak, this is not normally a matter for concern. The best course of action would be to first clean the engine thoroughly; then, after several more miles have been covered, the source of the leak can be identified and its severity assessed.

13 Hinge and lock lubrication

1 Refer to Chapter 1A, Section 12.

14 Roadwheel nut tightness check

1 Refer to Chapter 1A, Section 13.

15 Road test

1 Refer to Chapter 1A, Section 14.

16 Pollen filter renewal

1 Refer to Chapter 1A, Section 15.

17 Coolant strength check

1 Refer to Chapter 1A, Section 17.

18.3a Water draining nipple –
1.8 litre models . . .

18.3b . . . and 2.0 litre models (arrowed)

18.4a Slacken the bleed screw (arrowed) –
1.6 litre models . . .

18.4b . . . 1.8 litre models (arrowed) . . .

18.4c . . . and 2.0 litre models (arrowed)

18.7 Disconnect the sensor wiring plug

Every 37 500 miles or 3 years

18 Fuel filter water draining and renewal

Water draining

1 The fuel filter is located at the front of the engine compartment on 2.0 litre models, and at the left-hand end of the cylinder head on 1.6 and 1.8 litre models. Remove the plastic cover on the top of the engine (where fitted).
2 To improve access on 1.8 litre models, remove the air filter assembly as described in Chapter 4.
3 Position a container or cloth beneath the filter, then attach a length of plastic/rubber hose to the drain nipple, with the other end of the hose in a container (see illustrations).
4 Slacken the drain nipple and the top bleed screw a few turns, and allow the fuel to drain until it appears clean and free from water droplets. Tighten the bleed screw and drain nipple (see illustrations). Note that the bleed screw on the top of the filter on 1.6 litre models controls the flow through the drain nipple on its underside.
5 Remove the hose, and bleed the fuel system as described in Chapter 4.

Filter renewal

6 Proceed as described in paragraphs 1 and 2 of this Section.

1.6 litre engine

7 Disconnect the wiring plug from the water sensor on the top of the filter (see illustration).
8 Undo the bolts and remove the metal shield around the filter assembly (see illustration).
9 Disconnect the fuel supply and return pipes from the filter (see illustration). Plug the openings to prevent contamination.
10 Disconnect the fuel heater wiring plug from the side of the filter (where fitted).
11 Slide the filter assembly upwards from the bracket (see illustration).
12 Slide the new filter into the bracket.
13 Reconnect the fuel supply and return pipes.
14 The remainder of fitting is a reversal of removal. Bleed the fuel system as described in Chapter 4.

18.8 Undo the bolts and remove the metal shield

18.9 Depress the release buttons and disconnect the fuel pipes from the filter

18.11 Slide the fuel filter up from place

18.15 Undo the bolts (arrowed) and remove the metal shield

18.17a Depress the release button and disconnect the fuel supply pipe

18.17b Prise out the locking catch (1), push in or pull out the clip (2), and disconnect the fuel return pipe

18.19a Unscrew the collar . . .

18.19b . . . then lift the cover and element from the filter housing

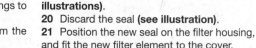

18.20 Renew the seal

1.8 litre engine

15 Undo the bolts and remove the metal shield over the top of the filter (see illustration).
16 Disconnect the wiring plug from the side of the filter housing.

18.22 Ensure the arrows align (arrowed)

18.27 Unscrew the filter head

17 Disconnect the fuel supply and return pipes (see illustrations). Plug the openings to prevent contamination.
18 Slide the filter housing upwards from the mounting bracket.
19 Unscrew the collar and lift the filter

18.26 Depress the release buttons and disconnect the fuel hoses from the filter head

18.29 Renew the filter element and the O-ring seal

cover and element from the housing (see illustrations).
20 Discard the seal (see illustration).
21 Position the new seal on the filter housing, and fit the new filter element to the cover.
22 Fit the new element and cover to the housing, ensuring the alignment arrows are aligned correctly (see illustration). Tighten the collar securely.
23 Refit the filter housing to the bracket, and reconnect the pipes/wiring plug.
24 The remainder of refitting is a reversal of removal. Bleed the fuel system as described in Chapter 4.

2.0 litre engine

25 Release the wiring harnesses from the cable ties on the fuel filter bracket, then disconnect the filter wiring plug, release the fuel pipe from the clip, undo the bolts, then remove the bracket (see illustrations 3.10a and 3.10b).
26 Depress the locking tabs and disconnect the fuel hoses from the filter head (see illustration). Be prepared for fuel spillage. Use the plugs supplied in the filter kit to seal the hose openings.
27 Unscrew the filter head using a 27 mm socket or spanner, and lift it from place (see illustration).
28 Remove the filter element, and discard the O-ring seal.
29 Fit the new filter element and O-ring seal to the filter head (see illustration), then position the filter head and tighten it by rotating it clockwise until the stop on the filter housing abuts the stop on the filter head.

19.3 Slacken the clamp (arrowed) securing the air outlet hose to the filter cover

19.4a Filter cover bolts (arrowed) – 1.6 litre models . . .

19.4b . . . 1.8 litre models (arrowed) . . .

19.4c . . . and 2.0 litre models (arrowed)

19.5a Lift the element from place – 1.6 litre models . . .

19.5b . . . 1.8 and 2.0 litre models

30 The remainder of refitting is a reversal of removal, but bleed the fuel system as described in Chapter 4.

19 Air filter element renewal

Caution: Never drive the vehicle with the air cleaner filter element removed. Excessive engine wear could result, and backfiring could even cause a fire under the bonnet.

1 The air filter element is located in the air cleaner assembly on the left-hand side of the engine compartment.

2 Remove the plastic cover (where fitted) from the top of the engine.

3 On 1.8 and 2.0 litre models, disconnect the wiring plug from the mass airflow meter, and slacken the clamp securing the air outlet hose to the filter cover **(see illustration)**.

4 Undo the bolts, and lift the filter cover from place **(see illustrations)**.

5 Note which way round it's fitted, then lift the air filter element from the housing **(see illustrations)**

6 Wipe clean the inner surfaces of the cover and main housing, then locate the new element in the housing, making sure that the sealing lip is correctly engaged with the edge of the housing.

7 Refit the filter cover and tighten the bolts securely.

8 Reconnect the outlet hose and the wiring plug where applicable. Tighten the hose clamp securely, then refit the plastic cover over the engine.

20 Exhaust particulate filter additive tank refilling

Note: An exhaust particulate filter is only fitted to some 1.6 and 2.0 litre models.

Note: Although refilling the additive tank is straightforward, after topping it up the tank level counter in the control module must be reset in order for the system to function correctly. If the MIL (Malfunction Indicator Lamp) or PCL (Powertrain Control Light) are lit because of an empty or low fluid level in the additive tank, then system can only be reset with Ford test equipment. If you do not have access to this equipment, entrust this task to a Ford dealer or suitably-equipped specialist. If the MIL or PCL is not lit, then the system can be manually reset as described below.

1 Chock the front wheels, raise the rear of the vehicle and support it securely on axle stands (see *Jacking and vehicle support*). Remove the right-hand rear wheel.

Caution: Do not allow the additive to come into contact with skin, eyes or vehicle paintwork.

2 Release the locking tang and remove the additive tank overflow pipe quick-release coupling blanking plug.

3 Fit the fuel additive refill kit overflow pipe – follow the manufacturer's information supplied with the kit.

4 Release the locking tang and remove the additive tank filler pipe quick-release coupling blanking cap **(see illustration)**.

5 Ensure the filling kit additive container valve is in the closed position, then connect the filling kit filler pipe to the tank filler pipe.

6 Attach the fuel additive tank filling kit hook, net and overflow container to the underside of the vehicle, then insert the additive tank overflow pipe into the container.

7 Using a transmission jack or suitable platform, with the refilling container in the horizontal position, raise the container until it's higher than the additive tank. Open the container valve until additive can be seen emerging from the overflow pipe, then close the valve.

8 Lower the filling container, and open the valve to allow the additive in the pipe to return to the container.

9 Disconnect the pipes, refit the blanking plugs/caps, refit the roadwheel and lower the vehicle to the ground.

10 With reference to the note at the beginning of this Section, the system must now be reset.

J46787

20.4 Remove the additive tank filler pipe coupling blanking plug (arrowed)

Resetting

11 Ensure the ignition switch is in position 0, and the fuel filler flap is closed. The following procedure must be completed within 60 seconds of the ignition switch being turned to position II:

Turn the ignition switch to position II.
Open and close the fuel filler flap.
Open and close the fuel filler flap.
Turn the ignition switch to position 0.
Turn the ignition switch to position II.

12 The following sequence must be started within 60 seconds of the ignition switch being turned to position II in the last paragraph, and must be completed within 10 seconds after the fuel filler flap being opened as described in this paragraph:

Open and close the fuel filler flap.
Open and close the fuel filler flap.
Open and close the fuel filler flap.

13 The following sequence must be started within 15 to 30 seconds after the fuel filler flap has be closed as described in the last paragraph, and completed within 10 seconds after the fuel filler flap has been opened as described in this paragraph:

Open and close the fuel filler flap.
Open and close the fuel filler flap.
Open and close the fuel filler flap.

14 The following must be carried out within 60 seconds of the fuel filler flap being closed as described in the last paragraph. Ensure the vehicle is in neutral:

Start the engine and allow it to idle for a minimum of 20 seconds.
After approximately 25 seconds the MIL or PCL should illuminate to indicate that resetting has been achieved.
Turn the ignition to position 0.
Turn the ignition to position II.
Neither the MIL or PCL light should now be illuminated.

15 If either the MIL or PCL are illuminated, repeat the procedure.

Every 62 500 miles or 5 years

21 Timing belt renewal

The procedure is described in the relevant part of Chapter 2.

Every 75 000 miles

22 Exhaust particulate filter renewal

Note: *An exhaust particulate filter is only fitted to some 1.6 and 2.0 litre models.*
1 The renewal of the particulate filter is described with the exhaust/catalytic converter renewal procedure – refer to Chapter 4.

Every 100 000 miles or 8 years

23 Auxiliary drivebelt renewal

1 To remove the drivebelt, first raise the front of the vehicle and support on axle stands (see *Jacking and vehicle support*). Undo the fasteners and remove the engine undershield (see illustration 3.12) and then remove the wheel arch liner.
2 Remove the plastic cover on the top of the engine (where fitted).

1.6 litre engines

3 Ford technicians use tool No 303-676 to rotate the belt tensioner. However, if the tool is not available, use a 15 mm spanner to rotate the tensioner, while an assistant lifts the belt from the pulleys (see illustration).
4 Fit the tool or spanner to the tensioner arm and rotate the tensioner clockwise until the tensioner arm passes the hose in the housing, and a 5.0 mm drill bit can be inserted, locking the tensioner in position (see illustration).
5 Note how the belt is routed, then remove the belt from the pulleys (see illustrations).

23.3 Use a 15 mm open-ended spanner to rotate the tensioner clockwise

23.4 Insert a 5.0 mm drill bit/rod into the hole (arrowed) in the tensioner housing

**23.5a Auxiliary belt routing –
1.6 litre without air conditioning**

1 Alternator pulley	3 Crankshaft pulley
2 Idler pulley	4 Tensioner

**23.5b Auxiliary belt routing –
1.6 litre with air conditioning**

1 Alternator pulley	3 Crankshaft pulley
2 Air conditioning compressor	4 Tensioner

6 Fit the new drivebelt onto the crankshaft, air conditioning compressor (where fitted), alternator and tensioner/idler pulleys. Fit the tool to the tensioner arm, hold the tensioner stationary with the tool and remove the locking drill bit. Slowly allow the tensioner arm to rotate and tension the belt. Remove the tool.

1.8 litre engines

7 Insert an M8 bolt, approximately 25 mm long into the bracket alongside the tensioner, and continue screwing in the bolt until the tension on the belt is relieved **(see illustrations)**.
8 Note how the belt is routed, then remove the belt from the pulleys **(see illustration 23.7a or 23.7b)**.

9 Fit the new belt to the pulleys, ensuring they are correctly seated in the pulley grooves.
10 Unscrew the bolt from the bracket and allow the tensioner to tension the belt.

2.0 litre engines

11 Using a spanner on the tensioner centre

**23.7a Insert the 8 x 25 mm bolt into the bracket (arrowed)
alongside the tensioner – 1.8 litre with air conditioning . . .**

23.7b . . . and without air conditioning

23.11 Rotate the tensioner bolt anti-clockwise, then insert a 5 mm drill bit/rod through the locking holes once they align (arrowed)

23.12 Auxiliary drivebelt routing – 2.0 litre models

1 Crankshaft pulley	3 Alternator
2 Air conditioning compressor	4 Tensioner

bolt, turn the tensioner anti-clockwise to release the drivebelt tension, then insert a 5 mm drill bit or rod through the holes in the arm/body when they align to lock the tensioner in this position **(see illustration)**.

12 Note how the drivebelt is routed, then remove the belt from the pulleys **(see illustration)**.

13 Fit the new drivebelt onto the crankshaft, air conditioning compressor, alternator, and tensioner pulleys. Use a spanner to hold the tensioner arm, then remove the locking drill bit/rod, and allow the tensioner to rotate clockwise and gently tension the belt.

All engines

14 Refit the engine top cover and undershield, then lower the car to the ground.

Every 2 years, regardless of mileage

24 Brake fluid renewal

1 Refer to Chapter 1A, Section 24.

25 Remote control battery renewal

1 Refer to Chapter 1A, Section 25.

26 Coolant renewal

⚠ *Warning: Do not allow antifreeze to come in contact with your skin or painted surfaces of the vehicle. Flush contaminated areas immediately with plenty of water. Don't store new coolant, or leave old coolant lying around, where it's accessible to children or pets – they're attracted by its sweet smell. Ingestion of even a small amount of coolant can be fatal. Wipe up garage-floor and drip-pan spills immediately. Keep antifreeze containers covered, and repair cooling system leaks as soon as they're noticed.*

⚠ *Warning: Never remove the expansion tank filler cap when the engine is running, or has just been switched off, as the cooling*

system will be hot, and the consequent escaping steam and scalding coolant could cause serious injury.

⚠ *Warning: Wait until the engine is cold before starting these procedures.*

Note: *If Ford pink/red antifreeze is used, the coolant can then be left indefinitely, providing the strength of the mixture is checked every year. If any antifreeze other than Ford's is to be used, the coolant must be renewed at regular intervals to provide an equivalent degree of protection; the conventional recommendation is to renew the coolant every two years.*

Coolant draining

1 To drain the system, first remove the expansion tank filler cap.

2 If the additional working clearance is required, raise the front of the vehicle and

26.4 Undo the coolant drain plug at the left-hand lower corner of the radiator

support it securely on axle stands (see *Jacking and vehicle support*).

3 Undo the fasteners **(see illustration 3.12)** and remove the engine undershield.

4 Place a large drain tray underneath, and unscrew the radiator drain plug **(see illustration)**; direct as much of the escaping coolant as possible into the tray.

5 Once the coolant has stopped draining from the radiator, close the drain plug.

System flushing

6 With time, the cooling system may gradually lose its efficiency, as the radiator core becomes choked with rust, scale deposits from the water, and other sediment. To minimise this, as well as using only good-quality antifreeze and clean soft water, the system should be flushed as follows whenever any part of it is disturbed, and/or when the coolant is renewed.

7 With the coolant drained, refit the drain plug and refill the system with fresh water. Refit the expansion tank filler cap, start the engine and warm it up to normal operating temperature, then stop it and (after allowing it to cool down completely) drain the system again. Repeat as necessary until only clean water can be seen to emerge, then refill finally with the specified coolant mixture.

8 If only clean, soft water and good-quality antifreeze (even if not to Ford's specification) has been used, and the coolant has been renewed at the suggested intervals, the above procedure will be sufficient to keep the system clean for a considerable length of time. If, however, the system has been neglected, a more thorough operation will be required, as follows.

9 First drain the coolant, then disconnect the radiator top and bottom hoses. Insert a garden hose into the radiator top hose connection, and allow water to circulate through the radiator until it runs clean from the bottom outlet.

10 To flush the engine, insert the garden hose into the radiator bottom hose, wrap a piece of rag around the garden hose to seal the connection, and allow water to circulate until it runs clear.

11 Try the effect of repeating this procedure in the top hose, although this may not be effective, since the thermostat will probably close and prevent the flow of water.

12 In severe cases of contamination, reverse-flushing of the radiator may be necessary. This may be achieved by inserting the garden hose into the bottom outlet, wrapping a piece of rag around the hose to seal the connection, then flushing the radiator until clear water emerges from the top hose outlet.

13 If the radiator is suspected of being severely choked, remove the radiator (Chapter 3), turn it upside-down, and repeat the procedure described in paragraph 12.

14 Flushing the heater matrix can be achieved using a similar procedure to that described in paragraph 12, once the heater intake and outlet hoses have been identified. These two hoses will be of the same diameter, and pass through the engine compartment bulkhead (refer to the heater matrix removal procedure in Chapter 3 for more details).

15 The use of chemical cleaners is not recommended, and should be necessary only as a last resort; the scouring action of some chemical cleaners may lead to other cooling system problems. Normally, regular renewal of the coolant will prevent excessive contamination of the system.

Coolant filling

16 With the cooling system drained and flushed, ensure that all disturbed hose unions are correctly secured, and that the radiator/engine drain plug(s) is securely tightened. Refit the engine undershield. If it was raised, lower the vehicle to the ground.

17 Prepare a sufficient quantity of the specified coolant mixture (see below); allow for a surplus, so as to have a reserve supply for topping-up.

18 On 1.8 and 2.0 litre models, slacken the bleed screw located on the EGR cooler hose at the rear of the engine **(see illustration)**.

19 Slowly fill the system through the expansion tank. Since the tank is the highest point in the system, all the air in the system should be displaced into the tank by the rising liquid. Slow pouring reduces the possibility of air being trapped and forming airlocks.

20 As soon as a steady stream of bubble-free coolant emerges from the bleed screw on the EGR hose, tighten the screw.

21 Continue filling until the coolant level reaches the expansion tank MAX level line (see *Weekly checks*), then cover the filler opening to prevent coolant splashing out.

22 Start the engine and run it at idle speed, until it has warmed-up to normal operating temperature and the radiator electric cooling fan has cut in; watch the temperature gauge to check for signs of overheating. If the level in the expansion tank drops significantly, top-up to the MAX level line to minimise the amount of air circulating in the system.

23 Stop the engine, wash off any spilt coolant from the engine compartment and bodywork, then leave the car to cool down *completely* (overnight, if possible).

24 With the system cool, uncover the expansion tank filler opening, and top-up the tank to the MAX level line. Refit the filler cap, tightening it securely, and clean up any further spillage.

25 After refilling, always check carefully all components of the system (but especially any unions disturbed during draining and flushing) for signs of coolant leaks. Fresh antifreeze has a searching action, which will rapidly expose any weak points in the system.

Antifreeze type and mixture

Note: *Do not use engine antifreeze in the windscreen/tailgate washer system, as it will damage the vehicle's paintwork. A screenwash additive should be added to the washer system in its maker's recommended quantities.*

26 If the vehicle's history (and therefore the quality of the antifreeze in it) is unknown, owners are advised to drain and thoroughly reverse-flush the system, before refilling with fresh coolant mixture.

27 If the antifreeze used is to Ford's specification, the levels of protection it affords are indicated in the coolant packaging.

28 To give the recommended *standard* mixture ratio for antifreeze, 50% (by volume) of antifreeze must be mixed with 50% of clean, soft water; if you are using any other type of antifreeze, follow its manufacturer's instructions to achieve the correct ratio.

29 You are unlikely to fully drain the system at any one time (unless the engine is being completely stripped), and the capacities quoted in Specifications are therefore slightly academic for routine coolant renewal. As a guide, only two-thirds of the system's total capacity is likely to be needed for coolant renewal.

30 As the drained system will be partially filled with flushing water, in order to establish the recommended mixture ratio, measure out 50% of the system capacity in antifreeze and pour it into the expansion tank as described above, then top-up with water. Any topping-up while refilling the system should be done with water – for *Weekly checks* use a suitable mixture.

31 Before adding antifreeze, the cooling system should be drained, preferably flushed, and all hoses checked for condition and

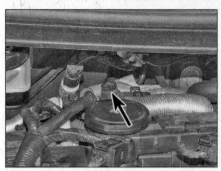

26.18 Slacken the bleed screw (arrowed) on the EGR cooler hose

security. As noted earlier, fresh antifreeze will rapidly find any weaknesses in the system.

32 After filling with antifreeze, a label should be attached to the expansion tank, stating the type and concentration of antifreeze used, and the date installed. Any subsequent topping-up should be made with the same type and concentration of antifreeze.

General cooling system checks

33 The engine should be cold for the cooling system checks, so perform the following procedure before driving the vehicle, or after it has been shut off for at least three hours.

34 Remove the expansion tank filler cap, and clean it thoroughly inside and out with a rag. Also clean the filler neck on the expansion tank. The presence of rust or corrosion in the filler neck indicates that the coolant should be changed. The coolant inside the expansion tank should be relatively clean and transparent. If it is rust-coloured, drain and flush the system, and refill with a fresh coolant mixture.

35 Carefully check the radiator hoses and heater hoses along their entire length; renew any hose which is cracked, swollen or deteriorated (see Section 5).

36 Inspect all other cooling system components (joint faces, etc) for leaks. A leak in the cooling system will usually show up as white- or antifreeze-coloured deposits on the area adjoining the leak **(see Haynes Hint)**.

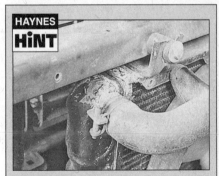

A leak in the cooling system will usually show up as white- or antifreeze-coloured deposits on the area adjoining the leak.

Where any problems of this nature are found on system components, renew the component or gasket with reference to Chapter 3.

37 Clean the front of the radiator with a soft brush to remove all insects, leaves, etc, embedded in the radiator fins. Be careful not to damage the radiator fins, or cut your fingers on them. To do a more thorough job, remove the radiator grille as described in Chapter 11.

Airlocks

38 If, after draining and refilling the system, symptoms of overheating are found which did not occur previously, then the fault is almost certainly due to trapped air at some point in the system, causing an airlock and restricting the flow of coolant; usually, the air is trapped because the system was refilled too quickly.

39 If an airlock is suspected, first try gently squeezing all visible coolant hoses. A coolant hose which is full of air feels quite different to one full of coolant when squeezed. After refilling the system, most airlocks will clear once the system has cooled, and been topped-up.

40 While the engine is running at operating temperature, switch on the heater and heater fan, and check for heat output. Provided there is sufficient coolant in the system, lack of heat output could be due to an airlock in the system.

41 Airlocks can have more serious effects than simply reducing heater output – a severe airlock could reduce coolant flow around the engine. Check that the radiator top hose is hot when the engine is at operating temperature – a top hose which stays cold could be the result of an airlock (or a non-opening thermostat).

42 If the problem persists, stop the engine and allow it to cool down **completely** before unscrewing the expansion tank filler cap or loosening the hose clips and squeezing the hoses to bleed out the trapped air. In the worst case, the system will have to be at least partially drained (this time, the coolant can be saved for re-use) and flushed to clear the problem. If all else fails, have the system evacuated and vacuum filled by a suitably-equipped garage.

Expansion tank pressure cap check

43 Wait until the engine is completely cold – perform this check before the engine is started for the first time in the day.

44 Place a wad of cloth over the expansion tank cap, then unscrew it slowly and remove it.

45 Examine the condition of the rubber seal on the underside of the cap. If the rubber appears to have hardened, or cracks are visible in the seal edges, a new cap should be fitted.

46 If the car is several years old, or has covered a large mileage, consider renewing the cap regardless of its apparent condition – they are not expensive. If the pressure relief valve built into the cap fails, excess pressure in the system will lead to puzzling failures of hoses and other cooling system components.

27 Manual transmission oil level check

1 Refer to Chapter 1A, Section 23.

Chapter 2 Part A:
1.6 litre petrol engine in-car repair procedures

Contents

	Section number
Camshaft oil seals – renewal	10
Camshafts and tappets – removal, inspection and refitting	11
Compression test – description and interpretation	2
Crankshaft oil seals – renewal	16
Crankshaft pulley/vibration damper – removal and refitting	6
Cylinder head – removal, inspection and refitting	12
Cylinder head cover – removal and refitting	4
Engine/transmission mountings – inspection and renewal	18
Flywheel/driveplate – removal, inspection and refitting	17
General information	1

	Section number
Oil pressure switch – removal and refitting	15
Oil pump – removal, inspection and refitting	14
Sump – removal and refitting	13
Timing belt – removal and refitting	8
Timing belt covers – removal and refitting	7
Timing belt tensioner and sprockets – removal, inspection and refitting	9
Top Dead Centre (TDC) for No 1 piston – locating	3
Valve clearances – checking and adjustment	5

Degrees of difficulty

Easy, suitable for novice with little experience 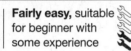	Fairly easy, suitable for beginner with some experience	Fairly difficult, suitable for competent DIY mechanic	Difficult, suitable for experienced DIY mechanic	Very difficult, suitable for expert DIY or professional

Specifications

General

Engine type	Four cylinder, in-line, double overhead camshafts, variable valve timing on Ti-VCT engine only
Designation	Duratec 16V or Duratec 16V Ti-VCT
Engine codes:	
Non-Ti-VCT engine	HWDA, HWDB, SHDA and SHDB
Ti-VCT engine	HXDA, HXDB, SHDA, SHDB and SIDA
Capacity	1596 cc
Bore	79.0 mm
Stroke	81.4 mm
Compression ratio	11.0:1
Output:	
Power:	
Non-Ti-VCT engine	74 kW (100 PS)
Ti-VCT engine	85 kW (115 PS)
Torque:	
Non-Ti-VCT engine	150 Nm
Ti-VCT engine	155 Nm
Firing order	1-3-4-2 (No 1 cylinder at timing belt end)
Direction of crankshaft rotation	Clockwise (seen from right-hand side of car)

Valves

	Intake	Exhaust
Valve clearances (cold):		
All engines	0.17 to 0.23 mm	0.31 to 0.37 mm

Camshafts

Camshaft bearing journal diameter	Unavailable at time of writing
Camshaft bearing journal-to-cylinder head running clearance	Unavailable at time of writing
Camshaft endfloat (typical)	0.05 to 0.13 mm

Lubrication

Oil pressure (minimum, warm engine):
Idling (800 rpm)...	1.0 bar
At 2000 rpm...	2.5 bars
Pressure relief valve opens at..............................	4.0 bars
Oil pump clearances	Not specified

Torque wrench settings

	Nm	lbf ft
Air conditioning compressor mounting bolts.....................	25	18
Alternator mounting bracket bolts	42	31
Camshaft bearing cap:		
Stage 1	7	5
Stage 2	Angle-tighten a further 45°	
Camshaft position sensor (Ti-VCT engine).......................	9	7
Camshaft pulley bolt (not Ti-VCT engine)*......................	60	44
Camshaft sensor ring (Ti-VCT engine)	21	15
Coolant outlet to cylinder head	20	15
Coolant pump pulley bolts (not Ti-VCT engine).................	24	18
Crankcase breather to cylinder block	9	7
Crankshaft oil seal carrier..................................	9	7
Crankshaft position sensor	9	7
Crankshaft pulley/vibration damper:*		
Stage 1	40	30
Stage 2	Angle-tighten a further 90°	
Crankshaft sprocket/timing belt retainer plate to cylinder block	9	7
Cross-brace bolts...	30	22
Cylinder head bolts:*		
Stage 1	15	11
Stage 2	30	22
Stage 3	Angle-tighten a further 90°	
Cylinder head cover...	10	7
Engine mountings:		
Right-hand mounting retaining bolts	90	66
Right-hand mounting bracket-to-engine bolts.................	56	41
Left-hand mounting nuts....................................	48	35
Left-hand mounting bracket to transmission	80	59
Left-hand mounting centre bolt	148	109
Lower-rear torque rod bolts	80	59
Exhaust flexible section-to-catalytic converter nuts	51	38
Exhaust manifold heat shield bolts	10	7
Exhaust manifold nuts/bolts.................................	54	40
Flywheel/driveplate bolts	85	63
Intake manifold-to-block bolt................................	15	11
Oil baffle to cylinder block	9	7
Oil drain plug	28	21
Oil filter connector	45	33
Oil pick-up pipe to oil baffle................................	9	7
Oil pressure switch...	15	11
Oil pump to cylinder block	9	7
Power steering fluid hose support bracket bolt.................	25	18
Spark plugs	15	11
Sump bolts:		
Sump-to-crankcase bolts:		
Stage 1	10	7
Stage 2	20	15
Sump-to-transmission bolts.................................	47	35
TDC pin hole blanking plug	20	15
Timing belt cover bolts......................................	9	7
Timing belt tensioner bolts..................................	20	15
Timing belt tensioner central bolt............................	25	18
Ti-VCT solenoid	8	6
Ti-VCT unit blanking plugs...................................	16	12
Ti-VCT unit retaining bolts:		
Stage 1	25	18
Stage 2	Angle-tighten a further 75°	

* Use new fasteners

1 General information

How to use this Chapter

This Part of Chapter 2 is devoted to in-car repair procedures on the 1.6 litre Duratec 16V petrol engine. All procedures concerning engine removal and refitting, and engine block/cylinder head overhaul can be found in Chapter 2F.

Refer to *Vehicle identification numbers* in the Reference Section at the end of this manual for details of engine code locations.

Most of the operations included in this Chapter are based on the assumption that the engine is still installed in the car. Therefore, if this information is being used during a complete engine overhaul, with the engine already removed, many of the steps included here will not apply.

Engine description

The Duratec engine (formerly the Zetec-SE), is a sixteen-valve, double overhead camshaft (DOHC), four-cylinder, in-line unit, mounted transversely at the front of the car, with the transmission on its left-hand end.

Apart from the plastic timing belt covers, plastic cylinder head cover, plastic intake manifold, and the cast-iron cylinder liners, the main engine components (including the sump) are manufactured entirely of aluminium alloy.

Caution: When tightening bolts into aluminium castings, it is important to adhere to the specified torque wrench settings, to avoid stripping threads.

The crankshaft runs in five main bearings, the centre main bearing's upper half incorporating thrustwashers to control crankshaft endfloat. Due to the very fine bearing clearances and bearing shell tolerances incorporated during manufacture, it is not possible to renew the crankshaft separate to the cylinder block; in fact it is not possible to remove and refit the crankshaft accurately using conventional tooling. This means that if the crankshaft is worn excessively, it must be renewed together with the cylinder block.

Caution: Do not unbolt the main bearing cap/ladder from the cylinder block, as it is not possible to refit it accurately using conventional tooling. Additionally, the manufacturers do not supply torque settings for the main bearing cap/ladder retaining bolts.

The connecting rods rotate on horizontally-split bearing shells at their big-ends, however the big-ends are of unusual design in that the caps are sheared from the rods during manufacture thus making each cap individually matched to its own connecting rod. The big-end bearing shells are also unusual in that they do not have any locating tabs and must be accurately positioned during refitting. The pistons are attached to the connecting rods by gudgeon pins which are an interference fit in the connecting rod small-end eyes. The aluminium alloy pistons are fitted with three piston rings: two compression rings and an oil control ring. After manufacture, the cylinder bores and pistons are measured and classified into three grades, which must be carefully matched together, to ensure the correct piston/cylinder clearance; no oversizes are available to permit reboring.

The intake and exhaust valves are each closed by coil springs; they operate in guides which are shrink-fitted into the cylinder head, as are the valve seat inserts.

Both camshafts are driven by the same toothed timing belt, each operating eight valves via bucket tappets. Each camshaft rotates in five bearings that are line-bored directly in the cylinder head and the (bolted-on) bearing caps; this means that the bearing caps are not available separately from the cylinder head, and must not be interchanged with caps from another engine.

The engines are available with variable valve timing on the both the intake and exhaust camshafts – this engine is known as the Ti-VCT (Twin Independent Variable Camshaft Timing). Engine oil pressure is used to vary the positions of the camshaft sprocket in relation to the camshafts, thus varying the valves' opening and closing times. Control of the oil flow is achieved using solenoid valves, which in turn are controlled by the engine management electronic control module (ECM). Varying the valve timing is this manner results in improved driveability and output, whist reducing fuel consumption and exhaust emissions.

The coolant pump is bolted to the right-hand end of the cylinder block, beneath the front run of the timing belt, and is driven by the auxiliary drivebelt from the crankshaft pulley.

Lubrication is by means of an eccentric-rotor trochoidal pump, which is mounted on the crankshaft right-hand end, and draws oil through a strainer located in the sump. The pump forces oil through an externally-mounted full-flow cartridge-type filter.

Operations with engine in car

The following work can be carried out with the engine in the car:

a) Cylinder head cover – removal and refitting.
b) Timing belt – renewal.
c) Timing belt tensioner and sprockets – removal and refitting.
d) Camshaft oil seals – renewal.
e) Camshafts, tappets and shims – removal and refitting.
f) Cylinder head – removal and refitting.
g) Sump – removal and refitting.
h) Crankshaft oil seals – renewal.
i) Oil pump – removal and refitting.
j) Flywheel/driveplate – removal and refitting.
k) Engine/transmission mountings – removal and refitting.

Note: *It is possible to remove the pistons and connecting rods (after removing the cylinder head and sump) without removing the engine. However, this is not recommended. Work of this nature is more easily and thoroughly completed with the engine on the bench, as described in Chapter 2F.*

2 Compression test – description and interpretation

1 When engine performance is down, or if misfiring occurs which cannot be attributed to the ignition or fuel systems, a compression test can provide diagnostic clues as to the engine's condition. If the test is performed regularly, it can give warning of trouble before any other symptoms become apparent.
2 The engine must be fully warmed-up to operating temperature, the oil level must be correct and the battery must be fully-charged. The help of an assistant will also be required.
3 Refer to Chapter 12 and remove the fuel pump relay from the engine compartment fusebox. Now start the engine and allow it to run until it stalls.
4 Disable the ignition system by disconnecting the multiplug from the DIS ignition coil. Remove all the spark plugs with reference to Chapter 1.
5 Fit a compression tester to the No 1 cylinder spark plug hole – the type of tester which screws into the spark plug thread is preferable.
6 Arrange for an assistant to hold the accelerator pedal fully depressed to the floor, while at the same time cranking the engine over for several seconds on the starter motor. Observe the compression gauge reading. The compression will build-up fairly quickly in a healthy engine. Low compression on the first stroke, followed by gradually-increasing pressure on successive strokes, indicates worn piston rings. A low compression on the first stroke which does not rise on successive strokes, indicates leaking valves or a blown head gasket (a cracked cylinder head could also be the cause). Deposits on the underside of the valve heads can also cause low compression. Record the highest gauge reading obtained, then repeat the procedure for the remaining cylinders.
7 Due to the variety of testers available, and the fluctuation in starter motor speed when cranking the engine, different readings are often obtained when carrying out the compression test. For this reason, actual compression pressure figures are not quoted by Ford. However, the most important factor is that the compression pressures are uniform in all cylinders, and that is what this test is mainly concerned with.
8 Add some engine oil (about three squirts from a plunger type oil can) to each cylinder through the spark plug holes, and then repeat the test.

3.7a Undo the blanking plug from the right-hand rear corner of the cylinder block . . .

9 If the compression increases after the oil is added, the piston rings are probably worn. If the compression does not increase significantly, the leakage is occurring at the valves or the head gasket. Leakage past the valves may be caused by burned valve seats and/or faces, or warped, cracked or bent valves.

10 If two adjacent cylinders have equally low compressions, it is most likely that the head gasket has blown between them. The appearance of coolant in the combustion chambers or on the engine oil dipstick would verify this condition.

11 If one cylinder is about 20 percent lower than the other, and the engine has a slightly rough idle, a worn lobe on the camshaft could be the cause.

12 On completion of the checks, refit the spark plugs and reconnect the HT leads and the DIS ignition coil plug. Refit the fuel pump relay to the fusebox.

3 Top Dead Centre (TDC) for No 1 piston – locating

1 Top dead centre (TDC) is the highest point of the cylinder that each piston reaches as the crankshaft turns. Each piston reaches its TDC position at the end of its compression stroke, and then again at the end of its exhaust stroke. For the purpose of engine timing, TDC on the compression stroke for No 1 piston is used. No 1 cylinder is at the timing belt end of the engine. Proceed as follows.

3.9 Locate the home-made camshaft setting tool (arrowed) in the slots

3.7b . . . and screw in the timing pin

2 Disconnect the battery negative (earth) lead (see Chapter 5). Remove the spark plugs as described in Chapter 1.

3 Apply the handbrake, then jack up the front of the vehicle and support it on axle stands (see *Jacking and vehicle support*). If the engine is to be turned using the right-hand front roadwheel with top gear engaged (manual transmission models only), it is only necessary to raise the right-hand front roadwheel off the ground.

4 Where necessary, undo the fasteners, remove the engine undershield, then remove the wheel arch liner, and auxiliary drivebelt lower cover for access to the crankshaft pulley and bolt.

Non-Ti-VCT engines

5 Remove the cylinder head cover as described in Section 4.

6 The piston of No 1 cylinder must now be positioned just before top dead centre (TDC). To do this, have an assistant turn the crankshaft until the slots in the left-hand ends of the camshafts are parallel with the upper surface of the cylinder head. Note that the slots are slightly offset so make sure that the lower edges of the slots are aligned with the cylinder head. Turn the crankshaft slightly anti-clockwise (viewed from the right-hand end of the engine).

7 Unscrew the blanking plug from the right-hand rear side of the engine cylinder block. A TDC timing pin must now be inserted and tightened into the hole. It is highly recommended that the special Ford timing pin 303-748 is obtained, or alternatively, a

3.14 Undo the nuts/bolts and remove the right-hand engine mounting

timing pin from a reputable tool manufacturer **(see illustrations)**. The diameter of the pin is critical as it determines the TDC point where the machined flat on the crankshaft web contacts the *shank* of the tool – note that the web does **not** contact the *end* of the tool.

8 With the timing pin in position, turn the crankshaft *slowly* clockwise until the specially-machined surface on the crank web just touches the timing pin. No 1 piston is now at TDC on its compression stroke. To confirm this, check that the camshaft lobes for No 4 cylinder are 'rocking' (ie, exhaust valves closing and intake valves opening).

9 It should now be possible to insert the camshaft setting bar into the slots in the left-hand ends of the camshafts. If the Ford setting tool 303-376B is unavailable, a home-made tool can be fabricated out of a length of flat metal bar 5.00 mm thick. The bar must be a good fit in the slots and should be approximately 180 to 230 mm long by 20 to 30 mm wide **(see illustration)**.

10 If the bar cannot be inserted in the slots with the crankshaft at TDC, the valve timing must be adjusted as described in Section 8 of this Chapter.

11 Once the work requiring the TDC setting has been completed, remove the metal bar from the camshaft slots then unscrew the timing pin and refit the blanking plug. Refit the spark plugs (Chapter 1), cylinder head cover (Section 4), auxiliary drivebelt lower cover, and where necessary the engine undershield. Lower the vehicle to the ground and reconnect the battery negative lead (see Chapter 5).

Ti-VCT engines

12 Remove the upper timing belt cover as described in Section 7.

13 Position a trolley jack under the engine. Use a block of wood on the jack head to prevent damage to the sump. Take the weight of the engine.

14 Make alignment marks between the right-hand engine mounting bracket and the cylinder head bracket/vehicle body, then undo the nuts/bolts and remove the mounting **(see illustration)**. Discard the nuts – new ones must be fitted.

15 Rotate the crankshaft pulley clockwise until the marks (dot on the intake sprocket, groove on the exhaust sprocket) of the camshaft VCT units are approaching the 11 o'clock position **(see illustrations)**.

16 Undo the blanking plug from the right-hand rear side of the engine cylinder block **(see illustration 3.7a)**. A TDC timing pin must now be inserted and tightened into the hole. It is highly recommended that the Ford timing pin 303-748 is obtained, or alternatively, a timing pin from a reputable tool manufacturer **(see illustration 3.7b)**. The diameter of the pin is critical as it determines the TDC point where the machined flat on the crankshaft web contacts the *shank* of the tool – note that the web does **not** contact the *end* of the tool.

17 With the timing pin in position, turn the crankshaft *slowly* clockwise until the specially machined surface on the crank web just touches the timing pin. No 1 piston is now at TDC on its compression stroke.

18 Now it is necessary to fit Ford special tool 303-1097 over the VCT units on the ends of the camshafts. Note that the tool is marked with a line to indicate the exhaust side, a dot to indicate the intake side, and an arrow which must point upwards **(see illustrations)**.

19 Once the work requiring the TDC setting has been completed, remove the special tool from the camshaft VCT units then unscrew the timing pin and refit the blanking plug. Refit the spark plugs (Chapter 1), upper timing belt cover, auxiliary drivebelt lower cover, and where necessary the engine undershield. Lower the vehicle to the ground and reconnect the battery negative lead (see Chapter 5).

4	Cylinder head cover – removal and refitting

Removal

1 Disconnect the battery negative (earth) lead (see Chapter 5).

2 Disconnect the breather pipe from the front of the cover **(see illustration)**.

3 Disconnect the HT leads from the spark plugs, unclip them from the cover, and position them to the left-hand side of the engine compartment.

4 On Ti-VCT engines, disconnect the wiring plugs from the camshaft position sensors and VCT solenoids on the cylinder head cover, clean around the area, then undo the retaining bolts and remove both VCT oil control solenoids from the top, right-hand end of the cylinder head **(see illustrations)**. Plug the openings to prevent contamination. Examine the O-ring seals, and renew if necessary.

5 Where fitted, undo the nut and bolt and move the wiring connector bracket at the left-hand rear corner of the cylinder head cover to one side.

6 On all engines, the cylinder head cover is secured by a total of twelve bolts. Note their fitted locations and remove the bolts. On

3.15a The intake camshaft sprocket is marked with a dot (arrowed) . . .

3.15b . . . and the exhaust camshaft sprocket with a groove (arrowed)

3.18a Fit the special tool over the Ti-VCT units

3.18b The tool is marked with a dot (1) for the intake camshaft, a line (2) for the exhaust camshaft, and an arrow (3) which must point upwards

Ti-VCT engines, the bolts are integral with the cover.

7 On non-Ti-VCT engines, remove the centre top bolt from the timing belt upper cover **(see illustration)**. This bolt secures the timing belt cover to the cylinder head cover.

4.2 Disconnect the breather pipe (arrowed)

4.4a Disconnect the camshaft position sensors wiring plugs

4.4b Disconnect the VCT solenoid wiring plugs (arrowed)

4.4c Undo the bolt (arrowed) . . .

4.4d . . . and pull the solenoids from place

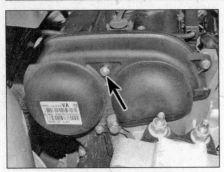

4.7 Remove the timing belt upper cover centre top bolt (arrowed)

8 Carefully lift the cover from the top of the cylinder head, unclipping any wiring as necessary. Recover the gasket – this may be re-used if it is not damaged.

Refitting

9 Clean the mating surfaces of the cylinder head and the cover gasket.
10 Lower the cover onto the cylinder head, ensuring that the gasket stays in place.
11 Progressively tighten all bolts to the specified torque.
12 The remainder of refitting is a reversal of removal.

---

5 Valve clearances – checking and adjustment

1 Remove the cylinder head cover as described in Section 4. **Note:** *If checking the valve clearances with the timing belt removed (eg, after refitting the camshafts), rotate the crankshaft 90° anti-clockwise back from TDC on No 1 cylinder so the pistons are halfway down the cylinder bores. Verify this by inserting a long screwdriver down the spark plug holes.*
2 Remove the spark plugs (Chapter 1) in order to make turning the engine easier. The engine may be turned using a spanner on the crankshaft pulley bolt or by raising the front right-hand roadwheel clear of the ground, engaging top gear and turning the wheel. If the former method is used, jack up and support the front of the car (see *Jacking and vehicle support*) then unbolt the lower cover for

5.10a Measure the thickness of the tappets with a micrometer

5.5 Insert a feeler gauge between the heel of the camshaft lobe and the tappet

access to the pulley bolt; if the latter method is used, apply the handbrake then jack up the front right-hand side of the car until the roadwheel is clear of the ground and support with an axle stand.
3 Draw the valve positions on a piece of paper, numbering them 1 to 8 intake and exhaust, from the timing belt (right-hand) end of the engine (ie, 1E, 1I, 2E, 2I and so on). As there are two intake and two exhaust valves for each cylinder, draw the cylinders as large circles and the four valves as smaller circles. The intake valves are at the front of the cylinder head, and the exhaust valves are at the rear. As the valve clearances are adjusted, cross them off.
4 Turn the engine in a clockwise direction until both intake valves of No 1 cylinder are fully shut and the apex of the camshaft lobes are pointing upwards away from the valve positions.
5 Insert a feeler blade of the correct thickness (see *Specifications*) between the heel of the camshaft lobe and the tappet **(see illustration)**. It should be a firm sliding fit. If this is the case, the clearance is correct and the valve position can be crossed off. If the clearance is not correct, use feeler blades to determine the exact clearance and record this on the drawing. From this clearance it will be possible to calculate the thickness of the new tappet to be fitted. Note that no shims are fitted between the camshaft and tappet – the complete tappet must be renewed.
6 Check the clearance of the second intake valve for No 1 cylinder, and if necessary record the existing clearance on the drawing.
7 Now turn the engine until the intake valves

5.10b The thickness of each tappet should be etched on its underside

of No 2 cylinder are fully shut and the camshaft lobes pointing away from the valve positions. Check the clearances as described previously, and record any that are incorrect.
8 After checking all of the intake valve clearances, check the exhaust valve clearances in the same way, but note that the clearances are different.
9 Where adjustment is required, the procedure is to remove the camshafts as described in Section 11.
10 If the recorded clearance was too small, a thinner tappet must be fitted, and conversely if the clearance was too large, a thicker tappet must be fitted. To calculate the thickness of the new tappet, first use a micrometer to measure the thickness of the existing tappet (C) and add this to the measured clearance (B) **(see illustrations)**. Deduct the desired clearance (A) to provide the thickness (D) of the new tappet. The thickness of the tappet should be etched on the downward facing surface, however use the micrometer to verify this. The formula is as follows.

New tappet thickness D

= *Existing tappet thickness C*
+ *Measured clearance B*
– *Desired clearance A*

Sample calculation

Desired clearance (A)	=	*0.20*
Measured clearance (B)	=	*0.15*
Existing tappet thickness (C)	=	*2.725*
Tappet thickness required (D)	=	*C+B–A = 2.675*

All measurements in mm

11 The tappets are available in varying thicknesses in increments of 0.025 mm.
12 It will be helpful for future adjustment if a record is kept of the thickness of the tappet fitted at each position.
13 When all the clearances have been checked and adjusted, refit the lower cover (where removed), lower the car to the ground and refit the cylinder head cover as described in Section 4.

---

6 Crankshaft pulley/ vibration damper – removal and refitting

Caution: Removal of the crankshaft pulley effectively loses the valve timing setting, and it will be necessary to reset the timing.
Note: The vibration damper retaining bolt may only be used once. Obtain a new bolt for the refitting procedure.

Removal

1 Remove the auxiliary drivebelt as described in Chapter 1.
2 Set the engine to the top dead centre (TDC) position as described in Section 3.
3 Remove the starter motor as described in Chapter 5, then use Ford tool 303-393 and 303-393-02 to lock the crankshaft in position.

6.3a Ford tool No 303-393 and 303-393-02

6.3b The assembled tools bolt across the starter motor aperture . . .

6.3c . . . and engages with the teeth on the flywheel ring gear

6.4 Using a home-made tool to hold the crankshaft pulley

6.5a If necessary, use a puller to free the pulley from the crankshaft . . .

6.5b . . . then withdrawn the pulley from the crankshaft

This tool bolts across the starter motor aperture in the transmission bellhousing, and engages with the teeth of the starter ring gear on the flywheel/driveplate (see illustrations).

4 Hold the crankshaft pulley stationary (see illustration). The bolt ends locate in the pulley holes, and an extension bar and socket can then be used to loosen the bolt. Do not allow the crankshaft to rotate, otherwise it will be more difficult to reset the valve timing – also, with the bolt loose, the crankshaft sprocket may not turn with the crankshaft.

5 With the bolt loosened several turns, use a suitable puller to free the pulley from the taper on the end of the crankshaft. Fully unscrew the bolt and withdraw the pulley (see illustrations).

6 Clean the end of the crankshaft and the pulley.

Refitting

7 The procedure in this paragraph is

necessary in order to be able to set the valve timing after the crankshaft/vibration pulley has been refitted.

Non Ti-VCT engines

8 Unbolt and remove the upper timing cover (see Section 7). While holding each of the camshaft sprockets stationary in turn using the home-made tool described in paragraph 4, loosen the sprocket retaining bolts until they are just finger-tight, to enable the sprockets to turn on the camshafts. Alternatively, the camshafts can be held stationary using a spanner on the special hexagon flats.

9 Locate the pulley on the end of the crankshaft, and press it onto the taper as far as it will go. This procedure must always be carried out before inserting and tightening the new bolt. Do not simply insert and tighten the new bolt, as in certain circumstances the torque will not be sufficient to press the pulley fully onto the end of the taper on the crankshaft. Ford technicians use

a special installer which consists of a threaded rod screwed into the crankshaft, together with a spacer which locates on the pulley. In the absence of this tool, use a long bolt or threaded rod together with washers and a nut (see illustration). As a last resort use the removed (old) bolt, however this is not recommended as the threads may be stretched (see Note at the beginning of this Section).

All engines

10 Temporarily remove the crankshaft timing pin.

11 Remove the pulley fitting tool (where applicable), then insert the new bolt and tighten it to the specified Stage 1 torque setting while holding the pulley stationary with the special tool. Note that two different bolts may be fitted: M12 x 29 mm or M12 x 44.5 mm. In order to determine which bolt is required, use a Vernier caliper to measure the depth of the hole in the end of the crankshaft (see illustrations).

6.9 Use a long bolt threaded into the crankshaft to draw the pulley onto the taper

6.11a Two different length crankshaft pulley bolts may be fitted – see text

6.11b Insert the new crankshaft pulley bolt

7.5 Timing belt upper cover bolts (arrowed)

A 42 mm depth requires a 29 mm bolt, whereas a 52 mm depth requires a 44.5 mm bolt.

12 Now angle-tighten the bolt through the specified Stage 2 angle. An angle gauge is useful for this, but 90° is a right-angle, which is quite easily judged by eye.

Non Ti-VCT engines

13 The valve timing must now be set and the camshaft sprocket bolts tightened as described in Section 8.

14 Refit the timing belt upper cover.

Ti-VCT engines

15 Remove the crankshaft and camshaft locking tools, then refit the timing belt cover, and engine mounting in the reverse of the procedure described in Section 3.

All engines

16 Fit a new auxiliary drivebelt as described in Chapter 1.

7 Timing belt covers – removal and refitting

Upper cover

Removal

1 Pull the coolant expansion tank upwards and move it to one side.

8.4 Slacken the camshaft sprocket retaining bolts whilst holding the sprockets with a home-made tool

2 Slacken the coolant pump pulley bolts, then remove the auxiliary drivebelt(s) as described in Chapter 1.

3 Unscrew the 4 bolts and remove the coolant pump pulley.

4 On non-Ti-VCT engines, undo the single bolt securing the upper timing belt cover to the cylinder head cover **(see illustration 4.7)**.

5 On all engines, unscrew the timing belt upper cover retaining bolts **(see illustration)**.

6 Manoeuvre the timing cover from the engine compartment.

Refitting

7 Refitting is a reversal of removal. Fit a new auxiliary drivebelt as described in Chapter 1.

Lower cover

Removal

8 The timing belt lower cover is located around the crankshaft. First remove the crankshaft pulley/vibration damper as described in Section 6.

9 Working beneath the right-hand wheel arch, unscrew the retaining bolts and withdraw the timing cover **(see illustration)**.

Refitting

10 Refitting is a reversal of removal.

8 Timing belt – removal and refitting

Caution: The camshaft sprockets are made from a type of plastic. Care must be taken to avoid damage to the sprockets during the following procedure.

Removal

1 Loosen the four bolts securing the coolant pump pulley.

2 Remove the crankshaft pulley/vibration damper as described in Section 6.

3 Remove the coolant pump pulley.

7.9 Timing belt lower cover bolts (arrowed)

Non-Ti-VCT engines

4 With the camshaft timing bar removed, loosen the camshaft sprocket bolts several turns while holding the sprockets with a suitable tool **(see illustration)**. Bearing in mind the caution at the start of this Section, release the sprockets from the tapers on the ends of the camshafts so that they are free to rotate.

All engines

5 Remove the timing belt covers as described in Section 7.

6 Where fitted, remove the timing belt guide disc from the end of the crankshaft. Note which way round the disc is fitted – the concave side faces outwards **(see illustration)**.

7 Remove the alternator as described in Chapter 5.

8 The engine must now be supported, as the right-hand mounting (right as seen from the driver's seat) must be removed. Supporting the engine should ideally be done from above, using an engine crane or a special engine lifting beam. However, in the absence of these tools, the engine can be supported from below, on the cast-aluminium sump, providing a piece of wood is used to spread the load **(see illustration)**.

9 With the engine securely supported, remove the nuts/bolts securing the right-hand mounting, and lift it off **(see illustration 3.14)**.

8.6 Remove the timing belt guide disc (where fitted)

8.8 Support the engine with a trolley jack and block of wood under the sump

8.11a Insert a 4 mm drill bit or rod (arrowed) into the pulley hub – engines up to 04/2005

8.11b Insert a 4 mm drill bit or rod into the tensioner arms (arrowed)

New nuts should be obtained for refitting the mounting.

10 Unbolt the lower half of the engine right-hand mounting bracket from the engine.

11 Push the timing belt eccentric tensioner pulley rearwards to de-tension the belt, then insert Ford tool No 303-1054 or a suitable equivalent into the pulley hub (engines up to April 2005) or arm (engines from April 2005) to lock it in position **(see illustrations)**.

12 Undo the bolt(s) and remove the tensioner and bracket assembly. **Note:** *It is recommended that the tensioner is renewed along with the timing belt.*

13 If the timing belt is to be re-used (this is not recommended), use white paint or similar to mark its direction of rotation, and note from the manufacturer's markings which way round it is fitted. Withdraw the belt from the sprockets and from over the tensioner **(see illustration)**. *Do not* attempt to turn the crankshaft or camshafts until the timing belt is refitted.

Inspection

14 If the belt is being removed for reasons other than routine renewal, check it carefully for any signs of uneven wear, splitting, cracks (especially at the roots of the belt teeth) or contamination with oil or coolant. Renew the belt if there is the slightest doubt about its condition. As a safety measure, the belt should be renewed irrespective of its apparent condition whenever the engine is overhauled.

15 Check the sprockets for signs of wear or damage, and ensure that the tensioner

pulley rotates smoothly on its bearings; renew any worn or damaged components. Ford dealers (and many motor factors) now supply 'cambelt kits', consisting of the belt itself and a new tensioner – for peace of mind, it is recommended that one of these is purchased.

16 If signs of oil or coolant contamination are found on the old belt, trace the source of the leak and rectify it, then wash down the engine timing belt area and related components to remove all traces of oil or coolant.

Refitting

Non-Ti-VCT engines

17 Ensure that the engine is still set to TDC. Remove the camshaft sprocket bolts and renew. Only finger-tighten the bolts at this stage, the camshaft sprockets must be free to rotate on their shafts.

18 Locate the timing belt on the crankshaft sprocket, then feed it over the two camshaft sprockets. If the original belt is being refitted, make sure that it is the correct way round as noted during removal **(see illustrations)**. Take care not to rotate the crankshaft.

19 Where applicable, refit the timing belt guide disc on the end of the crankshaft, making sure that the concave side faces outwards.

20 Ensure the tensioner is in the locked position (see paragraph 11), then fit the tensioner/bracket assembly, and tighten the bolt(s) to the specified torque.

21 Remove the locking pin from the tensioner, and allow it to tension the belt.

22 Refit the engine mounting bracket to the cylinder block, and tighten the bolts to the specified torque.

23 Refit the upper engine mounting bracket tighten the new nuts to the specified torque. Remove the jack from under the engine, or remove the hoist from above, as applicable.

24 Refit the timing belt lower cover, and tighten the bolts to the specified torque.

25 Locate the crankshaft pulley/vibration damper on the end of the crankshaft, and press it squarely onto the taper as far as it will go. Insert the new bolt and tighten it to the specified Stage 1 torque setting while holding the pulley stationary as described in Section 6.

26 Now tighten the crankshaft pulley bolt through the specified angle. The crankshaft sprocket is now effectively clamped to the crankshaft.

27 Moderately tighten the bolts retaining the camshaft sprockets to the camshafts, then remove the camshaft setting bar, crankshaft timing pin and flywheel/driveplate locking tool, then fully-tighten the bolts while holding the sprockets using the tool described in Section 6 or using a spanner on the hexagon flats provided **(see illustrations)**.

28 Rotate the crankshaft clockwise 1¾ turns approximately. Refit the crankshaft TDC timing pin then rotate the crankshaft clockwise until it stops against the timing pin. Check to see whether the setting bar will fit in the camshaft slots. If necessary, loosen the camshaft sprocket bolts, turn the camshafts slightly (without moving the timing belt) so the setting bar can be fitted, then retighten the camshaft

8.13 Note the belt may be marked with direction-of-rotation arrows

8.18a Fit the belt around the camshaft sprockets . . .

8.18b . . . and the crankshaft sprocket

8.27a Tighten the camshaft sprocket retaining bolts

8.27b Use an open-ended spanner on the hexagon section of the camshaft

8.30 Timing belt routing

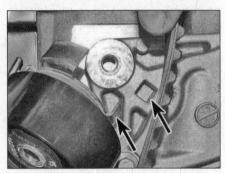

8.31 The lug on the tensioner mounting plate (arrowed) must locate in the square hole (arrowed) in the cylinder block

sprocket bolts. On completion, remove the timing pin and bar and refit the blanking plug.

29 Refit the timing belt upper cover, and the alternator. Refit the coolant pump pulley, and tighten the bolts as far as possible for now – once the auxiliary drivebelt has been fitted it will be easier to tighten the bolts to the specified torque.

Ti-VCT engines

30 Ensure the engine's still set to TDC on No 1 cylinder (Section 3), then working clockwise, locate the timing belt on the camshaft VCT units, then fit the belt over the crankshaft sprocket **(see illustration)**. If the original belt is being refitted, make sure that it is the correct way round as noted during removal. Take care not to rotate the crankshaft.

31 Fit the new tensioner (where applicable). Ensure the tensioner is in the locked position

(see paragraph 11), then fit the tensioner assembly, and tighten the bolt to the specified torque **(see illustration)**.

32 Remove the locking pin from the tensioner, and allow it to tension the belt.

33 Refit the lower timing belt cover and tighten the bolts to the specified torque.

34 Locate the crankshaft pulley/vibration damper on the end of the crankshaft, and press it squarely onto the taper as far as it will go. Insert the new bolt and tighten it to the specified Stage 1 torque setting while holding the pulley stationary as described in Section 6.

35 Now tighten the crankshaft pulley bolt through the specified angle. The crankshaft sprocket is now effectively clamped to the crankshaft.

36 Remove the locking tool from the camshaft VCT units, the crankshaft timing pin, and the flywheel/driveplate locking tool.

37 Rotate the crankshaft clockwise approximately 2 revolutions, until the marks on the camshaft VCT units are in the 11 o'clock position **(see illustration 3.15a and 3.15b)**.

38 Refit the crankshaft timing pin, and rotate the crankshaft clockwise until it stops against the timing pin. Refit the VCT units locking tool to check their positions. If the tool cannot be fitted, remove the belt, and carry out the fitting/tensioning procedure again. If the timing is correct, remove the timing pin and VCT locking tool. Refit the cylinder block blanking plug.

39 Refit the engine mounting, timing belt upper cover, and the alternator. Refit the coolant pump pulley, and tighten the bolts as far as possible for now – once the auxiliary drivebelt has been fitted it will be easier to tighten the bolts to the specified torque.

All engines

40 The remainder of refitting is a reversal of removal.

9 Timing belt tensioner and sprockets – removal, inspection and refitting

Tensioner pulley

1 Removal of the tensioner pulley is described within the timing belt procedure – see Section 8.

Camshaft sprockets

Caution: The camshaft sprockets are made from a type of plastic. Care must be taken to avoid damage to the sprockets during the following procedure.

2 Remove the timing belt as described in Section 8.

Non-Ti-VCT engines

3 Unscrew the bolts and remove the sprockets from the camshafts. If necessary, carefully use a soft-metal drift to release the sprockets from the taper on the camshafts **(see illustrations)**.

Ti-VCT engines

4 Remove the cylinder head cover as described in Section 4.

5 Counterhold the camshafts using an open-ended spanner on the hexagonal sections, then unscrew the blanking plugs from the centre of the VCT units **(see illustration)**.

6 Still counterholding the camshafts, slacken and remove the VCT units' centre Torx bolts **(see illustrations)**. Remove the VCT units from the ends of the camshafts.

All engines

7 Examine the teeth of the sprockets for wear and damage, and renew them if necessary.

Non-Ti-VCT engines

8 Locate the sprockets on the camshafts, and screw in the retaining bolts loosely.

9 Fit the timing belt as described in Section 8.

9.3a Unscrew the bolt . . .

9.3b . . . and remove the camshaft sprocket

9.5 Counterhold the camshaft with a spanner on the hexagonal section, then unscrew the blanking plug from the VCT unit

9.6a Unscrew the Torx bolt . . .

9.6b . . . and pull the VCT unit from the camshaft

Ti-VCT engines

10 Insert Ford tool No 303-376B into the slots in the left-hand ends of the camshafts. If the Ford setting tool 303-376B is unavailable, a home-made tool can be fabricated out of a length of flat metal bar 20 mm thick **(see illustrations)**.

11 Locate the VCT units on the ends of the camshafts, but only finger-tighten the retaining bolts at this stage. Ensure the timing marks on the VCT units (dot on the intake sprocket, groove on the exhaust sprocket) are at the 12 o'clock position **(see illustration)**.

12 Fit the VCT locking tool (No 303-1097) over the units **(see illustrations 3.18a and 3.18b)**. Note how the dots/holes on the VCT units align with the groove/dot on the sprockets **(see illustration)**.

13 Tighten each VCT unit retaining bolt to the specified Stage 1 torque.

14 Remove the camshaft setting bar and the VCT locking tool, then counterhold the camshafts using a spanner on the hexagonal section, and tighten each VCT unit retaining bolt to the specified Stage 2 angle setting. Do not allow the camshafts to rotate.

15 Refit the VCT locking tool, and check the marks on the sprockets align with the marks on the VCT units **(see illustration 9.12)**. If not, repeat the VCT unit refitting procedure.

16 If the timing is correct, counterhold the camshafts using a spanner on the hexagonal section, and fit the each VCT unit blanking plug. Tighten each plug to the specified torque. Renew the plug seal if necessary **(see illustrations)**.

9.10a Camshaft setting tool dimensions

Drawing not to scale

17 Fit the timing belt as described in Section 8, and the cylinder head cover as described In Section 4.

9.10b Fit the setting tool into the slots in the end of the camshafts

Crankshaft sprocket

18 Remove the timing belt as described in Section 8.

9.11 Ensure the groove (1) on the exhaust VCT unit and the dot (2) on the intake unit are at the 12 o'clock position

9.12 Note how the dots/holes on the VCT units align with the groove/dot on the sprockets (arrowed)

9.16a Renew the seal if necessary . . .

9.16b . . . then refit the plugs to the VCT units

9.19 Slide the crankshaft sprocket from place

10.3a Drill a small hole and insert a self-tapping screw . . .

10.3b . . . then pull out the oil seal using a pair of pliers

10.5 Locate the new oil seal into the cylinder/camshaft bearing cap

10.6 Drive the new seal into position with a socket

11 Camshafts and tappets – removal, inspection and refitting

Removal

1 Before removing the camshafts, it may be useful to check and record the valve clearances as described in Section 5. If any clearance is not within limits, new tappets can be obtained and fitted.

2 Remove the camshaft oil seals as described in Section 10.

3 The camshaft bearing caps are marked for position – the intake caps have the letter I and exhaust caps have the letter E. On the project car these were not very clear, and if this is the case, mark them using paint or a marker pen. Make sure they are identified for intake and exhaust camshafts **(see illustrations)**.

4 Position the crankshaft so that No 1 piston is approximately 25 mm before TDC. This can be done by starting from the TDC position; carefully insert a large screwdriver down No 1 cylinder spark plug hole until the tip touches the top of the piston, and turn the engine anti-clockwise until the screwdriver shaft has descended 25 mm.

5 Position the camshafts so that none of the valves are at full lift (ie, fully-open, being heavily pressed down by the cam lobes). To do this, turn each camshaft using a spanner on the hexagon flats provided.

6 Progressively loosen the camshaft

19 Slide the sprocket off the end of the crankshaft **(see illustration)**.

20 Examine the teeth of the sprocket for wear and damage, and renew if necessary.

21 Wipe clean the end of the crankshaft, then slide on the sprocket.

22 Refit the timing belt as described in Section 8.

10 Camshaft oil seals – renewal
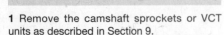

1 Remove the camshaft sprockets or VCT units as described in Section 9.

2 Note the fitted depths of the oil seals as a guide for fitting the new ones.

3 Using a screwdriver or similar tool, carefully prise the oil seals from the cylinder head/

camshaft bearing caps. Take care not to damage the oil seal contact surfaces on the ends of the camshafts or the oil seal seating. An alternative method of removing the seals is to drill a small hole, then insert a self-tapping screw and use pliers to pull out the seal **(see illustrations)**.

4 Wipe clean the oil seal seating and also the ends of the camshafts.

5 Apply a little clean engine oil to the seal lip, then locate it over the camshaft and into the cylinder head/camshaft bearing cap. Make sure that the closed end of the oil seal faces outwards **(see illustration)**.

6 Using a socket or length of metal tubing, drive the oil seals squarely into position to the previously-noted depths. Wipe away any excess oil **(see illustration)**.

7 Refit the camshaft sprockets as described in Section 9.

11.3a No 3 intake camshaft bearing cap

11.3b No 3 exhaust camshaft bearing cap

11.3c Number the bearing caps with paint if they are not clearly marked

11.6 Undo the camshaft bearing cap bolts . . .

11.7a . . . withdraw the caps . . .

11.7b . . . then remove the camshafts

bearing cap retaining bolts, working in the **same sequence** shown for tightening **(see illustration 11.19)**. Work only as described to release gradually and evenly the pressure of the valve springs on the caps **(see illustration)**.

7 Withdraw the caps, keeping them in order to aid refitting, then lift the camshafts from the cylinder head and withdraw their oil seals. The exhaust camshaft can be identified by the reference lobe for the camshaft position sensor on non-Ti-VCT engines, therefore, there is no need to mark the camshafts; on Ti-VCT engines, the intake camshaft is marked 7A and the exhaust marked 3A **(see illustrations)**. **Note:** *On Ti-VCT engines, renew the O-ring between the right-hand bearing cap and the cylinder head (see illustration).*

8 Obtain sixteen small, clean containers, and number them 1 to 8 for both the intake and exhaust camshafts. Lift the tappets one by one from the cylinder head.

Inspection

9 With the camshafts and tappets removed, check each for signs of obvious wear (scoring, pitting, etc) and for ovality, and renew if necessary.

10 Visually examine the camshaft lobes for score marks, pitting, and evidence of overheating (blue, discoloured areas). Look for flaking away of the hardened surface layer of each lobe. If any such signs are evident, renew the component concerned.

11 Examine the camshaft bearing journals and the cylinder head bearing surfaces for signs of obvious wear or pitting. If any such signs are evident, renew the component concerned.

12 To check camshaft endfloat, remove the tappets, clean the bearing surfaces carefully, and refit the camshafts and bearing caps. Tighten the bearing cap bolts to the specified torque wrench setting, then measure the endfloat using a dial gauge mounted on the cylinder head so that its tip bears on the camshaft right-hand end.

13 Tap the camshaft fully towards the gauge, zero the gauge, then tap the camshaft fully away from the gauge, and note the gauge reading. If the endfloat measured is found to be more than the typical value given, fit a

11.7c The exhaust camshaft is marked 3A (Ti-VCT engines)

new camshaft and repeat the check; if the clearance is still excessive, the cylinder head must be renewed.

Refitting

14 Lubricate the cylinder head tappet bores and the tappets with engine oil. Carefully refit the tappets to the cylinder head, ensuring each tappet is refitted to its original bore. Some care will be needed to enter the tappets squarely into their bores.

15 Liberally oil the camshaft bearings and lobes. Ensuring that each camshaft is in its original location, refit the camshafts, locating each so that the slot in its left-hand end is approximately parallel to, and just above, the cylinder head mating surface. At this stage, position the camshafts so that none of the

11.15 The slots in the end of the camshafts should be just above, and approximately parallel to, the cylinder head upper surface

11.7d On Ti-VCT engines, recover the O-ring seal under the right-hand (No 1) bearing cap

valves are at full lift – see paragraph 5 **(see illustration)**.

16 Clean the mating faces of the cylinder head and camshaft bearing caps.

17 Apply a thin smear of suitable sealant (Ford recommend WSK-M2G348-A5 or Loctite 518) to the No 1 camshaft bearing caps at the oil seal ends only **(see illustration)**. On Ti-VCT engines, renew the O-ring seal beneath the No 1 bearing cap **(see illustration 11.7d)**.

18 Oil the bearing surfaces, then locate the camshaft bearing caps on the camshafts and insert the retaining bolts loosely. Make sure that each cap is located in its previously-noted position **(see illustration)**.

19 Ensuring each cap is kept square to the cylinder head as it is tightened down, and working in sequence **(see illustration)**, tighten

11.17 Apply a thin bead of sealant (see text) to the underside of the No 1 bearing cap as shown

11.18 Oil the camshaft bearing surfaces

H32320

11.19 Camshaft bearing cap bolt slackening and tightening sequence

the camshaft bearing cap bolts slowly and by one turn at a time, until each cap touches the cylinder head. Next, go round again in the same sequence, tightening the bolts to the specified Stage 1 torque wrench setting specified.

20 Finally, still working in the tightening sequence, tightening the bolts further to the Stage 2 angle. It is recommended that an angle gauge is used for this, to ensure accuracy.

21 Wipe off all surplus sealant, and check the valve clearances as described in Section 5.

22 Fit new camshaft oil seals as described in Section 10.

12 Cylinder head –
removal, inspection and refitting

Removal

1 Depressurise the fuel system as described in Chapter 4.

2 Drain the cooling system as described in Chapter 1.

3 Disconnect the battery negative lead as described in Chapter 5.

4 Remove the intake manifold and exhaust manifold as described in Chapter 4.

12.18 Check the cylinder head gasket face for distortion using a straight-edge

5 Remove the camshafts and tappets as described in Section 11.

6 Remove the intake manifold support bolt from the front of the engine at the timing belt end.

7 Lower the car to the ground.

8 Make a note of their fitted locations and the harness routing, then disconnect any wiring plugs attached to components on the cylinder head. Label the plugs if necessary to aid refitting.

9 Unbolt the timing belt rear cover, which is secured by three bolts.

10 Release the spring-type clip and disconnect the coolant pipe from the left-hand rear of the cylinder head.

11 Undo the 4 bolts and detach the coolant housing from the left-hand end of the cylinder head.

12 Make a last check round the cylinder head, to ensure that nothing remains connected or attached which would prevent the head from being lifted off. Prepare a clean surface to lay the head down on once it has been removed.

13 Working in the **reverse** of the tightening sequence **(see illustration 12.27a or 12.27b)**, slacken the ten cylinder head bolts progressively and by half a turn at a time; a Torx key (TX 55 size) will be required. Remove all the bolts.

14 Lift the cylinder head away; use assistance if possible, as it is a heavy assembly. Remove the gasket, noting the two dowels. Although the gasket cannot be re-used, it is advisable to retain it for comparison with the new one, to confirm that the right part has been supplied.

Inspection

15 The mating faces of the cylinder head and cylinder block must be perfectly clean before refitting the head. Use a hard plastic or wood scraper to remove all traces of gasket and carbon; also clean the piston crowns. Take particular care during the cleaning operations, as aluminium alloy is easily damaged.

16 Make sure that the carbon is not allowed to enter the oil and coolant passages – this

is particularly important for the lubrication system, as carbon could block the oil supply to the engine's components. Using adhesive tape and paper, seal the coolant, oil and bolt holes in the cylinder block. To prevent carbon entering the gap between the pistons and bores, smear a little grease in the gap. After cleaning each piston, use a small brush to remove all traces of grease and carbon from the gap, then wipe away the remainder with a clean rag. Note that Ti-VCT engines have a filter fitted into the oil supply galleries feeding the VCT system. This filter is permanently installed and cannot be removed.

17 Check the mating surfaces of the cylinder block and the cylinder head for nicks, deep scratches and other damage. If slight, they may be removed carefully with a file, but if excessive, renewal is necessary as it is not permissible to machine the surfaces.

18 If warpage of the cylinder head gasket surface is suspected, use a straight-edge to check it for distortion **(see illustration)**. Refer to Part F of this Chapter if necessary.

19 If possible, clean out the bolt holes in the block using compressed air, to ensure no oil or coolant is present. Screwing a bolt into an oil- or coolant-filled hole can (in extreme cases) cause the block to fracture, due to the hydraulic pressure created.

20 Although not essential, if a suitable tap-and-die set is available, it's worth running the correct-size tap down the bolt threads in the cylinder block. This will clean the threads of any debris, and go some way to restoring any damaged threads. Make absolutely sure the tap is the right size and thread pitch, and lightly oil the tap before starting.

21 Ford insist that the cylinder head bolts must be renewed.

Refitting

22 Wipe clean the mating surfaces of the cylinder head and cylinder block, and check that the two locating dowels are in position in the block.

12.24 Locate the new cylinder head gasket over the dowels

23 Turn the crankshaft anti-clockwise so that pistons 1 and 4 are approximately 25 mm before TDC, in order to avoid the risk of valve/piston contact. Turn the crankshaft using a spanner on the pulley bolt.

24 If the old gasket is still available, check that it is identical to the new one – for instance, there are several different thicknesses of gasket, indicated by the number of small holes on one side. Position the new gasket over the dowels on the cylinder block surface. It can only be fitted one way round – check carefully that the holes in the gasket align with the holes in the block surface, and that none are blocked **(see illustration)**.

25 It is useful when refitting a cylinder head to have an assistant on hand to help guide the head onto the dowels. Take care that the gasket does not get moved as the head is lowered into position. To confirm that the head is aligned correctly, once it is in place, temporarily slide in two or more of the head bolts, and check that they fit into the block holes.

26 Fit the new head bolts carefully, and screw them in by hand only until finger-tight.

27 Working progressively and in sequence, tighten the cylinder head bolts to their Stage 1 torque setting **(see illustrations)**.

28 Next, go around again in the same sequence, and tighten the bolts to the Stage 2 setting.

29 Finally, the bolts should be angle-tightened further, by the specified Stage 3 amount. This means simply that each bolt in the sequence must be turned through the stated angle.

12.29 Use an angle-gauge for the final stage

J46823

12.27a Cylinder head bolt tightening sequence (non-Ti-VCT engines)

Special 'angle gauges' are available from tool suppliers for measuring this, but since 90° is a right-angle, it is possible to judge reasonably accurately by assessing the start and finish positions of the socket handle **(see illustration)**.

30 The remainder of refitting is a reversal of removal, noting the following points:

a) Refit the camshafts as described in Section 11, and the timing belt as described in Section 8.
b) Tighten all fasteners to the specified torque, where given.
c) Ensure that all hoses and wiring are correctly routed, and that hose clips and wiring connectors are securely refitted.
d) Refill the cooling system as described in Chapter 1.
e) Check all disturbed joints for signs of oil or coolant leakage once the engine has been restarted and warmed-up to normal operating temperature.

13 Sump – removal and refitting

Removal

1 Apply the handbrake, then jack up the front of the car and support it on axle stands (see *Jacking and vehicle support*).

2 Drain the engine oil, then check the drain plug sealing washer and renew if necessary. Clean and refit the engine oil drain plug together with the washer, and tighten it to the specified torque wrench setting. Although not strictly necessary, as the oil is being drained, it makes sense to fit a new oil filter at the same time (see Chapter 1).

3 Release the clip, undo the retaining bolt, and pull the engine oil level dipstick guide tube from the sump. Check the condition of the seal at the base of the tube, and renew it if necessary.

J46810

12.27b Cylinder head bolt tightening sequence (Ti-VCT engines)

4 Unscrew the bolts securing the transmission to the sump, then progressively unscrew the sump-to-block bolts **(see illustration)**.

5 On these models, a sump gasket is not used, and sealant is used instead. Unfortunately, the use of sealant makes removal of the sump more difficult. If care is taken not to damage the surfaces, the sealant can be cut around using a sharp knife.

6 On no account lever between the mating faces, as this will almost certainly damage them, resulting in leaks when finished. Ford technicians have a tool comprising a metal rod which is inserted through the sump drain hole, and a handle to pull the sump downwards. Providing care is taken not to damage the threads, a large screwdriver could be used in the drain hole to prise down the sump.

7 While the sump is removed, take the opportunity to remove the oil pump pick-up/strainer pipe, and clean it with reference to Section 14.

Refitting

8 Thoroughly clean the contact surfaces of the sump and crankcase. Take care not to damage the oil pump gasket or the crankshaft oil seal, both of which are partially exposed when the sump is removed. If necessary, use a cloth rag to clean inside the sump and crankcase. If the oil pump pick-up/strainer

13.4 Sump viewed from below, showing the engine and transmission bolts

13.9 Sump alignment stud positions (arrowed)

13.10 Apply the bead of sealant to the sump mating surface as shown

13.13 Sump bolt tightening sequence. Also shows sump-to-transmission bolts (A)

pipe was removed, fit a new O-ring and refit the pipe with reference to Section 14.

9 Ford state that, to refit the sump, five M8x20 studs must be screwed into the base of the engine **(see illustration)**. This not only helps to align the sump, ensuring that the bead of sealant is not displaced as the sump is fitted, but also ensures that the sealant does not enter the blind holes. Cut a slot across the end of each stud, to make removal easier when the sump is in place.

10 Apply a 3 to 4 mm diameter bead of sealant (Ford recommend WSE M4G323-A4, or equivalent) to the sump pan, to the inside of the bolt holes **(see illustration)**. The sump bolts must be fitted and tightened within 10 minutes of applying the sealant.

11 Offer the sump up into position over the studs, and fully refit the remaining bolts by hand. Unscrew the studs, and refit the sump bolts in their place. The sump should be fitted flush with the block at the transmission end.

12 Insert the four sump-to-transmission bolts and tighten them to the specified torque.

13 The sump-to-crankcase bolts are tightened in two stages. Working in sequence **(see illustration)**, tighten all the sump bolts to the specified Stage 1 torque, then go around again in sequence, and tighten them to the Stage 2 setting.

14 Refit the engine oil level dipstick guide tube, with a new seal where necessary, and tighten the retaining bolt securely. Refit the clip.

15 Lower the car to the ground. To be on the safe side, wait a further 30 minutes for the sealant to cure before filling the sump with fresh oil, as described in Chapter 1.

16 Finally start the engine and check for signs of oil leaks.

14 Oil pump – removal, inspection and refitting

Removal

1 Remove the crankshaft right-hand oil seal as described in Section 16.

2 Remove the sump as described in Section 13.

3 Undo the timing belt rear cover lower 2 bolts.

4 On models with air conditioning, remove the four bolts securing the air conditioning compressor, and tie it up clear of the engine without disconnecting any of the hoses.

5 Unscrew the bolts securing the oil pump pick-up/strainer pipe to the baffle plate/main bearing cap.

6 Unscrew the bolt securing the oil pump pick-up/strainer pipe to the oil pump, then withdraw the pipe and recover the sealing O-ring **(see illustration)**. Discard the O-ring.

7 Unscrew the bolts securing the oil pump to the cylinder block/crankcase **(see illustration)**. Withdraw the pump over the nose of the crankshaft.

8 Recover then discard the gasket **(see illustration)**.

9 If necessary, unbolt and remove the baffle plate from the main bearing cap/ladder **(see illustration)**. Thoroughly clean all components, particularly the mating surfaces of the pump, the sump, and the cylinder block/crankcase.

14.6 Remove the O-ring seal from the oil pump pick-up/strainer pipe

14.7 Remove the oil pump-to cylinder block/crankcase bolts

14.8 Remove the oil pump gasket

Inspection

10 It is not possible to obtain individual components of the oil pump, furthermore, there are no torque settings available for tightening the pump cover plate bolts. However, the following procedure is provided for owners wishing to dismantle the oil pump for examination.

11 Take out the bolts, and remove the pump cover plate; noting any identification marks on the rotors, withdraw the rotors.

12 Inspect the rotors for obvious signs of wear or damage, and renew if necessary; if either rotor, the pump body, or its cover plate are scored or damaged, the complete oil pump assembly must be renewed.

13 The oil pressure relief valve can be dismantled as follows.

14 Unscrew the threaded plug, and recover the valve spring and plunger. If the plug's sealing O-ring is worn or damaged, a new one must be obtained, to be fitted on reassembly.

15 Reassembly is the reverse of the dismantling procedure; ensure the spring and valve are refitted the correct way round, and tighten the threaded plug securely.

Refitting

16 If removed, refit the oil baffle plate to the crankcase and tighten the bolts.

17 The oil pump must be primed on installation, by pouring clean engine oil into it and rotating its inner rotor a few turns.

18 Use a little grease to stick the new gasket in place on the cylinder block/crankcase.

19 Offer the oil pump over the nose of the crankshaft, and turn the inner rotor as necessary to align its flats with the flats on the crankshaft. Locate the pump on the dowels, then insert the retaining bolts and progressively tighten them to the specified torque.

20 Locate a new O-ring (dipped in oil) on the pick-up/strainer pipe, then locate the pipe in the oil pump and insert the retaining bolts. Insert the bolts retaining the pipe on the baffle plate/main bearing cap. Tighten the bolts to the specified torque.

21 Where removed, refit the air conditioning compressor, tightening the bolts to the specified torque.

22 Refit the sump as described in Section 13.

23 Fit a new crankshaft oil seal as described in Section 16.

15 Oil pressure switch – removal and refitting

1 The oil pressure switch is a vital early warning of low oil pressure. The switch operates the oil warning light on the instrument panel – the light should come on with the ignition, and go out almost immediately when the engine starts.

2 If the light does not come on, there could be a fault on the instrument panel, the switch wiring, or the switch itself. If the light does not

14.9 Unbolt the baffle plate from the main bearing cap/ladder

go out, low oil level, worn oil pump (or sump pick-up blocked), blocked oil filter, or worn main bearings could be to blame – or again, the switch may be faulty.

3 If the light comes on while driving, the best advice is to turn the engine off immediately, and not to drive the car until the problem has been investigated – ignoring the light could mean expensive engine damage.

Removal

4 The oil pressure switch is located on the front face of the engine, above the oil filter **(see illustration)**.

5 Disconnect the wiring plug from the switch.

6 Unscrew the switch from the block, and remove it. There should only be a very slight loss of oil when this is done.

Inspection

7 Examine the switch for signs of cracking or splits. If the top part of the switch is loose, this is an early indication of impending failure.

8 Check that the wiring terminals at the switch are not loose, then trace the wire from the switch connector until it enters the main loom – any wiring defects will give rise to apparent oil pressure problems.

Refitting

9 Refitting is the reverse of the removal procedure, noting the following points:

a) Tighten the switch securely.
b) Reconnect the switch connector, making sure it clicks home properly. Ensure that the wiring is routed away from any hot or moving parts.

16.6 Locate the new right-hand oil seal over the crankshaft

15.4 Oil pressure switch (arrowed)

c) Check the engine oil level and top-up if necessary (see 'Weekly checks').
d) Check for signs of oil leaks once the engine has been restarted and warmed-up to normal operating temperature.

16 Crankshaft oil seals – renewal

Right-hand oil seal

1 Remove the crankshaft sprocket as described in Section 9.

2 As a safety precaution, refit the engine right-hand mounting upper section and mounting bracket, and tighten the mounting bolts/nuts.

3 Note the fitted depth of the oil seal as a guide for fitting the new one.

4 Using a screwdriver, prise the old oil seal from the oil pump housing. Take great care not to damage the seal contact surface on the nose of the crankshaft, or the seating in the housing.

5 Wipe clean the seating and the nose of the crankshaft.

6 Apply a little clean engine oil to the inner lip of the seal, then locate it over the crankshaft and into the oil pump housing. Make sure that the closed end of the oil seal faces outwards **(see illustration)**.

7 Using a socket or length of metal tubing, drive the oil seal squarely into position to the previously-noted depth. The Ford installation tool (303-395) is used together with an old crankshaft pulley bolt to press the oil seal into position. The same idea may be used with metal tubing and a large washer – do not use a new crankshaft pulley bolt, as it is only permissible to use the bolt once. With the oil seal in position, wipe away any excess oil.

8 With the weight of the engine once more supported, unscrew the nuts and bolts and remove the engine right-hand mounting upper section and mounting bracket.

9 Refit the crankshaft sprocket with reference to Section 9.

Left-hand oil seal

10 Remove the flywheel/driveplate as described in Section 17.

16.14 Locate the new oil seal housing (complete with fitting sleeve) over the end of the crankshaft

16.16 With the oil seal housing bolted into position, remove the fitting ring

11 Unscrew the six bolts and withdraw the oil seal carrier from the end of the crankshaft. Note that the seal and carrier are made as one unit – it is not possible to obtain the seal separately.

12 Clean the carrier contact surface on the cylinder block, and the end of the crankshaft.

13 The new oil seal carrier is supplied complete with a fitting sleeve, which ensures that the oil seal lips are correctly located on the crankshaft. Ford state that neither the crankshaft nor the new oil seal should be lubricated before fitting.

14 Locate the oil seal carrier and fitting sleeve over the end of the crankshaft. Press the carrier into position, noting that the centre bolt holes are formed into locating dowels **(see illustration)**.

15 Insert the retaining bolts and progressively tighten them to the specified torque.

16 Remove the fitting sleeve and check that the oil seal lips are correctly located **(see illustration)**.

17 Refit the flywheel/driveplate as described in Section 17.

---

17 Flywheel/driveplate –
removal, inspection and refitting

Removal

1 Remove the transmission as described in Chapter 7, and the clutch as described in Chapter 6.

2 Hold the flywheel/driveplate stationary using one of the following methods:
  a) *If an assistant is available, insert one of the transmission mounting bolts into the cylinder block and have the assistant engage a wide-bladed screwdriver with the starter ring gear teeth while the bolts are loosened. Alternatively, a piece of angle-iron can be engaged with the ring gear and located against the transmission mounting bolt.*
  b) *A further method is to fabricate a piece of flat metal bar with a pointed end to engage the ring gear – fit the tool to the transmission bolt and use washers and packing to align it with the ring gear, then tighten the bolt to hold it in position (see illustration).*

3 Unscrew and remove the bolts, then lift the flywheel/driveplate off the locating dowel on the crankshaft **(see illustration)**.

Inspection

4 Clean the flywheel/driveplate to remove grease and oil. Inspect the surface for cracks, rivet grooves, burned areas and score marks. Light scoring can be removed with emery cloth. Check for cracked and broken ring gear teeth. Lay the flywheel/driveplate on a flat surface, and use a straight-edge to check for warpage.

5 Clean and inspect the mating surfaces of the flywheel/driveplate and the crankshaft. If the crankshaft oil seal is leaking, renew it (see Section 16) before refitting the flywheel/driveplate. In fact, given the large amount

of work needed to remove the flywheel/driveplate, it's probably worth fitting a new seal anyway, as a precaution.

6 While the flywheel/driveplate is removed, clean carefully its inner face, particularly the recesses which serve as the reference points for the crankshaft speed/position sensor. Clean the sensor's tip, and check that the sensor is securely fastened. The sensor mounting may be removed if necessary by first removing the sensor, then unscrewing the bolt and withdrawing the mounting from the cylinder block **(see illustration)**.

Refitting

7 Make sure that the mating faces of the flywheel/driveplate and crankshaft are clean, then locate the flywheel/driveplate on the crankshaft and engage it with the locating dowel.

8 Insert the retaining bolts finger-tight.

9 Lock the flywheel/driveplate (see paragraph 2), then tighten the bolts in a diagonal sequence to the specified torque.

10 Refit the clutch with reference to Chapter 6, and the transmission as described in Chapter 7.

---

18 Engine/transmission mountings –
inspection and renewal

General

1 The engine/transmission mountings seldom require attention, but broken or deteriorated mountings should be renewed immediately, or the added strain placed on the driveline components may cause damage or wear.

2 While separate mountings may be removed and refitted individually, if more than one is disturbed at a time – such as if the engine/transmission unit is removed from its mountings – they must be reassembled and their fasteners tightened in the position marked on removal.

3 On reassembly, the complete weight of the engine/transmission unit must not be taken by the mountings until all are correctly aligned with the marks made on removal. Tighten the engine/transmission mounting fasteners to their specified torque wrench settings.

17.2 Home-made flywheel locking tool

17.3 Remove the flywheel retaining bolts. Note the dowel (arrowed) in the end of the crankshaft

17.6 Crankshaft position sensor mounting and retaining bolt

Inspection

4 During the check, the engine/transmission unit must be raised slightly, to remove its weight from the mountings.

5 Raise the front of the vehicle, and support it securely on axle stands. Position a jack under the sump, with a large block of wood between the jack head and the sump, then carefully raise the engine/transmission just enough to take the weight off the mountings.

 Warning: DO NOT place any part of your body under the engine when it is supported only by a jack.

6 Check the mountings to see if the rubber is cracked, hardened or separated from the metal components. Sometimes the rubber will split right down the centre.

7 Check for relative movement between each mounting's brackets and the engine/transmission or body (use a large screwdriver or lever to attempt to move the mountings). If movement is noted, lower the engine and check-tighten the mounting fasteners.

Renewal

Note: *The following paragraphs assume the engine is supported beneath the sump as described earlier.*

Right-hand mounting

8 Lift up the coolant expansion tank and position it to one side. Note there is no need to disconnect the coolant pipes.

9 Mark the position of the mounting on the

18.14 Left-hand mounting centre bolt (arrowed)

vehicle, right-hand inner wing panel, undo the nuts securing the upper mounting bracket **(see illustration 3.14)**. Discard the nuts, new ones must be fitted.

10 Undo the two retaining bolts to the vehicle inner wing panel and withdraw the mounting from the vehicle.

11 On refitting, tighten all fasteners to the torque wrench settings specified. Re-align the marks made on removal, then tighten the mounting bracket new retaining nuts.

Left-hand mounting

12 Remove the air cleaner assembly as described in Chapter 4.

13 Remove the battery as described in Chapter 5, then undo the 3 bolts and remove the battery tray. Disconnect any wiring as the tray is withdrawn.

18.17 Rear mounting/roll restrictor bolts (arrowed)

14 With the transmission supported, note the position of the mounting then unscrew the centre retaining bolt to release the mounting from the transmission **(see illustration)**.

15 Unscrew the four outer retaining nuts, and 2 bolts to dismantle the mounting from the mounting bracket.

16 On refitting, renew the self-locking nuts. Re-align the mounting in the position noted on removal, then tighten all fasteners to the specified torque wrench settings.

Rear mounting (roll restrictor)

17 Unbolt the mounting from the subframe and the transmission by unscrewing the mounting's centre bolts **(see illustration)**.

18 On refitting, ensure that the bolts are securely tightened to the specified torque wrench setting.

Notes

Chapter 2 Part B:
1.8 & 2.0 litre petrol engines in-car repair procedures

Contents

Section number

Camshafts and tappets – removal, inspection and refitting. 9
Compression test – description and interpretation 2
Crankshaft oil seals – renewal 10
Crankshaft pulley – removal and refitting. 6
Cylinder head – removal and refitting. 11
Cylinder head cover – removal and refitting. 4
Engine/transmission mountings – inspection and renewal 16
Flywheel/driveplate – removal, inspection and refitting 15
General information 1

Section number

Oil pressure warning light switch – removal and refitting. 14
Oil pump – removal, inspection and refitting 13
Sump – removal and refitting 12
Timing chain cover – removal and refitting. 7
Timing chain, tensioner and guides – removal, inspection and
    refitting 8
Top Dead Centre (TDC) for No 1 piston – locating. 3
Valve clearances – checking and adjustment 5

Degrees of difficulty

Easy, suitable for novice with little experience	**Fairly easy,** suitable for beginner with some experience	**Fairly difficult,** suitable for competent DIY mechanic	**Difficult,** suitable for experienced DIY mechanic	**Very difficult,** suitable for expert DIY or professional

Specifications

General

Engine type.	Four-cylinder, in-line, chain-driven double overhead camshafts, aluminium alloy cylinder head and engine block
Engine code:	
1.8 litre	QQDB and Q7DA
2.0 litre	AODA
Capacity:	
1.8 litre	1798 cc
2.0 litre	1998 cc
Bore:	
1.8 litre	83.0 mm
2.0 litre	87.5 mm
Stroke.	83.1 mm
Compression ratio	10.8:1
Output:	
Power:	
1.8 litre	82 kW (125 PS) @ 6000 rpm
2.0 litre	107 kW (145 PS) @ 6000 rpm
Torque:	
1.8 litre	165 Nm @ 4000 rpm
2.0 litre	185 Nm @ 4500 rpm
Firing order	1-3-4-2 (No 1 cylinder at timing chain end)
Direction of crankshaft rotation	Clockwise (seen from right-hand side of vehicle)

Camshafts

Camshaft endfloat	0.09 to 0.24 mm
Camshaft bearing journal diameter	24.96 to 24.98 mm

Valves

Valve clearances (cold):

	Intake	Exhaust
All engines	0.22 to 0.28 mm	0.27 to 0.33 mm

Lubrication

Oil pressure (engine at operating temperature):

At 1500 rpm	1.3 to 2.7 bar	
At 3000 rpm	2.3 to 5.2 bar	
Oil pressure relief valve opens at:	5.0 bar	

Torque wrench settings

	Nm	lbf ft
Air conditioning compressor	25	18
Camshaft bearing cap bolts:		
Stage 1	7	5
Stage 2	16	12
Camshaft position sensor	6	4
Camshaft sprocket	72	53
Crankshaft oil seal carrier bolts	10	7
Crankshaft pulley bolt:*		
Stage 1	100	74
Stage 2	Angle-tighten a further 90°	
Cylinder block blanking plug	20	15
Cylinder head bolts:*		
Stage 1	5	4
Stage 2	15	11
Stage 3	45	33
Stage 4	Angle-tighten a further 90°	
Stage 5	Angle-tighten a further 90°	
Cylinder head cover bolts	10	7
Engine mountings:		
Right-hand mounting retaining bolts	90	66
Right-hand mounting bracket-to-engine bolts	56	41
Left-hand mounting nuts	48	35
Left-hand mounting bracket to transmission	80	59
Left-hand mounting centre bolt	148	109
Lower-rear torque rod bolts	80	59
Flywheel/driveplate bolts:*		
Stage 1	30	22
Stage 2	Angle-tighten a further 90°	
Oil pick-up pipe bolts	10	7
Oil pressure switch	15	11
Oil pump chain guide	10	7
Oil pump chain tensioner	10	7
Oil pump sprocket bolt	25	18
Oil pump-to-cylinder block bolts:		
Stage 1	10	7
Stage 2	23	17
Sump drain plug	28	21
Sump pan to lower crankcase	25	18
Sump pan to transmission	50	37
Timing chain covers:		
M6	10	7
M8	48	35
Timing chain guide	10	7
Timing chain tensioner	10	7

* Do not re-use

1 General information

How to use this Chapter

This Part of Chapter 2 is devoted to repair procedures possible while the engine is still installed in the vehicle. Since these procedures are based on the assumption that the engine is installed in the vehicle, if the engine has been removed from the vehicle and mounted on a stand, some of the preliminary dismantling steps outlined will not apply.

Information concerning engine/transmission removal and refitting and engine overhaul can be found in Part F of this Chapter.

Engine description

The engine is of sixteen-valve, double overhead camshaft (DOHC), four-cylinder, in-line type, mounted transversely at the front of the vehicle, with the transmission on its left-hand end. It is available in 1.8 and 2.0 litre versions.

All major engine castings are of aluminium alloy, with cast-iron cylinder liners, and a crankshaft made from forged nodular iron.

The crankshaft runs in five main bearings, the centre main bearing's upper half incorporating thrustwashers to control crankshaft endfloat. The connecting rods rotate on horizontally-split bearing shells at their big-ends. The pistons are attached to the connecting rods by gudgeon pins which are an interference fit in the connecting rod small-end eyes. The aluminium alloy pistons are fitted with three piston rings: two compression rings and an oil control ring. After manufacture, the cylinder bores and piston skirts are measured and classified into three grades, which must be carefully matched together to ensure the correct piston/cylinder clearance; no oversizes are available to permit reboring. Cylinder blocks are supplied complete with crankshafts, pistons and connecting rods assembled. These components are not available separately.

The intake and exhaust valves are each closed by coil springs; they operate in guides which are shrink-fitted into the cylinder head, as are the valve seat inserts.

The two camshafts are driven by the same timing chain, each operating eight valves via solid tappets (cam followers). The tappets are graded for thickness, and are renewed in order to adjust the valve clearances. Each camshaft rotates in five bearings that are line-bored directly in the cylinder head and the (bolted-on) bearing caps; this means that the bearing caps are not available separately from the cylinder head, and must not be interchanged with caps from another engine.

The coolant pump is bolted to the right-hand end of the cylinder block, and is driven with the alternator by a multi-ribbed auxiliary drivebelt from the crankshaft pulley.

When working on this engine, note that Torx-type (both male and female heads) and hexagon socket (Allen head) fasteners are widely used; a good selection of bits, with the necessary adapters, will be required, so that these can be unscrewed without damage and, on reassembly, tightened to the torque wrench settings specified.

Lubrication system

Lubrication is by means of an eccentric-rotor pump, which is mounted at right-hand end of the cylinder block, and is driven by a chain from a sprocket on the crankshaft, and draws oil through a strainer located in the sump. The pump forces oil through an externally-mounted full-flow cartridge-type filter. From the filter, the oil is pumped into a main gallery in the cylinder block/crankcase, from where it is distributed to the crankshaft (main bearings) and cylinder head.

The big-end bearings are supplied with oil via internal drillings in the crankshaft. Each piston crown is cooled by a spray of oil

directed at its underside by a jet. These jets are fed by passages off the crankshaft oil supply galleries, with spring-loaded valves to ensure that the jets open only when there is sufficient pressure to guarantee a good oil supply to the rest of the engine components.

The cylinder head is provided with two oil galleries, one on the intake side and one on the exhaust, to ensure constant oil supply to the camshaft bearings and tappets. A retaining valve (inserted into the cylinder head's top surface, in the middle, on the intake side) prevents these galleries from being drained when the engine is switched off. The valve incorporates a ventilation hole in its upper end, to allow air bubbles to escape from the system when the engine is restarted.

While the crankshaft and camshaft bearings receive a pressurised supply, the camshaft lobes and valves are lubricated by splash, as are all other engine components.

Operations with engine in car

The following major repair operations can be accomplished without removing the engine from the vehicle. However, owners should note that any operation involving the removal of the sump requires careful forethought, depending on the level of skill and the tools and facilities available; refer to the relevant text for details.

a) Compression pressure – testing.
b) Cylinder head cover – removal and refitting.
c) Timing chain covers – removal and refitting.
d) Timing chain – renewal.
e) Timing chain tensioner and sprockets – removal and refitting.
f) Camshaft oil seals – renewal.
g) Camshafts and cam tappets – removal and refitting.
h) Cylinder head – removal, overhaul and refitting.
i) Cylinder head and pistons – decarbonising.
j) Sump – removal and refitting.
k) Crankshaft oil seals – renewal.
l) Oil pump – removal and refitting.
m) Flywheel/driveplate – removal and refitting.
n) Engine/transmission mountings – removal and refitting.

Clean the engine compartment and the exterior of the engine with some type of degreaser before any work is done (and/or clean the engine using a steam cleaner). It will make the job easier and will help to keep dirt out of the internal areas of the engine.

Depending on the components involved, it may be helpful to remove the bonnet to improve access to the engine as repairs are performed (refer to Chapter 11 if necessary). Cover the wings to prevent damage to the paint; special covers are available, but an old bedspread or blanket will also work.

2 Compression test – description and interpretation

1 When engine performance is down, or if misfiring occurs which cannot be attributed to the ignition or fuel systems, a compression test can provide diagnostic clues as to the engine's condition. If the test is performed regularly, it can give warning of trouble before any other symptoms become apparent.

2 The engine must be fully warmed-up to normal operating temperature, the oil level must be correct and the battery must be fully-charged. The aid of an assistant will also be required.

3 Referring to Chapter 12 identify and remove the fuel pump relay from the fusebox. Now start the engine and allow it to run until it stalls. If the engine will not start, at least keep it cranking for about 10 seconds. The fuel system should now be depressurised, preventing unburnt fuel from soaking the catalytic converter as the engine is turned over during the test.

4 Disable the ignition system by unplugging the crankshaft speed/position sensor (see Chapter 4). Remove the spark plugs as described in Chapter 1.

5 Fit a compression tester to the No 1 cylinder spark plug hole – the type of tester which screws into the plug thread is to be preferred.

6 Have the assistant hold the throttle wide open and crank the engine on the starter motor; after one or two revolutions, the compression pressure should build-up to a maximum figure and then stabilise. Record the highest reading obtained.

7 The compression will build-up fairly quickly in a healthy engine. Low compression on the first stroke, followed by gradually-increasing pressure on successive strokes, indicates worn piston rings. A low compression on the first stroke which does not rise on successive strokes, indicates leaking valves or a blown head gasket (a cracked cylinder head could also be the cause). Deposits on the underside of the valve heads can also cause low compression. Record the highest gauge reading obtained, then repeat the procedure for the remaining cylinders.

8 Due to the variety of testers available, and the fluctuation in starter motor speed when cranking the engine, different readings are often obtained when carrying out the compression test. For this reason, specific compression pressure figures are not quoted by Ford. However, the most important factor is that the compression pressures are uniform in all cylinders, and that is what this test is mainly concerned with.

9 If the pressure in any cylinder is considerably lower than the others, introduce a teaspoonful of clean oil into that cylinder through its spark plug hole and repeat the test.

10 If the addition of oil temporarily improves the compression pressure, this indicates that

3.8a These 2 holes (arrowed) will align at TDC – so this is about 45° before TDC

3.8b Remove the timing hole plug . . .

3.8c . . . and insert the timing pin

bore or piston wear is responsible for the pressure loss. No improvement suggests that leaking or burnt valves, or a blown head gasket, may be to blame.

11 A low reading from two adjacent cylinders is almost certainly due to the head gasket having blown between them; the presence of coolant in the engine oil will confirm this.

12 If one cylinder is about 20 percent lower than the others and the engine has a slightly rough idle, a worn camshaft lobe or faulty tappet could be the cause.

13 If the compression is unusually high, the combustion chambers are probably coated with carbon deposits. If this is the case, the cylinder head should be removed and decarbonised.

14 On completion of the test, refit the spark plugs, then reconnect the crankshaft speed/position sensor, and refit the fuel pump fuse. Note that carrying out this test as described may result in one or more fault codes being stored by the engine management ECM. Have these codes erased by a Ford dealer or suitably-equipped specialist.

3 Top Dead Centre (TDC) for No 1 piston – locating

Note: Only turn the engine in the normal direction of rotation – clockwise from the right-hand side of the vehicle.

General

1 Top Dead Centre (TDC) is the highest point

3.10 Insert an M6 bolt though the pulley into the hole in the casing – TDC position

in its travel up-and-down its cylinder bore that each piston reaches as the crankshaft rotates. While each piston reaches TDC both at the top of the compression stroke and again at the top of the exhaust stroke, for the purpose of timing the engine, TDC refers to the No 1 piston position at the top of its compression stroke.

2 It is useful for several servicing procedures to be able to position the engine at TDC.

3 No 1 piston and cylinder are at the right-hand (timing chain) end of the engine (right- and left-hand are always quoted as seen from the driver's seat).

Locating TDC

4 Remove all the spark plugs; this will make it easier to turn the engine (Chapter 1).

5 Disconnect the battery negative (earth) lead (refer to Chapter 5).

6 Apply the handbrake, then jack up the front of the vehicle and support it on axle stands (see *Jacking and vehicle support*). Remove the right-hand front roadwheel.

7 Undo the fasteners, then remove the right-hand front wheel arch liner.

8 There is a timing hole provided on the rear of the cylinder block (behind the TDC sensor) to position the crankshaft at TDC. Using a spanner or socket on the crankshaft pulley bolt, rotate the crankshaft clockwise until it is positioned approximately 45° before TDC **(see illustrations)**. Unscrew the timing hole plug and insert a timing peg obtainable from Ford dealers (303-507) – or a tool supplier.

3.12 Slide the tool/metal bar into the slots in the end of the camshafts

9 Rotate the crankshaft clockwise until it stops against the timing peg.

10 There is a bolt hole in the crankshaft pulley which should align with the thread in the timing chain cover, insert a bolt (M6 x 18 mm) to locate the pulley at TDC **(see illustration)**.

11 Number 1 and 4 pistons are now at TDC, one of them on the compression stroke. To determine which cylinder is on the compression stroke the camshaft cover will need to be removed (as described in Section 5).

12 Obtain Ford service tool 303-376A, or fabricate a substitute from a strip of metal 5 mm thick (while the strip's thickness is critical, its length and width are not, but should be approximately 180 to 230 mm by 20 to 30 mm). If number 1 cylinder is on the compression stroke – rest the tool on the cylinder head mating surface, and slide it into the slot in the left-hand end of both camshafts **(see illustration)**. The tool should slip snugly into both slots while resting on the cylinder head mating surface; if one camshaft is only slightly out of alignment, it is permissible to use an open-ended spanner to rotate the camshaft gently and carefully until the tool will fit.

13 If both camshaft slots (they are machined significantly off-centre) are below the level of the cylinder head mating surface, rotate the crankshaft through one full turn clockwise and fit the tool again; it should now fit as described in the previous paragraph. **Note:** *The timing peg and crankshaft pulley locking bolt will have to be removed before turning the engine.*

14 Do not use the locked camshafts to prevent the crankshaft from rotating – use only the locking methods described in Section 6 for removing the crankshaft pulley.

15 Once No 1 cylinder has been positioned at TDC on the compression stroke, TDC for any of the other cylinders can then be located by rotating the crankshaft clockwise 180° at a time and following the firing order (see Specifications).

16 Before turning the engine again, make sure that the timing peg and crankshaft pulley locating bolt have been removed.

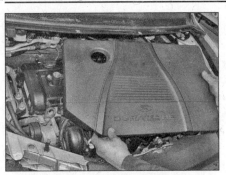

4.2 Pull the engine cover upwards

4.3 Disconnect the camshaft position sensor wiring plug (arrowed)

4.5 Squeeze together the sides of the collar (arrowed) and disconnect the breather hose

4 Cylinder head cover – removal and refitting

Removal

1 Disconnect the battery negative (earth) lead (refer to Chapter 5).
2 Remove the plastic cover on the top of the engine by pulling it straight up from its mountings **(see illustration)**.
3 Disconnect the electrical connector from the camshaft position sensor **(see illustration)**.
4 Detach the wiring harness from the camshaft cover.
5 Disconnect the positive crankcase ventilation (PCV) hose from the left-hand rear corner of the camshaft cover **(see illustration)**.
6 Unscrew the three engine upper plastic cover retaining pegs from the camshaft cover retaining studs, note the position of the retaining studs.
7 Undo the bolt securing the oxygen sensor wiring plugs bracket **(see illustration)**.
8 Carefully undo the retaining bolts and lift out the ignition coils above the spark plugs **(see illustration)**.
9 Working progressively, unscrew the cylinder head cover retaining bolts and withdraw the cover. Note that the bolts are integral with the cover.
10 Check the condition of the cover gasket, and renew it necessary.

Refitting

11 On refitting, clean the cover and cylinder head gasket faces carefully, then fit new gaskets to the cover where necessary, ensuring that they locate correctly in the cover grooves.
12 Apply a little silicone sealant (Ford No WSE-M4G323-A4) to the area where the upper edge of the timing chain cover contacts the cylinder head.
13 Refit the cover to the cylinder head. Start all bolts finger-tight, ensuring that the gasket remains seated in its groove.
14 Working in the sequence shown (see illustration), tighten the cover bolts to the specified torque wrench setting. Refit the three

4.7 Oxygen sensor wiring plugs bracket bolt (arrowed)

engine upper plastic cover retaining pegs to the cover retaining studs noted on removal.
15 The remainder of reassembly is the reverse of the removal procedure.

5 Valve clearances – checking and adjustment

Note: *Only turn the engine in the normal direction of rotation – clockwise viewed from the right-hand side of the vehicle.*

Checking

1 Remove the cylinder head cover as described in Section 4.

4.8 Undo the bolt and pull out the ignition coils

2 Set the engine to TDC on cylinder No 1 as described in Section 3. The intake and exhaust cam lobes of No 1 cylinder will be pointing upwards (though not vertical) and the valve clearances can be checked.
3 Working on each valve, measure the clearance between the base of the cam lobe and the bucket tappet using feeler blades **(see illustration)**. Record the thickness of the blade required to give a firm sliding fit on all the valves of No 1 cylinder. The desired clearances are given in the Specifications. Note that the clearances for intake and exhaust valves are different. The intake camshaft is at the front of the engine and the exhaust camshaft at the rear. Record all four clearances.

4.14 Cylinder head cover bolt tightening sequence

5.3 Measure the clearance between the base of the cam lobe and the tappet using feeler gauges

4 Now turn the crankshaft clockwise through 180° so that the valves of cylinder No 3 are pointing upwards. Check and record the four valve clearances for cylinder No 3. The clearances for cylinders 4 and 2 can be checked after turning the crankshaft through 180° each time.

Adjustment

5 If adjustment is required, the bucket tappets must be changed by removing the camshafts as described in Section 9.
6 If the valve clearance was too small, a thinner bucket tappet must be fitted. If the clearance was too large, a thicker bucket tappet must be fitted. The bucket tappet has a number engraved on the inside **(see illustration)**, if the marking is missing or illegible, a micrometer will be needed to establish bucket tappet thickness.
7 When the bucket tappet thickness and the valve clearance are known, the required thickness of the new bucket tappet can be calculated as follows:

New tappet thickness D

= *Existing tappet thickness C*
+ *Measured clearance B*
– *Desired clearance A*

Sample calculation

Desired clearance (A)   = 0.25
Measured clearance (B)   = 0.20
Existing tappet thickness (C) = 2.55
Tappet thickness required (D) = C+B-A = 2.50

All measurements in mm

6.3 Using a flywheel locking tool to prevent the flywheel from rotating

8 With the correct thickness bucket tappets fitted in the cylinder head, refit the camshafts as described in Section 9.
9 Check the valve clearances are now correct, as described in paragraphs 2 to 4. If any clearances are still not within specification then carry out the adjustment procedure again.
10 It will be helpful for future adjustment if a record is kept of the thickness of bucket fitted at each position. The buckets required can be purchased in advance once the clearances and the existing bucket thicknesses are known.
11 When all the clearances are correct, refit the cylinder head cover as described in Section 4.

5.6 The tappet bucket has a number engraved on the underside

6 Crankshaft pulley – removal and refitting

Note: *Only turn the engine in the normal direction of rotation – clockwise from the right-hand side of the vehicle.*
Caution: The pulley and crankshaft timing gear are not on a keyway, they are held in place by the crankshaft retaining bolt. Make sure the engine is set at TDC (see Section 3) before the pulley is removed.
Note: *The crankshaft pulley retaining bolt is very tight and Ford use special tools (205-072 and 205-072-02) to lock the pulley to prevent it from turning. A new pulley retaining bolt will be required on refitting.*

6.6 A new retaining bolt must be fitted

Removal

1 Remove the auxiliary drivebelts – either remove the drivebelts completely, or just secure them clear of the crankshaft pulley, depending on the work to be carried out (see Chapter 1).
2 Set the engine to TDC (see Section 3).
3 The crankshaft must now be locked to prevent its rotation while the pulley bolt is unscrewed. If the Ford special tools are not available proceed as follows:
 a) *Remove the rubber plug from the transmission bellhousing, and use a large screwdriver or similar to lock the flywheel/driveplate ring gear teeth while an assistant slackens the pulley bolt; take care not to damage the teeth or the surrounding castings when using this method.*
 b) *If the engine/transmission has been removed and separated, lock the flywheel/driveplate using a locking tool (see illustration).*
4 Unscrew the pulley bolt and remove the pulley.

Refitting

5 Refitting is the reverse of the removal procedure; making sure the engine has not moved from its setting at TDC (see Section 3).
6 Ensure that a new retaining bolt is used **(see illustration)**, and tightened to the torque specified at the beginning of this Chapter.

7 Timing chain cover – removal and refitting

Note: *Only turn the engine in the normal direction of rotation – clockwise from the right-hand side of the vehicle.*

Removal

1 Remove the cylinder head cover as described in Section 4.
2 Apply the handbrake, then jack up the front of the vehicle and support it on axle stands (see *Jacking and vehicle support*). Remove the right-hand front roadwheel and remove the cover from under the right-hand front wheel arch.
3 Slacken the water pump pulley retaining bolts by approximately three turns.
4 Remove the auxiliary drivebelts (Chapter 1).
5 Undo the bolts securing the protective cover over the air conditioning compressor, and remove the cover. Disconnect the wiring plug, then undo the compressor mounting bolts, and the refrigerant pipe bracket bolt, and move the compressor to one side **(see illustration)**. Suspend the compressor using wire or a strap from the vehicle bodywork/suspension. Note there is no need to disconnect any refrigerant pipes.
6 Remove the crankshaft pulley (Section 6).
7 Disconnect the crankshaft position (CKP) sensor wiring connector **(see illustration)**.
8 Unscrew the retaining bolts and remove the water pump pulley.

7.5 Compressor protective cover retaining bolts (arrowed)

7.7 Disconnect the crankshaft position sensor wiring plug

7.11 Undo the right-hand mounting bolts/ nuts (arrowed)

9 Detach the wiring harness from the studs on the lower edge of the timing chain cover.

10 Lift the coolant expansion tank from its mountings and move it to one side. If better access is required, drain sufficient coolant (see Chapter 1), then disconnect the lower coolant hose from the expansion tank.

11 Support the engine using a trolley jack and block of wood beneath the sump, then unscrew the nuts/bolts securing the engine/ transmission right-hand mounting bracket and remove the mounting from the engine **(see illustration)**. Unclip the air conditioning pipe as the mounting is removed.

12 Remove the auxiliary drivebelt tensioner lower bolt.

13 Unscrew the timing chain cover retaining bolts (noting their positions for refitting) and withdraw the cover from the engine.

Refitting

14 Refitting is the reverse of the removal procedure (using the relevant Sections). Note the following points:

a) *Clean the sealant from the timing cover, cylinder block and cylinder head mating surfaces. When using a scraper and solvent to remove all traces of old gasket/ sealant from the mating surfaces, be careful to ensure that you do not scratch or damage the material of either component – any solvents used must be suitable for this application. If the gasket was leaking, have the mating surfaces checked for warpage at an automotive engineering workshop.*

b) *Renew the crankshaft oil seal fitted into the timing chain cover as described in Section 10.*

c) *Ensure the drive shim is still fitted to the end of the crankshaft before the timing chain cover oil seal is fitted (see illustration).*

d) *Provided the relevant mating surfaces are clean and flat, apply a (3.0mm) bead of silicone sealant around the timing chain cover and the inner bolt holes (see illustration). Note: The cover must be fitted within 10 minutes of applying the sealant.*

e) *Tighten the timing chain cover bolts to the specified torque settings at the beginning of this Chapter, following the sequence shown (see illustration).*

7.14a Ensure the crankshaft pulley drive shim (arrowed) is fitted before fitting the new oil seal

7.14b Apply a 3.0 mm bead of sealant around the timing chain cover, including the inner bolt holes

7.14c Timing chain cover bolt tightening sequence

8.4 Press against the timing chain guide and insert a locking pin (approximately 1.5 mm diameter)

8.6 Use a spanner to hold the camshafts whilst undoing the retaining bolts

8.7a Withdraw the tensioner guide from the pivot pin . . .

8.7b . . . then undo the retaining bolts (arrowed) and remove the fixed guide

8.8 Timing chain tensioner bolts (arrowed)

---

8 Timing chain, tensioner and guides – removal, inspection and refitting

Note: *Only turn the engine in the normal direction of rotation – clockwise from the right-hand side of the vehicle.*

Removal

1 Remove the cylinder head cover as described in Section 4.

2 Set the engine to TDC as described in Section 3.

3 Remove the timing chain cover as described in Section 7.

4 Slacken the timing chain tensioner by inserting a small screwdriver into the access hole in the tensioner and releasing the pawl mechanism. Press against the timing chain guide to depress the piston into the tensioner

housing. When fully depressed, insert a locking pin (approximately 1.5 mm) to lock the piston in its compressed position **(see illustration)**.

5 Hold the camshafts by the hexagon sections on the shafts to prevent them from turning, using an open-ended spanner.

6 With the camshafts held in position, undo the camshaft sprocket retaining bolts and remove the camshaft sprockets and timing chain. Do not rotate the crankshaft until the timing chain is refitted **(see illustration)**.

7 If required, unbolt the fixed timing chain guide and withdraw the tensioner timing chain guide from its pivot pin on the cylinder head **(see illustrations)**.

8 To remove the tensioner, undo the two retaining bolts and remove the timing chain tensioner from the cylinder block, taking care not to remove the locking pin **(see illustration)**.

9 To remove the timing chain sprocket from the crankshaft, the oil pump drive chain will

need to be removed as described in Section 13. Note which way round it is fitted and mark the sprocket to ensure it is refitted the same way round.

Inspection

Note: *Keep all components identified for position to ensure correct refitting.*

10 Clean all components thoroughly and wipe dry.

11 Examine the chain tensioner and tensioner guide for excessive wear or other damage. Check the guides for deep grooves made by the timing chain. Renew them both if there is any doubt concerning their condition.

12 Examine the timing chain for excessive wear. Hold it horizontally and check how much movement exists in the chain links. If there is any doubt, compare it to a new chain. Renew as necessary.

13 Examine the teeth of the camshaft and crankshaft sprockets for excessive wear and damage.

14 Before refitting the timing chain tensioner, the piston must be compressed and locked until refitted (if not already done on removal). To do this, insert a small screwdriver into the access hole in the tensioner and release the pawl mechanism. Now lightly clamp the tensioner in a soft-jawed vice and slowly compress the piston. Do not apply excessive force and make sure that the piston remains aligned with its cylinder. When completely compressed, insert a locking pin/1.5 mm diameter wire rod into the special hole to lock the piston in its compressed position.

Refitting

15 If not already fitted, slide the crankshaft drive sprocket (and drive shim) onto the crankshaft. Ensure it is refitted the same way round as noted on removal (see Section 13 for further information on refitting the oil pump drive chain).

16 Refit the tensioner to the cylinder block and tighten the retaining bolts to the specified torque setting. Take care not to remove the locking pin **(see illustration)**.

17 Refit the fixed timing chain guide and tighten the two retaining bolts, then slide the tensioner timing chain guide back into place on the upper pivot pin **(see illustration)**.

8.16 Refit the timing chain tensioner (still in the locked position)

8.17 Refit the tensioner guides to the engine

8.19 Refit the camshaft sprockets into position, complete with timing chain

8.20 Press against the tensioner guide and withdraw the locking pin (arrowed)

8.22 Use a spanner on the camshaft hexagon section to prevent them from rotating

18 Refit the intake camshaft sprocket onto the camshaft, DO NOT tighten the retaining bolt at this stage.

19 With the timing chain around the exhaust camshaft sprocket refit the timing chain and sprocket, feeding the timing chain around the crankshaft drive sprocket and intake camshaft sprocket **(see illustration)**.

20 With the timing chain in place, press against the tensioner guide and withdraw the tensioner locking pin. This will then tension the timing chain **(see illustration)**.

21 Check that the engine is still set to TDC (as described in Section 3).

22 Tighten the both camshaft sprocket retaining bolts to the torque setting specified in the Specifications at the beginning of this Chapter. **Note:** *Use an open-ended spanner on the hexagon on the camshafts to stop them from turning* **(see illustration)**.

23 Refit the timing chain cover as described in Section 7.

24 Remove the camshaft locking plate and crankshaft timing peg and turn the engine (in the direction of engine rotation) two full turns. Refit the camshaft locking plate and crankshaft timing peg to make sure the engine is still set at TDC (see Section 3 for further information).

25 Refit the cylinder head cover as described in Section 4.

9 Camshafts and tappets –
removal, inspection and refitting

Note: *Only turn the engine in the normal direction of rotation – clockwise from the right-hand side of the vehicle.*

Removal

1 Remove the cylinder head cover as described in Section 4.

2 Set the engine to TDC on No 1 cylinder as described in Section 3.

3 Remove the timing chain cover lower and upper blanking plugs to gain access to the timing chain tensioner and guide **(see illustrations)**.

4 Slacken the timing chain tensioner by inserting a small screwdriver into the lower access hole in the timing chain cover and releasing the pawl mechanism in the tensioner **(see illustration)**.

5 Carefully turn the exhaust camshaft (by using an open-ended spanner on the hexagon on the shaft) in the normal direction of rotation (clockwise), to compress the timing chain tensioner **(see illustration)**.

6 Holding the exhaust camshaft in position, insert a bolt (M6 x 25 mm) into the upper access hole in the timing chain cover to lock the tensioner guide rail in position **(see illustration)**.

7 With the camshafts held in position (by using an open-ended spanner on the hexagon section on the shaft), slacken the camshaft sprocket retaining bolts.

8 Using a cable-tie or similar, fasten the timing chain to the camshaft sprockets.

9 Remove the camshaft sprocket retaining bolts and remove the sprockets, complete with timing chain, away from the camshafts. Using a suitable piece of wire secure the sprockets and timing chain to prevent them dropping into the timing cover.

9.3a Remove the timing chain cover lower . . .

9.3b . . . and upper blanking plugs

9.4 Insert a small screwdriver into the lower access hole to release the timing chain tensioner

9.5 Carefully turn the exhaust camshaft in the direction of the arrow

9.6 Whilst holding the exhaust camshaft in position, insert a bolt (M6 x 18 mm) to lock the tensioner guide rail

9.10 Sequence for slackening the camshaft bearing cap bolts

10 Working in sequence **(see illustration)**, slacken the camshaft bearing cap bolts progressively by half a turn at a time. Work only as described to release gradually and evenly the pressure of the valve springs on the caps.

11 Withdraw the camshaft bearing caps, noting their markings, then remove the camshafts. The intake camshaft can be identified by the reference lobe for the camshaft position

sensor; therefore, there is no need to mark the camshafts **(see illustrations)**.

12 Obtain sixteen small, clean containers, and number them 1 to 16. Using a rubber sucker, withdraw each bucket tappet in turn and place them in the containers. Do not interchange the bucket tappets as they are of different sizes; the shim is part of the bucket tappet **(see illustrations)**. Different sizes of bucket tappets are available in the event of

wear on the valves or repair on the cylinder head assembly.

Inspection

13 With the camshafts and tappets removed, check each for signs of obvious wear (scoring, pitting, etc) and for ovality, and renew if necessary.

14 Measure the outside diameter of each tappet **(see illustration)** – take measurements at the top and bottom of each tappet, then a second set at right-angles to the first; if any measurement is significantly different from the others, the tappet is tapered or oval (as applicable) and must be renewed. If the necessary equipment is available, measure the inside diameter of the corresponding cylinder head bore. If the tappets or the cylinder head bores are excessively worn, new tappets and/ or a new cylinder head will be required.

15 Visually examine the camshaft lobes for score marks, pitting, galling (wear due to rubbing) and evidence of overheating (blue, discoloured areas). Look for flaking away of the hardened surface layer of each lobe **(see illustration)**. If any such signs are evident, renew the component concerned.

16 Examine the camshaft bearing journals and the cylinder head bearing surfaces for signs of obvious wear or pitting. If any such signs are evident, renew the component concerned.

17 Using a micrometer, measure the diameter of each journal at several points **(see illustration)**. If any measurement is significantly different from the others, renew the camshaft.

9.11a Note the identification markings (arrowed) on the camshaft bearing caps . . .

9.11b . . . and the reference lobe (arrowed) on the intake camshaft for the position sensor

9.12a Remove the tappet bucket with a rubber sucker

9.12b Note the thickness number on the underside of the tappet bucket

9.14 Use a micrometer to measure the diameter of the tappets

9.15 Check the cam lobes for pitting, wear and score marks – if necessary, renew the camshaft

9.17 Measure each journal with a micrometer

9.20 Liberally oil the tappets when refitting

9.22 Apply clean engine oil to the cam lobes and journals

18 To check camshaft endfloat, remove the tappets, clean the bearing surfaces carefully, and refit the camshafts and bearing caps. Tighten the bearing cap bolts to the specified torque wrench setting, then measure the endfloat using a DTI (Dial Test Indicator, or dial gauge) mounted on the cylinder head so that its tip bears on the camshaft right-hand end.

19 Tap the camshaft fully towards the gauge, zero the gauge, then tap the camshaft fully away from the gauge, and note the gauge reading. If the endfloat measured is found to be at or beyond the specified service limit, fit a new camshaft and repeat the check; if the clearance is still excessive, the cylinder head must be renewed.

Refitting

20 On reassembly, liberally oil the cylinder head tappet bores and the tappets **(see illustration)**. Carefully refit the tappets to the cylinder head, ensuring that each tappet is refitted to its original bore. Some care will be required to enter the tappets squarely into their bores.

21 Turn the engine back approximately 45° so that there are no pistons at the top of the cylinders.

22 Liberally oil the camshaft bearings and lobes **(see illustration)**. Ensuring that each camshaft is in its original location, refit the camshafts, locating each so that the slot in its left-hand end is approximately parallel to, and just above, the cylinder head mating surface.

23 All camshaft bearing caps have an identifying number and letter etched on them. The exhaust camshaft's bearing caps are numbered in sequence E1 to E5 and the intake camshaft's bearing caps I1 to I5 **(see illustration 9.11a)**.

24 Ensuring that each cap is kept square to the cylinder head as it is tightened down, and working in sequence **(see illustration)**, tighten the camshaft bearing cap bolts slowly and by one turn at a time, until each cap touches the cylinder head. Next, go round again in the same sequence, tightening the bolts to the first stage torque wrench setting specified, then once more, tightening them to the second stage setting. Work only as described

to impose gradually and evenly the pressure of the valve springs on the caps.

25 Fit the camshaft aligning tool; it should slip into place as described in Section 3 **(see illustration)**.

26 Refit the camshaft sprockets, complete with timing chain to the ends of the camshafts. DO NOT tighten the camshaft sprocket retaining bolts at this stage. Remove the cable ties from the timing chain and camshaft sprockets.

27 Remove the tensioner guide rail locking bolt from the upper access hole in the timing chain cover. It may be necessary to hold some pressure against the tensioner guide rail to remove the locking bolt.

28 Turn the engine (in the direction of rotation) approximately 45° to TDC. For further information on setting the engine to TDC, see Section 3.

29 With the camshafts held in position (by using an open-ended spanner on the hexagon on the shaft), tighten the camshaft sprocket retaining bolts to the specified torque.

30 Remove the camshaft locking plate and crankshaft timing peg and turn the engine (in the direction of engine rotation) two full turns. Refit the camshaft locking plate and crankshaft timing peg to make sure the engine is still set at TDC (see Section 3 for further information).

31 Refit the timing chain cover upper and lower blanking plugs, coat the blanking plug threads with a suitable sealant to prevent leaks.

32 Refit the cylinder head cover as described in Section 4.

9.24 Camshaft bearing cap bolts tightening sequence

9.25 Fit the camshaft aligning tool to set TDC position

10.4a Ensure the oil seal remains square as it is being fitted

10.4b A socket of the correct size can be used for fitting the new seal

10.13 Oil seal carrier retaining bolts tightening sequence

10 Crankshaft oil seals – renewal

Timing chain end oil seal

1 Remove the crankshaft pulley as described in Section 6 of this Chapter.

2 Using a screwdriver, prise the old oil seal from the timing cover. Take care not to damage the surface of the timing cover and crankshaft. If the oil seal is tight, carefully drill two holes diagonally opposite each other in the oil seal, then insert self-tapping screws and use a pair of pliers to pull out the oil seal.

3 Wipe clean the seating in the timing cover and the nose of the crankshaft.

4 Smear clean engine oil on the outer periphery and sealing lips of the new oil seal, then start it into the timing cover by pressing it in squarely. Using a large socket or metal tubing, drive in the oil seal until flush with the outer surface of the timing cover. Make sure the oil seal remains square as it is being inserted. Wipe off any excess oil **(see illustrations)**.

5 Refit the crankshaft pulley as described in Section 6 of this Chapter.

Transmission end oil seal

Note: *The oil seal can only be renewed as a complete unit with the carrier.*

6 Remove the transmission (see the relevant part of Chapter 7).

7 On manual models, remove the clutch assembly (see Chapter 6).

8 Unbolt the flywheel/driveplate (Section 15).

9 Remove the sump (see Section 12).

10 Undo the six retaining bolts and remove the oil seal carrier from the cylinder block. Where applicable, remove and discard its gasket.

11 Clean the seal housing and crankshaft, polishing off any burrs or raised edges which may have caused the seal to fail in the first place. Where applicable, clean also the mating surfaces of the cylinder block/crankcase, using a scraper to remove all traces of the old gasket/sealant - be careful not to scratch or damage the material of either - then use a suitable solvent to degrease them.

12 Use a special sleeve to slide the seal over the crankshaft, if this is not available, make up a guide from a thin sheet of plastic or similar, lubricate the lips of the new seal and the crankshaft shoulder with oil, then offer up the oil seal carrier, with the guide feeding the seal's lips over the crankshaft shoulder.

13 Being careful not to damage the oil seal, move the carrier into the correct position, aligning the guide pins, and tighten its bolts in the correct sequence to the specified torque wrench setting **(see illustration)**.

14 Wipe off any surplus oil or grease; the remainder of the reassembly procedure is the reverse of dismantling, referring to the relevant text for details where required. Check for signs of oil leakage when the engine is restarted.

11 Cylinder head – removal and refitting

Note: *Only turn the engine in the normal direction of rotation – clockwise from the right-hand side of the vehicle.*

Removal

1 Remove the battery as described in Chapter 5.

2 Whenever you disconnect any vacuum lines, coolant and emissions hoses, wiring loom connectors, earth straps and fuel lines as part of the following procedure, always label them clearly so that they can be correctly reassembled.

3 Drain the cooling system as described in Chapter 1.

4 Remove the air cleaner assembly as described in Chapter 4.

5 Remove the starter motor as described in Chapter 5, then place it to one side.

6 Remove the exhaust manifold and heat shields as described in Chapter 4.

7 Place rags around the pipes, then depress the locking tab and disconnect the fuel feed pipe from the fuel rail.

8 Undo the two bolts and remove the fuel rail. Plug the openings to prevent dirt ingress. Refer to Chapter 4 for more information.

9 Remove the intake manifold as described in Chapter 4.

10 Note their fitted locations, then disconnect the various wiring plugs from the components on the cylinder head, and release any relevant wiring loom from any retaining clips.

11 Undo the four bolts and detach the coolant housing from the left-hand end of the cylinder head **(see illustration)**.

12 Undo the two bolts securing the EGR valve (where fitted). Discard the gasket **(see illustration)**.

13 Remove the cylinder head cover as described in Section 5.

14 Remove the timing chain as described in Section 8.

11.11 Remove the coolant outlet housing (arrowed) from the left-hand end of the cylinder head

11.12 Remove the EGR valve from the left-hand end of the cylinder head (arrowed)

15 Remove the camshafts and tappets as described in Section 9.

16 Make a final check to ensure that all relevant coolant/vacuum hoses and wiring connectors have been disconnected.

17 Working in sequence **(see illustration)**, slacken the ten cylinder head bolts progressively and by one turn at a time. Remove each bolt in turn, and ensure that new ones are obtained for reassembly; these bolts are subjected to severe stresses and so must be renewed, regardless of their apparent condition, whenever they are disturbed.

18 Lift the cylinder head away; use assistance if possible, as it is a heavy assembly. Remove the gasket and discard it, note the position of the dowels.

Refitting

19 The mating faces of the cylinder head and cylinder block must be perfectly clean before refitting the head. Use a hard plastic or wood scraper to remove all traces of gasket and carbon; also clean the piston crowns. Take particular care, as the soft aluminium alloy is easily damaged. Also, make sure that the carbon is not allowed to enter the oil and water passages – this is particularly important for the lubrication system, as carbon could block the oil supply to any of the engine's components. Using adhesive tape and paper, seal the water, oil and bolt holes in the cylinder block. Clean all the pistons in the same way.

20 Check the mating surfaces of the cylinder block and the cylinder head for nicks, deep scratches and other damage. If excessive, machining may be the only alternative to renewal.

21 If warpage of the cylinder head gasket surface is suspected, use a straight-edge to check it for distortion. Refer to Part F of this Chapter, if necessary.

22 Wipe clean the mating surfaces of the

11.17 Cylinder head bolt slackening sequence

cylinder head and cylinder block. Check that the locating dowels are in position in the cylinder block, and that all cylinder head bolt holes are free from oil.

23 Position a new gasket over the dowels on the cylinder block surface, making sure it is fitted the correct way around.

24 Rotate the crankshaft anti-clockwise so that No 1 cylinder's piston is lowered to approximately 20 mm before TDC, thus avoiding any risk of valve/piston contact and damage during reassembly.

25 Refit the cylinder head, locating it on the dowels. Lubricate the threads, then fit the new cylinder head bolts; carefully enter each into its hole and screw it in, by hand only, until finger-tight.

26 Working progressively and in sequence, use first a torque wrench, then an ordinary socket extension bar and an angle gauge to tighten the cylinder head bolts **(see illustrations)**. This is completed in stages given in the Specifications Section at the beginning of this Chapter. **Note:** *Once tightened correctly, following this procedure, the cylinder head bolts do not require check-tightening, and must not be retorqued.*

27 Refit the tappets, the camshafts, and the timing chain as described in Sections 8 and 9.

28 The remainder of reassembly is the reverse of the removal procedure, noting the following points:

a) *See the refitting procedures in the relevant Sections and tighten all nuts and bolts to the torque wrench settings specified.*

b) *Refill the cooling system, and top-up the engine oil.*

c) *Check all disturbed joints for signs of oil or coolant leakage, once the engine has been restarted and warmed-up to normal operating temperature.*

11.26a Cylinder head bolt tightening sequence

11.26b Use an angle-gauge for the final stages

12.6 Undo the sump-to-transmission bolts (arrowed)

12.9 Apply a 3.0 mm bead of sealant to the sump flange

12 Sump – removal and refitting

Note: *To carry out this task with the engine/transmission installed in the vehicle it requires the assistance of at least one person, plus the equipment necessary to raise and support the front of the vehicle (high enough that the sump can be withdrawn from underneath). It will also need a support bar across the top of the engine bay to hold the complete engine/transmission unit in place while the vehicle is raised. Precise details of the procedure will depend on the equipment available – the following is typical.*

Removal

1 Apply the handbrake, then jack up the front of the vehicle and support it on axle stands (see *Jacking and vehicle support*). Undo the fasteners and remove the engine undershield.
2 Drain the engine oil, then clean and refit the engine oil drain plug, tightening it to the specified torque wrench setting. **Note:** *If the drain plug seal is damaged, a new drain plug will be required. Although not strictly necessary as part of the dismantling*

procedure, owners are advised to remove and discard the oil filter, so that it can be renewed with the oil (see Chapter 1).
3 Remove the plastic cover from the top of the engine, then support the engine with a cross-beam or hoist.
4 Remove the timing chain cover as described in Section 7.
5 Undo the engine oil level dipstick guide tube retaining bolts, then pull the tube from the sump. Renew the seal at the base of the tube if necessary.
6 Unscrew and remove the sump-to-transmission bolts **(see illustration)**.
7 Progressively unscrew the sump retaining bolts. Use a scraper to break the sealant around the sump, taking care not to damage the mating surfaces of the sump and cylinder block. Lower the sump and withdraw it from the engine/transmission.

Refitting

8 On reassembly, thoroughly clean and degrease the mating surfaces of the cylinder block/crankcase and sump, then use a clean rag to wipe out the sump.
9 Apply a 3.0 mm bead of sealant (Ford No WSE-M4G323-A4) to the sump flange so that the bead is around the inside edge of the bolt holes **(see illustration)**. **Note:** *The sump must*

be refitted within 10 minutes of applying the sealant.
10 Offer up the sump and insert the retaining bolts, do not tighten them at this stage.
11 Using a straight-edge, align the sump to the cylinder block on the timing chain end. With the sump held in position, progressively tighten the retaining bolts to the specified torque in sequence **(see illustrations)**.
12 Refit the sump-to-transmission bolts and tighten them to the specified torque.
13 Refit the timing chain cover as described in Section 7.
14 Refit the engine undershield, then lower the car to the ground and refill the engine with oil (and fit new oil filter) and the cooling system with coolant (see Chapter 1).
15 Check for signs of oil or coolant leaks once the engine has been restarted and warmed-up to normal operating temperature.

13 Oil pump – removal, inspection and refitting

Note: *While this task is theoretically possible when the engine is in place in the vehicle, in practice, it requires so much preliminary dismantling, and is so difficult to carry out due to the restricted access, that owners are advised to remove the engine from the vehicle first. All the illustrations used in this Section are with the engine out of the vehicle and the engine upside down on a work bench.*
Note: *In addition to the new pump gasket and other parts required, read through this Section, and ensure that the necessary tools and facilities are available.*

Removal

1 Remove the timing chain as described in Section 8.
2 Remove the sump as described in Section 12.
3 Undo the two bolts securing the oil pump

12.11a Use a straight-edge to align the sump to the cylinder block

12.11b Sump bolt tightening sequence

H46409

13.3 Remove the oil pump pick-up pipe retaining bolts

13.4 Oil pump chain guide and tensioner retaining bolts (arrowed)

13.5 Hold the oil pump sprocket whilst undoing the sprocket bolt

13.7 Undo the 4 retaining bolts (arrowed) and remove the oil pump

13.11 Use one of the retaining bolts to locate the new gasket in place on the oil pump

13.12 Fit a new O-ring (arrowed) to the oil pump pick-up pipe

pick-up pipe to the pump (see illustration). Discard the O-ring/gasket.

4 Undo the two retaining bolts and remove the oil pump chain guide, then undo the retaining bolt and remove the oil pump chain tensioner (see illustration).

5 Hold the oil pump drive sprocket to prevent it from turning and slacken the sprocket retaining bolt (see illustration).

6 Undo the bolt and remove the oil pump sprocket complete with the oil pump drive chain.

7 Unbolt the pump from the cylinder block/crankcase (see illustration). Withdraw and discard the gasket.

Inspection

8 At the time of writing there were no parts for the pump, if there is any doubt in the operation of the oil pump, then the complete pump assembly should be renewed.

Refitting

9 Thoroughly clean and degrease all components, particularly the mating surfaces of the pump, the sump, and the cylinder block/crankcase. When using a scraper and solvent to remove all traces of old gasket/sealant from the mating surfaces, be careful to ensure that you do not scratch or damage the material of either component – any solvents used must be suitable for this application.

10 The oil pump must be primed on installation by pouring clean engine oil into it and rotating its inner rotor a few turns.

11 Fit the new gasket in place on the oil pump

using one of the retaining bolts to locate it, refit the pump to the cylinder block/crankcase and insert the retaining bolts, tightening them to the specified torque wrench setting (see illustration).

12 Fit the new O-ring/gasket in place and refit the pump pick-up pipe to the pump, tightening its retaining bolts securely (see illustration).

13 Refit the oil pump drive chain complete with oil pump sprocket (see illustration) and tighten the retaining bolt to the specified torque setting. Hold the oil pump drive sprocket (using the same method as removal) to prevent it from turning when tightening the sprocket retaining bolt.

14 Refit the oil pump chain tensioner to the cylinder block, making sure the spring is located correctly (see illustration). Tighten the retaining bolt to its specified torque setting.

15 Refit the oil pump chain guide to the

cylinder block, tightening the two retaining bolts to their specified torque setting.

16 Refit the timing chain as described in Section 8.

17 Refit the sump as described in Section 12.

14 Oil pressure warning light switch – removal and refitting

Removal

1 The switch is screwed into the oil filter housing on the front of the cylinder block (see illustration).

2 With the vehicle parked on firm level ground, open the bonnet and disconnect the battery negative (earth) lead (as described in Chapter 5).

13.13 Align the flats (arrowed) on the oil pump driveshaft and oil pump sprocket when refitting

13.14 Ensure the spring on the tensioner is hooked behind the bolt (arrowed) to tension the chain

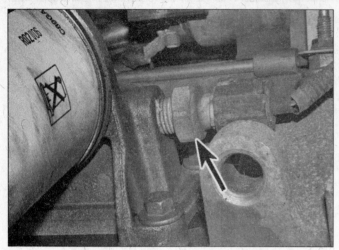

14.1 Oil pressure wiring light switch (arrowed)

14.3 Undo the fasteners (arrowed) and remove the engine undershield – where fitted

3 If required, raise the front of the vehicle, and support it securely on axle stands, this will give better access to the switch. Where fitted, undo the bolts and remove the engine undershield **(see illustration)**.

4 Disconnect the wiring connector from the switch, and unscrew it; be prepared for some oil loss.

Refitting

5 Refitting is the reverse of the removal procedure; apply a thin smear of suitable sealant to the switch threads, and tighten it to the specified torque wrench setting. Check the engine oil level, and top-up as necessary (see *Weekly checks*). Check for signs of oil leaks once the engine has been restarted and warmed-up to normal operating temperature.

15 Flywheel/driveplate – removal, inspection and refitting

Removal

1 Remove the transmission (see Chapter 7). Now is a good time to check components such as oil seals and renew them if necessary.

2 Where appropriate, remove the clutch (Chapter 6). Now is a good time to check or renew the clutch components.

3 Use a centre-punch or paint to make alignment marks on the flywheel/driveplate and crankshaft, to ensure correct alignment during refitting.

4 Prevent the flywheel/driveplate from turning by locking the ring gear teeth, or by bolting a strap between the flywheel/driveplate and the cylinder block/crankcase **(see illustration)**. Slacken the bolts evenly until all are free.

5 Remove each bolt in turn, and ensure that new ones are obtained for reassembly; these bolts are subjected to severe stresses, and so must be renewed, regardless of their apparent condition, whenever they are disturbed.

6 Withdraw the flywheel/driveplate from the end of the crankshaft. **Note:** *Take care when removing the flywheel/driveplate as it is a very heavy component.*

Inspection

7 Clean the flywheel/driveplate to remove grease and oil. Inspect the surface for cracks, rivet grooves, burned areas and score marks. Light scoring can be removed with emery cloth. Check for cracked and broken ring gear teeth. Lay the flywheel/driveplate on a flat surface, and use a straight-edge to check for warpage.

8 Clean and inspect the mating surfaces of the flywheel/driveplate and the crankshaft. If the crankshaft left-hand oil seal is leaking, renew it (see Section 10) before refitting the flywheel/driveplate.

9 While the flywheel/driveplate is removed, clean carefully its inboard (right-hand) face. Thoroughly clean the threaded bolt holes in the crankshaft – this is important, since if old sealer remains in the threads, the bolts will settle over a period and will not retain their correct torque wrench settings.

Refitting

10 On refitting, fit the flywheel/driveplate to the crankshaft so that all bolt holes align – it will fit only one way – check this using the marks made on removal. Apply suitable sealer to the threads of the new bolts then insert them **(see illustration)**.

11 Lock the flywheel/driveplate by the method used on dismantling. Working in a diagonal sequence to tighten them evenly, and increasing to the final amount in stages, tighten the new bolts to the specified torque wrench setting **(see illustration)**.

12 The remainder of reassembly is the reverse of the removal procedure, referring to the relevant text for details where required.

15.4 Lock the flywheel whilst the bolts (arrowed) are removed

15.10 Apply suitable locking fluid to the threads of the new bolts on fitting

15.11 Tighten the new bolts, using method used on dismantling for locking the flywheel

16 Engine/transmission mountings – inspection and renewal

General

1 The engine/transmission mountings seldom require attention, but broken or deteriorated mountings should be renewed immediately, or the added strain placed on the driveline components may cause damage or wear.

2 While separate mountings may be removed and refitted individually, if more than one is disturbed at a time – such as if the engine/transmission unit is removed from its mountings – they must be reassembled and their fasteners tightened in the position marked on removal.

3 On reassembly, the complete weight of the engine/transmission unit must not be taken by the mountings until all are correctly aligned with the marks made on removal. Tighten the engine/transmission mounting fasteners to their specified torque wrench settings.

Inspection

4 During the check, the engine/transmission unit must be raised slightly, to remove its weight from the mountings.

5 Raise the front of the vehicle, and support it securely on axle stands. Position a jack under the sump, with a large block of wood between the jack head and the sump, then carefully raise the engine/transmission just enough to take the weight off the mountings.

 Warning: DO NOT place any part of your body under the engine when it is supported only by a jack.

6 Check the mountings to see if the rubber is cracked, hardened or separated from the metal components. Sometimes the rubber will split right down the centre.

7 Check for relative movement between each mounting's brackets and the engine/transmission or body (use a large screwdriver

16.15 Undo the centre bolt (arrowed) to release the mounting from the transmission

or lever to attempt to move the mountings). If movement is noted, lower the engine and check-tighten the mounting fasteners.

Renewal

Note: *The following paragraphs assume the engine is supported beneath the sump as described earlier.*

Right-hand mounting

8 Pull the plastic cover on the top of the engine upwards from its mountings.

9 Lift up the coolant expansion tank and position it to one side. Note there is no need to disconnect the coolant pipes.

10 Mark the position of the mounting on the vehicle, right-hand inner wing panel, then unclip the refrigerant pipe from the clip on the mounting.

11 With the engine/transmission supported, unscrew the two locking nuts from the engine casing, then undo the two retaining bolts to the vehicle inner wing panel and withdraw the mounting from the vehicle **(see illustration 7.11)**.

12 On refitting, tighten all fasteners to the torque wrench settings specified. Tighten the two locking nuts to the engine casing first, then release the hoist or jack to allow the mounting bracket to rest on the vehicle

16.18 Undo the 2 bolts (arrowed) and remove the rear mounting

inner wing panel. Re-align the marks made on removal, then tighten the two mounting bracket-to-inner wing retaining bolts.

Left-hand mounting

13 Remove the air cleaner assembly as described in Chapter 4.

14 Remove the battery as described in Chapter 5, then undo the 3 bolts and remove the battery tray. Disconnect any wiring as the tray is withdrawn.

15 With the transmission supported, note the position of the mounting then unscrew the centre retaining bolt to release the mounting from the transmission **(see illustration)**.

16 Unscrew the 4 outer retaining nuts, and 2 bolts to dismantle the mounting from the mounting bracket.

17 On refitting, renew the self-locking nuts. Re-align the mounting in the position noted on removal, then tighten all fasteners to the specified torque wrench settings.

Rear mounting (roll restrictor)

18 Unbolt the mounting from the subframe and the transmission by unscrewing the mounting's centre bolts **(see illustration)**.

19 On refitting, ensure that the bolts are securely tightened to the specified torque wrench setting.

Notes

Chapter 2 Part C:
1.6 litre diesel engine in-car repair procedures

Contents

Section number

Camshaft, rocker arms and hydraulic tappets – removal, inspection
   and refitting 9
Compression and leakdown tests – description and interpretation . . 2
Crankshaft pulley – removal and refitting 5
Cylinder head – removal and refitting 10
Cylinder head cover/manifold – removal and refitting 4
Engine assembly/valve timing holes – general information and
   usage 3
Engine/transmission mountings – inspection and renewal 17
Flywheel – removal, inspection and refitting 16

Section number

General information 1
Oil cooler – removal and refitting 13
Oil pressure switch and level sensor – removal and refitting 15
Oil pump – removal, inspection and refitting 12
Oil seals – renewal 14
Sump – removal and refitting 11
Timing belt – removal, inspection, refitting and tensioning 7
Timing belt covers – removal and refitting 6
Timing belt sprockets and tensioner – removal and refitting 8

Degrees of difficulty

Easy, suitable for novice with little experience	**Fairly easy,** suitable for beginner with some experience	**Fairly difficult,** suitable for competent DIY mechanic	**Difficult,** suitable for experienced DIY mechanic	**Very difficult,** suitable for expert DIY or professional

Specifications

General

Designation	Duratorq-TDCi (DV)
Engine codes*	G8DA and G8DB
Capacity	1560 cc
Bore	75.0 mm
Stroke	88.3 mm
Direction of crankshaft rotation	Clockwise (viewed from the right-hand side of vehicle)
No 1 cylinder location	At the transmission end of block
Maximum power output	80 kW @ 4000 rpm
Maximum torque output	230 Nm @ 2000 rpm
Compression ratio	18.0 :1

* The engine code is stamped on a plate attached to the front of the cylinder block, next to the oil filter

Compression pressures (engine hot, at cranking speed)

Normal	20 ± 5 bar
Minimum	15 bar
Maximum difference between any two cylinders	5 bar

Camshaft

Drive	Toothed belt

Lubrication system

Oil pump type	Gear-type, driven directly by the right-hand end of the crankshaft, by two flats machined along the crankshaft journal

Minimum oil pressure at 80°C:
Idle speed	1.0 to 2.0 bar
2000 rpm	2.3 to 3.7 bar

Torque wrench settings

	Nm	lbf ft
Ancillary drivebelt tensioner roller	20	15
Big-end bolts:*		
Stage 1	10	7
Stage 2	Slacken 180°	
Stage 3	10	7
Stage 4	Angle-tighten a further 130°	
Camshaft bearing caps	10	7
Camshaft cover/bearing ladder:		
Studs	10	7
Bolts	10	7
Camshaft position sensor bolt	5	4
Camshaft sprocket	43	32
Coolant outlet housing bolts	8	6
Crankshaft position/speed sensor bolt	5	4
Crankshaft pulley/sprocket bolt:*		
Stage 1	35	26
Stage 2	Angle-tighten a further 180°	
Cylinder head bolts:*		
Stage 1	20	15
Stage 2	40	30
Stage 3	Angle-tighten a further 260°	
Cylinder head cover/manifold	10	7
EGR valve	10	7
Engine mountings:		
Right-hand mounting retaining bolts	90	66
Right-hand mounting bracket-to-engine bolts	56	41
Left-hand mounting nuts	48	35
Left-hand mounting bracket to transmission	80	59
Left-hand mounting centre bolt	148	109
Lower-rear torque rod bolts	80	59
Engine-to-transmission fixing bolts	47	35
Flywheel bolts:*		
Stage 1	30	22
Stage 2	Angle-tighten a further 90°	
Fuel pump sprocket	50	37
Main bearing ladder outer seam bolts:		
Stage 1	5	4
Stage 2	10	7
Main bearing ladder to cylinder block:		
Stage 1	10	7
Stage 2	Slacken 180°	
Stage 3	30	22
Stage 4	Angle-tighten a further 140°	
Piston oil jet spray tube bolt	20	15
Oil cooler retaining bolts	10	7
Oil filter cover	25	18
Oil pick-up pipe	10	7
Oil pressure switch	30	22
Oil pump to cylinder block	10	7
Sump drain plug	34	25
Sump bolts/nuts	10	7
Timing belt idler pulley	35	26
Timing belt tensioner pulley	30	22
Timing chain tensioner	10	7
Vacuum pump:		
Stage 1	18	13
Stage 2	Angle-tighten a further 5°	

* Do not re-use

1 General information

How to use this Chapter

This Part of Chapter 2 describes the repair procedures that can reasonably be carried out on the engine while it remains in the vehicle. If the engine has been removed from the vehicle and is being dismantled as described in Part F, any preliminary dismantling procedures can be ignored.

Note that, while it may be possible physically to overhaul items such as the piston/connecting rod assemblies while the engine is in the car, such tasks are not usually carried out as separate operations. Usually, several additional procedures are required (not to mention the cleaning of components and oilways); for this reason, all such tasks are classed as major overhaul procedures, and are described in Part F of this Chapter.

Part F describes the removal of the engine/ transmission from the car, and the full overhaul procedures that can then be carried out.

DV series engines

The 1.6 litre DV series engine is the result of development collaboration between Citroën/Peugeot and Ford. The engine is of double overhead camshaft (DOHC) 16-valve design. The direct injection, turbocharged, four-cylinder engine is mounted transversely, with the transmission mounted on the left-hand side.

A toothed timing belt drives the intake camshaft, high-pressure fuel pump and coolant pump. The intake camshaft drives the exhaust camshaft via a chain. The camshafts operate the intake and exhaust valves via rocker arms which are supported at their pivot ends by hydraulic self-adjusting tappets. The camshafts are supported by bearings machined directly in the cylinder head and camshaft bearing housing.

The high-pressure fuel pump supplies fuel to the fuel rail, and subsequently to the electronically-controlled injectors which inject the fuel directly into the combustion chambers. This design differs from the previous type where an injection pump supplies the fuel at high pressure to each injector. The earlier, conventional type injection pump required fine calibration and timing, and these functions are now completed by the high-pressure pump, electronic injectors and engine management ECM.

The crankshaft runs in five main bearings of the usual shell type. Endfloat is controlled by thrustwashers either side of No 2 main bearing.

The pistons are selected to be of matching weight, and incorporate fully-floating gudgeon pins retained by circlips.

Repair operations precaution

The engine is a complex unit with numerous accessories and ancillary components. The design of the engine compartment is such that every conceivable space has been utilised, and access to virtually all of the engine components is extremely limited. In many cases, ancillary components will have to be removed, or moved to one side, and wiring, pipes and hoses will have to be disconnected or removed from various cable clips and support brackets.

When working on this engine, read through the entire procedure first, look at the car and engine at the same time, and establish whether you have the necessary tools, equipment, skill and patience to proceed. Allow considerable time for any operation, and be prepared for the unexpected.

Because of the limited access, many of the engine photographs appearing in this Chapter were, by necessity, taken with the engine removed from the vehicle.

⚠️ **Warning: It is essential to observe strict precautions when working on the fuel system components of the engine, particularly the high-pressure side of the system. Before carrying out any engine operations that entail working on, or near, any part of the fuel system, refer to the special information given in Chapter 4.**

Operations with engine in vehicle

a) Compression pressure – testing.
b) Cylinder head cover – removal and refitting.
c) Crankshaft pulley – removal and refitting.
d) Timing belt covers – removal and refitting.
e) Timing belt – removal, refitting and adjustment.
f) Timing belt tensioner and sprockets – removal and refitting.
g) Camshaft oil seal – renewal.
h) Camshaft, rocker arms and hydraulic tappets – removal, inspection and refitting.
i) Sump – removal and refitting.
j) Oil pump – removal and refitting.
k) Crankshaft oil seals – renewal.
l) Engine/transmission mountings – inspection and renewal.
m) Flywheel – removal, inspection and refitting.

2 Compression and leakdown tests – description and interpretation

Compression test

Note: *A compression tester specifically designed for diesel engines must be used for this test.*

1 When engine performance is down, or if misfiring occurs which cannot be attributed to the fuel system, a compression test can provide diagnostic clues as to the engine's condition. If the test is performed regularly, it can give warning of trouble before any other symptoms become apparent.

2 A compression tester specifically intended for diesel engines must be used, because of the higher pressures involved. On this engine, an adapter suitable for use in the glow plug holes will be required, so as not to disturb the fuel system components. It is unlikely to be worthwhile buying such a tester for occasional use, but it may be possible to borrow or hire one – if not, have the test performed by a garage.

3 Unless specific instructions to the contrary are supplied with the tester, observe the following points:
a) The battery must be in a good state of charge, the air filter must be clean, and the engine should be at normal operating temperature.
b) All the glow plugs should be removed as described in Chapter 5 before starting the test.
c) Disconnect the fuel injector wiring plugs.

4 The compression pressures measured are not so important as the balance between cylinders. Values are given in the Specifications.

5 The cause of poor compression is less easy to establish on a diesel engine than on a petrol one. The effect of introducing oil into the cylinders ('wet' testing) is not conclusive, because there is a risk that the oil will sit in the swirl chamber or in the recess on the piston crown instead of passing to the rings. However, the following can be used as a rough guide to diagnosis.

6 All cylinders should produce very similar pressures; any difference greater than that specified indicates the existence of a fault. Note that the compression should build-up quickly in a healthy engine; low compression on the first stroke, followed by gradually-increasing pressure on successive strokes, indicates worn piston rings. A low compression reading on the first stroke, which does not build-up during successive strokes, indicates leaking valves or a blown head gasket (a cracked head could also be the cause). Deposits on the undersides of the valve heads can also cause low compression.

7 A low reading from two adjacent cylinders is almost certainly due to the head gasket having blown between them; the presence of coolant in the engine oil will confirm this.

8 If the compression reading is unusually high, the cylinder head surfaces, valves and pistons are probably coated with carbon deposits. If this is the case, the cylinder head should be removed and decarbonised.

Note: *After performing this test, a fault code may be generated and stored in the PCM memory. Have the PCM self-diagnosis facility interrogated by a Ford dealer or suitably-equipped specialist, and the fault code erased.*

3.9 Insert a 5.0 mm drill bit/bolt through the round hole in the sprocket flange into the hole in the oil pump housing (lower timing belt removed for clarity)

3.10 Insert an 8.0 mm drill bit/bolt through the hole in the camshaft sprocket into the corresponding hole in the cylinder head

Leakdown test

9 A leakdown test measures the rate at which compressed air fed into the cylinder is lost. It is an alternative to a compression test, and in many ways it is better, since the escaping air provides easy identification of where pressure loss is occurring (piston rings, valves or head gasket).

10 The equipment needed for leakdown testing is unlikely to be available to the home mechanic. If poor compression is suspected, have the test performed by a suitably-equipped garage.

3 Engine assembly/ valve timing holes – general information and usage

Note: *Do not attempt to rotate the engine whilst the crankshaft and camshaft are locked in position. If the engine is to be left in this state for a long period of time, it is a good*

3.11 Insert Ford tool No 303-732 or a 5.0 mm drill bit through the hole in the fuel pump sprocket into the fuel pump mounting bracket

idea to place suitable warning notices inside the vehicle, and in the engine compartment. This will reduce the possibility of the engine being accidentally cranked on the starter motor, which is likely to cause damage with the locking pins in place.

1 Timing holes or slots are located only in the crankshaft pulley flange and camshaft sprocket hub. The holes/slots are used to position the pistons halfway up the cylinder bores. This will ensure that the valve timing is maintained during operations that require removal and refitting of the timing belt. When the holes/slots are aligned with their corresponding holes in the cylinder block and cylinder head, suitable diameter bolts/pins can be inserted to lock the crankshaft and camshaft in position, preventing rotation.

2 Note that the fuel system used on these engines does not have a conventional diesel injection pump, but instead uses a high-pressure fuel pump. However, the fuel pump sprocket must be pegged in position in a similar fashion to the camshaft sprocket.

3 To align the engine assembly/valve timing holes, proceed as follows.

4 Apply the handbrake, then jack up the front of the vehicle and support it on axle stands (see *Jacking and vehicle support*). Remove the right-hand front roadwheel.

5 To gain access to the crankshaft pulley, to enable the engine to be turned, the wheel arch plastic liner must be removed. The liner is secured by several plastic expanding rivets/nut/bolts. To remove the rivets, push in the centre pins a little, then prise the clips from place. Remove the liner from under the front wing. The crankshaft can then be turned using a suitable socket and extension bar fitted to the pulley bolt.

6 Remove the upper and lower timing belt covers as described in Section 6.

7 Temporarily refit the crankshaft pulley bolt, remove the crankshaft locking tool, then turn the crankshaft until the timing hole in the

camshaft sprocket hub is aligned with the corresponding hole in the cylinder head. Note that the crankshaft must always be turned in a clockwise direction (viewed from the right-hand side of vehicle). Use a small mirror so that the position of the sprocket hub timing slot can be observed. When the slot is aligned with the corresponding hole in the cylinder head the camshaft is positioned correctly.

8 Remove the crankshaft drivebelt pulley as described in Section 5.

9 Insert a 5 mm diameter bolt, rod or drill through the hole in the crankshaft sprocket flange and into the corresponding hole in the oil pump (**see illustration**), if necessary, carefully turn the crankshaft either way until the rod enters the timing hole in the block.

10 Insert an 8 mm bolt, rod or drill through the hole in the camshaft sprocket hub and into engagement with the cylinder head (**see illustration**).

11 When refitting the timing belt, insert Ford tool No 303-732 through the hole in the fuel pump sprocket and into the corresponding hole in the fuel pump mounting bracket (**see illustration**). In the absence of this tool use a 5 mm bolt or drill bit.

12 The crankshaft and camshaft are now locked in position, preventing unnecessary rotation.

4 Cylinder head cover/manifold – removal and refitting

Removal

1 Disconnect the battery negative lead as described in Chapter 5.

2 Pull the plastic cover (where fitted) upwards from the top of the engine.

3 Remove the EGR cooler (where fitted) as described in Chapter 4. On models without an EGR cooler, undo the bolts, release the clamp and remove the pipe from the EGR

4.3 Undo the Torx bolts (arrowed) securing the EGR pipe

4.4a Slacken the clamp (arrowed) and pull the intake hose from the turbocharger . . .

4.4b . . . then release the clips and pull the breather hose from the manifold/cover

4.5a Depress the clip (arrowed) and disconnect the wiring plug from the injector

4.5b Undo the bolts (arrowed) and remove the wiring harness guide

valve to the cylinder head cover/manifold (see illustration).

4 Release the clamps and disconnect the air filter outlet hose from the turbocharger, and the breather hose from the cover/manifold (see illustrations).

5 Disconnect the wiring plugs from the top of each injector, undo the guide bolts, then make sure all wiring harnesses are freed from any retaining brackets on the cylinder head cover/ intake manifold (see illustrations). Disconnect any vacuum pipes as necessary, having first noted their fitted positions.

6 Depress the release buttons and disconnect the fuel feed and return hoses at the right-hand end of the cylinder head, then disconnect the fuel temperature sensor wiring plug, and move the pipe assembly to the rear (see illustrations). Plug the openings to prevent contamination.

7 Prise out the retaining clips and disconnect the fuel return pipes from the injectors, then undo the unions and remove the high-pressure fuel pipes from the injectors and the common fuel rail at the rear of the cylinder head – counterhold the unions with a second spanner (see illustrations). Plug the openings to prevent dirt ingress.

8 Disconnect the wiring plug from the Manifold Absolute Pressure (MAP) sensor (see illustration).

4.6a Depress the release buttons (arrowed) and disconnect the fuel hoses

4.6b Fuel temperature sensor (arrowed)

4.7a Prise out the clip and pull the return hose from the top of each injector

4.7b Use a second spanner to hold the injector port whilst slackening the fuel pipe unions

4.8 Disconnect the wiring plug from the MAP sensor (arrowed)

4.9a Remove the bolt (arrowed) . . .

4.9b . . . pull the tube from the mounting stud . . .

4.9c . . . then rotate the tube and disconnect it

4.9d Slacken the clamp (arrowed) and disconnect the hose from the anti-shudder valve

oil separator from the top of the cylinder head **(see illustration)**. Recover the rubber seal.

11 Undo the bolts securing the cylinder head cover/intake manifold. Lift the assembly away **(see illustration)**. Recover the manifold rubber seals.

Refitting

12 Refitting is a reversal of removal, bearing in mind the following points:

  a) *Examine the seals for signs of damage and deterioration, and renew if necessary. Smear a little clean engine oil on the manifold seals.*

  b) *Renew the fuel injector high-pressure pipes – see Chapter 4.*

9 Release the clamps, undo the bolts and remove the air ducting from the top of the turbocharger, and the anti-shudder valve attach to the manifold/cover. Make a note

of their fitted positions, then disconnect any wiring plugs as the assembly is withdrawn **(see illustrations)**.

10 Undo the retaining bolts and remove the

4.10 Undo the bolts and remove the oil separator (arrowed)

4.11 Undo the 2 remaining bolts (arrowed) and pull the cover/manifold upwards

5 Crankshaft pulley – removal and refitting

Removal

1 Remove the auxiliary drivebelt as described in Chapter 1.

2 To lock the crankshaft, working underneath the engine, insert Ford tool No 303-734 into the hole in the right-hand face of the engine block casting over the lower section of the flywheel. Rotate the crankshaft until the tool engages in the corresponding hole in the flywheel. In the absence of the Ford tool, insert a 12 mm rod or drill into the hole **(see illustration)**. **Note:** *The hole in the casting and the hole in the flywheel are provided purely to lock the crankshaft whilst the pulley bolt is undone, it does not position the crankshaft at TDC.*

3 Using a suitable socket and extension bar, unscrew the retaining bolt, remove the washer, then slide the pulley off the end of the crankshaft **(see illustration)**. If the pulley is tight fit, it can be drawn off the crankshaft using a suitable puller. If a puller is being used, refit the pulley retaining bolt without the washer, to avoid damaging the crankshaft as the puller is tightened.

Caution: Do not touch the outer magnetic sensor ring of the sprocket with your fingers, or allow metallic particles to come into contact with it.

5.2 The locking pin/bolt (arrowed) must locate in the hole in the flywheel (arrowed) to prevent rotation

5.3 Undo the crankshaft pulley retaining bolt (arrowed)

Refitting

4 Refit the pulley to the end of the crankshaft.

5 Thoroughly clean the threads of the pulley retaining bolt, then apply a coat of locking compound to the bolt threads. Ford recommend the use of Loctite (available from your Ford dealer or automotive store); in the absence of this, any good-quality locking compound may be used.

6 Refit the crankshaft pulley retaining bolt and washer. Tighten the bolt to the specified torque, then through the specified angle, preventing the crankshaft from turning using the method employed on removal.

7 Refit and tension the auxiliary drivebelt as described in Chapter 1.

6 Timing belt covers – removal and refitting

 Warning: Refer to the precautionary information contained in Section 1 before proceeding.

Removal

Upper cover

1 Remove the plastic cover from the top of the engine (where fitted).

2 Undo the 2 retaining bolts and move the brake master cylinder remote reservoir to one side (where fitted) **(see illustration)**.

3 Remove the wiper arms as described in Chapter 12.

4 Release the 5 clips and pull the windscreen cowl panel upwards from the moulding at the base of the windscreen **(see illustrations)**.

5 Undo the bolt at each end and pull the bulkhead extension panel forwards from the retaining clips **(see illustration)**.

6 Release the wiring harness and fuel pipes from the upper cover.

7 Undo the 5 bolts and remove the timing belt upper cover **(see illustration)**.

Lower cover

8 Remove the upper cover as described previously.

9 Drain the cooling system as described in Chapter 1.

10 Pull the coolant expansion tank upwards from its mountings, then release the clip and disconnect the supply hose from the coolant expansion tank **(see illustration)**.

11 Remove the crankshaft pulley as described in Section 5.

12 Position a trolley/workshop jack under the engine. Place a block of wood on the jack head, then take the weight of the engine.

13 Undo the nuts/bolts, and remove the right-hand engine mounting **(see illustration)**.

14 Undo the 4 bolts and remove the mounting bracket from the engine.

15 Undo the 5 bolts and remove the lower cover **(see illustration)**.

6.2 Undo the bolts securing the master cylinder remote reservoir (arrowed)

6.4b . . . and pull the scuttle cowl panel upwards from the moulding at the base of the windscreen

6.7 Upper timing cover bolts (arrowed)

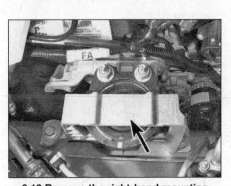

6.13 Remove the right-hand mounting assembly (arrowed)

6.4a Prise forwards the clips (arrowed) . . .

6.5 Undo the bolt (arrowed) at each end of the bulkhead extension panel

Refitting

16 Refitting of all the covers is a reversal of the relevant removal procedure, ensuring that each cover section is correctly located, and

that the cover retaining bolts are securely tightened. Ensure that all disturbed hoses are reconnected and retained by their relevant clips.

6.10 Disconnect the coolant hose from the base of the expansion tank (arrowed)

6.15 Lower timing belt cover bolts (arrowed)

7.4 Undo the fasteners (arrowed) and remove the engine undershield

7.6 Undo the bolt (arrowed) and remove the crankshaft position sensor

7.7 Remove the timing belt protection bracket

7 Timing belt –
removal, inspection, refitting and tensioning

General

1 The timing belt drives the camshaft, high-pressure fuel pump and coolant pump from a toothed sprocket on the end of the crankshaft. If the belt breaks or slips in service, the pistons are likely to hit the valve heads, resulting in expensive damage.

2 The timing belt should be renewed at the specified intervals, or earlier if it is contaminated with oil or at all noisy in operation (a 'scraping' noise due to uneven wear).

3 If the timing belt is being removed, it is a wise precaution to check the condition of the coolant pump at the same time (check for signs of coolant leakage). This may avoid the need to remove the timing belt again at a later stage, should the coolant pump fail.

Removal

4 Apply the handbrake, then jack up the front of the vehicle and support it on axle stands (see *Jacking and vehicle support*). Remove the front right-hand roadwheel, wheel arch liner (to expose the crankshaft pulley), and the engine undershield. The wheel arch liner is secured by several bolts. The engine undershield is retained by several fasteners **(see illustration)**.

5 Remove the upper and lower timing belt covers, as described in Section 6.

6 Undo the bolt and remove the crankshaft position sensor adjacent to the crankshaft sprocket flange, and move it to one side **(see illustration)**.

7 Undo the retaining bolt and remove the timing belt protection bracket, again, adjacent to the crankshaft sprocket flange **(see illustration)**.

8 Lock the crankshaft and camshaft in the correct position as described in Section 3. If necessary, temporarily refit the crankshaft pulley bolt to enable the crankshaft to be rotated.

9 Insert a hexagon key into the belt tensioner pulley centre, slacken the pulley bolt, and allow the tensioner to rotate, relieving the belt tension **(see illustration)**. With belt slack, temporarily tighten the pulley bolt.

10 Note its routing, then remove the timing belt from the sprockets.

Inspection

11 Renew the belt as a matter of course, regardless of its apparent condition. The cost of a new belt is nothing compared with the cost of repairs should the belt break in service. If signs of oil contamination are found, trace the source of the oil leak and rectify it. Wash down the engine timing belt area and all related components, to remove all traces of oil. Check that the tensioner and idler pulleys rotate freely without any sign of roughness, and also check that the coolant pump pulley rotates freely. If necessary, renew these items.

Refitting and tensioning

12 Commence refitting by ensuring that the crankshaft, camshaft and fuel pump sprocket timing pins are in position as described in Section 3.

13 Locate the timing belt on the crankshaft sprocket, then keeping it taut, locate it around the idler pulley, camshaft sprocket, high-pressure pump sprocket, coolant pump sprocket, and the tensioner roller **(see illustration)**.

14 Refit the timing belt protection bracket and tighten the retaining bolt securely.

15 Slacken the tensioner pulley bolt, and using a hexagonal key, rotate the tensioner arm anti-clockwise, which moves the index arm clockwise, until the index arm is aligned as shown **(see illustration)**.

7.9 Slacken the bolt and allow the tensioner to rotate, relieving the tension on the belt

7.13 Timing belt routing

7.15 The index arm must align with the lug (arrowed)

16 Remove the camshaft, crankshaft and fuel pump sprocket timing pins and, using a socket on the crankshaft pulley bolt, rotate the crankshaft clockwise 10 complete revolutions. Refit the crankshaft and camshaft locking pins.

17 Check that the tensioner index arm is still aligned between the edges of the area shown **(see illustration 7.15)**. If it is not, remove and belt and begin the refitting process again, starting at Paragraph 12.

18 The remainder of refitting is a reversal of removal. Tighten all fasteners to the specified torque where given.

8 Timing belt sprockets and tensioner – removal and refitting

Camshaft sprocket

Removal

1 Remove the timing belt as described in Section 7.

2 Remove the locking tool from the camshaft sprocket/hub. Slacken the sprocket hub retaining bolt. To prevent the camshaft rotating as the bolt is slackened, a sprocket holding tool will be required. In the absence of the special Ford tool, an acceptable substitute can be fabricated at home **(see Tool Tip 1)**. *Do not* attempt to use the engine assembly/valve timing locking tool to prevent the sprocket from rotating whilst the bolt is slackened.

3 Remove the sprocket hub retaining bolt,

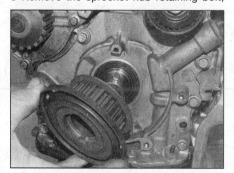

8.11a Slide the sprocket from the crankshaft . . .

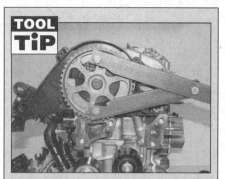

Tool Tip 1: A sprocket holding tool can be made from two lengths of steel strip bolted together to form a forked end. Drill holes and insert bolts in the ends of the fork to engage with the sprocket spokes.

and slide the sprocket and hub off the end of the camshaft.

4 Clean the camshaft sprocket thoroughly, and renew it if there are any signs of wear, damage or cracks.

Refitting

5 Refit the camshaft sprocket to the camshaft **(see illustration)**.

6 Refit the sprocket hub retaining bolt. Tighten the bolt to the specified torque, preventing the camshaft from turning as during removal.

7 Align the engine assembly/valve timing slot in the camshaft sprocket hub with the hole in the cylinder head and refit the timing pin to lock the camshaft in position.

8 Fit the timing belt around the pump sprocket and camshaft sprocket, and tension the timing belt as described in Section 7.

Crankshaft sprocket

Removal

9 Remove the timing belt as described in Section 7.

10 Check that the engine assembly/valve timing holes are still aligned as described in Section 3, and the camshaft sprocket and flywheel are locked in position.

11 Slide the sprocket off the end of the crankshaft and collect the Woodruff key **(see illustrations)**.

8.11b . . . and recover the Woodruff key

8.5 Ensure the lug on the sprocket hub engages with the slot on the end of the camshaft (arrowed)

12 Examine the crankshaft oil seal for signs of oil leakage and, if necessary, renew it as described in Section 14.

13 Clean the crankshaft sprocket thoroughly, and renew it if there are any signs of wear, damage or cracks. Recover the crankshaft locating key.

Refitting

14 Refit the key to the end of the crankshaft, then refit the crankshaft sprocket (with the flange facing the crankshaft pulley).

15 Fit the timing belt around the crankshaft sprocket, and tension the timing belt as described in Section 7.

Fuel pump sprocket

Removal

16 Remove the timing belt as described in Section 7.

17 Using a suitable socket, undo the pump sprocket retaining nut. The sprocket can be held stationary by inserting a suitably-sized locking pin, drill or rod through the hole in the sprocket, and into the corresponding hole in the backplate **(see illustration)**, or by using a suitable forked tool engaged with the holes in the sprocket **(see Tool Tip 1)**.

18 The pump sprocket is a taper fit on the pump shaft and it will be necessary to make up another tool to release it from the taper **(see Tool Tip 2)**.

19 Partially unscrew the sprocket retaining nut, fit the home-made tool, and secure it to the sprocket with two suitable bolts. Prevent the sprocket from rotating as before, and

8.17 Insert a suitable drill bit through the sprocket into the hole in the backplate

TOOL TiP

Tool Tip 2: Make a sprocket releasing tool from a short strip of steel. Drill two holes in the strip to correspond with the two holes in the sprocket. Drill a third hole just large enough to accept the flats of the sprocket retaining nut.

unscrew the sprocket retaining nut. The nut will bear against the tool as it is undone, forcing the sprocket off the shaft taper. Once the taper is released, remove the tool, unscrew the nut fully, and remove the sprocket from the pump shaft.

20 Clean the sprocket thoroughly, and renew it if there are any signs of wear, damage or cracks.

Refitting

21 Refit the pump sprocket and retaining nut, and tighten the nut to the specified torque. Prevent the sprocket rotating as the nut is tightened using the sprocket holding tool.
22 Refit the timing belt as described in Section 7.

9.5 Vacuum pump bolts (arrowed)

9.9a Undo the nut/bolts (arrowed) and remove the upper, outer section of the turbo heat shield . . .

8.31 Timing belt idler pulley retaining nut (arrowed)

Coolant pump sprocket

23 The coolant pump sprocket is integral with the pump, and cannot be removed. Coolant pump removal is described in Chapter 3.

Tensioner pulley

Removal

24 Remove the timing belt as described in Section 7.
25 Remove the tensioner pulley retaining bolt, and slide the pulley off its mounting stud.
26 Clean the tensioner pulley, but do not use any strong solvent which may enter the pulley bearings. Check that the pulley rotates freely, with no sign of stiffness or free play. Renew the pulley if there is any doubt about its condition, or if there are any obvious signs of wear or damage.
27 Examine the pulley mounting stud for signs of damage and if necessary, renew it.

9.7 Timing belt inner cover bolts (arrowed)

9.9b . . . followed by the inner section (bolts arrowed)

Refitting

28 Refit the tensioner pulley to its mounting stud, and fit the retaining bolt.
29 Refit the timing belt as described in Section 7.

Idler pulley

Removal

30 Remove the timing belt as described in Section 7.
31 Undo the retaining bolt/nut and withdraw the idler pulley from the engine **(see illustration)**.
32 Clean the idler pulley, but do not use any strong solvent which may enter the bearings. Check that the pulley rotates freely, with no sign of stiffness or free play. Renew the idler pulley if there is any doubt about its condition, or if there are any obvious signs of wear or damage.

Refitting

33 Locate the idler pulley on the engine, and fit the retaining bolt/nut. Tighten the bolt/nut to the specified torque.
34 Refit the timing belt as described in Section 7.

9 Camshafts, rocker arms and hydraulic tappets – removal, inspection and refitting

Removal

1 Remove the cylinder head cover/manifold as described in Section 4.
2 Remove the injectors as described in Chapter 4.
3 Remove the camshaft sprocket as described in Section 8.
4 Refit the right-hand engine mounting, but only tighten the bolts moderately; this will keep the engine supported during the camshaft removal.
5 Undo the bolts and remove the vacuum pump (see Chapter 9). Recover the pump O-ring seals **(see illustration)**.
6 Remove the fuel filter (see Chapter 1) then undo the bolts and remove the fuel filter mounting bracket.
7 Release the wiring harness clips, then undo the 3 bolts and remove the timing belt inner, upper cover **(see illustration)**.
8 Disconnect the wiring plug, unscrew the retaining bolt, and remove the camshaft position sensor from the camshaft cover/ bearing ladder.
9 Undo the bolts/nut and remove the upper rear sections of the turbocharger heat shield, then working gradually and evenly, slacken and remove the bolts securing the camshaft cover/bearing ladder to the cylinder head in sequence **(see illustrations)**. Lift the cover/ ladder from position complete with the camshafts.
10 Undo the retaining bolts and remove the bearing caps. Note their fitted positions,

as they must be refitted into their original positions (see illustration). Note that the bearing caps are marked A for intake, and E for exhaust and 1 to 4 from the flywheel end of the cylinder head.

11 Undo the bolts securing the chain tensioner assembly to the camshaft cover/ bearing ladder, then lift the camshafts, chain and tensioner from place (see illustrations). Discard the camshaft oil seal.

12 Obtain 16 small, clean plastic containers, and number them 1 to 8 intake and 1 to 8 exhaust; alternatively, divide a larger container into 16 compartments.

13 Lift out each rocker arm. Place the rocker arms in their respective positions in the box or containers.

14 A compartmentalised container filled with engine oil is now required to retain the hydraulic tappets while they are removed from the cylinder head. Withdraw each hydraulic follower and place it in the container, keeping them each identified for correct refitting. The tappets must be totally submerged in the oil to prevent air entering them.

Inspection

15 Inspect the cam lobes and the camshaft bearing journals for scoring or other visible evidence of wear. Once the surface hardening of the cam lobes has been eroded, wear will occur at an accelerated rate. **Note:** If these symptoms are visible on the tips of the camshaft lobes, check the corresponding rocker arm, as it will probably be worn as well.

16 Examine the condition of the bearing surfaces in the cylinder head and camshaft bearing housing. If wear is evident, the cylinder head and bearing housing will both have to be renewed, as they are a matched assembly.

17 Inspect the rocker arms and tappets for scuffing, cracking or other damage and renew any components as necessary. Also check the condition of the tappet bores in the cylinder head. As with the camshafts, any wear in this area will necessitate cylinder head renewal.

Refitting

18 Thoroughly clean the sealant from the mating surfaces of the cylinder head and camshaft bearing housing. Use a suitable liquid gasket dissolving agent (available from

9.9c Camshaft cover/bearing ladder bolt slackening sequence

Ford dealers) together with a soft putty knife; do not use a metal scraper or the faces will be damaged. As there is no conventional gasket used, the cleanliness of the mating faces is of the utmost importance. Prise out the oil injector oil seals from the camshaft bearing housing.

19 Clean off any oil, dirt or grease from both components and dry with a clean lint-free cloth. Ensure that all the oilways are completely clean.

20 Liberally lubricate the hydraulic tappet bores in the cylinder head with clean engine oil.

21 Insert the hydraulic tappets into their original bores in the cylinder head unless they have been renewed (see illustration).

22 Lubricate the rocker arms and place them over their respective tappets and valve stems (see illustration).

23 Engage the timing chain around the camshaft sprockets, aligning the black-coloured links with the marked teeth on the camshaft sprockets (see illustration). If the black colouring has been lost, there must be 12 chain link pins between the marks on the sprockets.

24 Fit the chain tensioner between the upper

9.10 The camshaft bearing caps are numbered 1 to 4 from the flywheel end – A for intake, and E for exhaust (arrowed)

9.11a Undo the tensioner bolts (arrowed) . . .

9.11b . . . then lift the camshafts, chain and tensioner from place

9.21 Refit the hydraulic tappets . . .

9.22 . . . and rocker arms to their original locations

9.23 Align the marks on the sprockets with the centre of the black-coloured chain links (arrowed). There must be 12 link pins between the sprocket marks

9.24a Assemble the chain tensioner between the upper and lower runs of the chain . . .

9.24b . . . and lower the camshaft, chain and tensioner into position

and lower runs of the chain, then lubricate the bearing surfaces with clean engine oil, and fit the camshafts into position on the underside of the camshaft cover/bearing ladder. Refit the bearing caps to their original positions and tighten the retaining bolts to the specified torque (see illustrations). Tighten the tensioner retaining bolts to the specified torque.

25 Apply a thin bead of silicone sealant (Ford part No WSE-M4G323-A4) to the mating surface of the camshaft cover/bearing ladder as shown (see illustration). Do not allow the sealant to obstruct the oil channels for the hydraulic chain tensioner.

26 Check that the black-coloured links on the chain are still aligned with the marks on the camshaft sprockets, then refit the camshaft cover/bearing ladder, and gradually and evenly tighten the retaining bolts until the cover/ladder is in contact with the cylinder head. Tighten the bolts to the specified torque in sequence (see illustration). **Note:** *Ensure the cover/ladder is correctly located by checking the bores of the vacuum pump and camshaft oil seal at each end of the cover/ladder.*

27 Fit a new camshaft oil seal as described in Section 14.

28 Refit the camshaft sprocket, and tighten the retaining bolt finger-tight.

9.25 Apply sealant to the camshaft cover/bearing ladder as indicated by the heavy block lines. Ensure sealant does not enter the tensioner oil holes marked A

9.26 Camshaft cover/bearing ladder bolt tightening sequence

29 Using a spanner on the camshaft sprocket bolt, rotate the camshafts approximately 40 complete revolutions clockwise. Check the black-coloured links on the chain still align with the marks on the camshaft sprockets.

30 If the marks still align, refit the camshaft sprocket as described in Section 8.

31 Refit and adjust the camshaft position sensor as described in Chapter 4.

32 Press the new oil seals into the bearing housing, using a tube/socket of approximately 20 mm outside diameter, ensuring the inner lip of the seal fits around the injector guide tube **(see illustrations)**. Refit the injectors as described in Chapter 4.

33 Refit the cylinder head cover/manifold as described in Section 4.

9.32a Fit the new seal around a 20 mm outside diameter socket . . .

9.32b . . . and push it into place

10 Cylinder head – removal and refitting

Removal

1 Apply the handbrake, then jack up the front of the vehicle and support it on axle stands (see *Jacking and vehicle support*). Remove the front right-hand roadwheel, the engine undershield, and the front wheel arch liner. The undershield is secured by several fasteners, and the wheel arch liner is secured by several plastic expanding rivets/nuts/plastic clips. Push the centre pins in a little, then prise the rivet from place.

2 Disconnect the battery negative lead as described in Chapter 5.

3 Drain the cooling system as described in Chapter 1.

4 Remove the camshafts, rocker arms and hydraulic tappets as described in Section 9.

5 Remove the turbocharger and exhaust manifold as described in Chapter 4.

6 Remove the glow plugs as described in Chapter 5.

7 Undo the upper mounting bolts, and pivot the alternator away from the engine, undo the oil dipstick guide tube bolt, then undo the bolts securing the alternator mounting bracket to the cylinder head/block **(see illustration)**.

8 Undo the coolant outlet housing (left-hand end of the cylinder head) retaining bolts, slacken the two bolts securing the housing support bracket to the top of the transmission bellhousing, and move the outlet housing away from the cylinder head a little **(see illustration)**. There is no need to disconnect the hoses.

9 Remove the brake vacuum pump as described in Chapter 9.

10 Disconnect the high-pressure fuel pipe from the common rail to the pump, and disconnect the fuel supply and return hoses. Remove the bracket at the rear of the pump, then undo the bolt/nut and remove the pump and mounting bracket as an assembly **(see illustrations)**. Note that a new high-pressure pipe must be fitted – see Chapter 4.

11 Working in the **reverse** of the sequence shown **(see illustration 10.30)** undo the cylinder head bolts. Discard the bolts – new ones must be fitted.

12 Release the cylinder head from the cylinder block and location dowels by rocking it. The Ford tool for doing this consists simply of two metal rods with 90-degree angled ends **(see illustration)**. Do not prise between the mating faces of the cylinder head and block, as this may damage the gasket faces.

10.7 The engine oil level dipstick guide tube is secured to the alternator bracket by a Torx bolt (arrowed)

10.8 Undo the bolts (arrowed) and pull the coolant outlet housing from the left-hand end of the cylinder head

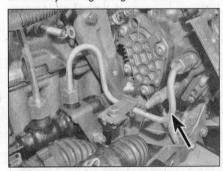

10.10a Remove the high-pressure pipe (arrowed) . . .

10.10b . . . and the bracket (arrowed)

10.10c Pump mounting bracket upper nut and lower mounting bolt (arrowed)

10.12 Free the cylinder head using angled rods

10.16a Pull the non-return valve from the cylinder head . . .

10.16b . . . and push a new one into place

10.21 Measure the piston protrusion using a DTI gauge

13 Lift the cylinder head from the block, and recover the gasket.

Preparation for refitting

14 The mating faces of the cylinder head and cylinder block must be perfectly clean before refitting the head. Ford recommend the use of a scouring agent for this purpose, but acceptable results can be achieved by using a hard plastic or wood scraper to remove all traces of gasket and carbon. The same method can be used to clean the piston crowns. Take particular care to avoid scoring or gouging the cylinder head/cylinder block mating surfaces during the cleaning operations, as aluminium alloy is easily damaged. Make sure that the carbon is not allowed to enter the oil and water passages – this is particularly important for the lubrication system, as carbon could block the oil supply to the engine's components. Using adhesive tape and paper, seal the water, oil and bolt holes in the cylinder block. To prevent carbon entering the gap between the pistons and bores, smear a little grease in the gap. After cleaning each piston, use a small brush

10.23 Cylinder head gasket thickness identification notches (arrowed)

to remove all traces of grease and carbon from the gap, then wipe away the remainder with a clean rag.

15 Check the mating surfaces of the cylinder block and the cylinder head for nicks, deep scratches and other damage. If slight, they may be removed carefully with a file, but if excessive, machining may be the only alternative to renewal. If warpage of the cylinder head gasket surface is suspected, use a straight-edge to check it for distortion. Refer to Part F of this Chapter if necessary.

16 Thoroughly clean the threads of the cylinder head bolt holes in the cylinder block. Ensure that the bolts run freely in their threads, and that all traces of oil and water are removed from each bolt hole. If required, pull the oil feed non-return valve from the cylinder head, and check the ball moves freely. Push a new valve into place if necessary **(see illustrations)**.

Gasket selection

17 The gasket thickness is indicated by notches/holes on the front edge of the gasket. If the crankshaft or pistons/connecting rods have

10.26 Ensure the gasket locates over the dowels (arrowed)

not been disturbed, fit a new gasket with the same number of notches/holes as the previous one. If the crankshaft/piston or connecting rods have been disturbed, it's necessary to work out the piston protrusion as follows:

18 Remove the crankshaft timing pin, then turn the crankshaft until pistons 1 and 4 are at TDC (Top Dead Centre). Position a dial test indicator (dial gauge) on the cylinder block adjacent to the rear of No 1 piston, and zero it on the block face. Transfer the probe to the crown of No 1 piston (10.0 mm in from the rear edge), then slowly turn the crankshaft back-and-forth past TDC, noting the highest reading on the indicator. Record this reading as protrusion A.

19 Repeat the check described in paragraph 18, this time 10.0 mm in from the front edge of the No 1 piston crown. Record this reading as protrusion B.

20 Add protrusion A to protrusion B, then divide the result by 2 to obtain an average reading for piston No 1.

21 Repeat the procedure described in paragraphs 18 to 20 on piston 4, then turn the crankshaft through 180° and carry out the procedure on the piston Nos 2 and 3 **(see illustration)**. Check that there is a maximum difference of 0.07 mm protrusion between any two pistons.

22 If a dial test indicator is not available, piston protrusion may be measured using a straight-edge and feeler blades or Vernier calipers. However, this is much less accurate, and cannot therefore be recommended.

23 Note the greatest piston protrusion measurement, and use this to determine the correct cylinder head gasket from the table below. The series of notches/holes on the side of the gasket are used for thickness identification **(see illustration)**.

Refitting

24 Turn the crankshaft and position Nos 1 and 4 pistons at TDC, then turn the crankshaft a quarter turn (90°) anti-clockwise.

25 Thoroughly clean the surfaces of the cylinder head and block.

26 Make sure that the locating dowels are in place, then fit the correct gasket the right way round on the cylinder block **(see illustration)**.

27 Carefully lower the cylinder head onto the gasket and block, making sure that it locates correctly onto the dowels.

Gasket selection table

Piston protrusion	Gasket identification	Gasket thickness
0.533 to 0.634 mm	2 notches	1.25 mm
0.634 to 0.684 mm	3 notches	1.30 mm
0.684 to 0.734 mm	1 notches	1.35 mm
0.734 to 0.784 mm	4 notches	1.40 mm
0.784 to 0.886 mm	5 notches	1.45 mm

28 Apply a smear of grease to the threads, and to the underside of the heads of the new cylinder head bolts.

29 Carefully insert the cylinder head bolts into their holes (*do not drop them in*) and initially finger-tighten them.

30 Working progressively and in sequence, tighten the cylinder head bolts to their Stage 1 torque setting, using a torque wrench and suitable socket **(see illustration)**.

31 Once all the bolts have been tightened to their Stage 1 torque setting, working again in the specified sequence, tighten each bolt to the specified Stage 2 setting. Finally, angle-tighten the bolts through the specified Stage 3 angle. It is recommended that an angle-measuring gauge is used during this stage of tightening, to ensure accuracy. **Note:** *Retightening of the cylinder head bolts after running the engine is not required.*

32 Refit the hydraulic tappets, rocker arms, and camshaft housing (complete with camshafts) as described in Section 9.

33 Refit the timing belt as described in Section 7.

34 The remainder of refitting is a reversal of removal, noting the following points.

a) *Use a new seal when refitting the coolant outlet housing.*

b) *When refitting a cylinder head, it is good practice to renew the thermostat.*

c) *Refit the camshaft position sensor and set the air gap with reference to Chapter 4.*

d) *Tighten all fasteners to the specified torque where given.*

e) *Refill the cooling system as described in Chapter 1.*

f) *The engine may run erratically for the first few miles, until the engine management ECM relearns its stored values.*

11 Sump –
removal and refitting

Removal

1 Drain the engine oil, then clean and refit the engine oil drain plug, tightening it securely. If the engine is nearing its service interval when the oil and filter are due for renewal, it is recommended that the filter is also removed, and a new one fitted. After reassembly, the engine can then be refilled with fresh oil. Refer to Chapter 1 for further information.

2 Apply the handbrake, then jack up the front of the vehicle and support it on axle stands (see *Jacking and vehicle support*). Undo the bolts and remove the engine undershield.

3 Remove the exhaust front pipe as described in Chapter 4.

4 Where necessary, disconnect the wiring connector from the oil temperature sender unit, which is screwed into the sump.

5 Progressively slacken and remove all the sump retaining bolts/nuts. Since the sump bolts vary in length, remove each bolt in turn,

10.30 Cylinder head bolt tightening sequence

and store it in its correct fitted order by pushing it through a clearly-marked cardboard template. This will avoid the possibility of installing the bolts in the wrong locations on refitting.

6 Try to break the joint by striking the sump with the palm of your hand, then lower and withdraw the sump from under the car. If the sump is stuck (which is quite likely) use a putty knife or similar, carefully inserted between the sump and block. Ease the knife along the joint until the sump is released. While the sump is removed, take the opportunity to check the oil pump pick-up/strainer for signs of clogging or splitting. If necessary, remove the pump as described in Section 12, and clean or renew the strainer.

Refitting

7 Clean all traces of sealant from the mating surfaces of the cylinder block/crankcase and sump, then use a clean rag to wipe out the sump and the engine's interior.

8 On engines where the sump was fitted without a gasket, ensure that the sump mating surfaces are clean and dry, then apply a thin coating of silicone sealant (Ford part No WSE-M4G323-A4) to the sump or crankcase mating surface **(see illustration)**. Note that the sump must be installed within

10 minutes of applying the sealant, and the bolts tightened within a further 5 minutes.

9 Offer up the sump to the cylinder block/crankcase. Refit its retaining bolts/nuts, ensuring that each bolt is screwed into its original location. Tighten the bolts evenly and progressively to the specified torque setting **(see illustration)**.

10 Reconnect the wiring connector to the oil temperature sensor (where fitted).

11 Lower the vehicle to the ground, then refill the engine with oil as described in Chapter 1.

12 Oil pump –
removal, inspection and refitting

Removal

1 Remove the sump as described in Section 11.

2 Remove the crankshaft sprocket as described in Section 8. Recover the locating key from the crankshaft.

3 Disconnect the wiring plug, undo the bolts and remove the crankshaft position sensor, located on the right-hand end of the cylinder block.

11.8 Apply a bead of sealant to the sump or crankcase mating surface. Ensure the sealant is applied to the inside of the retaining bolt holes

11.9 Refit the sump and tighten the bolts

12.4 Oil pick-up tube bolts (arrowed)

12.5 Oil pump retaining bolts (arrowed)

4 Undo the three bolts and remove the oil pump pick-up tube from the pump/block **(see illustration)**. Discard the oil seal, a new one must be fitted.

5 Undo the 8 bolts, and remove the oil pump **(see illustration)**.

Inspection

6 Undo and remove the Torx bolts securing the cover to the oil pump **(see illustration)**. Examine the pump rotors and body for signs of wear and damage. If worn, the complete pump must be renewed.

7 Remove the circlip, and extract the cap, valve piston and spring, noting which way

around they are fitted **(see illustrations)**. The condition of the relief valve spring can only be measured by comparing it with a new one; if there is any doubt about its condition, it should also be renewed.

8 Refit the relief valve piston and spring, then secure them in place with the circlip.

9 Refit the cover to the oil pump, and tighten the Torx bolts securely.

Refitting

10 Remove all traces of sealant, and thoroughly clean the mating surfaces of the oil pump and cylinder block.

11 Apply a 4 mm wide bead of silicone

sealant to the mating face of the cylinder block **(see illustration)**. Ensure that no sealant enters any of the holes in the block.

12 With a new oil seal fitted, refit the oil pump over the end of the crankshaft, aligning the flats in the pump drivegear with the flats machined in the crankshaft **(see illustrations)**. Note that new oil pumps are supplied with the oil seal already fitted, and a seal protector sleeve. The sleeve fits over the end of the crankshaft to protect the seal as the pump is fitted.

13 Install the oil pump bolts and tighten them to the specified torque.

14 Refit the oil pick-up tube to the pump/

12.6 Undo the Torx bolts and remove the pump cover

12.7a Remove the circlip . . .

12.7b . . . cap . . .

12.7c . . . spring . . .

12.7d . . . and piston

12.11 Apply a bead of sealant to the cylinder block mating surface

12.12a Fit a new seal . . .

12.12b . . . align the pump gear flats (arrowed) . . .

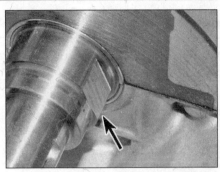

12.12c . . . with those of the crankshaft (arrowed)

cylinder block using a new O-ring seal. Ensure the oil dipstick guide tube is correctly refitted.
15 Refit the woodruff key to the crankshaft, and slide the crankshaft sprocket into place.
16 The remainder of refitting is a reversal of removal.

13 Oil cooler –
removal and refitting

Removal

1 Apply the handbrake, then jack up the front of the vehicle and support it on axle stands (see *Jacking and vehicle support*). Undo the fasteners and remove the engine undershield.
2 The oil cooler is fitted to the front of the oil filter housing. Drain the coolant as described in Chapter 1.
3 Drain the engine oil as described in Chapter 1, or be prepared for fluid spillage.
4 Undo the bolts/stud and remove the oil cooler. Recover the O-ring seals **(see illustrations)**.

Refitting

5 Fit new O-ring seals into the recesses in the oil filter housing, and refit the cooler. Tighten the bolts securely.
6 Refill or top-up the cooling system and engine oil level as described in Chapter 1 or *Weekly checks* (as applicable). Start the engine, and check the oil cooler for signs of leakage.

14 Oil seals –
renewal

Crankshaft

Right-hand oil seal

1 Remove the crankshaft sprocket and Woodruff key as described in Section 8.
2 Measure and note the fitted depth of the oil seal.
3 Pull the oil seal from the housing using a screwdriver. Alternatively, drill a small hole in the oil seal, and use a self-tapping screw and a pair of pliers to remove it **(see illustration)**.
4 Clean the oil seal housing and the crankshaft sealing surface.
5 The seal has a Teflon lip and must not be oiled or marked. The new seal should be

13.4a Undo the oil cooler bolts/stud (arrowed)

supplied with a protective sleeve, which fits over the end of the crankshaft to prevent any damage to the seal lip. With the sleeve in place, press the seal (open end first) into the pump to the previously-noted depth, using a suitable tube or socket **(see illustrations)**.
6 Where applicable, remove the plastic sleeve from the end of the crankshaft.
7 Refit the crankshaft sprocket as described in Section 8.

Left-hand oil seal

8 Remove the flywheel, as described in Section 16.
9 Measure and note the fitted depth of the oil seal.
10 Pull the oil seal from the housing using a screwdriver. Alternatively, drill a small hole in the oil seal, and use a self-tapping screw and a pair of pliers to remove it **(see illustration 14.3)**.

13.4b Renew the O-ring seals (arrowed)

14.3 Take great care not to mark the crankshaft whilst levering out the oil seal

14.5a Slide the seal and protective sleeve over the end of the crankshaft . . .

14.5b . . . and press the seal into place

14.12 Slide the seal and protective sleeve over the left-hand end of the crankshaft

14.16 Drill a hole, insert a self-tapping screw, and pull the seal from place using pliers

14.18 Fit the protective sleeve and seal over the end of the camshaft

11 Clean the oil seal housing and the crankshaft sealing surface.

12 The seal has a Teflon lip and must not be oiled or marked. The new seal should be supplied with a protective sleeve, which fits over the end of the crankshaft to prevent any damage to the seal lip **(see illustration)**. With the sleeve in place, press the seal (open end first) into the housing to the previously-noted depth, using a suitable tube or socket.

13 Where applicable, remove the plastic sleeve from the end of the crankshaft.

14 Refit the flywheel, as described in Section 16.

Camshaft

15 Remove the camshaft sprocket as described in Section 8. In principle there is no need to remove the timing belt completely, but remember that if the belt has been contaminated with oil, it must be renewed.

16 Pull the oil seal from the housing using a hooked instrument. Alternatively, drill a small hole in the oil seal and use a self-tapping screw and a pair of pliers to remove it **(see illustration)**.

17 Clean the oil seal housing and the camshaft sealing surface.

18 The seal has a Teflon lip and must not be oiled or marked. The new seal should be supplied with a protective sleeve. which fits over the end of the camshaft to prevent any damage to the seal lip **(see illustration)**. With the sleeve in place, press the seal (open end first) into the housing to the previously-noted

depth, using a suitable tube or socket which bears only of the outer edge of the seal.

19 Refit the camshaft sprocket as described in Section 8.

20 Where necessary, fit a new timing belt with reference to Section 7.

15 Oil pressure switch and level sensor – removal and refitting

Removal

Oil pressure switch

1 The oil pressure switch is located at the front of the cylinder block, adjacent to the oil dipstick guide tube. Note that on some models, access to the switch may be improved if the vehicle is jacked up and supported on axle stands, then undo the bolts and remove the engine undershield so that the switch can be reached from underneath (see *Jacking and vehicle support*).

2 Remove the protective sleeve from the wiring plug (where applicable), then disconnect the wiring from the switch.

3 Unscrew the switch from the cylinder block, and recover the sealing washer **(see illustration)**. Be prepared for oil spillage, and if the switch is to be left removed from the engine for any length of time, plug the hole in the cylinder block.

Oil level sensor

4 The oil level sensor is located at the rear of the cylinder block. Jack up the front of the vehicle and support it securely on axle stands (see *Jacking and vehicle support*). Undo the bolts and remove the engine undershield.

5 Reach up between the driveshaft and the cylinder block, and disconnect the sensor wiring plug **(see illustration)**.

6 Using an open-ended spanner, unscrew the sensor and withdraw it from position.

Refitting

Oil pressure switch

7 Examine the sealing washer for any signs of damage or deterioration, and if necessary renew.

8 Refit the switch, complete with washer, and tighten it to the specified torque.

9 Refit the engine undershield, and lower the vehicle to the ground.

Oil level sensor

10 Smear a little silicone sealant on the threads and refit the sensor to the cylinder block, tightening it securely.

11 Reconnect the sensor wiring plug.

12 Refit the engine undershield, and lower the vehicle to the ground.

16 Flywheel – removal, inspection and refitting

Removal

1 Remove the transmission as described in Chapter 7, then remove the clutch assembly as described in Chapter 6.

2 Prevent the flywheel from turning. *Do not* attempt to lock the flywheel in position using the crankshaft pulley locking tool described in Section 3. Insert a 12 mm diameter rod or drill bit through the hole in the flywheel cover casting, and into a slot in the flywheel **(see illustration 5.2)**

3 Make alignment marks between the flywheel and crankshaft to aid refitment. Slacken and remove the flywheel retaining bolts, and remove the flywheel from the end

15.3 The oil pressure switch is located on the front face of the cylinder block (arrowed)

15.5 The oil level sensor is located on the rear face of the cylinder block (arrowed)

16.9 Flywheel retaining Torx bolts

17.10 Undo the bolts (arrowed) and remove the battery tray

17.12 Left-hand mounting

of the crankshaft. Be careful not to drop it; it is heavy. If the flywheel locating dowel (where fitted) is a loose fit in the crankshaft end, remove it and store it with the flywheel for safe-keeping. Discard the flywheel bolts; new ones must be used on refitting.

Inspection

4 Examine the flywheel for scoring of the clutch face, and for wear or chipping of the ring gear teeth. If the clutch face is scored, the flywheel may be surface-ground, but renewal is preferable. Seek the advice of a Ford dealer or engine reconditioning specialist to see if machining is possible. If the ring gear is worn or damaged, the flywheel must be renewed, as it is not possible to renew the ring gear separately.

5 Note that on engines fitted with a dual-mass flywheel, the maximum travel of the primary mass in relation to the secondary must not exceed 15 teeth.

Refitting

6 Clean the mating surfaces of the flywheel and crankshaft. Remove any remaining locking compound from the threads of the crankshaft holes, using the correct size of tap, if available.

 HAYNES HiNT *If a suitable tap is not available, cut two slots along the threads of one of the old flywheel bolts, and use the bolt to remove the locking compound from the threads.*

7 If the new flywheel retaining bolts are not supplied with their threads already pre-coated, apply a suitable thread-locking compound to the threads of each bolt.

8 Ensure that the locating dowel is in position. Offer up the flywheel, locating it on the dowel (where fitted), and fit the new retaining bolts. Where no locating dowel is fitted, align the previously-made marks to ensure the flywheel is refitted in its original position.

9 Lock the flywheel using the method employed on dismantling, and tighten the retaining bolts to the specified torque **(see illustration)**.

10 Refit the clutch as described in Chapter 6. Remove the flywheel locking tool, and refit the transmission as described in Chapter 7.

17 Engine/transmission mountings – inspection and renewal

Inspection

1 If improved access is required, firmly apply the handbrake, then jack up the front of the car and support it on axle stands (see *Jacking and vehicle support*). Undo the bolts and remove the engine undershield.

2 Check the mounting rubbers to see if they are cracked, hardened or separated from the metal at any point; renew the mounting if any such damage or deterioration is evident.

3 Check that all the mountings' fasteners are securely tightened; use a torque wrench to check if possible.

4 Using a large screwdriver or a crowbar, check for wear in each mounting by carefully levering against it to check for free play. Where this is not possible, enlist the aid of an assistant to move the engine/transmission back-and-forth, or from side-to-side, while you watch the mounting. While some free play is to be expected even from new components, excessive wear should be obvious. If excessive free play is found, check first that the fasteners are correctly secured, then renew any worn components as described below.

Renewal

Right-hand mounting

5 Pull the coolant expansion tank upwards from its mountings, and move it to one side.
6 Undo the fasteners and remove the engine undershield, then place a jack beneath the engine, with a block of wood on the jack head.

Raise the jack until it is supporting the weight of the engine.
7 Undo the 2 bolts and 2 nuts and remove the mounting from place **(see illustration 6.13)**.
8 If required, undo the bolts/nuts securing the support bracket to the cylinder head/cylinder block.
9 Refitting is a reversal of removal, tightening all fittings to the specified torque where given.

Left-hand mounting

10 Remove the battery as described in Chapter 5, then undo the bolts and remove the battery tray **(see illustration)**.
11 Undo the fasteners and remove the engine undershield, then place a jack beneath the transmission, with a block of wood on the jack head. Raise the jack until it is supporting the weight of the transmission.
12 Undo the nuts/bolts and remove the mounting **(see illustration)**.
13 Check all components carefully for signs of wear or damage, and renew as necessary.
14 Refitting is a reversal of removal, tightening all fittings to the specified torque, where given.

Lower engine torque rod/ movement limiter link

15 If not already done, firmly apply the handbrake, then jack up the front of the vehicle and support it securely on axle stands (see *Jacking and vehicle support*). Undo the fasteners and remove the engine undershield.
16 Unscrew and remove the bolt securing the movement limiter link to the support bracket.
17 Remove the bolt securing the link to the subframe. Withdraw the link.
18 Check carefully for signs of wear or damage on all components, and renew them where necessary. The rubber bush fitted to the bearing housing is available as a separate item (at the time of writing), and can be pressed out and back into place.
19 Refit the movement limiter link, and tighten both its bolts to their specified torque settings. Refit the engine undershield.
20 Lower the vehicle to the ground.

Notes

Chapter 2 Part D:
1.8 litre diesel engine in-car repair procedures

Contents

Section number

Camshaft and cam followers – removal, inspection and refitting . . . 9
Camshaft oil seal – renewal 10
Compression and leakdown tests – description and interpretation. . 2
Crankshaft oil seals – renewal 16
Crankshaft pulley – removal and refitting. 6
Cylinder head – removal, inspection and refitting 11
Cylinder head cover – removal and refitting. 4
Engine/transmission mountings – inspection and renewal 18
Flywheel – removal, inspection and refitting 17
General information 1

Section number

Oil cooler – removal and refitting 15
Oil pressure warning light switch – removal and refitting. 14
Oil pump – removal, inspection and refitting 13
Setting the engine to Top Dead Centre (TDC) on No 1 cylinder. 3
Sump – removal and refitting 12
Timing belt – removal and refitting. 7
Timing belt tensioner and sprockets – removal, inspection and
  refitting 8
Valve clearances – checking and adjustment 5

Degrees of difficulty

Easy, suitable for novice with little experience	Fairly easy, suitable for beginner with some experience	Fairly difficult, suitable for competent DIY mechanic	Difficult, suitable for experienced DIY mechanic	Very difficult, suitable for expert DIY or professional

Specifications

General

Engine type.	Four cylinder, in-line, single overhead camshaft, cast-iron cylinder head and engine block
Designation	DuraTorq-TDCi
Engine code	KKDA
Power output	85 kW @ 3700 rpm
Torque output	280 Nm @ 1900 rpm
Capacity	1753 cc
Bore	82.5 mm
Stroke.	82.0 mm
Compression ratio	17.0:1
Firing order.	1-3-4-2 (No 1 cylinder at timing belt end)
Direction of crankshaft rotation	Clockwise (seen from right-hand side of vehicle)

Camshaft

Camshaft bearing journal diameter	27.96 to 27.98 mm
Camshaft endfloat	0.100 to 0.240 mm

Valves

Valve clearances (cold):

Intake	0.30 to 0.40 mm
Exhaust.	0.45 to 0.55 mm

Cylinder head

Camshaft bearing diameter (nominal)	30.500 to 30.525 mm
Maximum permissible gasket surface distortion	0.6 mm

Lubrication

Oil pressure – minimum (engine at operating temperature):

At idle	0.75 bars
At 2000 rpm	1.50 bars
Oil pump clearance (inner-to-outer rotors)......................	0.23 mm

Torque wrench settings

	Nm	lbf ft
Air conditioning compressor	25	18
Alternator bracket to block:		
M10 bolts..	23	17
M8 bolts...	15	11
Nuts..	15	11
Auxiliary drivebelt idler pulley bolt	48	35
Auxiliary drivebelt tensioner mounting bolts	23	17
Auxiliary shaft oil seal carrier	23	17
Big-end bearing cap bolts:*		
Stage 1	27	20
Stage 2	Angle-tighten a further 60°	
Stage 3	Angle-tighten a further 20°	
Camshaft bearing cap	20	15
Camshaft oil baffle...	20	15
Camshaft sprocket bolt	50	37
Coolant pump pulley bolts....................................	23	17
Crankcase ventilation oil separator	25	18
Crankshaft oil seal carrier*	20	15
Crankshaft position sensor bracket	10	7
Crankshaft pulley bolt:*		
Stage 1	100	74
Stage 2	Angle-tighten a further 180°	
Cylinder head bolts:*		
Stage 1	20	15
Stage 2	54	40
Stage 3	Angle-tighten a further 90°	
Stage 4:		
Short bolts	Angle-tighten a further 70°	
Long bolts.............................	Angle-tighten a further 90°	
Cylinder head cover bolts	5	4
Engine mountings:		
Right-hand mounting retaining bolts	90	66
Right-hand mounting bracket-to-engine bolts.........	56	41
Left-hand mounting nuts	48	35
Left-hand mounting bracket to transmission	80	59
Left-hand mounting centre bolt	148	109
Lower-rear torque rod bolts	80	59
Engine oil drain plug..	36	27
Flywheel bolts:*		
Stage 1	35	26
Stage 2	Angle-tighten a further 45°	
Fuel injection pump sprocket:		
Timing belt	42	31
Drive chain	33	24
Lower crankcase to cylinder block............................	11	8
Main bearing cap bolts:		
Stage 1..	45	33
Stage 2	70	52
Stage 2	Angle-tighten a further 60°	
Oil baffle plate nuts	20	15
Oil intake pipe bracket to block	10	7
Oil pressure switch..	20	15
Oil pump bolts/studs:		
Stage 1	10	7
Stage 2	23	17
Roadwheel nuts	130	96
Sump bolts...	11	8
TDC setting plug cover.......................................	24	18
Timing belt inner cover bolts:		
M6...	10	7
M8...	24	18

Torque wrench settings (continued)

	Nm	lbf ft
Timing belt outer covers...	7	5
Timing belt tensioner bolt...	50	37
Timing belt tensioner to cylinder head.............................	50	37
Timing chain guide retaining bolts.................................	23	17
Timing chain housing:		
M6...	10	7
M8...	23	17
Timing chain tensioner...	63	46
Transmission-to-engine bolts.......................................	48	35

* Do not re-use

1 General information

How to use this Chapter

This Part of Chapter 2 is devoted to repair procedures possible while the engine is still installed in the vehicle. Since these procedures are based on the assumption that the engine is installed in the vehicle, if the engine has been removed from the vehicle and mounted on a stand, some of the preliminary dismantling steps outlined will not apply.

Information concerning engine/transmission removal and refitting and engine overhaul, can be found in Part F of this Chapter.

Engine description

The DuraTorq-TDCi engine is a further development of the Endura-Di unit, and both units featured in previous Ford models. The engine is an eight-valve, single overhead camshaft (SOHC), four-cylinder, in-line type, mounted transversely at the front of the vehicle, with the transmission on its left-hand end.

All major engine castings are of cast-iron; the engine has a lower crankcase which is bolted to the underside of the cylinder block/crankcase, with a sump bolted under that. This arrangement offers greater rigidity than the normal sump arrangement, and helps to reduce engine vibration.

The crankshaft runs in five main bearings, the centre main bearing's upper half incorporating thrustwashers to control crankshaft endfloat. The connecting rods rotate on horizontally-split bearing shells at their big-ends. The pistons are attached to the connecting rods by gudgeon pins which are a floating fit in the connecting rod small-end eyes, secured by circlips. The aluminium alloy pistons are fitted with three piston rings: two compression rings and an oil control ring. After manufacture, the cylinder bores and piston skirts are measured and classified into two grades, which must be carefully matched together to ensure the correct piston/cylinder clearance; no oversizes are available to permit reboring.

The intake and exhaust valves are each closed by coil springs; they operate in guides which are shrink-fitted into the cylinder head, as are the valve seat inserts.

These engines are unusual in that the fuel injection pump/high-pressure pump is driven by an offset double-row ('gemini') chain from a sprocket on the crankshaft, with the camshaft being driven from the injection pump sprocket by a conventional toothed timing belt.

The camshaft operates the eight valves via conventional cam followers with shims. The camshaft rotates in five bearings that are line-bored directly in the cylinder head and the (bolted-on) bearing caps; this means that the bearing caps are not available separately from the cylinder head, and must not be interchanged with caps from another engine.

The vacuum pump (used for the brake servo and other vacuum actuators) is driven by a pushrod operated directly by a special lobe on the camshaft.

The coolant pump is bolted to the right-hand end of the cylinder block, and is driven with the steering pump and alternator by a multi-ribbed auxiliary drivebelt from the crankshaft pulley.

When working on this engine, note that Torx-type (both male and female heads) and hexagon socket (Allen head) fasteners are widely used; a good selection of bits, with the necessary adapters, will be required so that these can be unscrewed without damage and, on reassembly, tightened to the torque wrench settings specified.

Lubrication system

Lubrication is by means of a G-rotor pump, which is mounted on the crankshaft right-hand end, and draws oil through a strainer located in the sump. The pump forces oil through an externally-mounted full-flow cartridge-type filter. From the filter, the oil is pumped into a main gallery in the cylinder block/crankcase, from where it is distributed to the crankshaft (main bearings) and cylinder head. An oil cooler is fitted next to the oil filter, at the rear of the block. The cooler is supplied with coolant from the engine cooling system.

While the crankshaft and camshaft bearings receive a pressurised supply, the camshaft lobes and valves are lubricated by splash, as are all other engine components. The undersides of the pistons are cooled by oil, sprayed from nozzles fitted above the upper main bearing shells. The turbocharger receives its own pressurised oil supply.

Operations with engine in car

The following major repair operations can be accomplished without removing the engine from the vehicle. However, owners should note that any operation involving the removal of the sump requires careful forethought, depending on the level of skill and the tools and facilities available; refer to the relevant text for details.

a) Compression pressure – testing.
b) Cylinder head cover – removal and refitting.
c) Timing belt cover – removal and refitting.
d) Timing belt – renewal.
e) Timing belt tensioner and sprockets – removal and refitting.
f) Camshaft oil seals – renewal.
g) Camshaft and cam followers – removal and refitting.
h) Cylinder head – removal, overhaul and refitting.
i) Cylinder head and pistons – decarbonising.
j) Sump – removal and refitting.
k) Crankshaft oil seals – renewal.
l) Oil pump – removal and refitting.
m) Piston/connecting rod assemblies – removal and refitting (but see note below).
n) Flywheel – removal and refitting.
o) Engine/transmission mountings – removal and refitting.

Note: *It is possible to remove the pistons and connecting rods (after removing the cylinder head and sump) without removing the engine, however, this is not recommended. Work of this nature is more easily and thoroughly completed with the engine on the bench, as described in Chapter 2F.*

Clean the engine compartment and the exterior of the engine with some type of degreaser before any work is done (and/or clean the engine using a steam cleaner). It will make the job easier and will help to keep dirt out of the internal areas of the engine.

Depending on the components involved, it may be helpful to remove the bonnet, to improve access to the engine as repairs are performed (refer to Chapter 11 if necessary). Cover the wings to prevent damage to the paint; special covers are available, but an old bedspread or blanket will also work.

2.4 Glow plug relay (arrowed)

2 Compression and leakdown tests – description and interpretation

Compression test

Note: *A compression tester suitable for use with diesel engines will be required for this test.*

1 When engine performance is down, or if misfiring occurs which cannot be attributed to the fuel or emissions systems, a compression test can provide diagnostic clues as to the engine's condition. If the test is performed regularly, it can give warning of trouble before any other symptoms become apparent.

2 The engine must be fully warmed-up to normal operating temperature, the battery must be fully-charged and the glow plugs must be removed. The aid of an assistant will be required.

3 Make sure that the ignition is switched off (take out the key). Remove the plastic cover on the top of the engine, then disconnect the wiring plugs from the injectors.

4 Remove the glow plug relay **(see illustration)** from the central junction box/fusebox under the passenger's side of the facia (see Chapter 12).

5 Remove the glow plugs as described in Chapter 5.

6 Fit a compression tester to the No 1 cylinder glow plug hole. The type of tester which screws into the plug thread is preferred.

7 Crank the engine for several seconds on the starter motor. After one or two revolutions, the compression pressure should build-up to a maximum figure and then stabilise. Record the highest reading obtained.

8 Repeat the test on the remaining cylinders, recording the pressure in each.

9 The cause of poor compression is less easy to establish on a diesel engine than on a petrol engine. The effect of introducing oil into the cylinders (wet testing) is not conclusive, because there is a risk that the oil will sit in the recess on the piston crown, instead of passing to the rings. However, the following can be used as a rough guide to diagnosis.

10 All cylinders should produce very similar pressures. Any great difference indicates the existence of a fault. Note that the compression should build-up quickly in a healthy engine. Low compression on the first stroke, followed by gradually increasing pressure on successive strokes, indicates worn piston rings. A low compression reading on the first stroke, which does not build-up during successive strokes, indicates leaking valves or a blown head gasket (a cracked head could also be the cause).

11 A low reading from two adjacent cylinders is almost certainly due to the head gasket having blown between them and the presence of coolant in the engine oil will confirm this.

12 On completion, remove the compression tester, and refit the glow plugs, with reference to Chapter 5.

13 Take out the ignition key, then reconnect the injection pump wiring connector.

Leakdown test

14 A leakdown test measures the rate at which compressed air fed into the cylinder is lost. It is an alternative to a compression test, and in many ways it is better, since the escaping air provides easy identification of where pressure loss is occurring (piston rings, valves or head gasket).

15 The equipment required for leakdown testing is unlikely to be available to the home mechanic. If poor compression is suspected, have the test performed by a suitably-equipped garage.

3 Setting the engine to Top Dead Centre (TDC) on No 1 cylinder

General information

1 TDC is the highest point in the cylinder that each piston reaches as it travels up and down when the crankshaft turns. Each piston reaches TDC at the end of the compression stroke and again at the end of the exhaust stroke, but TDC generally refers to piston position on the compression stroke. No 1 piston is at the timing belt end of the engine.

2 Positioning No 1 piston at TDC is an essential part of many procedures, such as timing belt removal and camshaft removal.

3 The design of the engines covered in this Chapter is such that piston-to-valve contact may occur if the camshaft or crankshaft is turned with the timing belt removed. For this reason, it is important to ensure that the camshaft and crankshaft do not move in relation to each other once the timing belt has been removed from the engine.

Setting TDC on No 1 cylinder

Note: *Suitable tools will be required to lock the camshaft and the fuel injection pump sprocket in position during this procedure – see text.*

4 Disconnect the battery negative (earth) lead (refer to Chapter 5).

5 Remove the cylinder head cover as described in Section 4.

6 Remove the fuel filter as described in Chapter 1, then undo the bolts and remove the fuel filter mounting bracket **(see illustration)**.

7 Loosen the right-hand front wheel nuts, then firmly apply the handbrake. Jack up the front of the car, and support on axle stands (see *Jacking and vehicle support*). Remove the right-hand front wheel.

8 Undo the fasteners and remove the engine undershield **(see illustration)**.

3.6 Remove the fuel filter bracket (arrowed)

3.8 Undo the fasteners (arrowed) and remove the engine undershield

3.9a Offset slot in the camshaft aligned with the cylinder head

3.9b Flat bar engaged with the slot in the camshaft

3.11a Tool fabricated to locate the crankshaft at TDC . . .

3.11b . . . screw the tool into the cylinder block to locate with the crankshaft

3.13a Unscrew the blanking plug . . .

3.13b . . . and insert the timing pin

9 When No 1 cylinder is set to TDC on compression, an offset slot in the left-hand end of the camshaft (left as seen from the driver's seat) should align with the top surface of the cylinder head, to allow a special tool (Ford No 303-376) to be fitted. This tool can be substituted by a suitable piece of flat bar **(see illustrations)**. There is no need to fit this tool at this stage, but check that the slot comes into the required alignment while setting TDC – if the slot is above the level of the head, No 1 cylinder could be on the exhaust stroke.

10 If required, further confirmation that No 1 cylinder is on the compression stroke can be inferred from the positions of the camshaft lobes for No 1 cylinder. When the cylinder is on compression, the intake and exhaust lobes should be pointing upwards (ie, not depressing the cam followers). The camshaft lobes are only visible once the oil baffle plate is removed, and the securing nuts also retain two of the camshaft bearing caps – for more information, refer to Section 9.

11 A TDC timing hole is provided on the front of the cylinder block, to permit the crankshaft to be located more accurately at TDC. A timing pin (Ford service tool 303-193, obtainable from Ford dealers or a tool supplier) screws into the hole, and the crankshaft is then turned so that it contacts the end of the tool. A tool can be fabricated to set the timing at TDC, using a piece of threaded rod **(see illustrations)**. The fabricated tool has the following dimensions:
Thread diameter = 10 mm.
Length from 1st nut face to the point = 47 mm.
Point ground down to 8 mm.

12 To gain access to the blanking plug fitted

over the timing pin hole, remove the auxiliary drivebelt as described in Chapter 1, then unbolt and remove the alternator coupling, as described in the alternator removal procedure in Chapter 5.

13 Remove the camshaft setting tool from the slot, and turn the engine back slightly from the TDC position. Unscrew the timing pin blanking plug (which is located in a deeply-recessed hole), and screw in the timing pin **(see illustrations)**. Now carefully turn the crankshaft forwards until it contacts the timing pin (it should be possible to feel this point – the crankshaft cannot then be turned any further forward).

14 Once No 1 cylinder has been positioned at TDC on the compression stroke, TDC for any of the other cylinders can then be located by rotating the crankshaft clockwise 180° at a time and following the firing order (see Specifications).

15 Before rotating the crankshaft again,

make sure that the timing pin and camshaft setting bar are removed. When operations are complete, do not forget to refit the timing pin blanking plug.

4 Cylinder head cover –
removal and refitting

Removal

1 Pull the plastic cover on the top of the engine upwards to release the retaining clips **(see illustration)**.

2 Undo the 2 bolts and detach the Manifold Absolute Pressure (MAP) sensor from the cylinder head cover. Move the sensor to one side **(see illustration)**.

3 Noting their positions carefully for refitting, release the hose clips and detach the crankcase ventilation hoses from the cylinder

4.1 Pull the engine cover upwards

4.2 Undo the bolts and move the MAP sensor to one side (arrowed)

4.3a Disconnect the ventilation hoses (1), and the camshaft position sensor (2) . . .

4.3b . . . then disconnect the ventilation hose at the rear (arrowed)

4.5a Unscrew the securing bolts . . .

4.5b . . . and lift away the cylinder head cover

head cover **(see illustrations)**. There are two hoses at the front, and one at the rear. Move the hoses aside as far as possible.

4 Disconnect the camshaft position sensor wiring plug **(see illustration 4.3a)**.

5 Unscrew the three securing bolts, and lift the cylinder head cover off the engine **(see illustrations)**. Discard the gasket – a new one must be fitted.

6 If required, the baffle plate fitted below the cover can be removed by unscrewing the nuts and taking off the spacer plates and sleeves – note, however, that these nuts also secure Nos 2 and 4 camshaft bearing caps. Note the positions of all components carefully for refitting.

Refitting

7 Clean the sealing surfaces of the cover and the head, and check the condition of the rubber seals fitted to the cover bolts.

8 Before refitting the cover, check that the

crankcase ventilation holes are clear. The connection at the rear of the cover leads to the ventilation valve – if this appears to be blocked, use a suitable degreaser to wash out the valve (it is not advisable to use petrol, as this may damage the valve itself).

9 Lightly lubricate the surfaces of the gasket with fresh oil, then fit the gasket to the cover, making sure it is correctly located.

10 Lower the cover into position, ensuring that the gasket is not disturbed, then fit the three bolts and tighten them a little at a time, so that the cover is drawn down evenly to make a good seal.

11 Further refitting is a reversal of removal. Ensure that the pipes are routed as noted on removal, and that the ventilation hoses are correctly and securely reconnected.

12 When the engine has been run for some time, check for signs of oil leakage from the gasket joint.

Checking

1 Remove the cylinder head cover as described in Section 4.

2 Remove the baffle plate fitted below the cover by unscrewing the four nuts and taking off the spacer plates and sleeves. Note, however, that these nuts also secure Nos 2 and 4 camshaft bearing caps – refit the nuts temporarily, once the baffle plate has been removed **(see illustrations)**. Note the positions of all components carefully for refitting.

3 During the following procedure, the crankshaft must be turned in order to position the peaks of the camshaft lobes away from the valves. To do this, either turn the crankshaft on the pulley bolt or alternatively raise the front right-hand corner of the vehicle, engage 5th gear, and turn the front roadwheel. Access to the pulley bolt is gained by jacking up the front of the vehicle and supporting on axle stands, then removing the auxiliary drivebelt lower cover.

4 If desired, to enable the crankshaft to be turned more easily, remove the glow plugs as described in Chapter 5.

5 Draw the valve positions on a piece of paper, numbering them 1 to 8 from the timing belt end of the engine. Identify them as intake or exhaust (ie, 1I, 2E, 3I, 4E, 5I, 6E, 7I, 8E).

6 Turn the crankshaft until the valves of No 4 cylinder (flywheel end) are 'rocking' – the exhaust valve will be closing and the intake valve will be opening. The piston of No 1 cylinder will be at the top of its compression stroke, with both valves fully closed. The clearances for both valves of No 1 cylinder may be checked at the same time.

7 Use feeler blade(s) to measure the exact clearance between the heel of the camshaft lobe and the shim on the cam follower; the feeler blades should be a firm sliding fit **(see illustration)**. Record the measured clearance on the drawing. From this clearance it will be possible to calculate the thickness of the new shim to be fitted, where necessary. Note

5.2a Unscrew the 4 nuts (arrowed) . . .

5.2b . . . and lift off the baffle plate . . .

5.2c . . . then refit the camshaft bearing cap nuts temporarily

that the intake and exhaust valve clearances are different, so it is important that you know which valve clearance you are checking.

8 With No 1 cylinder valve clearances checked, turn the engine through half a turn so that No 2 valves are 'rocking', then measure the valve clearances of No 3 cylinder in the same way. Similarly check the valve clearances of No 4 cylinder with No 1 valves 'rocking' and No 2 cylinder with No 3 valves 'rocking'. Compare the measured clearances with the values give in the Specifications – any which fall within the range do not require adjustment.

Adjustment

9 If adjustment is required, turn the engine in the normal direction of rotation through approximately 90°, to bring the pistons to mid-stroke. If this is not done, the pistons at TDC will prevent the cam followers being depressed, and valve damage may result. Depress the cam followers and then either shim can be withdrawn if the peak of the cam does not prevent access. The Ford tools for this operation are Nos 303-195 and 303-196, but with care and patience a C-spanner or screwdriver can be used to depress the cam follower and the shim can be flicked out with a small screwdriver.

10 If the valve clearance was too small, a thinner shim must be fitted. If the clearance was too large, a thicker shim must be fitted. The thickness of the shim (in mm) is engraved on the side facing away from the camshaft. If the marking is missing or illegible, a micrometer will be needed to establish shim thickness.

11 When the shim thickness and the valve clearance are known, the required thickness of the new shim can be calculated as follows (all measurements in mm):

Sample calculation

Desired clearance (A) = 0.50
Measured clearance (B) = 0.35
Shim thickness found (C) = 3.95
Shim thickness required (D) = C+B-A = 3.80

12 With the correct shim fitted, release the cam follower depressing tool. Turn the engine back so that the cam lobes are again pointing upwards and check that the clearance is now correct.

13 Repeat the process for the remaining valves, turning the engine each time to bring a pair of cam lobes upwards.

14 It will be helpful for future adjustment if a record is kept of the thickness of shim fitted at each position. The shims required can be purchased in advance once the clearances and the existing shim thicknesses are known.

15 It is permissible to interchange shims between cam followers to achieve the correct clearances but it is not advisable to turn the camshaft with any shims removed, since there is a risk that the cam lobe will jam in the empty cam follower.

16 When all the clearances are correct, refit the glow plugs (Chapter 5), then refit the

5.7 Use feeler gauges to measure the exact clearance

oil baffle plate and tighten the nuts to the specified torque. Refit the cylinder head cover as described in Section 4.

---

6 Crankshaft pulley – removal and refitting

Removal

1 Disconnect the battery negative lead as described in Chapter 5.

2 Loosen the right-hand front roadwheel nuts, then raise the front of the vehicle, and support securely on axle stands (see *Jacking and vehicle support*). Remove the roadwheel.

3 Undo the fasteners and withdraw the engine undershield from under the car **(see illustration 3.8)**.

4 Remove the auxiliary drivebelt, as described in Chapter 1.

5 The centre bolt which secures the crankshaft pulley must now be slackened. This bolt is tightened to a very high torque, and it is first of all essential to ensure that the car is adequately supported, as considerable effort will be needed.

6 Ford technicians use a special holding tool (205-072) which locates in the outer holes of the pulley and prevents it from turning **(see illustration)**. If this is not available, select a gear, and have an assistant firmly apply the handbrake and footbrake as the bolt is loosened. If this method is unsuccessful, remove the starter motor as described in Chapter 5, and jam the flywheel ring gear,

6.6 Special tool used to stop the crankshaft from turning

using a suitable tool, to prevent the crankshaft from rotating.

7 Unscrew the bolt securing the pulley to the crankshaft, and remove the pulley. It is essential to obtain a new bolt for reassembly **(see illustration)**.

8 With the pulley removed, it is advisable to check the crankshaft oil seal for signs of oil leakage. If necessary, fit a new seal as described in Section 16.

Refitting

9 Refit the pulley to the crankshaft sprocket, then fit the new pulley securing bolt and tighten it as far as possible before the crankshaft starts to rotate.

10 Holding the pulley against rotation as for removal, first tighten the bolt to the specified Stage 1 torque.

11 Stage 2 involves tightening the bolt though an angle, rather than to a torque. The bolt must be rotated through the specified angle – special angle gauges are available from tool outlets. As a guide, a 180° angle is equivalent to a half-turn, and this is easily judged by assessing the start and end positions of the socket handle or torque wrench.

12 Refit and tension the auxiliary drivebelt as described in Chapter 1.

13 Refit the engine undershield.

14 Refit the roadwheel, lower the vehicle to the ground, and reconnect the battery negative lead as described in Chapter 5. Tighten the wheel nuts to the specified torque.

---

7 Timing belt – removal and refitting

Removal

1 Disconnect the battery negative lead as described in Chapter 5.

2 Remove the cylinder head cover as described in Section 4.

3 Referring to the information in Section 3, set the engine to TDC on No 1 cylinder. The timing pin described must be used, to ensure accuracy.

4 Remove the coolant expansion tank by pulling it up from its mountings, and move it to one side without disconnecting the hoses.

6.7 Renew the crankshaft pulley bolt when reassembling

7.5a Unclip the fuel pipes from the timing belt cover

7.5b Intercooler hose-to-throttle body clamp (arrowed)

7.9 Engine mounting nuts and bolts (arrowed)

5 Unclip the fuel pipes, then undo the nut, slacken the clamps and remove the intercooler outlet pipe from the right-hand end of the engine **(see illustrations)**.

6 Ford recommend that the engine is further prevented from turning by fitting another special tool to lock the flywheel ring gear (this prevents the injection pump sprocket from moving). This tool (Ford No 303-393) is also available from Ford dealers, and is quite simple. With the starter motor removed, as described in Chapter 5, the tool bolts across the starter motor aperture in the bellhousing, and a peg on the back of the tool engages and locks the flywheel ring gear. A substitute for this tool could be made, or the ring gear jammed using another suitable tool.

7 Before unbolting the engine mounting, it is recommended that the right-hand wheel is refitted, and the car lowered to the ground

(assuming the car has been raised as part of setting the engine to TDC).

8 The engine must now be supported before the right-hand mounting is removed. Ford technicians use an engine support bar, which locates in the channels at the top of each inner wing, and a further beam attached to this, which rests on the front crossmember. If such an arrangement is not available, use an engine crane; either way, use a suitable length of chain and hooks to attach the lifting gear to the engine lifting eye. If the engine must be supported from below (and this is not recommended), use a large piece of wood on a trolley jack to spread the load and reduce the chance of damage to the sump.

9 With the weight of the engine supported, unscrew the two nuts and two bolts securing the top half of the engine right-hand mounting, and lift the mounting off the two studs **(see illustration)**.

10 Before the timing belt outer cover can be removed, the stud fitted to the front of the engine mounting must be unscrewed and removed. This can be achieved using a socket on the Torx end fitting provided **(see illustrations)**.

11 Unscrew the three bolts (and one stud/bolt at the top), and remove the timing belt outer cover **(see illustration)**.

12 If the timing belt is not being fitted straight away (or if the belt is being removed as part of another procedure, such as cylinder head removal), temporarily refit the engine right-hand mounting and tighten the bolts securely.

13 Before proceeding further, check once more that the engine is positioned at TDC on No 1 cylinder, as described in Section 3.

14 Slacken the timing belt tensioner bolt, and remove the tensioner completely. Slip the timing belt from the sprockets, and remove it **(see illustrations)**.

15 The camshaft sprocket must be removed – this is necessary as part of setting up the new timing belt, to ensure that the correct valve timing is preserved. Not only will a method for holding the sprocket stationary be required, but the sprocket itself is mounted on a taper, so a puller will be needed to free it from the camshaft. Due to its design, the sprocket cannot readily be removed using an ordinary puller, so either the Ford tool (303-651) must be obtained, or a suitable alternative fabricated.

16 Holding the camshaft sprocket using a suitable tool, loosen the sprocket bolt **(see**

7.10a Using a suitable socket on the Torx end fitting . . .

7.10b . . . unscrew and remove the engine mounting front stud

7.11 Remove the timing belt outer cover

7.14a Slacken the tensioner bolt . . .

7.14b . . . and slip the timing belt from its sprockets

7.16 Using a forked holding tool, unscrew the camshaft sprocket bolt

7.17a Fit Ford tool 303-651 to the camshaft sprocket

7.17b Using the special Ford pulley, free the sprocket from its taper . . .

illustration). Note: *Do not rely on the TDC setting bar engaged in the slot at the opposite end of the camshaft to hold it stationary – not only is this dangerous, it could well result in damage to the camshaft.*

17 Using a suitable puller, release the camshaft sprocket from the taper, and remove it **(see illustrations)**.

18 Do not be tempted to re-use the old timing belt under any circumstances – even if it is known to have covered less mileage than the renewal interval indicated in Chapter 1. Ford state that, once a new timing belt has been run on the engine, it is considered worn, and should be discarded. In any case, given the potential expense involved should the belt fail in service, re-using an old belt would be a false economy.

19 Before disposing of the old belt, however, examine it for evidence of contamination by coolant or lubricant. If there are any signs of contamination, find the source of the contamination before progressing any further. If an oil leak is evident, this will most likely be from the camshaft seal. Cure the problem, then wash down the whole area (including the sprockets) with degreaser and allow to dry before fitting the new belt.

20 Spin the tensioner pulley, and check for signs of sticking or roughness, indicating bearing wear. Many professional mechanics will fit a new tensioner as a matter of course when fitting a new timing belt. This should be considered a good idea, especially if the engine has completed a large mileage.

Refitting

21 Ensure that the crankshaft and camshaft are still set to TDC on No 1 cylinder, as described in Section 3.

22 Refit the camshaft sprocket to the camshaft, tightening the bolt by hand only **(see illustration)**. The sprocket must be able to rotate independently of the camshaft.

23 Fit the timing belt tensioner into position, noting that the adjustment arm must be set pointing to the 9 o'clock position **(see illustration)**. Fit the retaining bolt, tightening it finger-tight only at this stage.

24 Fit the new timing belt over the sprockets and above the tensioner pulley, ensuring that the injection pump sprocket does not move

7.17c . . . then remove the sprocket bolt and washer . . .

(the camshaft sprocket must be free to turn – remember that the camshaft itself is locked by the tool fitted to its slotted end). Where applicable, ensure the arrow on the back of the belt points in the direction of engine rotation.

25 Using an Allen key in the adjuster arm,

7.22 Refit the camshaft sprocket bolt, hand-tight at first

7.25a Rotate the tensioner arm anti-clockwise . . .

7.17d . . . and finally remove the camshaft sprocket

maintain the tensioner's position whilst the retaining bolt is slackened, then rotate the adjuster arm anti-clockwise until the pointer is positioned between the sides of the adjustment 'window' **(see illustrations)**. Fully tighten the tensioner retaining bolt.

7.23 Note that the adjustment arm (arrowed) must be approximately pointing to the 9 o'clock position

7.25b . . . until the pointer is between the sides of the 'window' (arrowed)

26 Hold the camshaft sprocket against rotation, and tighten the sprocket retaining bolt.

27 Remove the locking tools from the engine so that it can be turned; these may include the timing pin, the plate fitted into the camshaft slot, and the tool used to lock the flywheel.

28 Mark the TDC position of the crankshaft pulley, using paint or typist's correction fluid, to give a rough indication of TDC, and so that the number of turns can be counted.

29 Using a spanner or socket on the crankshaft pulley centre bolt, turn the engine forwards (clockwise, viewed from the timing belt end) through six full turns, bringing the engine almost up to the TDC position on completion.

30 Using the information in Section 3, set the engine to TDC on No 1 cylinder. Make sure that the timing pin and camshaft locking tools are refitted – also lock the flywheel against rotation, using the same method used previously (see paragraph 6). If the special tools cannot be refitted, go back to paragraph 21 and repeat the setting procedure.

31 Check the position of the timing belt automatic tensioner pointer. If the pointer is still within the two sides of the 'window', proceed to next paragraph. If the pointer is outside the 'window', repeat the tensioning procedure.

32 Remove the locking tools from the engine; these may include the timing pin, the plate fitted into the camshaft slot, and the tool used to lock the flywheel.

33 If the engine right-hand mounting had been temporarily refitted as described in paragraph 12, support the engine once more, and remove the mounting.

34 Refit the timing belt outer cover, and tighten the retaining bolts securely.

35 Refit the front stud to the engine mounting, and tighten it securely, using a similar method to that used for the stud's removal.

36 Refit the top half of the engine right-hand mounting, and tighten the nuts and bolts to the specified torque's.

37 With the engine securely supported by its mounting once more, the engine supporting tools can be carefully removed.

38 Refit the cylinder head cover as described in Section 4.

9.6 Remove the camshaft bearing shells

39 Refit the coolant expansion tank to the inner wing.

40 Refit the intercooler outlet pipe and reclip the fuel pipes.

41 Reconnect the battery negative lead as described in Chapter 5.

8 Timing belt tensioner and sprockets – removal, inspection and refitting

Timing belt tensioner

1 The timing belt tensioner is removed as part of the timing belt renewal procedure, in Section 7.

Camshaft sprocket

2 The camshaft sprocket is removed as part of the timing belt renewal procedure, in Section 7.

Fuel injection pump sprocket

3 Removal of the injection pump sprocket is described as part of the injection pump removal procedure, in Chapter 4. Note that the sprocket is sealed to the pump using two types of sealant/locking compound.

9 Camshaft and cam followers – removal, inspection and refitting

Note: *A new camshaft oil seal will be required on refitting.*

Removal

1 Remove the timing belt and camshaft sprocket as described in Section 7.

2 Remove the camshaft oil seal. The seal is quite deeply recessed – Ford dealers have a special seal extractor for this (tool No 303-293). In the absence of this tool, do not use any removal method which might damage the sealing surfaces, or a leak will result when the new seal is fitted.

 HAYNES HiNT *One of the best ways to remove an oil seal is to carefully drill or punch two holes through the seal, opposite each other (taking care not to damage the surface behind the seal as this is done). Two self-tapping screws are then screwed into the holes; by pulling on the screw heads alternately with a pair of pliers, the seal can be extracted.*

3 Unscrew and remove the nuts securing the oil baffle plate to the top of the engine, noting that these nuts also secure Nos 2 and 4 camshaft bearing caps. Lift off the baffle plate, and recover the bearing caps – if no identification numbers are evident on the caps, mark them for position, as they must be refitted to the correct locations.

4 Progressively unscrew (by half a turn at a time) the nuts securing the remaining bearing caps (Nos 1, 3 and 5) until the camshaft is free.

5 Lift off each bearing cap and bearing shell in turn, and mark it for position if necessary – all the caps must be refitted in their original positions.

6 Carefully lift out the camshaft, and place it somewhere safe – the lobes must not be scratched. Remove the lower part of the bearing shells in turn, and mark them for position **(see illustration)**.

7 Before lifting out the cam followers and shims, give some thought to how they will be stored while they are removed. Unless new components are being fitted, the cam followers and shims must be identified for position. The best way to do this is to take a box, and divide it into eight compartments, each with a clearly-marked number; taking No 1 cam follower and shim as being that nearest the timing belt end of the engine, lift out each cam follower and shim, and place it in the box. Alternatively, keep the cam follower/shim assemblies in line, in fitted order, as they are removed – mark No 1 to avoid confusion.

Inspection

8 With the camshaft removed, examine the bearing caps and the bearing locations in the cylinder head for signs of obvious wear or pitting. If evident, a new cylinder head will probably be required. Also check that the oil supply holes in the cylinder head are free from obstructions. (New bearing shells should be used on reassembly.)

9 Visually inspect the camshaft for evidence of wear on the surfaces of the lobes and journals. Normally their surfaces should be smooth and have a dull shine; look for scoring, erosion or pitting and areas that appear highly polished, indicating excessive wear. Accelerated wear will occur once the hardened exterior of the camshaft has been damaged, so always renew worn items. **Note:** *If these symptoms are visible on the tips of the camshaft lobes, check the corresponding cam follower/shim, as it will probably be worn as well.*

10 If suitable precision measuring equipment (such as a micrometer) is available, the camshaft bearing journals can be checked for wear, by comparing the values measured with those specified.

11 If the machined surfaces of the camshaft appear discoloured or blued, it is likely that it has been overheated at some point, probably due to inadequate lubrication. This may have distorted the shaft, in which case the runout should be checked; Ford do not quote a runout tolerance, so if this kind of damage is suspected, an engine reconditioning specialist should be consulted. In the case of inadequate lubrication, distortion is unlikely to be the only damage which has occurred, and a new camshaft will probably be needed.

12 To measure the camshaft endfloat, temporarily refit the camshaft to the cylinder head, then fit Nos 1 and 5 bearing caps and tighten the retaining nuts to the specified torque setting. Anchor a DTI gauge to the timing belt end of the cylinder head. Push the camshaft to one end of the cylinder head as far as it will travel, then rest the DTI gauge probe on the end face of the camshaft, and zero the gauge. Push the camshaft as far as it will go to the other end of the cylinder head, and record the gauge reading. Verify the reading by pushing the camshaft back to its original position and checking that the gauge indicates zero again. **Note:** *The cam followers must **not** be fitted whilst this measurement is being taken.*

13 Check that the camshaft endfloat measurement is within the limit listed in the Specifications. If the measurement is outside the specified limit, wear is unlikely to be confined to any one component, so renewal of the camshaft, cylinder head and bearing caps must be considered.

14 Inspect the cam followers and shims for obvious signs of wear or damage, and renew if necessary.

Refitting

15 Make sure that the top surfaces of the cylinder head, and in particular the camshaft bearings and the mating surfaces for the camshaft bearing caps, are completely clean.

16 Smear some clean engine oil onto the sides of the cam followers, and offer each one into position in their original bores in the cylinder head, together with its respective shim **(see illustration)**. Push them down until they contact the valves, then lubricate the top surface of each shim.

17 Lubricate the camshaft and cylinder head bearing journals with clean engine oil. If the pushrod which operates the brake vacuum pump has been removed from the cylinder head **(see illustration)**, refit it now – once the camshaft is in position, the pushrod cannot be refitted.

18 Carefully lower the camshaft into position in the cylinder head, making sure that the cam lobes for No 1 cylinder are pointing upwards. Also use the position of the locking tool slot at the end of the camshaft as a guide to correct alignment when refitting – the slot should be flush to the top surface of the cylinder head (the larger 'semi-circle' created by the offset slot should be uppermost).

19 Prior to refitting the No 1 camshaft bearing cap, the front halves of the flat sealing surface must be coated with a smear of suitable sealant, as shown **(see illustration)**.

20 Lubricate Nos 1, 3 and 5 bearing caps and shells with clean oil (taking care not to get any on the sealant-coated surfaces of No 1 cap), then place them into their correct positions. Refit the bearing cap nuts, and tighten them progressively to the specified torque wrench setting.

21 The outer edges of No 1 bearing cap must now be sealed to the cylinder head surface with a thin bead of suitable sealant.

22 Clean out the oil seal housing and the sealing surface of the camshaft by wiping it with a lint-free cloth. Remove any swarf or burrs that may cause the seal to leak.

9.16 Lubricate the cam followers before refitting

23 Apply a little oil to the new camshaft oil seal, and fit it over the end of the camshaft, lips facing inwards. To avoid damaging the seal lips, wrap a little tape over the end of the camshaft. Ford dealers have a special tool (No 303-199) for fitting the seal, but if this is not available, a deep socket of suitable size can be used. It is important that the seal is fitted square to the shaft, and is fully-seated.

24 Refit the camshaft sprocket and timing belt as described in Section 7.

25 Check the valve clearances as described in Section 5.

26 Oil the bearing surfaces of Nos 2 and 4 bearing caps, then refit them and the oil baffle

9.17 Refit the brake vacuum pump pushrod before refitting the camshaft

plate to the engine. Tighten the bearing cap nuts to the specified torque.

27 Refit the cylinder head cover as described in Section 4.

28 Further refitting is a reversal of removal.

10 Camshaft oil seal – renewal

1 Remove the timing belt and camshaft sprocket as described in Section 7. Access to the seal is hampered by the presence of the timing belt backplate, but this can only be removed after taking off the injection pump

H45136

9.19 Camshaft refitting details

1 *Bearing caps (1 to 5)*	3 *Cylinder head*	A *Sealant application areas*
2 *Camshaft*	4 *Camshaft oil seal*	*on No 1 bearing cap*
	5 *Bearing shells*	

10.4a Lubricate the oil seal before fitting over the camshaft . . .

10.4b . . . and use a suitable socket to tap the seal in squarely

sprocket; it should not prove necessary to remove the backplate in practice.

2 Remove the camshaft oil seal. The seal is quite deeply recessed – Ford dealers have a special seal extractor for this (tool No 303-293). In the absence of this tool, do not use any removal method which might damage the sealing surfaces, or a leak will result when the new seal is fitted **(see Haynes Hint)**.

 HAYNES HINT *One of the best ways to remove an oil seal is to carefully drill or punch two holes through the seal, opposite each other (taking care not to damage the surface behind the seal as this is done). Two self-tapping screws are then screwed into the holes; by pulling on the screw heads alternately with a pair of pliers, the seal can be extracted.*

3 Clean out the seal housing and the sealing surface of the camshaft by wiping it with a lint-free cloth. Remove any swarf or burrs that may cause the seal to leak.

4 Apply a little oil to the new camshaft oil seal, and fit it over the end of the camshaft, lips facing inwards. To avoid damaging the seal lips, wrap a little tape over the end of the camshaft. Ford dealers have a special tool (No 303-199) for fitting the seal, but if this is not available, a deep socket of suitable size can be used. **Note:** *Select a socket that bears only on the hard outer surface of the seal, not the inner lip which can easily be damaged.* It is important that the seal is fitted square to the shaft, and is fully-seated **(see illustrations)**.

5 Refit the camshaft sprocket and timing belt as described in Section 7.

11.9a Remove the timing belt backplate bolt from the cylinder head . . .

11.9b . . . and the 7 nuts around the injection pump sprocket

11.10 Unscrew the nut securing the glow plug supply lead

11.11a Disconnect the breather hoses . . .

11 Cylinder head – removal, inspection and refitting

Note: *Ford technicians remove the cylinder head complete with the intake and exhaust manifolds. Whilst this may reduce the overall time spent, it makes the cylinder head assembly incredibly heavy and awkward to lift clear (the head is of cast iron, and is quite heavy enough on its own). We felt that, for the DIY mechanic at least, removing the manifolds would be the more sensible option.*

Removal

1 Remove the battery as described in Chapter 5, then unscrew the three bolts securing the battery tray, and remove the tray from the engine compartment.

2 Remove the air cleaner housing, as described in Chapter 4.

3 Remove the cylinder head cover as described in Section 4.

4 Using the information in Section 3, bring the engine round to just before the TDC position on No 1 cylinder. Do not insert any of the locking tools at this stage.

5 Apply the handbrake, then jack up the front of the car and support it on axle stands (see *Jacking and vehicle support*).

6 Drain the cooling system as described in Chapter 1.

7 Remove the turbocharger/exhaust manifold and the intake manifold as described in Chapter 4.

8 Remove the timing belt as described in Section 7.

9 Remove the bolt securing the timing belt backplate to the cylinder head, and the seven nuts around the injection pump sprocket **(see illustrations)**. While this does not allow the backplate to be removed, it makes it possible to bend the plate enough for the camshaft's tapered end to pass as the head is lifted. If the backplate is to be removed completely, this requires that the injection pump sprocket and its oil seal housing are also removed, as described in Chapter 4.

10 Disconnect the glow plug supply lead in front of the dipstick tube, and move the wiring harness to one side **(see illustration)**.

11 Release the clips from the crankcase ventilation hoses as necessary, and disconnect the wiring plug from the oil pressure switch, then unbolt and remove the oil separator from the left-hand end of the cylinder head **(see illustrations)**.

12 Unclip and disconnect the wiring plug for the cylinder head temperature sensor, next to the brake vacuum pump **(see illustration)**.

13 Disconnect the vacuum hose and the oil return pipe from the vacuum pump at the left-hand end of the cylinder head (left as seen from the driver's seat). Unscrew the top mounting bolt, and loosen the lower bolt – the lower mounting is slotted, to make removal easier – and lift off the pump. Recover the

11.11b . . . unscrew the mounting bolt . . .

11.11c . . . disconnect the oil pressure warning light switch . . .

11.11d . . . and remove the oil separator from the end of the cylinder head

large O-ring seal – a new one must be used on reassembly **(see illustrations)**.

14 Remove the screw securing the glow plug supply lead to the thermostat housing. Remove the two bolts securing the thermostat housing to the front of the head, then pull the housing forwards and rest it clear of the head without disconnecting any further pipework **(see illustrations)**. Note that a new thermostat housing gasket will be needed for reassembly.

15 Clean the area around the high-pressure fuel injection pipes from the pump to the supply manifold (common rail), and the from injectors to the supply manifold.

16 Disconnect the fuel return pipes from the injectors (see Chapter 4). Cover or plug the openings to prevent dirt ingress.

17 Disconnect the wiring plugs from each injector.

18 Make a note of their exact fitted positions,

11.12 Disconnect the cylinder head temperature sensor wiring plug

then remove the high-pressure pipe clamps **(see illustration)**.

19 Disconnect the wiring plug from the pressure sensor on the fuel supply manifold **(see illustration)**.

11.13a Unscrew the vacuum hose union . . .

20 Unscrew the union nuts and remove the high-pressure fuel injection pipes from the fuel supply manifold to the injectors. When unscrewing the unions, counterhold the adapters with one spanner, and loosen the

11.13b . . . release the hose clip and disconnect the oil return pipe . . .

11.13c . . . then unbolt . . .

11.13d . . . and remove the vacuum pump – recover the O-ring

11.14a Remove the glow plug supply lead securing bolt

11.14b Unscrew the thermostat housing bolts

11.18 Note their positions, then remove the pipe clamps

11.19 Disconnect the pressure sensor wiring plug

11.20a Use a second spanner to counterhold the adapters whilst undoing the union nuts at the injectors . . .

11.20b . . . and at the fuel supply manifold (common rail)

unions with another. Cover over the end fittings on the supply manifold and on the injectors, to keep the dirt out **(see illustrations)**. Ford insist that the fuel injection delivery pipes are not re-used – discard the pipes.

21 Undo the bolt/nut and remove the bracket supporting the high-pressure fuel pipe from the pump to the supply manifold **(see illustration)**.

22 Unscrew the union nuts and remove the high-pressure fuel pipe from the pump to the supply manifold – again, counterhold the adapters with a second spanner. Note its fitted position, then remove the clamp from the pipe, Cover or plug the openings to prevent dirt ingress. Ford insist that the pipe is not re-used – discard it.

23 Remove the three bolts securing the fuel supply manifold bracket to the engine, and withdraw the supply manifold complete with the bracket.

24 If not already done, it is recommended before removing the cylinder head that the engine right-hand mounting is refitted, and the engine supporting tools removed. This will improve working room if a hoist or engine support bar was used, and avoids the risk of the engine slipping if it was supported from below.

25 Remove the four nuts securing the oil baffle plate, and carefully lift the plate off the engine. Note that these nuts are also used to secure Nos 2 and 4 camshaft bearing caps, which will then be loose. Once the plate is removed, refit the nuts by hand, to keep the caps in place.

26 Check around the head and the engine bay that there is nothing still attached to the cylinder head, nor anything which would prevent it from being lifted away.

27 Working in the **reverse** order of the tightening sequence **(see illustration 11.53)**,

loosen the cylinder head bolts by half a turn at a time, until they are all loose. Remove the head bolts, and discard them – Ford state that they must not be re-used, even if they appear to be serviceable **(see illustrations)**. Note the fitted positions of the two shorter bolts, which should be the two nearest the timing belt end of the engine.

28 Bend the timing belt backplate gently away from the head sufficiently for the camshaft stub to clear it. Lift the cylinder head away; use assistance if possible, as it is a very heavy assembly.

29 If the head is stuck (as is possible), be careful how you choose to free it. Striking the head with tools carries the risk of damage, and the head is located on two dowels, so its movement will be limited. Do not, under any circumstances, lever the head between the mating surfaces, as this will certainly damage the sealing surfaces for the gasket, leading to leaks.

30 Once the head has been removed, recover the gasket from the two dowels. The gasket is manufactured from laminated steel, and cannot be re-used, but see paragraph 32.

Inspection

31 If required, dismantling and inspection of the cylinder head is covered in Part F of this Chapter.

Cylinder head gasket selection

32 Examine the old cylinder head gasket for manufacturer's identification markings. These will be in the form of notches (two to seven) on the front edge of the gasket, which indicate the gasket's thickness **(see illustration 11.49)**.

33 Unless new components have been fitted, or the cylinder head has been machined (skimmed), the new cylinder head gasket must be of the same type as the old one. Purchase the required gasket, and proceed to paragraph 40.

34 If the head has been machined, or if new pistons have been fitted, it is likely that a head gasket of different thickness to the original will be needed. Gasket selection is made on the basis of the measured piston protrusion above the cylinder head gasket surface. If the head has not been machined, and the pistons,

11.21 Remove the pipe support bracket (arrowed)

11.27a Working in the reverse of the tightening sequence, unscrew . . .

11.27b . . . and remove the cylinder head bolts

11.35 Measure piston projection with a dial test indicator (DTI)

connecting rods, and crankshaft have not been disturbed, use a new head gasket with the same number of notches as the old one.

35 To measure the piston protrusion, anchor a dial test indicator (DTI) to the top face (cylinder head gasket mating face) of the cylinder block, and zero the gauge on the gasket mating face **(see illustration)**.

36 Rest the gauge probe above No 1 piston crown, and turn the crankshaft slowly by hand until the piston reaches TDC (its maximum height). Measure and record the maximum piston projection at TDC.

37 Repeat the measurement for the remaining pistons, and record the results.

38 If the measurements differ from piston to piston, take the highest figure, and use this to determine the thickness of the head gasket required.

39 Note the greatest piston protrusion measurement, and use this to determine the correct cylinder head gasket from the table. The series of notches/holes on the side of the gasket are used for thickness identification **(see illustration 11.49)**.

Preparation for refitting

40 The mating faces of the cylinder head and cylinder block must be perfectly clean before refitting the head. Use a hard plastic or wooden scraper to remove all traces of gasket and carbon; also clean the piston crowns. **Note:** *The new head gasket has rubber-coated surfaces, which could be damaged from sharp edges or debris left by a metal scraper.*

41 Take particular care when cleaning the piston crowns, as the soft aluminium alloy is easily damaged.

42 Make sure that the carbon is not allowed to enter the oil and water passages – this is particularly important for the lubrication system, as carbon could block the oil supply to the engine's components. Using adhesive tape and paper, seal the water, oil and bolt holes in the cylinder block.

43 To prevent carbon entering the gap between the pistons and bores, smear a little grease in the gap. After cleaning each piston, use a small brush to remove all traces of grease and carbon from the gap, then wipe away the remainder with a clean rag. Clean all the pistons in the same way.

44 Check the mating surfaces of the cylinder block and the cylinder head for nicks, deep scratches and other damage (refer to the Note in paragraph 40). If slight, they may be removed carefully with a file, but if excessive, machining may be the only alternative to renewal.

45 If warpage of the cylinder head gasket surface is suspected, use a straight-edge to check it for distortion. Refer to Part F of this Chapter if necessary.

46 Ensure that the cylinder head bolt holes in the crankcase are clean and free of oil. Syringe or soak up any oil left in the bolt holes. This is most important in order that the correct

Gasket selection table		
Piston protrusion	**Gasket identification**	**Gasket thickness**
0.550 to 0.600 mm	*2 notches*	*1.27 mm*
0.601 to 0.650 mm	*3 notches*	*1.32 mm*
0.651 to 0.700 mm	*4 notches*	*1.37 mm*
0.701 to 0.750 mm	*5 notches*	*1.42 mm*
0.751 to 0.800 mm	*6 notches*	*1.47 mm*
0.801 to 0.850 mm	*7 notches*	*1.52 mm*

bolt tightening torque can be applied, and to prevent the possibility of the block being cracked by hydraulic pressure when the bolts are tightened.

Refitting

47 Turn the crankshaft anti-clockwise all the pistons at an equal height, approximately halfway down their bores from the TDC position (see Section 3). This will eliminate any risk of piston-to-valve contact as the cylinder head is refitted.

48 To guide the cylinder head into position, screw two long studs (or old cylinder head bolts with the heads cut off, and slots cut in the ends to enable the bolts to be unscrewed) into the end cylinder head bolt locations on the manifold side of the cylinder block.

49 Ensure that the cylinder head locating dowels are in place at the front corners of

the cylinder block, then fit the new cylinder head gasket over the dowels, ensuring that the OBEN/TOP marking is uppermost, and the notches are at the front (there is a further cut-out at the timing belt end of the gasket) **(see illustration)**. Take care to avoid damaging the gasket's rubber coating.

50 Lower the cylinder head into position on the gasket, ensuring that it engages correctly over the guide studs and dowels.

51 Fit the new cylinder head bolts to the eight remaining bolt locations (remember that the two shorter bolts are fitted at the timing belt end of the engine) and screw them in as far as possible by hand. Do not apply oil to the bolts.

52 Unscrew the two guide studs from the exhaust side of the cylinder block, then screw in the two remaining new cylinder head bolts as far as possible by hand.

H45137

11.49 Cylinder head bolt positions and gasket details

1 Cylinder head	4 Thickness markings (notches)
2 Longer bolts (eight, 177 mm long)	5 Position marking (cut-out)
3 Cylinder head gasket	6 Shorter bolts (two, 137 mm long)

11.53 Cylinder head bolt tightening sequence

11.55 The 2 shorter bolts are tightened through less of an angle than the longer bolts

53 Working in sequence **(see illustration)**, tighten all the cylinder head bolts to the specified Stage 1 torque.

54 Again working in sequence, tighten all the cylinder head bolts to the specified Stage 2 torque.

55 Stages 3 and 4 involve tightening the bolts though an angle, rather than to a torque **(see illustration)**. Each bolt in sequence must be rotated through the specified angle – special angle gauges are available from tool outlets. As a guide, a 90° angle is equivalent to a quarter-turn, and this is easily judged by assessing the start and end positions of the socket handle or torque wrench. **Note:** *The*

two shorter bolts at the timing belt end of the engine are tightened through a smaller angle than the remaining eight bolts – do not get confused when following the tightening sequence.

56 After finally tightening the cylinder head bolts, turn the crankshaft forwards to bring No 1 piston up to TDC, so that the crankshaft contacts the timing pin (see Section 3).

57 The remainder of the refitting procedure is a reversal of the removal procedure, bearing in mind the following points:

a) *Refit the timing belt with reference to Section 7.*

b) *Reconnect the exhaust front section to the exhaust manifold with reference to Chapter 4.*

c) *Refit the fuel supply manifold and new high-pressure fuel delivery pipes as described in Chapter 4.*

d) *Refit the cylinder head cover with reference to Section 4.*

e) *Refit the air cleaner and intercooler as described in Chapter 4.*

f) *Refill the cooling system as described in Chapter 1.*

g) *Check and if necessary top up the engine oil level and power steering fluid level as described in Weekly checks.*

h) *Before starting the engine, read through the section on engine restarting after overhaul, at the end of Chapter 2F.*

12 Sump – removal and refitting

Note: *The full procedure outlined below must be followed so that the mating surfaces can be cleaned and prepared to achieve an oil-tight joint on reassembly.*

Removal

1 Apply the handbrake, then jack up the front of the vehicle and support it on axle stands (see *Jacking and vehicle support*).

2 Referring to Chapter 1 if necessary, drain the engine oil, then clean and refit the engine oil drain plug, tightening it to the specified torque wrench setting. Although not strictly necessary as part of the dismantling procedure, owners are advised to remove and discard the oil filter, so that it can be renewed with the oil.

3 A conventional sump gasket is not used, and sealant is used instead.

4 Progressively unscrew the sump retaining bolts, and the two retaining nuts (the bolts are of different lengths, but it will be obvious where they fit on reassembly). Break the joint by striking the sump with the palm of the hand, then lower the sump away, turning it as necessary.

5 Unfortunately, the use of sealant can make removal of the sump more difficult. If care is taken not to damage the surfaces, the sealant can be cut around using a sharp knife. On no account lever between the mating faces, as this will almost certainly damage them, resulting in leaks when finished. Ford technicians have a tool comprising a metal rod which is inserted through the sump drain hole, and a handle to pull the sump downwards.

> **HAYNES HINT** *If the sump is particularly difficult to remove, extracting the two studs may prove useful – thread two nuts onto the stud, tightening them against each other, then use a spanner on the inner nut to unscrew the stud. Note the locations of the studs for refitting.*

Refitting

6 On reassembly, thoroughly clean and degrease the mating surfaces of the cylinder block/crankcase and sump, removing all traces of sealant, then use a clean rag to wipe out the sump and the engine's interior.

7 If the two studs have been removed, they must be refitted before the sump is offered up, to ensure that it is aligned correctly. If this is not done, some of the sealant may enter the

12.8 Sump bolt tightening sequence and sealant application details

Dotted line indicates 2.5 mm diameter bead of sealant

H45202

13.8 Undo the retaining bolts and remove the rotor cover

13.9 Check the condition of the pressure relief valve and clean out the oilways

13.10 Check the clearance between the inner and outer rotor

blind holes for the sump bolts, preventing the bolts from being fully fitted.

8 Referring to the accompanying illustration, apply silicone sealant (Ford part No WSE-M4G323-A4) to the sump flange. Do not allow sealant to enter the bolts holes. Ford specify that the sealant must be applied in a bead of 2.5 mm diameter **(see illustration)**. **Note:** *The sump must be refitted within 10 minutes of applying the sealant.*

9 Fit the sump over the studs, and insert the sump bolts and two nuts, tightening them by hand only at this stage.

10 Tighten all the bolts and nuts in the sequence shown **(see illustration 12.8)**.

11 Lower the car to the ground. Wait at least 1 hour for the sealant to cure (or whatever time is indicated by the sealant manufacturer) before refilling the engine with oil. If removed, fit a new oil filter with reference to Chapter 1.

13 Oil pump –
removal, inspection and refitting

Removal

1 Remove the crankshaft pulley as described in Section 6.

2 Unbolt the auxiliary drivebelt idler pulley in front of the crank pulley location.

3 Remove the timing belt and camshaft sprocket as described in Section 7.

4 Remove the injection pump sprocket and oil seal housing as described in Chapter 4.

5 Unbolt and remove the timing belt backplate from the engine.

6 The oil pump is secured by 7 studs and 12 bolts – note their positions carefully for refitting. The studs can be unscrewed using a spanner on the hex provided.

7 Once all the fasteners have been removed, carefully lift the pump from its location. Recover the main gasket, and the smaller spacer ring from below the injection pump. Neither gasket may be re-used – obtain new ones for reassembly.

Inspection

8 Undo the retaining screws and remove the cover from the oil pump **(see illustration)**. Note the location of the identification marks on the inner and outer rotors for refitting.

9 Unscrew the plug and remove the pressure relief valve, spring and plunger, clean out and check condition of components **(see illustration)**.

10 The clearance between the inner and outer rotors can be checked using feeler blades, and compared with the value given in the Specifications **(see illustration)**.

11 Check the general condition of the oil pump, and in particular, its mating face to the cylinder block. If the mating face is damaged significantly, this may lead to oil loss (and a resulting drop in oil pressure).

12 Inspect the rotors for obvious signs of wear or damage; it is not clear at the time of writing whether individual components are available separately. Lubricate the rotors with fresh engine oil and refit them into the body, making sure that the identification marks are positioned as noted on removal **(see illustration)**.

13 If the oil pump has been removed as part of a major engine overhaul, it is assumed that the engine will have completed a substantial mileage. In this case, it is often considered good practice to fit a new (or reconditioned) pump as a matter of course. In other words, if the rest of the engine is being rebuilt, the engine has completed a large mileage, or there is any question as to the old pump's condition, it is preferable to fit a new oil pump.

Refitting

14 Before fitting the oil pump, ensure that the mating faces on the pump and the engine block are completely clean.

15 Lay the main metal gasket and a new spacer ring in position on the engine – in the case of the spacer ring, 'stick' it in position with a little oil or grease if required **(see illustration)**.

13.12 Align the dots on the 2 rotors (arrowed)

13.15 Fit a new metal gasket and spacer ring (arrowed) in position

13.16 Oil pump nut/bolt tightening sequence – note special tool 303-652 used to align the pump

16 Offer the pump into position, and secure it with the studs and bolts, tightened only loosely at this stage **(see illustration)**.

17 Ford technicians use a special tool (303-652) to align the oil pump as it is being fitted and tightened **(see illustration)**. The tool is basically a circular socket, which fits over the end of the crankshaft, and ensures that the corresponding hole in the oil pump is centrally located over the end of the crankshaft. In the absence of the tool, this alignment could be confirmed visually, or a large socket/piece of tubing (perhaps wrapped with tape) could be used instead.

18 Ensuring that the correct alignment of the pump is maintained, tighten the pump securing studs and bolts to the specified Stage 1 torque, in sequence **(see illustration 13.16)**.

19 When all the fasteners have been tightened to the Stage 1 torque, go around again in the sequence, and tighten them all to the specified Stage 2 torque.

20 Refit the timing belt backplate to the engine.

21 Refit the injection pump sprocket and oil seal housing as described in Chapter 4.

22 Refit the timing belt and camshaft sprocket as described in Section 7.

23 Refit the auxiliary drivebelt idler pulley, and tighten the bolt to the specified torque.

24 Refit the crankshaft pulley as described in Section 6.

25 When the engine is next started, check for correct oil pump operation (at least, as indicated by the oil pressure warning light going out).

14 Oil pressure warning light switch – removal and refitting

Removal

1 The switch is screwed into the left-hand (flywheel) end of the cylinder head, behind the vacuum pump.

2 Open the bonnet and disconnect the battery negative (earth) lead as described in Chapter 5.

3 To improve access to the switch, it will be necessary to remove (or partially remove) the air cleaner intake duct and the intercooler right-hand air duct, using the information in Chapter 4. It will also be helpful to release the hoses and remove the crankcase ventilation system oil separator from the left-hand end of the cylinder head.

4 Unplug the wiring from the switch and unscrew it; be prepared for some oil loss **(see illustration)**.

Refitting

5 Refitting is the reverse of the removal procedure; apply a thin smear of suitable sealant to the switch threads, and tighten it to the specified torque wrench setting.

6 Refit all components removed for access to the switch.

7 Check the engine oil level and top-up as necessary (see *Weekly checks*).

8 Check for correct warning light operation, and for signs of oil leaks, once the engine has been restarted and warmed-up to normal operating temperature.

15 Oil cooler – removal and refitting

Note: *New sealing rings will be required on refitting.*

Removal

1 The oil cooler is mounted next to the oil filter on the rear of the cylinder block. Access to the oil cooler is best obtained from below – apply the handbrake, then jack up the front of the car and support it on axle stands. Undo the screws and remove the engine undershield.

2 Position a container beneath the oil filter to

13.17 Tool used to align the oil pump before tightening the bolts fully

14.4 Disconnect the wiring from the oil pressure warning switch

15.4 Disconnect the turbocharger oil supply union bolt (arrowed)

15.6 Renew the oil cooler gasket

catch escaping oil and coolant. To improve access to the coolant hoses, unscrew and remove the oil filter, making sure that the filter sealing ring is removed with the filter cartridge – anticipate a small loss of engine oil as the filter is removed. Provided the filter is not due for renewal, it can be refitted on completion.

3 Clamp the oil cooler coolant hoses to minimise spillage, then remove the clips, and disconnect the hoses from the oil cooler. Be prepared for coolant spillage.

4 Loosen the turbocharger oil supply union bolt at the top of the cooler **(see illustration)**, and separate the pipe (be prepared for oil spillage). Recover the copper washers from the union – new ones must be used on reassembly.

5 Unscrew the four bolts securing the oil cooler, noting their positions, as they are of different lengths. Remove the oil cooler from the engine, and recover the gasket (a new gasket must be used on refitting).

Refitting

6 Refitting is a reversal of removal, bearing in mind the following points:

a) Use a new gasket **(see illustration)**.

b) Fit the oil cooler mounting bolts to the positions noted on removal, and tighten them securely. Refit the oil filter

if removed – apply a little oil to the filter sealing ring, and tighten the filter securely by hand (do not use any tools).

c) Use new copper washers when reconnecting the oil supply union at the top of the cooler, and tighten the union bolt securely.

d) On completion, lower the car to the ground. Check and if necessary top-up the oil and coolant levels, then start the engine and check for signs of oil or coolant leakage.

16 Crankshaft oil seals – renewal

Timing belt end seal

1 Remove the crankshaft pulley (see Section 6).

2 Note the fitted depth of the oil seal as a guide for fitting the new one.

3 Using a screwdriver or similar tool, carefully prise the oil seal from its location. Take care not to damage the oil seal contact surfaces or the oil seal seating. An alternative method of removing the seals is to drill a small hole in the seal (taking care not to drill any deeper than necessary), then insert a self-tapping screw and use pliers to pull out the seal.

4 Wipe clean the oil seal contact surfaces and seating, and clean up any sharp edges or burrs which might damage the new seal as it is fitted, or which might cause the seal to leak once in place.

5 The new oil seal should be supplied fitted with a locating sleeve, which must **not** be removed prior to fitting. No oil should be applied to the oil seal, which is made of PTFE.

6 Ford technicians use a special seal-fitting tool (303-652), but an adequate substitute can be achieved using a large socket or piece of

tubing of sufficient size to bear on the outer edge of the new seal.

7 Locate the new seal (lips facing inwards) over the end of the crankshaft, using the tool **(see illustration)**, socket, or tubing to press the seal squarely and fully into position, to the previously-noted depth. Once the seal is fully fitted, remove the locating sleeve, if necessary.

8 The remainder of reassembly is the reverse of the removal procedure, referring to the relevant text for details where required. Check for signs of oil leakage when the engine is restarted.

Flywheel end seal

9 Remove the transmission as described in Chapter 7, and the clutch assembly as described in Chapter 6.

10 Unbolt the flywheel (see Section 17).

11 Unbolt and remove the oil seal carrier; the seal is renewed complete with the carrier, and is not available separately. A complete set of new carrier retaining bolts should also be obtained for reassembly **(see illustration)**.

12 Clean the end of the crankshaft, polishing off any burrs or raised edges, which may have caused the seal to fail in the first place. Clean also the seal carrier mating face on the engine block, using a suitable solvent for degreasing if necessary.

16.7 Use a locating tool to press the seal in squarely (locating sleeve not required when using this tool)

16.11 The oil seal is renewed complete with the carrier

16.14a Fit the new seal assembly, complete with guide sleeve over the end of the crankshaft . . .

16.14b . . . then remove the guide sleeve

17.12 Align the bolts holes in the crankshaft – they will only line up in one position

17.13 Tool (arrowed) fabricated to lock the flywheel

13 The new oil seal is supplied fitted with a locating sleeve, which must **not** be removed prior to fitting (it will drop out on its own when the carrier is bolted into position). No oil should be applied to the oil seal, which is made of PTFE.

14 Offer up the carrier into position, feeding the locating sleeve over the end of the crankshaft. Insert the new seal carrier retaining bolts, and tighten them all by hand **(see illustrations)**.

15 Ford technicians use a special tool (308-204) to centre the oil seal carrier around the end of the crankshaft. In the absence of the tool, this alignment could be confirmed visually, or a large socket/piece of tubing (perhaps wrapped with tape) could be used instead.

16 Ensuring that the correct alignment of the carrier is maintained, tighten the retaining bolts to the specified torque. If the seal locating sleeve is still in position, remove it now.

17 The remainder of the reassembly procedure is the reverse of dismantling, referring to the relevant text for details where required. Check for signs of oil leakage when the engine is restarted.

17 Flywheel –
removal, inspection and refitting

Removal

1 Remove the transmission as described in Chapter 7. Now is a good time to check components such as oil seals and renew them if necessary.

2 Remove the clutch as described in Chapter 6. Now is a good time to check or renew the clutch components and release bearing.

3 Use a centre-punch or paint to make alignment marks on the flywheel and crankshaft, to ensure correct alignment during refitting.

4 Prevent the flywheel from turning by locking the ring gear teeth, or by bolting a strap between the flywheel and the cylinder block/crankcase. Slacken the bolts evenly until all are free.

5 Remove each bolt in turn and ensure that new ones are obtained for reassembly; these bolts are subjected to severe stresses and so must be renewed, regardless of their apparent condition, whenever they are disturbed.

6 Withdraw the flywheel, remembering that it is very heavy – do not drop it.

Inspection

7 Clean the flywheel to remove grease and oil. Inspect the surface for cracks, rivet grooves, burned areas and score marks. Light scoring can be removed with emery cloth. Check for cracked and broken ring gear teeth. Lay the flywheel on a flat surface and use a straight-edge to check for warpage.

8 Clean and inspect the mating surfaces of the flywheel and the crankshaft. If the crankshaft seal is leaking, renew it (see Section 16) before refitting the flywheel. If the engine has covered a high mileage, it may be worth fitting a new seal as a matter if course, given the amount of work needed to access it.

9 While the flywheel is removed, clean carefully its inboard (right-hand) face, particularly the recesses which serve as the reference points for the crankshaft speed/position sensor. Clean the sensor's tip and check that the sensor is securely fastened.

10 Thoroughly clean the threaded bolt holes in the crankshaft, removing all traces of locking compound.

11 Note that on models fitted with a dual-mass flywheel, the maximum travel of the primary mass in relation to the secondary must not exceed 15 teeth.

Refitting

12 Fit the flywheel to the crankshaft so that all bolt holes align – it will fit only one way – check this using the marks made on removal **(see illustration)**. Apply suitable locking compound to the threads of the new bolts, then insert them.

13 Lock the flywheel by the method used on dismantling **(see illustration)**. Working in a diagonal sequence, tighten the bolts to the specified Stage 1 torque wrench setting.

14 Stage 2 involves tightening the bolts though an angle, rather than to a torque. Each bolt must be rotated through the specified angle – special angle gauges are available from tool outlets.

15 The remainder of reassembly is the reverse of the removal procedure, referring to the relevant text for details where required.

18 Engine/transmission mountings –
inspection and renewal

Refer to Chapter 2C, Section 17, but note the different torque wrench settings given at the beginning of this Chapter.

Chapter 2 Part E:
2.0 litre diesel engine in-car repair procedures

Contents

Section number

Camshaft, rocker arms and hydraulic adjusters – removal, inspection
   and refitting. 7
Camshaft oil seal – renewal 8
Compression and leakdown tests – description and interpretation. . 2
Crankshaft oil seals – renewal 14
Crankshaft pulley – removal and refitting. 4
Cylinder head – removal, inspection and refitting 9
Cylinder head cover – removal and refitting. 3
Engine/transmission mountings – inspection and renewal 16

Section number

Flywheel – removal, inspection and refitting 15
General information 1
Oil cooler – removal and refitting 13
Oil pressure warning light switch – removal and refitting. 12
Oil pump – removal, inspection and refitting 11
Sump – removal and refitting 10
Timing chain and tensioner – removal and refitting 6
Timing belt and tensioner – removal refitting 5

Degrees of difficulty

Easy, suitable for novice with little experience	Fairly easy, suitable for beginner with some experience	Fairly difficult, suitable for competent DIY mechanic	Difficult, suitable for experienced DIY mechanic	Very difficult, suitable for expert DIY or professional

Specifications

General

Engine type.	Four-cylinder, in-line, double overhead camshaft, aluminium cylinder head and cast-iron engine block with turbocharger
Designation	2.0 litre Duratorq-TDCi
Engine code	G6DA and G6DB
Power output	100 kW @ 4000 rpm
Torque output	320 Nm @ 1750 rpm
Capacity.	1998 cc
Bore	85.0 mm
Stroke.	88.0 mm
Compression ratio	18:1
Firing order.	1-3-4-2 (No 1 cylinder at transmission end)
Direction of crankshaft rotation	Clockwise (seen from right-hand side of vehicle)

Valves

Valve clearances.	Hydraulic adjusters – no adjustment necessary

Lubrication

Oil pressure – minimum (engine at operating temperature):

At 2000 rpm	2.0 bar
At 4000 rpm	4.0 bar

Torque wrench settings

	Nm	lbf ft
Air conditioning compressor	28	21
Big-end bearing cap bolts:*		
Stage 1	20	15
Stage 2	Angle-tighten a further 70°	
Camshaft bearing housing:		
Stage 1	5	4
Stage 2	10	7
Camshaft position sensor	10	7
Camshaft sprocket bolt:		
Stage 1	20	15
Stage 2	Angle-tighten a further 60°	
Crankshaft oil seal carrier	14	10
Crankshaft pulley bolt:*		
Stage 1	70	52
Stage 2	Angle-tighten a further 60°	
Cylinder head lower section-to-block bolts:*		
Stage 1	60	44
Stage 2	Angle-tighten a further 220°	
Cylinder head upper section-to-lower section bolts:		
Stage 1	5	4
Stage 2	10	7
Cylinder head cover/intake manifold:		
Stage 1	5	4
Stage 2	10	7
Engine mountings:		
Right-hand mounting retaining bolts	90	66
Right-hand mounting bracket-to-engine bolts	56	41
Left-hand mounting nuts	48	35
Left-hand mounting bracket to transmission	80	59
Left-hand mounting centre bolt	148	109
Lower-rear torque rod bolts	80	59
Engine oil drain plug	34	25
Engine-to-transmission bolts	48	35
Flywheel bolts*	48	35
Fuel high-pressure pump mounting bolts	20	15
Fuel high-pressure pipe unions	30	22
Fuel injector mounting studs	10	7
Main bearing bolts:		
Stage 1	25	18
Stage 2	Angle-tighten a further 60°	
Oil pressure switch	35	26
Oil pump bolts	16	12
Oil pump pick-up tube bolts	12	9
Piston cooling jet	10	7
Roadwheel nuts	130	96
Subframe mounting bolts:*		
Front	120	89
Rear	280	207
Subframe rear mounting brackets to body	25	18
Sump bolts	16	12
Thermostat housing to cylinder head	18	13
Timing belt tensioner	21	15
Timing chain tensioner	6	4

* Do not re-use

---

1 General information

How to use this Chapter

This Part of Chapter 2 is devoted to repair procedures possible while the engine is still installed in the vehicle. Since these procedures are based on the assumption that the engine is installed in the vehicle, if the engine has been removed from the vehicle and mounted on a stand, some of the preliminary dismantling steps outlined will not apply.

Information concerning engine/transmission removal and refitting and engine overhaul, can be found in Part F of this Chapter.

Engine description

The engine is a result of a joint venture between Ford and Peugeot. This DOHC (Double Overhead Camshaft) 16-valve engine features common rail direct injection, and a VNT (Variable Nozzle Turbine) turbocharger.

All major components are made from aluminium, apart from the cast-iron cylinder block – no liners are fitted, the cylinders are bored directly into the block. An aluminium main bearing ladder is fitted. This arrangement offers greater rigidity than the normal sump arrangement, and helps to reduce engine vibration.

The crankshaft runs in five main bearings, thrustwashers are fitting either side of the No 1 cylinder main bearings to control crankshaft endfloat. The connecting rods rotate on horizontally-split bearing shells at their big-ends. The pistons are attached to the connecting rods by gudgeon pins which are a floating fit in the connecting rod small-end eyes, secured by circlips. The aluminium alloy pistons are fitted with three piston rings: two compression rings and an oil control ring. After manufacture, the cylinder bores and piston skirts are measured and classified into four weight grades, which must be carefully matched together to ensure the correct piston/cylinder clearance; no oversizes are available to permit reboring.

The intake and exhaust valves are each closed by coil springs; they operate in guides which are shrink-fitted into the cylinder head, as are the valve seat inserts.

A rubber toothed-belt driven by the crankshaft sprocket rotates the coolant pump and the exhaust camshaft sprocket. The intake camshaft is driven by a short timing chain from the exhaust sprocket.

The camshafts operate the 16 valves via roller-rocker arms with hydraulic clearance adjusters. The camshafts rotate in five bearings that are line-bored directly into the two sections of the cylinder head.

The vacuum pump (used for the brake servo and other vacuum actuators) is driven from the end of the intake camshaft, whilst the fuel pump is driven from the end of the exhaust camshaft.

When working on this engine, note that Torx-type (both male and female heads) and hexagon socket (Allen head) fasteners are widely used; a good selection of bits, with the necessary adapters, will be required so that these can be unscrewed without damage and, on reassembly, tightened to the torque wrench settings specified.

Lubrication system

The oil pump is mounted under the cylinder block, and is chain driven from a crankshaft sprocket. The pump forces oil through an externally-mounted full-flow cartridge-type filter. From the filter, the oil is pumped into a main gallery in the cylinder block/crankcase, from where it is distributed to the crankshaft (main bearings) and cylinder head. An oil cooler is fitted next to the oil filter, at the rear of the block. The cooler is supplied with coolant from the engine cooling system.

While the crankshaft and camshaft bearings receive a pressurised supply, the camshaft lobes and valves are lubricated by splash, as are all other engine components. The undersides of the pistons are cooled by oil, sprayed from nozzles fitted above the upper main bearing shells. The turbocharger receives its own pressurised oil supply.

Operations with engine in car

The following major repair operations can be accomplished without removing the engine from the vehicle. However, owners should note that any operation involving the removal of the sump requires careful forethought, depending on the level of skill and the tools and facilities available; refer to the relevant text for details.

a) *Compression pressure – testing.*
b) *Cylinder head cover – removal and refitting.*
c) *Timing belt cover – removal and refitting.*
d) *Timing belt/chain – renewal.*
e) *Timing belt tensioner and sprockets – removal and refitting.*
f) *Camshaft oil seal – renewal.*
g) *Camshaft and cam followers – removal and refitting.*
h) *Cylinder head – removal, overhaul and refitting.*
i) *Cylinder head and pistons – decarbonising.*
j) *Sump – removal and refitting.*
k) *Crankshaft oil seals – renewal.*
l) *Oil pump – removal and refitting.*
m) *Piston/connecting rod assemblies – removal and refitting (but see note below).*
n) *Flywheel – removal and refitting.*
o) *Engine/transmission mountings – removal and refitting.*

Note: *It is possible to remove the pistons and connecting rods (after removing the cylinder head and sump) without removing the engine, however, this is not recommended. Work of this nature is more easily and thoroughly completed with the engine on the bench, as described in Chapter 2F.*

Clean the engine compartment and the exterior of the engine with some type of degreaser before any work is done (and/or clean the engine using a steam cleaner). It will make the job easier and will help to keep dirt out of the internal areas of the engine.

Depending on the components involved, it may be helpful to remove the bonnet, to improve access to the engine as repairs are performed (refer to Chapter 11 if necessary). Cover the wings to prevent damage to the paint; special covers are available, but an old bedspread or blanket will also work.

2 Compression and leakdown tests – description and interpretation

Compression test

Note: *A compression tester suitable for use with diesel engines will be required for this test.*

1 When engine performance is down, or if misfiring occurs which cannot be attributed to the fuel or emissions systems, a compression test can provide diagnostic clues as to the engine's condition. If the test is performed regularly, it can give warning of trouble before any other symptoms become apparent.

2 The engine must be fully warmed-up to normal operating temperature, the battery must be fully-charged and the glow plugs must be removed. The aid of an assistant will be required.

3 Pull the plastic cover on the top of the engine upwards to release it from its mountings.

4 Disconnect the wiring plugs from the injectors.

5 Remove the glow plugs as described in Chapter 5.

6 Raise the front of the vehicle and support it securely on axle stands (see *Jacking and vehicle support*).

7 Undo the fasteners and remove the engine undershield, then remove the splash shield under the radiator.

8 At the left-hand side of the radiator lower support bracket, unplug the glow plug relay.

9 Fit a compression tester to the No 1 cylinder glow plug hole. The type of tester which screws into the plug thread is preferred.

10 Crank the engine for several seconds on the starter motor. After one or two revolutions, the compression pressure should build-up to a maximum figure and then stabilise. Record the highest reading obtained.

11 Repeat the test on the remaining cylinders, recording the pressure in each.

12 The cause of poor compression is less easy to establish on a diesel engine than on a petrol engine. The effect of introducing oil into the cylinders (wet testing) is not conclusive, because there is a risk that the oil will sit in the recess on the piston crown, instead of passing to the rings. However, the following can be used as a rough guide to diagnosis.

13 All cylinders should produce very similar pressures. Any great difference indicates the existence of a fault. Note that the compression should build-up quickly in a healthy engine. Low compression on the first stroke, followed by gradually increasing pressure on successive strokes, indicates worn piston rings. A low compression reading on the first stroke, which does not build-up during successive strokes, indicates leaking valves or a blown head gasket (a cracked head could also be the cause).

14 A low reading from two adjacent cylinders is almost certainly due to the head gasket having blown between them and the presence of coolant in the engine oil will confirm this.

15 On completion, remove the compression tester, and refit the glow plugs.

16 Reconnect the injector wiring plugs, refit the glow plug relay and the engine/radiator undershields.

Leakdown test

17 A leakdown test measures the rate at which compressed air fed into the cylinder is lost. It is an alternative to a compression test, and in many ways it is better, since the escaping air provides easy identification of where pressure loss is occurring (piston rings, valves or head gasket).

18 The equipment required for leakdown testing is unlikely to be available to the home mechanic. If poor compression is suspected, have the test performed by a suitably-equipped garage.

3.1 Pull up at the front and remove the engine cover

3.4a Prise forwards the clips (arrowed) . . .

3.4b . . . then pull the scuttle cowling panel upwards from the base of the windscreen

3 Cylinder head cover – removal and refitting

Removal

1 The cylinder head cover is integral with the intake manifold. Begin by removing the plastic cover from the top of the engine by pulling it straight up from its mountings at the right-hand rear corner, right-hand front corner and left-hand front corner, then sliding it forwards (see illustration).

2 Undo the 2 bolts securing the brake fluid remote reservoir (where fitted) to the engine compartment bulkhead.

3 Remove the wiper arms as described in Chapter 12.

4 Release the 5 clips and remove the windscreen cowl panel, then undo the 2 bolts and remove the bulkhead extension panel (see illustrations).

5 Disconnect the battery negative lead as described in Chapter 5.

6 Disconnect the crankcase ventilation hoses from the intake manifold/cover, then release the clamp and disconnect the EGR pipe from the intake manifold (see illustrations).

7 Undo the bolts and remove the throttle body/anti-shudder valve and retaining bracket (see illustration).

8 Undo the remaining bolts and remove the EGR pipe.

9 Release the clips and detach the wiring harness and fuel pipes from the timing belt upper cover.

10 Undo the bolt and remove the wiring

bracket from the right-hand rear corner of the cylinder head.

11 Disconnect the wiring plug, undo the retaining bolt and remove the camshaft position sensor (see illustration).

12 Undo the bolts, slacken the nut, then remove the timing belt upper cover.

13 Disconnect the injector wiring plugs, then detach the harness duct from the intake manifold/cover and position it to one side (see illustration).

14 Release the glow plugs wiring harness from the 2 clips on the manifold.

15 Unclip the fuel temperature sensor (located on underside the intake manifold).

16 Undo the manifold/cover retaining bolts in the reverse of the sequence shown (see illustration 3.18). Discard the gaskets, new ones must be fitted.

3.4c Undo the bolt at each end (right-hand one arrowed) and pull the bulkhead extension panel forwards

3.6a Release the clamps and disconnect the breather hose (arrowed) from the cylinder head cover . . .

3.6b . . . the EGR pipe (arrowed) from the intake manifold . . .

3.6c . . . then depress the clip and disconnect the breather hose from the rear of the cylinder head cover

3.7 Anti-shudder valve/throttle body bolts (arrowed)

3.11 Undo the bolt (arrowed) and remove the camshaft position sensor

3.13 Release the clips (arrowed) and detach the injector wiring harness duct

Refitting

17 Clean the sealing surfaces of the manifold/cover and the head.

18 Fit the new seals to the intake manifold/cover, then fit it to the cylinder head. Use a little petroleum jelly on the manifold O-rings to ease assembly. Tighten the bolts to the specified torque in sequence **(see illustration)**.

19 The remainder of refitting is a reversal of removal, noting the following points:

  a) *Tighten all fasteners to their specified torque where given.*

  b) *The camshaft position sensor must be refitted in accordance with the instructions given in Chapter 4, otherwise it will not function correctly.*

4 Crankshaft pulley – removal and refitting

Removal

1 Loosen the right-hand front roadwheel nuts, then raise the front of the vehicle, and support securely on axle stands (see *Jacking and vehicle support*). Remove the roadwheel. Access is greatly improved once the wheel arch liner has been removed.

2 Release the fasteners and withdraw the engine undershield from under the car **(see illustration)**.

3 Remove the auxiliary drivebelt as described in Chapter 1.

4 The centre bolt which secures the crankshaft pulley must now be slackened.

3.18 Intake manifold/cylinder head cover bolt tightening sequence

Note that the 55 mm bolt is fitted to position 14, and 70 mm bolts are fitted to positions 16 and 17

This bolt is tightened to a very high torque, and it is first of all essential to ensure that the car is adequately supported, as considerable effort will be needed.

5 Ford technicians use a special holding tool (303-393/303-393-01) which bolts to the transmission housing and engages with the starter ring gear teeth once the starter motor has been removed. If this is not available, select a gear, and have an assistant firmly apply the handbrake and footbrake as the bolt is loosened.

6 Unscrew the bolt securing the pulley to the crankshaft, and remove the pulley. It is essential to obtain a new bolt for reassembly **(see illustrations)**. If required, remove the sensor ring/spacer. **Note:** *Do not touch the outer sensor ring.*

7 With the pulley removed, it is advisable to check the crankshaft oil seal for signs of oil leakage. If necessary, fit a new seal as described in Section 14.

Refitting

8 Refit the pulley to the crankshaft sprocket,

then fit the new pulley securing bolt and tighten it as far as possible before the crankshaft starts to rotate.

9 Holding the pulley against rotation as for removal, first tighten the bolt to the specified Stage 1 torque.

10 Stage 2 involves tightening the bolt though an angle, rather than to a torque. The bolt must be rotated through the specified angle – special angle gauges are available from tool outlets.

11 The remainder of refitting is a reversal of removal.

5 Timing belt and tensioner – removal and refitting

Removal

1 Disconnect the battery negative lead as described in Chapter 5.

2 Undo the 2 bolts securing the brake fluid remote reservoir (where fitted) to the engine compartment bulkhead.

4.2 Undo the fasteners (arrowed) and remove the engine undershield

4.6a Undo the bolt and remove the crankshaft pulley . . .

4.6b . . . followed by the TDC sensor ring/spacer

5.7 Pull the coolant expansion tank upwards from its mountings (arrowed)

5.9a Undo the 2 bolts (arrowed) . . .

5.9b . . . and slacken the nut (arrowed)

3 Remove the wiper arms as described in Chapter 12.

4 Release the 5 clips and remove the windscreen cowl panel, then undo the bolt at each end and pull the bulkhead extension panel forwards and remove it **(see illustrations 3.4a, 3.4b and 3.4c)**

5 Pull the plastic cover on top of the engine straight up from its mountings at the right-hand rear corner, right-hand front corner and left-hand front corner, then slide it forwards.

6 Remove the auxiliary drivebelt as described in Chapter 1.

7 Pull the coolant expansion tank up from its position, and move the tank to one side without disconnecting the hoses **(see illustration)**.

8 Release the wiring harness from the timing belt cover, then unclip the fuel pipes.

9 Undo the 2 bolts, slacken the nut, and remove the upper timing belt cover **(see illustrations)**.

10 Slacken the front right-hand roadwheel bolts, then jack up the front of the vehicle and support it securely on axle stands (see *Jacking and vehicle support*). Remove the roadwheel.

11 Release the fasteners and remove the engine undershield **(see illustration 4.2)**.

12 The engine must now be supported before the right-hand mounting is removed. Ford technicians use an engine support bar, which locates in the channels at the top of each inner wing, and a further beam attached to this, which rests on the front crossmember. If such an arrangement is not available, use an engine crane; either way, use a suitable length of chain and hooks to attach the lifting gear to the engine lifting eye. If the engine

must be supported from below (and this is not recommended), use a large piece of wood on a trolley jack to spread the load and reduce the chance of damage to the sump.

13 With the weight of the engine supported, unscrew the bolts/nuts, and remove the right-hand engine mounting **(see illustration)**.

14 Slacken the crankshaft pulley bolt as described in Section 4. Do not discard the old bolt yet – it is used during reassembly.

15 Two special tools are now required to set the engine at TDC (Top Dead Centre) for No1 cylinder (at the transmission end). Ford tool No 303-105 locates through a hole in the rear flange of the cylinder block into a corresponding hole in the rear of the flywheel, whilst tool No 303-735 locates through a hole in the exhaust camshaft sprocket into a hole in the cylinder head casting. In the absence of these tools, use an 8 mm drill bit to lock the camshaft sprocket, and an 8 mm rod to lock the flywheel. **Note:** *The flywheel locking bolt must be flat at the end (not tapered at all).*

16 Undo the starter motor bolts and position the motor to one side, to expose the crankshaft setting tool hole in the cylinder block flange. Refer to Chapter 5 if necessary.

17 Using a spanner or socket on the crankshaft pulley bolt, rotate the engine in a clockwise direction (viewed from the timing belt end of the engine) until the hole in the camshaft sprocket begins to align with the corresponding hole in the cylinder head.

18 Insert the crankshaft setting tool though the hole in the cylinder block flange and press it against the back of the flywheel. Have an assistant very slowly rotate the crankshaft clockwise, and the tool should slide into the flywheel as the holes align **(see illustrations)**.

19 It should now be possible to insert the camshaft locking tool (303-735) or equivalent through the hole in the camshaft sprocket into the hole in the cylinder head **(see illustration)**. Note that it may be necessary to rotate the camshaft sprocket backwards or forwards very slightly to be able to insert the tool.

20 At this point, Ford technicians use the tool described in paragraph 5 of Section 4 to lock the crankshaft in this position. The use of this tool or an equivalent is strongly recommended.

21 Disconnect the crankshaft position sensor

5.13 Undo the bolts (arrowed) and remove the right-hand engine mounting

5.18a The tool fits through the hole in the cylinder block flange . . .

5.18b . . . and into a hole in the rear of the flywheel

5.19 The tool fits through the hole in the exhaust camshaft sprocket, into the timing hole in the cylinder head

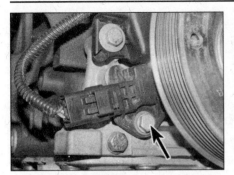

5.21 Crankshaft position sensor bolt (arrowed)

5.23 Timing belt lower cover bolts (arrowed)

5.24 Slacken the tensioner pulley bolt (arrowed)

wiring plug, then undo the bolt and remove the sensor **(see illustration)**.

22 Remove the crankshaft pulley, followed by the sensor ring/spacer **(see illustration 4.6a and 4.6b)**. Note: *Do not touch the outer sensor ring.*

23 Undo the bolts/nut and remove the lower timing belt cover **(see illustration)**.

24 Raise the engine slightly, then relieve the timing belt tension by slackening the bolt in the centre of the tensioning pulley **(see illustration)**.

25 Remove the timing belt from the sprockets. Note that the belt must not be re-used.

26 Slacken the bolts a few turns, remove the engine mounting bracket and the idler pulley, then undo the tensioner bolt **(see illustration)**. Discard both the tensioner and idler pulleys – new ones must be fitted.

27 If a new timing belt is not being fitted straight away (or if the belt is being removed as

part of another procedure, such as cylinder head removal), temporarily refit the engine right-hand mounting and tighten the bolts securely.

Refitting

28 Ensure that the crankshaft and camshaft are still set to TDC on No 1 cylinder.

29 Position the new idler pulley and insert the retaining bolt **(see illustration)**.

30 Refit the engine mounting bracket, then tighten the retaining bolts (including the idler pulley bolt) to the specified torque, where given.

31 Fit the new timing belt tensioner into position, but tighten the retaining finger-tight only at this stage.

32 Fit the new timing belt over the various sprockets in the following order: crankshaft, idler pulley, camshaft, tensioner and coolant pump **(see illustrations)**. Pay attention to any arrows on the belt indicating direction of rotation.

33 Using an Allen key in the tensioner arm, rotate the arm anti-clockwise until the pointer is positioned between the sides of the adjustment 'window' **(see illustrations)**. Fully tighten the tensioner retaining bolt.

34 Refit the timing belt lower cover and tighten the bolts securely.

35 Refit the sensor ring/spacer and the crankshaft pulley, then tighten the old pulley bolt to 50 Nm (37 lbf ft).

36 Remove the crankshaft and camshaft setting/locking tools, then rotate the crankshaft 2 complete revolutions clockwise, until the crankshaft setting tool can be re-inserted. Check that the camshaft locking tool can be inserted.

37 Check position of the tensioner pointer, and if necessary slacken the retaining bolt and use the Allen key to align the pointer in the centre of the adjustment 'window'. Tighten the retaining bolt securely.

5.26 Slacken the engine mounting bracket bolts and remove the idler pulley

5.29 Fit the new idler pulley

5.32a Timing belt routing

5.32b The arrows on the belt must point in the direction of rotation

5.33a Use an Allen key in the tensioner arm hole (arrowed)

5.33b Rotate the arm anti-clockwise until the pointer is between the sides of the adjustment 'window' (arrowed)

6.3 Lift up the chain upper guide rail and insert a 2.0 mm diameter rod/drill bit into the hole in the tensioner housing

38 Remove the old crankshaft pulley bolt, and fit the new one. Tighten the bolt to the specified torque, using the method employed during removal to prevent the crankshaft from rotating.

39 Remove the crankshaft and camshaft locking tools.

40 The remainder of refitting is a reversal of removal, remembering to tighten all fasteners to their specified torque where given.

6 Timing chain and tensioner – removal and refitting

Timing chain

1 Removal of the timing chain is included in the camshaft removal and refitment procedure, as described in Section 7.

6.4 Undo the tensioner retaining bolts (arrowed)

Tensioner

2 Remove the cylinder head cover as described in Section 3.

3 Press the tensioner upper guide rail upwards into the housing, then insert a 2.0 mm locking pin/drill bit to secure the rail in position **(see illustration)**.

4 Undo the 2 retaining bolts and withdrawn the tensioner **(see illustration)**.

5 Begin refitting by ensuring the tensioner and cylinder head mating faces are clean and free of debris.

6 Install the tensioner and tighten the retaining bolts to the specified torque.

7 Press the tensioner upper guide rail into the housing, pull out the locking pin/drill bit, then slowly release the guide rail.

8 Refit the cylinder head cover as described in Section 3.

7 Camshaft, rocker arms and hydraulic adjusters – removal, inspection and refitting

Note: *A new camshaft oil seal will be required on refitting.*

Removal

1 Remove the timing belt as described in Section 5.

2 Remove the timing chain tensioner as described in Section 6.

3 Remove the air cleaner assembly as described in Chapter 4.

4 Working at the left-hand end of the cylinder head, depress the release tab and disconnect the hose from the vacuum pump, undo the nut securing the EGR pipe and fuel supply hose, then undo the 3 Allen bolts and remove the pump from the cylinder head **(see illustrations)**. Check the condition of the pump O-ring seals and renew if necessary.

5 Undo the unions and remove the high-pressure fuel pipe between the fuel rail and the high-pressure pump located at the left-hand end of the cylinder head **(see illustration)**. Discard the pipe, a new one must be fitted. Plug or seal the openings to prevent contamination.

6 Slide off the retaining clip/depress the release tab and disconnect the fuel supply and return hoses from the high-pressure pump **(see illustrations)**. Plug or seal the openings to prevent contamination.

7.4a Depress the release tab (arrowed) and disconnect the servo hose from the pump

7.4b Undo the nut (arrowed) securing the EGR pipe and fuel hose

7.4c Vacuum pump securing bolts (arrowed)

7.5 Undo the unions (arrowed) and remove the high-pressure fuel pipe between the fuel rail and pump

7.6a Depress the release tab (arrowed) and disconnect the fuel return hose . . .

7.6b . . . and the fuel supply hose (arrowed)

7.8 High-pressure fuel pump retaining bolts (arrowed)

7 Note their fitted positions, and disconnect the wiring plug(s) from the high-pressure fuel pump.
8 Undo the 3 retaining bolts and pull the high-pressure fuel pump out from the cylinder head (**see illustration**). Be prepared for fuel spillage.
9 Remove the injectors as described in Chapter 4.
10 Undo the retaining bolt and pull the sprocket from the exhaust camshaft. Use a tool to prevent the camshaft and sprocket from rotating whilst the nut is released (**see Tool Tip**).
11 Undo the bolts and remove the engine mounting bracket from the right-hand end of the cylinder head/block.
12 Undo the bolts securing the timing belt inner cover to the cylinder head (**see illustration**).
13 Undo the 2 bolts and remove the EGR pipe from over the left-hand end of the cylinder head.
14 Unscrew the injector mounting studs using a Torx socket, in sequence (**see illustration**).
15 Working in the **reverse** of the sequence given (**see illustration 7.28**), gradually and evenly remove the bolts securing the upper section of the cylinder head.
16 Carefully tap around the edge of the cylinder head upper section and lift it from position. Note that the cover will probably be

To make a camshaft sprocket holding tool, obtain two lengths of steel strip about 6 mm thick by 30 mm wide or similar, one 600 mm long, the other 200 mm long (all dimensions are approximate). Bolt the two strips together to form a forked end, leaving the bolt slack so that the shorter strip can pivot freely. Drill holes and insert bolts of a suitable size in the ends of the fork to engage in the sprocket spokes. Hold the bolts at the ends firmly in place by using a nut on the other side of the steel strip.

reluctant to lift due to the sealant used, and possible corrosion around the two locating dowels at the front edge.
17 Lift the camshafts from position, disengage the timing chain from the sprockets, and remove the exhaust camshaft seal.
18 Have ready a box divided into 16 segments, or some containers or other means of storing and identifying the rockers arms and hydraulic adjusters after removal. It's essential that if they are to be refitted, they return to their original positions. Mark the segments in the box or the containers with the cylinder number for each rocker arm/adjuster, and left or right, for the particular cylinder.
19 Lift out the rockers arms and hydraulic

7.12 Remove the bolts (arrowed) securing the belt inner cover

adjusters, Keep them identified for position, and place them in their respective positions in the box or container (**see illustration**).

Inspection

20 With the camshaft removed, examine the bearing surfaces in the upper and lower sections of the cylinder head for signs of obvious wear or pitting. If evident, a new cylinder head will probably be required. Also check that the oil supply holes in the cylinder head are free from obstructions.
21 Visually inspect the camshaft for evidence of wear on the surfaces of the lobes and journals. Normally their surfaces should be smooth and have a dull shine; look for scoring, erosion or pitting and areas that appear highly polished, indicating excessive wear. Accelerated wear will occur once the hardened exterior of the camshaft has been damaged, so always renew worn items. **Note:** *If these symptoms are visible on the tips of the camshaft lobes, check the rocker arm, as it will probably be worn as well.*
22 If any doubt exists as to the condition of the camshafts or cylinder head, have them examined at a Ford dealer workshop or suitably-equipped automotive repair facility.
23 Inspect the rocker arms and hydraulic adjusters for obvious signs of wear or damage, and renew if necessary.

7.14 Injector mounting stud removal sequence

7.19 Lift out the rocker arms and hydraulic adjusters

7.24 Fit the secondary timing chain lower guide rail

7.25a Apply clean oil to the hydraulic adjusters . . .

7.25b . . . and refit them to their original positions

7.26a Align the coloured links on the chain (arrowed) with the marks on the camshaft sprockets . . .

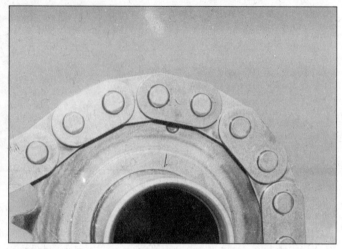

7.26b . . . the mark on the sprockets is a dot, and a line . . .

Refitting

24 Make sure that the top surfaces of the cylinder head, and in particular the camshaft bearings and the mating surfaces are completely clean. Ensure the secondary timing chain lower guide rail is in place **(see illustration)**.

25 Smear some clean engine oil onto the sides of the hydraulic adjusters, and offer each one into position in their original bores in the cylinder head, together with its rocker arm **(see illustrations)**.

26 Locate the timing chain on the camshaft sprockets, aligning the two coloured chain links

with the marks on the camshaft sprockets, then lubricate the camshaft and cylinder head bearing journals with clean engine oil, and lower the camshafts into position **(see illustrations)**. The mark on the intake camshaft must be in the 12 o'clock position.

27 Apply a thin bead of silicone sealant (Ford part No WSE-M4G323-A4) to the mating surface of the cylinder head. Take great care to ensure the chain tensioner oil supply hole is free from sealant **(see illustrations)**.

28 Lower the upper section of the cylinder head into place, and tighten the retaining bolts to the specified torque in sequence **(see illustration)**.

29 Refit the fuel injector mounting studs and tighten them to the specified torque.

30 Refit the camshaft timing chain tensioner assembly, and tighten the retaining bolts to the specified torque. Press the tensioner guide rail up into the housing and pull out the locking pin/drill bit. Slowly release the guide rail to tension the chain.

7.26c . . . then fit the camshafts with the mark on the intake camshaft (arrowed) in the 12 o'clock position

H46404

7.27a Apply a thin bead of sealant as indicated by the heavy black line

7.27b We inserted a tapered rod (arrowed) into the tensioner oil supply hole to prevent any sealant from entering

31 Fit a new exhaust camshaft oil seal as described in Section 8.

32 Refit the 2 bolts securing the timing belt inner cover to the cylinder head, and the single bolt to the cylinder block, then tighten the bolts securely.

33 Slide the exhaust camshaft sprocket into place, aligning the integral key with the camshaft and fit the camshaft sprocket locking tool **(see illustration 5.19)**.

34 Fit the sprocket retaining bolt and tighten it to the specified torque, preventing the sprocket from turning using the tool used during removal.

35 Refit the engine mounting bracket to the right-hand end of the cylinder head/block, and tighten the bolts to the specified torque.

36 The remainder of refitting is a reversal of removal, noting the following points:

a) Refit the injectors as described in Chapter 4.
b) Fit the new timing belt, tensioner and idler pulley as described in Section 5.
c) Tighten all fasteners to their specified torque, where given.
d) Check the engine oil and coolant levels as described in 'Weekly checks'.

8 Camshaft oil seal –
renewal

1 Remove the timing belt as described in Section 5, and the camshaft sprocket as described in paragraph 10 of the previous

7.28 Cylinder head upper section bolt tightening sequence

Section. Recover the sprocket locating key from the end of the camshaft.

2 Carefully prise or pull the seal from position.

 HAYNES HINT *One of the best ways to remove an oil seal is to carefully drill or punch two holes through the seal, opposite each other (taking care not to damage the surface behind the seal as this is done). Two self-tapping screws are then screwed into the holes; by pulling on the screw heads alternately with a pair of pliers, the seal can be extracted.*

3 Clean out the seal housing and the sealing surface of the camshaft by wiping it with a lint-free cloth. Remove any swarf or burrs that may cause the seal to leak.

4 Apply a little oil to the new camshaft oil seal, and fit it over the end of the camshaft, lips facing inwards. To avoid damaging the seal lips, wrap a little tape over the end of the camshaft. Ford dealers have a special tool (No 303-684/1) for fitting the seal, but if this is not available, a deep socket of suitable size can be used. **Note:** *Select a socket that*

bears only on the hard outer surface of the seal, not the inner lip which can easily be damaged. It is important that the seal is fitted square to the shaft, and is fully-seated **(see illustrations)**.

5 Refit the camshaft sprocket (and key – Section 7) and timing belt as described in Section 5.

9 Cylinder head –
removal, inspection and refitting

Removal

1 Remove the battery as described in Chapter 5, then unscrew the three bolts securing the battery tray, and remove the tray from the engine compartment.

2 Drain the coolant as described in Chapter 1.

3 Remove the camshafts, rocker arms and hydraulic adjusters as described in Section 7.

4 Undo the bolts, and remove the bracket over the fuel filter.

5 Undo the Torx bolt, lift out the filter housing, then undo the bolts and remove the fuel filter bracket. Refit the bolt securing the lifting bracket to the cylinder head **(see illustrations)**.

8.4a Apply a little clean oil to the oil seal inner lip . . .

8.4b . . . then use a socket (or similar) to drive the seal into place . . .

8.4c . . . until the seal is flush with the casing surface

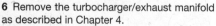

9.5a Undo the Torx bolt (arrowed) on the side and lift out the filter housing . . .

9.5b . . . then undo the bolts (arrowed) and remove the filter bracket

9.7 Thermostat housing studs (arrowed)

6 Remove the turbocharger/exhaust manifold as described in Chapter 4.

7 Disconnect the wiring plugs, then undo the 4 nuts, unscrew the 4 mounting studs and detach the thermostat housing from the left-hand of the cylinder head. Be prepared for coolant spillage **(see illustration)**.

8 Disconnect the wiring plug from the pressure sensor on the underside of the common fuel rail at the front of the cylinder head.

9 Undo the retaining bolt, and remove the oil filler pipe support bracket.

10 Working in the **reverse** of the sequence shown in paragraph 34, gradually and evenly slacken and remove the cylinder head bolts. Discard the bolts, new ones must be fitted.

11 Lift the cylinder head away; use assistance if possible, as it is a very heavy assembly. Do not place the cylinder head flat on its sealing surface, as the ends of the glow plugs may be damaged – support the ends of the cylinder head on wooden blocks.

12 If the head is stuck (as is possible), be careful how you choose to free it. Striking the head with tools carries the risk of damage, and the head is located on two dowels, so its movement will be limited. Do not, under any circumstances, lever the head between the mating surfaces, as this will certainly damage the sealing surfaces for the gasket, leading to leaks.

13 Once the head has been removed, recover the gasket from the two dowels.

14 Do not discard the gasket at this stage – it will be needed for correct identification of the new gasket.

9.20 Zero the DTI on the gasket face

Inspection

15 If required, dismantling and inspection of the cylinder head is covered in Part F of this Chapter.

Cylinder head gasket selection

16 Examine the old cylinder head gasket for manufacturer's identification markings. These will be in the form of holes on the front edge of the gasket, which indicate the gasket's thickness.

17 Unless new components have been fitted, or the cylinder head has been machined (skimmed), the new cylinder head gasket must be of the same type as the old one. Purchase the required gasket, and proceed to paragraph 24.

18 If the head has been machined, or if new pistons have been fitted, it is likely that a head gasket of different thickness to the original will be needed.

19 Gasket selection is made on the basis of the measured piston protrusion above the cylinder head gasket surface.

20 To measure the piston protrusion, anchor a dial test indicator (DTI) to the top face (cylinder head gasket mating face) of the cylinder block, and zero the gauge on the gasket mating face **(see illustration)**.

21 Rest the gauge probe above No 1 piston crown, and turn the crankshaft slowly by hand until the piston reaches TDC (its maximum height). Measure and record the maximum piston projection at TDC.

22 Repeat the measurement for the remaining pistons, and record the results.

23 If the measurements differ from piston to piston, take the highest figure, and use this to determine the thickness of the head gasket required (see table below).

Preparation for refitting

24 The mating faces of the cylinder head and cylinder block must be perfectly clean before refitting the head. Use a hard plastic or wooden scraper to remove all traces of gasket and carbon; also clean the piston crowns. **Note:** *The new head gasket has rubber-coated surfaces, which could be damaged from sharp edges or debris left by a metal scraper. Take particular care when cleaning the piston crowns, as the soft aluminium alloy is easily damaged.*

25 Make sure that the carbon is not allowed to enter the oil and water passages – this is particularly important for the lubrication system, as carbon could block the oil supply to the engine's components. Using adhesive tape and paper, seal the water, oil and bolt holes in the cylinder block.

26 To prevent carbon entering the gap between the pistons and bores, smear a little grease in the gap.

27 After cleaning each piston, use a small brush to remove all traces of grease and carbon from the gap, then wipe away the remainder with a clean rag. Clean all the pistons in the same way.

28 Check the mating surfaces of the cylinder block and the cylinder head for nicks, deep scratches and other damage (refer to the Note in paragraph 24). If slight, they may be removed carefully with a file, but if excessive, machining may be the only alternative to renewal.

29 If warpage of the cylinder head gasket surface is suspected, use a straight-edge to check it for distortion. Refer to Part F of this Chapter if necessary.

30 Ensure that the cylinder head bolt holes in the crankcase are clean and free of oil.

Cylinder head gasket selection

Piston protrusion	Gasket identification	Gasket thickness
0.55 to 0.60 mm	1 notch/hole	1.25 ± 0.04 mm
0.61 to 0.65 mm	2 notches/hole	1.30 ± 0.04 mm
0.66 to 0.70 mm	3 notches/hole	1.35 ± 0.04 mm
0.71 to 0.75 mm	4 notches/hole	1.40 ± 0.04 mm

9.31 Fit the new gasket over the dowels, with the thickness identification holes at the front (arrowed)

9.34 Cylinder head lower section bolt tightening sequence

Syringe or soak up any oil left in the bolt holes. This is most important in order that the correct bolt tightening torque can be applied, and to prevent the possibility of the block being cracked by hydraulic pressure when the bolts are tightened.

Refitting

31 Ensure that the cylinder head locating dowels are in place at the corners of the cylinder block, then fit the new cylinder head gasket over the dowels, ensuring that the identification holes are at the front **(see illustration)**. Take care to avoid damaging the gasket's rubber coating.

32 Lower the cylinder head into position on the gasket, ensuring that it engages correctly over the dowels.

33 Fit the new cylinder head bolts and screw them in as far as possible by hand.

34 Working in sequence **(see illustration)**, tighten all the cylinder head bolts to the specified Stage 1 torque using an E14 Torx socket.

35 Stage 2 involves tightening the bolts though an angle, rather than to a torque **(see illustration)**. Each bolt in sequence must be rotated through the specified angle – special angle gauges are available from tool outlets.

36 The remainder of the refitting procedure is a reversal of the removal procedure, bearing in mind the following points:

a) Refit the camshafts, rocker arms and hydraulic adjusters as described in Section 7.

b) Reconnect the exhaust front section to the exhaust manifold with reference to Chapter 4.

c) Fit new high-pressure fuel delivery pipes as described in Chapter 4.

d) Refit the intake manifold/cylinder head cover with reference to Section 3.

e) Refit the air cleaner as described in Chapter 4.

f) Refill the cooling system as described in Chapter 1.

g) Check and if necessary top-up the engine oil level and power steering fluid level as described in 'Weekly checks'.

h) Before starting the engine, read through the section on engine restarting after overhaul, at the end of Chapter 2F.

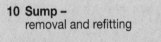

10 Sump –
removal and refitting

Note: The full procedure outlined below must be followed so that the mating surfaces can be cleaned and prepared to achieve an oil-tight joint on reassembly.

Removal

1 Apply the handbrake, then jack up the front of the vehicle and support it on axle stands (see Jacking and vehicle support). Undo the fasteners and remove the engine undershield **(see illustration 4.2)**.

2 Referring to Chapter 1 if necessary, drain the engine oil, then clean and refit the engine oil drain plug, tightening it to the specified torque wrench setting. We strongly advise renewing the oil filter element, also described in Chapter 1.

3 Pull the plastic cover on the top of the engine upwards from its mountings.

4 Slacken the hose clamps, undo the bracket bolt and remove the charge air pipe from the underside of the engine **(see illustration)**.

5 Remove the air conditioning compressor drivebelt as described in Chapter 1, then undo

9.35 Use an angle gauge for the Stage 2 torque setting

the mounting bolts and move the compressor to one side without disconnecting the refrigerant pipes. Suspend the compressor from the radiator crossmember using wires or straps.

6 Progressively unscrew the sump retaining bolts, including the 2 bolts securing the sump to the transmission housing. Don't forget the 4 bolts at the left-hand end accessed through the holes. Break the joint by carefully inserting a putty knife (or similar) between the sump and cylinder block **(see illustrations)**. Take care not to damage the sealing surfaces.

10.4 Undo the charge air pipe bracket bolt (arrowed)

10.6a Undo the 2 bolts securing the sump to the transmission (arrowed) . . .

10.6b . . . access to the sump end bolts is through the holes (arrowed)

10.8 Apply sealant around the inside of the bolt holes

edge of the bolt holes. Do not allow the sealant to enter the bolt holes **(see illustration). Note:** *The sump must be refitted within 4 minutes of applying the sealant.*

9 Refit the sump and fit the retaining bolts, tightening them by hand only at this stage.

10 Tighten the 2 bolts securing the sump to the transmission casing to the specified torque, then tighten the remaining bolts, gradually and evenly to the specified torque.

11 Lower the car to the ground. Wait at least 1 hour for the sealant to cure (or whatever time is indicated by the sealant manufacturer) before refilling the engine with oil. If removed, fit a new oil filter with reference to Chapter 1.

11 Oil pump – removal, inspection and refitting

Removal

1 Remove the timing belt as described in Section 5, then slide off the crankshaft sprocket **(see illustrations)**.

2 Remove the sump as described in Section 10.

3 Undo the retaining bolts and remove the cover and crankshaft seal. Note the original locations of the cover bolts – they are of different lengths.

4 Undo the bolt securing the oil level pipe **(see illustration)**.

5 Pull out the key from the crankshaft sprocket, then undo the pump mounting bolts, slide the pump, chain, and crankshaft sprocket from the end of the engine **(see illustrations)**. Recover the O-ring between the sprocket and crankshaft.

Inspection

6 Undo the retaining bolts and remove the cover from the oil pump **(see illustration)**. Note the location of any identification marks on the inner and outer rotors for refitting.

7 Unscrew the plug and remove the pressure relief valve, spring and plunger, clean out and check condition of components **(see illustration)**.

8 No specifications for the pump internal components are given by Ford.

9 Check the general condition of the oil

11.1a Slide off the crankshaft sprocket . . .

11.1b . . . and recover the crankshaft key

Refitting

7 On reassembly, thoroughly clean and degrease the mating surfaces of the cylinder block/crankcase and sump, removing all traces of sealant, then use a clean rag to

wipe out the sump and the engine's interior.

8 Apply a 3 mm thick bead of sealant (Ford part No WSE-M4G323-A4) to the sump flange, making sure the bead is around the inside

11.4 Oil level pipe bracket bolt (arrowed)

11.5a Remove the sprocket key . . .

11.5b . . . undo the oil pump mounting bolts (arrowed), slide the assembly from the crankshaft . . .

11.5c . . . and recover the O-ring between the sprocket and crankshaft (arrowed)

11.6 Oil pump cover bolts

pump, and in particular, its mating face to the cylinder block. If the mating face is damaged significantly, this may lead to oil loss (and a resulting drop in available oil pressure).

10 Inspect the rotors for obvious signs of wear or damage; at the time of writing, no new parts are available. If the pump is faulty, it must be renewed as a complete unit. Lubricate the rotors with fresh engine oil and refit them into the body, making sure that the identification marks are positioned as noted on removal.

11 If the oil pump has been removed as part of a major engine overhaul, it is assumed that the engine will have completed a substantial mileage. In this case, it is often considered good practice to fit a new (or reconditioned) pump as a matter of course. In other words, if the rest of the engine is being rebuilt, the engine has completed a large mileage, or there is any question as to the old pump's condition, it is preferable to fit a new oil pump.

Refitting

12 Before fitting the oil pump, ensure that the mating faces on the pump and the engine block are completely clean.

13 Fit the O-ring to the end of the crankshaft **(see illustration)**.

14 Engage the drive chain with the oil pump and crankshaft sprockets, then slide the crankshaft sprocket into place (aligning the slot in the sprocket with the keyway in the crankshaft) as the pump is refitted. Refit the crankshaft key.

15 Refit the mounting bolts and tighten them to the specified torque. Note that the front, left-hand bolt is slightly longer than the others.

16 Apply a 3 mm wide bead of silicone sealant (Ford part No WSE-M4G323-A4) to the oil seal carrier flange. Refit the cover and tighten the bolts to the specified torque. Note that the bolts must be tightened within 4 minutes of the sealant being applied.

17 Fit a new oil seal to the cover as described in Section 14.

18 Refit the bolt securing the oil level pipe.

19 The remainder of refitting is a reversal of removal, remembering to fit a new oil filter element, and replenish the engine oil.

12 Oil pressure warning light switch – removal and refitting

Removal

1 The switch is screwed into the oil filter housing **(see illustration)**. Access is from under the vehicle. Undo the fasteners and remove the engine undershield. To further improve access, undo the mounting bolts and move the air conditioning compressor to one side. Suspend the compressor from the radiator crossmember using wire or straps. There is no need to disconnect the refrigerant pipes.

11.7 Oil pressure relief valve plug

2 Disconnect the switch wiring plug.

3 Unscrew the switch from the housing; be prepared for some oil loss.

Refitting

4 Refitting is the reverse of the removal procedure; fit a new pressure switch sealing washer, and tighten the switch to the specified torque wrench setting.

5 Reconnect the switch wiring plug.

6 Refit all components removed for access to the switch.

7 Check the engine oil level and top-up as necessary (see *Weekly checks*).

8 Check for correct warning light operation, and for signs of oil leaks, once the engine has been restarted and warmed-up to normal operating temperature.

13 Oil cooler – removal and refitting

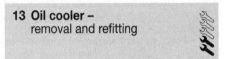

Note: *New sealing rings will be required on refitting – check for availability prior to commencing work.*

Removal

1 The cooler is fitted to the oil filter housing on the front of the cylinder block. Access is from under the vehicle. Undo the fasteners and remove the engine undershield. To further improve access, undo the mounting bolts and move the air conditioning compressor to one side. Suspend the compressor from the radiator crossmember using wire or straps.

12.1 Oil pressure warning switch (arrowed)

11.13 Fit the O-ring to the end of the crankshaft

There is no need to disconnect the refrigerant pipes.

2 Undo the 4 retaining bolts and detach the cooler from the housing **(see illustration)**. Recover the sealing rings and be prepared for oil/coolant spillage.

Refitting

3 Refitting is a reversal of removal, bearing in mind the following points:

a) *Use new sealing rings.*

b) *Tighten the cooler mounting bolts securely.*

c) *On completion, lower the car to the ground. Check and if necessary top-up the oil and coolant levels, then start the engine and check for signs of oil or coolant leakage.*

14 Crankshaft oil seals – renewal

Timing belt end seal

1 Remove the timing belt as described in Section 5.

2 Slide the belt sprocket from the crankshaft, and recover the locating key from the groove on the crankshaft **(see illustrations 11.1a and 11.1b)**.

3 Note the fitted depth of the oil seal as a guide for fitting the new one.

4 Using a screwdriver or similar tool, carefully prise the oil seal from its location. Take care not to damage the oil seal contact surfaces

13.2 Oil cooler retaining bolts (arrowed)

14.4a Drill a small hole in the seal . . .

14.4b . . . insert a self-tapping screw and pull out the seal

14.7a Locate the new seal and guide over the end of the crankshaft . . .

14.7b . . . then drive the seal home until it's flush with the cover

14.11a Drill a hole in the seal . . .

14.11b . . . then insert a self-tapping screw and pull out the seal

or crankshaft. Alternatively, drill a small hole in the seal (taking care not to drill any deeper than necessary), then insert a self-tapping screw and use pliers to pull out the seal **(see illustrations)**.

5 Wipe clean the oil seal contact surfaces and seating, and clean up any sharp edges or burrs which might damage the new seal as it is fitted, or which might cause the seal to leak once in place.

6 No oil should be applied to the oil seal, which is made of PTFE. Ford technicians use a special seal-fitting tool (303-255/303-395), but an adequate substitute can be achieved using a large socket or piece of tubing of sufficient size to bear on the outer edge of the new seal. Note that the new seal is supplied with a guide which fits over the end of the crankshaft.

7 Locate the new seal (with guide still fitted) over the end of the crankshaft, using the tool

(see illustrations), socket, or tubing to press the seal squarely and fully into position, to the previously-noted depth. Remove the guide from the end of the crankshaft.

8 The remainder of reassembly is the reverse of the removal procedure, referring to the relevant text for details where required. Check for signs of oil leakage when the engine is restarted.

Flywheel end seal

9 Remove the transmission as described in Chapter 7, and the clutch assembly as described in Chapter 6.

10 Unbolt the flywheel (see Section 15).

11 Using a screwdriver or similar, carefully prise the oil seal from place. Take great care not to damage the seal seating area or the crankshaft sealing surface. Alternatively, punch or drill two small holes opposite each other in the oil seal, then screw a self-tapping

screw into each hole, and pull the screws with pliers to extract the seal **(see illustrations)**.

12 Clean the end of the crankshaft, polishing off any burrs or raised edges, which may have caused the seal to fail in the first place. Clean also the seal mating face on the engine block, using a suitable solvent for degreasing if necessary.

13 The new oil seal is supplied fitted with a locating sleeve, which must **not** be removed prior to fitting (it will drop out on its own when the seal is fitted). Do not lubricate the seal.

14 Offer the new seal into position, feeding the locating sleeve over the end of the crankshaft **(see illustration)**.

15 Ford technicians use a special tool (205-307) to pull the seal into position. In the absence of the tool, use a large socket/piece of tubing which bears only on the hard outer edge of the seal, and carefully tap the seal into position **(see illustration)**.

16 If the seal locating sleeve is still in position, remove it now.

17 The remainder of the reassembly procedure is the reverse of dismantling, referring to the relevant text for details where required. Check for signs of oil leakage when the engine is restarted.

14.14 Locate the seal and locating sleeve over the end of the crankshaft

14.15 Press the seal in until it's flush with the surface

15 Flywheel – removal, inspection and refitting

Removal

1 Remove the transmission as described

15.5 Flywheel retaining bolts

15.10 Note the locating dowel and corresponding hole (arrowed)

15.11 A simple home-made tool to lock the flywheel

in Chapter 7. Now is a good time to check components such as oil seals and renew them if necessary.

2 Remove the clutch as described in Chapter 6. Now is a good time to check or renew the clutch components and release bearing.

3 Use a centre-punch or paint to make alignment marks on the flywheel and crankshaft, to ensure correct alignment during refitting.

4 Prevent the flywheel from turning by locking the ring gear teeth, or by bolting a strap between the flywheel and the cylinder block/crankcase. Slacken the Torx bolts evenly until all are free.

5 Remove each bolt in turn and ensure that new ones are obtained for reassembly; these bolts are subjected to severe stresses and so must be renewed, regardless of their apparent condition, whenever they are disturbed **(see illustration)**.

6 Withdraw the flywheel, remembering that it is very heavy – do not drop it.

Inspection

7 Clean the flywheel to remove grease and oil. Inspect the surface for cracks, rivet grooves, burned areas and score marks. Light scoring can be removed with emery cloth. Check for cracked and broken ring gear teeth. Lay the flywheel on a flat surface and use a straight-edge to check for warpage.

8 Clean and inspect the mating surfaces of the flywheel and the crankshaft. If the crankshaft seal is leaking, renew it (see Section 14) before refitting the flywheel. If the engine has covered a high mileage, it may be worth fitting a new seal as a matter if course, given the amount of work needed to access it.

9 Thoroughly clean the threaded bolt holes in the crankshaft, removing all traces of locking compound.

Refitting

10 Fit the flywheel to the crankshaft ensuring the dowel aligns with the hole in the crankshaft – it will fit only one way **(see illustration)**. Insert the new bolts.

11 Lock the flywheel by the method used on dismantling **(see illustration)**. Working in a diagonal sequence, tighten the bolts to the specified torque wrench setting.

12 Refit the clutch (Chapter 6) and the transmission (Chapter 7).

16 Engine/transmission mountings – inspection and renewal

Refer to Chapter 2C, Section 17, but use the torque wrench settings in this Chapter.

Notes

Chapter 2 Part F:
Engine removal and overhaul procedures

Contents

Section number

Crankshaft – inspection 11
Crankshaft – refitting 15
Crankshaft – removal 8
Cylinder block/crankcase – cleaning and inspection 9
Cylinder head – dismantling, cleaning, inspection and reassembly . . 5
Cylinder head – reassembly 8
Engine – initial start-up after overhaul 17
Engine and transmission – removal, separation and refitting 3
Engine overhaul – general information 2
Engine overhaul – preliminary information 4

Section number

Engine overhaul – reassembly sequence 13
Engine/transmission removal – preparation and precautions 2
Fuel injection pump drive chain (1.8 litre diesel engines) – removal,
    inspection and refitting 6
General information 1
Main and big-end bearings – inspection 12
Piston rings – refitting 14
Piston/connecting rod assembly – inspection 10
Piston/connecting rod assembly – refitting 16
Piston/connecting rod assembly – removal 7

Degrees of difficulty

Easy, suitable for novice with little experience	Fairly easy, suitable for beginner with some experience	Fairly difficult, suitable for competent DIY mechanic	Difficult, suitable for experienced DIY mechanic	Very difficult, suitable for expert DIY or professional

Specifications

Note: *At the time of writing, some specifications for certain engines were not available.*
Where the relevant specifications are not given here, refer to your Ford dealer for further information.

Cylinder head
Petrol engines:
  Warp limit – maximum acceptable for use:
    1.6 litre engines . . . .   0.03 mm
    1.8 litre and 2.0 litre engines . . . .   0.10 mm
  Diesel engines:
    1.6 litre engines . . . .   0.05 mm
    1.8 litre engines . . . .   0.06 mm
    2.0 litre engines . . . .   0.03 mm

Intake valves
Stem diameter:
  Petrol engines:
    1.6 litre engines . . . .   Not available
    1.8 litre and 2.0 litre engines . . . .   5.470 to 5.485 mm
  Diesel engines:
    1.6 litre engines . . . .   5.485 +0.0, -0.015 mm
    1.8 litre engines . . . .   Not available
    2.0 litre engines . . . .   5.978 ± 0.009 mm

Exhaust valves
Stem diameter:
  Petrol engines:
    1.6 litre engines . . . .   Not available
    1.8 litre and 2.0 litre engines . . . .   5.465 to 5.480 mm
  Diesel engines:
    1.6 litre engines . . . .   5.475 +0.0, -0.015 mm
    1.8 litre engines . . . .   Not available
    2.0 litre engines . . . .   5.968 ± 0.009 mm

Cylinder block

Cylinder bore diameter (nominal):
Petrol engines:

1.6 litre engines..	79.00mm
1.8 litre engines..	83.00mm
2.0 litre engines..	87.50mm

Diesel engines:

1.6 litre engines..	75.00 mm
1.8 litre engines..	82.50 mm
2.0 litre engines..	85.00 mm

Piston rings

End gaps:
1.6 litre engines:

Top compression ring.....................................	0.20 to 0.35 mm
Second compression ring................................	0.20 to 0.40 mm
Oil control ring	0.80 to 1.00 mm

1.8 litre engines:

Top compression ring.....................................	0.31 to 0.50 mm
Second compression ring................................	0.31 to 0.50 mm
Oil control ring	0.25 to 0.58 mm

2.0 litre engines:

Top compression ring.....................................	0.20 to 0.35 mm
Second compression ring................................	0.80 to 1.00 mm
Oil control ring	0.25 to 0.50 mm

Crankshaft

Endfloat:

1.6 litre engines thrustwasher thickness	2.4 ± 0.05 mm
1.8 litre engines	0.11 to 0.37 mm
2.0 litre engines	0.07 to 0.32 mm
Maximum bearing journal out-of-round (all engines)	0.007 mm

Torque wrench settings

Refer to the relevant sections of Chapter 2A, 2B, 2C, 2D, and 2E for torque wrench settings.

1 General information

Included in this part of Chapter 2 are details of removing the engine/transmission from the car and general overhaul procedures for the cylinder head, cylinder block and all other engine internal components.

Note: *On all petrol engines covered by this manual, it is not possible to remove the intermediate/main bearing section or to remove the crankshaft or pistons. No separate parts appear to be available, and new/exchange units are supplied with crankshaft, pistons, connecting rods, etc, already fitted. Consult a Ford dealer or parts specialist.*

2 Engine/transmission removal – preparation and precautions

If you have decided that an engine must be removed for overhaul or major repair work, several preliminary steps should be taken.

Locating a suitable place to work is extremely important. Adequate work space, along with storage space for the car, will be needed. If a workshop or garage is not available, at the very least, a flat, level, clean work surface is required.

If possible, clear some shelving close to the work area, and use it to store the engine components and ancillaries as they are removed and dismantled. In this manner, the components stand a better chance of staying clean and undamaged during the overhaul. Laying out components in groups together with their fixing bolts, screws, etc, will save time and avoid confusion when the engine is refitted.

Clean the engine compartment and engine/transmission before beginning the removal procedure; this will help visibility and help to keep tools clean.

The help of an assistant should be available; there are certain instances when one person cannot safely perform all of the operations required to remove the engine from the vehicle. Safety is of primary importance, considering the potential hazards involved in this kind of operation. A second person should always be in attendance to offer help in an emergency. If this is the first time you have removed an engine, advice and aid from someone more experienced would also be beneficial.

Plan the operation ahead of time. Before starting work, obtain (or arrange for the hire of) all of the tools and equipment you will need. Access to the following items will allow the task of removing and refitting the engine/transmission to be completed safely and with relative ease: an engine hoist – rated in excess of the combined weight of the engine/transmission, a heavy-duty trolley jack, complete sets of spanners and

sockets as described at the rear this manual, wooden blocks, and plenty of rags and cleaning solvent for mopping-up spilled oil, coolant and fuel. A selection of different-sized plastic storage bins will also prove useful for keeping dismantled components grouped together. If any of the equipment must be hired, make sure that you arrange for it in advance, and perform all of the operations possible without it beforehand; this may save you time and money.

Plan on the vehicle being out of use for quite a while. Read through the whole of this Section and work out a strategy based on your own experience and the tools, time and workspace available to you. Some of the overhaul processes may have to be carried out by a Ford dealer or an engineering works – these establishments often have busy schedules, so it would be prudent to consult them before removing or dismantling the engine, to get an idea of the amount of time required to carry out the work.

When removing the engine from the vehicle, be methodical about the disconnection of external components. Labelling cables and hoses as they removed will greatly assist the refitting process.

Always be extremely careful when lifting the engine/transmission assembly from the engine bay. Serious injury can result from careless actions. If help is required, it is better to wait until it is available rather than risk personal injury and/or damage to components

3.4a Remove the clips to release the upper panel...

3.4b ... and then unbolt ...

3.4c ... and remove the lower panel

by continuing alone. By planning ahead and taking your time, a job of this nature, although major, can be accomplished successfully and without incident.

On all models covered by this manual the engine and transmission can be removed as a complete assembly downwards and out of the engine bay. The engine and transmission are then separated with the assembly on the bench. Alternatively, the transmission can be removed as described in Chapter 7, and then the engine removed upwards.

3 Engine and transmission – removal, separation and refitting

Note: *This procedure describes removing the engine and transmission as a complete assembly downwards out the of the engine compartment. When raising the vehicle bear in mind that the front underside of the vehicle must be at least 700 mm above the ground to provide sufficient clearance.*

Removal

1 On petrol models remove the fuel pump relay from the fusebox, then start the engine (if possible) and allow it to run until it stops (having relieved the fuel pressure).
2 Open the bonnet and with the help of an assistant remove the bonnet as described in Chapter 11.
3 Remove the engine cover and battery cover and then disconnect and remove the battery with reference to Chapter 5.
4 Remove the wiper arms as described in Chapter 12. Release the clips and remove the windscreen cowl panel, then undo the bolt at each end, release the clips and where fitted remove the bulkhead extension panel **(see illustrations)**.
5 Apply the handbrake, then jack up the front of the vehicle and support it on axle stands (see *Jacking and vehicle support*). Remove both front roadwheels and wheel arch liners. Also remove the undershield from beneath the engine and transmission.
6 Drain the coolant as described in Chapter 1.
7 Drain the transmission oil as described in Chapter 7. Refit the drain plug, and tighten it to the specified torque setting.

8 Remove both front driveshafts as described in Chapter 8.
9 If the engine is to be dismantled, drain the engine oil and remove the oil filter as described in Chapter 1. Clean and refit the drain plug, tightening it to the specified torque.
10 Remove the radiator as described in Chapter 3.
11 Remove the air cleaner assembly as described in Chapter 4 and on diesel models remove the intercooler as described in Chapter 4.
12 On petrol models remove the exhaust manifold as described in Chapter 4.
13 On diesel models release the clamps and remove the throttle body intake pipe, then release the clamp, undo the mounting bolt and nut, then remove the turbocharger outlet pipe. With reference to Chapter 4, remove the front section of the exhaust pipe. On 2.0 litre models, undo the mounting nuts and remove the catalytic converter support bracket.

3.17a Press back the clip . . .

3.17c Disconnect the lead from the positive connection junction box (arrowed)

14 Remove the 'crash box' (where fitted) from the subframe behind the right-hand driveshaft location.
15 Remove the auxiliary drivebelt(s) as described in Chapter 1.
16 On models with air conditioning, disconnect the compressor wiring plug, undo the mounting bolts, and move the compressor to one side. Suspend the compressor from the vehicle bodywork using wire/cables ties, etc, to avoid placing any strain on the refrigerant pipes. On 1.8 and 2.0 litre petrol models, undo the bolts and remove the cover under the compressor prior to disconnecting the wiring plug.
17 Disconnect the engine wiring loom from the engine compartment fusebox, the positive connection junction box, and the earth leads from the left-hand suspension turret, transmission mounting and left-hand chassis member **(see illustrations)**. Disconnect the engine management PCM wiring connectors – see Chapter 4.

3.17b ... then pull the locking catch (arrowed) to disconnect the engine loom from the fusebox

3.17d Disconnect the earth lead from the suspension turret ...

3.17e . . . and the left-hand chassis member (arrowed)

3.18 Power steering fluid reservoir bolt (arrowed)

3.19a Prise out the catch . . .

3.19b . . . and depress the release button to disconnect the fuel hose

3.19c Depress the release button and disconnect the purge hose

3.19d The fuel pipes (arrowed) are on the right-hand side of the engine compartment on diesel models

18 On models fitted with conventional power steering, undo the bolt securing the power steering reservoir and secure it to the front panel using cable ties **(see illustration)**. Remove the power steering pump as described in Chapter 10.

19 Disconnect the fuel hoses at the quick-release connections **(see illustrations)**. Plug and seal the connections.
20 Rotate the collars approximately 30° anti-clockwise and disconnect the heater coolant hoses at the engine compartment bulkhead

(see illustrations). Note that when refitting the hoses, rotate the collars to the 'locked' position, then push the hoses onto the pipe stubs.
21 Disconnect the hoses from the coolant expansion tank to the engine. Note their fitted positions and routing. Pull the coolant tank upwards from its mountings and move it to one side.
22 Disconnect the transmission gearchange/ selector cable(s) from the transmission as described in Chapter 7.
23 On manual transmission models, prise up the wire clip and disconnect the clutch slave cylinder hydraulic pipe from the top of the transmission housing **(see illustration)**.
24 On automatic transmission models, disconnect the fluid cooling hoses from the transmission as described in Chapter 7.
25 Note their fitted positions and disconnect any vacuum hoses between the engine and

3.20a Rotate the collar (arrowed) 30° anti-clockwise . . .

3.20b . . . and pull the hose from the connection

3. 23 Prise out the clip and disconnect the clutch slave cylinder hose

3. 25a Push in the red collar (arrowed) and pull the servo vacuum hose from the manifold

3.25b On diesel models, press the tab (arrowed) and release the vacuum pipe

brake servo/EGR/EVAP valves. On diesel models depress the release button and disconnect the vacuum pipe from the brake vacuum pump **(see illustrations)**. On iB5 transmissions, disconnect the breather hose from the top of the transmission

26 Undo the bolts and remove the engine rear lower torque rod/movement limiter.

27 Attach lifting chains/straps to the engine/transmission lifting eyes, and position an engine hoist to take the weight of the engine/transmission assembly.

28 Undo the nuts and bolts, then remove the right-hand engine mounting assembly.

29 Remove the central bolt from the left-hand transmission mounting. The engine and transmission should now be suspended from the hoist. Check to ensure nothing will obstruct the engine/transmission assembly as it is lowered.

30 Make a final check to ensure all wiring connectors, coolant hoses, and vacuum hoses that would prevent the engine from being removed have been disconnected.

31 Enlist the help of an assistant, and lower the engine/transmission downwards onto a trolley jack or similar. Once the assembly is fully lowered, disconnect the engine hoist and pull the assembly from under the vehicle.

Separation

32 Remove the starter motor as described in Chapter 5.

Manual transmission models

33 Remove the bolts securing the transmission to the engine. Note the fitted positions of any brackets.

34 With the aid of an assistant, draw the transmission off the engine. Once it is clear of the dowels, do not allow it to hang on the input shaft.

Automatic transmission models

35 Rotate the crankshaft, using a socket on the pulley nut, until one of the torque converter-to-driveplate retaining bolts/nuts becomes accessible through the opening on the rear facing side of the engine. Working through the opening, undo the bolt. Rotate the crankshaft as necessary and remove the remaining bolts in the same way. Note that new bolts will be required for refitting.

36 Remove the bolts securing the transmission to the engine.

37 With the aid of an assistant, draw the transmission squarely off the engine dowels making sure that the torque converter remains in position on the transmission. Use the access hole in the transmission housing to hold the converter in place.

Refitting

Manual transmission models

38 Make sure that the clutch is correctly centred and that the clutch release components are fitted to the bellhousing. Do not apply any grease to the transmission input

J46811

3.42 The distance between the straight-edge (1) and the torque converter spigot must be 15 mm

shaft, the guide sleeve, or the release bearing itself, as these components have a friction-reducing coating which does not require lubrication.

39 Manoeuvre the transmission squarely into position, and engage it with the engine dowels. Refit the bolts securing the transmission to the engine, and tighten them to the specified torque. Refit the starter motor.

Automatic transmission models

40 Before refitting the transmission, flush out the fluid cooler with fresh transmission fluid. To do this, attach a hose to the upper union, pour ATF through the hose and collect it in a container positioned beneath the return hose.

41 Clean the contact surfaces on the torque converter and driveplate, and the transmission and engine mating faces. Lightly lubricate the torque converter guide projection and the engine/transmission locating dowels with grease.

42 Place a straight-edge across the bellhousing, and measure the distance between the torque converter spigot and the straight-edge. Position the torque converter so the distance is 15 mm **(see illustration)**.

43 Manoeuvre the transmission squarely into position, and engage it with the engine dowels. Refit the bolts securing the transmission to the engine and tighten lightly first in a diagonal sequence, then again to the specified torque.

44 Attach the torque converter to the driveplate using new bolts. Rotate the crankshaft for access to the bolts as was done for removal, then rotate the torque converter by means of the access hole in the transmission housing. Fit and tighten all the bolts hand-tight first, then tighten again to the specified torque.

All models

45 The remainder of refitting is essentially a reversal of removal, noting the following points:

a) Tighten all fastenings to the specified torque and, where applicable, torque angle. Refer to the relevant Chapters of this manual for torque wrench settings not directly related to the engine.

b) Reconnect and if necessary, adjust the manual transmission selector cables as described in Chapter 7.

c) On automatic transmission models,

reconnect and adjust the selector cable as described in Chapter 7.

d) Refit the air cleaner assembly as described in Chapter 4.

e) Refit the auxiliary drivebelts, then refill the engine with coolant and oil as described in Chapter 1.

f) Refill the transmission with lubricant if necessary as described in Chapter 7.

g) Refer to Section 17 before starting the engine.

4 Engine overhaul – preliminary information

It is much easier to dismantle and work on the engine if it is mounted on a portable engine stand. These stands can often be hired from a tool hire shop. Before the engine is mounted on a stand, the flywheel/driveplate should be removed so that the stand bolts can be tightened into the end of the cylinder block/crankcase.

If a stand is not available, it is possible to dismantle the engine with it suitably-supported on a sturdy, workbench or on the floor. Be careful not to tip or drop the engine when working without a stand.

If you intend to obtain a reconditioned engine, all ancillaries must be removed first, to be transferred to the new engine (just as they will if you are doing a complete engine overhaul yourself). These components include the following:

a) Engine mountings and brackets.

b) Alternator including accessories mounting bracket (Chapter 5).

c) Starter motor (Chapter 5).

d) The ignition system and HT components including all sensors, ignition coils, spark plugs, as applicable (Chapters 1 and 5).

e) Exhaust manifold (Chapter 4).

f) Intake manifold with fuel injection components (Chapter 4).

g) All electrical switches, actuators and sensors, and the engine wiring harness (Chapters 4 and 5).

h) Coolant pump, thermostat, hoses, and distribution pipe (Chapter 3).

i) Clutch components – manual transmission models (Chapter 6).

j) Flywheel/driveplate.

k) Oil filter (Chapter 1).

l) Dipstick, tube and bracket.

Note: When removing the external components from the engine, pay close attention to details that may be helpful or important during refitting. Note the fitting positions of gaskets, seals, washers, bolts and other small items.

If you are obtaining a 'short' engine (cylinder block/crankcase, crankshaft, pistons and connecting rods all assembled), then the cylinder head, timing belt/chain (together with tensioner, tensioner and idler pulleys and covers) and auxiliary drivebelt tensioner will have to be removed also.

5.4 Compress the valve spring with a suitable valve spring compressor

5.6 Special pliers are available specifically designed to remove valve stem seals

5.8 Keep groups of components together in labelled bags or boxes

If a complete overhaul is planned, the engine can be dismantled in the order given below:

a) Intake and exhaust manifolds and turbocharger (where applicable).
b) Timing belt/chain, sprockets, tensioner, pulleys and covers.
c) Cylinder head.
d) Oil pump.
e) Flywheel/driveplate.
f) Sump.
g) Oil pick-up pipe.

Note: On all petrol engines covered by this manual, it is not possible to remove the intermediate/main bearing section or to remove the crankshaft or pistons. No separate parts appear to be available, and new/exchange units are supplied with crankshaft, pistons, connecting rods, etc, already fitted. Consult a Ford dealer or parts specialist.

5 Cylinder head – dismantling, cleaning, inspection and reassembly

Note: New and reconditioned cylinder heads are available from the manufacturer and from engine overhaul specialists. Specialist tools are required for the dismantling and inspection procedures, and new components may not be readily available. It may, therefore, be more practical and economical for the home mechanic to purchase a reconditioned head rather than dismantle, inspect and recondition the original head.

5.12 Remove the camshaft drive chain guide – DOHC engines

Dismantling

Petrol engines

1 Remove the cylinder head as described in Chapter 2A or 2B.
2 According to components still fitted, remove the thermostat housing (Chapter 3), the spark plugs (Chapter 1), and any other unions, pipes, sensors or brackets as necessary.
3 Tap each valve stem smartly, using a light hammer and drift, to free the spring and associated items.
4 Fit a deep-reach type valve spring compressor to each valve in turn, and compress each spring until the collets are exposed **(see illustration)**. Lift out the collets; a small screwdriver, a magnet or a pair of tweezers may be useful. Carefully release the spring compressor and remove it.
5 Remove the valve spring upper seat and the valve spring. Pull the valve out of its guide.
6 Pull off the valve stem oil seal with a pair of long-nosed pliers **(see illustration)**. It may be necessary to use a tool such as a pair of electrician's wire strippers, the 'legs' of which will engage under the seal, if the seal is tight.
7 Recover the valve spring lower seat. If there is much carbon build-up round the outside of the valve guide, this will have to be scraped off before the seat can be removed.
8 It is essential that each valve is stored together with its collets, spring and seats. The valves should also be kept in their correct sequence, unless they are so badly worn or burnt that they are to be renewed. If they are going to be kept and used again, place each valve assembly in a labelled polythene bag or similar container **(see illustration)**.
9 Continue removing all the remaining valves in the same way.

Diesel engines

10 Remove the cylinder head as described in Part C, D or E of this Chapter (as applicable).
11 If not already done, remove the intake and exhaust manifolds with reference to Chapter 4. Remove any remaining brackets or housings as required.
12 Remove the camshaft(s), tappets and rockers (as applicable) as described in Part C, D or E of this Chapter. On the DOHC engines, remove the camshaft drive chain guide from the cylinder head **(see illustration)**.
13 If not already done so, remove the glow plugs as described in Chapter 5.
14 On all models, using a valve spring compressor, compress each valve spring in turn until the split collets can be removed. Release the compressor, and lift off the spring retainer, spring and, where fitted, the spring seat. Using a pair of pliers, carefully extract the valve stem oil seal from the top of the guide. On 16-valve engines, the valve stem oil seal also forms the spring seat and is deeply recessed in the cylinder head. It is also a tight fit on the valve guide making it difficult to remove with pliers or a conventional valve stem oil seal removal tool. It can be easily removed, however, using a self-locking nut of suitable diameter screwed onto the end of a bolt and locked with a second nut. Push the nut down onto the top of the seal; the locking portion of the nut will grip the seal allowing it to be withdrawn from the top of the valve guide. Access to the valves is limited, and it may be necessary to make up an adapter out of metal tube – cut out a 'window' so that the valve collets can be removed **(see illustrations)**.
15 If, when the valve spring compressor is screwed down the spring retainer refuses to free and expose the split collets, gently tap the top of the tool, directly over the retainer, with a light hammer. This will free the retainer.
16 Withdraw the valve from the combustion chamber. Remove the valve stem oil seal from the top of the guide, then lift out the spring seat where fitted.

5.14a Compress the valve spring using a spring compressor . . .

5.14b . . . then extract the collets and release the spring compressor

5.14c Remove the spring retainer . . .

5.14d . . . followed by the valve spring . . .

5.14e . . . and the spring seat (not all models)

5.14f Remove the valve stem oil seal using a pair of pliers

5.14g A fabricated metal tube for access to the valve collets

17 It is essential that each valve is stored together with its collets, retainer, spring, and spring seat. The valves should also be kept in their correct sequence, unless they are so badly worn that they are to be renewed. If they are going to be kept and used again, place each valve assembly in a labeled polythene bag or similar small container. Note that No 1 valve is nearest to the transmission (flywheel) end on the 1.6 and 2.0 litre engines.

Cleaning

18 Thoroughly clean all traces of old gasket material and sealing compound from the cylinder head upper and lower mating surfaces. Use a suitable liquid gasket dissolving agent together with a soft putty knife. Do not use a metal scraper, or the faces will be damaged.
19 Remove the carbon from the combustion chambers and ports, then clean all traces of oil and other deposits from the cylinder head, paying particular attention to the bearing journals, tappet bores, valve guides and oilways.
20 Wash the head thoroughly with paraffin or a suitable solvent. Take plenty of time and do a thorough job. Be sure to clean all oil holes and galleries very thoroughly, dry the head completely and coat all machined surfaces with light oil.
21 Scrape off any heavy carbon deposits that may have formed on the valves, then use a power-operated wire brush to remove deposits from the valve heads and stems.

Inspection

Note: *Be sure to perform all the following inspection procedures before concluding that the services of an engineering works are required. Make a list of all items that require attention.*

Cylinder head

22 Inspect the head very carefully for cracks, evidence of coolant leakage, and other damage. If cracks are found, a new cylinder head should be obtained.
23 Use a straight-edge and feeler blade to check that the cylinder head gasket surface is not distorted **(see illustration)**. If it is, it may be possible to resurface it; consult your dealer or engine overhaul specialist.

5.14h Secure a self-locking nut of suitable diameter to a long bolt, then use the tool to remove the valve stem oil seal

5.23 Measure the distortion of the cylinder head surface using a straight-edge and feeler gauges

5.30 Measure the valve stem diameter with a micrometer

24 Examine the valve seats in each of the combustion chambers. If they are severely pitted, cracked or burned, then they will need to be renewed or recut by an engine overhaul specialist. If they are only slightly pitted, this can be removed by grinding-in the valve heads and seats with fine valve-grinding compound, as described below.

25 If the valve guides appear worn, indicated by a side-to-side motion of the valve, new guides must be fitted. Measure the diameter of the existing valve stems and the bore of the guides, renew the valves or guides as necessary. The renewal of valve guides should be carried out by an engine overhaul specialist.

26 If the valve seats are to be recut, this must be done *only after* the guides have been renewed.

27 The threaded holes in the cylinder head must be clean to ensure accurate torque readings when tightening fixings during reassembly. Carefully run the correct size tap (which can be determined from the size of the relevant bolt which fits in the hole) into each of the holes to remove rust, corrosion, thread sealant or other contamination, and to restore damaged threads. If possible, use compressed air to clear the holes of debris produced by this operation. Do not forget to clean the threads of all bolts and nuts as well.

28 Any threads which cannot be restored in this way can often be reclaimed by the use of thread inserts. If any threaded holes are damaged, consult your dealer or engine overhaul specialist and have them install any thread inserts where necessary.

6.3 Unscrew the chain tensioner from the housing

5.41 Push the valve stem seal into place using a socket or tube

Valves

29 Examine the head of each valve for pitting, burning, cracks and general wear, and check the valve stem for scoring and wear ridges. Rotate the valve, and check for any obvious indication that it is bent. Look for pits and excessive wear on the tip of each valve stem. Renew any valve that shows any such signs of wear or damage.

30 If the valve appears satisfactory at this stage, measure the valve stem diameter at several points, using a micrometer **(see illustration)**. Any significant difference in the readings obtained indicates wear of the valve stem. Should any of these conditions be apparent, the valve(s) must be renewed.

31 If the valves are in satisfactory condition, they should be ground (lapped) into their respective seats, to ensure a smooth gas-tight seal. If the seat is only lightly pitted, or if it has been recut, fine grinding compound *only* should be used to produce the required finish. Coarse valve-grinding compound should *not* be used unless a seat is badly burned or deeply pitted; if this is the case, the cylinder head and valves should be inspected by an expert, to decide whether seat recutting, or even the renewal of the valve or seat insert, is required.

32 Valve grinding is carried out as follows. Place the cylinder head upside-down on a bench, with a block of wood at each end to give clearance for the valve stems.

33 Smear a trace of (the appropriate grade) valve-grinding compound on the seat face, and press a suction grinding tool onto the valve head. With a semi-rotary action, grind the valve head to its seat, lifting the valve occasionally to redistribute the grinding compound. A light spring placed under the valve head will greatly ease this operation.

34 If coarse grinding compound is being used, work only until a dull, matt even surface is produced on both the valve seat and the valve, then wipe off the used compound, and repeat the process with fine compound. When a smooth unbroken ring of light grey matt finish is produced on both the valve and seat, the grinding operation is complete. *Do not* grind in the valves any further than absolutely necessary, or the seat will be prematurely sunk into the cylinder head.

35 When all the valves have been ground-in, carefully wash off *all* traces of grinding compound, using paraffin or a suitable solvent, before reassembly of the cylinder head.

Valve components

36 Examine the valve springs for signs of damage and discoloration, and also measure their free length by comparing each of the existing springs with a new component.

37 Stand each spring on a flat surface, and check it for squareness. If any of the springs are damaged, distorted, or have lost their tension, obtain a complete set of new springs. It is normal to fit new springs as a matter of course if a major overhaul is being carried out.

38 Renew the valve stem oil seals regardless of their apparent condition.

Reassembly

39 Oil the stem of one valve and insert it into its guide then fit the spring lower seat.

40 The new valve stem oil seals may be supplied with a plastic fitting sleeve to protect the seal when it is fitted over the valve. If not, wrap a thin piece of polythene around the valve stem allowing it to extend about 10 mm above the end of the valve stem.

41 With the fitting sleeve, or polythene in place around the valve, fit the valve stem oil seal, pushing it onto the valve guide as far as it will go with a suitable socket or piece of tube **(see illustration)**. Once the seal is seated, remove the protective sleeve or polythene.

42 Fit the valve spring and upper seat. Compress the spring and fit the two collets in the recesses in the valve stem. Carefully release the compressor.

43 Cover the valve stem with a cloth and tap it smartly with a light hammer to verify that the collets are properly seated.

44 Repeat these procedures on all the other valves.

45 Refit the remainder of the disturbed components then refit the cylinder head.

---

6   Fuel injection pump drive chain (1.8 litre diesel engines) – removal, inspection and refitting

Removal

1 With the engine removed from the vehicle, proceed as follows.

2 Remove the oil pump as described in Chapter 2D.

3 At the rear of the engine block, locate the drive chain hydraulic tensioner (below and behind the coolant pump). Using the hex in the top of the tensioner body, unscrew and extract the tensioner from the block **(see illustration)**. Be prepared for a small amount of oil spillage as this is done.

4 Unscrew the two bolts securing the chain guides, then carefully slide the two sprockets simultaneously from their locations, and

6.5 Examine the chain guides for wear

6.8 Two chains ('Gemini') which run next to each other, offset by half a link

6.9 Tighten the chain guide retaining bolts

remove the complete chain, guide and sprocket assembly from the engine.

Inspection

5 Examine the guides for scoring or wear ridges, and for chipping or wear of the sprocket teeth **(see illustration)**.

6 Check the chains for wear, which will be evident in the form of excess play between the links. If the chains can be lifted at either 'end' of their run so that the sprocket teeth are visible, they have stretched excessively.

7 Check the chain tensioner for signs of wear, and renew if required.

8 At the time of writing, only the chain tensioner is available separately; if the chains or sprockets are worn, the complete assembly of sprockets, guides and chains must be purchased **(see illustration)**. If possible, compare the old items with new components, or seek the advice of an engineering works, before concluding that a renewal is necessary.

Refitting

9 Refitting is a reversal of removal, noting the following points:
  a) Tighten the chain guide retaining bolts securely to the specified torque **(see illustration)**.
  b) Especially if a new chain and sprocket assembly has been fitted, lubricate it thoroughly with fresh engine oil.
  c) Refit the chain tensioner, and tighten it to the specified torque.
  d) Refit the oil pump as described in Chapter 2D.

7 Piston/connecting rod assembly – removal

Note: *On all petrol engines covered by this manual it is not possible to remove the intermediate/main bearing section or to remove the crankshaft or pistons. No separate parts appear to be available, and new/exchange units are supplied with crankshaft, pistons, connecting rods, etc, already fitted. Consult a Ford dealer or parts specialist.*

1 Remove the cylinder head, sump and oil pump as described in Part C, D or E.

2 If there is a pronounced wear ridge at the top of any bore, it may be necessary to remove it with a scraper or ridge reamer, to avoid piston damage during removal. Such a ridge indicates excessive wear of the cylinder bore.

3 Using quick-drying paint, mark each connecting rod and big-end bearing cap with its respective cylinder number on the flat machined surface provided; if the engine has been dismantled before, note carefully any identifying marks made previously **(see illustration)**.

4 Turn the crankshaft to bring pistons 1 and 4 to BDC (bottom dead centre).

5 Unscrew the nuts or bolts, as applicable from No 1 piston big-end bearing cap. Take off the cap, and recover the bottom half bearing shell **(see illustration)**. If the bearing shells are to be re-used, tape the cap and the shell together.

6 Where applicable, to prevent the possibility of damage to the crankshaft bearing journals, tape over the connecting rod stud threads **(see illustration)**.

7 Using a hammer handle, push the piston up through the bore, and remove it from the top of the cylinder block. Recover the bearing shell, and tape it to the connecting rod for safe-keeping.

8 Loosely refit the big-end cap to the connecting rod, and secure with the nuts/bolts – this will help to keep the components in their correct order.

9 Remove No 4 piston assembly in the same way.

10 Turn the crankshaft through 180° to bring pistons 2 and 3 to BDC (bottom dead centre), and remove them in the same way.

8 Crankshaft – removal

Note: *On all petrol engines covered by this manual it is not possible to remove the intermediate/main bearing section or to remove the crankshaft or pistons. No separate parts appear to be available, and new/exchange units are supplied with crankshaft, pistons, connecting rods, etc, already fitted. Consult a Ford dealer or parts specialist.*

1 Remove the crankshaft sprocket and the oil pump as described in Part C, D or E of this Chapter (as applicable).

2 Remove the pistons and connecting rods,

7.3 Connecting rod and big-end bearing cap identification marks (No 3 shown)

7.5 Remove the big-end bearing shell and cap

7.6 To protect the crankshaft journals tape over the connecting rod stud threads

8.5 Prise up the two caps to expose the main bearing bolts at the flywheel end

8.6 Remove the crankshaft bearing cap housing

8.9 Main bearing caps are marked with cylinder number and arrowhead

as described in Section 7. If no work is to be done on the pistons and connecting rods, there is no need to remove the cylinder head, or to push the pistons out of the cylinder bores. The pistons should just be pushed far enough up the bores so that they are positioned clear of the crankshaft journals.

3 Check the crankshaft endfloat as described in Section 11, then proceed as follows.

1.6 litre engines

4 Working around the inner periphery of the crankcase, unscrew the small bolts securing the crankshaft bearing cap housing to the base of the cylinder block. Note the correct fitted depth of the left-hand crankshaft oil seal in the cylinder block/bearing cap housing.

5 Working in the **reverse** of the tightening sequence, evenly and progressively slacken the ten large bearing cap housing retaining bolts by a turn at a time **(see illustration 15.11)**. Once

all the bolts are loose, remove them from the housing. **Note:** *Prise up the two caps at the flywheel end of the housing to expose the two end main bearing bolts* **(see illustration)**.

6 With all the retaining bolts removed, tap around the outer periphery of the bearing cap housing using a soft-faced mallet to break the seal between the housing and cylinder block. Once the seal is released and the housing is clear of the locating dowels, lift it up and off the crankshaft and cylinder block **(see illustration)**. Recover the lower main bearing shells, and tape them to their respective locations in the housing. If the two locating dowels are a loose fit, remove them and store them with the housing for safe-keeping.

7 Lift out the crankshaft, and collect the left-hand oil seal.

8 Recover the upper main bearing shells, and store them along with the relevant lower bearing shell. Also recover the two

thrustwashers (one fitted either side of No 2 main bearing) from the cylinder block.

1.8 litre engines

9 Check the main bearing caps, to see if they are marked to indicate their locations. They should be numbered consecutively from the timing belt end of the engine – if not, mark them with number-stamping dies or a centre-punch. The caps will also have an embossed arrow pointing to the timing belt end of the engine **(see illustration)**. Noting, where applicable, the different fasteners (for the oil baffle nuts) used on caps 2 and 4, slacken the cap bolts a quarter-turn at a time each, starting with the left- and right-hand end caps and working toward the centre, until they can be removed by hand.

10 Gently tap the caps with a soft-faced hammer, then separate them from the cylinder block/crankcase. If necessary, use the bolts as levers to remove the caps. Try not to drop the bearing shells if they come out with the caps.

11 Carefully lift the crankshaft out of the engine. It may be a good idea to have an assistant available, since the crankshaft is quite heavy. With the bearing shells in place in the cylinder block/crankcase and main bearing caps, return the caps to their respective locations on the block, or refit the lower crankcase, and tighten the bolts finger-tight. Leaving the old shells in place until reassembly will help prevent the bearing recesses from being accidentally nicked or gouged. New shells should be used on reassembly.

2.0 litre engines

12 Slacken and remove the retaining bolts, and remove the oil seal carrier from the timing belt end of the cylinder block, along with its gasket (where fitted) **(see illustration)**.

13 Remove the oil pump drive chain, and slide the drive sprocket and spacer (where fitted) off the end of the crankshaft. Remove the Woodruff key, and store it with the sprocket for safe-keeping **(see illustrations)**.

14 The main bearing caps should be numbered 1 to 5, starting from the transmission (flywheel) end of the engine **(see illustration)**. If not, mark them accordingly using quick-drying paint. Also note the correct fitted depth of the crankshaft oil seal in the bearing cap.

8.12 remove the oil seal housing from the right-hand end of the cylinder block

8.13a Remove the oil pump drive chain . . .

8.13b . . . then slide off the drive sprocket . . .

8.13c . . . and remove the Woodruff key from the crankshaft

15 Slacken and remove the main bearing cap retaining bolts/nuts, and lift off each bearing cap. Recover the lower bearing shells, and tape them to their respective caps for safe-keeping. Also recover the lower thrust -washer halves from the side of No 2 main bearing cap **(see illustration)**. Remove the rubber sealing strips from the sides of No 1 main bearing cap, and discard them.

16 Lift out the crankshaft, and discard the oil seal **(see illustration)**.

17 Recover the upper bearing shells from the cylinder block, and tape them to their respective caps for safe-keeping **(see illustration)**. Remove the upper thrustwasher halves from the side of No 2 main bearing, and store them with the lower halves.

8.14 Main bearing cap Identification markings (arrowed)

8.15 Note the thrustwasher (arrowed) fitted to the No 2 main bearing cap

8.16 Lift out the crankshaft

8.17 Remove the upper main bearing shells

9 Cylinder block/crankcase – cleaning and inspection

Cleaning

1 Remove all external components and electrical switches/sensors from the block. For complete cleaning, the core plugs should ideally be removed **(see illustrations)**. Drill a small hole in the plugs, then insert a self-tapping screw into the hole. Pull out the plugs by pulling on the screw with a pair of grips, or by using a slide hammer.

2 Where applicable, undo the retaining bolts and remove the piston oil jet spray tubes from inside the cylinder block **(see illustration)**.

3 Scrape all traces of gasket from the cylinder block/crankcase, and from the main bearing ladder (where fitted), taking care not to damage the gasket/sealing surfaces.

4 Remove all oil gallery plugs (where fitted). The plugs are usually very tight – they may have to be drilled out, and the holes retapped. Use new plugs when reassembling.

5 If any of the castings are extremely dirty, all should be steam-cleaned.

6 After the castings are returned, clean all oil holes and oil galleries one more time. Flush all internal passages with warm water until the water runs clear. Dry thoroughly, and apply a light film of oil to all mating surfaces, to prevent rusting. On cast-iron block engines, also oil the cylinder bores. If you have access to compressed air, use it to speed up the drying process, and to blow out all the oil holes and galleries.

 Warning: Wear eye protection when using compressed air.

7 If the castings are not very dirty, you can do an adequate cleaning job with hot (as hot as you can stand), soapy water and a stiff brush. Take plenty of time, and do a thorough job. Regardless of the cleaning method used, be sure to clean all oil holes and galleries very thoroughly, and to dry all components well. On cast-iron block engines, protect the cylinder bores as described above, to prevent rusting.

8 All threaded holes must be clean, to ensure accurate torque readings during reassembly. To clean the threads, run the correct-size tap into each of the holes to remove rust, corrosion, thread sealant or sludge, and to restore damaged threads. If possible, use compressed air to clear the holes of debris produced by this operation.

9 Apply suitable sealant to the new oil gallery plugs, and insert them into the holes in the

9.1a Cylinder block core plugs (arrowed)

9.1b Remove the air conditioning compressor bracket

9.1c Remove the cylinder block ventilation/ oil separator

9.2 Piston cooling jets may be fitted to the base of each cylinder bore

10.2 Remove the piston rings with the aid of feeler gauges

block. Tighten them securely. Apply suitable sealant to the new core plugs, and insert them into the holes in the block. Tap them into place with a close-fitting tube or socket.

10 Where applicable, clean the threads of the piston oil jet retaining bolt, and apply a drop of thread-locking compound to the bolt threads. Refit the piston oil jet spray tube to the cylinder block, and tighten its retaining bolt to the specified torque setting.

11 If the engine is not going to be reassembled right away, cover it with a large plastic bag to keep it clean; protect all mating surfaces and the cylinder bores as described above, to prevent rusting.

Inspection

12 Visually check the castings for cracks and corrosion. Look for stripped threads in the threaded holes. If there has been any history of internal water leakage, it may be worthwhile having an engine overhaul specialist check the cylinder block/crankcase with special equipment. If defects are found, have them repaired if possible, or renew the assembly.

13 Check each cylinder bore for scuffing and scoring. Check for signs of a wear ridge at the top of the cylinder, indicating that the bore is excessively worn.

14 If wear is suspected, have the cylinder bores measured by an automotive engineering workshop, who will be able to carry out the reboring, and supply suitable pistons/rings, etc, as applicable.

15 At the time of writing, it was not clear whether oversize pistons were available. Consult your Ford dealer for the latest

10.15a Prise out the circlip . . .

information on piston availability. If oversize pistons are available, then it may be possible to have the cylinder bores rebored and oversize pistons fitted. If oversize pistons are not available, and the bores are worn, renewal of the block is the only option.

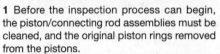

10 Piston/connecting rod assembly – inspection

1 Before the inspection process can begin, the piston/connecting rod assemblies must be cleaned, and the original piston rings removed from the pistons.

2 Carefully expand the old rings over the top of the pistons. The use of two or three old feeler blades will be helpful in preventing the rings dropping into empty grooves **(see illustration)**. Be careful not to scratch the piston with the ends of the ring. The rings are brittle, and will snap if they are spread too far. They are also very sharp – protect your hands and fingers. Note that the third ring incorporates an expander. Always remove the rings from the top of the piston.

3 Scrape away all traces of carbon from the top of the piston. A hand-held wire brush (or a piece of fine emery cloth) can be used, once the majority of the deposits have been scraped away.

4 Remove the carbon from the ring grooves in the piston, using an old ring. Break the ring in half to do this. Be careful to remove only the carbon deposits – do not remove any metal, and do not nick or scratch the sides of the ring grooves.

5 Once the deposits have been removed, clean the piston/connecting rod assembly with paraffin or a suitable solvent, and dry thoroughly. Make sure that the oil return holes in the ring grooves are clear.

6 If the pistons and cylinder bores are not damaged or worn excessively, and if the cylinder block does not need to be rebored, the original pistons can be refitted. Normal piston wear shows up as even vertical wear on the piston thrust surfaces, and slight looseness of the top ring in its groove. New piston rings should always be used when the engine is reassembled.

10.15b . . . and withdraw the gudgeon pin

7 Carefully inspect each piston for cracks around the skirt, around the gudgeon pin holes, and at the piston ring 'lands' (between the ring grooves).

8 Look for scoring and scuffing on the piston skirt, holes in the piston crown, and burned areas at the edge of the crown. If the skirt is scored or scuffed, the engine may have been suffering from overheating, and/or abnormal combustion which caused excessively high operating temperatures. The cooling and lubrication systems should be checked thoroughly. Scorch marks on the sides of the pistons show that blow-by has occurred. A hole in the piston crown, or burned areas at the edge of the piston crown, indicates that abnormal combustion (pre-ignition, knocking, or detonation) has been occurring. If any of the above problems exist, the causes must be investigated and corrected, or the damage will occur again.

9 Corrosion of the piston, in the form of pitting, indicates that coolant has been leaking into the combustion chamber and/or the crankcase. Again, the cause must be corrected, or the problem may persist in the rebuilt engine.

10 On aluminium-block engines with wet liners, it is not possible to renew the pistons separately; pistons are only supplied with piston rings and a liner, as a part of a matched assembly. On iron-block engines, pistons can be purchased from a Ford dealer.

11 Examine each connecting rod carefully for signs of damage, such as cracks around the big-end and small-end bearings. Check that the rod is not bent or distorted. Damage is highly unlikely, unless the engine has been seized or badly overheated. Detailed checking of the connecting rod assembly can only be carried out by a Ford dealer or engine repair specialist with the necessary equipment.

12 The big-end cap bolts/nuts must be renewed as a complete set prior to refitting. This should be done after the big-end bearing running clearance check has been carried out.

13 The gudgeon pins are of the floating type, secured in position by two circlips. The pistons and connecting rods can be separated as described in the following paragraphs.

14 Before separating the piston and connecting rod, check the position of the valve recesses or markings on the piston crown in relation to the connecting rod big-end bearing shell cut-outs and make a note of the orientation.

15 Using a small flat-bladed screwdriver, prise out the circlips, and push out the gudgeon pin **(see illustrations)**. Hand pressure should be sufficient to remove the pin. Identify the piston and rod to ensure correct reassembly. Discard the circlips – new ones *must* be used on refitting.

16 Examine the gudgeon pin and connecting rod small-end bearing for signs of wear or damage. Wear can be cured by renewing both the pin and bush. Bush renewal, however, is a specialist job – press facilities are required, and the new bush must be reamed accurately.

17 The connecting rods themselves should not be in need of renewal, unless seizure or some other major mechanical failure has occurred. Check the alignment of the connecting rods visually, and if the rods are not straight, take them to an engine overhaul specialist for a more detailed check.

18 Examine all components, and obtain any new parts from your Ford dealer. If new pistons are purchased, they will be supplied complete with gudgeon pins and circlips. Circlips can also be purchased individually.

19 Position the piston in relation to the connecting rod big-end bearing shell cut-outs as noted during separation.

20 Apply a smear of clean engine oil to the gudgeon pin and slide it into the piston and through the connecting rod small-end. Check that the piston pivots freely on the rod, then secure the gudgeon pin in position with two new circlips. Ensure that each circlip is correctly located in its groove in the piston.

11 Crankshaft – inspection

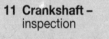

Checking endfloat

1 If the crankshaft endfloat is to be checked, this must be done when the crankshaft is installed in the cylinder block/crankcase, but is free to move.

2 Check the endfloat using a dial gauge in contact with the end of the crankshaft. Push the crankshaft fully one way, and then zero the gauge. Push the crankshaft fully the other way, and check the endfloat. The result can be compared with the specified amount, and will give an indication as to whether new thrustwashers are required **(see illustration)**.

3 If a dial gauge is not available, feeler gauges can be used. First push the crankshaft fully towards the flywheel end of the engine, then use feeler gauges to measure the gap between the web and the thrustwasher **(see illustration)**.

Inspection

4 Clean the crankshaft using paraffin or a suitable solvent, and dry it, preferably with compressed air if available. Be sure to clean the oil holes with a pipe cleaner or similar probe, to ensure that they are not obstructed.

Warning: Wear eye protection when using compressed air.

5 Check the main and big-end bearing journals for uneven wear, scoring, pitting and cracking.

6 Big-end bearing wear is accompanied by distinct metallic knocking when the engine is running (particularly noticeable when the engine is pulling from low speed) and by some loss of oil pressure.

11.2 Check the crankshaft endfloat using a dial gauge . . .

7 Main bearing wear is accompanied by severe engine vibration and rumble – getting progressively worse as engine speed increases – and again by loss of oil pressure.

8 Check the bearing journal for roughness by running a finger lightly over the bearing surface. Any roughness (which will be accompanied by obvious bearing wear) indicates that the crankshaft requires regrinding (where possible) or renewal.

9 If the crankshaft has been reground, check for burrs around the crankshaft oil holes (the holes are usually chamfered, so burrs should not be a problem unless regrinding has been carried out carelessly). Remove any burrs with a fine file or scraper, and thoroughly clean the oil holes as described previously.

10 Have the crankshaft inspected and measured by an automotive engineering workshop, who will be able to carry out any necessary repairs, and supply relevant parts.

11 Check the oil seal contact surfaces at each end of the crankshaft for wear and damage. If the seal has worn a deep groove in the surface of the crankshaft, consult an engine overhaul specialist; repair may be possible, but otherwise a new crankshaft will be required.

12 Ford produce a set of undersize bearing shells for both the main and big-end bearings on most engines. Where the crankshaft journals have not already been reground, it may be possible to have the crankshaft reconditioned, and to fit undersize shells. If no undersize shells are available and the crankshaft has worn beyond the specified limits, the crankshaft will have to be renewed. Consult your Ford dealer or engine specialist for further information on parts availability.

12 Main and big-end bearings – inspection

1 Even though the main and big-end bearings should be renewed during the engine overhaul, the old bearings should be retained for close examination, as they may reveal valuable information about the condition of the engine. The bearing shells are graded by thickness, the grade of each shell being indicated by the colour code marked on it.

11.3 . . . or with feeler gauges

2 Bearing failure can occur due to lack of lubrication, the presence of dirt or other foreign particles, overloading the engine, or corrosion **(see illustration)**. Regardless of the cause of bearing failure, the cause must be corrected (where applicable) before the engine is reassembled, to prevent it from happening again.

3 When examining the bearing shells, remove them from the cylinder block/crankcase, the main bearing ladder/caps (as appropriate), the connecting rods and the connecting rod big-end bearing caps. Lay them out on a clean surface in the same general position as their location in the engine. This will enable you to match any bearing problems with the corresponding crankshaft journal. *Do not* touch any shell's bearing surface with your fingers while checking it, or the delicate surface may be scratched.

4 Dirt and other foreign matter gets into the engine in a variety of ways. It may be left in the engine during assembly, or it may pass through filters or the crankcase ventilation system. It may get into the oil, and from there into the bearings. Metal chips from machining operations and normal engine wear are often present. Abrasives are sometimes left

FATIGUE FAILURE   IMPROPER SEATING

CRATERS OR POCKETS   BRIGHT (POLISHED) SECTIONS

SCRATCHED BY DIRT   LACK OF OIL

DIRT EMBEDDED INTO BEARING MATERIAL   OVERLAY WIPED OUT

EXCESSIVE WEAR   TAPERED JOURNAL

OVERLAY WIPED OUT   RADIUS RIDE

H 28395

12.2 Typical bearing failures

14.5 Measure the piston ring end gap with feeler gauges

in engine components after reconditioning, especially when parts are not thoroughly cleaned using the proper cleaning methods. Whatever the source, these foreign objects often end up embedded in the soft bearing material, and are easily recognised. Large particles will not embed in the bearing, and will score or gouge the bearing and journal. The best prevention for this cause of bearing failure is to clean all parts thoroughly, and keep everything spotlessly-clean during engine assembly. Frequent and regular engine oil and filter changes are also recommended.

5 Lack of lubrication (or lubrication breakdown) has a number of interrelated causes. Excessive heat (which thins the oil), overloading (which squeezes the oil from the bearing face) and oil leakage (from excessive bearing clearances, worn oil pump or high engine speeds) all contribute to lubrication breakdown. Blocked oil passages, which usually are the result of misaligned oil holes in a bearing shell, will also oil-starve a bearing, and destroy it. When lack of lubrication is the cause of bearing failure, the bearing material is wiped or extruded from the steel backing of the bearing. Temperatures may increase to the point where the steel backing turns blue from overheating.

14.10 Piston ring details (typical)

1 Top compression ring
2 2nd compression ring
3 Oil scraper ring assembly

6 Driving habits can have a definite effect on bearing life. Full-throttle, low-speed operation (labouring the engine) puts very high loads on bearings, tending to squeeze out the oil film. These loads cause the bearings to flex, which produces fine cracks in the bearing face (fatigue failure). Eventually, the bearing material will loosen in pieces, and tear away from the steel backing.

7 Short-distance driving leads to corrosion of bearings, because insufficient engine heat is produced to drive off the condensed water and corrosive gases. These products collect in the engine oil, forming acid and sludge. As the oil is carried to the engine bearings, the acid attacks and corrodes the bearing material.

8 Incorrect bearing installation during engine assembly will lead to bearing failure as well. Tight-fitting bearings leave insufficient bearing running clearance, and will result in oil starvation. Dirt or foreign particles trapped behind a bearing shell result in high spots on the bearing, which lead to failure.

9 *Do not* touch any shell's bearing surface with your fingers during reassembly; there is a risk of scratching the delicate surface, or of depositing particles of dirt on it.

10 As mentioned at the beginning of this Section, the bearing shells should be renewed as a matter of course during engine overhaul; to do otherwise is false economy.

13 Engine overhaul – reassembly sequence

1 Before reassembly begins, ensure that all new parts have been obtained and that all necessary tools are available. Read through the entire procedure to familiarise yourself with the work involved, and to ensure that all items necessary for reassembly of the engine are at hand. In addition to all normal tools and materials, thread-locking compound will be needed in most areas during engine reassembly. A tube of Ford liquid gasket solution together with a short-haired application roller will also be needed to assemble the main engine sections.

2 In order to save time and avoid problems, engine reassembly can be carried out in the following order:

a) Crankshaft.
b) Piston/connecting rod assemblies.
c) Oil pump.
d) Sump.
e) Flywheel.
f) Cylinder head.
g) Timing belt/chain tensioner and sprockets, and timing belt/chain.
h) Engine external components.

3 At this stage, all engine components should be absolutely clean and dry, with all faults repaired. The components should be laid out (or in individual containers) on a completely clean work surface.

14 Piston rings – refitting

1 Before fitting new piston rings, the ring end gaps must be checked as follows.

2 Lay out the piston/connecting rod assemblies and the new piston ring sets, so that the ring sets will be matched with the same piston and cylinder during the end gap measurement and subsequent engine reassembly.

3 Insert the top ring into the first cylinder, and push it down the bore using the top of the piston. This will ensure that the ring remains square with the cylinder walls. Position the ring near the bottom of the cylinder bore, at the lower limit of ring travel. Note that the top and second compression rings are different. The second ring is easily identified by the step on its lower surface, and by the fact that its outer face is tapered.

4 Measure the end gap using feeler gauges.

5 Repeat the procedure with the ring at the top of the cylinder bore, at the upper limit of its travel, and compare the measurements with the figures given in the Specifications **(see illustration)**. Where no figures are given, seek the advice of a Ford dealer or engine reconditioning specialist.

6 If the gap is too small (unlikely if genuine Ford parts are used), it must be enlarged, or the ring ends may contact each other during engine operation, causing serious damage. Ideally, new piston rings providing the correct end gap should be fitted. As a last resort, the end gap can be increased by filing the ring ends very carefully with a fine file. Mount the file in a vice equipped with soft jaws, slip the ring over the file with the ends contacting the file face, and slowly move the ring to remove material from the ends. Take care, as piston rings are sharp, and are easily broken.

7 With new piston rings, it is unlikely that the end gap will be too large. If the gaps are too large, check that you have the correct rings for your engine and for the particular cylinder bore size.

8 Repeat the checking procedure for each ring in the first cylinder, and then for the rings in the remaining cylinders. Remember to keep rings, pistons and cylinders matched up.

9 Once the ring end gaps have been checked and if necessary corrected, the rings can be fitted to the pistons.

10 Fit the piston rings using the same technique as for removal. Fit the bottom (oil control) ring first, and work up. When fitting the oil control ring, first insert the expander (where fitted), then fit the ring with its gap positioned 180° from the expander gap. Ensure that the second compression ring is fitted the correct way up, with its identification mark (either a dot of paint or the word TOP stamped on the ring surface) at the top, and the stepped surface at the bottom **(see illustration)**. Arrange the gaps of the top and

15.5 Main bearing shell fitment – 1.6 litre engine

1	Bearing shell	3	Ford tool No 303-245
2	Main bearing ladder	4	Aligning pins

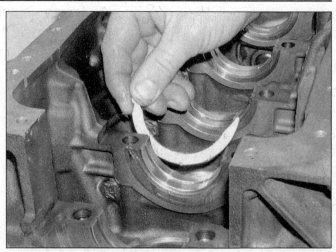

15.7 Place the thrustwashers each side of the No 2 bearing upper location

second compression rings 120° either side of the oil control ring gap. **Note:** *Always follow any instructions supplied with the new piston ring sets – different manufacturers may specify different procedures. Do not mix up the top and second compression rings, as they have different cross-sections.*

15 Crankshaft – refitting

New main bearing shells

1 To ensure that the main bearing running clearance is correct, the bearing shells are supplied in various thicknesses or grades. The grades are indicated by a colour-coding marked on the edge of each shell. The grade of the new bearing shells required (either standard size or undersize) is selected using the reference marks on the cylinder block and on the crankshaft. The cylinder block marks identify the diameter of the bearing bores in the block, and the crankshaft marks identify the diameter of the crankshaft journals.

2 Note that on the engines described in this Manual, the upper shells are all of the same size, and the running clearance is controlled by fitting a lower bearing shell of the required thickness.

3 Numerous grades of standard and oversize bearing shells are available, depending on the engine type, year of manufacture, and country of export. Using the cylinder block and crankshaft reference marks together with the crankshaft journal diameter, a Ford dealer or engine overhaul specialist will be able to supply the correct bearing shells to give the required bearing running clearance for each journal.

Final crankshaft refitting

4 Crankshaft refitting is the first major step

in engine reassembly. It is assumed at this point that the cylinder block/crankcase and crankshaft have been cleaned, inspected and repaired or reconditioned as necessary. Position the engine upside-down.

1.6 litre engines

5 Place the bearing shells in their locations. If new shells are being fitted, ensure that all traces of protective grease are cleaned off using paraffin. Wipe dry the shells with a lint-free cloth. The upper bearing shells all have a grooved surface, whereas the lower shells have a plain surface. It's essential that the lower bearing shells are centrally located in the bearing cap housing/ladder. To ensure this use a Ford tool (No 303-245) positioned over the housing/ladder, and insert the bearing shells through the slots in the tool **(see illustration)**.

6 Liberally lubricate each bearing shell in the cylinder block with clean engine oil then lower the crankshaft into position.

7 Insert the thrustwashers to either side of No 2 main bearing upper location and push them around the bearing journal until their edges are horizontal **(see illustration)**. Ensure that the oilway grooves on each thrustwasher face outwards (away from the bearing journal).

8 Thoroughly degrease the mating surfaces of

15.8 Apply a thin bead of RTV sealant to the bearing cap housing mating surface

the cylinder block and the crankshaft bearing cap housing. Apply a thin bead of silicone sealant (Ford part No WSE-M4G323-A4) to the bearing cap housing mating surface **(see illustration)**.

9 Lubricate the lower bearing shells with clean engine oil, then refit the bearing cap housing, ensuring that the shells are not displaced, and that the locating dowels engage correctly.

10 Install the ten large diameter, and sixteen smaller diameter crankshaft bearing cap housing retaining bolts, and screw them in until they are just making contact with the housing.

11 Working in sequence, tighten the bolts to the torque settings given in the Specifications **(see illustration)**.

12 With the bearing cap housing in place, check that the crankshaft rotates freely.

13 Refit the piston/connecting rod assemblies to the crankshaft as described in Section 16.

14 Refit the oil pump and sump.

15 Fit a new crankshaft left-hand oil seal, then refit the flywheel.

16 Where removed, refit the cylinder head, crankshaft sprocket and timing belt.

1.8 litre engines

17 If they're still in place, remove the old bearing shells from the block and the main

15.11 Main bearing cap housing/ladder retaining bolt tightening sequence

15.18a Ensure the tab (A) and oil hole (B) are correctly aligned when refitting the shells

15.18b Note the thrustwashers fitted to the No 3 main bearing shell

15.18c Make sure the tab on the cap bearing shell engages correctly

15.19 Oil the bearing shells before fitting the crankshaft

15.21 Lower the crankshaft gently into place

15.22 Tighten the main bearing cap bolts

bearing caps. Wipe the bearing recesses with a clean, lint-free cloth. They must be kept spotlessly clean.

18 Clean the backs of the new main bearing shells. Fit the shells with an oil groove in each main bearing location in the block. Note the thrustwashers integral with the No 3 (centre) upper main bearing shell, or the thrustwasher halves fitted either side of No 3 upper main bearing location. Fit the other shell from each bearing set in the corresponding main bearing cap. Make sure the tab on each bearing shell fits into the notch in the block or cap/lower crankcase. Also, the oil holes in the block must line up with the oil holes in the bearing shell **(see illustrations)**. Don't hammer the shells into place, and don't nick or gouge the bearing faces.

19 Clean the bearing surfaces of the shells in the block, then apply a thin, uniform layer of

15.26 Ensure the oil grooves on each thrustwasher are facing outwards from the No 2 main bearing location

clean molybdenum disulphide-based grease, engine assembly lubricant, or clean engine oil to each surface **(see illustration)**. Coat the thrustwasher surfaces as well.

20 Lubricate the crankshaft oil seal journals with molybdenum disulphide-based grease, engine assembly lubricant, or clean engine oil.

21 Make sure the crankshaft journals are clean, then lay the crankshaft back in place in the block **(see illustration)**.

22 Refit and tighten the main bearing caps as follows:

a) *Clean the bearing surfaces of the shells in the caps, then lubricate them. Refit the caps in their respective positions, with the arrows pointing to the timing belt end of the engine.*

b) *Working on one cap at a time, from the centre main bearing outwards (and ensuring that each cap is tightened down squarely and evenly onto the block), tighten the main bearing cap bolts to the specified torque wrench setting (see illustration).*

23 Rotate the crankshaft a number of times by hand, to check for any obvious binding.

24 Check the crankshaft endfloat (see Section 11). It should be correct if the crankshaft thrustwashers/thrust control bearing(s) aren't worn or damaged, or have been renewed.

25 Refit the crankshaft left-hand oil seal carrier and install a new seal (Chapter 2D).

2.0 litre engines

26 Using a little grease, stick the upper thrustwashers to each side of the No 2 main

bearing upper location. Ensure that the oilway grooves on each thrustwasher face outwards (away from the cylinder block) **(see illustration)**.

27 Place the bearing shells in their locations. If new shells are being fitted, ensure that all traces of protective grease are cleaned off using paraffin. Wipe dry the shells and connecting rods with a lint-free cloth. Liberally lubricate each bearing shell in the cylinder block/crankcase and cap with clean engine oil.

28 Lower the crankshaft into position so that Nos 2 and 3 cylinder crankpins are at TDC; Nos 1 and 4 cylinder crankpins will be at BDC, ready for fitting No 1 piston. Check the crankshaft endfloat, referring to Section 11.

29 Lubricate the lower bearing shells in the main bearing caps with clean engine oil. Make sure that the locating lugs on the shells engage with the corresponding recesses in the caps.

30 Fit main bearing caps Nos 2 to 5 to their correct locations, ensuring that they are fitted the correct way round (the bearing shell tab recesses in the block and caps must be on the same side). Insert the bolts/nuts, tightening them only loosely at this stage.

31 Apply a small amount of sealant to the No 1 main bearing cap mating face on the cylinder block, around the sealing strip holes **(see illustration)**.

32 Locate the tab of each sealing strip over the pins on the base of No 1 bearing cap, and press the strips into the bearing cap grooves. It is now necessary to obtain two thin metal strips, of 0.25 mm thickness or less, in order to prevent the strips moving when the cap is being fitted. Ford garages use the tool shown, which acts as a clamp. Metal strips (such as old feeler blades) can be used, provided all burrs which may damage the sealing strips are first removed **(see illustration)**.

33 Where applicable, oil both sides of the metal strips, and hold them on the sealing strips. Fit the No 1 main bearing cap, insert the bolts loosely, then carefully pull out the metal strips in a horizontal direction, using a pair of pliers **(see illustration)**.

34 Tighten all the main bearing cap bolts/nuts evenly to the specified torque. Using a sharp knife, trim off the ends of the No 1 bearing cap sealing strips, so that they protrude above the cylinder block/crankcase mating surface by approximately 1.0 mm **(see illustration)**.

35 Fit a new crankshaft left-hand oil seal as described in Part E of this Chapter.

36 Refit the piston/connecting rod assemblies to the crankshaft as described in Section 16.

37 Refit the Woodruff key, then slide on the oil pump drive sprocket and spacer (where fitted), and locate the drive chain on the sprocket.

38 Ensure that the mating surfaces of the right-hand oil seal carrier and cylinder block are clean and dry. Note the correct fitted depth of the oil seal then, lever or drive out the old oil seal from the housing. If preferred, a new oil seal can be pressed into the housing at this stage **(see illustrations)**.

39 Apply a smear of suitable silicone sealant (Ford part No WSE-M4G323-A4) to the oil seal carrier mating surface. Ensure that the locating dowels are in position, then slide the carrier over the end of the crankshaft and into position on the cylinder block **(see illustrations)**. Tighten the carrier retaining bolts to the specified torque.

40 If not already done, fit a new crankshaft right-hand oil seal as described in Part E of this Chapter.

41 Ensuring that the drive chain is correctly located on the sprocket, refit the oil pump and sump as described in Part E of this Chapter.

42 Where removed, refit the cylinder head as described in Part E of this Chapter.

16 Piston/connecting rod assembly – refitting

Note: *New big-end cap nuts/bolts must be used on refitting.*

1 Note that the following procedure assumes that the crankshaft and main bearing ladder/caps are in place.

2 Clean the backs of the bearing shells, and the bearing locations in both the connecting rod and bearing cap.

1.8 and 2.0 litre engines

3 Press the bearing shells into their locations, ensuring that the tab on each shell engages in the notch in the connecting rod and cap. Take

15.31 Apply sealant to the No 1 main bearing cap mating face on the cylinder block, around the sealing strip holes in the corners

15.33 Use 2 metal strips (arrowed) to hold the sealing strips in place as the bearing cap is fitted

care not to touch any shell's bearing surface with your fingers **(see illustration)**.

All engines

4 Lubricate the cylinder bores, the pistons,

15.38a Drive out the old oil seal . . .

15.39a Apply the sealant . . .

15.32 Fit the sealing strips to the No 1 main bearing cap

15.34 Trim off the ends of the bearing cap sealing strips, so that they protrude by approximately 1.0 mm

and piston rings, then lay out each piston/connecting rod assembly in its respective position.

5 Start with assembly No 1. Make sure that the piston rings are still spaced as described

15.38b . . . then press in the new one to the previously-noted depth

15.39b . . and refit the oil seal housing

16.3 Ensure the bearing shell tab (arrowed) locates correctly in the cut-out

16.8 Fit the big-end bearing cap, ensuring it is fitted the right-way around, and fit the new nuts

in Section 16, then clamp them in position with a piston ring compressor.

6 Insert the piston/connecting rod assembly into the top of cylinder/liner No 1, ensuring the piston is correctly positioned as follows.

a) *On 1.6 and 1.8 litre engines, ensure that the DIST mark or arrow on the piston crown is towards the timing belt end of the engine.*

b) *On 2.0 litre engines, ensure that the valve recesses on the piston crown are towards the rear of the cylinder block.*

7 Once the piston is correctly positioned, using a block of wood or hammer handle against the piston crown, tap the assembly into the cylinder/liner until the piston crown is flush with the top of the cylinder/liner **(see illustration)**.

1.8 and 2.0 litre engines

8 Ensure that the bearing shell is still correctly installed. Liberally lubricate the crankpin and both bearing shells. Taking care not to mark the cylinder/liner bores, pull the piston/connecting rod assembly down the bore and onto the crankpin. Refit the big-end bearing cap and fit the new nuts, tightening them finger-tight at first **(see illustration)**. Note that the faces with the identification marks must match (which means that the bearing shell locating tabs abut each other).

9 Tighten the bearing cap retaining nuts evenly and progressively to the specified torque setting.

16.7 Tap the piston into the bore using a hammer handle

H44712

16.11 Big-end bearing shell positioning – 1.6 litre engine

1   *Ford tool No 303-736*
2   *Bearing shell in the cap*

1.6 litre engines

10 On these engines, then connecting rod is made in one piece, then the big-end bearing cap is 'cracked' off. This ensures that the cap fits onto the connecting rod only in one position, and with maximum rigidity. Consequently, there are no locating notches for the bearing shells to fit into.

11 To ensure that the big-end bearing shells are centrally located in the connecting rod and cap, two special tools are available from Ford (part No 303-736). These half-moon shaped tools are pressed in from either side of the rod/cap and locate the shell exactly in the centre **(see illustration)**. Fit the shells into the connecting rods and big-end caps and lubricate them with plenty of clean engine oil.

12 Pull the connecting rods and pistons down the bores and onto the crankshaft journals. Fit the big-end caps – they will only fit properly one way round (see paragraph 10), and insert the new bolts.

13 Tighten the bolts to the specified torque settings.

All engines

14 Once the bearing cap retaining nuts have been correctly tightened, rotate the crankshaft. Check that it turns freely; some stiffness is to be expected if new components have been fitted, but there should be no signs of binding or tight spots.

15 Refit the cylinder head and oil pump as described in Part C, D or E of this Chapter (as applicable).

17 Engine – initial start-up after overhaul

1 Refit the remainder of the engine components, then refit the engine and transmission to the vehicle as described in Section 3 of this Part. Double-check the engine oil and coolant levels and make a final check that everything has been reconnected. Make sure that there are no tools or rags left in the engine compartment.

2 Remove the spark plugs and disable the ignition system by disconnecting the ignition coil wiring at the connector. Remove the fuel pump relay from the fusebox.

3 Turn the engine over on the starter motor until the oil pressure warning light goes out. If the light fails to extinguish after several seconds of cranking, check the engine oil level and that the oil filter is fitted securely. Assuming these are correct, check the security of the oil pressure sensor wiring – do not progress any further until you are sure that oil is being pumped around the engine at sufficient pressure.

4 Refit the spark plugs and ignition wiring (ignition coils and wiring), and refit the fuel pump fuse.

5 Start the engine, noting that this also may take a little longer than usual, due to the fuel system components being empty.

6 While the engine is idling, check for fuel, coolant and oil leaks. Don't be alarmed if there are some odd smells and smoke from parts getting hot and burning off oil deposits.

7 Keep the engine idling until hot water is felt circulating through the top hose, check that it idles reasonably smoothly and at the usual speed, then switch it off.

8 After a few minutes, recheck the oil and coolant levels, and top-up as necessary (see *Weekly checks*).

9 If new components such as pistons, rings or crankshaft bearings have been fitted, the engine must be run-in for the first 500 miles. Do not operate the engine at full-throttle, or allow it to labour in any gear during this period. It is recommended that the oil and filter be changed at the end of this period.

Chapter 3
Cooling, heating and air conditioning systems

Contents

	Section number		Section number
Air conditioning system – general information and precautions	11	Engine coolant (antifreeze) – general information	2
Air conditioning system components – removal and refitting	12	General information	1
Coolant pump – checking, removal and refitting	8	Heater/air conditioning controls – removal and refitting	10
Cooling system electronic components – removal and refitting	6	Heater/ventilation components – removal and refitting	9
Cooling system hoses – disconnection and renewal	3	Radiator and expansion tank – removal, inspection and refitting	7
Electric booster heater (diesel engines only) – general information,		Radiator electric cooling fan(s) – testing, removal and refitting	5
removal and refitting	13	Thermostat – removal, testing and refitting	4

Degrees of difficulty

Easy, suitable for novice with little experience	**Fairly easy,** suitable for beginner with some experience	**Fairly difficult,** suitable for competent DIY mechanic	**Difficult,** suitable for experienced DIY mechanic	**Very difficult,** suitable for expert DIY or professional

Specifications

System pressure

Pressure test	1.3 to 1.5 bars approximately – see cap for actual value

Expansion tank filler cap

Pressure rating	1.3 to 1.5 bars approximately – see cap for actual value

Thermostat

Petrol engines:
1.6 litre non-Ti-VCT:	
Starts to open	82°C
Fully-open	112°C
1.6 litre Ti-VCT (electronically-controlled)	98°C
1.8 litre and 2.0 litre:	
Starts to open	92°C
Fully-open	99°C

Diesel engines:
1.6 litre	88°C
1.8 and 2.0 litre:	
Starts to open	92°C
Fully open	99°C

Air conditioning system

Refrigerant	R134a
Refrigerant quantity:	
Vehicles built up to 19/07/2004	740 g
Vehicles built from 19/07/2004	600 g
Refrigerant oil	Ford WSH-M1C231-B
Refrigerant oil capacity:	
When refilling	200 ml
When renewing the condenser	30 ml
When renewing the evaporator	30 ml
When renewing the accumulator/dehydrator	90 ml
When renewing the compressor:	
If the oil drained from the faulty compressor is less than 150 ml	150 ml
If the oil drained from the faulty compressor is more than 150 ml	200 ml
When renewing the refrigerant pipes	200 ml

Torque wrench settings

	Nm	lbf ft
Air conditioning accumulator/dehydrator-to-subframe bolts.........	7	5
Air conditioning compressor mounting bolts......................	24	18
Air conditioning condenser mounting bolts......................	24	18
Air conditioning high-pressure cut-off switch	10	7
Auxiliary drivebelt tensioner bolts	25	18
Clutch pedal mounting nuts*	25	18
Compressor centre pulley bolt................................	13	10
Coolant by-pass pipe retaining bolts:		
1.8 litre engine	48	35
2.0 litre engine	18	13
Coolant by-pass valve bolts (2.0 litre engine only)...............	6	4
Coolant outlet connector	20	15
Coolant pump bolts		
Petrol engines...	9	7
Diesel engines:		
1.6 litre engines......................................	10	7
1.8 litre engines:		
Lower bolt..	23	17
Upper bolts..	10	7
2.0 litre engines......................................	16	12
Coolant pump pulley bolts...................................	24	18
Coolant temperature sensor..................................	12	9
Cylinder head temperature sensor (1.8 litre diesel engine only).......	20	15
Door check strap bolts......................................	23	17
Door hinge bolts...	15	11
Facia crossmember bolts:		
Inner	20	15
Outer..	25	18
Side bolts	80	59
Radiator mounting bracket-to-subframe bolts....................	25	18
Refrigerant line connection	8	6
Refrigerant line to compressor...............................	20	15
Refrigerant line to evaporator................................	20	15
Refrigerant line to expansion valve	25	18
Thermostat cover bolts (diesel engines):		
1.8 litre engine	9	7
2.0 litre engine	6	4
Thermostat housing bolts:		
Petrol engines...	9	7
Diesel engines:		
1.6 litre engine:		
Front bolts..	4	3
Rear bolts...	7	5
1.8 litre engine	23	17
2.0 litre engine	10	7

* Use new nuts

1 General information

Warning: DO NOT attempt to remove the expansion tank filler cap, or to disturb any part of the cooling system, while it or the engine is hot, as there is a very great risk of scalding. If the expansion tank filler cap must be removed before the engine and radiator have fully cooled down (even though this is not recommended) the pressure in the cooling system must first be released. Cover the cap with a thick layer of cloth, to avoid scalding, and slowly unscrew the filler cap until a hissing sound can be heard. When the hissing has stopped, showing that pressure is released, slowly unscrew the filler cap further until it can be removed; if more hissing sounds are heard, wait until they have stopped before unscrewing the cap completely. At all times, keep well away from the filler opening.

Warning: Do not allow coolant to come in contact with your skin, or with the painted surfaces of the vehicle. Rinse off spills immediately with plenty of water. Never leave coolant lying around in an open container, or in a puddle in the driveway or on the garage floor. Children and pets are attracted by its sweet smell, but coolant is fatal if ingested.

Warning: If the engine is hot, the electric cooling fan may start rotating even if the engine is not running, so be careful to keep hands, hair and loose clothing well clear when working in the engine compartment.

Engine cooling system

All vehicles covered by this manual employ a pressurised engine cooling system with thermostatically-controlled coolant circulation. The coolant is circulated by an impeller-type pump, bolted to the right-hand end of the cylinder block, inboard of the timing belt. On all models the pump is driven by the crankshaft pulley via the auxiliary drivebelt. The coolant flows through the cylinder block around each cylinder; in the cylinder head, cast-in coolant passages direct coolant around the intake and exhaust ports, near the spark plug areas and close to the exhaust valve guides.

A wax type thermostat is located in a housing attached to the engine. During warm-up, the closed thermostat prevents coolant from circulating through the radiator. Instead, it returns through the coolant pipe running across the front of the engine to the radiator or expansion bottle. The supply to the heater is made from the rear of the thermostat housing. As the engine nears normal operating temperature, the thermostat opens and allows hot coolant to travel through the radiator, where it is cooled before returning to the engine. On some models, an electrically-heated thermostat is fitted, where the engine management ECM controls the position of the thermostat to improve engine efficiency and reduce harmful exhaust emissions.

The radiator is of aluminium construction, and has plastic end tanks. On models with automatic transmission, the fluid cooler is located across the front of the radiator.

The cooling system is sealed by a pressure-type filler cap in the expansion tank. The pressure in the system raises the boiling point of the coolant, and increases the cooling efficiency of the radiator. When the engine is at normal operating temperature, the coolant expands, and the surplus is displaced into the expansion tank. When the system cools, the surplus coolant is automatically drawn back from the tank into the radiator.

The temperature gauge and cooling fan(s) are controlled by the engine coolant temperature sensor that transmits a signal to the engine electronic control module (ECM) to operate them.

Most diesel models have an oil cooler mounted on the sump/cylinder block – this is basically a heat exchanger with a coolant supply, to take heat away from the oil in the sump. Also available as options are additional electric and fuel-fired cabin and engine block heaters. These can be remotely operated, or programmed to operate for a suitable period before the vehicle is required.

Heating/ventilation system

The heating system consists of a blower fan and heater matrix (radiator) located in the heater unit, with hoses connecting the heater matrix to the engine cooling system. Hot engine coolant is circulated through the heater matrix. When the heater temperature control on the facia is operated, a flap door opens to expose the heater box to the passenger compartment. When the blower control is operated, the blower fan forces air through the unit according to the setting selected. The heater controls are linked to the flap doors by cables.

Incoming fresh air for the ventilation system passes through a pollen filter mounted at the front of the heater housing (see Chapter 1) – this ensures that most particles will be removed before the air enters the cabin. However, it is vital that the pollen filter is changed regularly, since a blocked filter will significantly reduce airflow to the cabin, leading to ineffective de-misting.

The ventilation system air distribution is controlled by flap doors on the heater housing. All the vehicles have a recirculated air function, with the flap being controlled by a servo motor.

Air conditioning system

See Section 11.

2 Engine coolant (antifreeze) – general information

⚠ **Warning: Engine coolant (antifreeze) contains mono-ethylene glycol and other constituents, which are toxic if taken internally. They can also be absorbed into the skin after prolonged contact.**

Note: *Refer to Chapter 1 for further information on coolant renewal.*

The cooling system should be filled with a water/monoethylene glycol-based coolant solution, of a strength which will prevent freezing down to at least –25°C, or lower if the local climate requires it. Coolant also provides protection against corrosion, and increases the boiling point.

The cooling system should be maintained according to the schedule described in Chapter 1. If the engine coolant used is old or contaminated it is likely to cause damage, and encourage the formation of corrosion and scale in the system. Use coolant which is to Ford's specification and to the correct concentration.

Before adding the coolant, check all hoses and hose connections, because coolant tends to leak through very small openings. Engines don't normally consume coolant, so if the level goes down, find the cause and correct it.

The engine coolant concentration should be between 40% and 55%. If the concentration drops below 40% there will be insufficient protection, this must then be brought back to specification. Hydrometers are available at most automotive accessory shops to test the coolant concentration.

3 Cooling system hoses – disconnection and renewal

Note: *Refer to the warnings given in Section 1 of this Chapter before starting work.*

1 If the checks described in Chapter 1 reveal a faulty hose, it must be renewed as follows.

2 First drain the cooling system (see Chapter 1); if the coolant is not due for renewal, the drained coolant may be re-used, if it is collected in a clean container.

3 To disconnect any hose, use a pair of pliers to release the spring clamps (or a screwdriver to slacken screw-type clamps), then move them along the hose clear of the union. Carefully work the hose off its stubs **(see illustration)**. The hoses can be removed with relative ease when new – on an older car, they may have stuck.

4 If a hose proves stubborn, try to release it by rotating it on its unions before attempting to work it off. Gently prise the end of the hose

3.3 You can buy special tools specifically designed to release spring-type hose clamps

with a blunt instrument (such as a flat-bladed screwdriver), but do not apply too much force, and take care not to damage the pipe stubs or hoses. Note in particular that the radiator hose unions are fragile; do not use excessive force when attempting to remove the hoses. If all else fails, cut the hose with a sharp knife, then slit it so that it can be peeled off in two pieces. While expensive, this is preferable to buying a new radiator. Check first, however, that a new hose is readily available.

5 When refitting a hose, first slide the clamps onto the hose, then work the hose onto its unions. If the hose is stiff, use soap (or washing-up liquid) as a lubricant, or soften it by soaking it in boiling water, but take care to prevent scalding.

6 Work each hose end fully onto its union, then check that the hose is settled correctly and is properly routed. Slide each clip along the hose until it is behind the union flared end, before tightening it securely.

7 Refill the system with coolant (see Chapter 1).

8 Check carefully for leaks as soon as possible after disturbing any part of the cooling system.

4 Thermostat – removal, testing and refitting

Note: *Refer to the warnings given in Section 1 of this Chapter before starting work.*

Removal

1 Disconnect the battery negative (earth) lead (see Chapter 5).

2 Drain the cooling system (see Chapter 1). If the coolant is relatively new or in good condition, drain it into a clean container and re-use it.

1.6 litre petrol engines

3 Remove the alternator as described in Chapter 5.

4 Disconnect the coolant hoses from the thermostat housing **(see illustration)**. On some 1.6 litre Ti-VCT engines, disconnect the wiring plug from the thermostat housing.

5 Unbolt the thermostat cover and withdraw the thermostat. Note the position of the air bleed valve (where fitted), and how the thermostat is

4.4 Release the clamps and disconnect the hoses from the thermostat housing – 1.6 litre Ti-VCT engine

4.5 Undo the bolts (arrowed) and remove the thermostat housing

4.8 Disconnect the coolant hoses from the thermostat housing – 1.8 and 2.0 litre engines

installed (ie, which end is facing outwards) **(see illustration). Note:** *On some 1.6 litre Ti-VCT engines, the electrically-heated thermostat is integral with the housing. If defective, the complete assembly must be renewed.*

1.8 and 2.0 litre petrol engines

6 Remove the auxiliary drivebelt as described in Chapter 1.

7 Unclip the wiring harness, then undo the 3 bolts and remove the auxiliary drivebelt tensioner assembly.

8 Release the clips and disconnect the coolant hoses from the thermostat cover **(see illustration)**

9 Slacken and remove the three bolts from the thermostat cover and withdraw from the thermostat housing. If improved access is required to the lower bolt, remove the alternator as described in Chapter 5. Note that

the thermostat is integral with the housing. If defective, the complete assembly must be renewed.

1.6 litre diesel engines

10 Remove the air cleaner assembly as described in Chapter 4.

11 The thermostat housing is located at the left-hand end of the cylinder head. Release the clips and disconnect the coolant hoses from the thermostat housing **(see illustration)**.

12 Disconnect the wiring plug from the engine coolant temperature sensor.

13 Undo the coolant bypass pipe retaining bolt.

14 Undo the 4 retaining bolts and remove the thermostat housing **(see illustration)**. Note that the thermostat is integral with the housing. If the thermostat is faulty, the housing must be renewed.

1.8 litre diesel engines

15 Remove the plastic cover from the top of the engine **(see illustration)**.

16 The thermostat cover is located at the front of the engine cylinder block. Undo the 3 retaining bolts and move the cover to one side **(see illustration)**.

17 Note the position of the air bleed valve (where fitted), and how the thermostat is installed (ie, which end is facing outwards), then pull the thermostat and rubber seal from place. Discard the rubber seal – a new one must be fitted.

2.0 litre diesel engines

18 Remove the plastic cover from the top of the engine. The thermostat housing is located at the left-hand end of the cylinder head.

19 Remove the battery as described in Chapter 5, then undo the bolts and remove the battery tray **(see illustration)**.

20 Undo the retaining nuts and remove the support bracket at the left-hand end of the thermostat housing **(see illustration)**.

21 Release the clamps and disconnect the hoses from the thermostat housing.

22 Disconnect the wiring plug(s) from the thermostat housing.

23 Undo the 4 retaining nuts and remove the housing **(see illustrations)**. Examine the rubber seal and renew if necessary. Note that the thermostat is integral with the housing – if faulty the complete assembly must be renewed.

4.11 Release the clips and disconnect the coolant hoses from the housing

4.14 Undo the bolts (arrowed) and detach the thermostat housing

4.15 Pull the plastic cover upwards to release it

4.16 Undo the thermostat cover bolts (arrowed)

4.19 Undo the 3 bolts (arrowed) and remove the battery tray

4.20 Undo the nuts and move the support bracket to one side

4.23a Thermostat housing retaining nuts (arrowed)

4.23b Renew the thermostat housing sealing ring

Testing

Note: *The following does not apply to 1.6 litre Ti-VCT engines with electrically-heated thermostats. If a fault develops with the cooling system of this model, have the engine management ECM interrogated using a diagnostic fault code reader.*

General

24 Before assuming the thermostat is to blame for a cooling system problem, check the coolant level (see *Weekly checks*), the auxiliary drivebelt tension and condition (see Chapter 1) and the temperature gauge operation.

25 If the engine seems to be taking a long time to warm up (based on heater output or temperature gauge operation), the thermostat may be stuck open. Renew the thermostat.

26 Equally, a lengthy warm-up period might suggest that the thermostat is missing – it may have been removed or inadvertently omitted by a previous owner or mechanic. Don't drive the vehicle without a thermostat – the engine management system's ECM will stay in warm-up mode for longer than necessary, causing emissions and fuel economy to suffer.

27 If the engine runs hot, use your hand to check the temperature of the radiator top hose. If the hose isn't hot, but the engine is, the thermostat is probably stuck closed, preventing the coolant inside the engine from escaping to the radiator – renew the thermostat.

28 If the radiator top hose is hot, it means that the coolant is flowing and the thermostat is open. Consult the *Fault finding* Section at the end of this manual to assist in tracing possible cooling system faults.

Thermostat test

29 If the thermostat remains in the open position at room temperature, it is faulty, and must be renewed as a matter of course.

30 To test it fully, suspend the (closed) thermostat on a length of string in a container of cold water, with a thermometer beside it; ensure that neither touches the side of the container.

31 Heat the water, and check the temperature at which the thermostat begins to open; compare this value with that specified.

Checking the fully-open temperature may not be possible in an open container if it is higher than the boiling point of water at atmospheric pressure. Remove the thermostat and allow it to cool down; check that it closes fully.

32 If the thermostat does not open and close as described, if it sticks in either position, or if it does not open at the specified temperature, it must be renewed.

Refitting

33 Refitting is the reverse of the removal procedure, noting the following points:
   a) *Clean the mating surfaces carefully, and renew the thermostat's sealing ring/ gasket.*
   b) *Fit the thermostat in the same position as noted on removal.*
   c) *Tighten the thermostat cover/housing bolts to the specified torque wrench setting.*
   d) *Remake all the coolant hose connections, then refill the cooling system as described in the relevant part of Chapter 1.*
   e) *Start the engine and allow it to reach normal operating temperature, then check for leaks and proper thermostat operation.*

5 Radiator electric cooling fan(s) – testing, removal and refitting

Note: *Refer to the warnings given in Section 1 of this Chapter before starting work.*

5.6a Remove the scrivets and . . .

Testing

1 The radiator cooling fan is controlled by the engine management system's ECM, acting on the information received from the cylinder head temperature sensor and engine coolant temperature sensor.

2 First, check the relevant fuses and relays (see Chapter 12).

3 To test the fan motor, unplug the electrical connector, and use fused jumper wires to connect the fan directly to the battery. If the fan still does not work, renew the motor.

4 If the motor proved sound, the fault lies in the engine coolant temperature sensor (see Section 6), in the wiring loom (see Chapter 12 for testing details) or in the engine management system (see Chapter 4).

Removal

Note: *On 1.6 litre diesel engines the cooling fan is removed with the radiator as described in Section 7.*

5 Disconnect the battery negative (earth) lead (see Chapter 5).

6 Undo the bolts and prise out the 6 scrivets, release the clips, then detach the air deflector panel from above the radiator grille **(see illustrations)**.

7 Release the clips and detach the lock cylinder from the radiator grille, then release the locating tangs and remove the radiator grille **(see illustrations)**.

8 Undo the fasteners and remove the engine undershield (where fitted), followed by the shield under the radiator.

5.6b . . . release the air deflector

5.7a Release the bonnet lock from the tabs (arrowed) . . .

5.7b . . . depress the grille tabs . . .

5.7c . . . and remove the grille

9 On diesel models slacken the clamps and remove the intake hose from the intercooler **(see illustration)**.

10 Unplug the cooling fan electrical connector, and release the wiring loom from the fan shroud. Unclip the lower radiator hose from the lower support bracket.

11 Undo the radiator support bracket front retaining bolts, and substitute them with M8 x 30 mm bolts, leaving at least 15 mm of thread exposed **(see illustration)**.

12 Remove the radiator support bracket rear retaining bolts and allow the bracket to drop onto the front bolts previously fitted **(see illustration)**.

13 On vehicles fitted with air conditioning, press in the retaining clips and slide the condenser upwards to release it. Secure it with cable-ties.

14 Unclip the shroud from its upper and lower mountings, then lift the assembly to disengage it from its mountings **(see illustration)**.

15 Withdraw the fan and shroud as an assembly from underneath the vehicle.

Refitting

16 Refitting is the reverse of the removal procedure, noting the following points:
 a) *When refitting the fan to the motor, make sure it has located correctly before refitting the retaining clip.*
 b) *Ensure that the shroud is settled correctly at all four mounting points before finally clipping into position.*

---

6 Coolant system electronic components – removal and refitting

Note: *Renewal of the cooling system sensors and controls does not require draining of the system, however considerable coolant loss should be anticipated. Refer to the warnings*

given in Section 1 of this Chapter before starting work.

⚠️ *Warning: Ensure the coolant is cold before removing cooling system components.*

Coolant temperature sensor

1 On all models, the sensor is located at the coolant outlet housing at the left-hand end of the cylinder head.

Petrol engines

2 Where applicable, remove the plastic cover from the top of the cylinder head.

3 Disconnect the wiring plug.

4 Two different types of sensor may be fitted. The first type is screwed into the coolant outlet housing, and the second type is clipped into place. Unscrew the sensor from the housing, or pull out the clip as applicable **(see illustrations)**. Be prepared for coolant spillage and have rag or a rubber plug handy to force

5.9 Slacken the clamp (arrowed) and release the intercooler hose

5.11 Substitute the front mounting bolts with M8 X 30 mm bolts

5.12 Radiator support bracket bolts (arrowed)

5.14 Depress the clip (arrowed) on each lower mounting and lift the cooling fan shroud upwards

6.4a Unscrew the engine coolant temperature sensor (arrowed) . . .

6.4b . . . or pull out the retaining clip (arrowed) followed by the sensor

into the sensor aperture. This way only a little coolant will be lost.

5 Refitting is the reverse of the removal procedure, noting the following points:

a) *Screw the sensor into position and tighten it to the specified torque, or refit the sensor and insert the clip, as applicable.*

b) *A new sensor seal should always be fitted.*

c) *Refill the cooling system as described in Chapter 1.*

1.6 and 1.8 litre diesel engines

6 Remove the air cleaner assembly as described in Chapter 4. Disconnect the sensor wiring plug, pull out the retaining clip, and remove the sensor **(see illustration)**.

7 Refitting is the reverse of the removal procedure, noting the following points:

a) *Refit the sensor and insert the clip.*

b) *A new sensor seal should always be fitted.*

c) *Refill the cooling system as described in the relevant section of Chapter 1.*

2.0 litre diesel engines

8 Remove the battery as described in Chapter 5, then undo the bolts and remove the battery tray. Prise out the retaining clip, and disconnect the coolant hose from the heater to the thermostat housing.

9 Disconnect the sensor wiring plug, pull out the retaining clip, and remove the engine coolant temperature sensor **(see illustration)**.

10 Refitting is the reverse of the removal procedure, noting the following points:

a) *Refit the sensor and insert the clip.*

b) *A new sensor seal should always be fitted.*

c) *Refill the cooling system as described in the relevant section of Chapter 1.*

Coolant degas shut-off valve

Note: *This valve is only fitted to some 1.6 litre Ti-VCT engines.*

11 This valve, located in the left-hand front corner of the engine compartment, controls the flow of coolant back to the expansion tank. In cold temperatures, whilst the engine is warming-up, the valve is closed, trapping the coolant in the cylinder head. This decreases warm-up time. When the coolant is warmed, the valve opens.

6.6 Slide out the clip (arrowed) and remove the coolant temperature sensor – 1.6 litre diesel engine

12 Use hose clamps on the coolant hoses to and from the shut-off valve, or be prepared for coolant spillage.

13 Disconnect the hoses and wiring connector from the valve.

14 Undo the bolts and remove the valve.

15 Refitting is a reversal of removal, remembering to refill the cooling system as described in Chapter 1.

Cylinder head temperature sensor

Note: *Only the 1.8 litre diesel engine is fitted with this sensor.*

16 Remove the plastic cover from the top of the engine.

17 Disconnect the hoses, then undo the retaining bolt and remove the crankcase vent oil separator from the end of the cylinder head **(see illustration)**.

18 Undo the 2 retaining bolts and remove the crash shield above the fuel filter **(see illustration)**.

19 Disconnect the fuel filter wiring plug, then release the clips securing the fuel hoses and move the fuel filter to one side.

20 Disconnect the wiring plug, unclip the plug from the bracket, then unscrew the cylinder head temperature sensor from place **(see illustration)**.

21 Refitting is a reversal of removal. Tighten the sensor to the specified torque.

Coolant shut-off valve

Note: *This valve is only fitted to the 2.0 litre diesel engine.*

6.9 Slide out the clip (arrowed) and remove the coolant temperature sensor – 2.0 litre diesel engine

22 The coolant shut-off valve is controlled by the engine management ECM, and limits coolant flow to the coolant expansion tank during the engine warm-up phase. It's located in the feed pipe from the thermostat housing to the tank.

23 Be prepared for coolant spillage as the hoses are disconnected.

24 Disconnect the valve wiring plug, then release the clips and disconnect the hoses from the valve.

25 Undo the retaining bolts and remove the valve.

26 Refitting is the reversal of removal, remembering to refill the cooling system as described in Chapter 1.

Coolant by-pass valve

Note: *This valve is only fitted to 2.0 litre diesel engine.*

27 The coolant by-pass valve is controlled by the engine management ECM, and limits the coolant flow to the coolant pump during the engine warm-up phase. It's located on the top of the thermostat housing.

28 Remove the brake vacuum pump as described in Chapter 9.

29 Disconnect the wiring plug, then undo the 2 retaining bolts and remove the by-pass valve. Renew the valve O-ring seals if necessary.

30 Refitting is a reversal of removal, remembering to refill the cooling system as described in Chapter 1.

6.17 Unbolt and remove the crankcase vent

6.18 Undo the two bolts and remove the crash shield (arrowed)

6.20 Disconnect the wiring plug and remove the sensor (arrowed)

7.7a Depress the clip (arrowed) on the lower condenser mountings

7 Radiator and expansion tank – removal, inspection and refitting

Note: *Refer to the warnings given in Section 1 of this Chapter before starting work.*
Note: *If leakage is the reason for removing the radiator, bear in mind that minor leaks can often be cured using a radiator sealant added to the coolant with the radiator in situ.*

Radiator removal

1 Drain the coolant system as described in Chapter 1.
2 To provide greater clearance for the radiator to be lowered and removed, ensure that the handbrake is firmly applied, then raise and support the front of the car on axle stands (see *Jacking and vehicle support*). Remove the radiator lower cover.

7.11 Intercooler mounting bolt (right-hand side bolt arrowed)

7.12b . . . lower hose . . .

7.7b Secure the condenser to the front panel using cable-ties

3 Whilst it is possible to remove the radiator complete with the cooling fan access will be improved by removing the fan and shroud as described in Section 5.
4 Undo the 4 scrivets and remove the air deflector panel behind the radiator grille.
5 Release the 2 clips securing the bonnet lock cylinder to the front grille.
6 Undo the scrivet at each end and remove the radiator grille.
7 On models with air conditioning remove the sponge padding at the base of the condenser. Release the clips at the condenser lower mountings, lift the condenser a little, then secure it to the front panel using cable-ties or similar (see illustrations).
8 Remove the headlights as described in Chapter 12.

Diesel models

9 Undo and remove the intercooler outlet pipe support bracket retaining bolt (see illustration).

7.12a Release the spring clamps and disconnect the radiator upper hose . . .

7.12c . . . and expansion tank hose

7.9 Undo the intercooler outlet hose bolt (arrowed) – viewed through the right-hand headlight aperture

10 Slacken the clamps and remove the intercooler outlet and intake hoses. Note that the clips are moulded into the hose. Do not attempt to separate them.
11 Undo the 2 retaining bolts, lift the intercooler upwards from the mounting brackets and remove it downwards (see illustration).

All models

12 Release the clamps, disconnect the radiator upper, lower and expansion tank hoses (see illustrations).
13 Undo the bolts and remove the radiator lower support bracket.
14 Slide the radiator downwards from place. If not already done so depress the clip each side, and lift the cooling fan shroud from the radiator

Radiator inspection

15 With the radiator removed, it can be inspected for leaks and damage. If it needs repair, have a radiator specialist or dealer service department perform the work, as special techniques are required.
16 Insects and dirt can be removed from the radiator with a garden hose or a soft brush. Take care not to damage the cooling fins as this is being done.

Radiator refitting

17 Refitting is the reverse of the removal procedure, noting the following points:
 a) *Be sure the mounting rubbers are seated properly at the base of the radiator.*
 b) *After refitting, refill the cooling system with the recommended coolant (see Chapter 1).*
 c) *Start the engine, and check for leaks. Allow the engine to reach normal operating temperature, indicated by the radiator top hose becoming hot. Once the engine has cooled (ideally, leave overnight), recheck the coolant level, and add more if required.*

Expansion tank

Removal

18 With the engine completely cool, remove the expansion tank filler cap to release any pressure, then refit the cap.
19 Disconnect the hoses from the tank (see illustration), upper hose first. As each hose is disconnected, drain the tank's contents into

a clean container. If the coolant is not due for renewal, the drained coolant may be re-used, if it is kept clean.

20 Pull the expansion tank upwards to release it from the mounting lugs **(see illustration)**.

21 Wash out the tank, and inspect it for cracks and chafing – renew it if damaged.

Refitting

22 Refitting is the reverse of the removal procedure. Refill the cooling system with the recommended coolant (see Chapter 1), then start the engine and allow it to reach normal operating temperature, indicated by the radiator top hose becoming hot. Recheck the coolant level and add more if required, then check for leaks.

7.19 Release the clips and disconnect the hoses from the expansion tank

7.20 Pull the expansion tank upwards from the mounting lugs (arrowed)

---

8 Coolant pump – checking, removal and refitting

Note: *Refer to the warnings given in Section 1 of this Chapter before starting work.*

Checking

1 A failure in the coolant pump can cause serious engine damage due to overheating.

2 There are three ways to check the operation of the coolant pump while it's installed on the engine. If the pump is defective, fit a new or rebuilt unit.

3 With the engine running at normal operating temperature, squeeze the radiator top hose. If the coolant pump is working properly, a pressure surge should be felt as the hose is released.

⚠ *Warning: Keep your hands away from the radiator electric cooling fan blades.*

4 Coolant pumps are equipped with weep or vent holes. If a failure occurs in the pump seal, coolant will leak from the hole. In most cases you'll need an electric torch to find the hole on the coolant pump from underneath to check for leaks.

5 If the coolant pump shaft bearings fail, there may be a howling sound at the drivebelt end of the engine while it's running. Shaft wear can be felt if the coolant pump pulley is rocked up and down.

6 Don't mistake drivebelt slippage, which

causes a squealing sound, for coolant pump bearing failure.

Removal

7 Drain the cooling system (see Chapter 1).

1.6 litre petrol engines up to April 2005

8 Remove the upper timing belt cover as described in Chapter 2A.

1.6 litre petrol engines from April 2005

9 Remove the timing belt and tensioner as described in Chapter 2A.

All 1.6 litre petrol engines

10 Undo the bolts and remove the coolant pump **(see illustration)**. On models pre-April 2005, protect the timing belt from coolant with rags, etc.

1.8 and 2.0 litre petrol engines

11 Remove the plastic cover on the top of the engine.

12 Slacken the coolant pump pulley bolts, then remove the auxiliary drivebelt as described in Chapter 1.

13 Unscrew the bolts and remove the coolant pump pulley.

14 Undo the 3 bolts and remove the coolant pump **(see illustrations)**. Remove the O-ring seal and discard it.

1.6 litre diesel engines

15 Remove the upper timing belt as described in Chapter 2C.

16 Undo the bolts and remove the coolant pump **(see illustrations)**.

1.8 litre diesel engines

17 Disconnect the battery negative lead with reference to Chapter 5.

18 Slacken the coolant pump pulley bolts, then remove the auxiliary drivebelt as described in Chapter 1.

19 Unbolt the coolant pump pulley and remove.

8.10 Undo the bolts (arrowed) and remove the coolant pump

8.14a Unscrew the mounting bolts (arrowed) . . .

8.14b . . . remove the coolant pump . . .

8.14c . . . and remove the O-ring seal

8.16a Undo the bolts (arrowed) and remove the coolant pump

8.16b Renew the coolant pump gasket

8.22 Remove the coolant pump from the cylinder block

8.24a Coolant pump retaining bolts (arrowed)

8.24b Renew the coolant pump gasket

8.25 Renew the coolant pump gasket – 1.6 litre Ti-VCT engine

20 Remove the timing belt cover and engine mounting as described in Chapter 2D. The engine must be supported as the engine front mounting is disconnected; support the engine from above with a hoist or engine support bar, if available. If the engine is supported from below with a trolley jack, use a wide block of wood between the jack head and the sump, to spread the load.

21 Remove the four bolts securing the engine front mounting bracket to the block, then lift the engine up by approximately 20 mm.

22 Unscrew the seven coolant pump securing bolts and withdraw the pump **(see illustration)**. Recover the gasket. *Note: Take care not to damage or contaminate the timing belt as the pump is removed. Place some stiff cardboard around the belt in the pump area.*

2.0 litre diesel engines

23 Remove the timing belt as described in Chapter 2E.

24 Undo the retaining bolts and remove the coolant pump **(see illustrations)**. Recover the gasket.

Refitting

25 Clean the pump mating surfaces carefully; the gasket/O-ring must be renewed whenever it is disturbed **(see illustration)**. Refit the pump and tighten the bolts to the specified torque wrench setting.

26 The remainder of the refitting procedure is the reverse of dismantling, noting the following points:
a) Tighten all fixings to the specified torque wrench settings (where given).
b) Where applicable, check the timing belt for contamination and renew if required, as described in the relevant section of Chapter 2.
c) On completion, refill the cooling system as described in Chapter 1.

9.6 Squeeze together the side of the fasteners (arrowed) and pull them downwards

9.8a Rotate the fasteners (arrowed) anti-clockwise . . .

9 Heater/ventilation components – removal and refitting

Heater blower motor

Note: *This is a difficult procedure requiring patience and dexterity to release the blower motor retaining clip. It's much easier if the facia is removed as described in Chapter 11.*

1 At first glance it would appear that the blower motor can be removed from the driver's side footwell, however in reality it must be removed from the passenger footwell after the left-hand side air recirculation flap housing has been removed. The motor must be unclipped from the driver's side, rotated and pushed back toward the passenger footwell from where it can be removed.

2 Disconnect the battery negative lead as described in Chapter 5.

3 Jack up and support the vehicle as described in the reference section of this manual, remove the undershield and then the clutch master cylinder supply and outlet pipes as described in Chapter 6. Prepare for some spillage of hydraulic fluid.

4 Lower the vehicle and remove the trim below the steering column, as described in Chapter 11.

5 Unplug the wiring connector from the clutch pedal position sensor and (where fitted) unhook the clutch pedal return spring. On vehicles fitted with an adjustable pedal assembly move the pedal toward the bulkhead. Unbolt and remove the clutch pedal, complete with the clutch master cylinder.

6 Unscrew and remove the lower passenger side footwell trim **(see illustration)**, and then withdraw the panel from the vehicle.

7 Remove the passenger glovebox and centre console side panels as described in Chapter 11.

8 Undo the 2 fasteners and pivot the central junction box/fusebox downwards, then lift it from place. Disconnect the engine wiring harness from the junction/fusebox, and move it to one side **(see illustrations)**.

9 Undo the 2 nuts securing the junction/fusebox support bracket **(see illustration)**.

10 Disconnect the flap wiring plug, then undo

9.8b . . . and lower the junction box/ fusebox

9.9 Undo the 2 nuts (arrowed) and remove the bracket

9.10 Recirculation flap housing bolts (arrowed)

9.11a The motor retaining clip is at the front edge of the housing (arrowed)

9.11b Depress the clip, rotate the housing (see text) . . .

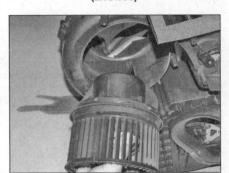

9.11c . . . and gently pull the motor from the other side of the housing

the 3 bolts and remove the air recirculation flap housing (see illustration). This is a difficult procedure as the bulkhead insulation effectively traps the housing in place. Cutting and removing some of the insulation may be the only way to release the housing.

11 Disconnect the blower motor wiring plug, then depress the release clip, and rotate the blower motor clockwise (RHD) or anti-clockwise (LHD) and pull the motor from the housing (see illustrations). Again this is a very difficult procedure as you will be working blind and high up above the now removed clutch pedal assembly. Take great care not to damage the motor fan – it's extremely delicate. Do not pull on the fan, or allow the motor to rest on the fan. Ford produce a special tool (412-131) that should be used to remove the fan, if available.

12 Refitting is the reverse of the removal procedure, but new nuts must be fitted to the clutch pedal assembly.

Blower motor resistor

Note: On vehicles fitted with dual climate control and built after October 2005 the entire facia must be removed (as described in Chapter 11) to access the blower motor resistor.

13 Disconnect the battery negative lead as described in Chapter 5, and then proceed as described in Paragraphs 6 to 9 in this Section.

14 Disconnect the wiring plug, undo the 2 bolts, and pull the resistor from the housing (see illustration).

15 Refitting is a reversal of removal.

Heater matrix

16 Disconnect the battery negative (earth) lead (see Chapter 5) and remove the engine cover.

17 Jack up the front of the vehicle and support it securely on axle stands. Undo

the fasteners and remove the engine under-shield.

18 Disconnect the clutch master cylinder supply and return pipes as described in Chapter 6.

19 Remove the right-hand lower trim panel and then remove the extension panels from the centre console. If the vehicle is fitted with a centre armrest, the entire console must be removed as described in Chapter 11.

20 On manual transmission vehicles, remove the clutch pedal assembly as described in paragraph 5 of this section. Be prepared for fluid spillage – wipe up any spills immediately – the fluid could damage paintwork.

21 Unbolt and remove the gear lever assembly, complete with the selector cables (see illustration).

22 Prise free the wiring loom, locate the bolts and remove the gearshift support bracket (see illustrations).

9.14 Heater blower motor resistor

9.21 Remove the bolts (arrowed with 1 bolt hidden) and lower the gear lever assembly

9.22a Note the position of the long bolts . . .

9.22b . . . and the earth connection (arrowed)

9.22c Remove the support bracket

24 Remove the rear air distribution tube, then undo the 6 bolts and remove the heater matrix upper cover **(see illustrations)**.

25 Undo the 2 bolts and remove the bulkhead aperture cover and spacer around the heater matrix pipes **(see illustrations)**.

26 On models up to 10/2004, release the clamps securing the two halves of the matrix pipes, and remove the matrix from the housing. On models after this date, cut through the matrix pipes as shown, and remove the matrix **(see illustration)**. In production, these later models were fitted with one-piece pipes, whereas new matrices are supplied with two-piece pipes and suitable clamps. Be prepared for fluid spillage.

27 Refitting is the reverse of the removal procedure, but new nuts should be fitted to the clutch pedal assembly. Note that new matrices are supplied with two-piece pipes and suitable clamps. Push the pipes into the aperture in the bulkhead before installing the matrix in the housing, then use the clamps and seals supplied to join the pipes.

28 Refill the cooling system with the recommended coolant (see Chapter 1). Start the engine and allow it to reach normal operating temperature, indicated by the radiator top hose becoming hot. Recheck the coolant level and add more if required, then check for leaks. Check the operation of the heater.

9.23a Rotate the collar (arrowed) 30° anti-clockwise . . .

9.23b . . . and pull the hose from the connection

23 If available fit hose clamps to the heater hoses. Alternatively drain the cooling system as described In Chapter 1. There is no need to drain the system entirely. Access to the hoses can be improved by first removing the wiper arms and cowl as described in Chapters 11 and 12. Rotate the collars anti-clockwise 30° and detach the heater hoses from the connections at the engine compartment bulkhead **(see illustrations)**.

Pollen filter

29 Refer to Chapter 1.

9.24a Remove the rear air distribution tube

9.24b Undo the heater matrix upper cover bolts (left-hand side ones arrowed) . . .

9.24c . . . and remove the upper cover

9.25a Undo the 2 bolts (arrowed) and remove the cover . . .

9.25b . . . followed by the spacer

9.26 Cut through the heater matrix pipes with a hacksaw (see text)

10.3a Undo the panel retaining bolts (arrowed)

10.3b Release the hazard warning electrical plug . . .

10.3c . . . pull the panel forward and release the remaining electrical connectors

10.4a Remove the heater control panel retaining bolts (arrowed) . . .

10.4b . . . the support panel bolts (arrowed) . . .

10.4c . . . and remove the support panel

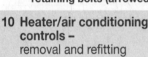

10 Heater/air conditioning controls –
removal and refitting

Heater control panel

1 Disconnect the battery negative (earth) lead (see Chapter 5).
2 Remove the facia-mounted audio unit as described in Chapter 12.

Manual temperature control

3 On models up to 03/2007, undo the 2 bolts and unclip the heater control panel trim. Disconnect the wiring plugs from the hazard warning switch, windscreen heater switches and (if fitted) the traction control switch (see illustrations).
4 Undo the 2 retaining screws to release the control panel and then unscrew and remove the support panel (see illustrations).
5 Taking careful note of all their locations, disconnect the various wiring connectors from the rear of the panel and unclip the heater operating cables from the temperature and direction controls (see illustration).
6 Make sure that nothing remains attached to the panel, then withdraw it from the facia.

Automatic temperature control

7 On models up to 01/2008, undo the 2 bolts and unclip the heater control panel trim (see illustrations 10.3a and 10.3b).
8 Undo the 2 retaining bolts and manoeuvre the control panel away from the facia a little (see illustration 10.4a).

9 Taking careful note of all their locations disconnect the various wiring connectors from the rear of the panel. Make sure that nothing remains attached to the panel, and then withdraw it from the facia.
10 On models built after 01/2008 the control panel is removed with the audio unit, as described in Chapter 12.

Climate control module

11 The climate control function is built-into the DVD navigation touch screen. Removal of the screen assembly is described in Chapter 12.
12 Undo the bolt each side and remove the climate control module from the unit.

Blower motor switch – manual control only

13 Remove the heater control panel as described above.
14 Ensure the switch control knob is in

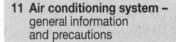

10.5 Squeeze together the sides of the clip (arrowed) and pull the outer cable fitting from the panel

position I during removal and refitting. Pull the control knob from the switch.
15 Cut through the retaining tabs and remove the switch cover from the rear of the panel (see illustration).
16 Pull the switch from place.
17 Refitting is the reverse of the removal procedure. Note that new switches are supplied with a cover that is retained by 2 bolts (also supplied). Check the operation of the controls on completion.

11 Air conditioning system –
general information and precautions

General information

The air conditioning system consists of a condenser mounted in front of the radiator, an evaporator mounted adjacent to the heater

10.15 Cut through the retaining tabs (arrowed) and remove the switch

11.3a Air conditioning refrigerant circuit high-pressure service port (arrowed) . . .

11.3b . . . and the low-pressure port (arrowed)

matrix, a compressor driven by an auxiliary drivebelt, an accumulator/dehydrator, and the plumbing connecting all of the above components – this contains a choke (or 'venturi') mounted in the intake to the evaporator, which creates the drop in pressure required to produce the cooling effect.

A blower fan forces the warmer air of the passenger compartment through the evaporator core (rather like a radiator in reverse), transferring the heat from the air to the refrigerant. The liquid refrigerant boils off into low-pressure vapour, taking the heat with it when it leaves the evaporator.

The refrigerant circuit high- and low-pressure service ports are located on the right-hand side of the engine compartment **(see illustrations)**.

Precautions

⚠ *Warning: The air conditioning system is under high pressure. Do not loosen any fittings or remove any components until after the system has been discharged. Air conditioning refrigerant should be properly discharged at a dealer service department or an automotive air conditioning repair facility capable of handling R134a refrigerant. Always wear eye protection when disconnecting air conditioning system fittings.*

When an air conditioning system is fitted, it is necessary to observe the following special precautions whenever dealing with any part of the system, its associated components, and any items which necessitate disconnection of the system:

a) *While the refrigerant used is less damaging to the environment than the previously-used R12, it is still a very dangerous substance. It must not be allowed into contact with the skin or eyes, or there is a risk of frostbite. It must also not be discharged in an enclosed space – while it is not toxic, there is a risk of suffocation. The refrigerant is heavier than air, and so must never be discharged over a pit.*

b) *The refrigerant must not be allowed to come in contact with a naked flame, otherwise a poisonous gas will be created – under certain circumstances, this can form an explosive mixture with air. For similar reasons, smoking in the presence*

of refrigerant is highly dangerous, particularly if the vapour is inhaled through a lighted cigarette.

c) *Never discharge the system to the atmosphere – R134a is not an ozone-depleting ChloroFluoroCarbon (CFC) like R12, but is instead a hydrofluorocarbon, which causes environmental damage by contributing to the 'greenhouse effect' if released into the atmosphere.*

d) *R134a refrigerant must not be mixed with R12; the system uses different seals (now green-coloured, previously black) and has different fittings requiring different tools, so that there is no chance of the two types of refrigerant becoming mixed accidentally.*

e) *If for any reason the system must be discharged, entrust this task to your Ford dealer or an air conditioning specialist.*

f) *It is essential that the system be professionally discharged prior to using any form of heat – welding, soldering, brazing, etc – in the vicinity of the system, before having the vehicle oven-dried at a temperature exceeding 70°C after repainting, and before disconnecting any part of the system.*

12 Air conditioning system components – removal and refitting

⚠ *Warning: The air conditioning system is under high pressure. Do not loosen any fittings or remove*

12.9 Depress the clip each side (arrowed) and lift the condenser upwards

any components until after the system has been discharged. Air conditioning refrigerant should be properly discharged into an approved type of container at a dealer service department or an automotive air conditioning repair facility capable of handling R134a refrigerant. Cap or plug the pipe lines as soon as they are disconnected to prevent the entry of moisture. Always wear eye protection when disconnecting air conditioning system fittings.

Note: *This Section refers to the components of the air conditioning system itself – refer to Sections 9 and 10 for details of components common to the heating/ventilation system.*

Condenser

1 Have the refrigerant discharged at a dealer service department or an automotive air conditioning repair facility.

2 Disconnect the battery negative (earth) lead (see Chapter 5).

3 Apply the handbrake, then raise the front of the vehicle and support on axle stands.

4 Undo the bolts and remove the engine undershield and the radiator undershield.

5 On diesel models remove the intercooler as described in Section 7 of this Chapter.

6 On automatic transmission models remove the radiator support front bolts and loosen the rear ones and then remove the air deflectors from the front bumper cover. Work the transmission fluid cooler free from its support and secure it with cable-ties.

7 Disconnect the refrigerant lines from the condenser. Immediately cap the open fittings, to prevent the entry of dirt and moisture.

8 Undo the nuts securing the power steering fluid cooler (where fitted) to the radiator crossmember.

9 On early models the condenser is bolted to the radiator, on later models the condenser is simply clipped to the radiator. Remove the bolts – where fitted – and push the condenser upwards to release it and then lower it from the vehicle. Have a jack or pair of axle stands ready to support the weight **(see illustration)**.

10 Refitting is the reverse of removal. Renew the O-rings and lubricate with refrigerant oil.

11 Have the system evacuated, charged and leak-tested by the specialist who discharged it.

Evaporator

12 The evaporator is mounted inside the heater housing with the heater matrix. In order to remove the evaporator, the complete heater housing must be removed.

13 Have the refrigerant discharged at a dealer service department or an automotive air conditioning repair facility.

14 Disconnect the battery negative (earth) lead (see Chapter 5).

15 Drain the cooling system as described in Chapter 1.

16 Remove both front doors as described in Chapter 11.

17 Remove the facia as described in Chapter 11.

18 Prise out the grommet then undo the bolt each end securing the facia crossmember to the door pillars **(see illustration)**.

19 Remove the plastic cover from the top of the engine, where fitted.

20 Remove the upper windscreen cowl extension.

21 Remove the front wiper arms as described Chapter 12 and then remove the cowl.

22 Unbolt and remove the lower bulkhead extension panel.

23 Rotate the collars anti-clockwise 30° approximately, and detach the heater hoses from the connections at the engine compartment bulkhead **(see illustrations 9.23a and 9.23b)**.

24 Undo the bolt and detach the refrigerant pipes at the engine compartment bulkhead **(see illustration)**. Plug or cover the openings to prevent contamination. Renew the O-ring seals.

25 Working in the footwell, unscrew and remove the steering column universal joint pinch-bolt **(see illustration)**. Discard the bolt, a new one must be fitted.

26 Disconnect the wiring plugs, undo the 4 mounting bolts, and remove the steering column – refer to Chapter 10 if necessary.

27 Undo the bolt and remove the footwell air duct each side **(see illustration)**.

28 Undo the bolt each side securing the heater/evaporator housing to the support brackets, then undo the nuts and remove the support bracket each side. Note the routing, then release any wiring harnesses from their clips as the brackets are withdrawn **(see illustrations 9.22a, 9.22b and 9.22c)**.

29 Unclip and remove the rear footwell air duct **(see illustration 9.24a)**, then undo the 6 bolts and remove the heater matrix upper cover **(see illustrations 9.24b and 9.24c)**.

30 Pull away the rubber weatherstrips from the door aperture adjacent to the A-pillar on each side, then remove both A-pillar trim panels as described in Chapter 11.

31 Pull up the door sill trim each side and then pull the footwell kick panel away from the A-pillar to release the retaining clips **(see illustrations)**.

32 Note their fitted positions, and the harness

12.18 Remove the grommet to access the crossmember bolts

12.25 Undo the steering column UJ pinch-bolt (arrowed)

routing, then unplug all electrical connectors that would prevent the facia crossmember assembly being removed.

33 Undo the 2 bolts securing the crossmember to the heater housing in the centre **(see illustration)**.

12.31a Pull the door sill trim upwards . . .

12.33 Undo the 2 bolts (arrowed) in the centre aperture

12.24 Undo the bolt (arrowed) and pull the refrigerant pipes from the bulkhead

12.27 Undo the bolt (arrowed) and remove the footwell air duct each side

34 Mark the position of the facia crossmember in relation to the door pillars, then remove the bolts, pull the crossmember rearwards and lift it from place. The help of an assistant during this procedure is absolutely essential **(see illustrations)**.

12.31b . . . then pull the footwell kick panel away from the pillar

12.34a Remove the crossmember . . .

12.34b . . . after marking its correct position

12.35 Disconnect the drain tube (arrowed) as the heater is withdrawn

12.37 Undo the evaporator cover bolts (arrowed)

12.38 Withdraw the heater matrix at the same time as the evaporator

35 Ensure all relevant electrical connectors are disconnected then lift the heater housing from position. Disconnect the evaporator drain tube as the housing is removed **(see illustration)**.

36 Undo the bolts securing the bulkhead aperture cover around the heater matrix and evaporator pipes **(see illustrations 9.25a and 9.25b)**.

37 Undo the retaining bolts and remove the evaporator cover **(see illustration)**.

38 Withdraw the heater matrix and evaporator from the heater housing at the same time **(see illustration)**.

39 Refitting is the reverse of removal, noting the following points:

a) Align the crossmember with the previously-made marks, then refit and tighten the four bolts securing it to the A-pillar before inserting the bolt each end from the sides.

b) A new bolt must be fitted to the steering column universal joint.

c) Apply thread locking compound to the door hinge bolts

d) Tighten all fasteners to the specified torque where given.

e) Have the system evacuated, charged and leak-tested by the specialist who discharged it.

Compressor

40 Have the refrigerant discharged at a dealer service department or an automotive air conditioning repair facility.

41 Disconnect the battery negative (earth) lead (see Chapter 5).

42 Apply the handbrake, then raise the front of the vehicle and support on axle stands. Remove the right-hand front roadwheel.

43 Remove the right-hand front wheel arch liner, and engine undershield.

44 On petrol models use a sharp knife and cut the compressor drivebelt and discard it. Obviously, a new belt will be required. On diesel models release the tension from the belt (as described in Chapter 1) and remove it.

45 Unscrew the clamping bolts to disconnect the refrigerant lines from the compressor **(see illustration)**. Plug the line connections to prevent entry of any dirt or moisture. Discard the O-ring seals, new ones must be fitted.

46 Unbolt the compressor from the cylinder block/crankcase, unplug its electrical connector, then withdraw the compressor from the vehicle. **Note:** *Keep the compressor level during handling and storage. If the compressor has seized, or if you find metal particles in the refrigerant lines, the system must be flushed out by an air conditioning technician, and the accumulator/dehydrator must be renewed.*

47 Prior to installation, turn the compressor clutch centre six times, to disperse any oil that has collected in the head.

48 Refit the compressor in the reverse order of removal; renew all seals disturbed.

49 If you are installing a new compressor, refer to the compressor manufacturer's instructions for adding refrigerant oil to the system.

50 On petrol models fit a new auxiliary drive-belt, as described in Chapter 1. On diesel models the old drivebelt can be refitted if in good condition.

51 Refit the wheel arch liner, undershield and roadwheel. Lower the vehicle to the ground.

52 Have the system evacuated, charged and leak-tested by the specialist that discharged it.

Accumulator/dehydrator

53 Have the refrigerant discharged at a dealer service department or an automotive air conditioning repair facility.

54 Apply the handbrake, then raise the front of the vehicle and support on axle stands.

55 Remove the right-hand front wheel. Unscrew the inner wheel arch liner and remove from the vehicle.

56 Remove the right-hand headlight as described in Chapter 12.

57 Undo the retaining nuts and detach the refrigerant pipes from the accumulator/dehydrator **(see illustration)**. Immediately cap the open fittings, to prevent the entry of dirt and moisture.

58 Undo the 3 mounting bolts/nuts (the rear one is accessible through the wheel arch) and withdraw the accumulator/dehydrator **(see illustration)**.

59 Refit the accumulator/dehydrator in the reverse order of removal; renew all seals disturbed.

60 If you are installing a new accumulator/dehydrator, top-up with new oil to the volume removed, plus 90 cc of extra refrigerant oil.

61 Refit the headlight and wheel arch liner.

62 Have the system evacuated, charged and leak-tested by the specialist that discharged it.

12.45 Undo the bolts and detach the refrigerant pipes from the compressor (arrowed)

12.57 Disconnect the refrigerant pipes from the accumulator/dehydrator

12.58 The rear mounting bolt (arrowed) is accessible through the wheel arch

12.65 Remove the cowl

12.66 Undo the bolt at each end and pull the bulkhead extension panel forwards to remove it

12.67 The high-pressure switch (arrowed)

12.68 The low-pressure switch (arrowed)

13.4a Undo the bolts (arrowed) . . .

13.4b . . . and slide out the booster heater element

High- and low-pressure cut-off switches

63 Have the refrigerant discharged at a dealer service department or an automotive air conditioning repair facility.

64 To access the high-pressure switch remove the wiper arms as described in Chapter 12.

65 Release the clips and remove the scuttle panel grille **(see illustration)**.

66 Undo the bolts securing the brake fluid reservoir to the bulkhead extension (where fitted), then undo the bolts at each end and remove the extension **(see illustration)**.

67 Unplug the relevant switch electrical connector, and unscrew the switch **(see illustration)**. Plug the openings to prevent contamination.

68 The low-pressure switched is adjacent to the coolant expansion tank **(see illustration)**.

Unplug the electrical connector and remove the switch

69 Refitting is the reverse of the removal procedure. Renew the O-rings and lubricate with refrigerant oil.

70 Have the system evacuated, charged and leak-tested by the specialist that discharged it. Check the operation of the air conditioning system.

13 Electric booster heater (diesel engines only) – general information, removal and refitting

General information

1 Because diesel engines give off low residual heat, an electric booster heating element is fitted into the heater housing. At engine coolant temperatures of less than 60°C and

ambient temperatures of less then 10°C, when the high temperature setting is selected, the GEM (see Chapter 12), provides power to the heating element. Power is cut to the element when the engine coolant temperature exceeds 70°C or the ambient temperature exceeds 20°C.

Removal

2 Remove the facia as described in Chapter 11.

3 Release the wiring harness retaining clips, then undo the bolts and remove the support bracket from the right-hand side of the heater housing

4 Disconnect the booster heater wiring plug and undo the bolts and slide the booster heater element from the heater housing **(see illustrations)**.

Refitting

5 Refitting is a reversal of removal.

Chapter 4 Part A:
Fuel and exhaust systems – petrol models

Contents

Accelerator pedal – removal and refitting. 6
Air cleaner assembly – removal and refitting 5
Exhaust system – general information, removal and refitting 14
Fuel injection system – checking 11
Fuel injection system components – removal and refitting 12
Fuel injection system shut-off (inertia) switch – removal and refitting 10
Fuel lines and fittings – general information. 4

Fuel pump/fuel gauge sender unit – removal and refitting. 8
Fuel system – depressurisation 2
Fuel tank – removal, inspection and refitting 7
Fuel tank roll-over valve – general 9
General information and precautions. 1
Manifolds – removal and refitting. 13
Unleaded petrol – general information and usage 3

Degrees of difficulty

| Easy, suitable for novice with little experience | Fairly easy, suitable for beginner with some experience | Fairly difficult, suitable for competent DIY mechanic | Difficult, suitable for experienced DIY mechanic | Very difficult, suitable for expert DIY or professional |

Specifications

General
System type	Sequential multiport fuel indirect injection
Fuel octane requirement	95 RON unleaded
Regulated fuel pressure (nominal)	380 kpa (55 psi)

Torque wrench settings
	Nm	lbf ft
Accelerator pedal assembly nuts	8	6
Camshaft position sensor	8	6
Catalytic converter support bracket bolts	25	18
Crankshaft position sensor	8	6
Exhaust heat shield bolts	25	18
Exhaust manifold:		
Manifold nuts (to cylinder head)	48	35
Manifold to exhaust flexible section	48	35
Floor panel brace bolts	30	22
Fuel pulse damper (1.6 litre engines only)	10	7
Fuel rail mounting bolts:		
1.6 litre engines	15	11
1.8 and 2.0 litre engines	25	18
Fuel tank strap retaining bolts	25	18
Intake manifold nuts/bolts:		
1.6 litre non-Ti-VCT engines	18	13
1.6 litre Ti-VCT engines	15	11
1.8 and 2.0 litre engines	Not available	
Oxygen sensors	48	35
Throttle body retaining bolts	10	7
Variable camshaft timing oil control solenoid (Ti-VCT engine only)	10	7

1 General information and precautions

General information

The fuel system consists of a fuel tank (mounted under the floor, beneath the rear seats), fuel hoses, an electric fuel pump mounted in the fuel tank, and a sequential electronic fuel injection system controlled by an engine management electronic control unit (Powertrain Control Module).

The electric fuel pump supplies fuel under pressure to the fuel rail, which distributes fuel to the injectors. A pressure regulator integral with the pump controls the system pressure. From the fuel rail, fuel is injected into the intake ports, just above the intake valves, by four fuel injectors. The fuel rail is mounted to the cylinder head, just above the plastic intake manifold.

The amount of fuel supplied by the injectors is precisely controlled by the Powertrain Control Module (PCM). The module uses the signals from the crankshaft position sensor and the camshaft position sensor to trigger each injector separately in cylinder firing order (sequential injection), with benefits in terms of better fuel economy and leaner exhaust emissions.

The Powertrain Control Module is the heart of the entire engine management system, controlling the fuel injection, ignition and emissions control systems. The module receives information from various sensors which is then computed and compared with preset values stored in its memory to determine the required period of injection.

Information on crankshaft position and engine speed is generated by a crankshaft position sensor. The inductive head of the sensor runs just above the engine flywheel and scans a series of protrusions on the flywheel periphery. As the crankshaft rotates, the sensor transmits a pulse to the system's ignition module every time a protrusion passes it. There is one missing protrusion in the flywheel periphery at a point corresponding to 90° BTDC. The ignition module recognises the absence of a pulse from the crankshaft position sensor at this point to establish a reference mark for crankshaft position. Similarly, the time interval between absent pulses is used to determine engine speed. This information is then fed to the Powertrain Control Module for further processing.

On all engines except the 1.6 litre Ti-VCT, the camshaft position sensor is located in the cylinder head so that it registers with a lobe on the camshaft. On 1.6 litre Ti-VCT engines, 2 camshaft position sensors are fitted, as each camshaft is fitted with variable timing units. The camshaft position sensor functions in the same way as the crankshaft position sensor, producing a series of pulses; this gives the Powertrain Control Module a reference point,

to enable it to determine the firing order and operate the injectors in the appropriate sequence.

Engine temperature information is supplied by the coolant temperature sensor. The sensor is an NTC (Negative Temperature Coefficient) thermistor – that is, a semi-conductor whose electrical resistance decreases as its temperature increases. The sensor provides the Powertrain Control Module with a constantly-varying (analogue) voltage signal, corresponding to the temperature of the engine coolant. This is used to refine the calculations made by the module when determining the correct amount of fuel required to achieve the ideal air/fuel mixture ratio.

Intake air temperature and density information for air/fuel mixture ratio calculations is provided by a temperature and manifold absolute pressure (TMAP) sensor. The TMAP sensor is located on the throttle housing, and consists of a pressure transducer and a temperature sensor which directly supersedes the mass airflow and intake air temperature sensors. The TMAP sensor provides information to the Powertrain Control Module relating to intake manifold vacuum and barometric pressure, and the temperature of the air in the intake manifold. When the ignition is switched on with the engine stopped, the sensor calculates barometric pressure and, when the engine is running, the sensor calculates intake manifold vacuum. Note that 1.6 litre Ti-VCT engines are fitted with a mass airflow sensor in the outlet duct from the air cleaner housing.

The throttle valve inside the throttle housing is controlled by the driver with the accelerator pedal. As the valve opens, the amount of air that can pass through the system increases. As the throttle valve opens further, the TMAP sensor signal alters, and the Powertrain Control Module opens each injector for a longer duration, to increase the amount of fuel delivered to the intake ports.

All models feature a throttle which is electronically-controlled – an accelerator cable is not fitted. Instead, a throttle position sensor fitted to the accelerator pedal provides the Powertrain Control Module with the throttle opening signal, and this is relayed to a motor-driven throttle valve. This system also enables the PCM to control the engine idle speed, varying the throttle opening as required by changes in engine temperature and load.

On all models, roadspeed is monitored by the ABS wheel sensors.

The clutch pedal position is monitored by a switch fitted to the pedal bracket. This sends a signal to the Powertrain Control Module.

A pressure-operated switch is screwed into the power steering system's high-pressure pipe. The switch sends a signal to the Powertrain Control Module to increase engine speed to maintain idle speed as pressure in the system rises – typically, when the steering is near full-lock.

Oxygen sensors in the exhaust system provides the module with constant feedback

– 'closed-loop' control – which enables it to adjust the mixture to provide the best possible operating conditions for the catalytic converter. A further sensor is fitted, downstream of the converter, to monitor the converter's operation, and this provides an even finer degree of emission control.

The air intake side of the system consists of an air cleaner housing, an intake hose and duct, and a throttle housing.

Both the idle speed and mixture are under the control of the Powertrain Control Module, and cannot be adjusted.

Precautions

Before disconnecting any of the fuel injection system sensor wiring plugs, ensure at least that the ignition is switched off (ideally, disconnect the battery). If this is not done, it could result in a fault code being logged in the system memory, and may even cause damage to the component concerned.

Residual pressure will remain in the fuel lines long after the car was last used. When disconnecting any fuel line, first depressurise the fuel system as described in Section 2.

⚠ *Warning: Many of the procedures in this Chapter require the removal of fuel lines and connections, which may result in some fuel spillage. Before carrying out any operation on the fuel system, refer to the precautions given in 'Safety first!' at the beginning of this manual, and follow them implicitly. Petrol is a highly-dangerous and volatile liquid, and the precautions necessary when handling it cannot be overstressed.*

2 Fuel system – depressurisation

⚠ *Warning: The following procedure will merely relieve the pressure in the fuel system – remember that fuel will still be present in the system components, and take precautions accordingly before disconnecting any of them.*

Note: *Refer to the warning note in Section 1 before proceeding.*

1 The fuel system referred to in this Chapter is defined as the fuel tank and tank-mounted fuel pump/fuel gauge sender unit, the fuel filter, the fuel injector, and the metal pipes and flexible hoses of the fuel lines between these components. All these contain fuel, which will be under pressure while the engine is running and/or while the ignition is switched on.

2 The pressure will remain for some time after the ignition has been switched off, and must be relieved before any of these components is disturbed for servicing work.

3 The simplest depressurisation method is to disconnect the fuel pump electrical supply by removing the fuel pump fuse (refer to the wiring diagrams or the label on the engine

compartment fusebox for exact location) and starting the engine; allow the engine to idle until it stops through lack of fuel. Turn the engine over once or twice on the starter to ensure that all pressure is released, then switch off the ignition; do not forget to refit the fuse when work is complete.

4 If an adapter is available to fit the Schrader-type valve on the fuel rail pressure test/release fitting (identifiable by its blue plastic cap, and located on the union of the fuel feed line and the fuel rail), this may be used to release the fuel pressure. The Ford adapter (tool number 23-033) operates like to a drain tap – turning the tap clockwise releases the pressure. If the adapter is not available, place cloth rags around the valve, then remove the cap and allow the fuel pressure to dissipate. Refit the cap on completion.

5 Note that, once the fuel system has been depressurised and drained (even partially), it will take significantly longer to restart the engine – perhaps several seconds of cranking – before the system is refilled and pressure restored.

3 Unleaded petrol – general information and usage

All petrol models are designed to run on fuel with a minimum octane rating of 95 (RON). All models have a catalytic converter, and so must be run on unleaded fuel **only**. Under no circumstances should leaded fuel (UK '4-star' or LRP) be used, as this will damage the converter.

Super unleaded petrol (98 octane) can also be used in all models if wished, though there is no advantage in doing so.

4 Fuel lines and fittings – general information

Note: *Refer to the warning note in Section 1 before proceeding.*

Quick-release couplings

1 Quick-release couplings are employed at many of the unions in the fuel feed and return lines.

2 Before disconnecting any fuel system component, relieve the residual pressure in the system (see Section 2), and equalise tank pressure by removing the fuel filler cap.

⚠ **Warning: This procedure will merely relieve the increased pressure necessary for the engine to run – remember that fuel will still be present in the system components, and take precautions accordingly before disconnecting any of them.**

3 Release the protruding locking lugs on each union by squeezing them together and carefully pulling the coupling apart **(see illustration)**. Use rag to soak up any spilt fuel.

4.3 Squeeze the quick-release connectors to release them

Where the unions are colour-coded, the pipes cannot be confused. Where both unions are the same colour, note carefully which pipe is connected to which, and ensure that they are correctly reconnected on refitting.

4 To reconnect one of these couplings, press them firmly together. Switch the ignition on and off five times to pressurise the system, and check for any sign of fuel leakage around the disturbed coupling before attempting to start the engine.

Checking fuel lines

5 Checking procedures for the fuel lines are included in Chapter 1.

Component renewal

6 If any damaged sections are to be renewed, use original-equipment hoses or pipes, constructed from exactly the same material as the section being renewed. Do not install

5.1 Release the clamps (arrowed) and remove the outlet tube

5.3 Pull the collar and disconnect the ventilation hose

substitutes constructed from inferior or inappropriate material; this could cause a fuel leak or a fire.

7 Before detaching or disconnecting any part of the fuel system, note the routing of all hoses and pipes, and the orientation of all clamps and clips. New sections must be installed in exactly the same manner.

8 Before disconnecting any part of the fuel system, be sure to relieve the fuel system pressure (see Section 2), and equalise tank pressure by removing the fuel filler cap. Also disconnect the battery negative (earth) lead – see Chapter 5. Cover the fitting being disconnected with a rag, to absorb any fuel that may spray out.

5 Air cleaner assembly – removal and refitting

1.6 litre engines

Non-Ti-VCT

1 Slacken the clamp at each end and remove the air cleaner outlet tube **(see illustration)**.

2 Unhook the rubber retaining ring **(see illustration)**.

3 Pull the collar away from the air cleaner assembly, and disconnect the crankcase ventilation hose from the air cleaner **(see illustration)**.

4 On later models, undo the 4 scrivets and remove the air deflector panel above the radiator grille **(see illustration)**.

5.2 Unhook the rubber ring (arrowed)

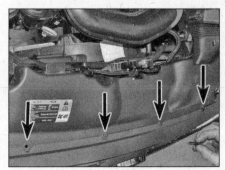

5.4 Undo the scrivets (arrowed) and remove the air deflector panel

5.7 Prise up the red locking catch and disconnect the wiring plug

5.8 Slacken the outlet hose clamps (arrowed)

5.10 Squeeze together the sides of the collar and pull the ventilation hose from the air cleaner

5.15 Use a small screwdriver to prise apart the hose clips

5.16 Release the rubber strap (arrowed)

5 Pull the air cleaner upwards to remove it. The pegs on the base of the cleaner fit into rubber grommets. These pegs may prove troublesome to release, and some effort may be needed – take care to avoid personal injury.

6 When refitting, locate the air cleaner pegs into the grommets and push down firmly to engage them in the grommets. Make sure the air cleaner duct clamps are securely refitted/tightened to prevent air leaks.

Ti-VCT

7 Disconnect the mass airflow sensor wiring plug, located in the outlet from the air cleaner cover **(see illustration)**.

8 Slacken the clamps and remove the air outlet hose from in between the air cleaner and the throttle body **(see illustration)**.

9 Disconnect the wiring plug from the coolant degas flow control valve (where fitted), then

6.3 Accelerator pedal/sensor assembly mounting nuts (arrowed)

unclip the pipes, remove the 2 retaining bolts, and move the valve to one side.

10 Squeeze together the sides of the collar and pull off the crankcase ventilation hose from the rear of the air cleaner **(see illustration)**.

11 Unhook the rubber retaining ring at the front right-hand corner of the air cleaner assembly **(see Illustration 5.2)**.

12 Pull the air cleaner upwards to remove it. The pegs on the base of the cleaner fit into rubber grommets. These pegs may prove troublesome to release, and some effort may be needed – take care to avoid personal injury.

13 When refitting, locate the air cleaner pegs into the grommets and push down firmly to engage them in the grommets. Make sure the air cleaner duct clamps are securely refitted/tightened to prevent air leaks.

1.8 and 2.0 litre engines

14 Remove the plastic cover from the top of the engine by pulling it upwards from its mountings.

15 Release the clips and remove the air cleaner outlet ducting **(see illustration)**.

16 Detach the rubber strap at the front of the housing **(see illustration)**.

17 Pull the air cleaner upwards from it rubber mountings. Squeeze together the sides of the collar and disconnect the crankcase ventilation hose from the air cleaner housing as it's withdrawn.

18 When refitting, locate the pegs on the base of the air cleaner housing into the mounting grommets and push the housing firmly downwards.

6 Accelerator pedal – removal and refitting

Removal

1 Remove the driver's side facia lower panel.

2 Disconnect the battery negative lead as described in Chapter 5.

3 Disconnect the wiring plug from the throttle position sensor, then unscrew the 3 mounting nuts and remove the pedal/sensor assembly from the bulkhead studs **(see illustration)**. Note that the sensor is not available separately from the pedal assembly. **Note:** *Ford insist that the sensor wiring plug can only be disconnected 10 times before is becomes irreversibly damaged. Use a marker pen to record each disconnection on the side of the connector. Only disconnect the plug if it is absolutely necessary.*

Refitting

4 Refit in the reverse order of removal. On completion, check the action of the pedal to ensure that the throttle has full unrestricted movement, and returns fully when released.

5 Reconnect the battery as described in Chapter 5.

7 Fuel tank – removal, inspection and refitting

Note: *Refer to the warning note in Section 1 before proceeding.*

Removal

1 Run the fuel level as low as possible prior to removing the tank. There is no drain plug fitted (and siphoning may prove difficult) but it may be possible to partially drain the tank.

2 Relieve the residual pressure in the fuel system (see Section 2), and equalise tank pressure by removing the fuel filler cap.

3 Disconnect the battery negative (earth) lead (see Chapter 5).

4 Chock the front wheels, then jack up the rear of the car and support it on axle stands

7.7 Undo the 3 bolts (arrowed) and remove the left-hand side air deflector shield

7.8 Undo the nuts and remove the heat shields beneath the fuel tank

7.9 Take care not to damage the filler pipe stub (arrowed) when removing the pipe

7.10 Depress the release button (arrowed) and disconnect the vent pipe from the rear of the tank

7.11a Disconnect the fuel supply and purge valve pipe at the front of the tank (arrowed)

7.11b The top part of the catch (arrowed) must be prised out before the release button can be depressed on the fuel supply pipe

(see *Jacking and vehicle support*). Remove the rear roadwheels.

5 Unhook the exhaust system mounting rubbers from the centre and rear hangers, and allow the exhaust system to rest on the rear suspension crossmember.

6 Undo the nuts securing the flange of the exhaust system rear section, then manoeuvre the rear section to one side, and secure it in place using cable-ties/wire/string.

7 Undo the 3 bolts and pull the left-hand side air deflector shield rearwards to release its retaining clip **(see illustration)**.

8 Undo the nuts and remove the exhaust centre and rear section heat shields from the vehicle underside **(see illustration)**.

9 Release the clips and disconnect the fuel tank filler pipes **(see illustration)**. Do not use any sharp-edged tools to release the pipes from their stub, as the pipe is easily damaged.

10 Depress the release button and disconnect the fuel tank vent pipe from the rear of the tank **(see illustration)**.

11 Disconnect the fuel supply pipe and EVAP canister purge valve pipe from the front of the tank **(see illustrations)**.

12 Support the tank using a trolley jack and a large sheet of wood to spread the load.

13 Note exactly how the fuel tank retaining straps are arranged to make refitting easier. In particular, note their fitted order under the retaining bolt heads, where applicable. The left-hand side strap is on top at the front fixing.

14 Unbolt and remove the fuel tank retaining straps **(see illustrations)**, but do not lower the tank at this stage.

15 Partially lower the tank on the jack, taking care that no strain is placed on any fuel lines or wiring. As soon as the wiring connector for the fuel pump/gauge sender

7.14a Undo the bolts at the rear (arrowed) . . .

7.15a Disconnect the wiring plug . . .

on top of the tank is accessible, reach in and disconnect it, then release the clip and disconnect the breather hose from the top of the tank **(see illustrations)**. Where

7.14b . . . and at the front (arrowed)

7.15b . . . then release the clip and disconnect the breather pipe (arrowed)

8.3 Using a home-made tool to slacken the retaining ring

8.5 Measure the resistance of the sender unit at full and zero float arm deflection

applicable, unclip the EVAP canister hose from the top of the tank.

16 Lower the fuel tank to the ground, checking all the way down that no pipes or wiring are under any strain. Remove the tank from under the car.

Inspection

17 Whilst removed, the fuel tank can be inspected for damage or deterioration. Removal of the fuel pump/fuel gauge sender unit (see Section 8) will allow a partial inspection of the interior. If the tank is contaminated with sediment or water, swill it out with clean fuel. Do not under any circumstances undertake any repairs on a leaking or damaged fuel tank; this work must be carried out by a professional who has experience in this critical and potentially-dangerous work.

18 Whilst the fuel tank is removed from the car, it should be placed in a safe area where sparks or open flames cannot ignite the fumes coming out of the tank. Be especially careful inside garages where a natural-gas type appliance is located, because the pilot light could cause an explosion.

19 Check the condition of the lower filler pipe and renew it if necessary.

Refitting

20 Refitting is a reversal of the removal procedure, noting the following points:

a) Ensure that all pipe and wiring connections are securely fitted.

b) When refitting the quick-release couplings, press them together until the locking lugs snap into their groove.

c) Tighten the tank strap retaining bolts to the specified torque.

d) If evidence of contamination was found, do not return any previously-drained fuel to the tank unless it is carefully filtered first.

8 Fuel pump/fuel gauge sender unit – removal and refitting

Note: Refer to the warning note in Section 1 before proceeding. Ford specify the use of their service tool 310-069 (a large socket with projecting teeth to engage the fuel pump/sender unit retaining rings raised edges) for this task. In practice, it was found that the ring could be loosened with conventional tools.

Removal

1 A combined fuel pump and fuel gauge

sender unit is located in the top face of the fuel tank. The combined unit can only be detached and withdrawn from the tank after the tank is released and lowered from under the car. Refer to Section 7 and remove the fuel tank, then proceed as follows.

2 With the fuel tank removed, disconnect the fuel supply pipe (if still attached to the tank) from the stub by squeezing the quick-release lugs.

3 Unscrew and remove the special retaining ring, either by unscrewing it with the Ford tool, or by carefully tapping it round until it can be unscrewed by hand. If care is taken, the ring could also be loosened using an oil filter removal chain- or strap-wrench **(see illustration)**.

4 Take out the rubber seal, then carefully lift out the fuel pump/gauge sender unit from the tank. Take care that the sender unit float and arm are not damaged as the unit is removed.

5 The level sender unit can be tested by connecting an ohmmeter across the sender terminals, and measuring its resistance. At full deflection (full tank) we measured a resistance of 9 ohms, and at zero deflection (empty tank) we measured 203 ohms **(see illustration)**.

Refitting

6 Refitting is a reversal of removal, but fit a new rubber seal and tighten the retaining ring securely, aligning the arrow on the top of the module with the mark on the top of the tank **(see illustrations)**. Refit the fuel tank as described in Section 7.

9 Fuel tank roll-over valve – general

1 The roll-over valve is built into the top of the fuel tank. It is not possible to access the valve. Its purpose is to prevent fuel loss if the car becomes inverted in a crash.

8.6a Renew the rubber seal

8.6b Align the arrow on the top of the module with the mark on the tank (arrowed)

10 Fuel injection system shut-off (inertia) switch – removal and refitting

1 The fuel injection system shut-off switch (also known as the inertia switch) is a safety feature, designed to reduce the loss of fuel following an accident. If a severe enough impact is detected by the switch, it will automatically shut off the car's high-pressure fuel pump, to reduce the chance of fuel escaping under pressure from the system.

2 It has been known for these switches to be triggered by non-life-threatening events, such as minor car parking bumps, or travelling over rough roads or potholes.

3 To reset the switch, depress the button on top of the switch. **Do not** reset the switch after an accident if fuel has escaped from the fuel system.

Removal

4 The fuel cut-off switch is located behind the driver's side footwell side trim panel. First disconnect the battery negative (earth) lead (see Chapter 5).

5 Remove the footwell side panel trim.

6 Unscrew and remove the switch retaining bolts, then disconnect the wiring plug and remove the switch (see illustration).

Refitting

7 Refitting is a reversal of removal, but make sure that the switch is reset. Start the engine to prove this.

11 Fuel injection system – checking

Note: *Refer to the warning note in Section 1 before proceeding.*

1 If a fault appears in the fuel injection system, first ensure that all the system wiring connectors are securely connected and free of corrosion – also refer to paragraphs 6 to 9 below. Check that the inertia switch has not been triggered (Section 10). Then ensure that the fault is not due to poor maintenance; ie, check that the air cleaner filter element is clean, the spark plugs are in good condition and correctly gapped, the cylinder compression pressures are correct, the ignition system wiring is in good condition and securely connected, and the engine breather hoses are clear and undamaged, referring to Chapter 1, Chapter 2 and Chapter 5.

2 If these checks fail to reveal the cause of the problem, the car should be taken to a suitably-equipped Ford dealer or specialist for testing. A diagnostic connector is fitted below the steering column, into which dedicated electronic test equipment can be plugged (**see illustration**). The test equipment is capable of 'interrogating' the engine management system PCM (Powertrain Control Module)

10.6 Fuel inertia shut-off switch

electronically and accessing its internal fault log (reading fault codes).

3 Fault codes can only be extracted from the PCM using a dedicated fault code reader. A Ford dealer will obviously have such a reader, but they are also available from other suppliers. It is unlikely to be cost-effective for the private owner to purchase a fault code reader, but a well-equipped local garage or auto-electrical specialist will have one.

4 Using this equipment, faults can be pinpointed quickly and simply, even if their occurrence is intermittent. Testing all the system components individually in an attempt to locate the fault by elimination is a time-consuming operation that is unlikely to be fruitful (particularly if the fault occurs dynamically), and carries a high risk of damage to the PCM's internal components.

5 Experienced home mechanics equipped with an accurate tachometer and a carefully-calibrated exhaust gas analyser may be able to check the exhaust gas CO content and the engine idle speed; if these are found to be out of specification, then the car must be taken to a suitably-equipped garage or Ford dealer for assessment. Neither the air/fuel mixture (exhaust gas CO content) nor the engine idle speed are manually adjustable; incorrect test results indicate the need for maintenance (possibly, injector cleaning) or a fault within the fuel injection system.

Limited Operation Strategy

6 Certain faults, such as failure of one of the engine management system sensors, will cause the system will revert to a backup (or

12.1a Slacken the clamp and disconnect the outlet tube (arrowed) – 1.6 litre non-Ti-VCT engines . . .

11.2 Diagnostic connector (arrowed)

'limp-home') mode, referred to by Ford as 'Limited Operation Strategy' (LOS). This is intended to be a 'get-you-home' facility only – the engine management warning light will come on when this mode is in operation.

7 In this mode, the signal from the defective sensor is substituted with a fixed value (it would normally vary), which may lead to loss of power, poor idling, and generally-poor running, especially when the engine is cold.

8 However, the engine may in fact run quite well in this situation, and the only clue (other than the warning light) would be that the exhaust CO emissions (for example) will be higher than they should be.

9 Bear in mind that, even if the defective sensor is correctly identified and renewed, the engine will not return to normal running until the fault code is erased, taking the system out of LOS. This also applies even if the cause of the fault was a loose connection or damaged piece of wire – until the fault code is erased, the system will continue in LOS.

12 Fuel injection system components – removal and refitting

Note: *Refer to the precautions in Section 1 before proceeding.*

Throttle body

1.6 litre engines

1 Slacken the clamps and remove the air cleaner outlet tube (see illustrations).

2 Slide up the red locking catch, and

12.1b . . . and Ti-VCT engines (arrowed)

12.2 Slide up the red locking catch

12.4 Undo the 4 bolts and remove the throttle body

12.7 Pull the engine cover upwards

12.10a Disconnect the throttle body wiring plug . . .

12.10b . . . then undo the 4 bolts (arrowed)

disconnect the wiring plug from the throttle body **(see illustration)**.

3 On non-Ti-VCT engines, detach the engine breather pipe from the cylinder head cover.

4 On all engines, undo the 4 bolts and remove the throttle body **(see illustration)**.

5 Refitting is a reversal of removal. Use a new gasket/seal, and tighten the mounting bolts to the specified torque.

1.8 and 2.0 litre engines

6 Drain the cooling system as described in Chapter 1, or use hose clamps to prevent coolant loss when the hoses are disconnected from the throttle body.

7 Remove the plastic cover on the top of the engine **(see illustration)**.

8 Release the clamps and remove the ducting between the air cleaner and the throttle body **(see illustration 5.15)**.

9 Release the clamps and disconnect the

coolant hoses from the throttle body. Use hose clamps if the system has not been drained (see Paragraph 6).

10 Disconnect the wiring plug, then undo the 4 bolts and remove the throttle body **(see illustrations)**.

11 Refitting is a reversal of removal. Use a new seal, and tighten the mounting bolts to the specified torque.

All engines

12 After refitting the throttle body, turn the ignition key to position II and wait for 1 minute for the throttle body to initialise, then turn the ignition off. Do not press the accelerator pedal during this procedure.

Fuel rail and injectors

13 Relieve the residual pressure in the fuel system (see Section 2), and equalise tank pressure by removing the fuel filler cap.

⚠️ **Warning: This procedure will merely relieve the increased pressure necessary for the engine to run – remember that fuel will still be present in the system components, and take precautions accordingly before disconnecting any of them.**

14 Disconnect the battery negative (earth) lead (see Chapter 5).

1.6 litre engines

15 Disconnect the engine breather hose from the cylinder head cover.

16 Unclip the fuel supply pipe from the support bracket, then prise out the locking catch, depress the release button and disconnect the pipe from the fuel rail **(see illustration)**.

17 Depress the wire locking clips and pull the wiring connectors assembly up from the injectors **(see illustrations)**. If necessary, disconnect the wiring plug from the oil pressure switch to allow the harness assembly to be moved to one side.

18 On 1.6 litre Ti-VCT engines, disconnect the wiring plugs from the throttle body, camshaft variable timing oil control solenoid at the right-hand end of the cylinder head, and the intake camshaft position sensor at the left-hand end of the cylinder head.

19 On all engines, unscrew and remove the two fuel rail mounting bolts. Carefully pull the fuel rail upwards to release the injectors from place – there will be some resistance from the injector O-ring seals **(see illustrations)**.

20 Remove the retaining clips and carefully

12.16 Prise out the locking catch (arrowed) then depress the release button

12.17a Push the locking clips (arrowed) forwards . . .

12.17b . . . and gently pull the connector assembly from the injectors

12.19a Undo the fuel rail mounting bolts (arrowed) . . .

12.19b . . . and pull the fuel upwards from place

12.20a Release the retaining clips from the rail . . .

12.20b . . . and pull the injector from the rail

12.21 Renew the injector O-rings seals (arrowed)

12.22 Prise out the clip and remove the fuel pulse damper

pull the injectors from the fuel rail **(see illustrations)**.

21 Using a screwdriver, prise the O-rings from the grooves at each end of the injectors **(see illustration)**. Note that the green seal is fitted to the injector nozzle end. Discard the O-rings and obtain new ones.

22 If required, the fuel pulse damper can be removed after the retaining clip/bolts have been removed **(see illustration)**. When refitting the damper, lubricate the new O-ring seals with clean engine oil.

23 Refitting is the reverse of the removal procedure, noting the following points:

a) Fit new injector O-rings, and lubricate them with clean engine oil to aid refitting.
b) Tighten the fuel rail mounting bolts to the specified torque.
c) Ensure that the hoses and wiring are routed correctly, and secured on reconnection by any clips or ties provided.
d) On completion, switch the ignition on to activate the fuel pump and pressurise the system, without cranking the engine. Check for signs of fuel leaks around all disturbed unions and joints before attempting to start the engine.

1.8 and 2.0 litre engines

24 Remove the plastic cover from the top of the engine.

25 Disconnect the vacuum hose from the fuel pulse damper on the fuel rail (where fitted).

26 Depress the clips and disconnect the wiring plugs from the injectors, then unclip the wiring harness.

27 Disconnect the fuel supply pipe from

the fuel rail by pushing the collar into the connector **(see illustration)**.

28 Unscrew the mounting nuts, then lift the fuel rail from the cylinder head – there will be some resistance from the injector O-ring seals **(see illustration)**.

29 To remove the injectors, first lift the retaining clips at the top, then slide them off sideways. Now pull the injectors out of the fuel rail.

30 Refitting is the reverse of the removal procedure, noting the following points:

a) Fit new injector O-rings, and lubricate them with clean engine oil to aid refitting.
b) Tighten the fuel rail mounting bolts to the specified torque.
c) Ensure that the hoses and wiring are routed correctly, and secured on reconnection by any clips or ties provided.
d) On completion, switch the ignition on to

12.27 Push in the collar (arrowed) and pull the connector from the fuel rail

activate the fuel pump and pressurise the system, without cranking the engine. Check for signs of fuel leaks around all disturbed unions and joints before attempting to start the engine.

TMAP sensor

Non-Ti-VCT engines

31 The sensor is located beneath the throttle body. Remove the plastic cover from the top of the engine – where fitted.

32 With the ignition switched off, disconnect the sensor wiring plug, then remove the mounting bolt and withdraw it from the manifold. Check the condition of the sensor O-ring seal, and obtain a new one if necessary **(see illustrations)**.

33 Refitting is a reversal of removal. Use a new seal if necessary, and tighten the mounting bolt securely, to prevent air leaks.

12.28 Undo the fuel rail mounting nuts (arrowed)

12.32a TMAP sensor (arrowed) – shown with the throttle body removed for clarity

Mass airflow sensor

Ti-VCT engines

34 Disconnect the wiring plug from the mass airflow sensor on the air cleaner cover (see illustration 12.2).

35 Undo the 2 bolts and pull the sensor from the air cleaner cover.

36 Refitting is a reversal of removal. Note the arrow on the top of the sensor indicating airflow.

Powertrain Control Module

Note: *The module is fragile. Take care not to drop it, or subject it to any other kind of impact. Do not subject it to extremes of temperature, or allow it to get wet.*

Note: *If a new PCM is to be fitted, the configuration information stored within the module must be uploaded to Ford diagnostic*

12.32b The TMAP sensor is located at the lower, left-hand edge of the manifold (arrowed)

equipment prior to the module being removed, and downloaded to the new PCM once installed. Entrust this task to a Ford dealer or suitably-equipped specialist.

37 Disconnect the battery negative lead as described in Chapter 5.

1.6 litre engines

38 Disconnect the wiring plug from the ignition coil assembly.

39 Depress the retaining clips and remove the cover over the PCM (see illustration).

40 Undo the PCM retaining bolts. Take care not to damage the cylinder head cover. Note the upper rear bolt has a plastic spacer between the PCM and the battery tray.

41 Place the module squarely on the cylinder head cover, and drill out the shear-bolt securing the module wiring connector (see illustration). A 6 mm drill bit will be required, and the hole must be drilled centrally, to avoid

damaging the module – Ford dealers use a special guide tool (418-537) to ensure this, which is a short tube with a 6 mm hole down the centre. Alternatively, use suitable socket, and a centre-punch to mark the centre of the bolt, and drill a smaller pilot hole first.

42 Once the module connector starts to come free, indicating that the shear-bolt has been released, clean up all the swarf from the drilling operations before removing the connector completely.

43 Remove the module connector, and extract the remains of the shear-bolt with some grips. The module itself can now be removed from the car.

44 Refitting is a reversal of removal. A new shear-bolt should be obtained for refitting, and tightened until the head shears off. Note that the O-ring seal fits onto the bolt before it's inserted into the connector, then fit the retaining washer on the threads of the bolt before refitting the connector (see illustrations).

1.8 and 2.0 litre engines up to 03/2007

45 Remove the plastic cover on the top of the engine, then depress the retaining clips and remove the cover over the PCM (see illustration).

46 In order to remove the security shield, the retaining shear-bolts must be drilled out. Centre-punch the holes, then drill out the bolts using a 6 mm drill (see illustration). Remove the shield.

47 Lever over the locking catches and disconnect the wiring plugs from the PCM.

48 Undo the 3 retaining bolts, and slide the PCM from the bracket.

12.39 Release the clips (arrowed) and remove the cover over the PCM

12.41 Drill out the wiring connector shear-bolt

12.44a Fit the O-ring (arrowed) onto the new shear-bolt . . .

12.44b . . . then insert the bolt and fit the retaining washer

12.45 Unclip the PCM cover

12.46 Drill out the security shield shear-bolts (arrowed)

49 Refitting is a reversal of removal. New shear-bolts should be obtained for refitting, and tightened until the heads shear off.

1.8 and 2.0 litre engines from 03/2007

50 Raise the front of the vehicle and support it securely on axle stands (see *Jacking and vehicle support*). Remove the left-hand front roadwheel.

51 Release the fasteners and remove the left-hand front wheel arch liner.

52 The PCM is fitted behind the front bumper. There may be a security shield fitted over the PCM. If this the case, remove the 4 retaining shear-bolts using an 8 mm drill. Where no shield is fitted, simply undo the 4 retaining bolts and remove the cover **(see illustrations)**.

53 Pull the PCM from place to release the retaining clips **(see illustration)**.

54 Lever over the locking catches and disconnect the wiring plugs from the PCM **(see illustration)**, then manoeuvre the PCM from position.

55 Refitting is a reversal of removal. New shear-bolts (where fitted) should be obtained for refitting, and tightened until the heads shear off.

Crankshaft position sensor

1.6 litre engines

56 The sensor is located on the front left-hand side of the engine, close to the transmission **(see illustration)**. For improved access, apply the handbrake, then jack up the front of the car and support it on axle stands (see *Jacking and vehicle support*). Remove the engine undershield.

57 With the ignition switched off, disconnect the wiring plug, then unscrew the mounting bolt and withdraw the sensor.

58 Refitting is a reversal of removal. Ensure that the sensor is clean when refitting, and tighten the bolt to the specified torque.

1.8 and 2.0 litre engines

59 The sensor is located adjacent to the crankshaft pulley. Raise the front of the vehicle and support it securely on axle stands (see *Jacking and vehicle support*). Remove the engine undershield **(see illustration)**.

60 Disconnect the sensor wiring plug **(see illustration)**.

61 Undo the 2 retaining bolts and remove the sensor.

62 Refitting is a reversal of removal. Tighten the sensor retaining bolts securely.

Camshaft position sensor

1.6 litre engines

63 On the 1.6 litre non-Ti-VCT engines, one sensor is fitted, located on the right-hand rear of the cylinder head. On 1.6 litre Ti-VCT engines, there are 2 sensors fitted – one over each of the camshafts at the left-hand end of the cylinder head cover.

64 With the ignition switched off, disconnect the wiring from the camshaft position sensor(s) **(see illustration)**.

12.52a Undo the 4 bolts (arrowed) and remove the PCM cover

12.53 Pull the PCM from the retaining clips

65 Unscrew the mounting bolt(s) and withdraw the sensor(s) from the cylinder head or cylinder head cover (as applicable).

66 Refitting is a reversal of removal, but use a new seal. Smear a little engine oil on the seal

12.56 Crankshaft position sensor (arrowed)

12.60 Crankshaft position sensor – 1.8 and 2.0 litre models

12.52b Drill out the shear-bolt (arrowed) and remove the security shield (where fitted)

12.54 Lever over the locking catches to disconnect the PCM wiring plugs

before fitting the sensor, and tighten the bolt(s) to the specified torque.

1.8 and 2.0 litre engines

67 Remove the plastic cover on the top of the engine.

12.59 Undo the fasteners (arrowed) and remove the engine undershield

12.64 Disconnect the camshaft position sensor wiring plug – 1.6 litre engines

12.68 Camshaft position sensor (arrowed) – 1.8 and 2.0 litre engines

12.71 Camshaft timing oil control solenoids (arrowed)

12.72 Undo the bolt and pull the solenoid from place

68 Disconnect the wiring plug, then undo the retaining bolt and remove the sensor (**see illustration**).
69 Refitting is a reversal of removal. Tighten the retaining bolt to the specified torque.

13.5 Undo the engine oil level dipstick guide tube bolt (arrowed)

13.6 Disconnect the breather hose (arrowed) – 1.6 litre Ti-VCT engine

12.75 Clutch pedal position switch (arrowed)

Coolant temperature sensor

70 See Chapter 3.

Variable camshaft timing oil control solenoids

71 The solenoids are located at the front, right-hand end of the cylinder head cover. Disconnect the solenoid wiring plug (**see illustration**).
72 Undo the retaining bolt and pull the solenoid from place (**see illustration**).
73 Refitting is a reversal of removal. Ensure the solenoid and aperture are scrupulously clean prior to refitting. Tighten the bolt to the specified torque.

Clutch pedal position switch

74 Remove the driver's side facia lower panel.
75 With the ignition switched off; disconnect the wiring from the clutch switch (**see illustration**).

13.7 Renew the manifold-to-cylinder head seals

76 Rotate the switch anti-clockwise and remove it.
77 Refitting is a reversal of removal.

Power steering pressure switch

78 Refer to Chapter 10.

Oxygen sensor

79 Refer to Chapter 4C.

13 Manifolds – removal and refitting

Note: *Refer to the warning note in Section 1 before proceeding.*

Intake manifold

1 Depressurise the fuel system as described in Section 2. On completion, disconnect the battery negative lead (refer to Chapter 5).

1.6 litre engines

2 Remove the alternator as described in Chapter 5.
3 Remove the fuel rail with injectors as described in Section 12.
4 Remove the throttle body as described in Section 12.
5 Undo the bolt securing the engine oil level dipstick guide tube to the manifold (**see illustration**).
6 Note their fitted locations and disconnect any vacuum hoses/pipes/wiring harnesses attached to the manifold (**see illustration**).
7 Undo the retaining bolts and remove the manifold. Renew the manifold-to-cylinder head seals/gasket (**see illustration**).
8 Refitting is a reversal of removal, noting the following points:
  a) Ensure that the mating faces are clean, and use a new manifold-to-cylinder head seals/gasket.
  b) Tighten all fixings to the specified torque.
  c) On completion, switch the ignition on to activate the fuel pump and pressurise the system, without cranking the engine. Check for signs of fuel leaks around all disturbed unions and joints before attempting to start the engine.

1.8 and 2.0 litre engines

9 Remove the plastic cover on the top of the engine.
10 Disconnect the battery as described in Chapter 5.
11 Remove the throttle body as described in Section 12.
12 Remove the engine oil level dipstick guide tube upper and lower retaining bolts (**see illustrations**).
13 Remove the intake manifold lower retaining bolt (**see illustration**).
14 Disconnect the wiring plugs from the left-hand knock sensor, MAP sensor (on the manifold), and unclip the harness from the manifold.

13.12a Oil level dipstick guide tube upper bolt (arrowed) . . .

13.12b . . . and lower bolt (arrowed)

13.13 Manifold lower retaining bolt (arrowed)

15 For improved access, undo the bolts and move the bonnet catch to one side.

16 Disconnect the following around the manifold:
a) *Crankcase breather hose at the base of the manifold.*
b) *Brake servo vacuum pipe from the manifold.*
c) *Fuel pulse damper vacuum hose (where fitted).*

17 Check carefully around the manifold, unclipping any remaining wiring or pipework which may still be attached to it.

18 Remove the retaining bolts, and withdraw the manifold from the front of the engine. Recover the gaskets **(see illustration)**.

19 Refitting is a reversal of removal, noting the following points:
a) *Ensure that the mating faces are clean, and use new manifold gaskets if necessary.*
b) *Tighten all fixings to the specified torque.*
c) *On completion, switch the ignition on to activate the fuel pump and pressurise the system, without cranking the engine. Check for signs of fuel leaks around all disturbed unions and joints before attempting to start the engine.*

Exhaust manifold

20 Disconnect the battery negative lead as described in Chapter 5.

⚠️ *Warning: Do not attempt this procedure until the engine is completely cool – ideally, the car should be left overnight before starting work.*

21 The exhaust manifold is integral with the front catalytic converter. Remove the front subframe as described in Chapter 10.

1.8 and 2.0 litre models

22 Remove the plastic cover on the top of the engine, then remove the oil filler cap.

All models

23 Undo the bolts and detach the brake fluid reservoir (where fitted) from the scuttle cowl panel.

24 Remove the wiper arms as described in Chapter 12.

25 Remove the 5 clips and remove the scuttle cowl panel.

26 Undo the 2 bolts, release the clips and remove the bulkhead extension panel **(see illustration)**.

27 Disconnect the oxygen sensors' wiring connectors behind the left-hand side of the engine **(see illustration)**.

13.18 Renew the intake manifold seals

28 Remove the bolts securing the exhaust manifold heat shield **(see illustration)**.

29 Working in a diagonal sequence, loosen and remove the exhaust manifold nuts. The manifold will remain in position for now, located on the cylinder head studs – do not try and slide it off the studs yet. **Note:** *If all of the studs come out with the nuts, leave two of them in place to support the manifold.*

30 Undo the bolts and remove the floor panel brace beneath the front of the exhaust system **(see illustration)**.

31 Undo the 2 bolts securing the catalytic converter to the support bracket on its underside, and with the help of an assistant, slide the manifold off the cylinder head studs (or completely unscrew any remaining studs), and lower it down to remove it, taking care not to damage the sensors or their wiring. Recover and discard the gasket **(see illustration)**.

13.26 Undo the bolt at each end (left-hand one shown) and pull the bulkhead extension panel forwards

13.27 Disconnect the oxygen sensor wiring plugs (arrowed)

13.28 Remove the heat shield from over the exhaust manifold (arrowed)

13.30 Remove the floor panel brace (arrowed)

13.31 Undo the bolts and remove support bracket under the catalytic converter

14.5 Make a 'splint' to support the flexible section of the exhaust

14.6 Undo the flange nuts (arrowed)

32 Unscrew the oxygen sensors from the manifold and catalytic converter.

33 Refitting is a reversal of removal, noting the following points:

a) Ensure that the mating faces are clean, and use new manifold gaskets.

b) Use new manifold/catalytic converter nuts/bolt.

c) Do not fully-tighten the manifold/catalytic converter mounting nuts/bolts until the front subframe has been refitted as described in Chapter 10.

d) Tighten the manifold nuts in a diagonal sequence.

e) Tighten all fixings to the specified torque.

---

14 Exhaust system –
general information, removal and refitting

Caution: Any work on the exhaust system should only be attempted once the system is completely cool – this may take several hours, especially in the case of the forward sections, such as the manifold and catalytic converter.

General information

1 The exhaust system consists of the exhaust manifold with integral catalytic converter, the centre section, and a separate rear silencer. At the front, where the centre section joins the manifold, a flexible ('mesh') section is fitted, to allow for engine movement.

2 The system is suspended throughout its entire length by rubber mountings.

Removal

3 To remove a part of the system, first jack up the front or rear of the car, and support it on axle stands (see *Jacking and vehicle support*). Alternatively, position the car over an inspection pit, or on car ramps.

Manifold and catalytic converter

4 Refer to Section 13.

Centre section

5 To prevent damage to the exhaust flexible section, support it by attaching a pair of splints either side (two scrap strips of wood, plant canes, etc) using some cable-ties **(see illustration)**. If a new centre section is being fitted, this precaution only applies to the new section of exhaust.

6 Unscrew the nuts securing the centre section to the flexible joint, and separate the joint. Recover the gasket **(see illustration)**.

7 Even if just the centre section is being removed, it still has to be separated from the rear silencer. Unbolt the clamp where the centre section joins the silencer, and separate the pipes (bear in mind that a corroded rear silencer may be damaged during removal – see paragraph 9).

8 Unhook the centre section's two rubber mountings, and remove it from under the car.

Rear silencer

9 When fitted in the factory, the exhaust system from the front section flange to the end of the tail pipe is one piece. However, if the rear silencer is to be renewed, new silencers should be available – check with your parts supplier. Using a hacksaw, cut through the exhaust pipe 150 mm behind the mounting, in front of the rear silencer.

10 Unhook the silencer rubber mountings, and remove it from under the car.

Heat shields

11 The heat shields are secured to the underside of the body by special nuts. Each shield can be removed separately, but note that they may overlap, making it necessary to loosen another section first. If a shield is being removed to gain access to a component located behind it, it may prove sufficient in some cases to remove the retaining nuts and/ or bolts, and simply lower the shield, without disturbing the exhaust system. Otherwise, remove the exhaust section as described earlier.

Refitting

12 In all cases, refitting is a reversal of removal, but note the following points:

a) Always use new gaskets, nuts and clamps (as applicable), and coat all threads with copper grease. Make sure any new clamps are the same size as the original – overtightening a clamp which is too big will not seal the joint.

b) On a sleeved joint (such as that between the centre section and rear silencer), use a smear of exhaust jointing paste to achieve a gas-tight seal.

c) If any of the exhaust mounting rubbers are in poor condition, fit new ones.

d) Make sure that the exhaust is suspended properly on its mountings, and will not come into contact with the floor or any suspension parts. The rear silencer especially must be aligned correctly before tightening the clamp nuts.

e) Tighten all nuts/bolts to the specified torque, where given.

Chapter 4 Part B:
Fuel and exhaust systems – diesel models

Contents

Section number

Accelerator pedal – removal and refitting. 4
Air cleaner assembly – removal and refitting 2
Engine management system components – removal and refitting . . 11
Exhaust system – general information and component renewal 17
Fuel gauge sender unit – removal and refitting 7
Fuel injection pump – removal and refitting 9
Fuel injection system – general information. 5
Fuel injection system – testing and adjustment 8
Fuel injectors – removal and refitting 10

Section number

Fuel system – priming and bleeding. 6
Fuel tank – removal and refitting 3
General information and precautions. 1
Intercooler – removal and refitting 15
Manifolds – removal and refitting. 16
Turbocharger – description and precautions 12
Turbocharger – examination and overhaul. 14
Turbocharger – removal and refitting 13

Degrees of difficulty

Easy, suitable for novice with little experience	**Fairly easy,** suitable for beginner with some experience	**Fairly difficult,** suitable for competent DIY mechanic	**Difficult,** suitable for experienced DIY mechanic	**Very difficult,** suitable for expert DIY or professional

Specifications

General
System type:

1.6 litre engines . . . .   Bosch direct injection common rail, with timing belt-driven high-pressure delivery pump, variable nozzle turbocharger and intercooler

1.8 litre engines . . . .   Siemens direct injection common rail with a chain-driven high-pressure delivery pump, variable nozzle turbocharger and intercooler

2.0 litre engines . . . .   Siemens direct injection common rail with a camshaft-driven high-pressure delivery pump, variable nozzle turbocharger and intercooler

Torque wrench settings

	Nm	lbf ft
Camshaft position sensor	10	7
Common rail mounting bolts/nuts:		
1.6 litre engines	22	16
1.8 litre engines	24	18
2.0 litre engines	22	16
Crankshaft position sensor:		
1.6 litre engines	8	6
1.8 litre engines	6	4
2.0 litre engines	8	6
Exhaust manifold to cylinder head:		
1.6 litre engines	25	18
1.8 litre engines	25	18
2.0 litre engines	30	22
Fuel high-pressure pipe union nuts:*		
To fuel rail:		
1.6 litre engines	25	18
1.8 litre engines	38	28
2.0 litre engines	23	17
To fuel pump:		
1.6 litre engines	25	18
1.8 litre engines	25	18
2.0 litre engines	23	17
To fuel injectors:		
1.6 litre engines	25	18
1.8 litre engines	25	18
2.0 litre engines	23	17
Fuel injector clamp nuts/bolts:		
1.6 litre engines:		
Stage 1	4	3
Stage 2	Angle-tighten a further 45°	
1.8 litre engines:		
Stage 1	5	4
Stage 2	Angle-tighten a further 90°	
2.0 litre engines:		
Stage 1	4	3
Stage 2	Angle-tighten a further 45°	
Fuel injection pump mounting bolts:		
1.6 litre engines	22	16
1.8 litre engines	20	15
2.0 litre engines	20	15
Fuel injection pump sprocket:		
1.6 litre engines	50	37
1.8 litre engines:		
Timing belt	42	31
Drive chain	33	24
Fuel tank sender unit collar	85	63
Throttle body bolts:		
1.6 litre engines	8	6
Turbocharger oil supply banjo bolt:		
1.6 litre engines	30	22
1.8 litre engines	18	13
2.0 litre engines:		
To engine block	40	30
To turbocharger	28	21
Turbocharger support bracket bolt:		
1.6 litre engines	25	18
1.8 litre engines	45	33
2.0 litre engines	15	11
Turbocharger to exhaust manifold:		
1.6 litre engines	25	18
1.8 litre engines	10	7
2.0 litre engines	25	18
Turbocharger-to-turbocharger support bracket bolt:		
1.8 litre engines	25	18
2.0 litre engines	30	22

* Do not re-use

2.2a Slacken the clamp (arrowed) and pull the air outlet hose from the turbocharger

2.2b Release the clips and disconnect the breather hose

1 General information and precautions

General information

The operation of the fuel injection system is described in more detail in Section 5.

Fuel is drawn from a tank under the rear of the vehicle by a tank-immersed electric pump, and then forced through a filter to the injection pump.

The camshaft-driven injection pump is a tandem pump – a low pressure vane-type pump which supplies the high-pressure pump with fuel at a constant pressure, and a high-pressure piston-type pump which supplies fuel to the common fuel rail at variable pressure.

Fuel is supplied from the common fuel rail to the injectors. Also inside the injection pump assembly is a pressure control valve which regulates the pressure of fuel from the high-pressure pump, and a fuel volume control valve which regulates the fuel flow to the high-pressure side of the pump. The injectors are operated by solenoids controlled by the PCM, based on information supplied by various sensors. The engine PCM also controls the preheating side of the system – refer to Chapter 5 for more details.

The engine management system fitted incorporates a 'drive-by-wire' system, where the traditional accelerator cable is replaced by an accelerator pedal position sensor. The position and rate-of-change of the accelerator pedal is reported by the position sensor to the PCM, which then adjusts the fuel injectors and fuel pressure to deliver the required amount of fuel and optimum combustion efficiency.

The exhaust system incorporates a turbocharger and an EGR system. Further detail of the emission control systems can be found in Chapter 4D.

Precautions

• When working on diesel fuel system components, scrupulous cleanliness must be observed, and care must be taken not to introduce any foreign matter into fuel lines or components.

• After carrying out any work involving disconnection of fuel lines, it is advisable to check the connections for leaks; pressurise the system by cranking the engine several times.

• Electronic control modules are very sensitive components, and certain precautions must be taken to avoid damage to these units.

• When carrying out welding operations on the vehicle using electric welding equipment, the battery and alternator should be disconnected.

• Although the underbonnet-mounted modules will tolerate normal underbonnet conditions, they can be adversely affected by excess heat or moisture. If using welding equipment or pressure-washing equipment in the vicinity of an electronic module, take care not to direct heat, or jets of water or steam at the module. If this cannot be avoided, remove the module from the vehicle, and protect its wiring plug with a plastic bag.

• Before disconnecting any wiring, or removing components, always ensure that the ignition is switched off.

• Do not attempt to improvise PCM fault diagnosis procedures using a test lamp or multimeter, as irreparable damage could be caused to the module.

• After working on fuel injection/engine management system components, ensure that all wiring is correctly reconnected before reconnecting the battery or switching on the ignition.

2 Air cleaner assembly – removal and refitting

Removal

1.6 litre engines

1 Pull the plastic cover (where fitted) on the top of the engine upwards from its mountings.
2 Slacken the clamps and remove the air cleaner outlet hose. Disconnect the engine breather hose at the same time (**see illustrations**).
3 Slide up the red locking clip, then disconnect the mass airflow sensor wiring plug.
4 Release the rubber retaining strap and pull the air cleaner assembly upwards from place. Disconnect the intake hose and vacuum hose as the assembly is removed (**see illustrations**).

2.4a Release the rubber strap . . .

2.4b . . . disconnect the vacuum hose . . .

2.4c . . . and the intake hose

2.5 Pull the engine cover upwards to release the clips in the order shown – 1.8 litre models

1.8 litre engines

5 Pull the plastic cover on the top of the engine upwards to release its mountings in the order shown (**see illustration**). Take care to manoeuvre the cover around the MAP sensor.
6 Disconnect the mass airflow meter wiring plug, release the harness clip, slacken the clamp and disconnect the outlet hose from the mass airflow meter (**see illustration**).
7 Release the rubber retaining strap at the front of the housing (**see illustration**).
8 Pull the housing upwards sharply to release it from the mounting grommets.

2.0 litre engines

9 Disconnect the mass airflow sensor wiring plug.
10 Slacken the clamp and disconnect the outlet hose from the mass airflow sensor (**see illustration**).
11 Release the rubber retaining strap at the front of the housing (**see illustration**).
12 Pull the housing upwards sharply to release it from the mounting grommets.

Refitting

13 Refitting is a reversal of removal.

2.6 Slacken the clamp (arrowed) and disconnect the hose from the airflow meter

2.7 Release the rubber strap at the front of the air filter housing

2.10 Slacken the clamp (arrowed) and disconnect the outlet hose

2.11 Release the strap at the front of the air filter housing

3 Fuel tank – removal and refitting

Note: *Observe the precautions in Section 1 before working on any component in the fuel system.*

Removal

1 Run the fuel level as low as possible prior to removing the tank. There is no drain plug fitted (and siphoning may prove difficult). It is preferable to keep as much fuel in the pipes as possible, to reduce the need for bleeding the system when restarting the engine.
2 Equalise tank pressure by removing the fuel filler cap.
3 Disconnect the battery negative (earth) lead (see Chapter 5).
4 Chock the front wheels, then jack up the rear of the car and support it on axle stands (see *Jacking and vehicle support*). Remove the rear roadwheels.
5 Unhook the exhaust system mounting rubbers from the centre and rear hangers, and allow the exhaust system to rest on the rear suspension crossmember.
6 Undo the nuts securing the flange of the exhaust system rear section, then manoeuvre the rear section to one side, and secure it in place using cable-ties/wire/string.
7 Undo the fasteners and remove the left-hand side rear air deflector shield (**see illustration**).
8 Undo the fasteners and remove the exhaust centre and rear section heat shields from the vehicle underside (**see illustration**).
9 Release the clips and disconnect the fuel tank filler and vent pipes at the rear of the tank. Do not use any sharp-edged tools to release the pipes from their stubs, as the pipes are easily damaged. If crimp-type clips are fitted, discard the pipe clips and obtain some worm-type/Jubilee clips for refitting. **Note:** *It's important to note the fitted positions of the original clips, and fit the new clips in exactly the same place/orientation.*
10 On models equipped with a particulate filter, depress the release buttons, and disconnect the additive pipes from the rear of the fuel tank.

3.7 Undo the bolts and remove the air deflector panel (arrowed)

11 Disconnect the fuel supply and return hoses at the front of the tank **(see illustration)**.
12 Support the tank using a trolley jack and a large sheet of wood to spread the load.
13 Note exactly how the fuel tank retaining straps are arranged, to make refitting easier. In particular, note their fitted order under the retaining bolt heads, where applicable.
14 Unbolt and remove the fuel tank retaining straps **(see illustrations)**.
15 Partially lower the tank on the jack, taking care that no strain is placed on any fuel lines or wiring. As soon as the wiring connector for the fuel pump/gauge sender on top of the tank is accessible, reach in and disconnect it.
16 Lower the fuel tank to the ground, checking all the way down that no pipes or wiring are under any strain. Remove the tank from under the car.

Inspection

17 Whilst removed, the fuel tank can be inspected for damage or deterioration. Removal of the fuel pump/fuel gauge sender unit (see Section 7) will allow a partial inspection of the interior. If the tank is contaminated with sediment or water, swill it out with clean fuel. Do not under any circumstances undertake any repairs on a leaking or damaged fuel tank; this work must be carried out by a professional who has experience in this critical and potentially-dangerous work.
18 Whilst the fuel tank is removed from the car, it should be placed in a safe area where sparks or open flames cannot ignite the fumes coming out of the tank. Be especially careful inside garages where a natural-gas type appliance is located, because the pilot light could cause an explosion.
19 Check the condition of the lower filler pipe and renew it if necessary.

Refitting

20 Refitting is a reversal of the removal procedure, noting the following points:
  a) *Ensure that all pipe and wiring connections are securely fitted.*
  b) *When refitting the quick-release couplings, press them together until the locking lugs snap into their groove.*
  c) *Tighten the tank strap retaining bolts securely.*
  d) *If evidence of contamination was found, do not return any previously-drained fuel to the tank unless it is carefully filtered.*

4 Accelerator pedal – removal and refitting

Removal

1 Remove the driver's side facia lower panel.
2 Disconnect the battery negative lead as described in Chapter 5.

3.8 Remove the heat shield under the fuel tank

3.14a Fuel tank strap rear bolts (arrowed) . . .

3 Disconnect the wiring plug from the throttle position sensor, then unscrew the 3 mounting nuts and remove the pedal/sensor assembly from the bulkhead studs **(see illustration)**. Note that the sensor is not available separately from the pedal assembly. **Note:** *Ford insist that the sensor wiring plug can only be disconnected 10 times before is becomes irreversibly damaged. Use a marker pen to record each disconnection on the side of the connector. Only disconnect the plug if it's absolutely necessary.*

Refitting

4 Refit in the reverse order of removal. On completion, check the action of the pedal to ensure that the throttle has full unrestricted movement, and fully returns when released.
5 Reconnect the battery as described in Chapter 5.

4.3 Accelerator pedal assembly retaining nuts (arrowed)

3.11 Prise up the catches (arrowed), depress the buttons on the other side and disconnect the fuel supply and return hoses

3.14b . . . and front bolt (arrowed)

5 Fuel injection system – general information

The system is under the overall control of the engine management PCM (Powertrain Control Module), which also controls the preheating system (see Chapter 5).

Fuel is supplied from the rear-mounted fuel tank, via an electrically-powered lift pump and the fuel filter, to the fuel injection pump. The fuel injection pump supplies fuel under high pressure to the common fuel rail. The fuel rail provides a reservoir of fuel under pressure ready for the injectors to deliver direct to the combustion chamber. The individual fuel injectors incorporate piezoelectrical/electromagnetic elements, which when operated, allow the high-pressure fuel to be injected. The elements are controlled by the PCM. The fuel injection pump purely provides high-pressure fuel. The timing and duration of the injection is controlled by the PCM, based on the information received from the various sensors. In order to increase combustion efficiency and reduce combustion noise (diesel 'knock'), a small amount of fuel is injected before the main injection takes place – this is known as Pre- or Pilot-injection. The fuel filter incorporates a heater element.

Additionally, the engine management PCM activates the preheating system (Chapter 5), and the exhaust gas recirculation (EGR) system (see Chapter 4D).

5.9 The diagnostic connector is below the driver's side of the facia (arrowed)

The system uses the following sensors.

a) *Crankshaft sensor – informs the PCM of the crankshaft speed and position.*

b) *Coolant/cylinder head temperature sensor – informs the PCM of engine temperature.*

c) *Mass airflow sensor – informs the PCM of the mass air entering the intake tract.*

d) *Wheel speed sensor – informs the PCM of the vehicle speed.*

e) *Accelerator pedal position sensor – informs the PCM of throttle position, and the rate of throttle opening/closing.*

f) *Fuel high-pressure sensor – informs the PCM of the pressure of the fuel in the common rail.*

g) *Camshaft position sensor – informs the PCM of the camshaft position so that the engine firing sequence can be established.*

h) *Stop-light switch – informs the PCM when the brakes are being applied*

i) *Boost pressure sensor – informs the PCM of the boost pressure generated by the turbocharger.*

j) *Air conditioning pressure sensor – informs the PCM of the high-pressure side of the air conditioning circuit, in case a raised idle speed is required to compensate for compressor load.*

k) *Intake air temperature sensor – informs the PCM of the intake air temperature.*

l) *Clutch pedal switch – informs the PCM of the clutch pedal position.*

m) *Turbocharger position sensor – informs the PCM of the position of the variable in take nozzle guide rails.*

On all models, a 'drive-by-wire' throttle control system is used. The accelerator pedal is not physically connected to the fuel injection pump with a traditional cable, but instead is monitored by a dual potentiometer mounted on the pedal assembly, which provides the powertrain control module (PCM) with a signal relating to accelerator pedal movement.

The signals from the various sensors are processed by the PCM, and the optimum fuel quantity and injection timing settings are selected for the prevailing engine operating conditions.

Catalytic converters and an exhaust gas recirculation (EGR) system are fitted, to reduce harmful exhaust gas emissions. Details of this and other emissions control system equipment are given in Chapter 4D.

If there is an abnormality in any of the readings obtained from any sensor, the PCM enters its back-up mode. In this event, the PCM ignores the abnormal sensor signal, and assumes a preprogrammed value which will allow the engine to continue running (albeit at reduced efficiency). If the PCM enters this back-up mode, the warning light on the instrument panel will come on, and the relevant fault code will be stored in the PCM memory.

If the warning light comes on, the vehicle should be taken to a Ford dealer or specialist at the earliest opportunity. A complete test of the system can then be carried out, using a special electronic test unit which is simply plugged into the system's diagnostic connector. The connector is located below the driver's side of the facia above the pedals **(see illustration)**.

6 Fuel system – priming and bleeding

1 After disturbing the fuel system before the high-pressure fuel injection pump, the system must be bled. To do this, Ford technicians use a hand pump (No 310-110) that sucks fuel from the tank, and forces it through the filter. In the absence of this tool, use a hand-held vacuum pump.

2 Remove the plastic cover on the top of the engine.

Using the Ford pump

3 Disconnect the fuel supply pipe quick-release connector from the high-pressure fuel injection pump, and place the end of the pipe in a suitable container to catch the emerging fuel.

4 Disconnect the fuel supply hose to the fuel filter, and connect the hand pump (or equivalent) between the hose and the filter. Ensure the arrow on the pump is pointing towards the fuel filter.

5 Operate the pump until there is a continuous flow of fuel into the container. Squeeze and hold the hand pump for 10 seconds.

6 Release the pump, then squeeze and hold the pump for a further 10 seconds.

7 Reattach the pipe to the high-pressure pump, then operate the pump until strong resistance is felt.

8 Operate the starter motor and run the engine until it reaches normal operating temperature. *Caution: Do not operate the starter motor for more than 10 seconds, then wait 30 seconds before trying again.*

9 Stop the engine, and remove the hand pump. Wipe up any fuel spillage, and refit the engine cover.

Using a hand-held vacuum pump

10 Depress the release tab(s) and disconnect the fuel outlet hose from the fuel filter **(see illustrations)**.

11 Connect the vacuum pump pipe to the outlet on the filter, and continue to pull a vacuum until bubble-free fuel emerges from the hose **(see illustration)**.

12 Reconnect the fuel hose.

6.10a Depress the button and disconnect the fuel outlet hose – 1.6 litre models . . .

6.10b . . . prise out the clip on 1.8 litre models . . .

6.10c . . . and depress the clip (arrowed) on 2.0 litre models

6.11 Attach the hand-held vacuum pump hose to the filter outlet, and continue to pull a vacuum until bubble-free fuel emerges

13 Operate the starter motor and run the engine until it reaches normal operating temperature.
Caution: Do not operate the starter motor for more than 10 seconds, then wait 30 seconds before trying again.
14 Stop the engine. Wipe up any fuel spillage, and refit the engine cover.

7 Fuel gauge sender unit – removal and refitting

Note: Observe the precautions in Section 1 before working on any component in the fuel system.

Removal

1 Remove the fuel tank as described in Section 3.
2 Depress the release buttons, and disconnect the fuel supply and return hoses from the sender unit **(see illustration)**.
3 Unscrew the sender unit plastic retaining collar using a pair of large, crossed-screwdrivers, or improvise a tool **(see illustration)**.
4 Lift the sender unit from the tank **(see illustrations)**. Discard the O-ring seal, a new one must be fitted. Note that on models with a fuel-fired auxiliary heater, undo the plug for the suction pipe on the underside of the level sensor, and transfer the pipe to the new sensor (if renewed). No separate parts are available.
5 If required, attach the leads from a multimeter to the sender unit wires, and measure the resistance at full float deflection and zero deflection. The resistance of the unit we tested was 200 ohms at full deflection, and 10 ohms at zero deflection **(see illustration)**.

Refitting

6 Refitting is a reversal of removal, bearing in mind the following points:
 a) Use a new O-ring seal smeared with petroleum jelly.
 b) Position the sender unit so the arrow on the cover aligns with the marks on the fuel tank align **(see illustration)**.
 c) Tighten the sender unit retaining collar to the specified torque, where tools permit.

8 Fuel injection system – testing and adjustment

Testing

1 If a fault appears in the fuel injection system, first ensure that all the system wiring connectors are securely connected and free from corrosion. Ensure that the fault is not due to poor maintenance; ie, check that the air cleaner filter element is clean, that the cylinder compression pressures are correct (see Chapter 2), and that the engine breather hoses are clear and undamaged (see Chapter 4D).

7.2 Depress the locking collars and disconnect the supply and return hoses from the tank sender unit

7.4a Lift the sender unit from the tank . . .

2 If the engine will not start, check the condition of the glow plugs (see Chapter 5).
3 If these checks fail to reveal the cause of the problem, the vehicle should be taken to a Ford dealer or specialist for testing using special electronic equipment which is plugged into the diagnostic connector (see Section 5). The tester should locate the fault quickly and simply, avoiding the need to test all the system components individually, which is time consuming, and also carries a risk of damaging the PCM.

Adjustment

4 The engine idle speed, maximum speed and fuel injection pump timing are all controlled by the PCM. Whilst in theory it is possible to check the settings, if they are found to be in need of adjustment, the car will have to

7.5 Use a multimeter to measure the sender unit resistance at full and zero float arm deflection

7.3 We used a home-made tool to unscrew the sender unit plastic collar

7.4b . . . discard the seal (arrowed) a new one must be fitted

be taken to a suitably-equipped Ford dealer or specialist. They will have access to the necessary diagnostic equipment required to test and (where possible) adjust the settings.

9 Fuel injection pump – removal and refitting

Caution: Cleanliness is essential. Be careful not to allow dirt into the injection pump or injector pipes during this procedure.
Note: Any rigid high-pressure fuel pipes disturbed must be renewed.

1.6 litre engines

Removal

1 Disconnect the battery (see Chapter 5) and

7.6 The arrow on the sender cover must align with the marks on the fuel tank (arrowed)

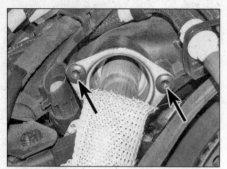

9.3a Undo the 2 bolts (arrowed) securing the EGR pipe to the manifold/cover . . .

9.3b . . . then the bolt (arrowed) securing the pipe to the head . . .

9.3c . . . then release the clamp (arrowed) and remove the EGR pipe

Tool Tip 1: *A sprocket holding tool can be made from two lengths of steel strip bolted together to form a forked end. Bend the ends of the strip through 90° to form the 'prongs'.*

Tool Tip 2: *Make a sprocket releasing tool from a short strip of steel. Drill two holes in the strip to correspond with the two holes in the sprocket. Drill a third hole just large enough to accept the flats of the sprocket retaining nut.*

remove the timing belt as described in Chapter 2. After removal of the timing belt, temporarily refit the right-hand engine mounting but do not fully tighten the bolts.

2 Remove the air filter assembly as described in Section 2.

3 Remove the EGR cooler as described in Chapter 4D, or on models without a cooler, undo the bolts, release the clamps and remove the EGR pipe **(see illustrations)**.

4 Undo the bolts/nuts and remove the support brackets above the fuel common rail and the high-pressure pump.

5 Undo the union nuts and remove the high-pressure fuel pipe between the fuel common rail and the high-pressure pump. Plug the openings to prevent contamination.

6 Disconnect the wiring plug from the high-pressure fuel pump.

7 Depress the release buttons and disconnect the fuel supply and return hoses from the pump. Note that the hoses may have a release button on each side of the fitting. Plug the openings to prevent contamination.

8 Hold the pump sprocket stationary, and loosen the centre nut securing it to the pump shaft **(see Tool Tip 1)**.

9 The fuel pump sprocket is a taper fit on the pump shaft and it will be necessary to make up a tool to release it from the taper **(see Tool Tip 2)**. Partially unscrew the sprocket retaining

nut, fit the home-made tool, and secure it to the sprocket with two 7.0 mm bolts and nuts. Prevent the sprocket from rotating as before, and screw down the nuts, forcing the sprocket off the shaft taper.

10 Once the taper is released, remove the tool, unscrew the nut fully, and remove the sprocket from the pump shaft.

11 Undo the three bolts, and remove the pump from the mounting bracket.

Caution: The high-pressure fuel pump is manufactured to extremely close tolerances and must not be dismantled in any way. Do not unscrew the fuel pipe male

9.16 Remove the seal housing retaining nuts

union on the rear of the pump, or attempt to remove the sensor, piston de-activator switch, or the seal on the pump shaft. No parts for the pump are available separately and if the unit is in any way suspect, it must be renewed.

Refitting

12 Refitting is a reversal of removal, noting the following points:
a) *Always renew the pump-to-common rail high-pressure pipe.*
b) *With everything reassembled and reconnected, and observing the precautions listed in Section 1, start the engine and allow it to idle. Check for leaks at the high-pressure fuel pipe unions with the engine idling. If satisfactory, increase the engine speed to 3000 rpm and check again for leaks.*
c) *Take the car for a short road test and check for leaks once again on return. If any leaks are detected, obtain and fit another new high-pressure fuel pipe.* **Do not** *attempt to cure even the slightest leak by further tightening of the pipe unions.*

1.8 litre engines

Removal

13 Disconnect the battery negative lead as described in Chapter 5.

14 Remove the timing belt as described in Chapter 2.

15 Slacken the three bolts securing the injection pump timing belt sprocket, and remove the sprocket from the pump. The sprocket may need to be prevented from turning as this is done – it should prove sufficient to select a gear and apply the hand- brake, but it may be necessary to jam the flywheel ring gear as described in Chapter 2. The sprocket is sealed to the inner pulley using RTV sealant, and may need to be prised free; recover the metal gasket.

16 Remove the 7 nuts which secure the injection pump oil seal housing, and withdraw the seal housing from around the pump inner pulley **(see illustration)**. Withdraw the timing belt backplate from the oil pump housing studs, noting which way round it fits.

17 Undo the bolt/nut and remove the

9.17 Undo the support bracket bolts (arrowed)

9.18 Place the spanner on the thickest section of the union nut (arrowed)

9.20 Remove the support bracket bolts at the rear of the pump (arrowed)

high-pressure fuel supply pipe support bracket from the pump (**see illustration**). **Note:** *Place rags over the alternator to prevent fuel damaging the unit.*

18 Ensure the area around fuel pipes connections on the pump and supply manifold are absolutely clean, place rags over the top of the alternator to protect it from fuel spillage. Slacken the unions and the clamp bolt, clean the pipes once the unions nuts have been moved along the pipe, then remove the pump-to-supply manifold rigid metal fuel pipe (**see illustration**). Plug or cap the openings to prevent dirt ingress. Make a note of the exact position of the pipe clamp, to enable it to be fitted in exactly the same place on the new pipe.

19 Note their fitted positions, then disconnect all wiring plugs from the pump.

20 Undo the 2 bolts securing the support bracket to the rear of the pump (**see illustration**).

21 Depress the locking tabs and disconnect the fuel return pipe from the pump (**see illustration**). Plug or cap the opening to prevent dirt ingress.

22 Prise out the locking catch, then using a small screwdriver, prise out the clip and disconnect the fuel supply pipe from the pump (**see illustration**). Plug or cap the opening to prevent dirt ingress.

23 Unscrew and remove the 4 bolts securing the drive chain sprocket to the injection pump. As with removal of its timing belt sprocket, it may be necessary to prevent the pulley from turning as the bolts are loosened.

24 Undo the 3 bolts securing the pump to the engine casing. It may not be possible to remove the bolts completely.

25 Manoeuvre the pump from the engine.

Refitting

26 Align the hole in the fuel pump drive flange with the etched mark on the pump body (**see illustration**).

27 With a new gasket and seal, refit the pump to the front engine casing, and tighten the bolts to the specified torque.

28 Refit the 4 chain sprocket bolts and tighten them to the specified torque.

29 Before reconnecting the return and supply pipes, the injection pump should

9.21 Depress the clip and disconnect the fuel return pipe

9.22 Prise out the locking catch, then prise out the clip and disconnect the fuel supply pipe

be primed with fuel, to reduce the length of time spent cranking the engine at start-up. If a new pump has been fitted (or the old pump has been off the engine for some time), priming with fuel is essential, as the fuel lubricates the pump internals, which may otherwise be dry. Follow the procedures in Section 6. If a vacuum pump is not available, a new pump can be partially primed by pouring in clean fuel via the fuel supply and return connections – take precautions against fuel spillage on delicate components by covering the surrounding area with clean rags, and be very careful not to introduce dirt into the pump.

30 Remove the blanking plugs/cap (if not already done so), and reconnect the fuel return and supply pipes to the pump.

31 If removed, refit the fuel pump rear support bracket to the pump, and tighten the bolts securely.

32 Reconnect the wiring plugs to the pump.

33 Fit the clamp to the new rigid pump-to-supply manifold metal pipe in exactly the same position as it was fitted to the original.

34 Spray the threads of the pump and supply manifold unions with a lubricant (eg, WD40, etc), then remove the blanking plugs and fit the pipe in place, but only finger-tighten the unions at this stage.

35 Refit the pump rear support bracket, and tighten the bolts securely.

36 Using a crow's-foot spanner tighten the rigid metal pipe unions to the specified torque, starting at the supply manifold first. Ensure the spanner acts upon the part of the union where

there is the most metal, to avoid damage to the union (**see illustration 9.18**).

37 Refit the support bracket to the ridged metal pipe at the pump, and tighten the bolt/nut securely.

38 Fit a new metal gasket to the pump drive chain sprocket. Apply a coating of Loctite RTV 5910 sealant to the sprocket (avoiding the three sprocket bolt holes). The three bolts should be cleaned, then lightly-coated with Loctite 518 locking fluid. Offer up the timing belt sprocket, aligning the bolt holes carefully, then fit the three bolts and tighten to the specified torque.

39 Refit the timing belt as described in Chapter 2.

40 Start the engine, and let it idle, noting that it may take a while before a stable idle speed is achieved, as the engine management module (PCM) may have to relearn some of

9.26 Align the hole in the drive flange with the mark on the pump body (arrowed)

9.43 Remove the pipe (arrowed) between the high-pressure pump and the fuel rail

9.44a Depress the release tabs (arrowed) and disconnect the fuel supply . . .

9.44b . . . and return hoses from the pump (arrowed)

9.46 Undo the 3 bolts and remove the pump (arrowed)

9.48 Ensure the pump drive dog (arrowed) is aligned with the slot in the end of the camshaft

between the pump and common rail, then tighten to the specified torque, using a crow's-foot adapter.

51 The remainder of refitting is a reversal of removal, bearing in mind the following points:

a) *Bleed the fuel system as described in Section 6.*

b) *Once the engine has started, thoroughly check for fuel leaks from the disturbed pipes/hoses.*

10 Fuel injectors –
  removal and refitting

Caution: The injectors are manufactured to extremely close tolerances and must not be dismantled in any way. Do not unscrew the fuel pipe union on the side of the injector, or separate any parts of the injector body. Do not attempt to clean carbon deposits from the injector nozzle or carry out any form of ultrasonic or pressure testing. Always store the injectors in cylinder order and keep them mounted vertically at all times.

Caution: Be careful not to allow dirt into the injection pump or injector pipes during this procedure.

Removal

1.6 litre engines

1 Disconnect the battery negative lead as described in Chapter 5.

2 Pull the plastic cover (where fitted) on the top of the engine upwards to release it from the mountings.

3 Undo the 2 retaining bolts and move the brake master cylinder remote reservoir (where fitted) to one side (see illustration).

4 Remove the wiper arms as described in Chapter 12.

5 Release the 5 clips and remove the windscreen cowl panel by pulling it up from the base of the windscreen (see illustrations).

6 Undo the bolt at each end, release the 2 clips and remove the bulkhead extension panel (see illustration).

7 Undo the 3 bolts, lift the injector wiring guide from place, then disconnect the wiring plugs from the top of each injector (see illustrations).

the 'adaptive' values. As the engine warms-up, check for signs of leakage from the fuel unions. If no leakage is evident, take the car for a short journey (of at least 5 miles) to allow the PCM to complete its 'learning' process.

2.0 litre engines

Removal

41 Remove the plastic cover from the top of the engine, by pulling it straight up from its mountings at the front and right-hand edges, then pull it forwards.

42 Remove the air cleaner assembly as described in Section 2.

43 Undo the unions and remove the high-pressure fuel pipe between the pump and the fuel rail (see illustration). Discard the pipe, a new one must be fitted.

44 Note their fitted positions, depress the release tabs, and disconnect the fuel

supply and return pipes from the pump (see illustrations). Be prepared for fuel spillage. Plug the openings to prevent contamination.

45 Note their fitted positions, and disconnect the wiring plugs from the pump.

46 Undo the 3 retaining bolts and pull the pump from the cylinder head (see illustration). Discard the gasket.

Refitting

47 Ensure that the mating surfaces of the pump and cylinder head are clean and dry, and fit the new gasket.

48 Ensure the slot in the end of the camshaft and the pump drive dog are aligned, then refit the pump, tightening the mounting bolts to the specified torque (see illustration).

49 Reconnect the fuel supply and return pipes to the pump, and the wiring plugs.

50 Fit the new high-pressure fuel pipe

10.3 Undo the bolts (arrowed) and move the remote reservoir to one side

10.5a Prise forwards the clips (arrowed) on each side . . .

8 Extract the retaining circlip and disconnect the leak-off pipe from each fuel injector **(see illustration)**.

9 Clean the area around the high-pressure fuel pipes between the injectors and the common rail, then unscrew the pipe unions. Use a second spanner to counterhold the union screwed into the injector body **(see illustration)**. The injectors screwed-in unions must not be allowed to move. Remove the bracket above the common rail unions, then remove the pipes. Plug the openings in the common rail and injectors to prevent dirt ingress.

10 Unscrew the injector retaining bolts, and carefully pull or lever the injector from place. If necessary, use an open-ended spanner and twist the injector to free it from position **(see illustrations)**. Do not lever against or pull on the solenoid housing at the top of the injector. Note down the injector's position – if the injectors are to be refitted, they must be refitted to their original locations. If improved access is required, undo the bolts and remove the oil separator housing from the front of the cylinder head cover.

11 Remove the copper washer and the upper seal from each injector, or from the cylinder head if they remained in place during injector removal. New copper washers and upper seals will be required for refitting. Cover the injector hole in the cylinder head to prevent dirt ingress.

12 Examine each injector visually for any signs of obvious damage or deterioration. If any defects are apparent, renew the injector(s).

1.8 litre engines

13 Remove the plastic cover on the top of the engine **(see illustration 2.5)**. Take care to manoeuvre the cover around the MAP sensor.

14 Disconnect the battery negative lead as described in Chapter 5.

15 Release the clamps and disconnect the breather hoses from the cylinder head cover **(see illustration)**.

16 Disconnect the wiring plugs from the high-pressure fuel pump and the common rail.

17 Disconnect the wiring plug from the fuel temperature sensor, then disconnect the wiring plug from each injector **(see illustrations)**. Move the wiring harness to one side.

10.5b . . . and pull the windscreen cowl panel upwards from the base of the windscreen

10.7a Undo the injector wiring guide bolts (arrowed)

18 Ensure the areas around the injection pipes and unions is absolutely clean. If possible, use a vacuum cleaner to remove all debris from the vicinity.

19 Slacken and unscrew the pipe unions

10.8 Prise out the clip and pull the return pipe from each injector

10.10a Injector retaining bolts (arrowed)

10.10b Use a spanner to twist the injector and free it from position

10.6 Undo the bolt at each end (arrowed) and pull the bulkhead extension panel forwards

10.7b Depress the clip and disconnect the wiring plugs from the injectors

at the injectors and the fuel supply manifold (common rail), but keep the metal pipes in contact with the injectors and manifold until the unions have been moved along the pipe and the areas at the ends of the pipes cleaned.

10.9 Use a second spanner to counterhold the high-pressure pipe union nuts

10.15 Disconnect the breather hoses (arrowed) from the cylinder head cover

10.17a Disconnect the fuel temperature sensor wiring plug (arrowed)

10.17b Depress the clip (arrowed) and disconnect the injector wiring plugs

10.22a Slacken the injector clamp bolts . . .

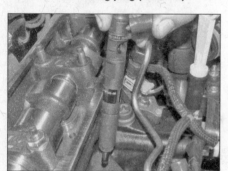

10.22b . . . and pull the injectors from place

10.26a Prise down the lower edge of the retaining clip (shown with the return hose disconnected for clarity) . . .

10.26b . . . then pull the return hoses from the injectors

Use a second spanner to counterhold the unions at the injectors. Be prepared for fuel spillage.

20 With any dirt/debris removed, detach the pipes from the injectors and manifold, then plug the openings to prevent dirt ingress. Discard the pipes – Ford insist that new ones must be fitted.

21 Ensure the area around the injectors is absolutely clean and free from debris. If possible, use a vacuum cleaner to remove any dirt.

22 Slacken the injector clamps retaining bolts, and pull the injectors from place **(see illustrations)**. Discard the clamp bolts – new ones must be fitted. If the original injectors are to be refitted, it is absolutely essential that they are refitted in to their original positions.

23 Discard the injectors sealing washers – new ones must be fitted.

2.0 litre engines

24 Remove the cylinder head cover/intake manifold as described in Chapter 2.

25 Make sure the areas around the high-pressure fuel pipe unions from the fuel rail to the injectors is scrupulously clean and free from debris, etc. If possible, use a vacuum cleaner and a degreaser to clean the area.

26 Carefully prise down the lower edge of the retaining clips, then disconnect the fuel return hoses from the injectors **(see illustrations)**. Take care not to drop the retaining clips as they are removed, and check the condition of the O-ring seals – renew if necessary.

27 Undo the unions, then remove the high-pressure fuel pipes from the fuel rail to the injectors. Discard the fuel pipes, new ones must be fitted. Use a second open-ended spanner on the injector port to counterhold when slackening the pipe union **(see**

illustration). Be prepared for fuel spillage and plug/cover the ports in the injectors and fuel rail to prevent dirt ingress.

28 Unscrew the two bolts securing each injector clamp, and carefully remove the injectors. Slide the copper sealing washer from the end of each injector. Discard the sealing washers – new ones must be fitted **(see illustration)**.

Refitting

29 Locate a new upper seal (1.6 and 2.0 litre) on the body of each injector, and place a new copper washer on the injector nozzle **(see illustration)**.

30 Refit the injector clamp locating dowels (where fitted) to the cylinder head.

1.6 litre engines

31 Ensure the injector clamps are in place over their respective circlips on the injector

10.27 Use a second spanner to counterhold the injector port when slackening the union nut

10.28 Injector clamp bolts (arrowed)

10.29 Upper seal (A) and copper washer (B)

10.31 Fit the injectors into their original locations

10.33 Note the injector classification number

10.34 Take note of the identification numbers of the new injectors, these need to be uploaded into the PCM

bodies, then fit the injectors into place in the cylinder head. If the original injectors are being refitted, ensure they are fitted into their original positions **(see illustration)**.

32 Fit the injector retaining bolts/nuts, but only finger-tighten them at this stage. When tightening the nuts/bolts, ensure the clamps stay horizontal.

33 If new injectors have been fitted, note down the new 8-digit injector classification number – this will be need to be entered into the PCM memory using dedicated Ford test equipment **(see illustration)**.

1.8 litre engines

34 If new injectors are being fitted, take of note of the identification numbers **(see illustration)**. These need to be uploaded into the PCM on completion of the work.

35 Fit a new sealing washer onto each injector **(see illustration)**.

36 Fit the injectors and clamps into the cylinder head, then tighten the new clamps bolts finger-tight only at this stage.

2.0 litre engines

37 Place the injector clamp in the slot on each injector body and refit the injectors to the cylinder head. Guide the clamp over the mounting stud and onto the locating dowel as each injector is inserted. Ensure the upper injector seals are correctly located in the cylinder head.

38 Fit the washer and a new injector clamp retaining nut to each mounting stud. Tighten the nuts finger-tight only at this stage.

All engines

39 Working on one fuel injector at a time, remove the blanking plugs from the fuel pipe unions on the common rail and the relevant injector. Locate a new high-pressure fuel pipe over the unions and screw on the union nuts. Take care not to cross-thread the nuts or strain the fuel pipes as they are fitted. Once the union nut threads have started, finger-tighten the nuts only at this stage, to the ends of the threads.

40 When all the fuel pipes are in place, tighten the injector clamp retaining nuts/bolts to the specified torque and angle.

41 Using an open-ended spanner, hold each fuel pipe union in turn and tighten the

10.35 Fit a new sealing washer onto each injector

union nut to the specified torque using a torque wrench and crow's-foot adapter **(see illustration)**. Tighten all the disturbed union nuts in the same way.

42 If new injectors have been fitted, their classification numbers must be programmed into the engine management PCM using dedicated diagnostic equipment/scanner. If this equipment is not available, entrust this task to a Ford dealer or suitably-equipped repairer. Note that it should be possible to drive the vehicle, albeit with reduced performance/increased emissions, to a repairer for the numbers to be programmed.

43 The remainder of refitting is a reversal of removal, noting the following points:

a) *Ensure all wiring connectors and harnesses are correctly refitting and secured.*

b) *Reconnect the battery as described in Chapter 5.*

11.3 Crankshaft position sensor (arrowed) – 1.6 litre

10.41 Tighten the high-pressure pipe union nuts using a 'crow's-foot' adapter

c) *Observing the precautions listed in Section 1, start the engine and allow it to idle. Check for leaks at the high-pressure fuel pipe unions with the engine idling. If satisfactory, increase the engine speed to 3000 rpm and check again for leaks. Take the car for a short road test and check for leaks once again on return. If any leaks are detected, obtain and fit additional new high-pressure fuel pipes as required. **Do not** attempt to cure even the slightest leak by further tightening of the pipe unions.*

11 Engine management system components – removal and refitting

Crankshaft position/ speed sensor

1.6 litre engines

1 The crankshaft position sensor is located adjacent to the crankshaft pulley on the right-hand end of the engine. Slacken the right-hand front roadwheel bolts, then jack the front of the vehicle up and support it on axle stands (see *Jacking and vehicle support*). Remove the right-hand front roadwheel.

2 Release the fasteners and remove the right-hand front wheel arch liner.

3 Disconnect the sensor wiring plug **(see illustration)**.

4 Undo the bolt and remove the sensor.

5 Refitting is a reversal of removal, tightening the sensor retaining bolt to the specified torque.

11.7 Crankshaft position sensor – 1.8 litre

11.9 Undo the bolt (arrowed), then slide the sensor from place

11.15 Slide up the red locking clip (arrowed) and disconnect the mass airflow sensor

1.8 litre engines

6 Before removing the sensor, set the crankshaft at TDC on No 1 cylinder, as described in Chapter 2.
7 The sensor is located at the flywheel end of the engine, low down at the rear **(see illustration)**. For improved access, apply the handbrake then jack up the front of the vehicle and support it on axle stands (see *Jacking and vehicle support*).
8 Disconnect the wiring plug from the sensor.
9 Unscrew the mounting bolt, then slide the sensor towards the timing belt end of the engine and withdraw it **(see illustration)**.
10 Refitting is a reversal of removal, but ensure that the sensor and the block mounting face is clean and free from debris, and tighten the bolt to the specified torque.

2.0 litre engines

11 Remove the crankshaft pulley as described in Chapter 2.
12 The sensor is located adjacent to the crankshaft pulley. Disconnect the sensor wiring plug.
13 Slacken and remove the retaining bolt and carefully remove the sensor.
14 Refitting is the reverse of removal, tightening the retaining bolt to the specified torque.

Mass airflow sensor

1.6 and 1.8 litre engines

15 On these engines, a combined Intake Air Temperature (IAT) and Mass AirFlow (MAF) sensor is fitted to the air cleaner cover outlet.

Slacken the clamp and disconnect the air outlet hose from the sensor **(see illustration)**.
16 Disconnect the sensor wiring plug.
17 Undo the bolts then remove the airflow sensor from the air cleaner housing, along with its sealing ring.
18 Refitting is the reverse of removal, lubricating the sealing ring.

2.0 litre engines

19 Disconnect the sensor wiring plug.
20 Slacken the clamp and disconnect the air outlet hose from the sensor **(see illustration 2.10)**.
21 Undo the bolts then remove the airflow sensor from the air cleaner housing, along with its sealing ring.
22 Refitting is the reverse of removal, lubricating the sealing ring.

Coolant temperature sensor

23 Refer to Chapter 3 for removal and refitting details.

Accelerator pedal position sensor

24 The sensor is secured to the accelerator pedal. Refer to Section 4 of this Chapter for pedal removal. Note that at the time of writing, the sensor was not available separately from the pedal assembly.

Manifold absolute pressure (MAP) sensor

1.6 and 2.0 litre engines only

25 The sensor is mounted on the intake manifold/throttle body **(see illustrations)**.

26 Pull the plastic cover (where fitted) on the top of the engine straight up from its mountings at the front and right-hand edges, then pull it forwards.
27 Ensure the ignition is switched off then disconnect the wiring connector from the sensor.
28 Slacken and remove the retaining bolt and remove the sensor from the vehicle.
29 Refitting is the reverse of removal, tightening the sensor retaining securely.

Stop-light switch

30 The powertrain control module receives a signal from the stop-light switch which indicates when the brakes are being applied. Stop-light switch removal and refitting details can be found in Chapter 9.

Powertrain control module (PCM)

Note: *If a new control module is fitted, it must be programmed using dedicated Ford test equipment. Entrust this task to a Ford dealer or suitably-equipped specialist.*
31 Disconnect the battery negative lead (see Chapter 5), then wait at least 2 minutes before commencing work, to allow any stored electrical energy to dissipate.
32 Slacken the left-hand front roadwheel nuts, then raise the front of the vehicle and support it securely on axle stands (see *Jacking and vehicle support*). Remove the roadwheel.
33 Remove the bolts and remove the left wheel arch liner **(see illustrations)**.

11.25a MAP sensor (arrowed) – 1.6 litre . . .

11.25b . . . and 2.0 litre (arrowed)

11.33a Undo the bolts at the front of the wheel arch liner (arrowed) . . .

11.33b . . . and the rear (arrowed)

11.34 PCM cover bolts (arrowed)

11.35 Pull the PCM to release the clips

34 Undo the 4 Torx bolts and remove the PCM cover **(see illustration)**.

35 Pull the PCM from place to release the retaining clips **(see illustration)**.

36 On models fitted with a security bracket over the PCM, drill a hole in the end and remove the shear bolt **(see illustration)**. Slide the bracket from the PCM.

37 Pivot over the locking catches, and disconnect the 3 wiring plugs from the PCM **(see illustration)**.

38 Refitting is a reversal of removal, ensuring the cover's rubber seal (where fitted) is correctly positioned in the groove.

Intake air temperature sensor

1.8 and 2.0 litre engines only

39 Remove the plastic cover from over the top of the engine by pulling it straight up from its mountings at the front and right-hand edges, then pull it forwards.

40 Disconnect the sensor wiring plug **(see illustrations)**.

41 Undo the retaining bolt and pull the sensor from position.

42 Apply a little petroleum jelly to ease the sensor in to place, then tighten the retaining bolt securely.

43 Reconnect the sensor wiring plug and refit the engine cover.

Fuel pressure sensor

44 It is not possible to renew the sensor separately from the fuel rail. Ford advise that no attempt should be made to remove it. If the sensor is faulty, renew the fuel rail as described in this Section.

Fuel (common) rail

1.6 litre engines

45 Remove the cylinder head cover/intake manifold as described in Chapter 2.

46 Drain the cooling system as described in Chapter 1.

47 Remove the EGR cooler or pipe as described in Chapter 4D.

48 Undo the mounting bolts, slacken the clamps, and move aside the coolant pump outlet assembly **(see illustration)**.

49 Clean around the pipe, then undo the unions and remove the high-pressure pipe from

11.36 Drill out the shear bolt (arrowed)

11.37 Pivot over the locking catches and disconnect the wiring plugs

the common rail to the high-pressure pump. Plug the openings to prevent contamination.

50 Disconnect the pressure sensor wiring plug from the common rail **(see illustration)**.

11.40a Intake air temperature sensor – 1.8 litre . . .

11.48 Undo the bolts (arrowed) and move aside the coolant outlet assembly

51 Unscrew the two rail mounting bolts and manoeuvre it from place **(see illustration)**. **Note:** *Ford insist that the fuel pressure sensor on the common rail must not be removed.*

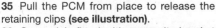

11.40b . . . and 2.0 litre (arrowed)

11.50 The pressure sensor is located at the end of the common rail (arrowed)

11.51 Common rail mounting bolt/stud (arrowed)

11.62 Undo the two bolts (arrowed) and remove the common rail

11.70 Undo the 3 bolts (arrowed) and remove the fuel filter bracket

Caution: Do not attempt to remove the four high-pressure fuel pipe male unions from the common rail. These parts are not available separately and if disturbed are likely to result in fuel leakage on reassembly.

52 Locate the common rail in position, refit and finger-tighten the mounting bolts.

53 Reconnect the common rail wiring plug(s).

54 Fit the new pump-to-rail high-pressure pipe. Use a second spanner to counterhold the union screwed into the pump body.

55 Tighten the common rail mounting bolts/nuts to the specified torque.

56 The remainder of refitting is a reversal of removal, noting the following points:

a) *Ensure all wiring connectors and harnesses are correctly refitting and secured.*

b) *Reconnect the battery as described in Chapter 5.*

c) *Observing the precautions listed in Section 1, start the engine and allow it to idle. Check for leaks at the high-pressure fuel pipe unions with the engine idling. If satisfactory, increase the engine speed to 3000 rpm and check again for leaks. Take the car for a short road test and check for leaks once again on return. If any leaks are detected, obtain and fit additional new high-pressure fuel pipes as required. Do not attempt to cure even the slightest leak by further tightening of the pipe unions.*

1.8 litre engines

57 Disconnect the high-pressure fuel pipes from the common rail as described in Section 10. Discard the pipes, new ones must be fitted.

11.73 The fuel pressure sensor (arrowed) is located on the underside of the common fuel rail

58 Ensure the area around the pump-to-fuel common rail pipe is absolutely clean. If possible, use a vacuum cleaner to remove any debris.

59 Slacken the nut/bolt securing the pipe support bracket to the pump. Make a note of the fitted position of the clamp on the pipe – it will need to be transferred to the new pipe.

60 Slacken and undo the pump-to-common rail pipe unions, then clean the area at the ends of the pipe before removing and discarding it. Plug or cover the openings in the pump and rail to prevent dirt ingress.

61 Disconnect the wiring plug from the fuel pressure sensor on the common rail.

62 Undo the two bolts and remove the fuel common rail **(see illustration)**.

63 No further dismantling of the common rail is advised, no parts are available separately.

64 Locate the common rail in position, refit and finger-tighten the mounting bolts.

65 Reconnect the common rail wiring plug(s).

66 Fit the new pump-to-rail high-pressure pipe. Use a second spanner to counterhold the union screwed into the pump body.

67 Tighten the common rail mounting bolts to the specified torque.

68 The remainder of refitting is a reversal of removal, noting the following points:

a) *Ensure all wiring connectors and harnesses are correctly refitting and secured.*

b) *Reconnect the battery as described in Chapter 5.*

c) *Observing the precautions listed in Section 1, start the engine and allow it to idle. Check for leaks at the high-pressure*

11.80 Use a 'crow's-foot' adapter to tighten the union nuts

fuel pipe unions with the engine idling. If satisfactory, increase the engine speed to 3000 rpm and check again for leaks. Take the car for a short road test and check for leaks once again on return. If any leaks are detected, obtain and fit additional new high-pressure fuel pipes as required. Do not attempt to cure even the slightest leak by further tightening of the pipe unions.

2.0 litre engines

69 Remove the intake manifold/cylinder head cover as described in Chapter 2.

70 Remove the fuel filter as described in Chapter 1, then undo the bolts and remove the fuel filter bracket **(see illustration)**.

71 Make sure the areas around the high-pressure fuel pipe unions from the fuel rail to the injectors and the high-pressure pump is scrupulously clean and free from debris, etc. If possible, use a vacuum cleaner and a degreaser to clean the area.

72 Undo the unions, then remove the high-pressure fuel pipes from the fuel rail to the injectors, and from the fuel rail to the high-pressure pump. Discard the fuel pipes, new ones must be fitted. Use a second open-ended spanner on the ports to counterhold when slackening the pipe union **(see illustration 10.27)**. Be prepared for fuel spillage and plug/cover the ports in the injectors, high-pressure pump and fuel rail to prevent dirt ingress.

73 Disconnect the fuel pressure sensor wiring plug **(see illustration)**.

74 Undo the nuts and remove the fuel rail.

75 Locate the common rail in position, refit and finger-tighten the mounting nuts.

76 Reconnect the common rail wiring plug(s).

77 Fit the new pump-to-rail high-pressure pipe. Use a second spanner to counterhold the union screwed into the pump body.

78 Fit the new set of rail-to-injector high-pressure pipes, and finger-tighten the unions. If it's not possible to fit the new pipes to the injector unions, remove and refit the injectors as described in Section 10, and try again.

79 Tighten the common rail mounting bolts/nuts to the specified torque.

80 Tighten the rail-to-injector pipe unions. Use a second spanner to counterhold the injector unions. Use a crow's-foot adapter to tighten the union nuts **(see illustration)**.

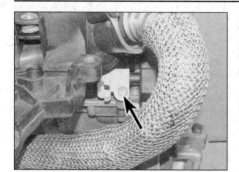

11.85a Camshaft position sensor bolt (arrowed) – 1.6 litre

11.85b Camshaft position sensor (arrowed) – 2.0 litre

11.89 Camshaft position sensor – 1.8 litre

81 The remainder of refitting is a reversal of removal, noting the following points:

a) *Ensure all wiring connectors and harnesses are correctly refitting and secured.*

b) *Reconnect the battery as described in Chapter 5.*

c) *Observing the precautions listed in Section 1, start the engine and allow it to idle. Check for leaks at the high-pressure fuel pipe unions with the engine idling. If satisfactory, increase the engine speed to 3000 rpm and check again for leaks. Take the car for a short road test and check for leaks once again on return. If any leaks are detected, obtain and fit additional new high-pressure fuel pipes as required.* **Do not** *attempt to cure even the slightest leak by further tightening of the pipe unions.*

Camshaft position sensor

1.6 and 2.0 litre engines

82 The camshaft position sensor is mounted on the right-hand end of the cylinder head cover, directly behind the camshaft sprocket.

83 Remove the upper timing belt cover, as described in Chapter 2.

84 Unplug the sensor wiring connector.

85 Undo the bolt and pull the sensor from position **(see illustrations)**.

86 Upon refitting, position the sensor so that the nipple of the sensor is just in contact with the camshaft signal wheel. Tighten the sensor retaining bolt to the specified torque.

87 The remainder of refitting is a reversal of removal.

1.8 litre engines

88 Carefully pull the plastic cover on the top of the engine upwards from place.

89 The sensor is located on the cylinder head cover. Disconnect the sensor wiring plug **(see illustration)**.

90 Undo the bolt and pull the sensor from position.

91 Refitting is a reversal of removal.

Turbocharger boost pressure regulator valve

1.6 and 2.0 litre engines only

92 Remove the plastic cover (where fitted) from over the top of the engine

11.93a Turbocharger boost pressure control valve (arrowed) – 1.6 litre . . .

93 Disconnect the wiring plug, then undo the 2 regulator retaining nuts **(see illustrations)**.

94 Note their fitted locations and disconnect the vacuum hoses as the regulator is withdrawn.

95 Refitting is a reversal of removal.

Fuel pressure control valve and fuel volume control valve

96 These valves are fitted to the high-pressure injection pump. They are not available as separate items, and can only be renewed along with the pump. Ford advise that no attempt should be made to remove the valves.

Anti-shudder control valve

97 On some engines, an anti-shudder valve is fitted to the intake manifold to reduce vibration when the engine is turned off. It achieves this by closing the intake port, preventing any air from being drawn into the cylinders. The valve

11.98 Anti-shudder valve (arrowed) – 1.6 litre

11.93b . . . and at the left-hand end of the cylinder head on the 2.0 litre (arrowed)

body is fitted between the intake manifold and the intercooler. Remove the plastic cover from the top of the engine.

98 To remove the valve body, note their fitted positions, and disconnect wiring plugs from the various sensors/motors fitted to the valve body **(see illustration)**.

99 Slacken the clamps, and disconnect the air intake hoses from the valve body.

100 Undo the mounting bolts and remove the valve body **(see illustration)**.

101 Refitting is a reversal of removal, tightening the bolts securely.

---

12 Turbocharger – description and precautions

Description

A turbocharger increases engine efficiency by

11.100 Anti-shudder valve bolts (arrowed) – 2.0 litre

13.3a Slacken the clamp (arrowed) and disconnect the turbocharger intake hose

13.3b Slacken the clamp (arrowed) and disconnect the outlet hose

13.3c Undo the outlet pipe bolt (arrowed) . . .

13.3d . . . pull the pipe up from the mounting stud (arrowed) . . .

13.3e . . . and rotate it to remove it

raising the pressure in the intake manifold above atmospheric pressure. Instead of the air simply being sucked into the cylinders, it is forced in. Additional fuel is supplied by the injection pump in proportion to the increased air intake.

Energy for the operation of the turbocharger comes from the exhaust gas. The gas flows through a specially-shaped housing (the turbine housing) and in so doing spins the turbine wheel. The turbine wheel is attached to a shaft, at the end of which is another vaned wheel known as the compressor wheel. The compressor wheel spins in its own housing and compresses the inducted air on the way to the intake manifold.

The compressed air passes through an intercooler. This is an air-to-air heat exchanger, mounted with the radiator at the front of the vehicle. The purpose of the intercooler is to remove from the inducted air some of the heat gained in being compressed. Because cooler

air is denser, removal of this heat further increases engine efficiency.

The turbocharger has adjustable guide vanes controlling the flow of exhaust gas into the turbine. On 1.6 and 2.0 litre engines, the vanes are swivelled by a vacuum unit on the turbocharger, controlled by the boost pressure regulator valve, controlled in turn by the engine management PCM. On 1.8 litre engines, the position of the vanes is controlled by an electric motor attached to the turbocharger, again, controlled by the PCM. At lower engine speeds, the vanes close together, giving a smaller exhaust gas entry port, and therefore higher gas speed, which increases boost pressure at low engine speed. At high engine speed, the vanes are turned to give a larger exhaust gas entry port, and therefore lower gas speed, effectively maintaining a reasonably constant boost pressure over the engine rev range. This is known as a Variable Nozzle Turbocharger (VNT).

The turbo shaft is pressure-lubricated by an oil feed pipe from the main oil gallery. The shaft 'floats' on a cushion of oil. A drain pipe returns the oil to the sump.

Precautions

The turbocharger operates at extremely high speeds and temperatures. Certain precautions must be observed to avoid premature failure of the turbo or injury to the operator.
• **Do not** operate the turbo with any parts exposed. Foreign objects falling onto the rotating vanes could cause excessive damage and (if ejected) personal injury.
• **Do not** race the engine immediately after start-up, especially if it is cold. Give the oil a few seconds to circulate.
• **Always** allow the engine to return to idle speed before switching it off – do not blip the throttle and switch off, as this will leave the turbo spinning without lubrication.
• Allow the engine to idle for several minutes before switching off after a high-speed run.
• Observe the recommended intervals for oil and filter changing, and use a reputable oil of the specified quality (see *Lubricants and fluids*). Neglect of oil changing, or use of inferior oil, can cause carbon formation on the turbo shaft and subsequent failure.

13 Turbocharger – removal and refitting

1.6 litre engines

Removal

1 Apply the handbrake, then jack up the front of the vehicle and support it on axle stands (see *Jacking and vehicle support*). Undo the bolts and remove the engine undershield.
2 Place a sheet of cardboard over the rear of the radiator to protect it from accidental damage.
3 Slacken the clamps, undo the bolts, and remove the air ducts to and from the turbocharger and air filter assembly **(see illustrations)**. Note their fitted positions and disconnect the various wiring plugs as the assembly is withdrawn.
4 Slacken the clamps, undo the bolts and remove the intercooler intake pipe **(see illustrations)**.

13.4a Intercooler intake pipe bolt on the transmission housing (arrowed) . . .

13.4b . . . and above the oil filter (arrowed)

13.5 Undo the bolts and remove the heat shield above the turbocharger

13.7 Disconnect the vacuum hose (arrowed)

13.8 Turbocharger oil supply and return pipes (arrowed)

5 Undo the mounting bolts **(see illustration)**, and remove the heat shield from above turbocharger/catalytic converter.

6 Undo the 2 bolts and remove the heat shield above the exhaust manifold.

7 Disconnect the vacuum hose from the turbocharger wastegate control assembly **(see illustration)**.

8 Undo the oil supply pipe banjo bolts and recover the sealing washers **(see illustration)**. **Note:** *Ford insist that any strainer fitted to the banjo bolt at the lower end of the oil supply pipe must be removed, using pliers, and discarded.*

9 Slacken the retaining clip and disconnect the oil return pipe from the turbocharger and cylinder block.

10 Make a note of its fitted position, then slacken the clamp securing the catalytic converter to the turbocharger **(see illustration)**.

11 Unscrew the four nuts, and the nut securing the support bracket, then remove the turbocharger from the exhaust manifold **(see illustration)**.

Inspection

12 With the turbocharger removed, inspect the housing for cracks or other visible damage.

13 Spin the turbine or the compressor wheel, to verify that the shaft is intact and to feel for excessive shake or roughness. Some play is normal, since in use the shaft is 'floating' on a film of oil. Check that the wheel vanes are undamaged.

14 If oil contamination of the exhaust or induction passages is apparent, it is likely that turbo shaft oil seals have failed.

15 No DIY repair of the turbo is possible and none of the internal or external parts are available separately. If the turbocharger is suspect in any way a complete new unit must be obtained.

Refitting

16 Refitting is a reverse of the removal procedure, bearing in mind the following points:

 a) *Renew the turbocharger retaining nuts and gaskets.*
 b) *When refitting the oil supply pipe, it's absolutely essential that the banjo bolts*

13.10 Slacken the clamp (arrowed) securing the catalytic converter to the turbocharger

 are tightened without placing the pipe under stress.
 c) *If a new turbocharger is being fitted, change the engine oil and filter.*
 d) *Prime the turbocharger by injecting clean engine oil through the oil feed pipe union before reconnecting the union.*

1.8 litre engines

Removal

17 The turbocharger should only be removed with the engine completely cool. Disconnect the battery negative lead (see Chapter 5).

18 Remove the catalytic converter as described in Section 17.

19 Remove the air cleaner and intake duct as described in Section 2.

20 Remove the EGR tube or cooler, as described in Chapter 4D.

21 Using the information in Section 15 if necessary, disconnect the intercooler air ducts

13.23 Turbocharger wastegate actuator wiring plug (arrowed)

13.11 Turbocharger upper retaining nuts (arrowed)

from the turbocharger and intake manifold, and remove them from the top of the engine – there is no need to remove the intercooler itself.

22 Undo the nuts and remove the turbocharger to exhaust manifold retaining clamp.

23 Disconnect the turbocharger wastegate actuator wiring plug **(see illustration)**.

24 Undo the nut securing the turbocharger oil supply pipe support bracket, then undo the banjo bolt and disconnect the oil supply pipe from the cylinder block. Note that the banjo bolt cannot be removed from the pipe.

25 Slacken the 3 nuts securing the turbocharger support bracket to the cylinder block.

26 Undo the bolts and remove the oil return pipe from the underside of the turbocharger. Discard the gaskets.

27 Undo the 2 bolts securing the turbocharger to the support bracket, and manoeuvre it from position.

28 No further dismantling of the turbocharger is recommended. Interfering with the wastegate setting may lead to a reduction in performance, or could result in engine damage. No parts appear to be available separately for the turbocharger.

29 If on inspection there are any signs of internal oil contamination on the turbine or compressor wheels, this indicates failure of the turbocharger oil seals. Renewing these seals is a job best left to a turbocharger specialist. In the event of any problem with the turbocharger, one of these specialists will usually be able to rebuild a defective unit, or offer a rebuilt unit on an exchange basis, either of which will prove cheaper than a new unit.

13.39 Turbocharger intake hose support bracket bolt (arrowed)

Refitting

30 Refitting is a reversal of removal, noting the following points:

a) Clean the mating surfaces, use a new exhaust manifold gasket, and tighten the manifold bolts to the specified torque.

b) Refit and tighten the engine rear mounting bolt to the specified torque (see Chapter 2).

c) Use new gaskets for the turbocharger oil return connections.

d) When refitting the EGR tube/cooler, offer it into position, and hand-tighten the bolts. Position the new clamp as noted on removal, tighten the clamp nut/bolt securely, then tighten the remaining bolts.

e) Refer to Section 17 when refitting the catalytic converter.

f) On models with the EGR cooler, top-up the cooling system as necessary (see 'Weekly checks').

13.45 Undo the two bolts (arrowed) securing the intake hose

13.48 The oil feed banjo bolt incorporates a filter

13.43 Undo the bolts/nuts and remove the bracket under the turbocharger (arrowed)

2.0 litre engines

Removal

31 Drain the cooling system as described in Chapter 1.

32 Remove the plastic cover from the top of the engine, then undo the bolts securing the brake master cylinder remote reservoir to the engine compartment bulkhead (where fitted).

33 Remove the wiper arms as described in Chapter 12.

34 Release the clips and remove the windscreen cowl panel (see illustrations 10.5a and 10.5b).

35 Undo the bolt at each end, release the clips and remove the bulkhead extension panel (see illustration 10.6).

36 Depress the release button and disconnect the engine breather hose from the intake manifold.

37 Remove the right-hand driveshaft as described in Chapter 8.

13.47 Coolant bypass pipe bolt (arrowed)

13.49 Turbocharger oil return hose retaining bolts (arrowed)

13.44 Turbocharger position sensor/ actuator wiring plug and vacuum hose (arrowed)

38 Undo the 2 bolts securing the right-hand engine mounting to the inner wing.

39 Undo the bolt securing the turbocharger intake hose support bracket (see illustration).

40 Slacken the clamp and disconnect the outlet pipe from the turbocharger.

41 Remove the catalytic converter as described in Section 17.

42 Remove the catalytic converter support bracket.

43 Undo the nuts/bolts and remove the support bracket from the underside of the turbocharger (see illustration).

44 Note their fitted positions, then disconnect the vacuum hose and wiring plug from the wastegate control assembly (see illustration).

45 Undo the bolts and detach the intake hose from the turbocharger. Depress the release clip and detach the pipe from the cylinder head cover (see illustration).

46 Release the clamp and disconnect the heater core-to-bypass coolant hose.

47 Slacken the clamp, remove the support bracket bolt, undo the connection bolts and remove the bypass hose (see illustration). Recover the O-ring seal, and renew if necessary.

48 Undo the banjo bolts and securing the oil supply pipe to the cylinder block. Renew the sealing washers. Note that a small filter is fitted into the banjo bolt – renew it (see illustration).

49 Undo the 2 bolts securing the oil return hose to the underside of the turbocharger (see illustration). Renew the gasket.

50 Undo the nuts and separate the turbocharger from the manifold (see illustration).

13.50 Undo the nuts (arrowed) securing the turbocharger to the manifold

15.2a Engine undershield fasteners (arrowed)

15.2b Radiator splash shield left-hand bolts (arrowed)

15.3 The intercooler outlet pipe bolt (arrowed) is accessed through the right-hand headlight aperture

15.4a Slacken the intercooler intake hose clamp (arrowed) . . .

15.4b . . . and the outlet hose clamp (arrowed)

15.5 Undo the retaining bolt (arrowed) each side

51 If required, undo the banjo bolt and detach the oil supply pipe from the turbocharger. Renew the seals.

Refitting

52 Refitting is a reversal of removal, noting the following points:

a) *Ensure all mating surfaces are clean and dry.*
b) *Renew all O-rings, seals and gaskets.*
c) *Tighten all fasteners to the specified torque where available.*

14 Turbocharger – examination and overhaul

With the turbocharger removed, inspect the housing for cracks or other visible damage.

Spin the turbine or the compressor wheel to verify that the shaft is intact and to feel for excessive shake or roughness. Some play is normal since in use the shaft is 'floating' on a film of oil. Check that the wheel vanes are undamaged.

The wastegate and actuator are integral with the turbocharger, and cannot be checked or renewed separately. Consult a Ford dealer or other specialist if it is thought that the wastegate may be faulty.

If the exhaust or induction passages are oil-contaminated, the turbo shaft oil seals have probably failed. (On the induction side, this will also have contaminated the intercooler, which if necessary should be flushed with a suitable solvent.)

No DIY repair of the turbo is possible. A new unit may be available on an exchange basis.

15 Intercooler – removal and refitting

Removal

1 Raise the front of the vehicle and support it securely on axle stands (see *Jacking and vehicle support*).

2 Undo the fasteners and remove the engine undershield, followed by the splash shield under the radiator (see illustrations).

3 Remove the right-hand headlight as described in Chapter 12, then undo the Torx bolt securing the intercooler outlet pipe to the radiator fan shroud (see illustration)

4 Slacken the clamps and disconnect the intake and outlet hoses from the intercooler (see illustrations). Note that the clamps are integral with the hoses.

16.6 Undo the nuts and recover the manifold spacers – 2.0 litre

5 Undo the 2 retaining bolts, lift the intercooler upwards to disengage the upper mounting lugs, and lower the intercooler from position (see illustration).

Refitting

6 Refitting is a reversal of removal. Ensure the inside of the intake and outlet hoses is clean where they attach to the intercooler.

16 Manifolds – removal and refitting

Intake manifold

1.6 litre engines

1 The intake manifold is integral with the cylinder head cover – refer to Chapter 2.

1.8 litre engines

2 The manifold is integral with the EGR valve – refer to Chapter 4D.

2.0 litre engines

3 The manifold is integral with the cylinder head cover – refer to Chapter 2.

Exhaust manifold

Removal

4 Remove the turbocharger as described in Section 13.

5 On 2.0 litre models, pull the manifold heat shield upwards to release the 2 retaining clips.

6 Undo the nuts securing the exhaust manifold to the cylinder head, and recover the spacers (see illustration). Pull the manifold

17.11 Undo the bolts (arrowed) securing the catalytic converter to the bracket – viewed from underneath

17.14a Unscrew the pressure take-off union from the side of the catalyst/filter . . .

17.14b . . . and the one at the base

from the mounting studs. If the manifold is being removed to renew the gasket, no further dismantling is required. Remove the gasket.

Refitting

7 Examine the studs for signs of damage and corrosion; remove traces of corrosion, and repair or renew any damaged studs.

8 Ensure the mating surfaces of the exhaust manifold and cylinder head are clean and dry. Position the new gasket, and refit the exhaust manifold to the cylinder head. Tighten the nuts to the specified torque.

9 The remainder of refitting is a reversal of removal, noting the following points:

a) Tighten all fasteners to their specified torque where available.

b) Apply a little high-temperature anti-seize grease (Copperslip) to the manifold studs.

c) Top-up the coolant system as described in 'Weekly checks'.

d) Check and, if necessary, top-up the oil level.

17 Exhaust system – general information and component renewal

1 The exhaust system consists of several sections: the front pipe with the catalytic converter(s), and the rear section with the intermediate and rear silencers. A particulate filter is available as standard or optional fitment on 1.6 and 2.0 litre models, depending on the market the vehicle is sold in. If required, the rear silencer can be renewed independently

17.19 Undo the clamp (arrowed) and slide the particulate filter from the catalytic converter

of the remainder of the system, by cutting the old silencer from the pipe, and slipping the new one over the cut end – details are given in this Section.

2 The exhaust system is joined together by a mixture of flanged, or sliding joints. Apply plenty of penetrating fluid to the fasteners prior to removal, undo the fasteners, unhook the rubber mountings, and manoeuvre the system from under the vehicle.

3 Each section is refitted by reversing the removal sequence, noting the following points:

a) Ensure that all traces of corrosion have been removed from the flanges and renew all gaskets.

b) Inspect the rubber mountings for signs of damage or deterioration, and renew as necessary.

c) Prior to tightening the exhaust system fasteners, ensure that all rubber mountings are correctly located, and that there is adequate clearance between the exhaust system and vehicle underbody.

Catalytic converter – 1.6 litre engines

4 Remove the plastic cover from the top of the engine (where fitted).

5 Raise the front of the vehicle and support it securely on axle stands (see Jacking and vehicle support).

6 Remove the cooling fan and shroud as described in Chapter 3.

7 Undo the bolt securing the intercooler intake pipe bracket to the cylinder block.

17.22 Undo the bolts and remove the underfloor brace (arrowed)

8 Slacken the clamps and remove the intercooler intake pipe assembly.

9 Attach wooden 'splints' each side of the exhaust flexible section using cable-ties. This is to prevent excessive bending of the section as it's disconnected. Undo the 2 nuts securing the flexible section to the catalytic converter/particulate filter.

10 On models without a particulate filter, undo the bolts and remove the heat shield **(see illustration 13.5)**

11 Undo the 2 nuts securing the catalytic converter to the support bracket, and the bolts securing the support bracket to the cylinder block **(see illustration)**.

12 Undo the nut securing the catalytic converter bracket to the transmission casing.

Models with a particulate filter

13 Disconnect the wiring plug, and unscrew the temperature sensor from the catalytic converter/particulate filter.

14 Note their fitted positions, and disconnect the pressure take-off hoses from the catalytic converter/particulate filter **(see illustrations)**.

15 Undo the bolts and remove the heat shield over the catalytic converter.

All models

16 Slacken the clamp securing the catalytic converter to the turbocharger. Note its fitted position to aid refitment.

17 Remove the heat shield bracket.

18 Manoeuvre the catalytic converter from place.

19 If required, note its fitted position, then slacken the clamp and detach the particulate filter from the base of the catalytic converter **(see illustration)**.

Catalytic converter – 1.8 litre engines

20 Raise the front of the vehicle and support it securely on axle stands (see Jacking and vehicle support).

21 Undo the fasteners and remove the engine undershield.

22 Undo the bolts and remove the underfloor brace adjacent to the front exhaust mounting **(see illustration)**.

23 Attach wooden 'splints' each side of the exhaust flexible section using cable-ties. This is to prevent excessive bending of the section

17.24 Catalytic converter-to-turbocharger nuts (arrowed)

17.31 Catalytic converter-to-turbocharger clamp (arrowed)

17.32 Undo the support bracket nuts

as it's disconnected. Undo the nuts securing the flexible section to the intermediate section.

24 Undo the nuts securing the catalytic converter to the turbocharger (see illustration).

25 Undo the catalytic converter support bracket nuts, release the mounting rubbers, and manoeuvre the catalytic converter from position.

Catalytic converter – 2.0 litre engines

26 Raise the front of the vehicle and support it securely on axle stands (see *Jacking and vehicle support*).

27 Undo the fasteners and remove the engine undershield.

28 Undo the bolts and remove the underfloor brace adjacent to the front exhaust mounting (see illustration 17.22).

29 Attach wooden 'splints' each side of the exhaust flexible section using cable-ties. This is to prevent excessive bending of the section as it's disconnected. Undo the nuts securing the flexible section to the intermediate section. Pull the intermediate section rearwards, and allow the exhaust to hang down.

30 Disconnect the wiring plug, then unscrew the temperature sensor (where fitted) from the front section of the catalytic converter.

31 Slacken the clamp securing the catalytic converter to the turbocharger (see illustration).

17.36 Disconnect the pressure sensor hoses (arrowed) from the particulate filter

32 Undo the catalytic converter support bracket nuts, release the mounting rubbers, and manoeuvre the catalytic converter from position (see illustration).

Particulate filter

1.6 litre engines

33 Remove the catalytic converter as described in this Section, then slacken the clamp and detach the filter from the base of the catalytic converter (see illustration 17.19).

2.0 litre engines

34 Raise the front of the vehicle and support it securely on axle stands (see *Jacking and vehicle support*).

35 Attach wooden 'splints' each side of the

17.37 Exhaust temperature sensor (arrowed)

exhaust flexible section using cable-ties. This is to prevent excessive bending of the section as it's disconnected. Undo the nuts securing the flexible section to the particulate filter.

36 Note their fitted positions, and disconnect the pressure pipes from the front of the particulate filter (see illustration).

37 Unscrew the temperature sensor from the front of the filter (see illustration).

38 Undo the nuts securing the rear exhaust section to the particulate filter, and manoeuvre the filter from position.

Rear silencer

39 Slacken the various clamps securing the exhaust pipe/silencer, then release it from the rubber mountings.

Chapter 4 Part C:
Emission control systems – petrol models

Contents

Section number

Catalytic converter – general information and precautions 2
Crankcase emission control system – checking and component
   renewal 3
Evaporative emission control system – checking and component
   renewal 4

Section number

Exhaust emission control systems – checking and component
   renewal 5
General information 1

Degrees of difficulty

Easy, suitable for novice with little experience	**Fairly easy,** suitable for beginner with some experience	**Fairly difficult,** suitable for competent DIY mechanic	**Difficult,** suitable for experienced DIY mechanic	**Very difficult,** suitable for expert DIY or professional

Specifications

Torque wrench setting	Nm	lbf ft
Oxygen sensor	42	31

1 General information

All models covered by this manual have various features built into the fuel and exhaust systems to help minimise harmful emissions. These features fall broadly into three categories; crankcase emission control, evaporative emission control, and exhaust emission control. The main features of these systems are as follows.

Crankcase emission control

To reduce the emissions of unburned hydrocarbons from the crankcase into the atmosphere, a Positive Crankcase Ventilation (PCV) system is used. The engine is sealed, and the blow-by gases and oil vapour are drawn from inside the crankcase, through an oil separator, into the intake tract, to be burned by the engine during normal combustion.

Under conditions of high manifold depression (idling, deceleration) the gases will be sucked positively out of the crankcase. Under conditions of low manifold depression (acceleration, full-throttle running) the gases are forced out of the crankcase by the (relatively) higher crankcase pressure; if the engine is worn, the raised crankcase pressure (due to increased blow-by) will cause some of the flow to return under all manifold conditions.

Evaporative emission control

The evaporative emission control (EVAP) system is used to minimise the escape of unburned hydrocarbons into the atmosphere. To do this, the fuel tank filler cap is sealed, and a carbon canister is used to collect and store petrol vapours generated in the tank. When the engine is running, the vapours are cleared from the canister by an PCM-controlled electrically-operated EVAP purge valve into the intake tract, to be burned by the engine during normal combustion.

To ensure that the engine runs correctly when idling, the valve only opens when the engine is running under load; the valve then opens to allow the stored vapour to pass into the intake tract.

Exhaust emission control

Oxygen (lambda) sensors

To minimise the amount of pollutants which escape into the atmosphere, all models are fitted with a catalytic converter in the exhaust system. The system is of the closed-loop type, in which two heated oxygen sensors in the exhaust system provide the engine management PCM with constant feedback on the oxygen content of the exhaust gases. This enables the PCM to adjust the mixture by altering injector opening time, thus providing the best possible conditions for the converter to operate. The system functions in the following way.

The oxygen sensors (also known as a lambda sensors) have built-in heating elements, activated by the PCM to quickly bring the sensor's tip to an efficient operating temperature. The sensor's tip is sensitive to oxygen, and sends the control module a

3.4 PCV valve location – 1.6 litre engines

varying voltage depending on the amount of oxygen in the exhaust gases; if the intake air/ fuel mixture is too rich, the exhaust gases are low in oxygen, so the sensor sends a voltage signal proportional to the oxygen detected, the voltage altering as the mixture weakens and the amount of oxygen in the exhaust gases rises. Peak conversion efficiency of all major pollutants occurs if the intake air/ fuel mixture is maintained at the chemically-correct ratio for complete combustion of petrol – 14.7 parts (by weight) of air to 1 part of fuel (the stoichiometric ratio). The sensor output voltage alters in a large step at this point, the PCM using the signal change as a reference point, and correcting the intake air/ fuel mixture accordingly, by altering the fuel injector opening time.

Exhaust gas recirculation (EGR)

This system is only fitted to some 1.8 and 2.0 litre models, and is designed to recirculate small quantities of exhaust gas into the intake tract, and therefore into the combustion process. This reduces the level of oxides of nitrogen present in the final exhaust gas which is released into the atmosphere.

The volume of exhaust gas recirculated is controlled by an electrically-operated solenoid valve. The solenoid and valve is mounted at the left-hand end of the cylinder head. The EGR system is controlled by the engine management PCM, which receives information on engine operating parameters from its various sensors.

Catalytic converters

Catalytic converters are fitted to all models.

3.5 Oil separator – 1.8 and 2.0 litre engines

The catalytic converter is integral with the exhaust manifold.

2 Catalytic converter – general information and precautions

On all models, a three-way catalytic converter is incorporated into the exhaust manifold. The catalytic converter is a reliable and simple device, which needs no maintenance in itself, but there are some facts of which an owner should be aware if the converter is to function properly for its full service life.

a) *DO NOT use leaded petrol or LRP – the lead will coat the precious metals, reducing their converting efficiency, and will eventually destroy the converter.*

b) *Always keep the ignition and fuel systems well-maintained in accordance with the manufacturer's schedule (see Chapter 1).*

c) *If the engine develops a misfire, do not drive the vehicle at all (or at least as little as possible) until the fault is cured.*

d) *DO NOT push- or tow-start the vehicle – this will soak the catalytic converter in unburned fuel, causing it to overheat when the engine does start.*

e) *DO NOT switch off the ignition at high engine speeds, ie, do not blip the throttle immediately before switching off.*

f) *DO NOT use fuel or engine oil additives – these may contain substances harmful to the catalytic converter.*

g) *DO NOT continue to use the vehicle if the engine burns oil to the extent of leaving a visible trail of blue smoke.*

h) *Remember that the catalytic converter operates at very high temperatures. DO NOT, therefore, park the vehicle in dry undergrowth, over long grass or piles of dead leaves, after a long run.*

i) *Remember that the catalytic converter is FRAGILE. Do not strike it with tools during servicing work.*

j) *In some cases, a sulphurous smell (like that of rotten eggs) may be noticed from the exhaust. This is common to many catalytic converter-equipped vehicles. Once the vehicle has covered a few*

4.5 The carbon canister (arrowed) is attached to the rear subframe

thousand miles, the problem should disappear – in the meantime, try changing the brand of petrol used.

k) *The catalytic converter used on a well-maintained and well-driven vehicle should last for between 50 000 and 100 000 miles. If the converter is no longer effective, it must be renewed.*

3 Crankcase emission control system – checking and component renewal

Checking

1 The components of this system require no attention other than to check that the hoses are clear and undamaged.

Oil separator renewal

2 Remove the intake manifold as described in Chapter 4A.

3 The oil separator is located on the front facing side of the cylinder block, below the intake manifold. Disconnect the breather hose from the top of the separator.

4 Pull the PCV valve from the top of the separator **(see illustration)**. Note: *On 1.8 and 2.0 litre models, depress the clip each side of the valve before pulling it from place.*

5 Undo the bolts and remove the separator **(see illustration)**. Recover the gasket.

6 On reassembly, fit a new gasket and tighten the bolts securely.

4 Evaporative emission control system – checking and component renewal

Checking

1 Poor idle, stalling and poor driveability can be caused by an inoperative canister vacuum valve, a damaged canister, split or cracked hoses, or hoses connected to the wrong fittings. Check the fuel filler cap for a damaged or deformed gasket.

2 Fuel loss or fuel odour can be caused by liquid fuel leaking from fuel lines, a cracked or damaged canister, an inoperative canister vacuum valve, and disconnected, misrouted, kinked or damaged vapour or control hoses.

3 Inspect each hose attached to the canister for kinks, leaks and cracks along its entire length. Repair or renew as necessary.

4 Inspect the canister. If it is cracked or damaged, renew it. Look for fuel leaking from the bottom of the canister. If fuel is leaking, renew the canister, and check the hoses and hose routing.

Component renewal

Carbon canister

5 The canister is located under the rear of the vehicle, attached to the rear subframe **(see illustration)**.

4.6 Depress the release buttons (arrowed) and disconnect the hoses

4.10a Canister purge valve (arrowed) – 1.6 litre engines . . .

4.10b . . . and 1.8 and 2.0 litre engines (arrowed)

6 Note their fitted locations, then press in the release buttons, and disconnect the hoses from the canister **(see illustration)**.

7 Undo the two retaining screws and lower the canister from place.

8 Refitting is a reversal of removal.

Canister purge valve (EVAP)

9 The canister purge valve is mounted in the engine compartment, on the left-hand end of the cylinder head. Remove the battery and battery tray as described in Chapter 5.

10 Note their fitted positions, then disconnect the vacuum pipes and wiring plug from the valve **(see illustrations)**.

11 Unclip the valve from the bracket.

12 Refitting is a reversal of removal.

---

5 Exhaust emission control systems – checking and component renewal

---

Checking

1 Checking of the system as a whole entails a close visual inspection of all hoses, pipes and connections for condition and security. Apart from this, any known or suspected faults should be attended to by a Ford dealer or suitably-equipped specialist.

Component renewal

Heated oxygen (lambda) sensors

Note: *The sensor is delicate, and will not work*

if it is dropped or knocked, if its power supply is disrupted, or if any cleaning materials are used on it.

2 Disconnect the oxygen sensor wiring plugs at the rear of the engine **(see illustrations)**.

3 Unscrew the sensors from place **(see illustrations)**.

4 On refitting, clean the sealing washer (where fitted) and renew it if it is damaged or worn. Apply a smear of anti-seize compound to the sensor's threads, then refit the sensor, tightening it to the specified torque. Reconnect the wiring and secure with cable-ties where applicable.

Catalytic converter(s)

5 The catalytic converter(s) is part of the exhaust manifold. Refer to Part A of this Chapter for renewal procedures and additional information.

5.2a Oxygen sensor wiring plugs (arrowed) at the left-hand rear corner of the cylinder head – 1.6 litre engines . . .

5.3a An oxygen sensor is fitted to the exhaust manifold . . .

5.3b . . . and the front section of the exhaust pipe

EGR solenoid/valve

6 Remove the plastic cover on the top of the engine by pulling it straight up from its mountings.

7 Remove the air cleaner assembly as described in Chapter 4A.

8 Drain the coolant as described in Chapter 1. Alternatively, use hose clamps prior to disconnecting the coolant hoses from the EGR valve.

9 Slacken the clamps and remove the air cleaner outlet pipe.

10 Disconnect the EGR valve solenoid wiring plug **(see illustration)**.

11 Release the clamps and disconnect the coolant hoses from the EGR valve.

12 Undo the 2 bolts and remove the EGR valve/solenoid. Recover the gasket.

13 Refitting is a reversal of removal, renewing the gasket where applicable.

5.2b . . . and 1.8 and 2.0 litre engines (arrowed)

5.10 The EGR valve (arrowed) is located at the left-hand end of the cylinder head

Chapter 4 Part D:
Emission control systems – diesel engines

Contents

Section number

Catalytic converter – general information and precautions 2
Crankcase emission control system – checking and component
   renewal 3

Section number

Exhaust emission control systems – checking and component
   renewal 4
General information 1

Degrees of difficulty

Easy, suitable for novice with little experience	Fairly easy, suitable for beginner with some experience	Fairly difficult, suitable for competent DIY mechanic	Difficult, suitable for experienced DIY mechanic	Very difficult, suitable for expert DIY or professional

1 General information

All models covered by this manual have various features built into the fuel and exhaust systems to help minimise harmful emissions. These features fall broadly into two categories; crankcase emission control and exhaust emission control. The main features of these systems are as follows.

Crankcase emission control

To reduce the emission of unburned hydrocarbons from the crankcase into the atmosphere, the engine is sealed and the blow-by gases and oil vapour are drawn from inside the crankcase, through a wire mesh oil separator, into the intake tract to be burned by the engine during normal combustion.

Under all conditions, the gases are forced out of the crankcase by the (relatively) higher crankcase pressure. All diesel engines have a ventilation valve in the camshaft cover, to control the flow of gases from the crankcase.

Exhaust emission control

EGR system

An oxidation catalyst is fitted in the exhaust system of all diesel-engined models. This has the effect of removing a large proportion of the gaseous hydrocarbons, carbon monoxide and particulates present in the exhaust gas.

An Exhaust Gas Recirculation (EGR) system is fitted to all models. This reduces the level of nitrogen oxides produced during combustion by introducing a proportion of the exhaust gas back into the intake manifold, under certain engine operating conditions, via a plunger valve. The system is controlled electronically by the engine management system. On some models, a cooler is fitted to the EGR, through which engine coolant is passed. This lowers the temperature of the recirculated gas, thus reducing the formation of NOx (oxides of nitrogen) in the exhaust gases.

Particulate filter

A particulate filter is also available as standard or as an option on 1.6 and 2.0 litre models, depending on the vehicle's country market.

This device is designed to trap carbon particulates produced by the combustion process. In order for the particulate filter to function correctly, and not to block up, an additive is injected into the fuel tank. As this additive passes through the combustion process, it reacts with the elements of the particulate filter, causing them to heat up and burn off the particles. The additive is automatically added to the tank whenever more than 5 litres of fuel is added. The whole process is controlled by an additive system module (ASM), which also informs the driver when the additive level is low. Replenishing the additive can only be performed by a dealer or specialist, as the ASM must be reset using specialist equipment. The consumption of additive is such that refilling should only be necessary every 3 years/37 500 miles approximately.

Catalytic converters

Catalytic converters are fitted to all diesel models. The catalytic converter is fitted between the turbocharger and the particulate filter.

2 Catalytic converter – general information and precautions

An oxidation catalytic converter is fitted downstream from the turbocharger.

The catalytic converter is a reliable and simple device, which needs no maintenance in itself, but there are some facts of which an owner should be aware if the converter is to function properly for its full service life.

a) *DO NOT use fuel or engine oil additives – these may contain substances harmful to the catalytic converter.*

b) *DO NOT continue to use the vehicle if the engine burns oil to the extent of leaving a visible trail of blue smoke.*

c) *Remember that the catalytic converter operates at very high temperatures. DO NOT, therefore, park the vehicle in dry undergrowth, over long grass or piles of dead leaves, after a long run.*

d) *Remember that the catalytic converter is FRAGILE. Do not strike it with tools during servicing work.*

e) *The catalytic converter used on a well-maintained and well-driven vehicle should last for between 50 000 and 100 000 miles. If the converter is no longer effective, it must be renewed.*

3.5a Unscrew the mounting bolts . . .

3.5b . . . and remove the oil separator from the engine

3 Crankcase emission control system – checking and component renewal

Checking

1 The components of this system require no attention other than to check that the hoses are clear and undamaged.

Oil separator

1.6 litre engines

2 The oil separator is integral with the cylinder head cover/intake manifold – refer to Chapter 2C.

1.8 litre engines

3 The oil separator is located at the left-hand end of the cylinder head. Pull the plastic cover on the top of the engine upwards from its

mountings at the front and right-hand edges, then pull it forwards.
4 Release the clamps and disconnect the breather hoses from the separator.
5 Undo the retaining bolts and remove the oil separator **(see illustrations)**.
6 Refitting is a reversal of removal.

2.0 litre engines

7 The oil separator is integral with the cylinder head cover/intake manifold – refer to Chapter 2E.

4 Exhaust emission control systems – checking and component renewal

Checking

1 Checking of the system as a whole entails a close visual inspection of all hoses, pipes and connections for condition and security.

Apart from this, any known or suspected faults should be attended to by a Ford dealer or suitably-equipped specialist.

Catalytic converter

2 Removal of the catalytic converter is described in Chapter 4B – Exhaust system.

EGR solenoid/valve

1.6 litre engines

3 Disconnect the battery negative lead as described in Chapter 5.
4 Remove the plastic cover from the top of the engine (where fitted) by pulling it upwards at the right-hand and front edges, then pull it forwards.
5 Remove the wiper arms as described in Chapter 12, then undo the 2 bolts and move the remote brake fluid reservoir (where fitted) to one side **(see illustration)**.
6 Release the clips and remove the windscreen cowl panel by pulling it upwards from the moulding at the base of the windscreen **(see illustrations)**.
7 Undo the bolt at each end, then release the clips and remove the bulkhead extension panel from the engine compartment **(see illustration)**.
8 Disconnect the EGR valve wiring plug.
9 Make a note of its fitted position, then remove the clamp securing the pipe to the EGR valve **(see illustration)**.
10 Undo the 2 bolts and remove the valve. Note that if a new valve is fitted, the base setting must be programmed using Ford specialist diagnostic equipment (IDS).
11 Refitting is a reversal of removal.

1.8 litre engines

12 Proceed as described in Paragraphs 3 to 7 in this Section.
13 Remove the exhaust manifold as described in Chapter 4B.
14 Disconnect the vacuum hose from the MAP sensor on the intake manifold.
15 Note their fitted positions, then disconnect the various wiring plugs from the EGR valve/intake manifold **(see illustration)**.
16 Unclip the EGR cooler coolant hose from the support bracket.
17 Slacken the clamp and disconnect the air hose from the intake manifold **(see illustration)**.
18 Undo the retaining nuts/bolts and remove

4.5 Undo the bolts (arrowed) and move the remote reservoir to one side

4.6a Prise forwards the clips (right-hand clips arrowed) . . .

4.6b . . . and pull the windscreen cowl panel upwards from the base of the windscreen

4.7 Undo the bolt (arrowed) at each end of the bulkhead extension panel

4.9 Release the EGR pipe clamp (arrowed)

4.15 Disconnect the wiring plug from the EGR valve (arrowed)

4.17 Air intake hose clamp (1) and MAP sensor vacuum hose (2)

4.21 Undo the nut (arrowed) and remove the stud securing the EGR pipe support bracket

4.22a Release the EGR pipe clamp (arrowed) . . .

4.22b . . . and undo the 2 bolts securing the pipe to the valve

4.24 EGR cooler-to-valve bolts (arrowed)

the intake manifold. Note that the EGR valve is integral with the manifold.

19 Refitting is a reversal of removal.

2.0 litre engines

20 Proceed as described in Paragraphs 3 to 7 in this Section.

21 Undo the EGR pipe support bracket retaining nut **(see illustration)**.

22 Release the clamp securing the EGR pipe to the intake manifold, and the 2 bolts securing the pipe to the EGR valve **(see illustrations)**.

23 Disconnect the wiring plug from the EGR valve.

24 Undo the bolts securing the EGR cooler to the valve **(see illustration)**.

25 Slacken the EGR valve lower retaining bolt

26 Undo the 2 remaining retaining bolts and remove the valve. Note that if a new valve is fitted, the base setting must be programmed using Ford specialist diagnostic equipment (WDS).

27 Refitting is a reversal of removal.

EGR cooler

28 Drain the cooling system as described in Chapter 1.

1.6 litre engines

29 Proceed as described in Paragraphs 3 to 7 in this Section.

30 Disconnect the injector wiring plugs, then undo the bolts and move the injector wiring harness guide to one side **(see illustration)**.

31 Release the clamps and disconnect the coolant hoses from the EGR cooler **(see illustration)**.

32 Release the clamp securing the EGR pipe to the cooler, then undo the 2 bolts securing the pipe to the intake manifold **(see illustration)**. Remove the pipe.

33 Release the clamp securing the EGR cooler to the EGR valve, then undo the nut/bolt and remove the cooler **(see illustration)**.

34 Refitting is a reversal of removal.

4.30 Injector wiring harness bolts (arrowed)

4.32 EGR pipe-to-manifold bolts (arrowed)

4.31 Release the EGR cooler hose clamps (arrowed)

4.33 Release the clamp (arrowed) securing the EGR cooler to the valve

4.45 EGR cooler pipe clamp and coolant hose clamps (arrowed)

4.47 EGR elbow-to-manifold nuts (arrowed)

1.8 litre engines

35 Proceed as described in Paragraphs 3 to 7 in this Section.

36 Release the clamps and disconnect the coolant hoses from the EGR cooler.

37 Undo the bolts securing the cooler to the exhaust manifold and intake manifold, then manoeuvre it from position.

38 Refitting is a reversal of removal.

2.0 litre engines

39 Proceed as described in Paragraphs 3 to 7 in this Section.

40 Pull the coolant expansion tank upwards to release its mountings. Move it to one side.

41 Raise the front of the vehicle and support it securely on axle stands (see *Jacking and vehicle support*). Remove the engine undershield.

42 Position a trolley jack under the engine, with a block of wood between the jack head and take the weight of the engine.

43 Undo the bolts securing the right-hand engine mounting to the inner wing, then carefully pull the engine forwards a little.

44 Release the clamp and disconnect the turbocharger intake pipe breather hose.

45 Prise out the wire clip and disconnect the heater-to-EGR cooler hose, then release the clamp and disconnect the coolant bypass-to-EGR cooler hose **(see illustration)**.

46 Undo the nuts and remove the EGR tube heat shield.

47 Release the clamp, undo the 2 retaining nuts, and remove the EGR cooler 'elbow' connecting pipe **(see illustration)**. Renew the gasket.

48 Undo the 2 retaining bolts, and remove the EGR cooler.

Particulate filter

49 Particulate filter renewal is described in Chapter 4B – Exhaust system.

Particulate filter additive system module (ASM)

50 Disconnect the battery negative lead (see Chapter 5), then remove the rear seat as described in Chapter 11.

51 Remove the rear right-hand side door sill trim as described in Chapter 11.

52 Lift up the carpet on the right-hand side under the seat, undo the 2 nuts and remove the ASM. Disconnect the ASM wiring plug as the unit is withdrawn.

53 Refitting is a reversal of removal. Note that if the ASM has been renewed, the new unit must be programmed using software downloaded from Ford. Consult a Ford dealer or specialist.

Chapter 5 Part A:
Starting and charging systems

Contents

	Section number		Section number
Alternator – removal and refitting	5	General information and precautions	1
Battery – removal and refitting	3	Starter motor – removal and refitting	7
Battery – testing and charging	2	Starter motor – testing and overhaul	8
Charging system – testing	4	Starting system – testing	6

Degrees of difficulty

Easy, suitable for novice with little experience	**Fairly easy,** suitable for beginner with some experience	**Fairly difficult,** suitable for competent DIY mechanic	**Difficult,** suitable for experienced DIY mechanic	**Very difficult,** suitable for expert DIY or professional

Specifications

System type	12 volt, negative earth

Battery

Type	Silver-calcium (marked Ca), low-maintenance or maintenance-free sealed for life
Capacity	43, 50, 60 or 70 Ah (depending on model)
Charge condition:	
Poor	12.5 volts
Normal	12.6 volts
Good	12.7 volts

Alternator

Output	120 or 150 A

Torque wrench settings	Nm	lbf ft
Alternator mounting bolts:		
Petrol engines:		
1.6 litre models	45	33
1.8 and 2.0 litre models	25	18
Diesel engines:		
1.6 litre models	45	33
1.8 litre models	27	20
2.0 litre models	45	33
Alternator pulley	80	59
Starter motor mounting bolts:		
Petrol engines	35	26
Diesel engines:		
1.6 litre models	25	18
1.8 litre models	35	26
2.0 litre models	35	26

1 General information and precautions

General information

The engine electrical system consists mainly of the charging and starting systems. Because of their engine-related functions, these components are covered separately from the body electrical devices such as the lights, instruments, etc (which are covered in Chapter 12). Information on the ignition system is covered in Part B of this Chapter.

The electrical system is of the 12 volt negative earth type.

The battery is of the low-maintenance or maintenance-free (sealed for life) type, and is charged by the alternator, which is belt-driven from the crankshaft pulley.

The starter motor is of the pre-engaged type, incorporating an integral solenoid. On starting, the solenoid moves the drive pinion into engagement with the flywheel ring gear before the starter motor is energised. Once the engine has started, a one-way clutch prevents the motor armature being driven by the engine until the pinion disengages from the flywheel.

Further details of the various systems are given in the relevant Sections of this Chapter. While some repair procedures are given, the usual course of action is to renew the component concerned.

Precautions

⚠️ *Warning: It is necessary to take extra care when working on the electrical system to avoid damage to semi-conductor devices (diodes and transistors), and to avoid the risk of personal injury. In addition to the precautions given in Safety first!, observe the following when working on the system:*

• *Always remove rings, watches, etc, before working on the electrical system.* Even with the battery disconnected, capacitive discharge could occur if a component's live terminal is earthed through a metal object. This could cause a shock or nasty burn.

• *Do not reverse the battery connections.* Components such as the alternator, electronic control modules, or any other components having semi-conductor circuitry could be irreparably damaged.

• Never disconnect the battery terminals, the alternator, any electrical wiring or any test instruments when the engine is running.

• Do not allow the engine to turn the alternator when the alternator is not connected.

• Never test for alternator output by 'flashing' the output lead to earth.

• Always ensure that the battery negative lead is disconnected when working on the electrical system.

• If the engine is being started using jump leads and a slave battery, connect the batteries *positive-to-positive* and *negative-to-negative* (see *Jump starting*). This also applies when connecting a battery charger.

• *Never* use an ohmmeter of the type incorporating a hand-cranked generator for circuit or continuity testing.

• Before using electric-arc welding equipment on the car, *disconnect the battery, alternator and components such as the electronic control modules* (where applicable) to protect them from the risk of damage.

2 Battery – testing and charging

Testing

Standard and low-maintenance battery

1 If the vehicle covers a small annual mileage, it is worthwhile checking the specific gravity of the electrolyte every three months to determine the state of charge of the battery. Use a hydrometer to make the check, and compare the results with the following table. Note that the specific gravity readings assume an electrolyte temperature of 15°C; for every 10°C below 15°C subtract 0.007. For every 10°C above 15°C add 0.007.

| | Ambient temperature | |
	Above 25°C	Below 25°C
Fully-charged	1.210 to 1.230	1.270 to 1.290
70% charged	1.170 to 1.190	1.230 to 1.250
Discharged	1.050 to 1.070	1.110 to 1.130

2 If the battery condition is suspect, first check the specific gravity of electrolyte in each cell. A variation of 0.040 or more between any cells indicates loss of electrolyte or deterioration of the internal plates.

3 If the specific gravity variation is 0.040 or more, the battery should be renewed. If the cell variation is satisfactory but the battery is discharged, it should be charged as described later in this Section.

Maintenance-free battery

4 In cases where a sealed for life maintenance-free battery is fitted, topping-up and testing of the electrolyte in each cell may not be possible. The condition of the battery can therefore only be tested using a battery condition indicator or a voltmeter.

5 Certain models my be fitted with a maintenance-free battery, with a built-in charge condition indicator. The indicator is located in the top of the battery casing, and indicates the condition of the battery from its colour. The charge conditions denoted by the colour of the indicator should be printed on a label attached to the battery – if not, consult a Ford dealer or automotive electrician for advice.

All types

6 If testing the battery using a voltmeter, connect the voltmeter across the battery and note the voltage. The test is only accurate if the battery has not been subjected to any kind of charge for the previous six hours. If this is not the case, switch on the headlights for 30 seconds, then wait four to five minutes before testing the battery after switching off the headlights. All other electrical circuits must be switched off, so check that the doors and tailgate are fully shut when making the test.

7 If the voltage reading is less than 12.2 volts, then the battery is discharged, whilst a reading of 12.2 to 12.4 volts indicates a partially-discharged condition.

8 If the battery is to be charged, remove it from the vehicle and charge it as described later in this Section.

Charging

Note: The following is intended as a guide only. Always refer to the manufacturer's recommendations (often printed on a label

3.2 Release the clip and remove the battery cover

attached to the battery) before charging a battery.

Note: Silver-calcium (Ca) batteries require a dedicated battery charger. Check that your charger is suitable for these batteries.

Standard and low-maintenance battery

9 Charge the battery at a rate equivalent to 10% of the battery capacity (eg, for a 45 Ah battery charge at 4.5 A) and continue to charge the battery at this rate until no further rise in specific gravity is noted over a four-hour period.

10 Alternatively, a trickle charger charging at the rate of 1.5 amps can safely be used overnight.

11 Special rapid boost charges which are claimed to restore the power of the battery in 1 to 2 hours are not recommended, as they can cause serious damage to the battery plates through overheating. If the battery is completely flat, recharging should take at least 24 hours.

12 While charging the battery, note that the temperature of the electrolyte should never exceed 38°C.

Maintenance-free battery

13 This battery type takes considerably longer to fully recharge than the standard type, the time taken being dependent on the extent of discharge, but it can take anything up to three days.

14 A constant voltage type charger is required, to be set, when connected, to 13.9 to 14.9 volts with a charger current below 25 amps. Using this method, the battery should be useable within three hours, giving a voltage reading of 12.5 volts, but this is for a partially-discharged battery and, as mentioned, full charging can take far longer.

15 If the battery is to be charged from a fully-discharged state (condition reading less than 12.2 volts), have it recharged by your Ford dealer or local automotive electrician, as the charge rate is higher, and constant supervision during charging is necessary.

3 Battery – removal and refitting

Caution: Wait at least 5 minutes after turning off the ignition switch before disconnecting the battery. This is to allow sufficient time for the various control modules to store information.

Note: Ensure you have the audio unit security code. This code will need to be inputted after reconnecting the battery – refer to the owner's handbook supplied with the vehicle.

Removal

1 The battery is located on the left-hand side of the engine compartment. Begin by removing the air cleaner assembly as described in Chapter 4.

2 Release the clip and remove the battery cover **(see illustration)**.

3 Slacken the clamp nut and disconnect the battery negative lead terminal (see illustration).

4 Slacken the clamp nut and disconnect the battery positive lead terminal (see illustration).

5 Using a screwdriver release the clips securing the cables to the battery box, then unclip and remove the front wall of the battery box (see illustrations).

6 Unscrew the nuts and remove the battery retaining clamp (see illustration).

7 Lift the battery out of the engine compartment.

8 To remove the battery tray, begin by removing the air cleaner assembly as described in Chapter 4.

9 On all 1.6 litre models, and 1.8 and 2.0 litre models up to 03/2007, unclip the cover, then undo the 3 Torx bolts and move the engine management PCM from its location on the side of the battery tray and lay it over the engine – refer to Chapter 4 if necessary.

10 Undo the 3 bolts and remove the battery tray (see illustration).

Refitting

11 Position the battery in the battery box.

12 Refit the retaining clamp and tighten the retaining nuts securely.

13 Reconnect the battery positive lead, followed by the negative lead. Smear a little petroleum jelly on the terminals. Ensure no-one is inside the vehicle whilst the battery is reconnected.

14 Refit the battery cover.

15 After reconnecting the battery, the engine may run erratically until it's been driven for a few minutes to allow the PCM to relearn. Also the electric windows must be re-initialised as follows:

a) Press and hold the window control close button until the window is fully closed.

b) Release the button, then press it again for 3 seconds.

c) Briefly press the open button to the second detent, then release it. The window should open automatically.

d) Briefly press the close button to the second detent, then release it. If the window does not close automatically, repeat the complete procedure.

e) Repeat this procedure on each electric window.

4   Charging system –
      testing

Note: Refer to the warnings given in 'Safety first!' and in Section 1 of this Chapter before starting work.

1 The charging system uses Ford's smart charge technology. The output of the alternator is controlled by the main engine control module (ECM) in conjunction with the electronics incorporated in the alternator itself. 'Smart' charge has several advantages over a traditional alternator system:

3.3 Slacken the nut and disconnect the battery negative terminal . . .

a) There will be no output from the alternator until the ECM sees an engine running condition. This leaves more battery power available for the starter motor.

b) All batteries can be charged more efficiently when cold. By monitoring the air temperature and coolant temperature the ECM can calculate the battery temperature and adjust the alternator output accordingly. This allows for higher charge rates than those associated with a traditional system.

c) Idle speed and output can be controlled when the electrical demand is high.

d) Heavy electrical consumers, eg, screen heaters can be turned off, or their output reduced when a low battery charge is detected by the ECM.

e) In the event of a failure of the smart charge electronics the alternator will operate in the traditional manner.

3.5a Release the clip (where applicable) . . .

3.6 Undo the battery clamp nuts (arrowed)

3.4 . . . followed by the positive terminal

2 If the charge warning light fails to illuminate when the ignition is switched on, first check the 15 amp fuse in the fusebox. This is normally fuse number 17. If satisfactory, check that the warning light bulb has not blown, and that the bulbholder is secure in its location in the instrument panel. If the light still fails to illuminate, check the continuity of the warning light feed wire from the fuse to the bulbholder and then from the bulbholder to the ECM. If all is satisfactory the ECM or the wiring between the ECM and the alternator maybe at fault.

3 To check the wiring at the alternator remove the 3 pin multiplug and check for battery voltage at the outer pin. Do this with the ignition on, but the engine not running. If battery voltage is not available check fuse number 26 in the fusebox. If this is intact check for continuity between the fuse and the alternator electrical connector.

4 The other two wires at the multiplug are the control system from the ECM. These can only

3.5b . . . and slide up the front cover

3.10 Battery tray bolts (arrowed)

5.2 Power steering fluid reservoir bolt (arrowed)

5.4 Alternator upper mounting nut (arrowed)

5.5 Alternator lower mounting bolt (arrowed)

be tested with an oscilloscope since they are a modulated square wave. However continuity between these wires and the ECM can be checked. Disconnect the battery negative lead, and position the lead away from the battery before checking for continuity.

5 If the ignition warning light illuminates when the engine is running, stop the engine and check that the drivebelt is intact and correctly tensioned (see Chapter 1) and that the alternator connections are secure.

6 If the alternator output is suspect even though the warning light functions correctly, the regulated voltage may be checked as follows.

7 Connect a voltmeter across the battery terminals and note the battery voltage. Start the engine.

8 Increase the engine speed to 1500 rpm. The voltmeter should read 2.5 volts above the starting voltage. The reading should be within the range of 14.1 volts to 15.1 volts. The

standard output for a 'smart' alternator system is 14.8 volts, but this will vary depending on ambient temperature, electrical demand and battery voltage.

9 Switch on as many electrical accessories (eg, the headlights, heated rear window and heater blower) as possible and increase the engine speed to approximately 2000 rpm. Check that the alternator maintains the regulated voltage between 14.1 and 15.1 volts. Repeat this test at the main (B+) wire at the alternator. This will eliminate a wiring fault between the alternator and battery.

10 If the regulated voltage is not as stated, and all other tests have proved satisfactory, the fault may be due to worn brushes, weak brush springs, a faulty voltage regulator, a faulty diode, a severed phase winding or worn or damaged slip-rings. The alternator should be renewed or taken to an auto-electrician for testing and repair.

5 Alternator – removal and refitting

Petrol engines

1 Disconnect the battery negative lead (see Section 3).

2 Undo the bolt and move the power steering reservoir to one side (models with conventional power steering only) **(see illustration)**.

3 Remove the auxiliary drivebelt as described in Chapter 1.

1.6 litre engines

4 Undo and remove the alternator upper mounting nut **(see illustration)**.

5 Undo the alternator lower retaining bolt **(see illustration)**.

6 Undo the remaining upper mounting bolt and remove the splash shield **(see illustration)**.

7 Unclip the alternator wiring harness, then disconnect the power steering pressure switch, and the plug from the rear of the alternator.

8 Prise off the plastic cap, then undo the nut and disconnect the remaining cable from the rear of the alternator.

9 Unscrew the alternator upper mounting stud. This can be done using two nuts locked together on the stud's threads, or pull the alternator forwards a little and use a pair of self-locking pliers to unscrew the stud. Support the alternator as the stud is removed, then lift the alternator from place.

10 Refitting is a reversal of removal. Remembering to tighten the various fasteners to their specified torque where given.

1.8 and 2.0 litre engines

11 Remove the plastic cover on the top of the engine by pulling it straight upwards from its mountings. Remove the right-hand side headlight assembly as described in Chapter 12.

12 Undo the upper bolt securing the engine oil level dipstick guide tube to the manifold **(see illustration)**.

13 Undo and remove the alternator upper mounting bolt **(see illustration)**.

14 Raise the vehicle and support it securely on axle stands (see *Jacking and vehicle support*). Where fitted, undo the fasteners and remove the engine undershield.

5.6 Alternator upper mounting bolt (arrowed)

5.12 Undo the engine oil level dipstick guide tube bolt (arrowed)

5.13 Alternator upper mounting bolt (arrowed) – viewed through the headlight aperture

5.16 Engine oil level dipstick guide tube lower bolt (arrowed)

5.17 Disconnect the wiring plug, then pull away the rubber cap and disconnect the lead from the terminal stud (arrowed)

15 Working from underneath, unclip the refrigerant pipe (where applicable) and move it to one side. There's no need to disconnect the refrigerant pipe.

16 Undo the lower retaining bolt and pull the engine oil level dipstick tube from place **(see illustration)**.

17 Disconnect the wiring plug, then prise out the rubber cap and disconnect the lead from the rear of the alternator **(see illustration)**.

18 Undo the 2 lower mounting bolts and lower the alternator **(see illustration)**.

19 Refitting is a reversal of removal. Remembering to tighten the various fasteners to their specified torque where given.

Diesel engines

20 Disconnect the battery negative lead (see Section 3). Remove the auxiliary drivebelt as described in Chapter 1.

5.18 Alternator lower mounting bolts (arrowed)

1.6 litre engines

21 Slacken the clamp and disconnect the air intake hose from the air intake tube above the alternator **(see illustration)**.

22 Disconnect the sensor(s) wiring plug(s), then undo the retaining bolts and remove the air intake tube/anti-shudder valve **(see illustration)**. Recover the O-ring seal, and renew if necessary.

23 Disconnect the wiring plug from the alternator, then prise up the rubber cap, undo the nut and disconnect the battery cable from the alternator **(see illustration)**.

24 Undo the retaining bolts and remove the auxiliary drivebelt tensioner **(see illustration)**. Remove the alternator upper rear and front retaining bolts.

25 On models with air conditioning, disconnect the wiring plug, undo the 4 bolts and lower the air conditioning compressor

5.21 Slacken the intake hose clamp (arrowed)

from place. Use string or wire to suspend the compressor from the vehicle bodywork. There's no need to disconnect the refrigerant pipes.

26 Remove the lower retaining bolt and lower the alternator from position.

27 Refitting is a reversal of removal. Remembering to tighten the various fasteners to their specified torque where given.

1.8 litre models with air conditioning

28 Remove the plastic cover, unscrew the nut and disconnect the wiring from the alternator **(see illustration)**.

29 Undo the four bolts from the air conditioning compressor and remove to one side. *Caution: Do not disconnect the refrigerant pipes.*

30 Undo the pulley bracket bolts, then slacken the three generator coupling bolts and remove the coupling **(see illustrations)**.

5.22 Anti-shudder valve bolts (arrowed)

5.23 Disconnect the alternator wiring connections (arrowed)

5.24 Auxiliary drivebelt tensioner bolts (arrowed)

5.28 Prise up the cover (arrowed) and disconnect the wiring

5.30a Undo the two pulley bolts . . .

5.30b . . . slacken the three coupling bolts . . .

5.30c . . . and remove the coupling from the alternator

Unscrew the alternator mounting bolts and carefully lift the alternator from the engine

31 Refitting is a reversal of removal. Remembering to tighten the various fasteners to their specified torque where given.

1.8 litre models without air conditioning

32 Remove the plastic cover, unscrew the nut and disconnect the wiring from the alternator **(see illustration 5.28)**.
33 Undo the Torx bolt, and remove the auxiliary drivebelt idler pulley from above the alternator. Undo the 2 retaining bolts and remove the alternator **(see illustration)**.
34 Refitting is a reversal of removal. Remembering to tighten the various fasteners to their specified torque where given.

2.0 litre models

35 Undo the retaining bolts and remove the auxiliary drivebelt tensioner. Undo and

5.36 Slacken the air pipe clamp (arrowed)

5.39 Undo the bolt (arrowed) on the right-hand side of the filter

5.33 Alternator mounting bolts and idler pulley bolt

remove the alternator lower retaining bolt **(see illustration)**.
36 Slacken the clamp and disconnect the intercooler outlet pipe from the anti-shudder valve **(see illustration)**.
37 Undo the bolts and remove the crash shield over the fuel filter **(see illustration)**.
38 Note their fitted positions, then disconnect the various wiring plugs from the fuel filter assembly.
39 Undo the retaining bolt, then lift the fuel filter upwards from the bracket and position it to one side **(see illustration)**. There's no need to disconnect the fuel pipes, but release them from the various retaining clips.
40 Undo the 3 retaining bolts and remove the fuel filter bracket **(see illustration)**.
41 Disconnect the wiring plug, then undo the nut and disconnect the cable from the alternator.
42 Slacken the alternator lower mounting

5.37 Undo the bolts (arrowed) and remove the crash shield

5.40 Fuel filter bracket bolts (arrowed)

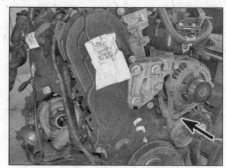

5.35 Alternator lower bolt (arrowed) – engine removed for clarity

clamp bolt, then undo the upper mounting bolts, slide the alternator to the right, and manoeuvre it from place **(see illustration)**.
43 Refitting is a reversal of removal. Remembering to tighten the various fasteners to their specified torque where given.

6 Starting system – testing

Note: *Refer to the precautions given in Safety first! and in Section 1 of this Chapter before starting work.*

1 If the starter motor fails to operate when the ignition key is turned to the appropriate position, the following possible causes may be to blame:
a) *The battery is faulty.*
b) *The electrical connections between the switch, solenoid, battery and starter motor are somewhere failing to pass the necessary current from the battery through the starter to earth.*
c) *The solenoid is faulty.*
d) *The starter motor is mechanically or electrically defective.*

2 To check the battery, switch on the headlights. If they dim after a few seconds, this indicates that the battery is discharged – recharge (see Section 2) or renew the battery. If the headlights glow brightly, operate the ignition switch and observe the lights. If they dim, then this indicates that current is reaching the starter motor; therefore the fault must lie in the starter motor. If the lights continue to glow

5.42 Undo the upper bolts and slacken the lower Allen bolt (arrowed)

brightly (and no clicking sound can be heard from the starter motor solenoid), this indicates that there is a fault in the circuit or solenoid – see following paragraphs. If the starter motor turns slowly when operated, but the battery is in good condition, then this indicates that either the starter motor is faulty, or there is considerable resistance somewhere in the circuit.

3 If a fault in the circuit is suspected, disconnect the battery leads (including the earth connection to the body), the starter/solenoid wiring and the engine/transmission earth strap. Thoroughly clean the connections, and reconnect the leads and wiring, then use a voltmeter or test light to check that full battery voltage is available at the battery positive lead connection to the solenoid, and that the earth is sound. Smear petroleum jelly around the battery terminals to prevent corrosion – corroded connections are amongst the most frequent causes of electrical system faults.

4 If the battery and all connections are in good condition, check the circuit by disconnecting the wire from the solenoid blade terminal. Connect a voltmeter or test light between the wire end and a good earth (such as the battery negative terminal), and check that the wire is live when the ignition switch is turned to the start position. If it is, then the circuit is sound – if not, the circuit wiring can be checked as described in Chapter 12.

5 The solenoid contacts can be checked by connecting a voltmeter or test light between the battery positive feed connection on the starter side of the solenoid, and earth. When the ignition switch is turned to the start position, there should be a reading or lighted bulb, as applicable. If there is no reading or lighted bulb, the solenoid is faulty and should be renewed.

6 If the circuit and solenoid are proved sound, the fault must lie in the starter motor. In this event, it may be possible to have the starter motor overhauled by a specialist, but check on the cost of spares before proceeding, as it may prove more economical to obtain a new or exchange motor.

7 Starter motor – removal and refitting

Petrol engines

1 Disconnect the battery negative lead (see Section 3).

1.6 litre engines

2 Remove the air cleaner assembly as described in Chapter 4.
3 On 1.6 litre Ti-VCT engines, remove the throttle body as described in Chapter 4.
4 Disconnect the starter motor wiring connections **(see illustration)**.
5 Support the starter motor, then undo the 3 retaining bolts and manoeuvre it from place **(see illustration)**. Note the earth connection

7.4 Undo the 2 nuts (arrowed) and disconnect the starter motor wiring

7.7 Undo the nut (arrowed) and slide the wiring terminal from the stud

on the rearmost bolt and the bracket on the lower bolt.
6 Refitting is a reversal of removal. Tighten all fasteners to their specified torque where given.

1.8 and 2.0 litre engines

7 Raise the front of the vehicle and support it securely on axle stands (see *Jacking and vehicle support*). Where fitted, undo the fasteners and remove the engine undershield. Disconnect the wiring from the starter solenoid **(see illustration)**.
8 Undo the retaining nuts and move the wiring bracket to one side **(see illustration)**.
9 Undo the mounting studs and remove the starter motor. Discard the gasket.
10 Refitting is a reversal of removal. Tighten all fasteners to their specified torque where given.

Diesel engines

1.6 litre engines

11 Remove the battery as described in Section 3, then undo the 3 bolts and remove the battery tray.
12 Note their fitted positions, then disconnect the wiring connections from the starter motor, which is located on the rear of the cylinder block.
13 Raise the front of the vehicle and support it securely on axle stands (see *Jacking and vehicle support*). Undo the bolts and remove the engine undershield.
14 Undo the starter motor lower mounting bolt from underneath. Remove the upper mounting bolts, and remove the starter motor.

7.5 Note the earth connection on the rearmost starter mounting bolt (arrowed)

7.8 Remove the wiring harness bracket from the starter motor retaining studs/bolts

15 Refitting is a reversal of removal. Tighten all fasteners to their specified torque where given.

1.8 litre engines

16 Disconnect the battery negative lead as described in Section 3. Remove the air cleaner assembly as described in Chapter 4.
17 Undo the upper starter motor retaining bolts.
18 Raise the front of the vehicle and support it securely on axle stands (see *Jacking and vehicle support*). Undo the fasteners and remove the engine undershield.
19 Undo the nuts, and disconnect the wiring connections from the starter motor **(see illustration)**.
20 Undo the mounting bolt and remove the starter downwards.
21 Refitting is a reversal of removal. Tighten all fasteners to their specified torque where given.

7.19 Remove the wiring connectors from the starter motor

7.23 Undo the nuts (arrowed) and disconnect the wiring

7.24 Starter motor bolts (arrowed)

2.0 litre engines

22 Disconnect the battery negative lead as described in Section 3. Pull the plastic cover on the top of the engine upwards to release its mountings.

23 Undo the nuts and disconnect the wiring from the starter motor solenoid **(see illustration)**.

24 Undo the 3 mounting bolts, and remove the starter motor **(see illustration)**. Check the locating dowel is still in place in the starter motor mounting face.

25 Refitting is a reversal of removal. Tighten all fasteners to their specified torque where given.

8 Starter motor –
   testing and overhaul

If the starter motor is thought to be suspect, it should be removed from the vehicle and taken to an auto-electrician for testing. Most auto-electricians will be able to supply and fit brushes at a reasonable cost. However, check on the cost of repairs before proceeding, as it may prove more economical to obtain a new or exchange motor.

Chapter 5 Part B:
Ignition system – petrol engines

Contents

Section number

Electronic ignition HT coil(s) – removal and refitting 3
Ignition system – general information and precautions 1
Ignition system – testing 2

Section number

Ignition timing – checking and adjustment 4
Knock sensor – removal and refitting 5

Degrees of difficulty

Easy, suitable for novice with little experience	Fairly easy, suitable for beginner with some experience	Fairly difficult, suitable for competent DIY mechanic	Difficult, suitable for experienced DIY mechanic	Very difficult, suitable for expert DIY or professional

Specifications

General

System type	Electronic distributorless ignition system controlled by engine management system (Powertrain Control Module)
Firing order	1-3-4-2
Location of No 1 cylinder	Timing chain/belt end

Ignition system data

Ignition timing	Controlled by the Powertrain Control Module (PCM)
Ignition coil resistances	Not available

Torque wrench settings

	Nm	lbf ft
Ignition coil:		
1.6 litre engines	6	4
1.8 and 2.0 litre engines	10	7
Knock sensors	20	15

1 Ignition system – general information and precautions

General information

The ignition system is integrated with the fuel injection system to form a combined engine management system under the control of the Powertrain Control Module (PCM) (see Chapter 4 for further information). The main ignition system components include the ignition switch, the battery, the crankshaft speed/position sensor, the ignition coil, the camshaft position sensor(s), the knock sensor(s), and the spark plugs.

A Distributorless Ignition System (DIS) is fitted where the main functions of the conventional distributor are superseded by a computerised module within the Powertrain Control Module. On 1.6 litre engines, the remote ignition coil unit combines a double-ended pair of coils

– each time a coil receives an ignition signal, two sparks are produced, one at each end of the secondary windings. One spark goes to a cylinder on its compression stroke and the other goes to the corresponding cylinder on its exhaust stroke. The first will give the correct power stroke, but the second spark will have no effect (a 'wasted spark'), occurring as it does during exhaust conditions. On 1.8 and 2.0 litre engines, one coil is fitted for each spark plug. The coil fits above the spark plug, and has an integral power stage and HT cap. This system is often referred to as a 'COP' (coil on plug) ignition system.

The information contained in this Chapter concentrates on the ignition-related components of the engine management system. Information covering the fuel, exhaust and emission control components can be found in Chapter 4.

Precautions

The following precautions must be observed, to prevent damage to the ignition

system components and to reduce risk of personal injury.

a) Do not keep the ignition on for more than 10 seconds if the engine will not start.

b) Ensure that the ignition is switched off before disconnecting any of the ignition wiring.

c) Ensure that the ignition is switched off before connecting or disconnecting any ignition test equipment, such as a timing light.

d) Do not earth the coil primary or secondary circuits.

 Warning: Voltages produced by an electronic ignition system are considerably higher than those produced by conventional ignition systems. Extreme care must be taken when working on the system with the ignition switched on. Persons with surgically-implanted cardiac pacemaker devices should keep well clear of the ignition circuits, components and test equipment.

3.2 Disconnect the ignition coil wiring plug (arrowed)

3.3 Pull the HT leads (arrowed) from the terminals on the coil

Engine misfires

5 An irregular misfire is probably due to a loose connection to one of the ignition coils or system sensors.

6 With the ignition switched off, check carefully through the system, ensuring that all connections are clean and securely fastened.

7 Regular misfiring indicates a problem with one of the ignition coils or spark plugs. As no resistance values are available, testing the coils is best left to a Ford dealer or suitably-equipped specialist.

8 Any further checking of the system components should be carried out after first checking the PCM for fault codes.

2 Ignition system – testing

> ⚠ **Warning: Voltages produced by an electronic ignition system are considerably higher than those produced by conventional ignition systems. Extreme care must be taken when working on the system if the ignition is switched on. Persons with surgically-implanted cardiac pacemaker devices should keep well clear of the ignition circuits, components and test equipment.**

General

1 The components of the ignition system are normally very reliable; most faults are far more likely to be due to loose or dirty connections, or to tracking of HT voltage due to dirt, dampness or damaged insulation, than to the failure of any of the system's components. **Always** check all wiring thoroughly before condemning an electrical component, and work methodically to eliminate all other possibilities before deciding that a particular component is faulty.

2 The old practice of checking for a spark by holding the live end of an HT cap a short distance away from the engine is **not** recommended; not only is there a high risk of a powerful electric shock, but the PCM or HT coil may be damaged. Similarly, **never** try to diagnose misfires by pulling off one HT coil at a time.

3 The following tests should be carried out when an obvious fault such as non-starting or a clearly detectable misfire exists. Some faults, however, are more obscure and are often disguised by the fact that the PCM will adopt an emergency program (limp-home) mode to maintain as much driveability as possible. Faults of this nature usually appear in the form of excessive fuel consumption, poor idling characteristics, lack of performance, knocking or pinking noises from the engine under certain conditions, or a combination of these conditions. Where problems such as this are experienced, the best course is to refer the car to a suitably-equipped garage for diagnostic testing using dedicated test equipment.

Engine will not start

Note: *Remember that a fault with the anti-theft alarm or immobiliser will give rise to apparent starting problems. Make sure that the alarm or immobiliser has been deactivated, referring to the vehicle handbook for details.*

4 If the engine either will not turn over at all, or only turns very slowly, check the battery and starter motor. Connect a voltmeter across the battery terminals (meter positive probe to battery positive terminal) then note the voltage reading obtained while turning the engine over on the starter for (no more than) ten seconds. If the reading obtained is less than approximately 9.5 volts, first check the battery, starter motor and charging system as described in Part A of this Chapter.

3 Electronic ignition HT coil(s) – removal and refitting

Removal

1.6 litre engines

1 The ignition coil is bolted to the coolant outlet elbow on the left-hand end of the cylinder head.

2 Make sure the ignition is switched off, then disconnect the main wiring plug from the coil **(see illustration)**.

3 Identify the HT leads for position (mark the leads and the coil terminals) then carefully pull them from the terminals on the coil **(see illustration)**.

4 Unscrew the four mounting bolts and remove the ignition coil from the engine compartment. Where applicable, recover the heat shield/mounting plate.

1.8 and 2.0 litre engines

5 Remove the plastic cover from the top of the engine, by pulling it upwards from the mountings.

6 Disconnect the ignition coil(s) wiring plug(s) **(see illustration)**. It is safest to work on one coil at a time. However, if the coils and the wiring plugs are marked for position, all 4 could be removed at once.

7 Each coil is secured by 1 bolt. Undo the bolt and pull the coil from the cylinder head **(see illustration)**.

Refitting

8 Refitting is a reversal of removal. Tighten the retaining bolts to the specified torque.

4 Ignition timing – checking and adjustment

Due to the nature of the ignition system, the ignition timing is constantly being monitored and adjusted by the engine management PCM, and nominal values cannot be given. Therefore, it is not possible for the home mechanic to check the ignition timing.

3.6 Press down the clip and disconnect the coil wiring plug

3.7 Undo the bolt and pull the coil from place

The only way in which the ignition timing can be checked is using special electronic test equipment, connected to the engine management system diagnostic connector (refer to Chapter 4). No adjustment of the ignition timing is possible. Should the ignition timing be incorrect, then a fault must be present in the engine management system.

5 Knock sensor – removal and refitting

Removal

1.6 litre models

1 Remove the alternator as described in Chapter 5A.
2 The knock sensor is located on the front facing side of the cylinder block under the intake manifold.
3 Trace the wiring back from the sensor to the connector, then slide the retaining clip down and disconnect the wiring plug.
4 Note its fitted position, then undo the bolt and remove the sensor **(see illustration)**.

5.4 The knock sensors (arrowed) are located under the intake manifold – 1.6 litre Ti-VCT engine

1.8 and 2.0 litre models

5 The knock sensors are located on the front facing side of the cylinder block under the intake manifold.
6 Refer to Chapter 4 and remove the intake manifold.
7 Disconnect the wiring connector from the knock sensor(s).
8 Note the fitted position of the sensor(s), it is essential that it is refitted to its original positions. Undo the retaining bolt and remove the sensor **(see illustration)**.

5.8 Knock sensor (arrowed) – 1.8 and 2.0 litre engines

Refitting

9 Refitting is a reversal of removal, noting the following points:
a) *The sensor(s) must be refitted in their original positions, with the wiring harness angle exactly as before.*
b) *Tightening the retaining bolt to the specified torque is absolutely essential. Failure to do so could impair the performance of the sensor, causing engine damage.*

Chapter 5 Part C:
Pre/post-heating system – diesel engines

Contents

	Section number			Section number
Glow plugs – removal, inspection and refitting	3		Pre/post-heating – testing	2
Pre/post-heating system – general information	1			

Degrees of difficulty

Easy, suitable for novice with little experience	**Fairly easy,** suitable for beginner with some experience	**Fairly difficult,** suitable for competent DIY mechanic	**Difficult,** suitable for experienced DIY mechanic	**Very difficult,** suitable for expert DIY or professional

Specifications

Torque wrench settings	Nm	lbf ft
Glow plugs:		
1.6 litre engine	8	6
1.8 litre engine	15	11
2.0 litre engine	10	7

1 Pre/post-heating system – general information

To assist cold starting and to control emission levels, diesel engine models are fitted with a pre/post- heating system, which comprises a relay, and four glow plugs. The system is controlled by the engine management PCM (Powertrain Control Module), using information provided by the coolant temperature sensor, air temperature sensor and cylinder head temperature sensors (see Chapter 3).

The glow plugs are miniature electric heating elements, encapsulated in a metal case with a probe at one end, and an electrical connection at the other. The combustion chambers have a glow plug threaded into it. When the glow plug is energised, it heats up rapidly causing the temperature of the air charge drawn into each of the combustion chambers to rise. Each glow plug probe is positioned directly in line with the incoming spray of fuel from the injector. Hence the fuel passing over the glow plug probe is also heated, allowing its optimum combustion temperature to be achieved more readily.

The duration of the preheating period is governed by the engine management powertrain control module (PCM), using information provided by the coolant temperature sensor (see Chapter 3). The PCM alters the preheating time (the length for which the glow plugs are supplied with current) to suit the prevailing conditions. Post start heating of the glow plugs is also controlled by the PCM to control the exhaust gas emissions during the warm-up phase.

A warning light informs the driver that preheating is taking place. The lamp extinguishes when sufficient preheating has taken place to allow the engine to be started. If no attempt is made to start the engine, the power supply to the glow plugs is switched off to prevent battery drain and glow plug burn-out.

2 Pre/post-heating system – testing

1 Full testing of the system can only be carried out using specialist diagnostic equipment which is connected to the engine management system diagnostic wiring connector (see Chapter 4). If the preheating system is thought to be faulty, some preliminary checks of the glow plug operation may be made as described in the following paragraphs.

2 Connect a voltmeter or 12 volt test lamp between the glow plug supply cable, and a good earth point on the engine.

Caution: Make sure that the live connection is kept well clear of the engine and bodywork.

3 Have an assistant activate the preheating system by turning the ignition key to the second position, and check that battery voltage is applied to the glow plug electrical connection. **Note:** *The supply voltage will be less than battery voltage initially, but will rise and settle as the glow plug heats up. It will then drop to zero when the preheating period ends and the safety cut-out operates.*

4 If no supply voltage can be detected at the glow plug, then the glow plug relay or the supply cable may be faulty.

5 To locate a faulty glow plug, measure the electrical resistance between the glow plug terminal and the engine earth, and compare it with the resistance of the other glow plugs, or known working example. If the reading is significantly different, the glow plug is probably defective.

6 If no problems are found, take the vehicle to a Ford dealer or specialist for testing using the appropriate diagnostic equipment.

3 Glow plugs – removal, inspection and refitting

Removal

1 Disconnect the battery negative lead as described in Section 3.

1.6 litre engines

2 Pull the plastic cover (where fitted) on the top of the engine upwards to release it from the mountings.

3 Undo the 2 bolts and move the brake fluid remote reservoir (where fitted) to one side **(see illustration)**.

3.3 Undo the remote reservoir bolts (arrowed)

3.5a Prise forwards the clips (right-hand side clips arrowed) . . .

3.5b . . . then pull the windscreen cowl panel upwards from the base of the windscreen

3.6 Undo the bolt (arrowed) at each end of the bulkhead extension panel

3.7 Pull the electrical connector from each glow plug

3.12 Undo the nuts (right-hand side glow plugs arrowed) and disconnect the supply cable

4 Remove the wiper arms as described in Chapter 12.

5 Prise forwards the 5 retaining clips, then pull the windscreen cowl panel upwards from the base of the windscreen **(see illustrations)**.

6 Undo the bolt at each end, then release the clips and remove the bulkhead extension panel from the engine compartment **(see illustration)**.

7 Reach down the back of the engine, pull the electrical connector from each glow plug, and move the supply cable to one side **(see illustration)**. Access to No 1 glow plug is extremely limited – if improved access is required, remove the EGR cooler as described in Chapter 4.

8 Using a deep socket, carefully unscrew each glow plug from the cylinder head.

1.8 litre engines

9 Pull the plastic cover on the top of the engine upwards to release it from the mountings.

10 Release the clamps and disconnect the 2 engine breather hoses from the front of the cylinder head cover.

11 Undo the bolt securing the engine oil level dipstick guide tube.

12 Undo the nuts and disconnect the electrical supply cable from the top of each glow plug **(see illustration)**.

13 Using a deep socket, carefully unscrew each glow plug from the cylinder head.

2.0 litre engines

14 Remove the EGR valve and cooler as described in Chapter 4.

15 Undo the nuts (1 per plug) and disconnect the wiring harness from the glow plugs **(see illustration)**.

16 Unscrew each glow plug from the cylinder head using a deep socket **(see illustration)**.

Inspection

17 Inspect the glow plugs for signs of damage. Burt or eroded glow plug tips can be caused by a bad injector spray pattern. Have the injectors checked if this sort of damage is found.

18 If the glow plugs are in good condition, check them electrically.

19 The glow plugs can be energised by applying 12 volts to them to verify that they heat up evenly and in the required time. Observe the following precautions:

a) Support the glow plug by clamping it carefully in a vice or self-locking pliers. Remember it will be red hot.

b) Make sure that the power supply or test lead incorporates a fuse or overload trip to protect against damage from a short-circuit.

c) After testing, allow the glow plug to cool for several minutes before attempting to handle it.

20 A glow plug in good condition will start to glow red at the tip after drawing current for 5 seconds or so. Any plug which takes much longer to start glowing, or which starts glowing in the middle instead of at the tip, is probably defective.

Refitting

21 Thoroughly clean the glow plugs, and the glow plug seating areas in the cylinder head.

22 Do not apply anti-seize compound or lubricant to the glow plug threads before refitting.

23 Reconnect the wiring to the glow plug and tighten the nut securely.

24 The remainder of refitting is a reversal of removal.

3.15 Undo the nuts (arrowed) securing the electrical connections to the glow plugs

3.16 Unscrew the glow plugs from the cylinder head

Chapter 6
Clutch

Contents
Section number

Clutch assembly – removal, inspection and refitting 6
Clutch hydraulic system – bleeding 5
Clutch master cylinder – removal and refitting. 3
Clutch pedal – removal and refitting. 2
Clutch release bearing – removal, inspection and refitting 7
Clutch slave cylinder – removal and refitting 4
General information 1

Degrees of difficulty

Easy, suitable for novice with little experience	Fairly easy, suitable for beginner with some experience	Fairly difficult, suitable for competent DIY mechanic	Difficult, suitable for experienced DIY mechanic	Very difficult, suitable for expert DIY or professional

Specifications

General
Clutch type . . . .   Single dry plate, diaphragm spring, hydraulic actuation

Driven plate
Warp limit . . . .   0.2 mm

Torque wrench settings

	Nm	lbf ft
Pressure plate retaining bolts.	29	21
Release bearing and slave cylinder mounting bolts.	10	7

---

1 General information

A single dry plate diaphragm spring clutch is fitted to all manual transmission models. The clutch is hydraulically-operated via a master and slave cylinder. All models have an internally-mounted slave cylinder and release bearing combined into one unit.

The main components of the clutch are the pressure plate, the driven plate (sometimes called the friction plate or disc) and the release bearing. The pressure plate is bolted to the flywheel, with the driven plate sandwiched between them. The centre of the driven plate carries female splines which mate with the splines on the transmission input shaft. The release bearing acts on the diaphragm spring fingers of the pressure plate.

When the engine is running and the clutch pedal is released, the diaphragm spring clamps the pressure plate, driven plate and flywheel firmly together. Drive is transmitted through the friction surfaces of the flywheel and pressure plate to the linings of the driven plate, and thus to the transmission input shaft.

The slave cylinder is incorporated into the release bearing – when the slave cylinder operates, the release bearing moves against the diaphragm spring fingers. As the spring pressure on the pressure plate is relieved, the flywheel and pressure plate spin without moving the driven plate. As the pedal is released, spring pressure is restored and the drive is gradually taken up.

The clutch hydraulic system consists of a master cylinder, a slave cylinder and the associated pipes and hoses. The fluid reservoir is shared with the brake master cylinder.

2 Clutch pedal – removal and refitting

⚠ *Warning: Hydraulic fluid is poisonous; wash off immediately and thoroughly in the case of skin contact, and seek immediate medical advice if any fluid is swallowed or gets into the eyes. Certain types of hydraulic fluid are inflammable, and may ignite when allowed into contact with hot components; when servicing any hydraulic system, it is safest to assume that the fluid IS inflammable, and to take precautions against the risk of fire as though it is petrol that is being handled. Hydraulic fluid is also an effective paint stripper, and will attack plastics; if any is spilt, it should be washed off immediately, using copious quantities of clean water. Finally, it is hygroscopic (it absorbs moisture from the air) – old fluid may be contaminated and unfit for further use. When topping-up or renewing the fluid, always use the recommended type, and ensure that it comes from a freshly-opened sealed container.*

Removal

1 Remove the trim panel below the steering wheel and unclip the diagnostic socket (as described in Chapter 11).

2 Remove the windscreen cowl extension **(see illustration)** and then remove the wiper arms as described In Chapter 12.

2.2 Remove the cowl extension panel

2.3 Unbolt and move to one side the remote reservoir (where fitted)

2.5a Remove the bolts . . .

2.5b . . . and lift out the panel

2.6 Undo the 2 inner bolts, slacken the outer bolt, undo the 2 nuts and pivot the strut brace (arrowed) away from the engine compartment bulkhead

2.7a Prise down the clip and pull the pressure pipe from the clutch master cylinder

3 Where fitted unbolt the brake master cylinder remote reservoir and move it to one side **(see illustration)**.

4 Prise out the 6 plastic clips securing the plastic panel to the engine compartment bulkhead, pull the panel forward and remove it.

5 Undo the 2 retaining bolts, pull forward and then remove the lower bulkhead panel **(see illustrations)**. Access can be further improved by removing the wiper motor and linkage (as described in Chapter 12) if required.

6 Remove the 2 inner bolts, slacken the outer bolt, remove the nuts and pivot the cross-stay each side away from the bulkhead **(see illustration)**. Refit the bolts to secure the tops of the suspension struts to the vehicle body.

7 Depress the release buttons/prise out the clip and disconnect the pressure pipe from the clutch master cylinder connection at the engine compartment bulkhead, then disconnect the fluid supply hose from the master cylinder **(see illustrations)**. Be prepared for fluid spillage – wipe up any spills immediately – the fluid could damage paintwork, etc.

8 Disconnect the clutch pedal position sensor wiring plug **(see illustration)**.

9 Undo the retaining nuts and manoeuvre the clutch pedal complete with the bracket and master cylinder from place **(see illustration)**.

10 To separate the master cylinder from the pedal bracket, begin by squeezing the sides of the retaining clip and pull the pushrod from the pedal **(see illustration)**.

11 Rotate the master cylinder 60° clockwise and pull it from the bracket **(see illustration)**.

2.7b Pull back the collar (arrowed) and disconnect the fluid supply pipe

2.8 Disconnect the wiring plug (arrowed) from the clutch pedal position sensor

2.9 Undo the nuts (arrowed) and remove the pedal/master cylinder assembly

2.10 Squeeze the sides of the clip (arrowed) and pull the pushrod from the pedal

2.11 Rotate the master cylinder 60° clockwise and pull it from the bracket

4.3 Slave cylinder mounting bolts (arrowed)

Refitting

12 Refit by reversing the removal operations. Note the following points:
  a) Tighten all fasteners securely.
  b) Renew the seal between the master cylinder and the bulkhead if necessary.
  c) Bleed the clutch hydraulic system as described in Section 5.
  d) Check the operation of the clutch before refitting the lower facia panel.

3 Clutch master cylinder – removal and refitting

Note: At the time of writing, it would appear that master cylinder internal components are not available separately, and therefore no repair or overhaul of the cylinder is possible. In the event of a hydraulic system fault, or any sign of visible fluid leakage on or around the master cylinder or clutch pedal, the unit should be renewed – consult a Ford dealer or specialist.
1 Removal and refitting of the master cylinder is included in the pedal removal and refitting procedure described previously.

4 Clutch slave cylinder – removal and refitting

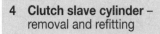

Note 1: Slave cylinder internal components are not available separately, and no repair

or overhaul of the cylinder is possible. In the event of a hydraulic system fault, or any sign of fluid leakage, the unit should be renewed.
Note 2: Refer to the warning at the beginning of Section 2 before proceeding.

Removal

1 Remove the transmission as described in Chapter 7. The internal slave cylinder cannot be removed with the transmission in place.
2 Release the rubber seal from the transmission.
3 Remove the mounting bolts securing the cylinder and release bearing assembly to the transmission, and remove the assembly, feeding the fluid pipe in through the transmission aperture **(see illustration)**.

Refitting

4 Ensure the release bearing/slave cylinder and transmission casing mating surfaces are clean. Apply a bead of sealant (Ford No ESK-M4G269-A) to the rear of the bearing/ cylinder as shown **(see illustration)**.
5 Lubricate the inner lips of the seal with a little grease, then position the release bearing/slave cylinder on the input shaft, and tighten the bolts to the specified torque. Take care not to damage the seal lips with the input shaft splines – wrap adhesive tape around the splines prior to fitting the cylinder.
6 Refit the rubber seal around the pipes, ensuring it is correctly positioned.
7 The remainder of refitting is a reversal of removal, noting the following points:

  a) Remove the adhesive tape from the input shaft splines.
  b) Refit the transmission as described in Chapter 7.
  c) Bleed the clutch hydraulic system on completion (Section 5).

5 Clutch hydraulic system – bleeding

Note: Refer to the warning at the beginning of Section 2 before proceeding.
1 Top-up the hydraulic fluid reservoir on the brake master cylinder with fresh clean fluid of the specified type (see Lubricants and fluids).
2 Remove the air cleaner assembly as described in Chapter 4.
3 Remove the dust cover, and fit a length of clear hose over the bleed nipple on the slave cylinder **(see illustration)**. Place the other end of the hose in a jar containing a small amount of hydraulic fluid.
4 Slacken the bleed nipple half a turn, then have an assistant depress the clutch pedal. Tighten the bleed screw when the pedal is depressed. Have the assistant release the pedal, then slacken the bleed screw again.
5 Repeat the process until clean fluid, free of air bubbles, emerges from the bleed nipple. Tighten the nipple at the end of a pedal downstroke, and remove the hose and jar. Refit the dust cover.
6 Top-up the hydraulic fluid reservoir.
7 Pressure bleeding equipment may be used if preferred.

4.4 Apply a bead of sealant to the slave cylinder around the edge (arrowed)

5.3 Connect the hose to the bleed nipple on the top of the transmission housing

6.3a Undo the pressure plate retaining bolts

6.14a The clutch driven plate should be marked to indicate which side faces the transmission or flywheel

6.3b Using a home-made tool to lock the flywheel

6.14b Position the driven plate using a clutch aligning tool

6 Clutch assembly – removal, inspection and refitting

> ⚠ **Warning: Dust created by clutch wear and deposited on the clutch components may contain asbestos, which is a health hazard. DO NOT blow it out with compressed air or inhale any of it. DO NOT use petrol or petroleum-based solvents to clean off the dust. Brake system cleaner or methylated spirit should be used to flush the dust into a suitable receptacle. After the clutch components are wiped clean with rags, dispose of the contaminated rags and the used cleaner in a sealed, marked container.**

Removal

1 Access to the clutch may be gained in one

6.19 Check the stop-pin (arrowed) is moveable as the bolts are tightened

of two ways. Either the engine/transmission assembly can be removed as described in Chapter 2F, and the transmission then separated from the engine, or the engine may be left in the car and the transmission removed independently as described in Chapter 7.

2 Having separated the transmission from the flywheel, check if there are any marks identifying the relation of the pressure plate to the flywheel. If not, make your own marks using a dab of paint or a scriber. These marks will be used if the original pressure plate is refitted, and will help to maintain the balance of the unit. A new pressure plate may be fitted in any position allowed by the locating dowels.

3 Unscrew and remove the 6 pressure plate retaining bolts, working in a diagonal sequence, and slackening the bolts only a turn at a time. If necessary, the flywheel may be held stationary using a home-made locking tool **(see illustrations)**.

4 Ease the pressure plate off its locating dowels. Be prepared to catch the driven plate, which will drop out as the pressure plate is removed. Note which way round the driven plate is fitted.

Inspection

Note: *On models equipped with a self-adjusting clutch, Ford insist that if a new driven plate is fitted, the pressure plate must also be renewed.*

5 With the clutch assembly removed, clean off all traces of clutch dust using a dry cloth. This is best done outside or in a well-ventilated area.

6 Examine the linings of the driven plate for wear and loose rivets, and the rim for distortion, cracks, broken torsion springs and worn splines. The surface of the friction linings may be highly glazed, but, as long as the friction material pattern can be clearly seen, this is satisfactory.

7 If there is any sign of oil contamination, indicated by a continuous or patchy, shiny black discolouration, the plate must be renewed and the source of the contamination traced and rectified. This will be either a leaking crankshaft oil seal or transmission input shaft oil seal – or both.

8 The driven plate must also be renewed if the lining thickness has worn down to, or just above, the level of the rivet heads. Given the amount of dismantling work necessary to gain access to the driven plate, it may be wise to fit a new plate regardless of the old one's condition.

9 Check the machined faces of the flywheel and pressure plate. If either is grooved, or heavily scored, renewal is necessary. Providing the damage is not too serious, the flywheel can be removed as described in the relevant sections of Chapter 2 and taken to an engineering works, who may be able to clean up the surface by machining.

10 The pressure plate must be renewed if any cracks are apparent, if the diaphragm spring is damaged or its pressure suspect, or if there is excessive warpage of the pressure plate face.

11 With the transmission removed, check the condition of the release bearing, as described in Section 7.

Refitting

12 It is advisable to refit the clutch assembly with clean hands, and to wipe down the pressure plate and flywheel faces with a clean dry rag before assembly begins.

13 Fit an appropriate centering tool into the hole at the end of the crankshaft. The tool must be a sliding fit in the crankshaft hole and the driven plate centre. Ford centering tool No 308-204 may also be available, or a suitable equivalent may be fabricated.

14 Place the driven plate in position with the longer side of the centre boss towards the flywheel (1.6 and 1.8 litre models), or with the spring hub assembly facing away from the flywheel (2.0 litre models), or as noted on removal. Note that the new driven plate will be marked to indicate which side faces the flywheel **(see illustrations)**.

15 Place the pressure plate over the dowels. Refit the retaining bolts, and tighten them finger-tight so that the driven plate is gripped lightly, but can still be moved.

16 The driven plate must now be centralised so that, when the engine and transmission are mated, the splines of the gearbox input shaft will pass through the splines in the centre of the driven plate hub.

17 Centralisation can be carried out by inserting a round bar through the hole in the centre of the driven plate, so that the end of the bar rests in the hole in the rear end of the crankshaft. Move the bar sideways or up-and-down, to move the plate in whichever direction is necessary to achieve centralisation. Centralisation can then be checked by removing the bar and viewing the driven plate hub in relation to the diaphragm spring fingers, or by viewing through the side apertures of the pressure plate, and checking that the driven plate is central in relation to the outer edge of the pressure plate.

18 An alternative and more accurate method of centralisation is to use a commercially available clutch-aligning tool, obtainable from most accessory shops **(see illustration 6.14b)**.

19 Once the clutch is centralised, progressively tighten the pressure plate bolts in a diagonal sequence to the specified torque setting. **Note:** *On models with a self-adjusting clutch, check that the 'stop-pin' is moveable during the tightening of the bolts (see illustration)*.

20 The engine and/or transmission can now be refitted by referring to the appropriate Chapters of this manual.

7 Clutch release bearing – removal, inspection and refitting

Removal

1 Access to the clutch release bearing may be gained in one of two ways. Either the engine/transmission assembly can be removed as described in Chapter 2F and the transmission then separated from the engine, or the engine may be left in the car and the transmission removed independently as described in Chapter 7.

2 The release bearing and slave cylinder are combined into one unit, and cannot be separated. Refer to the slave cylinder removal procedure in Section 4.

Inspection

3 Check the bearing for smoothness of operation, and renew it if there is any roughness or harshness as the bearing is spun. It is a good idea to renew the bearing as a matter of course during clutch overhaul, regardless of its apparent condition, considering the amount of dismantling work necessary to gain access to it.

Refitting

4 Refer to Section 4.

Chapter 7 Part A:
Manual transmission

Contents

Section number

Gearchange cables – adjustment............................ 2
Gearchange cables and gear lever – removal and refitting 3
General information 1
Oil seals – renewal 5

Section number

Reversing light switch – removal and refitting 4
Transmission – removal and refitting 7
Transmission oil – draining and refilling 6
Transmission overhaul – general information................. 8

Degrees of difficulty

Easy, suitable for novice with little experience 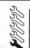	**Fairly easy,** suitable for beginner with some experience	**Fairly difficult,** suitable for competent DIY mechanic	**Difficult,** suitable for experienced DIY mechanic	**Very difficult,** suitable for expert DIY or professional

Specifications

General

Transmission type.. Five or six forward speeds, one reverse. Synchromesh on all forward gears (and reverse gear on MTX75 transmission). Gearchange linkage operated by twin cables

Transmission code:
  Petrol models:
    1.6 litre iB5
    1.8 litre .... iB5 or MTX75
    2.0 litre MTX75
  Diesel models:
    1.6 litre and 1.8 litre MTX75
    2.0 litre MMT6
Transmission oil capacity:
  iB5 transmission...................................... 2.3 litres
  MTX75 .... 1.9 litres
  MMT6.. 1.75 litres

Gear ratios (typical)

	iB5 transmission	MTX75 transmission	MMT6 transmission
1st..	3.58:1	3.417:1	3.077:1
2nd.......................................	2.04:1	2.136:1	1.864:1
3rd..	1.41:1	1.448:1	1.241:1
4th..	1.11:1	1.028:1	0.842:1
5th..	0.88:1	0.805:1	0.886:1
6th..	N/A	N/A	0.711:1
Reverse	3.62:1	3.737:1	1.360:1

Final drive ratios

iB5 transmission.. 4.06:1
MTX75 transmission...................................... 4.06:1
MMT6 transmission 4.07:1

Torque wrench settings

	Nm	lbf ft
Battery tray bolts	25	18
Crashbox-to-subframe bolts	40	30
Engine mountings:		
Right-hand mounting retaining bolts	90	66
Right-hand mounting bracket-to-engine bolts	56	41
Left-hand mounting nuts	48	35
Left-hand mounting bracket to transmission	80	59
Left-hand mounting centre bolt	148	109
Lower-rear torque rod bolts	80	59
Gearchange cable bracket bolts	20	15
Gearchange cable bushing	9	7
Gearchange mechanism to floor	9	7
Oil filler/level plug (MMT6 transmission)	35	26
Reversing light switch	18	13
Selector lever securing bolt	25	18
Slave cylinder pressure pipe bracket	28	21
Transmission to engine	48	35

* Do not re-use

1 General information

The transmission is contained in a cast-aluminium alloy casing bolted to the engine's left-hand end, and consists of the gearbox and final drive differential – often called a transaxle. The transmission unit type is stamped on a plate attached to the transmission. The 5-speed manual transmissions used in the C-MAX are the iB5 and MTX75 types – refer to the Specifications for application details. 2.0 litre diesel models are fitted with the six-speed MMT6 transmission. All transmissions feature a cable-operated gearchange linkage.

Drive is transmitted from the crankshaft via the clutch to the input shaft, which has a splined extension to accept the clutch driven plate. From the input shaft, drive is transmitted to the output shaft, from where the drive is transmitted to the differential crownwheel, which rotates with the differential and planetary gears, thus driving the sun gears and driveshafts. The rotation of the planetary gears on their shaft allows the inner roadwheel to rotate at a slower speed than the outer roadwheel when the car is cornering.

The input and output shafts are arranged side-by-side, parallel to the crankshaft and driveshafts, so that their gear pinion teeth are in constant mesh. In the neutral position, the output shaft gear pinions rotate freely, so that drive cannot be transmitted to the crownwheel.

The transmission selector mechanism causes the appropriate selector fork to move its respective synchro-sleeve along the output shaft, to lock the gear pinion to the synchro-hub. Since the synchro-hubs are splined to the output shaft, this locks the pinion to the shaft, so that drive can be transmitted. To ensure that gearchanging can be made quickly and quietly, a synchromesh system is fitted to all forward gears, consisting of baulk rings and spring-loaded fingers, as well as the gear pinions and synchro-hubs. The synchromesh cones are formed on the mating faces of the baulk rings and gear pinions.

Transmission overhaul

Because of the complexity of the assembly, possible unavailability of new parts and special tools necessary, internal repair procedures for the transmission are not recommended for the home mechanic. The bulk of the information in this Chapter is devoted to removal and refitting procedures.

2.5 Unclip the cover from the front of the transmission

2.7 Prise out the locking insert

2 Gearchange cables – adjustment

iB5 and MTX75 transmissions

Note: *Ford special tool 308-451 will be required for this procedure.*

1 Inside the car, move the gear lever to neutral.

2 Carefully unclip the surround panel at the base of the gear lever gaiter, and move the panel aside for access to the base of the gear lever, disconnecting the switch wiring if necessary.

3 Move the gear lever to the 4th gear position, then install the special tool to hold the gear lever in the 4th gear position. If the Ford special tool is not available a suitable plate can be fabricated from sheet aluminum. Alternatively an assistant may be able to hold the lever in the correct position whilst adjustment is made.

4 For vehicles fitted with the iB5 transmission, apply the handbrake, then jack up the front of the car, supporting it on axle stands (see *Jacking and vehicle support*). Where applicable, remove the engine undershield.

5 On the iB5 transmission remove the selector mechanism cover by working around the edge, releasing a total of seven clips **(see illustration)**. On the MTX75 transmission remove the air filter assembly as described in Chapter 4.

6 Only the selector cable is to be adjusted during this procedure – this is the cable which comes to the lowest point on the front of the transmission, with its end fitting nearest the engine.

7 Unlock the selector cable by pressing the coloured insert towards the engine, and move the transmission selector lever (**not** the gear lever inside the car) to the 4th gear position by moving it up or down as necessary **(see illustration)**.

2.12 Prise out the locking catch on the side of the selector cable

2.13 Insert a 2.5 mm drill bit, set the vertical height of the drill bit to 25mm by pulling or pushing the preload sleeve, then rotate it to the position shown

8 Lock the selector cable in position by moving the coloured insert away from the engine.

9 Refit the selector mechanism cover, ensuring that the clips engage correctly, and lower the car to the ground.

10 Inside the car, remove the special tool from the gear lever base mechanism, and refit the gaiter.

11 Start the engine, keeping the clutch pedal depressed, and check for correct gear selection.

MMT6 transmission

Note: *For models built up to October 2005, Ford special tool 308-451 will be required.*

Vehicles built after November 2005 will require special tool 308-666.

12 Disconnect both gearchange cables from the levers on the transmission, then prise up the locking catch on the end fitting of the selector cable **(see illustration)**.

13 Insert a 2.5 mm drill bit into the centre of the roll-pin securing the selector mechanism preload sleeve, set the vertical distance of 25 mm, and turn the selector arm to engage 4th gear as shown **(see illustration)**.

14 Carefully prise up the gear lever gaiter from the console.

15 Ford technicians now use a special tool to hold the gearchange lever in the 4th

gear position. In the absence of these tools, make a tool from thin aluminium plate to the dimensions shown **(see illustrations)**. If none of the tools are available, the only option is to have an assistant attempt to hold the gearchange lever in the 4th gear position.

16 Re-attach the selector lever cable to the balljoint, and press down the locking catch. Re-attach the shift cable end fitting.

17 Remove the drill bit and special tools (where applicable) and check the operation of the gearchange mechanism. If all appears satisfactory, refit the air cleaner assembly, and the gear lever gaiter.

2.15a Fit the fabricated plate around the gear lever to hold it in 4th gear

16mm · 16mm · 13mm · 12mm · 35mm · 44mm

J46792

2.15b Fabricate a gear lever holding tool from aluminium plate to the dimensions shown

3.3 Twist the knurled collar anti-clockwise

3.6 Remove the gearchange trim

3 Gearchange cables and gear lever – removal and refitting

Removal

1 Remove the air cleaner assembly as described in Chapter 4.

2 Apply the handbrake, then jack up the front of the car, supporting it on axle stands (see *Jacking and vehicle support*). Where applicable, remove the engine undershield.

3 At the transmission, unclip the cover (where fitted) from the selector mechanism. Remove the cables from the support brackets by twisting the spring-loaded knurled collars anti-clockwise. Depress the release button and detach the selector cable from the lever on the transmission, then prise the shift cable end fitting from the its lever on the transmission – note their fitted locations **(see illustration)**. Unclip the cables from the clips on the transmission casing.

4 Remove the washer-type fasteners, and slide the exhaust heat shield rearwards.

5 Unclip the cables from the vehicle body underside.

6 Remove the centre console as described in Chapter 11 and then remove the trim panel to access the gear lever assembly **(see illustration)**.

3.7 Unbolt and lower the gearchange assembly

3.9 Remove the lower bracket from each side of the crossmember supports

7 Where fitted remove the support bracket and then unbolt and lower the gearchange assembly **(see illustration)**.
8 Press the release buttons and disconnect the shift (white) and selector (black) inner cables from the gear lever **(see illustration)**. Disconnect the cable outers from the gear lever assembly by twisting the collars and sliding them from the housing. Remove the gear lever assembly from the vehicle.
9 To remove the cables first undo the bolts and remove the bracket each side between the facia crossmember centre supports and the floor **(see illustration)**. Take care as the edges of the brackets are extremely sharp.
10 Fold back the carpet and insulation material under the centre part of the facia for access to the selector cable floor grommet. Use a sharp knife to cut the insulation if necessary. Remove the two nuts and release

4.3 Unscrew the reversing light switch – iB5 transmission

3.8 Depress the release button (arrowed)

3.10 Undo the nuts (arrowed) to release the grommet – shown with the heater removed for clarity

the grommet from the floor **(see illustration)**.
11 Pass the cables up through the floor.
12 If required, the gear lever knob simply unscrews from place.

Refitting

13 Refitting is a reversal of removal. Use new clips when reconnecting the gearchange cables, and adjust the cables as described in Section 2.

4   Reversing light switch –
     removal and refitting

iB5 transmission

1 The switch is located on the front of the transmission, next to the selector cable front cover. To improve access, jack up the front

4.6 Reversing light switch (arrowed) – MTX75 transmission

left-hand side of the car (see *Jacking and vehicle support*). Where fitted, remove the engine undershield.
2 Disconnect the wiring plug from the switch.
3 Unscrew and remove the switch from the front of the transmission – anticipate a little oil spillage as this is done **(see illustration)**.
4 Refitting is a reversal of removal. Tighten the switch to the specified torque.

MTX75 and MMT6 transmissions

5 The switch is located on top of the transmission. Remove the air cleaner as described in Chapter 4. Remove the battery and tray, as described in Chapter 5.
6 Disconnect the wiring leading to the reversing light switch on the top of the transmission **(see illustration)**.
7 Unscrew the mounting bolts and remove the reversing light switch from the cover housing on the transmission.
8 Refitting is a reversal of the removal procedure.

5   Oil seals –
     renewal

1 Oil leaks frequently occur due to wear or deterioration of the driveshaft oil seals, or the selector shaft oil seal (iB5 transmission). Renewal of these seals is relatively easy, since the repairs can be performed without removing the transmission from the vehicle.

Driveshaft oil seals

2 The driveshaft oil seals are located at the sides of the transmission, where the driveshafts enter the transmission. If leakage at the seal is suspected, raise the vehicle and support it securely on axle stands. If the seal is leaking, oil will be found on the side of the transmission below the driveshaft.
3 Refer to Chapter 8 and remove the appropriate driveshaft.
4 Using a large screwdriver or lever, carefully prise the oil seal out of the transmission casing, taking care not to damage the transmission casing **(see illustration)**.
5 Wipe clean the oil seal seating in the transmission casing.
6 Dip the new oil seal in clean oil, then press

5.4 Prise the driveshaft oil seal from place

5.7 Drive the oil seal into place using a tube or socket

5.25 Insert a self-tapping screw and pull the seal from place

5.26 Drive the new seal squarely into place to its original depth

it a little way into the casing by hand, making sure that it is square to its seating.

7 Using suitable tubing or a large socket carefully drive the oil seal fully into the casing until it contacts the seating **(see illustration)**.

8 When refitting the left-hand driveshaft on the iB5 transmission, use the protective sleeve which should be provided with Ford parts. The sleeve is fitted into the seal, and the driveshaft is then fitted through it – the sleeve is then withdrawn and cut free.

9 Refit the driveshaft (see Chapter 8).

Selector shaft oil seal (iB5 transmission)

10 Apply the handbrake, then jack up the front of the car, supporting it on axle stands (see *Jacking and vehicle support*). Where fitted, remove the engine undershield.

11 At the front face of the transmission housing, remove the selector mechanism cover by working around the edge, releasing a total of seven clips.

12 Prise off the retaining clips, then pull the shift and selector cables from the transmission levers, and detach them from the cable support brackets by turning the knurled collars clockwise.

13 Unscrew and remove the four bolts securing the selector mechanism rear cover to the transmission housing.

14 Remove the transmission shift lever by prising off the protective cap and extracting the retaining clip.

15 With the shift lever removed, unscrew the securing bolt and take off the selector lever and dust cover.

16 The selector shaft oil seal can now be prised out of its location. If using a screwdriver or similar sharp tool, take great care not to mark or gouge the selector shaft or the seal housing as this is done, or the new seal will also leak.

17 Before fitting the new oil seal, carefully clean the visible part of the selector shaft, and the oil seal housing. Wrap a little tape around the end of the shaft, to protect the seal lips as they pass over it.

18 Smear the new oil seal with a little oil, then carefully fit it over the end of the selector shaft, lips facing inwards (towards the transmission).

19 Making sure that the seal stays square to the shaft, press it fully along the shaft (if

available, a 16 mm ring spanner is ideal for this).

20 Press the seal fully into its housing, again using the ring spanner or perhaps a deep socket. Remove the tape from the end of the shaft.

21 Further refitting is a reversal of removal. Tighten the selector lever securing bolt to the specified torque, and use new clips when reconnecting the gearchange cables.

22 On completion, check and if necessary adjust the cables as described in Section 2.

Input shaft oil seal

iB5 and MTX75 transmissions

23 The input shaft seal is integral with the clutch slave cylinder/release bearing. Renew the cylinder/bearing as described in Chapter 6.

MMT6 transmission

24 Remove the clutch release bearing/slave cylinder as described in Chapter 6.

25 Note its fitted depth, then drill a small hole in the hard outer surface of the seal, insert a self-tapping screw, and use pliers to extract the seal **(see illustration)**.

26 Lubricate the new seal with grease and fit it to the bellhousing, lips pointing to the gearbox side. Use a deep socket or suitable tubing to seat it **(see illustration)**.

27 Refit the release bearing/slave cylinder using a reversal of removal.

6 Transmission oil – draining and refilling

Note: *Although not included in the maintenance schedule by the manufacturers, it is a good idea to drain and renew the manual transmission oil on a regular basis. The frequency with which this needs to carried out can be left to the individual, but it is certainly advisable on a vehicle that has covered a high mileage.*

iB5 transmission

1 The iB5 transmission has no drain plug; the most effective way to drain the oil is to remove one or both driveshafts, as described in Chapter 8.

2 When refilling the transmission, remember

that the vehicle must be level for the oil level to be correct. Refill the transmission using the information in Chapter 1 – refer to *Lubricants and fluids* for the type of oil to be used.

MTX75 transmission

3 The drain plug is located in the base of the differential housing – like the oil filler/level plug, a special hexagonal socket (or large Allen key) will be required for removal.

4 The oil is best drained when the transmission is hot, but bear in mind the risk of burning yourself on hot exhaust components, etc. Apply the handbrake, then jack up the front of the car, and support it on axle stands (see *Jacking and vehicle support*).

5 Where applicable, remove the engine undershield. Position a suitable container under the transmission drain plug, then unscrew and remove it, and allow the oil to drain.

6 When the flow of oil stops, clean and refit the drain plug, and tighten it securely.

7 When refilling the transmission, remember that the vehicle must be level for the oil level to be correct. Refill the transmission using the information in Chapter 1 – refer to *Lubricants and fluids* for the type of oil to be used.

MMT6 transmission

8 The drain plug is located on the left-hand side of the transmission.

9 Unscrew and remove the drain plug and allow the oil to drain into the container **(see illustration)**. Check the condition of the drain plug sealing washer (where fitted), and renew if necessary.

6.9 Transmission drain plug (arrowed) – MMT6 transmission

6.10 Oil filler/level plug (arrowed) – MMT6 transmission

10 Wipe clean the area around the filler/level plug, and unscrew the plug from the casing **(see illustration)**.

11 Fill the transmission through the filler plug orifice with the correct type of oil (see *Lubricants and fluids*) until the oil begins to run out of the orifice.

12 Refit the filler/level plug with a new seal (where fitted), and tighten it to the specified torque.

7 Transmission – removal and refitting

⚠️ *Warning: The hydraulic fluid used in the clutch system is brake fluid, which is poisonous. Take care to keep it off bare skin, and in particular out of your eyes. The fluid also attacks paintwork,* and may discolour carpets, etc – keep spillages to a minimum, and wash any off immediately with cold water. Finally, brake fluid is highly inflammable, and should be handled with the same care as petrol.
Note: Read through this procedure before starting work to see what is involved, particularly in terms of lifting equipment. Depending on the facilities available, the home mechanic may prefer to remove the engine and transmission together, then separate them on the bench, as described in Chapter 2F. The help of an assistant is highly recommended if the transmission is to be removed (and later refitted) on its own.

Removal

1 Remove the plastic cover from the top of the engine (where fitted).

2 Remove the air cleaner and intake duct as described in Chapter 4.

3 Remove the battery and starter motor as described in Chapter 5.

4 Remove the engine management PCM as described in Chapter 4.

5 Undo the 3 bolts and remove the battery tray **(see illustration)**.

6 On diesel models slacken the clamp and remove the intercooler outlet pipe.

7 Remove both headlights as described Chapter 12 and then secure the radiator to the bonnet slam panel with cable-ties.

8 Remove the radiator undershield, then undo the bolts and remove the radiator support bracket **(see illustration)**.

9 On 1.8 and 2.0 litre models, undo the bolts and remove the crashbox from the front subframe (where fitted).

10 Undo the 2 upper transmission-to-engine retaining bolts, and on diesel models remove the intercooler intake pipe.

11 Disconnect the reversing light wiring plug, and transmission earth cable(s), then unclip the wiring harness **(see illustrations)**.

12 Disconnect the gearchange cables from the transmission as described in Section 3.

13 Make sure that the gear lever is in neutral. Taking adequate precautions against brake fluid spillage (refer to the *Warning* at the start of this Section), pull out the securing clip, then pull the pipe fitting out of the clutch slave cylinder at the top of the transmission **(see illustration)**. Plug or tape over the pipe end, to avoid losing fluid, and to prevent dirt entry.

14 Unclip the slave cylinder fluid pipe from the support bracket, and move it clear of the transmission.

15 Remove both driveshafts from the transmission as described in Chapter 8, and on diesel models disconnect the wiring to the glow plug relay.

16 Unscrew and remove the two nuts/bolts, and separate the exhaust front pipe at the first flange joint under the car. Unhook the exhaust pipe from the rubber mountings. Support the flexible section with splints.

17 On diesel models remove the catalytic converter as described in Chapter 4 and then undo and remove the support bracket **(see illustration)**.

18 Where fitted, undo the bolts and remove

7.5 Undo the 3 bolts and remove the battery tray

7.8 Undo the bolts and remove the radiator support bracket

7.11a Disconnect the reversing light wiring plug earth cable . . .

7.11b . . . and the transmission earth cable

7.13 Pull out the securing clip

7.17 Remove the catalytic convertor support bracket (arrowed)

the floor brace from beneath the front section of the exhaust system.

19 Unscrew the two through-bolts and remove the engine/transmission rear mounting from the subframe and (where fitted) remove the cover from the clutch housing.

20 The engine/transmission must now be supported, as the left-hand mounting must be dismantled and removed. Ford technicians use a support bar which locates in the tops of the inner wings – proprietary engine support bars are available from tool outlets.

21 If a support bar is not available, an engine hoist can be used. With an engine hoist, the engine/transmission can be manoeuvred more easily and safely. In the workshop, we found the best solution was to move the engine to the required position, and support it from below. Using the hoist on the transmission then gave excellent manoeuvrability, and total control for lowering out.

22 Supporting both the engine and transmission from below should be considered a last resort, and should only be done if a heavy-duty hydraulic ('trolley') jack is used, with a large, flat piece of wood on the jack head to spread the load and avoid damage to the sump. A further jack will be needed to lower the transmission out. **Note:** *Always take care when using a hydraulic jack, as it is possible for this type to collapse under load – generally, a scissor-type jack avoids this problem, but is also less stable, and offers no manoeuvrability.*

23 With the engine securely supported, progressively unscrew and remove the left-hand mounting central bolt **(see illustration)**.

24 Remove three further nuts/bolts, and remove the lower section of the engine left-hand mounting.

25 Taking care that nothing which is still attached to the engine is placed under strain, lower the transmission as far as possible.

26 Remove the lower transmission-to-engine bolts, noting that, on some models, one of the bolts also retains the power steering pipe support bracket. The flange bolts are of different lengths, so note their positions carefully for refitting.

27 On 1.6 litre engines, swing the transmission forwards, and wedge it in position with a stout piece of wood, about 300 mm long, between the engine and the subframe.

28 Check that, apart from the remaining flange bolts, there is nothing preventing the transmission from being lowered and removed. Make sure that any wiring or hoses lying on top of the transmission are not going to get caught up and stretched as the transmission is lowered.

29 Unscrew the remaining flange bolts. If the transmission does not separate on its own, it must be rocked from side-to-side, to free it from the locating dowels. As the transmission is withdrawn from the engine, make sure its weight is supported at all times – the transmission input shaft (or the clutch) may otherwise be damaged as it

is withdrawn through the clutch assembly bolted to the engine flywheel. Recover the adapter plates fitted between the engine and transmission, as they may fall out when the two are separated.

30 Keeping the transmission steady, carefully lower it down and remove it from under the car. On 1.8 litre engine models, the transmission will have to be moved forwards to clear the subframe as it is lowered – if the transmission is being supported from below, take care that it is kept steady.

31 The clutch components can now be inspected with reference to Chapter 6, and renewed if necessary. Unless they are virtually new, it is worth renewing the clutch components as a matter of course, even if the transmission has been removed for some other reason.

Refitting

32 If removed, refit the clutch components (see Chapter 6). Also ensure that the engine-to-transmission adapter plates (where fitted) are in position on the engine.

33 Lightly lubricate the splines of the transmission input shaft with engine oil, or ideally a lubricant formulated for such an application (Ford SA-M1C9107-A is ideal). Take care not to apply too much or the clutch plates may become contaminated. Do not use multipurpose grease or anti-seize compound.

34 Where a block of wood was used to wedge the engine forwards for transmission removal, make sure that it is in place for refitting.

35 With the transmission secured to the hoist/trolley jack as on removal, raise it into position, and then carefully slide it onto the engine, at the same time engaging the input shaft with the clutch driven plate splines. If marks were made between the transmission and engine on removal, these can be used as a guide to correct alignment.

36 Do not use excessive force to refit the transmission – if the input shaft does not slide into place easily, readjust the angle of the transmission so that it is level, and/or turn the input shaft so that the splines engage properly with the plate. If problems are still experienced, check that the clutch driven plate is correctly centred (see Chapter 6).

37 Once the transmission is successfully mated to the engine, insert as many of the flange bolts as possible, and tighten them progressively to draw the transmission fully onto the locating dowels.

38 Refit the lower section of the engine left-hand mounting, and tighten the nuts to the specified torque. On the iB5 transmission, refit the mounting pipe support bracket, and tighten the mounting bolts.

39 Where applicable, remove the wedge fitted between the engine and subframe. Raise the transmission into position, then refit the upper section of the engine left-hand mounting. Tighten the nuts/bolt to the specified torque, noting that the centre one

7.23 Unscrew and remove the left-hand mounting central bolt (arrowed)

is tightened considerably more than the four outer ones.

40 Refit the remaining transmission-to-engine bolts, and tighten all of them to the specified torque.

41 Refit the engine/transmission rear mounting to the subframe, and tighten the through-bolts to the specified torque.

42 Once the engine/transmission mountings have been refitted, the support bar, engine hoist or supporting jack can be removed.

43 Further refitting is a reversal of removal, noting the following points:

a) *Refit the starter motor as described in Chapter 5.*

b) *Refit the driveshafts as described in Chapter 8.*

c) *On completion, adjust the gearchange cables as described in Section 2.*

8 Transmission overhaul – general information

The overhaul of a manual transmission is a complex (and often expensive) engineering task for the DIY home mechanic to undertake, which requires access to specialist equipment. It involves dismantling and reassembly of many small components, measuring clearances precisely and if necessary, adjusting them by the selection shims and spacers. Internal transmission components are also often difficult to obtain and in many instances, extremely expensive. Because of this, if the transmission develops a fault or becomes noisy, the best course of action is to have the unit overhauled by a specialist repairer or to obtain an exchange reconditioned unit.

Nevertheless, it is not impossible for the more experienced mechanic to overhaul the transmission if the special tools are available and the job is carried out in a deliberate step-by-step manner, to ensure that nothing is overlooked.

The tools necessary for an overhaul include internal and external circlip pliers, bearing pullers, a slide hammer, a set of pin punches, a dial test indicator, and possibly a hydraulic press. In addition, a large, sturdy workbench and a vice will be required.

During dismantling of the transmission, make careful notes of how each component is fitted to make reassembly easier and accurate.

Before dismantling the transmission, it will help if you have some idea of where the problem lies. Certain problems can be closely related to specific areas in the transmission which can make component examination and renewal easier. Refer to *Fault finding* at the end of this manual for more information.

Chapter 7 Part B:
Automatic transmission

Contents

	Section number		Section number
Automatic transmission – removal and refitting	9	General information	1
Automatic transmission overhaul – general information	10	Oil seals – renewal	6
Fault finding – general	2	Selector cable – removal, refitting and adjustment	3
Fluid cooler – removal and refitting	8	Selector components – removal and refitting	4
Fluid pan – removal and refitting	7	Transmission sensors – removal and refitting	5

Degrees of difficulty

Easy, suitable for novice with little experience	**Fairly easy,** suitable for beginner with some experience	**Fairly difficult,** suitable for competent DIY mechanic	**Difficult,** suitable for experienced DIY mechanic	**Very difficult,** suitable for expert DIY or professional

Specifications

General

Transmission type	Electronically-controlled automatic, four forward speeds (one overdrive) and reverse. Selectable overdrive function, torque converter lock-up in 3rd and 4th gears
Transmission code	4F27E

Gear ratios

1st	2.816:1
2nd	1.498:1
3rd	1.000:1
4th	0.726:1
Reverse	2.649:1

Torque wrench settings

	Nm	lbf ft
Engine mountings:		
Right-hand mounting retaining bolts	90	66
Right-hand mounting bracket-to-engine bolts	56	41
Left-hand mounting nuts	48	35
Left-hand mounting bracket to transmission	80	59
Left-hand mounting centre bolt	148	109
Lower-rear torque rod bolts	80	59
Fluid cooler union nuts	25	18
Fluid pan bolts	7	5
Torque converter to driveplate (use new nuts)	37	27
Transmission lever bolt	10	7
Transmission range sensor bolts	10	7
Transmission to engine	48	35

1 General information

Available on 2.0 litre petrol models, the 4F27E automatic transmission is controlled electronically by the engine management electronic control module. This is a four-speed unit, featuring an overdrive top gear and a lock-up torque converter. This unit, which was developed by Mazda and is built in the USA, has been designed specifically for front-wheel-drive applications, and is particularly light and compact.

The transmission control module (TCM) is located on the engine bulkhead on the left-hand side of the engine compartment. The electronic control system has a fail-safe mode, which gives the transmission limited operation in order to drive the vehicle home or to a repair garage. A warning light on the instrument panel tells the driver when this occurs. The module uses all the information available from the various transmission and engine management-related sensors (also see Chapters 4 and 5) to determine the optimum gearshift points for smoothness, performance and economy. Depending on throttle position and vehicle speed, the module can 'lock-up' the torque converter in 3rd and 4th gear, eliminating torque converter 'slip' and improving fuel consumption.

1.8 Press down to release the locking lever

The transmission features a selectable overdrive top gear. When this is enabled (using a pushbutton on the underside of the selector lever), a fourth, extra-high ratio can be selected automatically; otherwise, the transmission will only use three forward speeds. An O/D OFF warning light is illuminated when the overdrive function is disabled.

The unit has been designed to have a low maintenance requirement, the fluid level being checked periodically (see Chapter 1). The fluid is intended to last the life of the transmission, and is cooled by a separate cooler located next to the radiator.

There is no kickdown switch, as kickdown is controlled by the throttle position sensor in the engine management system.

The gear selector includes the normal P, R, N, D, 2, and 1 positions.

As is normally the case with automatic transmissions, a starter inhibitor relay is fitted, which prevents the engine from being started (by interrupting the supply to the starter solenoid) when the selector is in any position other than P or N. The intention is to prevent the car moving, which might otherwise happen if the engine were started in position D, for example. The inhibitor system is controlled by the module, based on signals received from the engine and transmission sensors. For more details on relay locations, see Chapter 12.

As a further safety measure, the ignition key can only be removed from the ignition switch when the selector is in P; it is also necessary for the ignition to be on, and for the brake pedal and selector lever locking button (on the side of the lever) to be depressed in order to move the selector from position P. If the vehicle battery is discharged, the selector lever release solenoid will not function. If it is required to move the vehicle in this state, prise up the flap, and insert a pen or a similar small instrument into the aperture on the right-hand side of the centre console **(see illustration)**. Push the locking lever downwards and move the selector lever to the required position.

2 Fault finding – general

In the event of a fault occurring on the transmission, first check that the fluid level is correct (see Chapter 1). If there has been a loss of fluid, check the oil seals as described in Section 6. Also check the hoses to the fluid cooler in the radiator for leaks. The only other tasks possible for the home mechanic are the renewal of the various transmission sensors (Section 5); however, it is not advisable to go ahead and renew any sensor until the fault has been positively identified by reading the transmission fault codes.

Any serious fault which occurs will result in the transmission entering the fail-safe mode, and a fault code (or several codes) will be logged in the control module. The transmission can generate over 90 different fault codes and these codes can be read using an electronic fault code reader. A Ford dealer will obviously have such a reader, but they are also available from other suppliers. It is unlikely to be cost-effective for the private owner to purchase a fault code reader, but a well-equipped local garage or auto-electrical specialist will have one.

If the fault still persists, it is necessary to determine whether it is of an electrical, mechanical or hydraulic nature; to do this, special test equipment is required. It is therefore essential to have the work carried out by an automatic transmission specialist or Ford dealer if a transmission fault is suspected.

Do not remove the transmission from the vehicle for possible repair before professional fault diagnosis has been carried out, since most tests require the transmission to be in the vehicle.

3 Selector cable – removal, refitting and adjustment

Removal

1 Loosen the left-hand front wheel nuts. Apply the handbrake, jack up the front of the vehicle and support it on axle stands. Remove the left-hand front wheel. Where applicable, remove the engine undershield.
2 Remove the 'flat nut' fasteners, and slide the exhaust heat shield rearwards.
3 Locate the end of the selector cable, which is on the front of the transmission.
4 Disconnect the cable end fitting by prising it off the transmission selector lever **(see illustration)**.
5 Lift the locking tab, slide up the locking catch, then squeeze together the sides of the clip and slide the cable outer from the bracket on the transmission **(see illustrations)**.
6 Trace the cable back from the selector lever, releasing it from the various clips attaching it to the transmission and underside of the car.
7 Remove the centre console as described in Chapter 11.
8 Unscrew the bolts securing the left-hand side brackets fitted between the centre section of the facia panel and the floor, and remove the brackets. Release the wiring harness from any clips.
9 Move the selector lever to P. Working through the front of the selector housing, disconnect the cable inner from the lever by

3.4 Prise the cable end fitting from the lever on the transmission

3.5a Prise out the locking catch (arrowed) . . .

3.5b . . . squeeze together the clips (arrowed) . . .

3.5c . . . and slide the cable from the bracket

prising the end fitting sideways, then pull the collar forwards, and lift the cable outer from the bracket (see illustrations).

10 Fold back the carpet and insulation material under the centre part of the facia, for access to the selector cable floor grommet. Remove the two nuts and release the grommet from the floor.

11 Pass the cable down through the vehicle floor, and remove it from under the car.

Refitting

12 Refitting is a reversal of removal, noting the following points:

a) Once the cable has been reconnected to the selector lever, shift the lever to position D before reconnecting the cable end fitting at the transmission lever.

b) Before securing the cable to the transmission bracket or transmission lever, check the cable adjustment as described below.

Adjustment

13 Inside the vehicle, move the selector lever to position D.

14 With the inner cable disconnected from the lever on the transmission, check that the transmission lever is in the D position. To do this, it will be necessary to move the lever slightly up and down until it is positioned correctly. A further check can be made by observing that the D mark on the selector lever position sensor is correctly aligned with the mark on the transmission lever (see illustration).

15 Unclip the cable locking catch at the transmission end (see illustration).

16 With both the selector levers inside the vehicle and on the side of the transmission in position D, refit the cable end fitting to the transmission lever, then press the catch on the cable into place to lock it.

17 Refit the left-hand front wheel, then lower the vehicle to the ground. Tighten the wheel nuts to the specified torque.

18 Road test the vehicle to check the operation of the transmission.

4 Selector components – removal and refitting

Selector assembly

Removal

1 Remove the centre console as described in Chapter 11.

2 Remove the trim panel and support bracket (where fitted). Disconnect the cable inner from the lever as described in Section 3.

3 Disconnect the multiplug wiring connector at the rear of the assembly and move the wiring harness clear.

4 Unscrew the four mounting nuts, and withdraw the selector lever assembly.

5 If required, the assembly can be further

3.9a Prise the end fitting (arrowed) from the lever

3.14 Selector lever position sensor/ transmission lever alignment markings

dismantled (after removing the selector lever knob, as described below) by unclipping the top cover and removing the illumination bulb and inner cover.

Refitting

6 Refitting is a reversal of the removal procedure, but adjust the selector cable as described in Section 3.

Selector lever knob

Removal

7 Remove the centre console as described in Chapter 11.

8 Disconnect the multiplug connector for the overdrive switch (where fitted), at the base of the selector lever.

9 Remove the grub screw at the rear of the knob, below the overdrive button, then pull the knob upwards off the lever.

Refitting

10 Refitting is a reversal of removal.

5 Transmission sensors – removal and refitting

Transmission range sensor

1 The transmission range sensor is effectively a selector position sensor, the signal from which is used by the engine management module to modify the operation of the transmission, dependent on which 'gear' is selected. For example, besides controlling gearshift points, depending on the signal received, the module

3.9b Pull the outer cable collar (arrowed) forwards

3.15 Prise up the cable locking catch

may actuate the starter inhibitor relay, the reversing lights, or the ignition key lock. **Note:** *To set the range sensor in its working position, Ford special tool 307-415 is required. If this tool is not available, the sensor position must be carefully marked before removal.*

2 Access to the range sensor is easiest from below – the sensor is at the front of the transmission, near the transmission selector lever (see illustration). Apply the handbrake, then jack up the front of the car and support it on axle stands (see *Jacking and vehicle support*). Remove the engine undershield (where fitted).

3 Prise the selector cable end fitting off the transmission lever, and disconnect the wiring plug from the sensor.

4 Hold the transmission lever against rotation, then unscrew the lever retaining bolt, and remove the lever from the sensor.

5.2 Transmission range sensor location

5.13 Turbine (output) shaft speed sensor location

5.22 Output shaft speed sensor location

Caution: If the lever is not held as its bolt is undone, the force required to loosen the bolt will be transmitted to the sensor itself, which may well lead to the sensor being damaged. The same applies when retightening the bolt on completion.

5 Before removing the sensor make alignment marks between the sensor and the transmission, for use when refitting.

6 Take precautions against the possible spillage of transmission fluid. Unscrew the two sensor retaining bolts, and withdraw the sensor from the transmission.

7 Clean the sensor location in the transmission, and the sensor itself. If a new sensor is being fitted, transfer the alignment marks from the old unit to the new one – this will provide an approximate setting, which should allow the car to be driven.

8 Refit the sensor, and secure it loosely in position with the two bolts, tightened by hand only at this stage.

9 Ford special tool 307-415 must now be used to set the sensor in its working position. If the tool is not available, realign the marks made prior to removal. When correctly aligned, tighten the two sensor retaining bolts to the specified torque.

10 Refit the transmission lever. Tighten the lever retaining bolt to the specified torque, holding the lever against rotation as the bolt is tightened (refer to the *Caution* earlier in this Section).

11 Reconnect the selector cable to the transmission lever, and check the cable adjustment as described in Section 3.

12 On completion, lower the car to the ground.

Turbine (input) shaft speed sensor

13 The turbine shaft speed sensor is located on top of the transmission, and is an inductive pick-up sensor which senses the speed of rotation of the input shaft **(see illustration)**.

This information is used by the TCM to control gearchanging and the torque converter lock-up clutch. Removal and refitting details are similar to the output shaft speed sensor described later in this Section.

Brake pedal position switch

14 The signal from the switch is used by the TCM to disengage the torque converter lock-up, and to allow the selector lever to be moved from the P position when starting the engine. Removal and refitting details for the switch is the same as for the stop-light switch in Chapter 9.

Brake pedal shift interlock actuator

15 This unit part of the system used to lock the selector lever in P when the ignition key is removed, and is incorporated in the selector lever itself.

16 Remove the selector knob as described in Section 4. With the knob removed, push down the clip and remove the manual selector cover and then remove the selector lock upper and lower plungers complete with their springs.

17 If required remove the selector indicator cover and the cover plate by releasing the securing tabs.

18 Refitting is a reversal of removal. Check the operation of the system on completion.

Selector lever shift interlock solenoid

19 The main solenoid controlling the shift interlock system (used to lock the selector lever in P when the ignition key is removed) is located at the base of the selector lever. For access to the solenoid, remove the centre console as described in Chapter 11. At the time of writing, no further removal details were available from Ford.

Transmission fluid temperature sensor

20 The fluid temperature sensor signal is used

by the TCM to determine whether to allow the operation the torque converter lock-up clutch, and the selection of the overdrive 4th gear. The sensor is located among the transmission solenoid valves inside the fluid pan – no renewal procedure is suggested by Ford, so any suspected problems should be referred to a Ford dealer.

Output shaft speed sensor

21 Access to the speed sensor is easiest from below. Apply the handbrake, then loosen the left-hand front wheel nuts. Jack up the front of the car and support it on axle stands (see *Jacking and vehicle support*). Remove the engine undershield (where fitted).

22 Remove the left-hand front wheel and the wheel arch liner – the sensor is located at the rear of the transmission, behind the driveshafts **(see illustration)**.

23 Disconnect the wiring plug from the sensor, then position a suitable container below the sensor to catch any transmission fluid which may be spilt as the sensor is removed.

24 Unscrew the sensor securing bolt, and slowly withdraw the sensor from its location.

25 Check the condition of the O-ring seal fitted to the sensor body – fit a new seal if the old one is in poor condition.

26 Refitting is a reversal of the removal procedure, but clean the sensor location and lightly oil the O-ring before inserting the assembly in the transmission casing. Check the transmission fluid level as described in Chapter 1 on completion.

Transmission control module

27 Disconnect the battery negative lead as described in Chapter 5.

28 Remove the battery as described in Chapter 5, then undo the 3 bolts and slide the battery tray forward a little.

29 Remove the windscreen cowl extension panel and the lower panel as described in Chapter 12.

30 Release the retaining clips and pull the TCM from the bulkhead bracket **(see illustration)**

31 Pivot down the locking catch, and disconnect the wiring plug and remove the TCM **(see illustration)**.

32 Refitting is a reversal of removal. Note that if a new TCM is fitted, it must be programmed to the vehicle using Ford diagnostic equipment (IDS). Entrust this task to a Ford dealer or suitably-equipped specialist.

5.30 Release the clips (arrowed)

5.31 Pivot down the locking catch and disconnect the wiring plug

6 Oil seals – renewal

Driveshaft oil seals

The procedure is the same as that for the manual transmission (refer to Chapter 7A).

Output shaft speed sensor seal

The procedure is covered in Section 5.

7 Fluid pan – removal and refitting

Note: *This procedure is provided principally to cure any leak developing from the fluid pan joint. It is not advisable for the DIY mechanic to remove the fluid pan for any other reason, since it gives access to internal transmission components, servicing of which is considered beyond the scope of this Manual.*

Removal

1 Apply the handbrake, then jack up the front of the car and support it on axle stands (see *Jacking and vehicle support*). Remove the engine undershield (where fitted)

2 Place a suitable container below the pan, as most of the contents of the transmission will drain when the pan is removed.

3 Progressively unscrew and remove the fluid pan bolts.

4 The fluid pan is 'stuck' to the base of the transmission by a bead of sealant, so it is unlikely that the pan will fall off once the bolts are removed. Care must now be taken to break the sealant without damaging the mating surfaces. Do not prise the pan down, as this may bend it, or damage the sealing surfaces. The most successful method found is to run a sharp knife around the joint – this should cut through sufficiently to make removal possible without excess effort.

Refitting

5 With the fluid pan removed, clean off all traces of sealant from the pan and the mating face on the transmission. Again, take care not to mark either mating surface.

6 Apply a 1.5 mm thick bead of suitable sealant (Ford recommend Loctite 5699, or equivalent) to the fluid pan mating face, running the bead on the inside of the bolt holes. Do not apply excess sealant, or a bead much thicker than suggested, since the excess could end up inside the pan, and contaminate the internal components.

7 Offer the pan up into position, and insert a few of the bolts to locate it. Refit all the remaining bolts, and tighten them progressively to the specified torque.

8 Give the sealant time to cure, then trim off any excess with a knife. Refill the transmission via the dipstick tube, with reference to Chapter 1.

9 On completion, take the car for a run of several miles to get the fluid up to operating temperature, then recheck the fluid level, and check for signs of leakage.

8 Fluid cooler – removal and refitting

Removal

1 This procedure should only be attempted when the engine and transmission are completely cool; otherwise there is a great risk of scalding. The fluid cooler is mounted in front of the radiator **(see illustration)**.

2 Apply the handbrake, then jack up the front of the car and support it on axle stands (see *Jacking and vehicle support*).

3 Remove the engine undershield (where fitted).

4 Remove the three screws securing the radiator lower splash shield, and remove the shield from under the car.

5 Undo the fasteners and remove the air deflector panels under the right- and left-hand sides of the radiator.

6 Place a container below the fluid cooler connections to catch the escaping fluid; also note that, if the engine is still warm, the fluid may be extremely hot. Note the positions of the hose connections for refitting, then push the quick-release connector towards the cooler, press together the retaining tabs and pull the hose from the cooler. Tie the hoses up out of the way, and plug the hose ends to prevent the ingress of dirt.

7 Pull the retaining clip forwards and lift each side of the cooler upwards from the brackets. Manoeuvre the cooler from place.

H48216

8.1 Fluid cooler details

1 Fluid cooler	2 Supply hose	3 Return hose

Refitting

8 Clean the fluid cooler fins of any debris as necessary, using a small brush – do not use any other tools, as the fins can easily be damaged.

9 Refitting is a reversal of removal, noting the following points:

 a) *Top-up the transmission fluid level using the information in Chapter 1.*

 b) *Start the engine and check for signs of fluid leakage from the disturbed connections.*

9 Automatic transmission – removal and refitting

Removal

1 Remove the plastic cover from the top of the engine (where fitted).

2 Remove the air cleaner and intake duct as described in Chapter 4.

3 Remove the battery and starter motor as described in Chapter 5. Note that one of the mounting bolts also secures the transmission earth strap.

4 Remove the engine management PCM as described in Chapter 4.

5 Undo the 3 bolts and remove the battery tray.

6 Remove both front headlights as described in Chapter 12.

7 Before jacking up the front of the car, loosen the front wheel nuts, and if possible, the driveshaft retaining bolts.

8 Apply the handbrake, and chock the rear wheels. Jack up the front of the car, and support it on axle stands (see *Jacking and vehicle support*). There must be sufficient clearance below the car for the transmission to be lowered and withdrawn. Remove the front wheels and the engine undershield.

9 Undo the fasteners and remove the splash shield beneath the radiator.

10 Remove the wiring harness and electrical connector from the fluid level indicator tube.

11 Disconnect the selector cable end fitting from the transmission lever as described in Section 3.

12 Disconnect the wiring plugs from the

vehicle/output shaft speed sensor, turbine shaft speed sensor and transmission range sensor, as described in Section 5.

13 Unbolt and remove the floor panel brace and then remove the front section of the exhaust pipe, referring to Chapter 4 as necessary. Note particularly that the flexible section of the exhaust must not be bent too far during removal.

14 Remove both driveshafts from the transmission as described in Chapter 8.

15 Slacken the left-hand radiator lower support bracket front bolt 3 turns, then remove the rear bolt.

16 Wipe clean around the fluid supply and return pipes on the front of the transmission. It is essential that no dirt is introduced into the transmission. Undo the bolts and remove the crashbox (where fitted) from the front subframe.

17 Noting their respective positions, disconnect the fluid pipes from the transmission. The connectors are released by pushing the connector towards the transmission, squeezing together the retaining tags, and pulling the connector away **(see illustrations)**. Be prepared for loss of fluid, and cover the pipe ends and transmission pipe fittings to prevent further loss or dirt entry.

18 Working from below, unscrew the through-bolts and remove the engine/transmission rear mounting **(see illustration)**.

19 The engine/transmission must now be supported, as the left-hand mounting must be dismantled and removed. Ford technicians use a support bar which locates in the tops of the inner wings – proprietary engine support bars are available from tool outlets.

20 If a support bar is not available, an engine hoist should be used. Supporting the engine from below should be considered a last resort, and should only be done if a heavy-duty hydraulic ('trolley') jack is used, with a large, flat piece of wood on the jack head to spread the load and avoid damage to the sump. Note that a further jack will be needed to lower the transmission out.

21 With the engine securely supported, progressively unscrew the centre bolt, and remove the nuts securing the top section of the engine/transmission left-hand mounting, and lift it off.

22 Remove three further nuts/bolts, and remove the lower section of the engine left-hand mounting.

23 Locate the transmission fluid filler tube, and remove the screw at its base where it enters the transmission. Pull the tube out of its location, and remove it.

24 Remove the cover (where fitted) from the base of the transmission bellhousing, for access to the four large torque converter nuts. It will be necessary to turn the engine (using a spanner or socket on the crankshaft pulley bolt) in order to bring each of the nuts into view. It may also prove necessary to jam the driveplate ring gear with a suitable tool to prevent the engine turning as the nuts are unscrewed. Before removing the last nut, paint an alignment mark between the converter and driveplate to use when refitting. New nuts must be obtained for refitting.

25 Swing the transmission forwards, and wedge it in position with a stout piece of wood, about 300 mm long, between the engine and the subframe.

26 Support the transmission from below, ideally using a trolley jack (if one is not available, a sturdy jack with a large, flat piece of wood on top of the jack head will suffice).

27 Have an assistant ready to help steady the transmission as the flange bolts are removed – attempting to remove the transmission single-handed is not recommended, as it is a heavy assembly which can be awkward to handle.

28 Check that, apart from the remaining flange bolts, there is nothing preventing the transmission from being lowered and removed. Make sure that any wiring or hoses lying on top of the transmission are not going to get caught up and stretched as the transmission is lowered.

29 Unscrew and remove the flange bolts – there are three inserted from the transmission side, and six from the engine side **(see illustration)**. Note the bolt locations carefully, as they are of different lengths.

30 If the transmission does not separate on its own, it must be rocked from side-to-side, to free it from the locating dowels. As the transmission is withdrawn from the engine, make sure its weight is supported at all times – care must be taken that the torque converter

9.17a Fluid pipe at the left-hand end . . .

9.17b . . . and right-hand front face of the transmission

9.18 Remove the through-bolts (arrowed)

9.29 Engine-to-transmission bolts

1 *Three bolts inserted from the transmission side*

2 *Six bolts inserted from the engine side*

9.32 Check the torque converter is fully entered into the transmission

1 *Straight-edge*
2 *Depth = 25 mm*
3 *Torque converter centre spigot*

(which is a large, heavy, circular component) does not fall out.

31 Keeping the transmission steady on the jack head, and maintaining a supporting hand on the torque converter, carefully lower it and remove it from under the car.

32 Once the transmission has been fully lowered and steadied, bolt a strip of wood or metal across the bellhousing face, with suitable packing, to secure the torque converter firmly in position. The converter centre spigot should be 25 mm below the bellhousing face – this can be determined by placing a straight-edge across the bellhousing, and measuring between it and the centre of the converter **(see illustration)**.

Refitting

33 Prior to refitting, clean the contact surfaces of the driveplate and torque converter.

34 Check that the torque converter is fully entered in the transmission, as described in paragraph 32.

Caution: This procedure is important, to ensure that the torque converter is engaged with the fluid pump. If it is not fully engaged, serious damage will occur.

35 As for removal, use a block of wood to wedge the engine forwards for refitting.

36 With the help of an assistant, raise the transmission, and locate it on the rear of the driveplate. The torque converter must remain in full engagement during the fitting procedure. Use the markings made prior to removal to help align the transmission.

37 Refit the transmission-to-engine flange bolts to the locations noted on removal, and tighten them progressively to draw the transmission fully onto the locating dowels.

38 Align the mark made on removal between the torque converter and driveplate. Refit and tighten the torque converter-to-driveplate nuts to the specified torque – new nuts must be used. Turn the engine as necessary to bring each nut into view, and lock the ring gear to prevent it turning as the nuts are tightened.

39 Refit the lower section of the engine left-hand mounting, and tighten the nuts to the specified torque.

40 Remove the wedge fitted between the engine and subframe. Raise the transmission into position, then refit the upper section of the engine left-hand mounting. Tighten the nuts/bolt to the specified torque, noting that the centre one is tightened considerably more than the four outer ones.

41 Working from below, refit the through-bolts to the engine/transmission rear mounting, and tighten them to the specified torque.

42 Once the engine/transmission mountings have been refitted, the support bar, engine hoist or supporting jack can be removed.

43 Further refitting is a reversal of removal, noting the following points:

a) *Refit the starter motor as described in Chapter 5.*

b) *Refit the driveshafts as described in Chapter 8.*

c) *Tighten all fasteners to the specified torque (where given).*

d) *On completion, adjust the selector cable as described in Section 3, and top-up the fluid level as described in Chapter 1.*

e) *Recheck the transmission fluid level once the car has been driven.*

f) *Note that, since the battery has been disconnected, the TCM will take time to 'relearn' various settings which will have an adverse effect on how the transmission performs. After the car has completed a few miles of varied driving, however, the TCM's adaptive values should have been re-established.*

10 Automatic transmission overhaul – general information

Overhaul of the automatic transmission should be left to an automatic transmission specialist or a Ford dealer. Refer to the information given in Section 2 before removing the unit.

Note that, if the vehicle is still within the warranty period, in the event of a fault it is important to take it to a Ford dealer who will carry out a comprehensive diagnosis procedure using specialist equipment. Failure to do this will invalidate the warranty.

Chapter 8
Driveshafts

Contents

Section number

Driveshaft overhaul – general information 6
Driveshafts – removal and refitting. 2
General information 1

Section number

Inner constant velocity joint gaiter – renewal 4
Outer constant velocity joint gaiter – renewal 3
Right-hand driveshaft support bearing – removal and refitting 5

Degrees of difficulty

Easy, suitable for novice with little experience	**Fairly easy,** suitable for beginner with some experience	**Fairly difficult,** suitable for competent DIY mechanic	**Difficult,** suitable for experienced DIY mechanic	**Very difficult,** suitable for expert DIY or professional

Specifications

General

Driveshaft type . . . . Equal-length solid-steel shafts, splined to inner and outer constant velocity joints. Intermediate shaft incorporated in right-hand driveshaft assembly

Outer constant velocity joint type. . . . . Ball-and-cage

Inner constant velocity joint type . . . . Tripod

Lubrication

Lubricant type . . . . Special grease supplied in repair kit, or suitable molybdenum disulphide grease – consult a Ford dealer or parts specialist

CV joint grease capacity (approximate):	Outboard joint	Inboard joint
1.6 litre models	100 g	100 g
1.8 litre models	100 g	170 g
2.0 litre models:		
Petrol.	100 g	170 g
Diesel	140 g	170 g

Torque wrench settings

	Nm	lbf ft
Crashbox bolts.	40	30
Driveshaft bolt:*		
Stage 1	45	33
Stage 2	Angle-tighten a further 90°	
Headlight levelling sensor bracket to lower arm	8	6
Lower arm balljoint to hub carrier*	70	52
Right-hand driveshaft support bearing cap nuts*	25	18
Roadwheel nuts	130	96

* Do not re-use

---

1 General information

Drive is transmitted from the differential to the front wheels by means of two solid-steel, equal-length driveshafts equipped with constant velocity (CV) joints at their inner and outer ends. Due to the position of the transmission, an intermediate shaft and support bearing are incorporated into the right-hand driveshaft assembly.

A ball-and-cage type CV joint is fitted to the outer end of each driveshaft. The joint has an outer member, which is splined at its outer end to accept the wheel hub, and is threaded so that it can be fastened to the hub by a large bolt. The joint contains six balls within a cage, which engage with the inner member. The complete assembly is protected by a flexible gaiter secured to the driveshaft and joint outer member.

At the inner end, the driveshaft is splined to engage a tripod type CV joint, containing needle roller bearings and cups. On the left-hand side, the driveshaft inner CV joint engages directly with the differential sunwheel. On the right-hand side, the inner joint is integral with the intermediate shaft, the inner end of which engages with the differential sunwheel. As on the outer joints, a flexible gaiter secured to the driveshaft and CV joint outer member protects the complete assembly.

2.3a Slacken the driveshaft retaining bolt (arrowed)

2.3b On some models, prise out the centre cap and slacken the bolt

2.4 Undo the bolts (arrowed) and remove the engine undershield

2 Driveshafts –
removal and refitting

Removal

1 Firmly apply the handbrake and chock the rear wheels. When the driveshaft bolt is to be loosened (or tightened), it is preferable to do so with the car resting on its wheels. If the car is jacked up, this places a high load on the jack, and the car could slip off.

2 If the car has steel wheels, remove the wheel trim on the side being worked on – the driveshaft bolt can then be loosened with the wheel on the ground. On models with alloy wheels, the safest option is to remove the wheel on the side being worked on, and to fit the temporary spare (see *Wheel changing* at the front of this Manual. Note

that not all models have a spare wheel) this wheel allows access to the driveshaft bolt.

3 With an assistant firmly depressing the brake pedal, slacken the driveshaft retaining bolt using a socket and a long extension bar **(see illustrations)**. Note that this bolt is extremely tight – ensure that the tools used to loosen it are of good quality, and a good fit.

4 Loosen the front wheel nuts, then jack up the front of the car and support it on axle stands (see *Jacking and vehicle support*). Remove the appropriate front roadwheel, then undo the 7 Torx bolts and remove the engine undershield (where fitted) **(see illustration)**.

5 Remove the previously-slackened driveshaft retaining bolt. Discard the bolt – a new one must be fitted.

6 Tap the end of the driveshaft approximately 15 to 20 mm into the wheel hub.

7 Undo the bolt/nut and detach the headlight

levelling sensor bracket from the lower arm (where applicable).

8 Undo the bolts and remove the crashbox from the subframe (where fitted).

9 Slacken the lower control arm balljoint nut until the end of the balljoint shank is level with the top of the nut.

10 Detach the lower control arm balljoint from the hub carrier using a balljoint separator tool **(see illustration)**.

11 Push down on the suspension arm using a stout bar to release the balljoint shank from the hub carrier. Take care not to damage the balljoint dust cover during and after disconnection.

12 Swivel the suspension strut and hub carrier assembly outwards, and withdraw the driveshaft CV joint from the hub flange **(see illustration)**.

13 If removing the left-hand driveshaft, free the inner CV joint from the transmission by levering between the edge of the joint and the transmission casing with a large screwdriver or similar tool. Take care not to damage the transmission oil seal or the inner CV joint gaiter. Withdraw the driveshaft from under the wheel arch.

14 If removing the right-hand driveshaft, undo the two nuts and remove the cap from the intermediate shaft support bearing **(see illustration)**. Pull the intermediate shaft out of the transmission, and remove the driveshaft assembly from under the wheel arch. **Note:** *Do not pull the outer shaft from the intermediate shaft – the coupling will separate.*

Refitting

15 Refitting is a reversal of removal, but observe the following points.

  a) *Prior to refitting, remove all traces, rust, oil and dirt from the splines of the outer CV joint, and lubricate the splines of the inner joint with wheel bearing grease.*

  b) *Apply a little grease to the driveshaft seal lips in the transmission casing.*

  c) *If working on the left-hand driveshaft, ensure that the inner CV joint is pushed fully into the transmission, so that the retaining circlip locks into place in the differential gear.*

  d) *Always use a new driveshaft-to-hub retaining bolt* **(see illustration)**.

  e) *Fit the same wheel as was used for*

2.10 Use a balljoint separator tool to detach the balljoint from the hub carrier

2.12 Push the lower control arm downwards, pull the hub carrier outwards, and withdraw the driveshaft

2.14 Undo the 2 nuts (arrowed) and remove the intermediate bearing cap

2.15 Always renew the driveshaft retaining bolt

3.3 Cut the gaiter retaining clips

3.7 Pack the outer CV joint with about half the grease supplied

3.10a Locate the outer clip on the gaiter . . .

3.10b . . . then using a special pair of pliers . . .

3.10c . . . remove any slack in the clip

3.11 Lift the inner edge of the gaiter to equalise the air pressure

loosening the driveshaft bolt, and lower the car to the ground.

f) Tighten all nuts and bolts to the specified torque (see Chapters 9 and 10 for brake and suspension component torque settings). When tightening the driveshaft bolt, tighten first using a torque wrench, then further, through the specified angle, using an angle-tightening gauge.

g) Ford insist that when refitting the right-hand driveshaft the intermediate shaft bearing cap nuts must be renewed.

h) Where applicable, refit the alloy wheel on completion. Tighten the roadwheel nuts to the specified torque.

3 Outer constant velocity joint gaiter – renewal

1 Dismantle the inner constant velocity joint as described in Section 4.

Automatic models with a vibration damper fitted

2 On these vehicles, after removing the inner CV joint, measure and note the distance from the end of the shaft to the edge of the damper. The damper must then be pressed from the shaft, the outer joint boot renewed, then the damper pressed back into its original position using the dimensions previously-noted. If access to a hydraulic press in not available, most engineering workshops (automotive or otherwise) would be prepared to carry out this task for a modest fee.

All models

3 Cut off the gaiter retaining clips, then slide the gaiter down the shaft to expose the outer constant velocity joint (see illustration).
Caution: Do not disassemble the outer CV joint.

4 Scoop out as much grease as possible from the joint.

5 Inspect the ball tracks on the inner and outer members. If the tracks have widened, the balls will no longer be a tight fit. At the same time, check the ball cage windows for wear or cracking between the windows. If the joints appear worn, complete renewal may be the only option – check with a Ford dealer or specialist.

6 If the joint is in satisfactory condition, obtain a repair kit from your Ford dealer, consisting of a new gaiter, retaining clips, driveshaft bolt, circlip and grease.

7 Pack the joint with the half of the grease supplied, working it well into the ball tracks, and into the driveshaft opening in the inner member (see illustration).

8 Slide the rubber gaiter onto the shaft.

9 Apply the remaining grease to the joint and the inside of the gaiter.

10 Locate the outer lip of the gaiter in the groove on the joint outer member, then fit the retaining clip. Remove any slack in the clips by carefully compressing the raised section using a special pair of pincers (see illustrations).
Note: Ensure no grease is on the surfaces between the gaiter and the joint housing.

11 Use a small screwdriver to lift the inner lip of the gaiter, allowing the air pressure inside

the gaiter to equalise, then fit the inner clip to the gaiter (see illustration).

12 Where applicable, press the damper into its original position.

13 Reassembly the inner constant velocity joint as described in Section 4.

4 Inner constant velocity joint gaiter – renewal

1 Remove the driveshaft(s) as described in Section 2.

2 Cut through the metal clips, and slide the gaiter from the inner CV joint.

3 Clean out some of the grease from the joint, then make alignment marks between the housing and the shaft, to aid reassembly (see illustration).

4 Carefully pull the housing from the tripod,

4.3 Make alignment marks between the shaft and housing

4.6a Remove the circlip from the end of the shaft . . .

4.6b . . . then carefully drive the tripod from the shaft

4.7 Slide the new gaiter and smaller diameter clip onto the shaft

4.8a Fit the tripod with the bevelled edge (arrowed) towards the shaft . . .

4.8b . . . then fit the new circlip

twisting the housing so the tripod rollers come out one at a time. If necessary, use a soft-faced hammer or mallet to tap the housing off.

5 Clean the grease from the tripod and housing.

6 Remove the circlip, and carefully drive the tripod from the end of the shaft **(see illustrations)**. Discard the circlip, a new one (supplied in the repair kit) must be fitted. Remove the gaiter if still on the shaft.

7 Slide the new gaiter onto the shaft along with the smaller clip **(see illustration)**.

8 Refit the tripod with the bevelled edge towards the driveshaft, and drive it fully into place, until the new circlip can be installed **(see illustrations)**.

9 Lubricate the tripod rollers with some of the

grease supplied in the gaiter kit, then fill the housing and gaiter with the remainder.

10 Refit the housing to the tripod, tapping it gently into place using a soft-hammer or mallet if necessary.

11 Slide the new gaiter into place ensuring the smaller diameter of the gaiter locates over the grooves in the shaft **(see illustration)**.

12 Fit the new retaining clips **(see illustration)**.

13 Fit the new circlip to the end of the shaft **(see illustration)**.

5   Right-hand driveshaft support bearing – removal and refitting

Note: *At the time of writing, it would appear*

the support bearing was not available as a separate part. If the bearing is worn of damaged, the complete driveshaft must be renewed. Exchange driveshafts may be available – check with a Ford dealer or specialist.

6   Driveshaft overhaul – general information

Road test the car, and listen for a metallic clicking from the front as the car is driven slowly in a circle with the steering on full-lock. Repeat the check on full-left and full-right lock. This noise may also be apparent when pulling away from a standstill with lock applied. If a clicking noise is heard, this indicates wear in the outer constant velocity joints.

If vibration, consistent with roadspeed, is felt through the car when accelerating, there is a possibility of wear in the inner constant velocity joints.

If the joints are worn or damaged, it would appear at the time of writing that no parts are available, other then boot renewal kits, and the complete driveshaft must be renewed. Exchange driveshafts may be available – check with a Ford dealer or specialist.

4.11 The smaller diameter of the gaiter must locate over the groove in the shaft (arrowed)

4.12 Equalise the air pressure before tightening the gaiter clip

4.13 The circlip on the end of the shaft must be renewed

Chapter 9
Braking system

Contents

Section number

ABS hydraulic unit – removal and refitting 17
ABS wheel sensor – testing, removal and refitting. 18
Brake pedal – removal and refitting 12
Brake switches – removal, refitting and adjustment 21
Electric parking brake – removal, refitting and adjustment 24
Electronic stability control components – removal and refitting 19
Front brake caliper – removal, overhaul and refitting. 3
Front brake disc – inspection, removal and refitting 4
Front brake pads – renewal 2
General information 1
Handbrake cables – removal and refitting 23
Handbrake lever – removal and refitting. 22
Hydraulic pipes and hoses – inspection, removal and refitting 13
Hydraulic system – bleeding 14

Section number

Master cylinder – removal and refitting 11
Rear brake caliper – removal, overhaul and refitting 9
Rear brake disc – inspection, removal and refitting 10
Rear brake drum – removal, inspection and refitting 5
Rear brake pads – renewal. 8
Rear brake shoes – renewal 6
Rear wheel cylinder – removal, overhaul and refitting 7
Traction control system – general information 20
Vacuum pump – removal and refitting 25
Vacuum pump – testing and overhaul 26
Vacuum servo unit – testing, removal and refitting 15
Vacuum servo unit vacuum hose and non-return valve – removal,
   testing and refitting. 16

Degrees of difficulty

| **Easy,** suitable for novice with little experience | | **Fairly easy,** suitable for beginner with some experience | | **Fairly difficult,** suitable for competent DIY mechanic | | **Difficult,** suitable for experienced DIY mechanic | | **Very difficult,** suitable for expert DIY or professional | |

Specifications

Front brakes
Type	Ventilated disc, with single sliding piston caliper
Disc diameter:	
1.6 and 1.8 litre models	278 mm
2.0 litre models.	300 mm
Disc thickness:	
New	25.0 mm
Minimum.	23.0 mm
Maximum disc thickness variation.	0.020 mm
Maximum disc/hub run-out (installed)	0.050 mm
Caliper piston diameter	54.0 mm
Brake pad friction material minimum thickness.	1.5 mm

Rear drum brakes
Type	Leading and trailing shoes, with automatic adjusters
Drum diameter:	
New	228.3 mm
Maximum	230.2 mm
Shoe width	38.0 mm
Brake shoe friction material minimum thickness	1.0 mm

Rear disc brakes
Type	Solid disc, with single-piston floating caliper
Disc diameter:	
1.6 and 1.8 litre models	265 mm
2.0 litre models.	280 mm
Disc thickness:	
New	11.0 mm
Minimum.	9.0 mm
Maximum disc thickness variation.	0.020 mm
Maximum disc/hub run-out (installed)	0.050 mm
Brake pad friction material minimum thickness.	1.5 mm

Torque wrench settings

	Nm	lbf ft
ABS wheel sensor securing bolts	5	4
Brake pipe to hydraulic control unit	11	8
Brake pipe to master cylinder	17	13
Brake pipe unions	15	11
Front caliper guide bolts	28	21
Front caliper mounting bracket bolts	120	89
Handbrake lever mountings	35	26
Master cylinder to servo mountings	25	18
Pedal bracket to servo mountings	23	17
Rear caliper bracket	70	52
Rear caliper guide bolts	35	26
Rear wheel cylinder bolts	10	7
Roadwheel nuts	130	96
Vacuum pump:		
1.6 litre models	18	13
1.8 and 2.0 litre models	22	16
Yaw rate sensor bracket to body	5	4

1 General information

The braking system is of diagonally-split, dual-circuit design, with ventilated discs at the front, and drum or disc brakes (according to model) at the rear. The front calipers are of single sliding piston design, and (where fitted) the rear calipers are of a single-piston floating design, using asbestos-free pads. The rear drum brakes are of the leading and trailing shoe type, and are self-adjusting during footbrake operation. The rear brake shoe linings are of different thicknesses, in order to allow for the different proportional rates of wear.

On petrol models, the vacuum servo unit uses intake manifold depression to boost the effort applied by the driver at the brake pedal and transmits this increased effort to the master cylinder pistons. On diesel models, the servo action is supplemented by a vacuum pump.

The handbrake is cable-operated, and acts on the rear brakes. On rear drum brake models, the cables operate on the rear trailing brake shoe operating levers; on rear disc brake models, they operate on levers on the rear calipers. The handbrake lever incorporates an automatic adjuster, which will adjust the cable when the handbrake is operated several times. Some higher specification models are fitted with an electric parking brake (EPB). On these models a rear mounted electric motor operates the parking cables.

The anti-lock braking system (ABS) uses the basic conventional brake system, together with an ABS hydraulic unit fitted between the master cylinder and the four brake units at each wheel. The hydraulic unit consists of a hydraulic actuator, an ABS brake pressure pump, and an ABS module. Braking at each of the four wheels is controlled by separate solenoid valves in the hydraulic actuator. If wheel lock-up is detected by one of the wheel sensors, when the vehicle speed is above 3 mph, the valve opens; releasing pressure to the relevant brake until the wheel regains a rotational speed corresponding to the speed of the vehicle. The cycle can be repeated many times a second. In the event of a fault in the ABS system, the conventional braking system is not affected. Diagnosis of a fault in the ABS system requires the use of special equipment, and this work should therefore be left to a Ford dealer or suitably-equipped specialist. The wheel speed sensor signal rings are built-into the oil seals of the wheel bearings.

Where fitted, the traction control systems are integrated with the ABS, and use the same wheel sensors. The hydraulic control unit has additional solenoid valves incorporated to enable control of the wheel brake pressure. The system is only active at speeds up to 53 mph – when the system is active the warning light on the instrument panel illuminates to warn the driver. This uses controlled braking of the spinning driving wheel when the grip at the driven wheels are different. The spinning wheel is braked by the ABS system, transferring a greater proportion of the engine torque through the differential to the other wheel, which increases the use of the available traction control.

On several models in the range, there is an Electronic Stability Program (ESP) available. This system supports the vehicle's stability and steering through a combination of ABS and traction control operations. There is a switch on the centre console, so that if required the system can be switched off. This will then illuminate the warning light on the instrument panel, to inform the driver that the ESP is not in operation. The stability of the vehicle is measured by Yaw rate and Accelerometer sensors, which sense the movement of the vehicle about its vertical axis, and also lateral acceleration.

Note: *When servicing any part of the system, work carefully and methodically; also observe scrupulous cleanliness when overhauling any part of the hydraulic system. Always renew components (in axle sets, where applicable) if in doubt about their condition, and use only genuine Ford parts, or at least those of known good quality. Note the warnings given in 'Safety first!' and at relevant points in this Chapter concerning the dangers of asbestos dust and hydraulic fluid.*

2 Front brake pads – renewal

⚠ *Warning: Renew both sets of front brake pads at the same time – never renew the pads on only one wheel, as uneven braking may result. Note that the dust created by wear of the pads may contain asbestos, which is a health hazard. Never blow it out with compressed air, and don't inhale any of it. An approved filtering mask should be worn when working on the brakes. DO NOT use petrol or petroleum-based solvents to clean brake parts; use brake cleaner or methylated spirit only.*

1 Apply the handbrake, then slacken the front roadwheel nuts. Jack up the front of the vehicle and support it on axle stands. Remove both front roadwheels.

2 Follow the accompanying photos **(illustrations 2.2a to 2.2p)** for the actual pad renewal procedure. Be sure to stay in order and read the caption under each illustration, and note the following points:

a) *New pads may have an adhesive foil on the backplates. Remove this foil prior to installation.*

b) *Thoroughly clean the caliper guide surfaces, and apply a little brake assembly (polycarbamide) grease.*

c) *When pushing the caliper piston back to accommodate new pads, keep a close eye on the fluid level in the reservoir.*

Caution: Pushing back the piston causes a reverse-flow of brake fluid, which has been known to 'flip' the master cylinder rubber seals, resulting in a total loss of braking. To avoid this, clamp the caliper flexible hose and open the bleed screw – as the piston is pushed back, the fluid can be directed into a suitable container using a hose attached to the bleed screw. Close the screw just before the piston is pushed fully back, to ensure no air enters the system.

2.2a Use a flat-bladed screwdriver to carefully prise off the caliper retaining spring

2.2b Prise out the rubber caps . . .

2.2c . . . and use an Allen key to undo the caliper guide bolts (arrowed)

2.2d Slide the caliper and inner pad from the disc

2.2e Pull the inner brake pad from the caliper piston . . .

2.2f . . . and lift the outer pad from the caliper bracket

2.2g If you're fitting new pads, push the piston back into the caliper using a piston retraction tool or G-clamp

2.2h Clean the pad mounting surfaces with a wire brush

2.2i Measure the thickness of the pad's friction material. If it's 1.5 mm or less, renew all the front pads

2.2j Fit the outer pad to the caliper mounting bracket . . .

2.2k . . . then fit the inner pad to the caliper piston

2.2l Slide the caliper with the inner panel fitted over the disc and outer pad

2.2m Refit the caliper guide bolts and tighten them to the specified torque

2.2n Press the rubber caps into position

2.2o Use a pair of pliers . . .

2.2p . . . to refit the caliper retaining spring

3 Depress the brake pedal repeatedly, until the pads are pressed into firm contact with the brake disc, and normal (non-assisted) pedal pressure is restored.

4 Repeat the above procedure on the remaining front brake caliper.

3.2 Use a hose clamp on the flexible hoses

3.3 Slacken the flexible hose union (arrowed)

5 Refit the roadwheels, then lower the vehicle to the ground and tighten the roadwheel nuts to the specified torque.

6 Check the hydraulic fluid level as described in *Weekly checks*.

Caution: New pads will not give full braking efficiency until they have bedded-in. Be prepared for this, and avoid hard braking as far as possible for the first hundred miles or so after pad renewal.

| 3 | Front brake caliper – removal, overhaul and refitting |

Note: *Refer to the warning at the beginning of the previous Section before proceeding.*

Removal

1 Apply the handbrake. Loosen the front wheel nuts, then jack up the front of the

3.6 Caliper bracket bolts (arrowed)

vehicle and support it on axle stands. Remove the appropriate front wheel.

2 Fit a brake hose clamp to the flexible hose leading to the caliper **(see illustration)**. This will minimise brake fluid loss during subsequent operations.

3 Loosen the union on the caliper end of the flexible brake hose **(see illustration)**. Once loosened, do not try to unscrew the hose at this stage.

4 Remove the brake pads as described in Section 2.

5 Support the caliper in one hand, and prevent the hydraulic hose from turning with the other hand. Unscrew the caliper from the hose, making sure that the hose is not twisted unduly or strained. Once the caliper is detached, plug the open hydraulic unions in the caliper and hose, to keep out dust and dirt.

6 If required, the caliper bracket can be unbolted from the hub carrier **(see illustration)**.

Overhaul

Note: *Before starting work, check on the availability of parts (caliper overhaul kit/seals).*

7 With the caliper on the bench, brush away all traces of dust and dirt, but take care not to inhale any dust, as it may be harmful to your health.

8 Pull the dust cover rubber seal from the end of the piston.

9 Apply low air pressure to the fluid intake union, to eject the piston. Only low air pressure is required for this, such as is produced by a foot-operated tyre pump.

Caution: The piston may be ejected with some force. Position a thin piece of wood between the piston and the caliper body to prevent damage to the end face of the piston in the event of it being ejected suddenly.

10 Using a suitable blunt instrument, prise the piston seal from the groove in the cylinder bore. Take care not to scratch the surface of the bore.

11 Clean the piston and caliper body with methylated spirit, and allow to dry. Examine the surfaces of the piston and cylinder bore for wear, damage and corrosion. If the piston alone is unserviceable, a new piston must be obtained, along with seals. If the cylinder bore is unserviceable, the complete caliper must be renewed. The seals must be renewed, regardless of the condition of the other components.

12 Coat the piston and seals with clean brake fluid, then manipulate the piston seal into the groove in the cylinder bore.

13 Push the piston squarely into its bore, taking care not to damage the seal.

14 Fit the dust cover rubber seal onto the piston and caliper, then depress the piston fully.

Refitting

15 If removed, refit the caliper bracket and tighten the bolts to the specified torque.

4.2 Suspend the caliper from the spring using wire or string

4.4 Measure the thickness of the disc using a micrometer

4.10 Lift the brake disc from the studs

16 Refit the brake pads as described in Section 2, but screw the caliper onto the flexible hose before refitting it to the caliper bracket.

17 Tighten the flexible hose union ensuring the hose is not kinked or twisted.

18 Bleed the brake circuit according to the procedure given in Section 14, remembering to remove the brake hose clamp from the flexible hose. Make sure there are no leaks from the hose connections. Test the brakes carefully before returning the vehicle to normal service.

| 4 | Front brake disc – inspection, removal and refitting | |

Note: *To prevent uneven braking, BOTH front brake discs should be renewed or reground at the same time.*

Inspection

1 Apply the handbrake. Loosen the relevant wheel nuts, jack up the front of the vehicle and support it on axle stands. Remove the appropriate front wheel.

2 Remove the front brake caliper from the disc with reference to Section 3, and undo the two caliper bracket securing bolts. Do not disconnect the flexible hose. Support the caliper on an axle stand, or suspend it out of the way with a piece of wire, taking care to avoid straining the flexible hose **(see illustration)**.

3 Temporarily refit two of the wheel nuts to diagonally-opposite studs, with the flat sides of the nuts against the disc. Tighten the nuts progressively, to hold the disc firmly.

4 Scrape any corrosion from the disc. Rotate the disc, and examine it for deep scoring, grooving or cracks. Using a micrometer, measure the thickness of the disc in several places **(see illustration)**. The minimum thickness is stamped on the disc hub. Light wear and scoring is normal, but if excessive, the disc should be removed, and either reground by a specialist, or renewed. If regrinding is undertaken, the minimum thickness must be maintained. Obviously, if the disc is cracked, it must be renewed.

5 Using a dial gauge or a flat metal block and

feeler gauges, check that the disc run-out 10 mm from the outer edge does not exceed the limit given in the Specifications. To do this, fix the measuring equipment, and rotate the disc, noting the variation in measurement as the disc is rotated. The difference between the minimum and maximum measurements recorded is the disc run-out.

6 If the run-out is greater than the specified amount, check for variations of the disc thickness as follows. Mark the disc at eight positions 45° apart then, using a micrometer, measure the disc thickness at the eight positions, 15 mm in from the outer edge. If the variation between the minimum and maximum readings is greater than the specified amount, the disc should be renewed.

7 The hub face run-out can also be checked in a similar way. First remove the disc as described later in this Section, fix the measuring equipment, then slowly rotate the hub, and check that the run-out does not exceed the amount given in the Specifications. If the hub face run-out is excessive, this should be corrected (by renewing the hub bearings – see Chapter 10) before rechecking the disc run-out.

Removal

8 With the wheel, caliper and bracket removed, remove the wheel nuts which were temporarily refitted in paragraph 3.

9 Mark the disc in relation to the hub, if it is to be refitted.

10 Remove the washer/retaining clip(s) (where fitted), and withdraw the disc over the wheel studs **(see illustration)**.

5.2a Prise off the clip (arrowed)

Refitting

11 Make sure that the disc and hub mating surfaces are clean, then locate the disc on the wheel studs. Align the previously-made marks if the original disc is being refitted.

12 Refit the washer/retaining clip(s), where fitted.

13 Refit the brake caliper and bracket with reference to Section 2.

14 Refit the wheel, and lower the vehicle to the ground. Tighten wheel nuts to their specified torque.

15 Test the brakes carefully before returning the vehicle to normal service.

| 5 | Rear brake drum – removal, inspection and refitting | |

Note: *Refer to the warning at the beginning of Section 6 before proceeding.*

Note: *To prevent uneven braking, BOTH rear brake drums should be renewed at the same time.*

Removal

1 Chock the front wheels, release the handbrake and engage 1st gear (or P). Loosen the relevant wheel nuts, jack up the rear of the vehicle and support it on axle stands. Remove the appropriate rear wheel.

2 Prise off the spring clip (where fitted), and pull the drum from place. If the drum is reluctant to move, use two 8.0 mm bolts screwed into the threaded holes provided, and draw the drum from place **(see illustrations)**.

5.2b Use 2 x 8 mm bolts to force the drum from place

6.3 Clean the components with brake cleaner

6.4 Depress the hold-down spring, and slide it from under the head of the pin

6.5 Pull the top end of the shoe assembly outwards from the wheel cylinder

6.7a Pull the bottom end of the shoes from the anchor . . .

6.7b . . . then pivot the whole brake shoe assembly outwards

3 With the brake drum removed, clean the dust from the drum, brake shoes, wheel cylinder and backplate, using brake cleaner or methylated spirit. Take care not to inhale the dust, as it may contain asbestos.

Inspection

4 Clean the inside surfaces of the brake drum, then examine the internal friction surface for signs of scoring or cracks. If it is cracked, deeply scored, or has worn to a diameter greater than the maximum given in the Specifications, then it should be renewed, together with the drum on the other side.
5 Regrinding of the brake drum is not recommended.

Refitting

6 Refitting is a reversal of removal, tightening relevant bolts to their specified torque. Where necessary, adjust the handbrake as described in Section 22.

6.8 Pull the spring back and disengage the handbrake lever cable end fitting from the lever on the shoe

7 Test the brakes carefully before returning the vehicle to normal service.

6 Rear brake shoes – renewal

⚠ *Warning: Drum brake shoes must be renewed on BOTH rear wheels at the same time – never renew the shoes on only one wheel, as uneven braking may result. Also, the dust created by wear of the shoes may contain asbestos, which is a health hazard. Never blow it out with compressed air, and don't inhale any of it. An approved filtering mask should be worn when working on the brakes. DO NOT use petroleum-based solvents to clean brake parts; use brake cleaner or methylated spirit only.*

1 Chock the front wheels, release the

6.9 Unhook the lower return spring

handbrake and engage 1st gear (or P). Loosen the relevant wheel nuts, jack up the rear of the vehicle and support it on axle stands. Remove the rear wheels. Work on one brake assembly at a time, using the assembled brake for reference if necessary.
2 Remove the rear brake drum as described in Section 5.
3 Note the fitted position of the springs and the brake shoes, then clean the components with brake cleaner and allow to dry **(see illustration)**. Position a tray beneath the backplate, to catch the cleaner and residue.
4 Remove the two shoe hold-down springs; use a pair of pliers to depress the ends so that they can be withdrawn off the pins. If required, remove the hold-down pins from the backplate **(see illustration)**. Note that on some models, it's not possible to remove the rearmost hold-down pin with the backplate in place.
5 Disconnect the top ends of the shoes from the wheel cylinder, taking care not to damage the rubber boots **(see illustration)**.
6 To prevent the wheel cylinder pistons from being accidentally ejected, fit a suitable elastic band or wire lengthways over the cylinder/pistons. DO NOT press the brake pedal while the shoes are removed.
7 Pull the bottom end of the brake shoes from the bottom anchor **(see illustrations)**. Use pliers or an adjustable spanner over the edge of the shoe to lever it away, if required.
8 Pull the handbrake cable spring back from the operating lever on the rear of the trailing shoe. Unhook the cable end from the cut-out in the lever, and remove the brake shoes **(see illustration)**.
9 Working on a clean bench, move the bottom ends of the brake shoes together, and unhook the lower return spring from the shoes, noting the location holes **(see illustration)**.
10 Pull the leading shoe from the strut and brake shoe adjuster **(see illustration)**.
11 Pull the adjustment strut to release it from the trailing brake shoe, then unhook the upper return spring from the shoes, noting the location holes **(see illustrations)**. Ford insist that the upper return spring is renewed.
12 If the wheel cylinder shows signs of fluid

6.10 Pull the shoe from the strut and brake shoe adjuster

6.11a Pull the adjustment strut from the trailing shoe . . .

6.11b . . . then unhook the upper return spring

6.15a Set the adjustment strut so the diameter of the shoe assembly is 228 mm

6.15b When reassembled, the top of the assembly should look like this . . .

6.15c . . . and the lower end should look like this

leakage, or if there is any reason to suspect it of being defective, inspect it now, as described in the next Section.

13 Clean the backplate, and apply small amounts of high melting-point brake grease to the brake shoe contact points. Be careful not to get grease on any friction surfaces.

14 Lubricate the sliding components of the brake shoe adjuster with a little high melting-point brake grease.

15 Fit the new brake shoes using a reversal of the removal procedure, but set the adjustment strut so the diameter of the shoe assembly is 228 mm **(see illustrations)**.

16 Before refitting the brake drum, it should be inspected as described in Section 5.

17 With the drum in position and all the securing bolts and nuts tightened to their specified torque, refit the wheel, then carry out the renewal procedure on the remaining rear brake.

18 Lower the vehicle to the ground, and tighten the wheel nuts to the specified torque.

19 Depress the brake pedal several times, in order to operate the self-adjusting mechanism and set the shoes at their normal operating position.

20 Make several forward and reverse stops, and operate the handbrake fully two or three times (adjust the handbrake as required). Give the vehicle a road test, to make sure that the brakes are functioning correctly, and to bed-in the new shoes to the contours of the drum. Remember that the new shoes will not give full braking efficiency until they have bedded-in.

7 Rear wheel cylinder – removal, overhaul and refitting

Note: *Before starting work, check on the availability of parts (wheel cylinder, or overhaul kit/seals). Also bear in mind that if the brake shoes have been contaminated by fluid leaking from the wheel cylinder, they must be renewed. The shoes on BOTH sides of the vehicle must be renewed, even if they are only contaminated on one side.*

Removal

1 Remove the brake drum as described in Section 5.

2 Minimise fluid loss either by removing the master cylinder reservoir cap, and then tightening it down onto a piece of polythene to obtain an airtight seal, or by using a brake hose clamp, a G-clamp, or similar tool, to clamp the flexible hose at the nearest convenient point to the wheel cylinder.

3 Pull the brake shoes apart at their top ends, so that they are just clear of the wheel cylinder. The automatic adjuster will hold the shoes in this position, so that the cylinder can be withdrawn.

4 Wipe away all traces of dirt around the hydraulic union at the rear of the wheel cylinder, then undo the union nut.

5 Unscrew the two bolts securing the wheel cylinder to the backplate **(see illustration)**.

6 Withdraw the wheel cylinder from the backplate so that it is clear of the brake shoes.

Plug the open hydraulic unions, to prevent the entry of dirt, and to minimise further fluid loss whilst the cylinder is detached.

Overhaul

7 No overhaul procedures or parts were available at the time of writing, check availability of spares before dismantling. Renewing a wheel cylinder as a unit is recommended.

Refitting

8 Wipe clean the backplate and remove the plug from the end of the hydraulic pipe. Fit the cylinder onto the backplate and screw in the hydraulic union nut by hand, being careful not to cross-thread it.

9 Tighten the mounting bolts, then fully tighten the hydraulic union nut.

10 Retract the automatic brake adjuster mechanism, so that the brake shoes engage

7.5 Undo the 2 bolts (arrowed) and remove the wheel cylinder

with the pistons of the wheel cylinder. To do this, prise the shoes apart slightly, turn the automatic adjuster to its minimum position, and release the shoes.

11 Remove the clamp from the flexible brake hose, or the polythene from the master cylinder (as applicable).

12 Refit the brake drum with reference to Section 5.

13 Bleed the hydraulic system as described in Section 14. Providing suitable precautions were taken to minimise loss of fluid, it should only be necessary to bleed the relevant rear brake.

14 Test the brakes carefully before returning the vehicle to normal service.

8.2a Prise away the retaining spring

8.2b Pull out the rubber caps . . .

8.2c . . . and use a 7 mm Allen key or bit to unscrew the guide bolts

8.2d Unclip the brake hose from the bracket

8.2e Lift away the caliper . . .

8.2f . . . and suspend it from the suspension using cable-ties/string

8.2g Remove the outer brake pad . . .

8.2h . . . and the inner pad

8 Rear brake pads – renewal

8.2i Measure the thickness of the pad friction material

> **Warning: Renew both sets of rear brake pads at the same time – never renew the pads on only one wheel, as uneven braking may result. Note that the dust created by wear of the pads may contain asbestos, which is a health hazard. Never blow it out with compressed air, and don't inhale any of it. An approved filtering mask should be worn when working on the brakes. DO NOT use petrol or petroleum-based solvents to clean brake parts; use brake cleaner or methylated spirit only.**

1 Chock the front wheels, slacken the rear road-wheel nuts, then jack up the rear of the vehicle and support it on axle stands (see *Jacking and vehicle support*). Remove the rear wheels.

2 With the handbrake lever fully released, follow the accompanying photos **(see illustrations 8.2a to 8.2u)** for the actual pad renewal procedure. Be sure to stay in order and read the caption under each illustration, and note the following points:

a) If re-installing the original pads, ensure they are fitted to their original position.

b) Thoroughly clean the caliper guide surfaces and guide bolts.

c) If new pads are to be fitted, use a piston retraction tool to push the piston back and twist it clockwise at the same time – keep an eye on the fluid level in the reservoir whilst retracting the piston.

Caution: Pushing back the piston causes a reverse-flow of brake fluid, which has been known to 'flip' the master cylinder rubber seals, resulting in a total loss of braking. To avoid this, clamp the caliper flexible hose and open the bleed screw – as the piston is pushed back, the fluid can be directed into a suitable container using a hose attached to the bleed screw. Close the screw just before the piston is pushed fully back, to ensure no air enters the system.

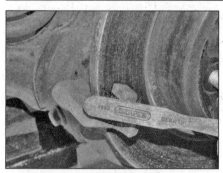

8.2j Use a wire brush to clean the pad mounting bracket

8.2k Note that the inner pad has an anti-rattle spring (arrowed)

8.2l Apply a little high-temperature anti-seize grease (Copperslip) to the rear of the pad . . .

8.2m . . . and the areas where the pad backing plate contacts the mounting bracket

8.2n Fit the inner pad – friction material side against the disc . . .

8.2o . . . followed by the outer pad

8.2p If new pads have been fitted, use a retraction tool to rotate the caliper piston clockwise, at the same time as pushing it into the caliper

8.2q Refit the caliper over the pads . . .

8.2r . . . then refit and tighten the guide bolts to the specified torque

8.2s Refit the rubber caps

8.2t Clip the brake hose back into the bracket

8.2u Use pliers to refit the caliper retaining spring

9.4 Unclip the cable end fitting (arrowed) from the caliper lever

3 Depress the brake pedal repeatedly, until the pads are pressed into firm contact with the brake disc, and normal (non-assisted) pedal pressure is restored.

4 Repeat the above procedure on the remaining brake caliper.

5 If necessary, adjust the handbrake as described in Section 22.

6 Refit the roadwheels, then lower the vehicle to the ground and tighten the roadwheel nuts to the specified torque.

7 Check the hydraulic fluid level as described in *Weekly checks*.

Caution: New pads will not give full braking efficiency until they have bedded-in. Be prepared for this, and avoid hard braking as far as possible for the first hundred miles or so after pad renewal.

9 Rear brake caliper – removal, overhaul and refitting

Removal

1 Chock the front wheels, and engage 1st gear (or P). Loosen the rear wheel nuts, jack up the rear of the vehicle and support it on axle stands. Remove the appropriate rear wheel.

2 Fit a brake hose clamp to the flexible hose leading to the caliper **(see illustration 3.2)**. This will minimise brake fluid loss during subsequent operations.

3 Slacken (but do not completely unscrew)

10.3 Pull the rear brake disc over the wheel studs

9.6 Undo the caliper mounting bracket bolts (arrowed)

the union on the caliper end of the flexible hose.

4 Unclip the handbrake inner cable fitting from the lever on the caliper, then detach the outer cable from the bracket **(see illustration)**.

5 Unscrew the caliper from the hydraulic brake hose, making sure that the hose is not twisted or strained unduly. Plug the open hydraulic unions to keep dust and dirt out.

6 If necessary, unbolt the caliper bracket from the hub carrier **(see illustration)**.

Overhaul

7 No overhaul procedures, or parts, were available at the time of writing. Check the availability of spares before dismantling the caliper. Do not attempt to dismantle the handbrake mechanism inside the caliper; if the mechanism is faulty, the complete caliper assembly must be renewed.

Refitting

8 Refit the caliper, and where applicable the bracket, by reversing the removal operations. Refer to the points made in Section 22 when reconnecting the handbrake cable. Tighten the mounting bolts and wheel nuts to the specified torque, and do not forget to remove the brake hose clamp from the flexible brake hose.

9 Bleed the brake circuit according to the procedure given in Section 14. Make sure there are no leaks from the hose connections. Test the brakes carefully before returning the vehicle to normal service.

11.4 Battery tray retaining bolts (arrowed)

10 Rear brake disc – inspection, removal and refitting

Removal

1 Remove the rear caliper and pads as described in Section 8.

2 Unbolt the caliper carrier bracket from the hub **(see illustration 9.6)**, then mark the disc in relation to the hub, if it is to be refitted.

3 Remove the retaining clip from the wheel stud (where fitted), and withdraw the disc over the wheel studs **(see illustration)**.

4 Procedures for inspection of the rear brake discs are the same as the front brake discs as described in Section 4.

Refitting

5 Refitting is a reversal of removal, as described in the relevant Sections. Apply a little thread-locking compound to the caliper bracket-to-hub carrier bolts.

11 Master cylinder – removal and refitting

⚠️ *Warning: Brake fluid is poisonous. Take care to keep it off bare skin, and in particular not to get splashes in your eyes. The fluid also attacks paintwork and plastics – wash off spillages immediately with cold water. Finally, brake fluid is highly inflammable, and should be handled with the same care as petrol.*

Removal

1 Exhaust the vacuum in the servo by pressing the brake pedal a few times, with the engine switched off.

2 Disconnect the battery negative lead. **Note:** *Before disconnecting the battery, refer to Chapter 5 for precautions.*

⚠️ *Warning: Do not siphon the fluid by mouth; it is poisonous. Any brake fluid spilt on paintwork should be washed off with clean water, without delay – brake fluid is also a highly-effective paint-stripper.*

3 Where fitted, undo the 2 bolts securing the brake fluid reservoir extension to the bulkhead extension panel, then depress the release button and detach the reservoir extension hose from the reservoir above the master cylinder.

4 Remove the battery as described in Chapter 5, then undo the 3 bolts and slide the battery tray forward a little **(see illustration)**.

5 Prise out the 4 plastic clips securing the plastic panel to the engine compartment bulkhead, then undo the inner 2 retaining bolts, slacken the outer bolt, remove the nuts and pivot the cross-stay each side away from

11.7 Depress the release button (on the reverse of the connector – 1), and disconnect the clutch fluid supply hose, then disconnect the level warning sensor wiring plug (2)

11.10 Undo the brake pipe unions (arrowed)

the bulkhead. Lift the plastic panel (where fitted) from place. Refit the bolts to secure the tops of the suspension struts to the vehicle body.

6 Raise the front of the vehicle and remove the wheels. Slacken the caliper bleed nipples, attach a rubber hose to the nipple, and place the other end of the hose in a suitable container. Operate the brake pedal until the fluid level is down to the base of the reservoir.

7 Depress the release button and detach the clutch master cylinder fluid supply hose from the side of the brake fluid reservoir **(see illustration)**. Plug the openings to prevent contamination.

8 Disconnect the wiring plug from the fluid level sensor on the side of the reservoir **(see illustration 11.7)**.

9 Identify the locations of each brake pipe on the master cylinder, then place rags beneath the master cylinder to catch spilt hydraulic fluid.

10 Clean around the hydraulic union nuts. Unscrew the nuts, and disconnect the hydraulic lines from the master cylinder; a split ring spanner should be used in preference to an open-ended spanner **(see illustration)**.

Cap the end of the pipes and the master cylinder to prevent any dirt contamination.

11 Undo the master cylinder securing nuts, and withdraw the master cylinder from the studs on the servo unit **(see illustration)**.

12 Recover the gasket/seal from the master cylinder.

13 If the master cylinder is faulty, it must be renewed. At the time of writing, no overhaul kits were available.

Refitting

14 Refitting is a reversal of the removal procedure, noting the following points:

a) Clean the contact surfaces of the master cylinder and servo, and locate a new gasket on the master cylinder.

b) Refit and tighten the nuts to the specified torque.

c) Carefully insert the brake pipes in the apertures in the master cylinder, then tighten the union nuts. Make sure that the nuts enter their threads correctly.

d) Fill the reservoir with fresh brake fluid.

e) Bleed the brake hydraulic system as described in Section 14.

f) Test the brakes carefully before returning the vehicle to normal service.

Brake fluid reservoir

15 Carry out the procedure described in Paragraph 3 to 7 of this Section.

16 Disconnect the wiring plug from the fluid level sensor on the side of the reservoir.

17 Remove the retaining pin and detach the reservoir from the master cylinder **(see illustration)**.

12 Brake pedal – removal and refitting

Removal

1 Working inside the vehicle move the driver's seat fully to the rear, to allow maximum working area.

2 Remove the driver's side lower facia panel.

3 Remove the accelerator pedal as described in Chapter 4.

4 Disconnect the electrical connectors to the brake pedal switches. Remove the switches by turning them, then pulling them out of the pedal bracket **(see illustration)**.

5 Prise out the pin securing the servo pushrod

11.11 Master cylinder retaining nuts (arrowed)

11.17 Pull out the reservoir retaining pin (arrowed – viewed from underneath)

12.4 Disconnect the wiring plugs from the brake pedal switches

12.5 Prise out and discard the servo pushrod pin

to the pedal (see illustration). Discard the pin – a new one must be fitted.

6 Slacken the 5 retaining nuts on the pedal bracket assembly (see illustration).

7 Manoeuvre the pedal assembly rearwards, and down from under the facia. No further dismantling of the assembly is recommended – it would appear that only the complete assembly is available.

Refitting

8 Refitting is a reversal of the removal procedure.

9 Refit the brake pedal switches as described in Section 21.

13 Hydraulic pipes and hoses – inspection, removal and refitting

Note: Refer to the warning at the start of Section 14 concerning the dangers of brake fluid.

Inspection

1 Jack up the front and rear of the vehicle, and support on axle stands (see Jacking and vehicle support). Making sure the vehicle is safely supported on a level surface.

2 Check for signs of leakage at the pipe unions, then examine the flexible hoses for signs of cracking, chafing and fraying.

3 The brake pipes should be examined carefully for signs of dents, corrosion or other damage. Corrosion should be scraped off, and if the depth of pitting is significant, the pipes

13.7 Use a brake pipe spanner to slacken the union nuts

renewed. This is particularly likely in those areas underneath the vehicle body where the pipes are exposed and unprotected.

4 Renew any defective brake pipes and/or hoses.

Removal

5 If a section of pipe or hose is to be removed, loss of brake fluid can be reduced by unscrewing the filler cap, and completely sealing the top of the reservoir with cling film or adhesive tape. Alternatively, the reservoir can be emptied (see Section 11).

6 To remove a section of pipe, hold the adjoining hose union nut with a spanner to prevent it from turning, then unscrew the union nut at the end of the pipe, and release it. Repeat the procedure at the other end of the pipe, then release the pipe by pulling out the clips attaching it to the body.

7 Where the union nuts are exposed to the full force of the weather, they can sometimes be quite tight. If an open-ended spanner is used, burring of the flats on the nuts is not uncommon, and for this reason, it is preferable to use a split ring (brake) spanner (see illustration), which will engage all the flats. If such a spanner is not available, self-locking grips may be used as a last resort; these may well damage the nuts, but if the pipe is to be renewed, this does not matter.

8 To further minimise the loss of fluid when disconnecting a flexible brake line from a rigid pipe, clamp the hose as near as possible to the pipe to be detached, using a brake hose clamp or a pair of self-locking grips with protected jaws.

9 To remove a flexible hose, first clean the ends of the hose and the surrounding area, then unscrew the union nuts from the hose ends. Remove the spring clip, and withdraw the hose from the serrated mounting in the support bracket. Where applicable, unscrew the hose from the caliper.

10 Brake pipes supplied with flared ends and union nuts can be obtained individually or in sets from Ford dealers or accessory shops. The pipe is then bent to shape, using the old pipe as a guide, and is ready for fitting. Be careful not to kink or crimp the pipe when bending it; ideally, a proper pipe-bending tool should be used.

12.6 Brake pedal bracket assembly retaining nuts (arrowed)

Refitting

11 Refitting of the pipes and hoses is a reversal of removal. Make sure that all brake pipes are securely supported in their clips, and ensure that the hoses are not kinked. Check also that the hoses are clear of all suspension components and underbody fittings, and will remain clear during movement of the suspension and steering.

12 On completion, bleed the hydraulic system as described in Section 14.

14 Hydraulic system – bleeding

⚠ **Warning: Brake fluid contains polyglycol ethers and polyglycols which are poisonous. Take care to keep it off bare skin, and in particular not to get splashes in your eyes. Wash hands thoroughly after handling and if fluid contacts the eyes, flush out with cold running water. If irritation persists get medical attention immediately. The fluid also attacks paintwork and plastics – wash off spillages immediately with cold water. Finally, brake fluid is highly inflammable, and should be handled with the same care as petrol.**

1 If the master cylinder has been disconnected and reconnected, then the complete system (all circuits) must be bled of air. If a component of one circuit has been disturbed, then only that particular circuit need be bled.

2 Bleeding should commence on the furthest bleed nipple from the master cylinder, followed by the next one until the bleed nipple remaining nearest to the master cylinder is bled last.

3 There are a variety of do-it-yourself 'one-man' brake bleeding kits available from motor accessory shops, and it is recommended that one of these kits be used wherever possible, as they greatly simplify the brake bleeding operation. Follow the kit manufacturer's instructions in conjunction with the following procedure. If a pressure-bleeding kit is obtained, then it will not be necessary to depress the brake pedal in the following procedure.

4 During the bleeding operation, do not allow the brake fluid level in the reservoir to drop below the minimum mark. If the level is allowed to fall so far that air is drawn in, the whole procedure will have to be started again from scratch. Only use new fluid for topping-up, preferably from a freshly-opened container. Never re-use fluid bled from the system.

5 Before starting, check that all rigid pipes and flexible hoses are in good condition, and that all hydraulic unions are tight. Take great care not to allow hydraulic fluid to come into contact with the vehicle paintwork, otherwise the finish will be seriously damaged. Wash

off any spilt fluid immediately with cold water.

6 If a brake bleeding kit is not being used, gather together a clean jar, a length of plastic or rubber tubing which is a tight fit over the bleed screw, and a new container of the specified brake fluid (see *Lubricants and fluids*). The help of an assistant will also be required.

7 Clean the area around the bleed screw on the rear brake unit to be bled (it is important that no dirt be allowed to enter the hydraulic system), and remove the dust cap. Connect one end of the tubing to the bleed screw, and immerse the other end in the jar **(see illustrations)**. The jar should be filled with sufficient brake fluid to keep the end of the tube submerged.

8 Open the bleed screw by half a turn, and have the assistant depress the brake pedal to the floor. Tighten the bleed screw at the end of the down stroke, then have the assistant release the pedal. Continue this procedure until clean brake fluid, free from air bubbles, can be seen flowing into the jar. Finally tighten the bleed screw with the pedal in the fully-depressed position.

9 Remove the tube, and refit the dust cap. Top-up the master cylinder reservoir if necessary, then repeat the procedure on the opposite rear brake.

10 Repeat the procedure on the front brake furthest from the master cylinder, followed by the brake nearest to the master cylinder.

11 Check the feel of the brake pedal – it should be firm. If it is spongy, there is still some air in the system, and the bleeding procedure should be repeated.

12 When bleeding is complete, top-up the master cylinder reservoir and refit the cap.

13 On models with manual transmission check the clutch operation on completion; it may be necessary to bleed the clutch hydraulic system as described in Chapter 6.

---

15 Vacuum servo unit – testing, removal and refitting

Testing

1 To test the operation of the servo unit, depress the footbrake four or five times to dissipate the vacuum, then start the engine while keeping the footbrake depressed. As the engine starts, there should be a noticeable give in the brake pedal as vacuum builds-up. Allow the engine to run for at least two minutes, and then switch it off. If the brake pedal is now depressed again, it should be possible to hear a hiss from the servo when the pedal is depressed. After four or five applications, no further hissing should be heard, and the pedal should feel harder.

2 Before assuming that a problem exists in the servo unit itself, inspect the non-return valve as described in the next Section.

14.7a Prise off the dust cap from the bleed screw (arrowed)

Removal

RHD models

3 On models with air-conditioning, have the refrigerant circuit evacuated as described in Chapter 3. When disconnecting the air conditioning pipes, cap the ends to prevent any contamination.

4 Refer to Section 11 and remove the master cylinder.

5 Remove the right-hand headlight assembly as described in Chapter 12.

6 Detach the coolant expansion tank from the right-hand side inner wing and move it to one side.

7 Disconnect the wiring plugs from the high- and low-pressure cut-off switches in the refrigerant pipes, then undo the bolt securing the pipes to the connection at the engine compartment bulkhead **(see illustrations)**. Discard the O-ring seals – new ones must be fitted.

8 Undo the bolts securing the refrigerant pipes to the connections at the condenser and accumulator/dehydrator, and unclip the pipes from the inner wing. Discard the O-ring seals – new ones must be fitted. Plug the openings to prevent contamination.

9 Carefully prise the vacuum non-return valve from the servo **(see illustration 16.5)**.

10 Remove the driver's side lower facia panel.

11 Disconnect their wiring plugs, then remove the brake pedal position switch (coloured blue/white) and brake light switch (coloured black) from the bracket. Rotate the position switch anti-clockwise, and the light switch clockwise.

15.7a Undo the bolt securing the refrigerant pipes (arrowed)

14.7b Connect the kit and open the bleed screw

Do not move the brake pedal during this procedure.

12 Carefully prise the pin from the servo actuator rod **(see illustration 12.5)**. Discard the pin – a new one must be fitted

13 Undo the 4 nuts securing the servo to the bulkhead/pedal bracket and manoeuvre it from the engine compartment.

14 Note that the servo unit cannot be dismantled for repair or overhaul and, if faulty, must be renewed.

LHD models

15 Remove the brake master cylinder as described in Section 11.

16 Undo the brake pipes to the hydraulic control unit. Cap the end of the pipes and the hydraulic unit to prevent any dirt contamination.

17 Disconnect the vacuum pipe from the servo.

18 Remove the driver's side lower facia panel.

19 Disconnect their wiring plugs, then remove the brake pedal position switch (coloured blue/white) and brake light switch (coloured black) from the bracket. Rotate the position switch anti-clockwise, and the light switch clockwise. Do not move the brake pedal during this procedure.

20 Carefully prise the pin from the servo actuator rod **(see illustration 12.5)**. Discard the pin – a new one must be fitted

21 Undo the 4 nuts securing the servo to the bulkhead/pedal bracket and manoeuvre it from the engine compartment.

22 Note that the servo unit cannot be dismantled for repair or overhaul and, if faulty, must be renewed.

15.7b Renew the refrigerant pipe O-ring seals (arrowed)

16.5 The vacuum non-return valve is located in the pipe between the intake manifold and the servo (arrowed)

Refitting

23 Refitting is a reversal of the removal procedure, noting the following points:
a) *Refer to the relevant Sections/ Chapters for details of refitting the other components removed.*
b) *Compress the actuator rod into the brake servo, before refitting.*
c) *Make sure the gasket is correctly positioned on the servo.*
d) *Test the brakes carefully before returning the vehicle to normal service.*

16 Vacuum servo unit vacuum hose and non-return valve –
removal, testing and refitting

Removal

1 With the engine switched off, depress the brake pedal four or five times, to dissipate any remaining vacuum from the servo unit.
2 Disconnect the vacuum hose adapter at the servo unit, by pulling it free from the rubber grommet. If it is reluctant to move, prise it free, using a screwdriver with its blade inserted under the flange.
3 Detach the vacuum hose from the intake manifold or vacuum pump connection, pressing in the collar to disengage the tabs, then withdrawing the collar slowly.
4 If the hose or the fixings are damaged or in poor condition, they must be renewed.

Testing

5 Examine the non-return valve **(see illus-**

18.4 Front ABS sensor mounting bolt (arrowed)

17.3 Release the clips (arrowed) and disconnect the ABS unit wiring plug

tration) for damage and signs of deterioration, and renew it if necessary. The valve may be tested by blowing through its connecting hoses in both directions. It should only be possible to blow from the servo end.

Refitting

6 Refitting is a reversal of the removal procedure. If fitting a new non-return valve, ensure that it is fitted the correct way round.

17 ABS hydraulic unit –
removal and refitting

Note: *At the time of writing, no parts for the ABS hydraulic unit were available, and it must therefore be renewed as an assembly. Refer to the warning at the start of Section 14 concerning the dangers of brake fluid.*

Removal

1 Remove the battery (see Chapter 5) and the PCM (Chapter 4), then undo the bolts and remove the battery tray **(see illustration 11.4).**
2 Raise the front of the vehicle and remove the wheels. Slacken the caliper bleed nipples, attach a rubber hose to the nipple, and place the other end of the hose in a suitable container. Operate the brake pedal until the fluid level is down to the base of the reservoir.

⚠️ *Warning: Do not siphon the fluid by mouth; it is poisonous. Any brake fluid spilt on paintwork should be washed off with clean water, without delay – brake fluid is also a highly-effective paint-stripper.*

18.7 Rear ABS sensor retaining bolt (arrowed) – disc brake model

3 Depress the retaining clips, release the retainer and disconnect the wring plug from the ABS control unit **(see illustration)**. Cover the disconnected plug and socket to prevent contamination.
4 Undo the six brake pipes to the hydraulic control unit. Cap the end of the pipes and the hydraulic unit to prevent any dirt contamination. Unclip the brake lines from the retaining clips.
5 Undo the securing bolts from the brake hydraulic unit, and withdraw from the bulkhead. Remove it from the engine compartment, taking care not to damage any other components.

Refitting

6 Refitting is a reversal of removal. Ensure that the multiplug is securely connected, and that the brake pipe unions are tightened to the specified torque. On completion, bleed the hydraulic system as described in Section 14.

18 ABS wheel sensor –
testing, removal and refitting

Testing

1 Checking of the sensors is done either by substitution for a known good unit, or interrogating the ABS ECM for stored fault codes, using dedicated test equipment found at Ford dealers or suitably-equipped specialists.

Removal

Front wheel sensor

2 Apply the handbrake and loosen the relevant front wheel nuts. Jack up the front of the vehicle and support it on axle stands. Remove the wheel.
3 Disconnect the sensor wiring plug.
4 Unscrew the sensor mounting bolt from the hub carrier and withdraw the sensor **(see illustration)**. Withdraw the O-ring seal.

Rear wheel sensor

5 Chock the front wheels, and engage 1st gear (or P). Jack up the rear of the vehicle and support it on axle stands. Remove the relevant wheel.
6 Disconnect the sensor wiring plug.
7 Unscrew the sensor mounting bolt, and withdraw the sensor **(see illustration)**. Withdraw the O-ring seal.

Refitting

8 Refitting is a reversal of the removal procedure. Fit a new O-ring seal to the hub carrier – not the sensor.

19 Electronic stability control components –
removal and refitting

Note: *This system uses the same components as the ABS and Traction control system. The only additional components are the 'yaw rate' sensor and 'accelerometer sensor', which are*

mounted on the same bracket on the floor crossmember, and the steering wheel rotation sensor.

Yaw rate and accelerometer sensor

Removal

1 Remove the driver's side front seat as described in Chapter 11.
2 Open the relevant door, then pull the trim upwards from along the sill.
3 Remove the driver's side B-pillar trim panel as described in Chapter 11.
4 Pull the carpet back to gain access to the sensors.
5 Disconnect the sensor wiring plug.
6 Undo the two retaining bolts and remove the sensor and bracket.

Refitting

7 Refitting is a reversal of the removal procedure. Ensure the sensor and bracket is correctly positioned.

Steering wheel rotation sensor

8 The steering wheel rotation sensor is integral with the driver's airbag contact unit, beneath the steering wheel. Removal of the unit is described in Chapter 12.

20 Traction control system – general information

1 The Traction control system is an expanded version of the ABS system. It is integrated with the ABS, and uses the same wheel sensors. It also uses the hydraulic control unit, which incorporates additional internal solenoid valves.
2 To remove the hydraulic unit or wheel sensors, carry out the procedures as described in Sections 17 and 18.

21 Brake switches – removal, refitting and adjustment

Removal

Brake pedal position switch

1 Disconnect the battery negative (earth) lead (see Chapter 5).
2 Remove the driver's side lower facia panel.
3 Disconnect the wiring connector from the brake pedal position switch. This is the upper of the two switches, and is coloured blue and white **(see illustration 12.4)**.
4 Rotate the switch anti-clockwise by a quarter-turn, and withdraw it from the pedal bracket. Do not depress the brake pedal during the removal or refitting procedure – the pedal must be 'at rest'.

Brake light switch

5 Proceed as described in Paragraphs 1 and 2 in this Section.

6 Disconnect the wiring connector from the brake light switch. This is the lower of the two switches, and is coloured black **(see illustration 12.4)**.
7 Rotate the switch *clockwise* by a quarter-turn, and withdraw it from the pedal bracket **(see illustration)**. Do not depress the brake pedal during the removal or refitting procedure – the pedal must be 'at rest'.

Refitting and adjustment

8 Refitting is a reversal of the removal procedure. **Note:** *If both switches have been removed, the brake pedal position switch must be installed before the light switch.*
9 Both switches are automatically adjusted/calibrated by the vehicle system.

22 Handbrake lever – removal and refitting

Removal

1 Chock the front wheels, and engage 1st gear (or P).
2 Remove the centre console as described in Chapter 11.
3 Disconnect the electrical connector from the handbrake warning switch **(see illustration)**.
4 Slacken the locknut, then undo the handbrake adjusting nut **(see illustration)**.
5 Unscrew the mounting bolts securing the handbrake lever to the floor **(see illustration)**.
6 Withdraw the handbrake from inside the vehicle.

22.3 Disconnect the handbrake warning light switch (arrowed)

22.5 Handbrake lever bracket bolts (arrowed)

21.7 Rotate the brake light switch clockwise to remove it

Refitting

7 Refitting is a reversal of removal, ensuring the cable retaining tab is positioned away from the cable.
8 When refitting the lever, it will be necessary to adjust the mechanism, as follows. **Note:** *The handbrake should only be adjusted when the brakes are cool.*
9 Tighten the cable adjustment nut finger-tight, then raise the handbrake lever 12 notches.
10 Fully release the handbrake, then slacken the adjustment nut to the end of the threads.

Disc brake models

11 Insert a 0.7 mm feeler gauge between the handbrake lever and the caliper abutment on both sides **(see illustration)**.
12 With the help of an assistant, tighten the adjustment nut until movement is observed on one of the caliper handbrake levers.
13 Remove the feeler gauges from both

22.4 Handbrake adjusting nut (arrowed)

22.11 Insert a 0.7 mm feeler gauge between the caliper lever and the abutment (stop)

sides, then check the wheels rotate freely with no excess friction or drag caused by the brake. Tighten the adjustment locknut.

Drum brake models

14 Remove the brake drums as described in Section 5.

15 Ensure the handbrake lever is fully released, then insert a 2.0 mm feeler gauge between the handbrake lever end stop and the rear brake shoe on each side (see illustration).

16 With the help of an assistant, tighten the cable adjustment nut until movement is observed on one of the handbrake levers.

17 Remove the feeler gauges, and refit the drum brakes as described in Section 5.

18 Check the wheels rotate freely with no excess friction or drag caused by the brake. Tighten the cable locknut.

23 Handbrake cables – removal and refitting

Removal

1 Starting at the rear, prise up and remove the gaiter/trim around the handbrake lever.

2 Slacken the handbrake adjustment nut to the end of the threads.

3 Chock the front wheels and engage 1st gear (or P). Loosen the wheel nuts on the relevant rear wheel, then jack up the rear of the vehicle and support it on axle stands. Fully release the handbrake lever.

22.15 Insert a 2.0 mm feeler gauge between the lever end stop and the side of the shoe

4 Release the fasteners and remove the air deflector panel on each side (see illustration).

5 Remove the exhaust system as described in Chapter 4.

6 Undo the fasteners and remove the exhaust front and centre heat shields.

7 Remove the relevant rear wheel and unclip the handbrake outer cable from its retaining clips (see illustration).

Disc brake models

8 Unbolt the cable guide from the arm on both sides (see illustration).

9 Use a pair of pliers to detach the handbrake cable inner fitting from the lever on each caliper (see illustration 9.4).

10 Detach each outer cable from the bracket on the vehicle underbody, then disengage them from the equaliser bracket (see illustrations). Note that the left-hand cable has a black sleeve, and the right-hand cable has a white sleeve.

Drum brake models

11 Unbolt the outer cable guide from the tie-bar on both sides (see illustration).

12 Unclip the handbrake cable from the arm both sides. Pull the cable through the tie-bar on both sides.

13 Unclip the cable from the support hangers. Note that there are marks on the cable outer sleeve to indicate the clip positions.

14 Rotate each cable through 90° and detach them from the equaliser, then depress the clips and pull the outer cables from the bracket (see illustrations 23.10a and 23.10b). Withdraw the cables from beneath the vehicle. Note that the left-hand cable has a black sleeve, whilst the right-hand cable has a white sleeve.

Refitting

15 Refitting is a reversal of the removal procedure, noting the following points:
a) *Adjust the cable as described in Section 22.*
b) *Make sure that the cable end fittings are correctly located*
c) *Check the operation of the handbrake. Make sure that both wheels are locked, then free to turn, as the handbrake is operated.*

24 Electric parking brake – removal, refitting and adjustment

1 Some high specification models are fitted with an electrically operated handbrake –

23.4 Remove the air deflector panel each side (arrowed)

23.7 Release the handbrake cable from the retaining clips

23.8 Undo the bolt (arrowed) securing the cable guide to the tie-bar

23.10a Disconnect the cables from the equaliser bracket

23.10b Note that the cables cross over when fitted correctly

23.11 Undo the bolt (arrowed) securing the handbrake cable to the tie-bar

often referred to as an electronic or electric parking brake (EPB). This supersedes the conventional handbrake with an electric motor to operate the cables to the conventional rear disc brakes. A simple switch is in place of the handbrake lever.

Removal

2 Jack up and support the rear of the vehicle (see *Jacking and vehicle support*) and remove both rear wheels.

3 The EPB must now be released by holding down the switch as the ignition is turned off. On vehicles fitted with the keyless system hold down the switch as the ignition switch is pulled out.

4 Working inside the vehicle remove the coin tray and the cover from the emergency release **(see illustrations)**. Pull up the handle and free it from the housing. Work the cable free from the handle and remove the handle.

5 Working under the vehicle, release the emergency cable **(see illustration)** and unhook the handbrake cables from both calipers.

6 Remove the right-hand deflector and the exhaust heat shield. Work the cables free from the support brackets.

7 Remove the end cover from the control unit and (after disconnecting the battery) unplug the wiring connector **(see illustrations)**.

8 Remove the single bolt and gently bend the support bracket to gain access to the control unit and motor. Undo the nuts and remove the complete assembly **(see illustration)**.

Refitting

9 Refitting is a reversal of the removal procedure, noting the following points:

a) *Check carefully the condition of the 'cotton reel' rubber mountings as they are prone to splitting*

b) *At the time of writing no separate parts were available – the complete unit must be renewed.*

c) *New units must be programmed to the vehicle with suitable diagnostic equipment. At the time of writing only the Ford diagnostic tool (IDS) was able to do this.*

---

25 Vacuum pump –
removal and refitting

Removal

1.6 litre models

1 Remove the plastic cover from the top of the engine (where fitted).

2 Undo the bolt and remove the crash shield around the fuel filter (where fitted).

3 Disconnect the hose from the vacuum pump **(see illustration)**.

4 Undo the 2 retaining bolts and remove the vacuum pump Discard the O-ring seals, new ones must be fitted.

24.4a Remove the small tray . . .

24.4c . . . to expose the emergency release handle

1.8 litre models

5 Remove the plastic cover from the top of the engine.

6 Unscrew the union nut and disconnect the

24.7a Remove the cover . . .

24.8 Recover the rubber mountings (arrowed)

24.4b . . . and the lower tray . . .

24.5 Unclip the emergency cable guide tube (arrowed)

vacuum line from the top of the pump **(see illustration)**.

7 Release the retaining clips and disconnect the oil separator/return hose(s) from the cylinder head cover.

24.7b . . . and disconnect the wiring

25.3 Depress the button (arrowed) and pull the hose from the vacuum pump

25.6 Undo the vacuum line from the top of the pump

25.13 Slacken the bolts evenly, then remove the top bolt

25.14 Renew the sealing ring when refitting the brake vacuum pump

25.18 Vacuum pump retaining bolts (arrowed)

25.19a Renew the pump O-ring seals (arrowed)

25.19b Ensure the drive lugs engage with the slot in the end of the camshaft (arrowed)

8 Unbolt the air intake hoses from the top of the cylinder head cover, and detach the breather hoses.

9 Unbolt and remove the cylinder head cover.

10 Using a suitable socket or spanner on the crankshaft pulley bolt, turn the crankshaft until the vacuum pump pushrod (operated by the eccentric on the camshaft end) is fully retracted into the cylinder head.

11 Disconnect the electrical connectors from the glow plug, the engine temperature sensor and the oil pressure switch.

12 Release the retaining clips and disconnect the oil separator/return hose(s) from the pump. Be prepared for some oil spillage as the hose is disconnected and mop-up any spilt oil.

13 Evenly and progressively slacken the bolts securing the pump to the front of the cylinder head **(see illustration)**. Note that there is no need to remove the lower bolt completely, as the lower end of the pump is slotted.

14 Remove the pump from the engine compartment, along with its sealing ring **(see illustration)**. Discard the sealing ring, a new one should be used on refitting.

2.0 litre models

15 Remove the plastic cover from the top of the engine.

16 Unclip the fuel pipe from the support bracket above the vacuum pump – located at the left-hand end of the cylinder head.

17 Undo the stud/nut and detach the EGR pipe from the pump.

18 Undo the bolts/nut and remove the vacuum pump **(see illustration)**. Discard the O-ring seals, new ones must be fitted.

Refitting

19 Refitting is a reversal of removal, noting the following points:
a) *Ensure the pump and cylinder head mating surfaces are clean and dry. Fit the new sealing ring to the pump recess.*
b) *On 1.6 and 2.0 litre models, ensure the drive coupling is aligned with the slot in the camshaft (see illustrations).*
c) *Start the engine and check for correct operation of the pump (check brakes have servo action) as described in Section 15.*
d) *Make sure all the hose connections are secure, and check for leaks.*

26 Vacuum pump – testing and overhaul

Note: *A vacuum gauge will be required for this check.*

1 The operation of the braking system vacuum pump can be checked using a vacuum gauge.

2 Disconnect the vacuum pipe from the pump, and connect the gauge to the pump union using a suitable length of hose.

3 Start the engine and allow it to idle, then measure the vacuum created by the pump. As a guide, after one minute, a minimum of approximately 500 mm Hg should be recorded. If the vacuum registered is significantly less than this, it is likely that the pump is faulty. However, seek the advice of a Ford dealer before condemning the pump.

4 Overhaul of the vacuum pump is not possible, since no components are available separately. If faulty, the complete pump assembly must be renewed.

Chapter 10
Suspension and steering

Contents

Section number

Front anti-roll bar – removal and refitting 6
Front hub carrier and bearing – removal and refitting 2
Front subframe – removal and refitting 21
Front suspension control arm and balljoint – removal, overhaul and
   refitting 5
Front suspension strut – dismantling, inspection and reassembly . . 4
Front suspension strut – removal and refitting 3
General information 1
Power steering pump – removal and refitting 18
Rear anti-roll bar – removal and refitting 12
Rear coil spring – removal and refitting 10

Section number

Rear hub bearings – renewal 7
Rear shock absorber – removal and refitting 9
Rear hub carrier/lateral link – removal and refitting 8
Rear suspension link arms – removal and refitting 11
Steering column – removal and refitting 14
Steering rack – removal and refitting 15
Steering rack gaiters – renewal 16
Steering system – bleeding 17
Steering wheel – removal and refitting 13
Track rod end – removal and refitting 19
Wheel alignment and steering angles – general information 20

Degrees of difficulty

Easy, suitable for novice with little experience	Fairly easy, suitable for beginner with some experience	Fairly difficult, suitable for competent DIY mechanic	Difficult, suitable for experienced DIY mechanic	Very difficult, suitable for expert DIY or professional

Specifications

Front suspension

Type . . . . Independent, with MacPherson struts incorporating coil springs and telescopic shock absorbers. Anti-roll bar fitted to all models

Rear suspension

Type . . . . Fully-independent, multi-link with separate coil springs and hydraulic telescopic shock absorbers. Anti-roll bar fitted to all models

Steering

Type . . . . Power-assisted rack-and-pinion. Electro-hydraulic on some models

Wheel alignment and steering angles

	Vehicles built up to 07/2005	Vehicles built from 07/2005
Front wheel:		
Camber angle:		
Standard chassis	0.35° to -1°56'	0.25° to -2°07'
Sports chassis	0.25° to -2°0.6'	0.25° to -2°07'
Castor angle:		
Standard chassis	4°29' to 2°28'	4°27' to 2°27'
Sports chassis	4°32' to 2°31'	4°32' to 2°29'
Toe setting	0°06' ± 0°09' toe-in	0°06' ± 0°15' toe-in
Rear wheel:		
Camber angle:		
Standard chassis	-0°20' to -2°50'	-0°19' to -2°49'
Sports chassis	-0°29' to -2°59'	-0°22' to -2°52'
Toe setting	0°38' to 0°08' toe-in	0°38' to 0°08' toe-in

Torque wrench settings

	Nm	lbf ft
Front suspension		
ABS sensor	10	7
Anti-roll bar clamp bolts*	50	37
Anti-roll bar connecting link nuts*	50	37
Balljoint nut to hub carrier*	70	52
Balljoint-to-control arm bolts	70	52
Brake caliper mounting bracket bolts*	120	89
Control arm to subframe:*		
Rear bolt	115	85
Front bolt	175	129
Driveshaft bolt	See Chapter 8	
Lower balljoint to control arm	70	52
Lower torque rod bolts:		
M10	60	44
M12	80	59
Subframe front and rear mounting bolts:*		
Front	120	89
Rear	280	207
Subframe rear mounting brackets	70	52
Suspension strut piston nut*	50	37
Suspension strut to hub carrier*	90	66
Suspension strut upper mounting/brace to body	32	24
Suspension upper mount brace-to-bulkhead nuts	20	15
Rear suspension		
Anti-roll bar link to anti-roll bar (link with balljoints)	70	52
Anti-roll bar link to lower arm (solid link)	25	18
Anti-roll bar link to lower control arms (link with balljoints)	50	37
Anti-roll bar-to-subframe bolts	50	37
Lateral link/hub carrier to body	115	85
Lower control arm to hub carrier	115	85
Lower control arm to subframe	90	66
Rear hub bearing assembly	55	41
Shock absorber lower mounting bolt	115	85
Shock absorber upper mounting nut:*		
Normal suspension	25	18
Self-levelling suspension (Nivomat)	60	44
Shock absorber upper mounting bolts	25	18
Tie-rod bolts	115	85
Upper control arm to hub carrier/lateral link and subframe	115	85
Steering		
Steering column mounting bolts*	25	18
Steering pump bolts	23	17
Steering rack mounting bolts	90	66
Steering wheel bolt	48	35
Steering shaft universal joint pinch-bolt*	28	21
Track rod end balljoint nuts*	50	37
Track rod locknuts	62	46
Roadwheels		
Wheel nuts	130	96

* Do not re-use

1 General information

The independent front suspension is of the MacPherson strut type, incorporating coil springs and integral telescopic shock absorbers. The struts are located by transverse control arms, which are attached to the front subframe via rubber bushes at their inner ends, and incorporate a balljoint at their outer ends. The hub carriers, which carry the hub bearings, brake calipers and the hub/disc assemblies, are bolted to the MacPherson struts, and connected to the control arms through the balljoints. A front anti-roll bar is fitted to all models, and is attached to the subframe and to the MacPherson struts via link arms **(see illustration)**.

The rear suspension is of the fully independent, multi-link type, consisting of an upper and lower control arm mounted via rubber bushes, to the lateral link/hub carrier and rear subframe. The lateral link is attached to the vehicle body at the front end and incorporate the hub carrier at the rear. The

1.1 Front suspension

1 Upper bearing, mounting and spring seat	4 Anti-roll bar	9 Front bush
	5 Spring	10 Control arm
2 Rear bush	6 Lower spring seat	11 Balljoint
3 Clamp	7 Hub carrier	12 MacPherson strut
	8 Front subframe	

H46425

1.2 Rear suspension

1 Lower control arm	3 Anti-roll bar	6 Tie rod
	4 Wheel speed sensor	7 Lateral link/hub carrier
2 Subframe	5 Upper control arm	

H46424

assembly is located by a tie rod each side. Coil springs are fitted between the lower control arm and the subframe. Separate hydraulic telescopic shock absorbers are fitted between the hub carrier between the lower control arm and the vehicle body **(see illustration)**.

Power-assisted rack and pinion steering is fitted as standard equipment. On some models, power assistance is derived from a hydraulic pump, driven by an electric motor, controlled by the Electro-Hydraulic Power Steering module (EHPS). On other models, the hydraulic pump is driven by the auxiliary drivebelt.

2 Front hub carrier and bearing – removal and refitting

Note: *The hub bearing is a sealed, pre-adjusted and pre-lubricated, double-row ball type, and is intended to last the car's entire service life without maintenance or attention. The hub flange and bearing are serviced as a complete assembly, and these components cannot be dismantled or renewed individually.*

Removal

1 Loosen the appropriate front wheel nuts, then jack up the front of the car and support it on axle stands (see *Jacking and vehicle support*). Remove the appropriate front roadwheel.

2 Undo the bolt securing the headlight levelling sensor bracket to the right-hand front lower arm (where applicable).

3 Slacken and remove the bolt securing the driveshaft to the hub **(see illustration)**. Have an assistant depress the brake pedal to prevent the hub from rotating. Discard the bolt, a new one must be used.

4 Remove the front brake disc as described in Chapter 9.

5 Disconnect the wiring plug, undo the bolt and remove the ABS wheel sensor from the hub carrier – refer to Chapter 9 if necessary.

6 Undo the retaining nut, then disconnect the steering track rod end balljoint from the hub carrier. If necessary, use a balljoint separator tool **(see illustrations 19.3a and 19.3b)**.

7 Undo the bolt and remove the lower arm balljoint heat shield.

2.3 Slacken the driveshaft bolt (arrowed)

2.8 Use a balljoint separator tool to detach the lower arm balljoint from the hub carrier

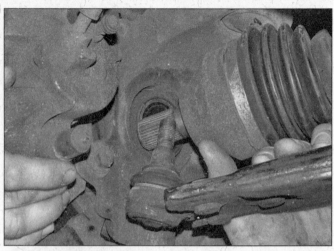

2.10 Lever the control arm downwards, pull the hub carrier outwards, and withdraw the end of the driveshaft from the hub flange

2.11a With the bolt removed, spread the hub carrier slightly using a large screwdriver . . .

2.11b . . . then gently tap the hub carrier downwards from the shock absorber

8 Slacken the nut until it is level with the end of the balljoint shank, then using a balljoint separator tool, detach the suspension control arm balljoint from the hub carrier. Use a 6.0 mm Allen key in the end of the balljoint shank to prevent it from rotating as the nut is slackened (see illustration).

9 Use a stout bar to lever the control arm downwards and move the hub carrier over the end of the balljoint shank. Take care not to damage the balljoint dust cover during and after disconnection.

10 Swivel the hub carrier assembly outwards, and withdraw the driveshaft CV joint from the hub flange (see illustration).

11 Remove the bolt securing the hub carrier to the shock absorber. Insert a flat-bladed tool into the gap and very slightly spread the hub carrier where it clamps onto the lower end of the shock absorber. Tap the hub carrier downwards from the shock absorber at the same time. Note which way the bolt is inserted – from the front (see illustrations).

12 The hub and bearing must now be removed from the hub carrier as an assembly. Due to the design of the assembly, we found it impossible to press the new hub/bearing into the carrier without using Ford special tool No 204-348 (see illustrations). The bearing will be rendered unserviceable by removal and cannot be re-used.

2.12a Using the Ford special tool to support the hub carrier, press the hub flange and bearing out . . .

2.12b . . . then assemble the special tool around the new bearing/flange assembly . . .

2.12c . . . position the hub carrier over the new bearing, and the special tool in place on the hub carrier . . .

2.12d . . . then press the hub carrier . . .

2.12e . . . fully onto the bearing

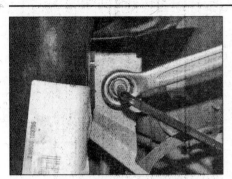

3.7 Use an Allen key to counterhold the anti-roll bar link balljoint nut

3.10a Remove the strut bolts (arrowed) . . .

3.10b . . . and the bulkhead nuts (arrowed)

Refitting

13 Prior to refitting, remove all traces of metal adhesive, rust, oil and dirt from the splines and threads of the driveshaft outer CV joint and the bearing housing mating surface on the hub carrier.

14 The remainder of refitting is a reversal of removal, but observe the following points:

a) *Ensure that the hub and brake disc mating faces are spotlessly clean, and refit the disc with the orientation marks aligned.*

b) *A new driveshaft retaining bolt should be used.*

c) *Ensure that the ABS sensor, and the sensor location in the hub carrier, are perfectly clean before refitting.*

d) *Tighten all nuts and bolts to the specified torque (see Chapter 9 for brake component torque settings).*

3 Front suspension strut – removal and refitting

Removal

1 Loosen the appropriate front wheel nuts, then jack up the front of the car and support it on axle stands (see *Jacking and vehicle support*). Remove the appropriate front roadwheel.

2 Remove the plastic cover from the top of the engine (where fitted).

3 Undo the 2 bolts securing the brake fluid

remote reservoir (where fitted) to the cowl panel.

4 Remove the wiper arms as described in Chapter 12.

5 Release the 5 clips and remove the scuttle cowl panel.

6 Undo the 2 bolts at each end and pull the bulkhead extension panel forwards to release it from the clips release the clips and remove the bulkhead extension panel.

7 Undo the nut securing the anti-roll bar link balljoint to the suspension strut. Use an Allen key to counterhold the balljoint shank **(see illustration)**. A new nut will be required.

8 Unclip the brake hose from the bracket on the suspension strut.

9 Remove the bolt securing the hub carrier to the shock absorber. Insert a flat-bladed tool into the gap and very slightly spread the hub carrier where it clamps onto the lower end of the shock absorber. Tap the hub carrier downwards from the shock absorber at the same time. Note which way the bolt is inserted – from the front **(see illustrations 2.11a and 2.11b)**. A new bolt will be required.

10 Undo the 3 bolts and 2 nuts, and remove the brace between the suspension top mountings and the bulkhead **(see illustrations)**. Have an assistant support the strut assembly. If working on the right-hand side strut access is much easier with the wiper linkage and motor removed as described in Chapter 12.

11 Manoeuvre the strut out from underneath the wheel arch.

Refitting

12 Refitting is a reversal of removal, but tighten all nuts and bolts to the specified torque, using new nuts/bolts where necessary.

4 Front suspension strut – dismantling, inspection and reassembly

⚠ **Warning: Before attempting to dismantle the suspension strut, a suitable tool to hold the coil spring in compression must be obtained. Adjustable coil spring compressors which can be positively secured to the spring coils are readily available, and are recommended for this operation. Any attempt to dismantle the strut without such a tool is likely to result in damage or personal injury.**

Dismantling

1 Remove the strut from the car as described in Section 3.

2 Slacken the strut mounting nut 1/2 a turn, while holding the protruding portion of the piston rod with an Allen key **(see illustration)**. Do not remove the nut at this stage.

3 Fit the spring compressors to the coil springs, and tighten the compressors until the load is taken off the spring seats **(see illustration)**.

4 Remove the piston nut, then make alignment marks where the ends of the spring contact the upper and lower seats **(see illustration)**. Discard the nut – a new one must be fitted.

4.2 Hold the strut piston rod with an Allen key, and slacken the retaining nut

4.3 Fit the compressors to the springs

4.4 Make alignment marks between the spring and seats

4.5 With the springs fully compressed, remove the mounting/seat/bump stop and gaiter, followed by the spring

5 Remove the upper mounting/spring seat, bump stop and gaiter followed by the spring **(see illustration)**. Do not attempt to separate the spring seat from the mounting or the bearing balls will fall out.

Inspection

6 With the strut assembly now completely dismantled, examine all the components for wear, damage or deformation. Renew any of the components as necessary.

7 Examine the shock absorber for signs of fluid leakage, and check the strut piston for signs of pitting along its entire length. Test the operation of the shock absorber, while holding it in an upright position, by moving the piston through a full stroke and then through short strokes of 50 to 100 mm. In both cases, the resistance felt should be smooth and continuous. If the resistance is jerky, or uneven, or if there is any visible sign of wear or damage, renewal is necessary.

5.5a Drill out the 3 rivets . . .

5.7a The colour of the rubber band (arrowed) determines the diameter of the balljoint shank

4.11a Ensure the spring ends are correctly located in their seats

8 If any doubt exists about the condition of the coil spring, gradually release the spring compressor, and check the spring for distortion and signs of cracking. Since no minimum free length is specified by Ford, the only way to check the tension of the spring is to compare it to a new component. Renew the spring if it is damaged or distorted, or if there is any doubt as to its condition.

9 Inspect all other components for signs of damage or deterioration, and renew any that are suspect.

10 If a new shock absorber is being fitted, hold it vertically and pump the piston a few times to prime it.

Reassembly

11 Reassembly is a reversal of dismantling, but ensure that the spring is fully compressed before fitting. Make sure that the spring ends are correctly located in the upper and lower

5.5b . . . and pull the balljoint from the control arm

5.7b Insert the bolts from the underside of the control arm . . .

4.11b Tighten the new piston rod nut to the specified torque

seats, aligning the marks made on removal, then tighten the new shock absorber piston retaining nut and strut mounting bolts to the specified torque **(see illustrations)**.

---

5 Front suspension control arm and balljoint – removal, overhaul and refitting

Balljoint

Removal

1 Loosen the appropriate front wheel nuts. Chock the rear wheels and apply the handbrake, then jack up the front of the vehicle and support it on axle stands (see *Jacking and vehicle support*). Remove the appropriate front roadwheel, then release the fasteners and remove the engine undershield (where fitted).

2 Undo the bolt securing the headlight levelling sensor bracket to the control arm (where fitted).

3 Slacken the nut until it is level with the end of the balljoint shank, then using a balljoint separator tool, detach the suspension control arm balljoint from the hub carrier. Use an Allen key in the end of the balljoint shank to prevent it from rotating as the nut is slackened **(see illustration 2.8)**. Discard the nut – a new one must be fitted.

4 Use a stout bar to lever the control arm downwards and over the end of the balljoint shank. Take care not to damage the balljoint dust cover during and after disconnection.

5 If the original balljoint is being removed, use a drill to remove the 3 balljoint-to-control arm retaining rivets **(see illustrations)**. Pull the balljoint from the control arm.

6 If the balljoint being removed is not the original, undo the 3 bolts and pull the balljoint from the control arm.

Refitting

7 New balljoints may be supplied with suitable retaining bolts. If not, obtain 3 bolts, M10 x 30 mm, and 3 suitable self-locking nuts. Position the new balljoint in the end of the control arm, insert the bolts from underneath, and tighten the nuts to the specified torque. Note that 2 different balljoints may be available. The balljoints are

5.7c . . . and fit the self-locking nuts on the upper side

5.10a Control arm rear mounting bolts (arrowed) . . .

5.10b . . . and front mounting bolt (arrowed)

identical apart from the diameter of the taper of the balljoint shank. The shank with the larger diameter taper is identified by a blue band on the gaiter, and the smaller diameter taper by a yellow band **(see illustrations)**. Select the balljoint that matches the one to be renewed.

8 The remainder of refitting is a reversal of removal. Tighten all fasteners to their specified torque, where given.

Control arm

Removal

9 Proceed as described in Paragraphs 1 to 4.
10 Undo the two bolts securing the control arm rear mounting and the single bolt securing the front mounting and manoeuvre the control arm from under the vehicle **(see illustrations)**. Discard the bolts, new one must be fitted.

Overhaul

11 Thoroughly clean the control arm and the area around the control arm mountings. Inspect the arm for any signs of cracks, damage or distortion, and carefully check the inner pivot bushes for signs of swelling, cracks or deterioration of the rubber.

12 If either bush requires renewal, the work should be entrusted to a Ford dealer or specialist. A hydraulic press and suitable spacers are required to remove and refit the bushes and a setting gauge is needed for accurate positioning of the bushes in the arm.

Refitting

13 Locate the arm in its mountings, and starting at the rear, fit the new mounting bolts finger-tight only. Once all the bolts are in place, tighten the bolts to their specified torque. Do not allow the control arm to move during the tightening procedure.

14 Engage the balljoint shank in the control arm, then tighten the new nut to the specified torque.

15 The remainder of refitting is a reversal of removal. Have the front wheel alignment checked at the earliest opportunity.

---

6 Front anti-roll bar –
   removal and refitting

Removal

1 Loosen the appropriate front wheel nuts. Chock the rear wheels and apply the handbrake, then jack up the front of the vehicle and support it on axle stands (see *Jacking and vehicle support*). Remove the appropriate front roadwheel, then release the fasteners and remove the engine undershield (where fitted) **(see illustration)**

2 Slacken the nut until it is level with the end of the balljoint shank, then using a balljoint separator tool, detach the suspension control arm balljoint from the hub carrier. Use an Allen key in the end of the balljoint shank to prevent

it from rotating as the nut is slackened **(see illustration 2.8)**.

3 Use a stout bar to lever the control arm downwards and over the end of the balljoint shank. Take care not to damage the balljoint dust cover during and after disconnection.

4 Ensure the wheels are in the straight-ahead position, then working under the facia, undo and remove the steering column lower universal joint pinch-bolt **(see illustration 14.8)**. Discard the bolt – a new one must be fitted.

5 Undo the nut each side securing the lower end of the anti-roll bar links to the bar. Use a Torx bit to counterhold the nut.

6 Undo the nut and detach the track rod end balljoint from the hub carrier each side, using a balljoint separator tool as described in Section 19.

7 Undo the bolt at the lower rear of the engine securing the lower torque rod to the bracket on the transmission/engine.

8 Attach splints each side of the exhaust flexible section (two wooden strips secured by cable-tie will suffice) to prevent excessive bending, then undo the bolts/nuts securing the centre exhaust section to the front section.

9 Unhook the exhaust mounting rubbers at the front.

10 Position a sturdy trolley jack beneath, and in contact with, the rear of the subframe.

11 Undo the bolt each side securing the front of the subframe to the body approximately 6 turns **(see illustration)**. Note that new

6.1 Undo the fasteners (arrowed) and remove the engine undershield

6.11 Slacken the subframe front mounting bolt each side (arrowed) about 6 turns

6.12 Undo the subframe rear mounting bolts (arrowed)

6.14 Anti-roll bar clamp bolts (arrowed)

6.15 The anti-roll bar bushes are split to facilitate renewal, and are shaped to fit the bar profile

6.18 Align the front subframe by inserting aligning tools (arrowed) through the holes in the subframe into the corresponding holes in the vehicle body

subframe front mounting bolts will be required for refitting.

12 Undo the bolts each side securing the rear mounting brackets to the subframe and vehicle body, and recover the washers **(see illustration)**. Note that new subframe mounting bolts will be required for refitting.

13 Carefully lower the jack and allow the subframe to drop slightly at the rear, so that the anti-roll bar clamp bolts are accessible. Take care not to damage the power steering hoses.

14 Undo the bolts securing the anti-roll bar clamps on each side of the subframe, and manipulate the anti-roll bar out from under the car **(see illustration)**. Discard the bolts, new ones must be fitted.

15 Examine the anti-roll bar for signs of damage or distortion, and the connecting links

and mounting bushes for signs of deterioration of the rubber. The bushes are split along their length and must be fitted in their original positions **(see illustration)**.

Refitting

16 Manipulate the anti-roll bar into position on the subframe. Fit the new clamp bolts and tighten to the specified torque.

17 Raise the subframe at the rear, fit the rear mounting brackets to the body, and tighten the bolts (new where applicable) hand-tight only at this stage.

18 The alignment of the subframe must be checked by inserting round tools through the holes in the side members. Ford tools (part No 205-316) may be available. Alternatively, using two lengths of wooden dowel, 20 mm in

diameter, and approximately 150 mm in length **(see illustration)**.

19 With the subframe correctly aligned, fit new front subframe mounting bolts, and tighten all subframe bolts to the specified torque.

20 The remainder of refitting is a reversal of removal. Have the front wheel alignment checked at the earliest opportunity.

7 Rear hub bearings – renewal

1 The rear hub bearings cannot be renewed separately, and are supplied with the rear hub as a complete assembly.

2 Remove the brake disc or drum (as applicable) as described in Chapter 9.

3 Undo the bolt and remove the ABS wheel speed sensor from the hub carrier.

4 Undo the four Torx bolts and withdrawn the bearing assembly from the hub carrier.

5 Fit the new assembly to the hub carrier then insert and tighten the bolts to the specified torque.

6 Refit the ABS wheel speed sensor and brake disc or drum as described in Chapter 9.

8 Rear hub carrier/lateral link – removal and refitting

Removal

1 Remove the rear hub as described in the previous Section. On models with disc brakes, unbolt and remove the disc shield.

2 Undo the bolt securing the handbrake cable retaining clip to the lateral link, then unhook the cable from the connecting sleeve. Pull the cable through the lateral link/hub carrier.

3 Unclip the brake hose from the hub carrier.

4 Unclip the handbrake cable from the hub carrier.

5 Release the ABS wheel speed sensor wiring harness from the clips on the lateral link.

6 Remove the relevant rear coil spring as described in Section 10.

7 Fabricate a spacer, 20 mm in diameter and 113 mm long. Unscrew the suspension bump stop, insert the spacer between the lower control arm and the coil spring upper seat, then raise the lower control arm with a trolley jack until the spacer is lightly trapped **(see illustration)**. Ensure the spacer is vertical.

8 Undo the fasteners and remove the air baffle plate from the relevant side **(see illustration)**.

9 Undo the retaining bolt and withdraw the ABS wheel sensor from hub carrier/lateral link. Do not disconnect the wheel sensor wiring plug.

10 Undo the bolts securing the upper control arm and tie rod to the lateral link/hub carrier.

11 Undo the bolt and detach the lower control arm from the lateral link/hub carrier.

8.7 Remove the bump stop (B), and insert the spacer (A) between the lower control arm (D) and the spring upper seat (C)

J46819

8.8 Remove the air baffle plate (arrowed)

8.12 Lateral link/hub carrier front mounting bolts

12 Undo the 2 bolts securing the front mounting to the vehicle body, and withdrawn the lateral link from under the vehicle (**see illustration**).

13 Renewal of the bush at the front of the lateral link requires the use of Ford special tools and a hydraulic press. Therefore it is recommended that this task should be entrusted to a Ford dealer or suitably-equipped specialist.

Refitting

14 Manoeuvre the lateral link into position and tighten the 2 front mounting bolts to the specified torque.

15 Refit the ABS wheel speed sensor wiring harness clips to the link.

16 Position the handbrake cable and refit the cable retaining clip.

17 Refit the upper control arm, lower control arm and tie rod, but don't tighten the bolts yet.

18 Ensure the fabricated spacer (paragraph 7) is still in place between the lower control arm and the spring seat (**see illustration 8.7**).

19 Tighten the upper control arm, lower control arm and tie rod bolts to their specified torque. Remove the spacer, and refit the bump stop.

20 The remainder of refitting is a reversal of removal. Have the rear wheel alignment checked at the earliest opportunity.

9 Rear shock absorber – removal and refitting

Removal

1 Slacken the rear roadwheel nuts, then chock the front wheels then jack up the rear of the vehicle and support it on axle stands (see *Jacking and vehicle support*). Remove the rear wheels.

2 Place a trolley jack under the hub carrier and raise the suspension a little to take the load off the shock absorber.

3 Undo the 2 bolts securing the upper end of the shock absorber to the vehicle body (**see illustration**).

4 Undo the lower mounting bolt, and pull the shock absorber from the hub carrier (**see illustration**).

5 If required, undo the nut and pull the upper mounting from the shock absorber (**see illustration**).

6 Check the condition of the shock absorber and renew as necessary.

Refitting

7 Refitting is a reversal of removal, tightening all nuts and bolts to the specified torques.

10 Rear coil spring – removal and refitting

Removal

1 Slacken the roadwheel nuts, then chock the front wheels and raise the rear of the vehicle. Support it securely on axle stands (see *Jacking and vehicle support*). Remove the roadwheels.

2 Undo the nut securing the anti-roll bar link to the lower control arm (**see illustration 12.2**).

3 Position a trolley jack under the hub carrier, and take the weight.

4 Remove the shock absorber lower mounting bolt.

5 Attach spring compressors to the spring and compress the spring. Ford specify tools No 204-215 and 204-167. Alternative spring compressors may be available (**see illustration**).

6 Remove the trolley jack, and remove the spring.

7 Examine all the components for wear or damage, and renew as necessary.

Refitting

8 Refit the rubbers seats to the control arm and spring, ensuring the ends of the spring locate correctly (**see illustrations**).

9.3 Shock absorber upper mounting bolts (arrowed)

9.4 Shock absorber lower mounting bolt (arrowed)

9.5 Undo the shock absorber upper mounting nut (arrowed)

10.5 Remove the rear springs using spring compressors

10.8a The lug (arrowed) on the underside of the seat must locate in the hole in the arm

10.8b The end of the spring must fit against the stop in the rubber seat (arrowed)

11.4 Tie-rod mounting bolts (arrowed)

11.7a Upper control arm inner bolt (arrowed) . . .

11.7b . . . and outer bolt (arrowed)

11.9a Undo the lower control arm outer bolt (arrowed) . . .

11.9b . . . then mark the position of the eccentric washer (arrowed) and remove the bolt

9 Refit the compressed spring onto the seat in the lower control arm. Rotate the spring until the spring engages correctly in the control arm grooves.

10 Raise the control arm by means of the jack, and engage the upper end of the spring in its recess in the body.

11 Refit the shock absorber lower mounting bolt, securing it in place before removing the jack. Tighten all nuts and bolts to the specified torque.

12 Release and remove the spring compressor.

13 Remainder of refitting is a reversal of removal.

11 Rear suspension link arms – removal and refitting

Removal

1 Loosen the rear wheel bolts. Chock the front

12.2 Rear anti-roll bar-to-control arm bolt (arrowed)

wheels, then jack up the rear of the vehicle and support it on axle stands (see *Jacking and vehicle support*). Remove the appropriate rear roadwheel(s).

Tie-rod

2 Remove the rear spring as described in Section 10.

3 Fabricate a spacer, 20 mm in diameter and 113 mm long. Unscrew the suspension bump stop, insert the spacer between the lower control arm and the coil spring upper seat, then raise the lower control arm with a trolley jack until the spacer is lightly trapped **(see illustration 8.7)**. Ensure the spacer is vertical.

4 Undo the outer and inner bolts, then remove the tie-rod **(see illustration)**. Note that the tie-rod is marked FRONT on one side.

Upper control arm

5 Remove the rear spring as described in Section 10.

12.3 Undo the bolts (arrowed) securing the anti-roll bar clamps

6 Fabricate a spacer, 20 mm in diameter and 113 mm long. Unscrew the suspension bump stop, insert the spacer between the lower control arm and the coil spring upper seat, then raise the lower control arm with a trolley jack until the spacer is lightly trapped **(see illustration 8.7)**. Ensure the spacer is vertical.

7 Undo the outer and inner bolts, then remove the control arm **(see illustrations)**.

Lower control arm

8 Remove the coil spring as described in Section 10.

9 Mark the position of the inner bolt eccentric washer in relation to the arm, then undo the inner and outer control arm bolts, rotate the anti-roll bar approximately 30° and remove the control arm **(see illustrations)**.

10 Examine the condition of the metal-elastic bushes in the control arm. If renewal is necessary, the bushes must be pressed from the arm and new ones pressed into place. This necessitates the use of a hydraulic press. Entrust this task to a Ford dealer or suitably-equipped garage.

Refitting

11 Refitting is essentially a reversal of removal, noting the following points:

a) Tighten all fasteners to their specified torque where given, using a little thread-locking compound.

b) Before tightening any control arm/tie rod mounting bolts, ensure the suspension is in the 'normal' position using the fabricated spacers as described in the removal procedures.

12 Rear anti-roll bar – removal and refitting

Removal

1 Chock the front wheels, then jack up the rear of the vehicle and support it on axle stands (see *Jacking and vehicle support*).

2 Undo the nuts securing the outer ends of the anti-roll bar to the links **(see illustration)**. Take care not to damage the rubber boots.

3 Undo the bolts securing the anti-roll bar clamps to the subframe, manoeuvre the anti-roll bar from under the vehicle **(see illustration)**.

4 Examine the anti-roll bar for signs of damage or distortion, and the connecting links and mounting bushes for signs of deterioration of the rubber. The bushes are split along their length and must be fitted in their original positions.

Refitting

5 Position the anti-roll bar, then fit and tighten the bolts securing the anti-roll bar clamps to the subframe.

6 Refit the anti-roll bar links and tighten the nuts to the specified torque, using a Torx bit to counterhold the nuts.

7 The remainder of refitting is a reversal of removal.

13 Steering wheel –
removal and refitting

⚠️ **Warning: Handle the airbag unit with extreme care as a precaution against personal injury, and always hold it with the cover facing away from the body. If in doubt concerning any proposed work involving the airbag unit or its control circuitry, consult a Ford dealer.**

Removal

1 Drive the car forwards and park it with the front wheels in the straight-ahead position.

2 Remove the driver's airbag as described in Chapter 12. Secure the rotary contact unit in place using tape to prevent any rotation.

3 Disconnect the wiring plug at the top of the steering wheel aperture.

4 Undo the steering wheel centre retaining bolt **(see illustration)**.

5 On vehicles built up to 01/2005, if a new steering wheel is being fitted, but the original driver's airbag is to be used, undo the bolt and remove the earth spring from the wheel. This must be fitted to the new wheel.

6 Make alignment marks between the steering wheel centre and the column shaft, then lift the steering wheel off the column shaft, and feed the wiring and plastic strip through the hole in the wheel.

Refitting

7 Ensure that the front wheels are still in the straight-ahead position.

14.5 Undo the bolts (arrowed) securing the column lower shroud

8 On vehicles built up to 01/2005, if a new steering wheel is being fitted, but the original driver's airbag is to be used, undo the bolt and remove the earth cable from the new wheel, then attach the old earth spring.

9 Check the airbag rotary contact unit is still aligned. Refer to Chapter 12 if necessary. Remove the securing tape.

10 Feed the wiring through the hole in the steering wheel, then engage the wheel with the steering column shaft. Ensure that the marks made on removal are aligned, and that the pegs on the contact reel engage with the recesses on the steering wheel hub.

11 Refit the steering wheel retaining bolt, and tighten it to the specified torque.

12 Refit the airbag unit to the steering wheel as described in Chapter 12.

14 Steering column –
removal and refitting

Removal

1 Disconnect the battery negative lead – see Chapter 5.

2 Fully extend the steering column, then on models with an audio control switch fitted to the column shroud, release the locking tang, pull the switch from place and disconnect the wiring plug **(see illustration)**.

3 Undo the fasteners and remove the lower facia panel on the driver's side.

4 Turn the steering wheel for access, then release the retaining clips and remove

14.2 Release the clip and pull the audio control switch from the column shroud

14.8 Steering column lower pinch-bolt (arrowed)

13.4 Steering wheel retaining bolt (arrowed)

the steering column upper shroud **(see illustration)**. Turn the steering wheel back to the straight-ahead position.

5 Undo the 2 retaining bolts, and remove the steering column lower shroud **(see illustration)**. Release the steering column locking lever to remove the shroud completely.

6 Remove the steering wheel as described in Section 13.

7 Note their fitted positions and routing, then disconnect the various column wiring plugs and release the loom retaining clips.

8 Undo the steering column lower pinch-bolt and pull the joint upwards from the pinion **(see illustration)**. Ensure the column adjustment lever is released before detaching the joint from the pinion. Discard the pinch-bolt, a new one must be fitted.

9 Undo the 4 retaining bolts and manoeuvre the column from the vehicle **(see illustration)**. Discard the bolts, new ones must be fitted.

14.4 Release the clip each side securing the column upper shroud to the lower

14.9 Steering column upper mounting bolts (arrowed)

14.10 Drill out the security bolt (arrowed) each side

10 If required, drill out the security bolts, and remove the steering lock from the column **(see illustration)**. No further dismantling of the assembly is recommended.

Refitting

11 Refitting is a reversal of removal, bearing in mind the following points:

a) *Lubricate universal joint splines with grease before engaging the steering column.*

b) *When fitting the new column retaining bolts, the shortest bolts are nearest the bulkhead.*

c) *Use a new universal joint pinch-bolt.*

d) *If refitting the steering lock, tighten the new security bolts until their heads snap off.*

e) *If the steering column has been rotated, or the front wheels turned from straight-ahead, reset the airbag contact reel as described in Chapter 12.*

15 Steering rack – removal and refitting

Removal

1 Drive the car forwards and park it with the steering wheels in the straight-ahead position. Remove the ignition key to lock the steering in this position.

2 Remove the lower facia panel (where fitted) on the driver's side.

3 Remove the steering column lower gaiter (where fitted), then undo the pinch-bolt

and pull the joint upwards from the pinion **(see illustration 14.8)**. Ensure the column adjustment lever is released before detaching the joint from the pinion. Discard the pinch-bolt, a new one must be fitted.

4 Loosen the front wheel nuts. Chock the rear wheels then jack up the front of the vehicle and support it on axle stands (see *Jacking and vehicle support*). Remove both front roadwheels.

5 Undo the fasteners and remove the engine undershield (where fitted) **(see illustration 6.1)**.

6 Undo the bolt securing the headlight levelling sensor bracket to the lower control arm (where applicable).

7 On some models, disconnect the steering angle sensor wiring plug (located at the steering column pinion in the engine compartment).

8 Attach splints each side of the exhaust flexible section (two wooden strips secured by cable-tie will suffice) to prevent excessive bending, then undo the bolts/nuts securing the centre exhaust section to the front section.

9 Unhook the exhaust mounting rubbers at the front.

10 Slacken the nut until it is level with the end of the balljoint shank, then using a balljoint separator tool, detach the suspension control arm balljoint from the hub carrier. Use an Allen key in the end of the balljoint shank to prevent it from rotating as the nut is slackened **(see illustration 2.8)**.

11 Use a stout bar to lever the control arm downwards and over the end of the balljoint shank. Take care not to damage the balljoint dust cover during and after disconnection.

12 Undo the nut each side securing the lower end of the anti-roll bar links to the bar. Use a Torx bit to counterhold the nut.

13 Undo the nut and detach the track rod end balljoint from the hub carrier each side, using a balljoint separator tool as described in Section 19.

14 Undo the bolt at the lower rear of the engine securing the lower torque rod to the bracket on the transmission/engine.

15 Remove the bolt, unclip the power steering pipes from the steering rack, then undo the bolt, rotate the clamp plate and disconnect the pipes from the steering rack pinion **(see illustration)**.

16 Position a sturdy trolley jack beneath, and in contact with, the rear of the subframe.

17 Undo the bolt each side securing the front of the subframe **(see illustration 6.11)**. Note that new subframe front mounting bolts will be required for refitting.

18 Undo the bolts each side securing the rear mounting brackets to the subframe and vehicle body, and recover the washers **(see illustration 6.12)**. Note that new subframe mounting bolts will be required for refitting.

19 Carefully lower the jack and subframe. Take care not to damage the power steering hoses.

20 Undo the bolts and remove the anti-roll bar **(see illustration 6.14)**. Discard the bolts – new ones must be fitted.

21 Undo the bolts and remove the steering rack heat shield **(see illustration)**.

22 Undo the retaining bolts, and lift the steering rack from the subframe **(see illustration)**.

Refitting

23 Manipulate the steering rack into position and tighten the bolts to the specified torque.

24 Refit the steering rack heat shield and tighten the bolts securely.

25 Refit the anti-roll bar to the subframe and tighten the new bolts to the specified torque.

26 Ensure the steering rack pinion bulkhead seal is in place, then raise the subframe into position.

27 Fit the subframe rear mounting brackets to the body, then insert the new front and rear subframe mounting bolts. Only hand-tighten them at this stage.

28 The alignment of the subframe must be checked by inserting round tools though the holes in the side members. Ford tools (part No 205-316) may be available. Alternatively, using two lengths of wooden dowel, 20 mm in diameter, and approximately 150 mm in length **(see illustration 6.18)**.

29 With the subframe correctly aligned, tighten all subframe bolts to the specified torque.

30 Engage the steering shaft universal joint with the pinion shaft, and push it fully home.

31 Fit the new universal joint pinch-bolt and tighten it to the specified torque.

32 Refit the fluid pipes to the steering rack

15.15 Steering rack pipes clamp bolts (arrowed)

15.21 Steering rack heat shield bolts (arrowed)

15.22 Steering rack retaining bolts (arrowed)

using new O-ring seals, and tighten the retaining bolt securely.

33 The remainder of refitting is a reversal of removal, noting the following points:

a) *Tighten all fasteners to their specified torque where given.*

b) *Bleed the power steering system as described in Section 17.*

c) *Have the front wheel alignment checked at the earliest opportunity.*

16 Steering rack gaiters – renewal

1 Remove the track rod end on the side concerned as described in Section 19. Unscrew the locknut from the track rod.

2 Release the two clips and peel off the gaiter. Disconnect the breather hose as the gaiter is withdrawn **(see illustration)**

3 Clean out any dirt and grit from the inner end of the track rod and (when accessible) the rack.

4 Wrap insulating tape around the track rod threads to protect the new gaiter whilst installing.

5 Refit the track rod end locknut.

6 Refit the track rod end as described in Section 19.

17 Steering system – bleeding

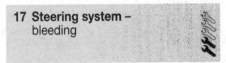

Belt-driven pump

1 Wipe clean the area around the reservoir filler neck, and unscrew the filler cap/dipstick from the reservoir.

2 If topping-up is necessary, use clean fluid of the specified type (see *Weekly checks*). Check for leaks if frequent topping-up is required. Do not run the engine without fluid in the reservoir.

3 After component renewal, or if the fluid level has been allowed to fall so low that air has entered the hydraulic system, bleeding must be carried out as follows.

4 Fill the reservoir to the MAX mark as described in *Weekly checks*. Note that the power steering fluid should be cold, and poured slowly to minimise aeration.

5 Raise the front of the vehicle until the tyres are just clear of the ground, then support the vehicle securely on axle stands (see *Jacking and vehicle support*).

6 Without starting the engine, slowly turn the steering wheel from lock to lock, and add power steering fluid until the fluid level ceases to drop.

7 Start the engine and turn the steering wheel repeatedly from full lock one way, to full lock the other way, then top-up the fluid level as necessary.

8 Turn the steering wheel slowly to the full right lock position, and hold it there for 2 seconds.

16.2 Steering rack gaiter clips and breather hose (arrowed) – shown with the rack removed for clarity

9 Now turn the steering wheel slowly to the full left lock position, and hold it there for 2 seconds.

10 Top-up the fluid level again if necessary.

11 Repeat paragraphs 8 and 9 until the steering operation is satisfactory.

12 If the steering is still noisy (indicating air in the system), leave the vehicle overnight, and then try again. If this still fails to remove the air, the vehicle must be taken to a Ford dealer or suitably-equipped specialist, who will be able to apply a vacuum to the reservoir using special tools.

13 On completion, stop the engine, lower the vehicle to the ground, and recheck the fluid level.

Electro-Hydraulic power steering

14 Remove the right-hand headlight as described in Chapter 12.

15 Wipe clean the area around the reservoir filler neck, and unscrew the filler cap/dipstick from the reservoir.

16 If topping-up is necessary, use clean fluid of the specified type (see *Weekly checks*). Check for leaks if frequent topping-up is required. Do not run the engine without fluid in the reservoir.

17 After component renewal, or if the fluid level has been allowed to fall so low that air has entered the hydraulic system, bleeding must be carried out as follows.

18 Fill the reservoir to the MAX mark as described in *Weekly checks*. Note that the power steering fluid should be cold, and

18.6 Power steering pump fluid supply hose (1) and lower mounting bolts (2)

poured slowly into the reservoir to minimise aeration.

19 Raise the front of the vehicle until the tyres are just clear of the ground, then support the vehicle securely on axle stands (see *Jacking and vehicle support*).

20 Start the engine, slowly turn the steering wheel from lock to lock, and add power steering fluid until the fluid level ceases to drop.

21 Switch off the engine and check the fluid level. Top-up if necessary.

22 Start the engine and turn the steering from lock to lock. If excessive noise is still apparent (indicating air in the system), leave the vehicle overnight, then try again.

23 If the steering is still noisy, it may be that the pump is faulty. Consult a Ford dealer or specialist.

24 On completion, stop the engine, lower the vehicle to the ground, and recheck the fluid level.

18 Power steering pump – removal and refitting

Removal

Belt-driven pump

1 Remove the auxiliary drivebelt as described in Chapter 1.

2 Jack up the front of the vehicle and support it securely on axle stands (see *Jacking and vehicle support*).

3 Undo the fasteners and remove the splash shield under the radiator.

4 Undo the bolts and remove the right-hand wheel arch liner.

5 On models with a fluid cooler, release the clamp and disconnect the hose from the power steering cooler to the pump. Be prepared for fluid spillage. Plug the openings to prevent contamination.

6 On models without a fluid cooler, release the clamp and disconnect the hose from the power steering reservoir to the pump **(see illustration)**. Be prepared for fluid spillage. Plug the openings to prevent contamination.

7 Disconnect the fluid supply hose from the pump. Be prepared for fluid spillage. Plug the openings to prevent contamination.

8 Undo the 2 lower mounting bolts from the pump **(see illustration 18.6)**.

9 Remove the alternator as described in Chapter 5.

10 Disconnect the power steering pump pressure switch wiring plug.

11 Slacken the power steering pump pressure pipe union nut.

12 Undo the upper mounting bolts and remove the pump. Disconnect the pressure pipe as the pump is withdrawn.

Electro-Hydraulic power steering

Note: *If a new EHPS pump/module is to be fitted, the relevant programme code needs*

18.14 Disconnect the wiring plugs from the EHPS module

18.19 Disconnect the fluid return and pressure pipes

18.21 EHPS module retaining bolts (arrowed)

to be extracted and reloaded to the module. Entrust this task to a Ford dealer or suitably-equipped specialist.

13 Remove the right-hand side headlight as described in Chapter 12.

14 Disconnect the pump wiring plugs **(see illustration)**.

15 Jack up the front of the vehicle and support it securely on axle stands (see *Jacking and vehicle support*).

16 Undo the fasteners and remove the splash shield under the radiator and the engine undershield.

17 Undo the Torx bolts and remove the right-hand wheel arch liner.

18 Use a syringe to extract as much fluid as possible from the pump reservoir.

19 Undo the union nut and disconnect the pump pressure pipe **(see illustration)**. Be prepared for fluid spillage. Plug the openings to prevent contamination.

20 Release the clamp and disconnect the fluid return hose from the pump **(see illustration 18.19)**. Be prepared for fluid spillage. Plug the openings to prevent contamination.

21 Undo the 3 bolts and remove the assembly **(see illustration)**.

22 No individual parts are available. If faulty, exchange units are available from Ford.

Refitting

23 Refitting is a reversal of removal, bearing in mind the following points:

a) Use a new O-ring on pressure pipe union.

b) Tighten the mounting bolts to the specified torque.

c) If a new EHPS has been fitted, suitable software will need to be downloaded from Ford. Consult your local dealer or specialist.

d) Refill/top-up the fluid reservoir, and bleed the system as described in Section 17.

19 Track rod end – removal and refitting

Removal

1 Loosen the appropriate front wheel nuts. Chock the rear wheels, then jack up the front of the vehicle and support it on axle stands (see *Jacking and vehicle support*). Remove the appropriate front roadwheel.

2 Counterhold the track rod, and slacken the track rod end locknut by half a turn **(see illustration)**. If the locknut is now left in this position, it will act as a further guide for refitting.

3 Unscrew the track rod end balljoint nut, using an Allen key to counterhold the balljoint shank. Separate the balljoint from the steering arm with a proprietary balljoint separator, then remove the nut and disengage the balljoint from the arm **(see illustrations)**.

4 Unscrew the track rod end from the track rod, counting the number of turns needed to remove it. Make a note of the number of turns, so that the tracking can be reset (or at least approximated) on refitting.

Refitting

5 Screw the track rod end onto the track rod by the same number of turns noted during removal.

6 Engage the balljoint in the steering arm. Fit a new nut and tighten it to the specified torque.

7 Counterhold the track rod and tighten the locknut.

8 Refit the front wheel, lower the car and tighten the wheel bolts in a diagonal sequence to the specified torque.

9 Have the front wheel toe-in (tracking) checked and adjusted by a Ford dealer or suitably-equipped repairer.

20 Wheel alignment and steering angles – general information

1 A car's steering and suspension geometry is defined in four basic settings – all angles are expressed in degrees (toe settings are also expressed as a measurement); the relevant settings are camber, castor, steering axis inclination, and toe setting **(see illustration)**. On the models covered by this manual, only the front and rear wheel toe settings are adjustable.

2 Camber is the angle at which the front wheels are set from the vertical when viewed from the front or rear of the car. Negative camber is the amount (in degrees) that the wheels are tilted inward at the top from the vertical.

19.2 Slacken the track rod end locknut (arrowed)

19.3a Use an Allen key to counterhold the track rod end balljoint shank

19.3b Use a separator tool to detach the track rod end from the hub carrier

3 The front camber angle is adjusted by slackening the steering knuckle-to-suspension strut mounting bolts and repositioning the hub carrier assemblies as necessary.

4 Castor is the angle between the steering axis and a vertical line when viewed from each side of the car. Positive castor is when the steering axis is inclined rearward at the top.

5 Steering axis inclination is the angle (when viewed from the front of the vehicle) between the vertical and an imaginary line drawn through the front suspension strut upper mounting and the control arm balljoint.

6 Toe setting is the amount by which the distance between the front inside edges of the roadwheels (measured at hub height) differs from the diametrically opposite distance measured between the rear inside edges of the roadwheels. Toe-in is when the roadwheels point inwards, towards each other at the front, while toe-out is when they splay outwards from each other at the front.

7 The front wheel toe setting is adjusted by altering the length of the steering track rods on both sides. This adjustment is normally referred to as the tracking.

8 The rear wheel toe setting is adjusted by rotating the lateral link front mounting bolt in the chassis. The bolt incorporates an eccentric

washer, and the pivot point for the link varies as the bolt is rotated.

9 All other suspension and steering angles are set during manufacture, and no adjustment is possible. It can be assumed, therefore, that unless the vehicle has suffered accident damage, all the preset angles will be correct.

10 Special optical measuring equipment is necessary to accurately check and adjust the front and rear toe settings and front camber angles, and this work should be carried out by a Ford dealer or similar expert. Most tyre fitting centres have the expertise and equipment to carry out at least a front wheel toe setting (tracking) check for a nominal charge.

21 Front subframe –
removal and refitting

1 The front subframe removal and refitting is described within the steering rack removal and refitting procedure, as described in Section 15. If the subframe is to be removed as part of another procedure (eg, catalytic converter renewal), the steering rack and anti-roll bar can be left in place on the subframe.

20.1 Front wheel geometry

Chapter 11
Bodywork and fittings

Contents

Section number

Body side-trim mouldings and adhesive emblems – removal and
  refitting 22
Bonnet – removal, refitting and adjustment 8
Bonnet lock – removal, refitting and adjustment 9
Bumpers – removal and refitting 6
Central locking system – testing, reprogramming, removal and
  refitting 20
Centre console – removal and refitting. 27
Door – removal and refitting. 14
Door handle and lock components – removal and refitting 13
Door inner trim panel – removal and refitting 10
Door window glass – removal and refitting 11
Door window regulator – removal and refitting 12
Exterior mirror and glass – removal and refitting 15
Facia – removal and refitting 30
General information 1
Glovebox – removal and refitting 29

Section number

Interior mirror – removal and refitting. 16
Interior trim panels – removal and refitting 26
Maintenance – bodywork and underframe. 2
Maintenance – upholstery and carpets 3
Major body damage – repair 5
Minor body damage – repair 4
Overhead console – removal and refitting 28
Radiator grille – removal and refitting. 7
Seat belts – removal and refitting. 25
Seats – removal and refitting 24
Sunroof – general information and adjustment 23
Support struts – removal and refitting 18
Tailgate – removal and refitting. 17
Tailgate lock components – removal and refitting 19
Wheel arch liner – removal and refitting. 31
Windscreen and fixed windows – removal and refitting. 21

Degrees of difficulty

Easy, suitable for novice with little experience	Fairly easy, suitable for beginner with some experience	Fairly difficult, suitable for competent DIY mechanic	Difficult, suitable for experienced DIY mechanic	Very difficult, suitable for expert DIY or professional

Specifications

Torque wrench settings

	Nm	lbf ft
Bumper bar mounting:		
Front bolts	25	18
Rear bolts	20	15
Front seat mounting bolts	35	26
Passenger's airbag module lower support bracket:		
Bolts	9	7
Nuts	7	5
Rear seat backrest catch retaining bolts	23	17
Rear seat hinge	35	26
Seat belt mounting nuts and bolts:		
Front inertia reel bolt.	38	28
Front lower anchorage	38	28
Front seat belt buckle stake	47	35
Front seat bolts shoulder height adjuster.	35	26
Front upper anchorage.	38	28
Rear centre belt buckle stalk	55	41
Rear centre inertia reel	35	26
Rear centre lower anchorage	55	41
Rear outer inertia reel	40	30
Rear outer lower anchorage.	38	28

1 General information

The bodyshell and underframe on all models feature variable thickness steel. Achieved by laser-welded technology, used to join steel panels of different gauges. This gives a stiffer structure, with mounting points being more rigid, which gives an improved crash performance.

An additional safety crossmember is incorporated between the A-pillars in the upper area of the bulkhead, and the facia and steering column are secured to it. The lower bulkhead area is reinforced by additional systems of members connected to the front of the vehicle. The body side rocker panels (sills) have been divided along the length of the vehicle by internal reinforcement, this functions like a double tube which increases its strength. All doors are reinforced and incorporate side impact protection, which is secured in the door structure. There are additional impact absorbers to the front and rear of the vehicle, behind the bumper assemblies.

All sheet metal surfaces which are prone to corrosion are galvanised. The painting process includes a base colour which closely matches the final topcoat, so that any stone damage is not as noticeable. The front wings are of a bolt-on type to ease their renewal if required.

Automatic seat belts are fitted to all models, and the front seat safety belts are equipped with a pyrotechnic pretension seat belt buckle, which is attached to the seat frame of each front seat. In the event of a serious front impact, the system is triggered and pulls the stalk buckle downwards to tension the seat belt. It is not possible to reset the tensioner once fired, and it must therefore be renewed. The tensioners are fired by an explosive charge similar to that used in the airbag, and are triggered via the airbag control module. The safety belt retractor, which is fitted in the base of the B-pillar, has a device to control the seat belt, if the deceleration force is enough to activate the airbags.

In the UK, central locking is standard on all models. In other countries, it is available on certain models only. Where double-locking is fitted, the lock mechanism is disconnected (when the system is in use) from the interior door handles, making it impossible to open any of the doors or the tailgate from inside the vehicle. This means that, even if a thief should break a side window, he will not be able to open the door using the interior handle. In the event of a serious accident, a crash sensor unlocks all doors if they were previously locked.

Many of the procedures in this Chapter require the battery to be disconnected; refer to Chapter 5.

2 Maintenance – bodywork and underframe

The general condition of a vehicle's bodywork is the one thing that significantly affects its value. Maintenance is easy, but needs to be regular. Neglect, particularly after minor damage, can lead quickly to further deterioration and costly repair bills. It is important also to keep watch on those parts of the vehicle not immediately visible, for instance the underside, inside all the wheel arches, and the lower part of the engine compartment.

The basic maintenance routine for the bodywork is washing – preferably with a lot of water, from a hose. This will remove all the loose solids which may have stuck to the vehicle. It is important to flush these off in such a way as to prevent grit from scratching the finish. The wheel arches and underframe need washing in the same way, to remove any accumulated mud, which will retain moisture and tend to encourage rust. Paradoxically enough, the best time to clean the underframe and wheel arches is in wet weather, when the mud is thoroughly wet and soft. In very wet weather, the underframe is usually cleaned of large accumulations automatically, and this is a good time for inspection.

Periodically, except on vehicles with a wax-based underbody protective coating, it is a good idea to have the whole of the underframe of the vehicle steam-cleaned, engine compartment included, so that a thorough inspection can be carried out to see what minor repairs and renovations are necessary. Steam-cleaning is available at many garages, and is necessary for the removal of the accumulation of oily grime, which sometimes is allowed to become thick in certain areas. If steam-cleaning facilities are not available, there are some excellent grease solvents available which can be brush-applied; the dirt can then be simply hosed off. Note that these methods should not be used on vehicles with wax-based underbody protective coating, or the coating will be removed. Such vehicles should be inspected annually, preferably just prior to Winter, when the underbody should be washed down, and any damage to the wax coating repaired. Ideally, a completely fresh coat should be applied. It would also be worth considering the use of such wax-based protection for injection into door panels, sills, box sections, etc, as an additional safeguard against rust damage, where such protection is not provided by the vehicle manufacturer.

After washing paintwork, wipe off with a chamois leather to give an unspotted clear finish. A coat of clear protective wax polish will give added protection against chemical pollutants in the air. If the paintwork sheen has dulled or oxidised, use a cleaner/polisher combination to restore the brilliance of the shine. This requires a little effort, but such dulling is usually caused because regular washing has been neglected. Care needs to be taken with metallic paintwork, as special non-abrasive cleaner/polisher is required to avoid damage to the finish. Always check that the door and ventilator opening drain holes and pipes are completely clear, so that water can be drained out. Brightwork should be treated in the same way as paintwork. Windscreens and windows can be kept clear of the smeary film which often appears, by the use of proprietary glass cleaner. Never use any form of wax or other body or chromium polish on glass.

3 Maintenance – upholstery and carpets

Mats and carpets should be brushed or vacuum-cleaned regularly, to keep them free of grit. If they are badly stained, remove them from the vehicle for scrubbing or sponging, and make quite sure they are dry before refitting. Seats and interior trim panels can be kept clean by wiping with a damp cloth. If they do become stained (which can be more apparent on light-coloured upholstery), use a little liquid detergent and a soft nail brush to scour the grime out of the grain of the material. Do not forget to keep the headlining clean in the same way as the upholstery. When using liquid cleaners inside the vehicle, do not over-wet the surfaces being cleaned. Excessive damp could get into the seams and padded interior, causing stains, offensive odours or even rot.

Caution: If the inside of the vehicle gets wet accidentally, it is worthwhile taking some trouble to dry it out properly, particularly where carpets are involved. Do not leave oil or electric heaters inside the vehicle for this purpose.

4 Minor body damage – repair

Minor scratches

If the scratch is very superficial, and does not penetrate to the metal of the bodywork, repair is very simple. Lightly rub the area of the scratch with a paintwork renovator, or a very fine cutting paste, to remove loose paint from the scratch, and to clear the surrounding bodywork of wax polish. Rinse the area with clean water.

Apply touch-up paint to the scratch using a fine paint brush; continue to apply fine layers of paint until the surface of the paint in the scratch is level with the surrounding paintwork. Allow the new paint at least two weeks to harden, then blend it into the surrounding paintwork by rubbing the scratch area with a paintwork renovator or a very fine cutting paste. Finally, apply wax polish.

Where the scratch has penetrated right through to the metal of the bodywork, causing the metal to rust, a different repair technique is required. Remove any loose rust from the bottom of the scratch with a penknife, then apply rust-inhibiting paint to prevent the formation of rust in the future. Using a rubber or nylon applicator, fill the scratch with bodystopper paste. If required, this paste can be mixed with cellulose thinners to provide a very thin paste which is ideal for filling narrow scratches. Before the stopper-paste in the scratch hardens, wrap a piece of smooth cotton rag around the top of a finger. Dip the finger in cellulose thinners, and quickly sweep it across the surface of the stopper-paste in the scratch; this will ensure that the surface of the stopper-paste is slightly hollowed. The scratch can now be painted over as described earlier in this Section.

Dents

When deep denting of the vehicle's bodywork has taken place, the first task is to pull the dent out, until the affected bodywork almost attains its original shape. There is little point in trying to restore the original shape completely, as the metal in the damaged area will have stretched on impact, and cannot be reshaped fully to its original contour. It is better to bring the level of the dent up to a point which is about 3 mm below the level of the surrounding bodywork. In cases where the dent is very shallow anyway, it is not worth trying to pull it out at all. If the underside of the dent is accessible, it can be hammered out gently from behind, using a mallet with a wooden or plastic head. Whilst doing this, hold a suitable block of wood firmly against the outside of the panel, to absorb the impact from the hammer blows and thus prevent a large area of the bodywork from being 'belled-out'.

Should the dent be in a section of the bodywork which has a double skin, or some other factor making it inaccessible from behind, a different technique is called for. Drill several small holes through the metal inside the area – particularly in the deeper section. Then screw long self-tapping screws into the holes, just sufficiently for them to gain a good purchase in the metal. Now the dent can be pulled out by pulling on the protruding heads of the screws with a pair of pliers.

The next stage of the repair is the removal of the paint from the damaged area, and from an inch or so of the surrounding 'sound' bodywork. This is accomplished most easily by using a wire brush or abrasive pad on a power drill, although it can be done just as effectively by hand, using sheets of abrasive paper. To complete the preparation for filling, score the surface of the bare metal with a screwdriver or the tang of a file, or alternatively, drill small holes in the affected area. This will provide a really good 'key' for the filler paste.

To complete the repair, see the Section on filling and respraying.

Rust holes or gashes

Remove all paint from the affected area, and from an inch or so of the surrounding 'sound' bodywork, using an abrasive pad or a wire brush on a power drill. If these are not available, a few sheets of abrasive paper will do the job most effectively. With the paint removed, you will be able to judge the severity of the corrosion, and therefore decide whether to renew the whole panel (if this is possible) or to repair the affected area. New body panels are not as expensive as most people think, and it is often quicker and more satisfactory to fit a new panel than to attempt to repair large areas of corrosion.

Remove all fittings from the affected area, except those which will act as a guide to the original shape of the damaged bodywork (e.g. headlight shells etc). Then, using tin snips or a hacksaw blade, remove all loose metal and any other metal badly affected by corrosion. Hammer the edges of the hole inwards, in order to create a slight depression for the filler paste.

Wire-brush the affected area to remove the powdery rust from the surface of the remaining metal. Paint the affected area with rust-inhibiting paint, if the back of the rusted area is accessible, treat this also.

Before filling can take place, it will be necessary to block the hole in some way. This can be achieved by the use of aluminium or plastic mesh, or aluminium tape.

Aluminium or plastic mesh, or glass-fibre matting, is probably the best material to use for a large hole. Cut a piece to the approximate size and shape of the hole to be filled, then position it in the hole so that its edges are below the level of the surrounding bodywork. It can be retained in position by several blobs of filler paste around its periphery.

Aluminium tape should be used for small or very narrow holes. Pull a piece off the roll, trim it to the approximate size and shape required, then pull off the backing paper (if used) and stick the tape over the hole; it can be overlapped if the thickness of one piece is insufficient. Burnish down the edges of the tape with the handle of a screwdriver or similar, to ensure that the tape is securely attached to the metal underneath.

Filling and respraying

Before using this Section, see the Sections on dent, deep scratch, rust holes and gash repairs.

Many types of bodyfiller are available, but generally speaking, those proprietary kits which contain a tin of filler paste and a tube of resin hardener are best for this type of repair. A wide, flexible plastic or nylon applicator will be found invaluable for imparting a smooth and well-contoured finish to the surface of the filler.

Mix up a little filler on a clean piece of card or board – measure the hardener carefully (follow the maker's instructions on the pack), otherwise the filler will set too rapidly or too slowly. Using the applicator, apply the filler paste to the prepared area; draw the applicator across the surface of the filler to achieve the correct contour and to level the surface. As soon as a contour that approximates to the correct one is achieved, stop working the paste – if you carry on too long, the paste will become sticky and begin to 'pick-up' on the applicator. Continue to add thin layers of filler paste at 20-minute intervals, until the level of the filler is just proud of the surrounding bodywork.

Once the filler has hardened, the excess can be removed using a metal plane or file. From then on, progressively-finer grades of abrasive paper should be used, starting with a 40-grade production paper, and finishing with a 400-grade wet-and-dry paper. Always wrap the abrasive paper around a flat rubber, cork, or wooden block – otherwise the surface of the filler will not be completely flat. During the smoothing of the filler surface, the wet-and-dry paper should be periodically rinsed in water. This will ensure that a very smooth finish is imparted to the filler at the final stage.

At this stage, the 'dent' should be surrounded by a ring of bare metal, which in turn should be encircled by the finely 'feathered' edge of the good paintwork. Rinse the repair area with clean water, until all of the dust produced by the rubbing-down operation has gone.

Spray the whole area with a light coat of primer – this will show up any imperfections in the surface of the filler. Repair these imperfections with fresh filler paste or bodystopper, and once more smooth the surface with abrasive paper. Repeat this spray-and-repair procedure until you are satisfied that the surface of the filler, and the feathered edge of the paintwork, are perfect. Clean the repair area with clean water, and allow to dry fully.

The repair area is now ready for final spraying. Paint spraying must be carried out in a warm, dry, windless and dust-free atmosphere. This condition can be created artificially if you have access to a large indoor working area, but if you are forced to work in the open, you will have to pick your day very carefully. If you are working indoors, dousing the floor in the work area with water will help to settle the dust which would otherwise be in the atmosphere. If the repair area is confined to one body panel, mask off the surrounding panels; this will help to minimise the effects of a slight mis-match in paint colours. Bodywork fittings (e.g. chrome strips, door handles etc) will also need to be masked off. Use genuine masking tape, and several thicknesses of newspaper, for the masking operations.

Before commencing to spray, agitate the aerosol can thoroughly, then spray a test area (an old tin, or similar) until the technique is mastered. Cover the repair area with a thick coat of primer; the thickness should be built up

6.4a Undo the bolts at the front of the wheel arch liner (arrowed) . . .

6.4b . . . and at the rear

using several thin layers of paint, rather than one thick one. Using 400-grade wet-and-dry paper, rub down the surface of the primer until it is really smooth. While doing this, the work area should be thoroughly doused with water, and the wet-and-dry paper periodically rinsed in water. Allow to dry before spraying on more paint.

Spray on the top coat, again building up the thickness by using several thin layers of paint. Start spraying at one edge of the repair area, and then, using a side-to-side motion, work until the whole repair area and about 2 inches of the surrounding original paintwork is covered. Remove all masking material 10 to 15 minutes after spraying on the final coat of paint.

Allow the new paint at least two weeks to harden, then, using a paintwork renovator, or a very fine cutting paste, blend the edges of the paint into the existing paintwork. Finally, apply wax polish.

Plastic components

With the use of more and more plastic body components by the vehicle manufacturers (e.g. bumpers. spoilers, and in some cases major body panels), rectification of more serious damage to such items has become a matter of either entrusting repair work to a specialist in this field, or renewing complete components. Repair of such damage by the DIY owner is not really feasible, owing to the cost of the equipment and materials required for effecting such repairs. The basic technique involves making a groove along the line of the crack in the plastic, using a

rotary burr in a power drill. The damaged part is then welded back together, using a hot-air gun to heat up and fuse a plastic filler rod into the groove. Any excess plastic is then removed, and the area rubbed down to a smooth finish. It is important that a filler rod of the correct plastic is used, as body components can be made of a variety of different types (e.g. polycarbonate, ABS, polypropylene).

Damage of a less serious nature (abrasions, minor cracks etc) can be repaired by the DIY owner using a two-part epoxy filler repair material. Once mixed in equal proportions, this is used in similar fashion to the bodywork filler used on metal panels. The filler is usually cured in twenty to thirty minutes, ready for sanding and painting.

If the owner is renewing a complete component himself, or if he has repaired it with epoxy filler, he will be left with the problem of finding a suitable paint for finishing which is compatible with the type of plastic used. At one time, the use of a universal paint was not possible, owing to the complex range of plastics encountered in body component applications. Standard paints, generally speaking, will not bond to plastic or rubber satisfactorily. However, it is now possible to obtain a plastic body parts finishing kit which consists of a pre-primer treatment, a primer and coloured top coat. Full instructions are normally supplied with a kit, but basically, the method of use is to first apply the pre-primer to the component concerned, and allow it to dry for up to 30 minutes. Then the primer is applied, and left to dry for about an hour

before finally applying the special-coloured top coat. The result is a correctly coloured component, where the paint will flex with the plastic or rubber, a property that standard paint does not normally posses.

5 Major body damage – repair

Where serious damage has occurred, or large areas need renewal due to neglect, it means that complete new panels will need welding-in; this is best left to professionals. If the damage is due to impact, it will also be necessary to check completely the alignment of the bodyshell; this can only be carried out accurately by a Ford dealer, using special jigs. If the body is left misaligned, it is primarily dangerous, as the car will not handle properly, and secondly, uneven stresses will be imposed on the steering, suspension and possibly transmission, causing abnormal wear or complete failure, particularly to items such as the tyres.

6 Bumpers – removal and refitting

Removal

Front bumper

1 Apply the handbrake, jack up the front of the vehicle and support it on axle stands. Undo the fasteners and remove the engine undershield.

2 Undo the fasteners and remove the splash shield under the radiator.

3 Remove the front headlights as described in Chapter 12.

4 Undo the bolts securing the wheel arch liners to the front bumper (see illustrations).

5 Working inside the wheel arch, undo the 2 bolts each side securing the bumper to the front wing (see illustration).

6 Remove the radiator grille (as described in Section 7) and then release the clips from the bumper backing panel (see illustration).

7 Pull the headlight washer jets forwards (where fitted), then release the clips and detach the jet assembly from the pipe.

8 Release the clips at the upper and outer edges, then with the help of an assistant to support one end of the bumper, withdraw it forwards from the vehicle. Disconnect the foglight connectors as the bumper is withdrawn.

Rear bumper

9 Chock the front wheels, jack up the rear of the vehicle and support it on axle stands (see *Jacking and vehicle support*). Open up the tailgate.

10 Remove the 2 retaining bolts and pull out

6.5 Remove the bumper mounting bolts (arrowed)

6.6 Release the tabs (arrowed)

6.10 Undo the bolts and prise out the plastic rivets (arrowed) – left-hand side shown

6.11a Prise the reflector free . . .

6.11b . . . and remove the bolt from each side

6.12 Wheel arch liner-to-bumper bolts (arrowed)

6.13 Undo the nut each side securing the bumper to the wing

6.14 Disconnect the parking sensor wiring plug

the plastic expanding rivets from the bumper underside **(see illustration)**.

11 Remove the reflector from each side of the bumper to access the hidden bolts **(see illustrations)**.

12 Undo the 2 bolts each side securing the bumper to the wheel arch liner **(see illustration)**.

13 Undo the nut each side in the wheel arch securing the bumper to the wing, and pull the front edges of the bumper outwards to release the guide pin each side **(see illustration)**.

14 Where fitted disconnect the wiring plug for the rear parking assistance sensors **(see illustration)**.

15 With the help of an assistant, pull the bumper rearwards.

16 If required, the parking distance sensors can be removed from the bumper cover, by depressing the retaining tangs and withdrawing the sensor.

Refitting

17 Refitting is a reversal of the removal procedure. Make sure that, where applicable, the bumper guides are located correctly. Check all electrical components that have been disconnected.

---

7   Radiator grille –
    removal and refitting

Removal

1 Support the bonnet in the open position.

Undo the 4 scrivets and remove the plastic panel above the radiator grille **(see illustrations)**.

2 Release the 2 clips securing the bonnet lock linkage to the radiator grille **(see illustration)**.

7.1a Undo the bolt and prise out the scrivets . . .

7.2 Prise apart the clip each side (arrowed) to release the bonnet lock linkage

3 Unscrew the 2 radiator grille upper mounting scrivets **(see illustration)**.

4 Pivot the grille forwards, then undo the 2 lower clips and remove the grille **(see illustrations)**.

7.1b . . . along the front edge (arrowed) of the air deflector panel

7.3 Remove the scrivet each side of the radiator grille (arrowed)

7.4a Release the radiator grille lower clips (arrowed) . . .

Refitting

5 Refitting is a reversal of the removal procedure.

8 Bonnet – removal, refitting and adjustment

Removal

1 Open the bonnet, and support it in the open position using the stay. Where fitted, release the clips and remove the bonnet insulation panel.
2 Disconnect the windscreen washer hoses from the bottom of the jets, and unclip them from the bonnet.
3 Disconnect the windscreen washer wiring connector from the bottom of the jets, and unclip from the bonnet.

8.4 Bonnet hinge retaining nuts (arrowed)

9.3 Release the clip (arrowed) each side of the link rod

7.4b . . . and remove the grille

4 To assist in correctly realigning the bonnet when refitting it, mark the outline of the hinges with a soft pencil. Loosen the two hinge retaining nuts on each side **(see illustration)**.
5 With the help of an assistant, unscrew the four nuts, release the stay, and lift the bonnet from the vehicle.

Refitting and adjustment

6 Refitting is a reversal of the removal procedure, noting the following points:
  a) *Position the bonnet hinges within the outline marks made during removal, and if necessary, alter its position to provide a uniform gap all round.*
  b) *Adjust the front height by repositioning the lock (see Section 9) and turning the rubber buffers on the engine compartment front cross panel up or down to support the bonnet.*

9.2 Undo the bonnet lock bolts (arrowed)

10.2 Starting at the front edge, carefully pull the interior handle bezel from place

9 Bonnet lock – removal, refitting and adjustment

Removal

1 Undo the 4 bolts, release the 2 clips and remove the air deflector panel over the bonnet lock **(see illustrations 7.1a and 7.1b)**.
2 Make alignment marks between the lock and panel, then undo the 2 bolts securing the lock assembly to the bonnet slam panel **(see illustration)**.
3 Note its fitted position, then detach the bonnet lock key cylinder link rod from the lock assembly **(see illustration)**.
4 Disconnect the wiring connector from the lock assembly, as it is being removed.
5 Push the lock cylinder from the housing, using a screwdriver to unclip it.

Refitting and adjustment

6 Refitting is a reversal of the removal procedure, starting by positioning the lock as noted before removal.
7 If the front of the bonnet is not level with the front wings, the lock may be moved up or down within the mounting holes. After making an adjustment, raise or lower the rubber buffers to support the bonnet correctly.

10 Door inner trim panel – removal and refitting

Removal

1 Disconnect the battery negative (earth) lead (Chapter 5).

Front door

2 Operate the inner door release handle, and carefully pull the bezel from place **(see illustration)**.
3 Gently work the electric window switch free and then disconnect the wiring connector from the rear **(see illustration)**.
4 Insert a blunt, flat-bladed tool under the door grab handle, then twist it to unclip the cover trim **(see illustration)**. Note that early models used a slightly different-shaped grab

10.3 Remove the switch panel and disconnect the switch wiring plug

10.4 Lever the handle cover free with a suitable tool

10.5 Use a forked tool to lever between the door panel retaining clips and their collars (arrowed) – panel removed for clarity

10.6 Carefully pull the handle bezel from place

10.7a Use a clean cloth and a sawing motion to release the regulator handle retaining clip

10.7b The edges of the clip (arrowed) must be pushed towards the handle

10.7c Recover the handle spacer

handle. Undo the two bolts from behind the cover inside the door pull handle.

5 Working around the outer edge, use a forked trim release tool to release the retaining clips securing the trim panel **(see illustration)**.

Rear door

6 Operate the inner door release handle, and carefully pull the bezel from place **(see illustration)**. Disconnect the window switch wiring plug as the bezel is withdrawn.

7 On models fitted with manual (ie, non-electric) rear windows, fully shut the window, and note the position of the regulator handle. Release the spring clip by inserting a clean cloth between the handle and the door trim. Using a 'sawing' action, pull the cloth

against the open ends of the clip to release it, at the same time pulling the handle from the regulator shaft splines. Withdraw the handle and the spacer **(see illustrations)**.

8 Carefully prise the cover from the door grab handle. Note that early models have a slightly different trim style. Undo the two bolts from behind the cover inside the door pull handle.

9 Working around the outer edge, use a forked trim release tool to release the retaining clips securing the trim panel **(see illustration)**. Disconnect the tweeter speaker wiring plug (where fitted) as the panel is withdrawn.

Refitting

10 Refitting is a reversal of the removal procedure. On the rear manual windows,

ensure the retaining clip is fitted to the winder handle before refitting the handle to the regulator shaft.

11 Door window glass –
removal and refitting

Removal

Front door

1 Remove the door inner trim panel as described in Section 10.

2 Prise the rubber grommet from the front and rear of the door panel to access the window clamps **(see illustration)**.

10.9 Rear inner door panel retaining clips (arrowed)

11.2 Prise the rubber grommets (arrowed) from the panel

11.3 Pull the inner weather strip up from the door

11.5 Align the window clamp bolts with the apertures in the panel

11.7 Lift the rear of the window and withdraw it from the outside of the door

7 Lift the window glass from the door while tilting it up at the rear, and withdraw it from the outside of the door frame **(see illustration)**.

Rear door

8 Remove the door window regulator panel as described in Section 12. Note that there is no need to drill out the rivets securing the regulator to the panel.
9 Lower the window, then prise out the lower sections of the window guide rubber at the front and rear of the window frame **(see illustrations)**.
10 Carefully prise the rubber inner weather strip from the door **(see illustration)**.
11 Lift the window glass from the door while tilting it up at the rear, and withdraw it from the outside of the door frame **(see illustration)**.

Refitting

12 Refitting is a reversal of the removal procedure, making sure that the glass is correctly located in the clamps.

11.9a Prise out the front . . .

11.9b . . . and rear window guide rubbers

3 Carefully prise the rubber inner weather strip from the door **(see illustration)**.
4 Reconnect the door window switch, and reconnect the battery negative lead.
5 Operate the window switch and align the

window clamps bolts with the apertures exposed by removing the grommets **(see illustration)**.
6 Slacken each of the window clamp bolts by 2 turns.

12 Door window regulator –
removal and refitting

Removal

Front door

1 Remove the front door window as described in Section 11.
2 Disconnect the wiring plugs, then undo the 3 bolts and remove the electric window motor **(see illustration)**.
3 Disconnect the cable from the door inner release handle **(see illustration)**.
4 Remove the exterior handle as described in Section 13.
5 Prise off the door mirror inner trim panel complete with the tweeter speaker cover **(see illustration)**.
6 Undo the 10 bolts securing the inner panel to the door frame **(see illustration)**.
7 Undo the 5 bolts securing the door lock to the door **(see illustrations)**.
8 Manoeuvre the panel from the door **(see illustration)**.

11.10 Prise up the door inner weather strip

11.11 Tilt it up at the rear, and remove the glass from the door

12.2 Window motor retaining bolts (arrowed)

12.3 Push the lock button into the door, then lift the release cable end fitting from the handle

12.5 Prise the trim free

12.6 Inner panel retaining bolts (arrowed)

9 Using a suitable-sized drill bit, remove the 4 rivets securing the window regulator to the door panel **(see illustration)**.

Rear door

10 Remove the rear door inner trim panel as described in Section 10.

11 Prise the foam/rubber grommet from the front and rear of the door panel to access the window clamps **(see illustration)**.

12 On models with manual windows, refit the window winder handle, and fully lower the window. On models with electric windows, reconnect the window switch and the battery negative lead, then fully lower the window.

13 Operate the window switch/handle and align the window clamp bolts with the apertures exposed by removing the grommets **(see illustration)**.

14 Slacken the clamp bolts two turns, then lift the window to the top of the door and secure it in place using tape.

15 On models with electric windows, undo the 3 bolts and remove the window regulator motor **(see illustration)**. Disconnect the wiring plug as the motor is withdrawn.

16 Set the handle in the 'Lock' position, then lift the interior door release handle operating cable end fitting upwards, and disconnect it **(see illustration 12.3)**.

12.7a Undo the 4 bolts (arrowed) at the end of the door . . .

12.7b . . . and the one (arrowed) on the outside of the door

12.8 Manoeuvre the panel from the door

12.9 Drill out the rivets (arrowed) securing the regulator to the panel

12.11 Prise out the grommets (arrowed) to access the window clamps

12.13 Raise the window until the clamp bolt is visible (arrowed)

12.15 Undo the bolts and pull the window motor from the panel

12.17a Release the 2 clips each side of the connector (arrowed) and pull it from the pillar

17 Close the door, prise away the rubber gaiter, release the 4 clips and pull the connector from the door pillar, then disconnect the door wiring plug **(see illustrations)**. Push the wiring harness into the door.
18 Open the door, and remove the exterior handle as described in Section 13.
19 Undo the 9 bolts securing the inner panel to the door frame **(see illustration)**.
20 Undo the 4 bolts securing the door lock at the rear edge of the door, and the single bolt securing the exterior handle frame to the door **(see illustrations)**. Manoeuvre the panel/regulator from the door.

21 Using a suitable-sized drill bit, remove the 5 rivets (manual windows) or 4 rivets (electric windows) securing the window regulator to the door panel **(see illustration)**.

Refitting

22 Refitting is a reversal of the removal procedure.

13 Door handle and lock components – removal and refitting

 Warning: before working on any electrical components, disconnect the battery negative (earth) lead (Chapter 5).

Removal

Front exterior handle

1 Prise out the rubber grommet from the end of the door adjacent to the exterior handle **(see illustration)**.
2 Working through the aperture, slacken the handle retaining bolt approximately 22 turns **(see illustration)**.
3 Carefully pull the trim and lock cylinder from the door **(see illustration)**. On models with the Keyless Entry system, remove the trim at

12.17b Disconnect the door wiring plug

the rear of the handle (where the lock cylinder would be on conventional systems).
4 Pull the exterior handle rearwards, and manoeuvre it from the door. Recover the seals between the handle and the door skin.
5 On models with the Keyless Entry system, gently pull the handle antenna wiring harness until an audible click is heard, and the harness connector is in the horizontal position. Disconnect the wiring plug.

Rear exterior handle

6 Prise out the rubber grommet from the end of the door adjacent to the exterior handle **(see illustration)**.

12.19 Rear door panel bolts (arrowed)

12.20a Undo the 4 bolts at the end of the door (arrowed) . . .

12.20b . . . and one on the outside of the door (arrowed)

12.21 Drill out the rivets (arrowed) securing the regulator to the panel – electric window model

13.1 Prise out the grommet at the end of the door

7 Working through the aperture, slacken the handle retaining bolt approximately 7 turns **(see illustration)**.

8 Pull the trim at the rear of the handle outwards **(see illustration)**.

9 Pull the exterior handle rearwards, and manoeuvre it from the door. Recover the seals between the handle and the door skin.

Interior handle

10 Remove the door inner trim panel as described Section 10.

11 Detach the door release handle from the door by undoing the bolt, unclipping the front end, then slide the handle out in a forwards direction **(see illustrations)**.

12 Set the handle in the 'Lock' position, then lift the operating cable end fitting upwards, and disconnect it **(see illustration 12.3)**.

Front lock motor/module

13 Proceed as described in paragraphs 1 to 8 of Section 12.

14 Press in the centre pins, prise out the plastic rivets securing the lock and latch retaining bracket to the door panel **(see illustration)**. Disconnect the lock wiring plugs as it's withdrawn.

15 Depress the retaining clips each side of the lock remote control cable outer fitting, and pull it from the support bracket, then rotate the cable end fitting 90° and detach it from the lever on the lock **(see illustration)**. Repeat this procedure on the exterior handle cable.

16 Using a suitable-sized drill bit remove the rivet securing the lock to the bracket **(see illustration)**.

13.2 Slacken the handle retaining bolt approximately 22 turns . . .

13.6 Prise out the grommet . . .

Lock cylinder

17 Prise out the rubber grommet from the end of the door adjacent to the exterior handle **(see illustration 13.1)**.

18 Working through the aperture, slacken the

13.3 . . . until the lock cylinder and trim can be pulled from the door

13.7 . . . undo the bolt approximately 7 turns . . .

handle retaining bolt approximately 22 turns **(see illustration 13.2)**.

19 Pull the trim and lock cylinder from the door **(see illustration 13.3)**. If required, release the clip each side with a small screwdriver,

13.8 . . . until the trim can be removed

13.14 Push in the centre pins of the 3 rivets (arrowed)

13.11a Undo the bolt (arrowed) . . .

13.15 Depress the clips (arrowed) and pull the fitting from the bracket

13.11b . . . and pull the front end of the handle assembly from the door

13.16 Drill out the rivet (arrowed) securing the lock to the bracket

13.19a Release the clip each side . . .

13.19b . . . and detach the cover from the lock cylinder

13.21 Rotate the end fitting and detach it from the lever

13.22 Press the centres from the 3 rivets . . .

13.23 . . . and drill out the rivet securing the lock to the bracket (arrowed)

and separate the lock cylinder from the trim **(see illustrations)**

Rear lock motor/module

20 Proceed as described in paragraphs 10 to 20 of Section 12.

21 Depress the retaining clips each side of the lock remote control cable outer fitting, and pull it from the support bracket **(see illustration 13.15)**, then rotate the cable end fitting and detach it from the lever on the lock

(see illustration). Repeat this procedure on the exterior handle cable.
22 Using a suitably-sized rod, drive out the centres of the 3 plastic rivets securing the lock and latch retaining bracket to the door panel **(see illustration)**. Disconnect the lock wiring plugs as it's withdrawn.
23 Using a suitable-sized drill bit remove the rivet securing the lock to the bracket **(see illustration)**.

Refitting

Handles (exterior and interior)

24 Refitting is a reversal of the removal procedure. When refitting the exterior handle on models with the Keyless Entry system reconnect the antenna wiring connector and push it into the holder.

Lock cylinder

25 Refitting is a reversal of removal.

Lock motor/modules

26 Refitting is a reversal of the removal procedure, but check that the door lock passes over the striker centrally. If necessary, reposition the striker before fully-tightening the mounting bolts.

14 Door –
   removal and refitting

Removal

1 Disconnect the battery negative (earth) lead (Chapter 5).
2 Use masking tape to protect the front edge of the door and the rear of the wing – or front door if removing the rear door **(see illustration)**.
3 Free off the seal and disconnect the wiring plug from the A-pillar – or B-pillar if removing the rear door.
4 Using a Torx key, unscrew and remove the check strap mounting bolt from the door pillar **(see illustration)**.
5 Have an assistant support the door, then undo the retaining bolts in the top and bottom hinges **(see illustrations)**.
6 Carefully lift the door from the hinges, and support it on a trolley jack or similar **(see illustration)**.

14.2 Protect the door and wing edges with masking tape

14.4 Remove the check strap retaining bolt

14.5 Undo the upper and lower hinge bolts

14.6 Use a block of wood and a clean cloth to support the door

15.2a Disconnect the speaker wiring . . .

15.2b . . . and the motor wiring

15.3a Release the mirror . . .

15.3b . . . and pull the electrical connector through the door

15.5a Lever the mirror free from the inboard end

15.5b The difficult to release locking tab (arrowed)

Refitting

7 Refitting is a reversal of the removal procedure, but check that the door lock passes over the striker centrally. If necessary, reposition the striker.

15 Exterior mirror and glass – removal and refitting

Removal

Mirror

1 Unclip the trim panel from the front of the window opening over the tweeter speaker and remove it **(see illustration 12.5)**.
2 Disconnect the wiring plugs from the mirror and the speaker **(see illustrations)**.

3 Undo the retaining bolts and lift the mirror from the door. Feed the electrical cable through the door aperture as the mirror is removed **(see illustrations)**.

Mirror glass

4 It is strongly recommended that gloves are worn. Also consider covering the glass with masking tape to avoid injury from glass shards.
5 Pull the outer edge of the glass rearwards, insert a plastic trim removal tool and gently lever the glass from place **(see illustrations)**. We found the mirror difficult to release from the locking tab. It would be very easy to slip and break the glass or the mirror frame.
6 Withdraw the mirror glass and disconnect the wiring connectors for the heated mirrors.

Refitting

7 Refitting is a reversal of the removal pro-

cedure. Take care not to drop the rubber grommet inside the door panel when removing the mirror, as the interior door trim will have to be removed to retrieve it **(see illustration)**.

16 Interior mirror – removal and refitting

Basic mirror

1 Press the retaining clip away from the windscreen, then slide the mirror up from the base **(see illustrations)**.
2 Refitting is a reversal of removal.

Auto-dimming mirror

3 Squeeze together the sides, and slide up the mirror base upper cover **(see illustration)**.

15.7 The mirror must be hooked into place (arrowed)

16.1a Push the clip at the base of the mirror rearwards, and slide it up from the windscreen mounting

16.1b Mirror retaining clip – viewed from the front face of the mirror base

16.3 Squeeze together the sides and slide up the upper cover

16.4 Pull apart the top edges (arrowed) and slide down the lower cover

16.6 Rotate the mirror 60° anti-clockwise to release it

4 Pull apart the top edges and slide down the mirror base lower cover **(see illustration)**.
5 Disconnect the mirror wiring plug (where applicable).
6 Rotate the mirror base 60° anti-clockwise and detach it from the mounting **(see illustration)**.
7 Refitting is the reversal of the removal procedure.

17 Tailgate –
removal and refitting

Removal

1 Disconnect the battery negative (earth) lead (Chapter 5).

2 The tailgate may be unbolted from the hinges and the hinges left in position.
3 Undo the bolts, remove the high-level brake light and disconnect the wiring plug. Prise out the washer jet and disconnect the hose **(see illustrations)**.
4 Undo the retaining bolts in the handle recesses, then pull trim panel away from the tailgate to release the retaining clips.
5 Carefully unclip the upper central tailgate trim and then pull the rear window side trims inwards to release the clips **(see illustration)**.
6 Unbolt the rear spoiler, disconnect the washer tube and feed the screen washer tube and the brake light wiring loom through the tailgate aperture **(see illustration)**.
7 Disconnect the wiring loom connectors to the tailgate lock, number plate light, screen heater and the rear wiper motor.

8 Attach a strong fine cord to the end of the wiring loom, to act as an aid to guiding the wiring through the tailgate when it is refitted. Unclip the wiring loom and feed it through the tailgate inner skin aperture. Disconnect the earth wiring.
9 Prise the rubber grommet from the tailgate aperture, and pull out the wiring loom. Untie the cord, leaving it in position in the tailgate for guiding the wire through on refitting.
10 Have an assistant support the tailgate in its open position.
11 Using a small screwdriver, prise off the clip securing the struts to the tailgate. Pull the sockets from the ball-studs, and move the struts downwards **(see illustration 18.2)**.
12 Unscrew and remove the hinge bolts (two each side) from the tailgate **(see illustration)**. Withdraw the tailgate from the body aperture, taking care not to damage the paintwork.
13 If the hinges are to be removed from the roof panel, remove the D-pillar trim panels as described in Section 26.
14 Carefully pull down the rear edge of the headlining for access to the nuts and bolts. Take care not to damage the headlining.
15 Unscrew the mounting nuts and bolts for the hinges from the rear roof panel.

Refitting

16 Refitting is a reversal of the removal procedure, but check that the tailgate is located centrally in the body aperture, and that the striker enters the lock centrally. If necessary, loosen the mounting nuts and reposition the tailgate as required.

17.3a Disconnect the wiring . . .

17.3b . . . and unclip the screen washer tube

17.5 Remove the trim panel

17.6 Disconnect the screen washer tube

17.12 Tailgate hinge bolts

18.2 Prise the clip from the end of the strut

19.2 Tailgate lock wiring plug (arrowed)

19.4 Remove the number plate light panel to access the tailgate release

18 Support struts – removal and refitting

Removal

1 Have an assistant support the tailgate, boot or bonnet in its open position.
2 Prise off the upper spring clip securing the strut to the tailgate or bonnet, then pull the socket from the ball-stud **(see illustration)**.
3 Similarly prise off the bottom clip, and pull the socket from the ball-stud. Withdraw the strut.

Refitting

4 Refitting is a reversal of the removal procedure, making sure that the strut is fitted the same way up as when it was removed.

19 Tailgate lock components – removal and refitting

Removal

1 Undo the 2 bolts at the lower edge, and pull the interior trim panel from the tailgate.
2 Disconnect the wiring plug from the lock assembly **(see illustration)**.
3 Using a Torx key, unscrew the lock mounting bolts, and withdraw the lock.
4 To remove the release button assembly, undo the 4 nuts and remove the panel from the tailgate **(see illustration)**. Unclip the button from the panel.

Refitting

5 Refitting is a reversal of the removal procedure.

20 Central locking system – testing, reprogramming, removal and refitting

Testing/reprogramming

1 Testing of the central locking/alarm system can only be carried out using Ford's IDS diagnostic tester.

2 Prior to reprogramming a remote locking transmitter, ensure the vehicle battery is fully-charged, and the alarm is not armed or triggered. Fasten all seat belts, and close all doors.
3 Turn the ignition switch from position I to position II four times within 6 seconds, then turn it to position 0 (off).
4 A chime will be heard to indicate that the 'learning mode' has begun.
5 Within 10 seconds of the previous step, press any button on the remote transmitter until a further chime is heard. This indicates the process has been successful. Turn the ignition switch to position II to exit the learning mode.

Removal

Generic electronic module (GEM)

Note: *If the GEM is to be renewed, the unit settings must be saved prior to removal, then initialised using the Ford IDS diagnostic tester.*
6 The GEM is fully integrated into the central junction box, located below the glovebox. Removal and refitting of the GEM is described in Chapter 12.

Keyless Entry system module

Note: *If the module is to be renewed, the unit settings must be saved prior to removal, then initialised using the Ford IDS diagnostic tester.*
7 Disconnect the battery negative lead as described in Chapter 5.
8 Remove the left-hand luggage compartment side panel, C-pillar panel and parcel shelf support as described in Section 26.

20.9 Keyless Entry module retaining bolts (arrowed)

9 Undo the 2 retaining bolts, and remove the module **(see illustration)**. Disconnect the wiring plugs as the module is withdrawn.

Door motors

10 The door lock motors are integral with the locks. Refer to Section 13.

Tailgate motor

11 The tailgate motor is integral with the lock. Refer to Section 19.

Refitting

12 In all cases, refitting is a reversal of the removal procedure.

21 Windscreen and fixed windows – removal and refitting

1 The windscreen and rear window on all models are bonded in place with special mastic, as are the rear side windows. Special tools are required to cut free the old units and fit new ones; special cleaning solutions and primer are also required. It is therefore recommended that this work is entrusted to a Ford dealer or windscreen replacement specialist.

22 Body side-trim mouldings and adhesive emblems – removal and refitting

Removal

1 Body side trims and mouldings are attached either by retaining clips or adhesive bonding. On bonded mouldings, insert a length of strong cord (fishing line is ideal) behind the moulding or emblem concerned. With a sawing action, break the adhesive bond between the moulding or emblem and the panel.
2 Thoroughly clean all traces of adhesive from the panel using methylated spirit, and allow the location to dry.
3 On mouldings with retaining clips, unclip the mouldings from the panel, taking care not to damage the paintwork.

Refitting

4 Renew any broken retaining clips before refitting trims or mouldings.

23.2 Sunroof glass panel details

1 Glass panel   2 Guide arm covers   3 Retaining bolts

5 Peel back the protective paper from the rear face of the new moulding or emblem. Carefully fit it into position on the panel concerned, but take care not to touch the adhesive. When in position, apply hand pressure to the moulding/emblem for a short period, to ensure maximum adhesion to the panel.

23 Sunroof – general information and adjustment

Note: *Some models have a bonded glass roof panel fitted. The repair and renewal of this panel should be entrusted to a Ford dealer or specialist glazing company.*

Glass panel

1 Slide back the sun blind, and set the glass panel in the closed position.

24.2 Undo the bolt (arrowed) and disconnect the seat wiring plug

2 Pull the panel guide arm covers inwards and remove them **(see illustration).**
3 Undo the 2 retaining bolts each side, then lift the sunroof glass panel out from the vehicle.
4 When refitting, adjust the position of the rear edge of the panel so that it is flush with the roof, then tighten the bolts.
5 The remainder of refitting is a reversal of removal.

Sun blind

6 Remove the glass panel as described in paragraphs 1 to 3.
7 Close the sun blind, then undo the bolts each side securing the blind.
8 Manoeuvre the blind from the vehicle.
9 Refitting is a reversal of removal.

Sunroof mechanism and motor

10 Removal of the sunroof mechanism and/or

24.3 Seat front retaining bolts (arrowed)

motor involves removal of the headlining. This is a complex task, which requires patience and dexterity, and is considered to be beyond the scope of the home mechanic. Consequently, we recommend this task be entrusted to a Ford dealer or upholstery specialist.

Adjustment

11 The sunroof should operate freely, without sticking or binding, as it is opened and closed. When in the closed position, check that the panel is flush with the surrounding roof panel.
12 If adjustment is required, slide back the sun blind, but leave the glass panel in the closed position.
13 Loosen the rear securing bolts (one each side). Adjust the glass panel up or down, so that it is flush at its back edge with the roof panel.
14 Loosen the front securing bolts (one each side). Adjust the glass panel up or down, so that it is flush at its front edge with the roof panel.
15 Retighten the four securing bolts.
16 Check the roof seal for wind noise and water leaks.

Drain tubes

17 There are four drain tubes, one located in each corner of the sunroof aperture.
18 To remove any obstruction, insert a length of suitable nylon wire down through the tubes. If the obstruction cannot be cleared, access the drain tubes as follows:
19 The front drain tubes go down the front A-pillars; remove the lower trim panel to gain access to the drain tube.
20 The rear drain tubes go down the D-pillars. Remove the load area rear side trims to gain access.

24 Seats – removal and refitting

Removal

Front seat

1 Disconnect the battery negative lead, and position the lead away from the battery (see Chapter 5).

 Warning: Before proceeding, wait a minimum of 5 minutes, as a precaution against accidental firing of the airbag unit or seat belt pretensioner. This period ensures that any residual electrical energy is dissipated.
2 Undo the security bolt and disconnect the wiring plug under the front of the seat **(see illustration).**
3 Undo the 4 seat retaining bolts and with the help of an assistant, manoeuvre the seat from the vehicle **(see illustration).** Note that the seat is extremely heavy.

Rear seats

4 The rear seats are all easily removable.

25.4 Front seat belt upper anchorage bolt
(arrowed)

25.5 Seat belt inertia reel bolt (arrowed)

25.6 Remove the lower bolt (arrowed)

5 Slide the seats fully forward and release the seat belts from the guides on the outer seats. Lower the outer headrests by depressing the catch at the base of the headrest and then raise the inner seat headrest.

6 Lower the seat backs and then tip the seats forwards to approximately 45 degrees. Release the red locking levers at the front of the seats and remove them.

Refitting

7 Refitting is a reversal of the removal procedure. Tighten the mounting bolts to the specified torque.

25 Seat belts –
removal and refitting

⚠️ *Warning: Be careful when handling the seat belt tensioning device, it contains a small explosive charge (pyrotechnic device) similar to the one used to deploy the airbag(s). Clearly, injury could be caused if these are released in an uncontrolled fashion. Once fired, the tensioner cannot be reset, and must be renewed. Note also that seat belts and associated components which have been subject to impact loads must be renewed.*

Removal

Front seat belt

1 Disconnect the battery negative lead, and position the lead away from the battery (see Chapter 5).

⚠️ *Warning: Before proceeding, wait a minimum of 5 minutes, as a precaution against accidental firing of the seat belt tensioner. This period ensures that any residual electrical energy is dissipated.*

⚠️ *Warning: There is a potential risk of the seat belt tensioning device firing during removal, so it should be handled carefully. Once removed, treat it with care – do not allow use chemicals on or near it, and do not expose it to high temperatures, or it may detonate.*

2 Undo and remove the bolt for the lower seat belt anchorage. Note that the spacer and washer are integral with the bolt.

3 Remove the B-pillar trim panel as described in Section 26.

4 Undo the seat belt upper anchorage bolt from the height adjuster (see illustration).

5 Unscrew the mounting bolt, and lift the seat belt reel from the base of the pillar (see illustration).

Rear side seat belt

6 Fold the rear seats and tip them forward. Unscrew the seat belt lower anchorage bolt (see illustration).

7 Remove the rear quarter trim panel and load area panel as described in Section 26.

8 Unscrew the upper seat belt upper anchor.

9 Unscrew the mounting bolt securing the seat belt reel unit, and withdraw it from the vehicle (see illustration).

Rear centre seat belt

10 The centre rear seat belt inertia reel is attached to the rear quarter panel. Remove the quarter panel trim as described in Section 26.

11 Unbolt the inertia reel and then lower the head liner slightly to access the upper guide rail (see illustration 25.9). Unbolt the guide.

12 Prise open the screw covers and remove the screws holding the trim panel in place (see illustration).

13 Unbolt and remove the upper anchor point. Feed the belt through the head liner and remove it.

Seat belt stalks

14 The seat belt stalks are bolted to the seat frame (see illustration) and can be removed after removing the seat as described in Section 24.

15 Note its routing, then unclip the pre-

25.9 Inertia seat belt reel mounting bolt

A Outer seat belt   B Centre seat belt

25.12 Remove the cover to access the bolt (arrowed)

25.14 Seat belt pretensioner retaining bolt (arrowed)

26.1 Sunvisor outer mounting bolts

26.3 Prise up the cover to expose the sunvisor inner mounting bolt (arrowed)

26.4 Prise up the covers to expose the grab handle bolts

26.6 Pull the A-pillar trim inwards to release the clips

26.8 Prise up the front edge of the rear door sill trim . . .

tensioner wiring harness from the under- side of the seat.

16 Unclip the pretensioner wiring plug from the seat frame.

17 Undo the Torx bolt and remove the pretensioner/stalk.

Refitting

18 Refitting is a reversal of the removal procedure, noting the following points:

a) Tighten the mounting nuts and bolts to the specified torque.

b) Make sure the seat belt reel locating dowel is correctly positioned.

c) Refit spacers in their correct position.

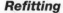

26 Interior trim panels –
removal and refitting

Note: *This section covers the removal and*

installation of the interior trim panels. It may be necessary to remove an overlapping trim before you can remove the one required. For more information on trim removal, look at relevant Chapters and Sections, where the trims may need to be removed to carry out any other procedures (eg, to remove the steering column you will need to remove the shrouds).

Removal

Sunvisor

1 Unscrew the mounting bolts and remove the visor **(see illustration)**.

2 Disconnect the wiring for the vanity mirror light, where fitted.

3 Prise up the cover, unscrew the inner bracket mounting bolts, and remove the bracket **(see illustration)**.

Passenger grab handle

4 Prise up the covers, then unscrew the

mounting bolts and remove the grab handle **(see illustration)**.

A-pillar trim

5 Pull the rubber weatherstrip away from the area adjacent to the pillar.

6 Starting at the top, carefully pull the A-pillar trim inwards to release the retaining clips **(see illustration)**. Note that it is quite likely that some of the clips will be damaged during the removal procedure.

B-pillar trim

7 Pull the rubber weatherstrip from the rear door aperture adjacent to the B-pillar trim.

8 Prise up the front edge of the rear door sill trim to access the B-pillar trim **(see illustration)**.

9 Pull up the rear edge of the front door sill scuff plate panel **(see illustration)**.

10 Prise out the cover and undo the bolts at the top section of the B-pillar trim **(see illustrations)**.

26.9 . . . and the rear edge of the front door sill trim

26.10a Prise out the cover . . .

26.10b . . . and undo the 2 retaining bolts

26.13a Undo the bolt, and prise out the scrivets . . .

26.13b . . . then pull the panel from the pillar

26.15 Prise out the cover . . .

11 Unscrew the seat belt mounting bolt from its lower anchorage point.
12 Carefully pull the upper B-pillar trim from the pillar.
13 Slacken the two bolts and prise out the scrivets from the top of the lower trim panel, then unclip it from the B-pillar **(see illustrations)**.

C-pillar trim

14 Pull the rubber weatherstrip from the door aperture adjacent to the C-pillar.
15 Starting at the lower edge, prise out the plastic cover at the top of the trim and undo the bolt **(see illustration)**.
16 Pull the C-pillar trim inwards to release the retaining clips **(see illustration)**.

D-pillar trim

17 Move the rear seats forward and then remove the parcel shelf.
18 Pull the rubber weatherstrip from the tailgate aperture adjacent to the D-pillar.
19 Carefully prise off the cover at the front, upper edge of the D-pillar **(see illustration)**.
20 To remove the panel completely unbolt the seat belt lower anchorage and feed the seat belt through the panel.

Luggage area side panel

21 Remove the parcel shelf and the luggage compartment floor covering.
22 Move all the rear seats forward and fold the seats back down.
23 Remove the C-pillar trim and D-pillar trim as described previously in this Section.
24 Pull the rubber weatherstrip from the tailgate aperture.
25 Prise the trim clips free from the load area scuff panel **(see illustration)** and remove the panel.
26 Open the storage compartment and unclip the retaining strap.
27 Remove the 2 screws **(see illustration)** and then prise the panel free.
28 As the panel is removed disconnect the wiring plugs from the load space light and the 12V power outlet **(see illustrations)**.

Steering column shrouds

29 To release the upper shroud from the lower

26.16 . . . and pull the C-pillar trim panel from position

shroud, turn the steering wheel 90°, insert a thin screwdriver into a hole at each side of the column **(see illustration)**. Lift the upper shroud from the column and unclip from the bottom of the instrument panel.

26.25 Prise the clips free

26.28a Disconnect the wiring plugs . . .

26.19 Prise the panel free

30 Using a thin screwdriver unclip the radio control switch from the lower shroud **(see illustration)**.
31 Release the steering column height lever. Undo the 2 securing bolts from the lower

26.27 Remove the screws

26.28b . . . and remove the panel

26.29 Rotate the steering wheel 90° and release the upper shroud clips

26.30 Depress the clip to release the audio switch from the shroud

26.31 Lower shroud retaining bolts (arrowed)

shroud, and remove from the column (see illustration).

Refitting

32 Refitting is a reversal of the removal procedure. Where seat belt fastenings have been disturbed, make sure that they are tightened to the specified torque. Renew any broken clips as required.

27 Centre console – removal and refitting

Removal

Models up to 03/2007

1 Prise out the covers, and remove the bolts at the front and rear of the console.

27.5 Remove the handbrake gaiter

27.6b . . . and rear inserts

2 Prise free the handbrake cover and either remove it or feed it through the centre console.
3 On vehicles fitted with the electronic parking brake (EPB) open the rear storage compartment to access the rear screws. Slide both front seats back wards to access the front screws
4 Disconnect the wiring plug from the 12V power outlet and handbrake warning light as the console is removed. On vehicles fitted with EPB disconnect the wiring to the operating switch.

Models from 03/2007 without an armrest

5 Prise free the handbrake cover and work it over the handbrake lever (see illustration).
6 Remove the inserts from the front and rear cup holders to access the bolts (see illustrations).

27.6a Remove the front . . .

27.7a Remove the bolts from the front (arrowed) . . .

7 Remove the bolts (see illustrations) and lift off the centre console. Disconnect the wiring plugs from the 12V power outlet and (where fitted) the auxiliary input socket as the console is lifted off the handbrake.

Models from 03/2007 with an armrest

8 The centre console panel extension must be removed before the console can be removed.
9 Prise free and remove the trim panel from below the glovebox and from below the steering column.
10 Remove the panels from the gearshift lever and the front of the armrest. Also remove the small filler panel from below the handbrake lever.
11 Open the glovebox and remove the 2 screws (or trim clips). Remove the screws from the driver's footwell and from in front of the gear shift.
12 Remove the fixings from the front of the armrest and lift off the centre console. Disconnect the wiring plugs as the console is removed.

Refitting

13 Refitting is a reversal of the removal procedure.

28 Overhead console – removal and refitting

Removal

1 Starting at the front edge, carefully prise the interior light unit from the console (see

27.7b . . . and the rear (arrowed)

28.1 Insert a plastic trim tool and release the interior light from the console

28.3a Remove the console retaining bolts (arrowed) . . .

28.3b . . . and lower the console

illustration). Disconnect the wiring plug as the light is removed.

2 On models with an electrically-operated sunroof, remove the sunroof switch (Chapter 12, Section 4).

3 Undo the 2 bolts in the light aperture, then starting at the front edge, prise down the console panel **(see illustrations)**. Disconnect any wiring plugs as the console is removed.

Refitting

4 Refitting is a reversal of the removal procedure.

---

29 Glovebox –
removal and refitting

1 On models with an air conditioned glovebox, undo the fasteners and lower the GEM/fusebox from below the passenger's side of the facia, then reach up to the right-hand side of the glovebox and pull the cool air pipe from the fitting on the side of the box.

2 Open the glovebox lid, undo the 7 retaining bolts and pull the glovebox from place **(see illustration)**. Prise down the covers to access the lower 3 bolts. Take care not to lose the lock striker from the top of the glovebox as its withdrawn.

3 Disconnect the wiring plugs as the glovebox is withdrawn. If required, the glovebox lid simply pulls from place.

4 Refitting is a reversal of the removal procedure, making sure that the glovebox is located correctly before tightening the bolts.

---

30 Facia –
removal and refitting

Note: *Remove of the facia is a major task. Proceed In a logical manner and label each component as it is removed. Whilst not strictly necessary the task is considerable easier if both seats are removed first.*

Removal

1 Disconnect the battery negative (earth) lead (Chapter 5).

2 Support and remove both front doors as described in Section 14 of this Chapter.

3 Remove the centre console as described in Section 27.

4 On vehicles built before October 2005 remove the passenger's airbag module as described in Chapter 12.

5 Squeeze together the sides and remove the fasteners, then remove the cover under the central junction box under the facia **(see illustration)**.

6 Rotate the fasteners anti-clockwise and detach the central junction box from the support bracket **(see illustration)**.

7 On models with air conditioning, reach up and disconnect the cooling hose from the glovebox.

8 Remove the glovebox as described in Section 29.

9 Undo the passenger's airbag module lower support bracket bolts/nuts and remove the bracket **(see illustration)**.

10 Disconnect the passenger's airbag module wiring plug.

11 Remove the A-post trim panels as described in Section 26.

12 Working along the top of the facia remove the outer trim panels, the upper centre panel and (where fitted) the storage compartment lid **(see illustrations)**. Disconnect the wiring to the aerial.

13 Remove both outer air distribution vents **(see illustration)**.

14 With reference to Chapter 7, unbolt and remove the gearshift lever and support bracket.

15 Remove the audio unit (Chapter 12) and the heater control panel as described in Chapter 3.

29.2 Remove the glovebox

30.5 Remove the fusebox cover

30.6 Lower and then remove the fusebox

30.9 Note the position of the earth tag (arrowed)

30.12a Remove the outer panels . . .

30.12b . . . and the centre panel

30.13 Lever the vent free with a suitable trim type tool

30.16a Remove the end trim panel

30.16b Remove the lower panel and release the diagnostic socket

30.20 Remove the air distribution ducting

16 Unclip and remove the facia lower quarter panels and then release the driver's side lower trim panel **(see illustrations)**.
17 Remove the centre air distribution vents and support panel.
18 With reference to Chapter 12 remove the instrument panel and the facia-mounted light switch.
19 Remove the steering column upper and lower shrouds – see Section 26 of this Chapter.
20 Unbolt and remove the central and rear air distribution ducting **(see illustration)**.
21 Unbolt and remove the steering column as described in Chapter 10.
22 At this point it is possible to remove the facia panel without the support bar, however access to the upper mounting points is extremely difficult. We recommend that the

facia is removed complete with the support bar. The facia can then be separated on the bench.
23 Mark the exact position of the facia support bar **(see illustration)** and then remove the 3 upper mounting bolts.
24 Remove the A-pillar mounting bolts and with the help of an assistant remove the facia from the vehicle **(see illustration)**.

Refitting

25 Refitting is a reversal of the removal procedure, noting the following points:
  a) *On completion, check the operation of all electrical components*
  b) *A new bolt must be fitted to the steering column lower universal joint.*
  c) *Apply a thread-locking compound to the door hinge bolts.*

31 Wheel arch liner – removal and refitting

Removal

Front

1 Apply the handbrake. If the wheel is to be removed (to improve access), loosen the wheel nuts. Jack up the front of the vehicle and support it on axle stands (see *Jacking and vehicle support*). Remove the front wheel.
2 Unscrew the bolts securing the liner to the inner wheel arch panel.
3 Remove the bolts and clips securing the liner to the outer edge of the wheel arch and bumper. Withdraw the liner from under the vehicle.

Rear

4 Chock the front wheels, and engage 1st gear (or P). If the wheel is to be removed (to improve access), loosen the wheel nuts. Jack up the rear of the vehicle and support it on axle stands (see *Jacking and vehicle support*). Remove the rear wheel.
5 Undo the bolts securing the liner to the outer edge of the wheel arch and bumper.
6 Remove the clips securing the liner to the inner wheel arch, and withdraw the liner from under the vehicle.

Refitting

7 Refitting is a reversal of the removal procedure. If the wheels were removed, tighten the wheel nuts to the specified torque.

30.23 Mark the position of the support bar (bar removed for clarity)

30.24 Remove the blanking plug to access the bolt

Chapter 12
Body electrical system

Contents

	Section number		Section number
Aerial – removal and refitting	19	Horns – removal and refitting	14
Airbag system – general information and precautions	21	Ignition switch – removal and refitting	4
Airbag system components – removal and refitting	22	Instrument panel – removal and refitting	10
Anti-theft alarm system – general information	23	Interior light bulbs – renewal	7
Audio/DVD units – removal and refitting	18	Parking aid components – general, removal and refitting	17
Central locking system – general information	16	Speakers – removal and refitting	20
Electrical fault finding – general information	2	Sunroof motor – removal and refitting	15
Electronic control modules – removal and refitting	24	Switches – removal and refitting	5
Exterior light bulbs – renewal	6	Tailgate wiper motor – removal and refitting	13
Exterior light units – removal, refitting and beam adjustment	8	Washer system – general	12
Fuel filler flap motor – removal and refitting	25	Windscreen wiper components – removal and refitting	11
Fuses and relays – general information	3	Xenon gas discharge headlight system – component removal, refitting	
General information and precautions	1	and adjustment	9

Degrees of difficulty

| Easy, suitable for novice with little experience | | Fairly easy, suitable for beginner with some experience | | Fairly difficult, suitable for competent DIY mechanic | | Difficult, suitable for experienced DIY mechanic | | Very difficult, suitable for expert DIY or professional | |

Specifications

System type	12 volt, negative earth

Bulbs

	Power rating (watts)
Brake light	21
Brake/tail light	21/5
Direction indicators	21
Direction indicator side repeaters	5 capless
Foglight:	
Front	35 H8
Rear	21
Headlight:	
Halogen:	
Dipped	55 H7
Main	55 H1
Gas discharge (Xenon):	
Dipped	35 DS2
Main	55 H1
Glovebox light	3 capless
High-level brake light	5
Interior light	10
Number plate light	5
Luggage compartment light	5 capless
Reading light	5
Reversing light	21
Sidelights	5
Vanity mirror	5

Torque wrench settings

	Nm	lbf ft
Airbag control unit nuts	7	5
Crash sensor bolts	6	4

1 General information and precautions

⚠️ **Warning: Before carrying out any work on the electrical system, read through the precautions given in 'Safety first!' at the beginning of this manual, and in Chapter 5.**

1 The electrical system is of 12 volt negative earth type. Power for the lights and all electrical accessories is supplied by a lead-acid type battery which is charged by the alternator.

2 This Chapter covers repair and service procedures for the various electrical components not associated with the engine. Information on the battery, alternator and starter motor can be found in Chapter 5.

3 It should be noted that prior to working on any component in the electrical system, the battery negative terminal should first be disconnected to prevent the possibility of electrical short-circuits and/or fires. **Note:** *If the vehicle has a security-coded radio, check that you have a copy of the code number before disconnecting the battery. Refer to your Ford dealer if in doubt.*

2 Electrical fault finding – general information

Note: *Refer to the precautions given in 'Safety first!' and in Chapter 5 before starting work. The following tests relate to testing of the main electrical circuits, and should not be used to test delicate electronic circuits (such as anti-lock braking systems), particularly where an electronic control module is used.*
Caution: *The Ford C-MAX electrical system is extremely complex. Many of the ECMs are connected via a 'Databus' system, where they are able to share information from the various sensors, and communicate with each other. For instance, as the automatic gearbox approaches a gear ratio shift point, it signals the engine management ECM via the Databus. As the gearchange is made by the transmission ECM, the engine management ECM retards the ignition timing, momentarily reducing engine output, to ensure a smoother transition from one gear ratio to the next. Due to the design of the Databus system, it is not advisable to backprobe the ECMs with a multimeter in the traditional manner. Instead, the electrical systems are equipped with a sophisticated self-diagnosis system, which can interrogate the various ECMs to reveal stored fault codes, and help pinpoint faults. In order to access the self-diagnosis system, specialist test equipment (fault code reader/scanner) is required.*

General

1 Typically, electrical circuit consists of an electrical component, any switches, relays, motors, fuses, fusible links or circuit breakers related to that component, and the wiring and connectors which link the component to both the battery and the chassis. To help to pinpoint a problem in an electrical circuit, wiring diagrams are included at the end of this Chapter.

2 Have a good look at the appropriate wiring diagram before attempting to diagnose an electrical fault, to obtain a complete understanding of the components included in the particular circuit concerned. The possible sources of a fault can be narrowed down by noting if other components related to the circuit are operating properly. If several components or circuits fail at one time, the problem is likely to be related to a shared fuse or earth connection.

3 An electrical problem will usually stem from simple cause, such as loose or corroded connections, a faulty earth connection, a blown fuse, a melted fusible link, or a faulty relay (refer to Section 3 for details of testing relays). Visually inspect the condition of all fuses, wires and connections in a problem circuit before testing the components. Use the wiring diagrams to determine which terminal connections will need to be checked in order to pinpoint the trouble-spot.

4 The basic tools required for electrical fault finding include a circuit tester or voltmeter (a 12 volt bulb with a set of test leads can also be used for certain tests); a self-powered test light (sometimes known as a continuity tester); an ohmmeter (to measure resistance); a battery and set of test leads; and a jumper wire, preferably with a circuit breaker or fuse incorporated, which can be used to bypass suspect wires or electrical components. Before attempting to locate a problem with test instruments, use the wiring diagram to determine where to make the connections.

5 Sometimes, an intermittent wiring fault (usually caused to a poor or dirty connection, or damaged wiring insulation) can be pinpointed by performing a wiggle test on the wiring. This involves wiggling the wiring by hand to see if the fault occurs as the wiring is moved. It should be possible to narrow down the source of the fault to a particular section of wiring. This method of testing can be used in conjunction with any of the tests described in the following sub-Sections.

6 Apart from problems due to poor connections, two basic types of fault can occur in an electrical circuit: open-circuit, or short-circuit.

7 Largely, open-circuit faults are caused by a break somewhere in the circuit, which prevents current from flowing. An open-circuit fault will prevent a component from working, but will not cause the relevant circuit fuse to blow.

8 Low resistance or short-circuit faults are caused by a 'short'; a failure point which allows the current flowing in the circuit to 'escape' along an alternative route, somewhere in the circuit. This typically occurs when a positive supply wire touches either an earth wire, or an earthed component such as the bodyshell. Such faults are normally caused by a breakdown in wiring insulation, A short circuit fault will normally cause the relevant circuit fuse to blow.

9 Fuses are designed to protect a circuit from being overloaded. A blown fuse indicates that there may be problem in that particular circuit and it is important to identify and rectify the problem before renewing the fuse. Always renew a blown fuse with one of the correct current rating; fitting a fuse of a different rating may cause an overloaded circuit to overheat and even catch fire.

Finding an open-circuit

10 One of the most straightforward ways of finding an open-circuit fault is by using a circuit test meter or voltmeter. Connect one lead of the meter to either the negative battery terminal or a known good earth. Connect the other lead to a connector in the circuit being tested, preferably nearest to the battery or fuse. Switch on the circuit, bearing in mind that some circuits are live only when the ignition switch is moved to a particular position. If voltage is present (indicated either by the tester bulb lighting or a voltmeter reading, as applicable), this means that the section of the circuit between the relevant connector and the battery is problem-free. Continue to check the remainder of the circuit in the same fashion. When a point is reached at which no voltage is present, the problem must lie between that point and the previous test point with voltage. Most problems can be traced to a broken, corroded or loose connection.

⚠️ **Warning: Under no circumstances may live measuring instruments such as ohmmeters, voltmeters or a bulb and test lead be used to test any of the airbag circuitry. Any testing of these components must be left to a Ford dealer or specialist, as there is a danger of activating the system if the correct procedures are not followed.**

Finding a short-circuit

11 Loading the circuit during testing will produce false results and may damage your test equipment, so all electrical loads must be disconnected from the circuit before it can be checked for short circuits. Loads are the components which draw current from a circuit, such as bulbs, motors, heating elements, etc.

12 Keep both the ignition and the circuit under test switched off, then remove the relevant fuse from the circuit, and connect a circuit test meter or voltmeter to the fuse connections.

13 Switch on the circuit, bearing in mind that some circuits are live only when the ignition switch is moved to a particular position. If voltage is present (indicated either by the

tester bulb lighting or a voltmeter reading, as applicable), this means that there is a short-circuit. If no voltage is present, but the fuse still blows with the load(s) connected, this indicates an internal fault in the load(s).

Finding an earth fault

14 The battery negative terminal is connected to 'earth': the metal of the engine/transmission and the car body – and most systems are wired so that they only receive a positive feed, the current returning through the metal of the car body. This means that the component mounting and the body form part of that circuit. Loose or corroded mountings can therefore cause a range of electrical faults, ranging from total failure of a circuit, to a puzzling partial fault. In particular, lights may shine dimly (especially when another circuit sharing the same earth point is in operation), motors (eg, wiper motors or the radiator auxiliary cooling fan motor) may run slowly, and the operation of one circuit may have an apparently unrelated effect on another. Note that on many vehicles, earth straps are used between certain components, such as the engine/transmission and the body, usually where there is no metal-to-metal contact between components due to flexible rubber mountings, etc **(see illustrations)**.

15 To check whether a component is properly earthed, disconnect the battery and connect one lead of an ohmmeter to a known good earth point. Connect the other lead to the wire or earth connection being tested. The resistance reading should be zero; if not, check the connection as follows.

16 If an earth connection is thought to be faulty, dismantle the connection and clean back to bare metal both the bodyshell and the wire terminal or the component earth connection mating surface. Be careful to remove all traces of dirt and corrosion, then use a knife to trim away any paint, so that a clean metal-to-metal joint is made. On reassembly, tighten the joint fasteners securely; if a wire terminal is being refitted, use serrated washers between the terminal and the bodyshell to ensure a clean and secure connection. When the connection is remade, prevent the onset of corrosion in the future by applying a coat of petroleum jelly or silicone-based grease or by spraying on (at regular intervals) a proprietary ignition sealer or a water dispersant lubricant.

3 Fuses and relays –
general information

Main fuses

1 The fuses are located on a single panel under the passenger's side of the facia (also known as the central junction box), and in a fusebox on the left-hand side of the engine compartment (also known as the engine junction box).

2.14a Earth connection on the left-hand side suspension turret in the engine compartment . . .

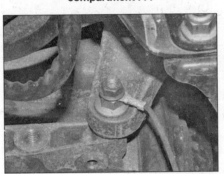
2.14c . . . left-hand transmission mounting (under the battery tray) . . .

2 Access to the passenger cabin fuses is gained by removing the trim panel concealing the fusebox. The panel is secured by 2 fasteners. Undo the fasteners and allow the panel to drop down. Rotate the fusebox

2.14e . . . right-hand facia support bracket (arrowed) . . .

2.14g . . . and passenger side airbag support bracket

2.14b . . . left-hand chassis member in the engine compartment (under the air filter) . . .

2.14d . . . transmission bellhousing (arrowed) . . .

fasteners anti-clockwise, lower the fusebox from place, and pull it towards you. Hook the fusebox into the rear part of the bracket **(see illustrations)**.

3 To access the engine compartment fusebox,

2.14f . . . left- and right-hand front door sills (under the sill trims)

3.2a Squeeze together the sides of the fasteners to release them (arrowed) and lower the panel

3.2b Rotate the fasteners anti-clockwise (arrowed) . . .

3.2c . . . then pull the fusebox rearwards

3.3 Release the clip at the rear then lift off the engine compartment fusebox cover

open the bonnet, pull up on the lever and open the fusebox cover **(see illustration)**.

4 Each fuse is numbered; the fuses' ratings and circuits they protect are listed on the rear face of the cover panel. A list of fuses is also given with the wiring diagrams.

5 To remove a fuse, first switch off the circuit concerned (or the ignition), then pull the fuse out of its terminals – a pair of tweezers provided specifically for this purpose are fitted on the underside of the engine compartment fusebox cover. The wire within the fuse should be visible; if the fuse is blown the wire will have a break in it, which will be visible through the plastic casing.

6 Always renew a fuse with one of an identical rating; never use a fuse with a different rating from the original or substitute anything else. Never renew a fuse more than once without tracing the source of the trouble. The fuse rating is stamped on top of the fuse; note that the fuses are also colour-coded for easy recognition.

7 If a new fuse blows immediately, find the cause before renewing it again; a short to earth as a result of faulty insulation is most likely. Where a fuse protects more than one circuit, try to isolate the defect by switching on each circuit in turn (if possible) until the fuse blows again. Always carry a supply of spare fuses of each relevant rating in the vehicle. A spare of each rating should be clipped into the base of the fusebox.

8 Note that some circuits are protected by 'maxi' fuses fitted in the engine compartment fusebox. These fuses are physically much

bigger than the normal fuses, and have correspondingly higher ratings. Should one of these fuses fail, have the circuit examined a Ford dealer or specialist prior to renewing the fuse.

9 Two fusible links are fitted to the battery positive lead. These are designed to protect the starter motor and alternator wiring harnesses from damage resulting from a major fault. If either of these two links should fail, do not renew them until the circuit concerned has been examined.

Relays

10 The main relays are located in the central junction box and the engine compartment fusebox. The location and function of the relays is given on the underside of the fusebox lid.

11 The relays are of sealed construction, and cannot be repaired if faulty. The relays are of the plug-in type, and may be removed by pulling directly from their terminals. In some cases, it will be necessary to prise the two plastic clips outwards before removing the relay.

12 If a circuit or system controlled by a relay develops a fault and the relay is suspect, operate the system; if the relay is functioning, it should be possible to hear it click as it is energised. If this is the case, the fault lies with the components or wiring of the system. If the relay is not being energised, then either the relay is not receiving a main supply or a switching voltage, or the relay itself is faulty. Testing is by the substitution of a known

good unit, but be careful; while some relays are identical in appearance and in operation, others look similar but perform different functions.

13 To renew a relay, first ensure that the ignition switch is off. The relay can then simply be pulled out from the socket and the new relay pressed in.

4 Ignition switch – removal and refitting

Removal

1 Ensure the battery negative lead has been disconnected as described in Chapter 5, then turn the ignition switch to position I.

2 Using a thin screwdriver, release the locking clip at the front edge, the remove then audio control switch from the steering column (where fitted) **(see illustration)**. Disconnect the wiring plug as the switch is withdrawn.

3 Rotate the steering wheel as necessary to access the column upper shroud retaining clips. Release the clips and remove the shroud **(see illustration)**.

4 Undo the bolts and remove the steering column lower shroud **(see illustration)**. Release the steering column adjustment lever to remove the shroud.

5 Disconnect the wiring plug, then depress the clips and remove the ignition switch **(see illustration)**. Do not turn the lock cylinder (key) from position I whilst the ignition switch is removed.

4.2 Depress the clip and remove the audio control switch from the column shroud

4.3 Rotate the steering wheel and release the upper shroud retaining clip each side

4.4 Lower steering column shroud bolts (arrowed)

4.5 Release the clips (arrowed) and pull the switch from the lock

4.6a Insert a thin rod into the hole on the underside of the lock to release the locking lug . . .

4.6b . . . and pull the lock cylinder from the housing

6 With the key still in position I, insert a thin rod into the hole in the lower part of the cylinder housing and depress the spring-loaded locking lug, and pull the cylinder from the housing **(see illustrations)**.

Refitting

7 Refitting is a reversal of removal. Note that the lock cylinder (key) must be in position I prior to refitting the ignition switch.

5 Switches – removal and refitting

Steering column switches

1 Using a thin screwdriver, release the locking clip at the front edge, the remove the audio control switch from the steering column (where fitted) **(see illustration 4.2)**. Disconnect the wiring plug as the switch is withdrawn.
2 Rotate the steering wheel as necessary to access the column upper shroud retaining clips. Release the clips and remove the shroud **(see illustration 4.3)**.
3 Undo the 2 bolts and remove the steering column lower shroud **(see illustration 4.4)**. Release the steering column adjustment lever to remove the shroud.
4 Undo the bolts and slide the relevant switch from the assembly **(see illustration)**.
5 If the multifunction switch/rotary contact carrier is to be removed, begin by removing the steering wheel as described in Chapter 10.
6 Disconnect the wiring plugs, undo the 4 bolts and slide the assembly from the steering column **(see illustrations)**.
7 Refitting is a reversal of removal.

Light switch

8 Remove the driver's side lower facia panel.
9 Reach up, squeeze together the switch upper and lower retaining clips, and pull the switch from the facia **(see illustration)**. Disconnect the wiring plug as the switch is withdrawn.
10 Refitting is a reversal of removal.

Glovebox light switch

11 Remove the glovebox as described in Chapter 11.
12 Disconnect the switch wiring plug.
13 Release the clips and remove the switch **(see illustration)**.
14 Refitting is a reversal of removal.

Door mirror adjuster switch

15 The door mirror adjusters are integral with the window switch assemblies fitted to the door panels.

5.4 Undo the bolts (arrowed) and slide the relevant switch from place

5.6a Undo the bolts (arrowed) on the top . . .

5.6b . . . and the ones underneath (arrowed), then slide the multifunction switch/contact carrier assembly from the column

5.9 Reach up behind the facia and squeeze together the light switch clips (arrowed)

5.13a Disconnect the wiring and pull the glovebox light switch from place

5.13b A small screwdriver helps to remove the bulb

5.16 Remove the switch

5.17 Disconnect the wiring plug

5.19 Audio unit surround trim bolts (arrowed)

16 Prise away the switch assembly using a suitable plastic trim tool **(see illustration)**.
17 Detach the wiring connector and remove the switch **(see illustration)**.
18 Refit in the reverse order of removal.

Facia centre panel switches

19 Remove the facia-mounted audio unit as described in Section 18, undo the 2 bolts and pull the surround trim from place **(see illustration)**.
20 Disconnect the wiring plugs as the panel is withdrawn **(see illustration)**. Release the switches from the panel as required.
21 If required, release the clips and pull the relevant switch from the panel.
22 Refitting is a reversal of removal.

Sunroof control switch

23 Remove the overhead console as described in Chapter 11.

24 Press out the retaining clips and pull the switch from the console.
25 Refit in the reverse order of removal.

Window switches

26 The front window switches are incorporated into the electric door mirror switch **(see illustrations 5.16 and 5.17)**.
27 On vehicles fitted with rear electric windows the switch is part of the door release handle trim **(see illustrations)**
28 Refit in the reverse order of removal.

Courtesy light switches

29 The courtesy lights are controlled by microswitches incorporated into the door locks. The switches are not available separately. If defective, the door lock assembly must be renewed (see Chapter 11).

Handbrake warning switch

30 Remove the centre console as described in Chapter 11.
31 Undo the single bolt and detach the switch **(see illustration)**.
32 Detach the wiring connector from the switch.
33 Refit in the reverse order of removal.

Brake light switch

34 Refer to Chapter 9.

Headlight control/foglight/ instrument illumination switches

35 These switches are integral with the light switch module. Removal is described earlier in this Section.

Hazard warning switch

36 Remove the facia-mounted audio unit as described in Section 18. Undo the 2 bolts and pull the surround trim from place **(see illustration 5.19)**.
37 Disconnect the wiring plug from the switch **(see illustration)**.
38 Depress the clips and push the switch from position.
39 Refitting is a reversal of removal.

Steering wheel switches

40 Remove the driver's airbag as described in Section 22.
41 Undo the bolts and remove the relevant switch pad **(see illustration)**. Disconnect the wiring plug as the switch pad is withdrawn.
42 Refitting is a reversal of removal.

5.20 Disconnect the wiring plugs as the panel is removed

5.27a Prise out the front edge, and remove the handle surround

5.27b Depress the clips (arrowed) and pull the switch from the surround

5.31 Handbrake warning switch retaining bolt (arrowed)

5.37 Unplug the hazard warning switch as the panel is removed

5.41 Steering wheel switch retaining bolts (arrowed)

6.3a Depress the tabs (arrowed) to release the clips around the edge . . .

6.3b . . . and remove the plastic cover from the rear of the headlight

Seat heating switches

43 Remove the facia centre switch panel as described in Paragraph 19 and 20.
44 Release the clips and slide the switch from the panel.

6 Exterior light bulbs – renewal

Note: *This section does not cover bulb renewal on models fitted with gas discharge headlights; refer to Section 9 for renewal details.*

1 Whenever a bulb is renewed, note the following points:

a) *Remember that if the light has just been in use, the bulb may be extremely hot.*
b) ***Do not*** *touch the bulb glass with the fingers, as the small deposits can cause the bulb to cloud over.*
c) *Always check the bulb contacts and holder, ensuring that there is clean metal-to-metal contact. Clean off any corrosion or dirt before fitting a new bulb.*
d) *Wherever bayonet-type bulbs are fitted, ensure that the live contacts bear firmly against the bulb contact.*
e) *Always ensure that the new bulb is of the correct rating and that it is completely clean before fitting it.*

Halogen main beam

2 Remove the headlight unit as described in Section 8.

Models up to 12/2007

3 Push the retaining clips inwards and remove the plastic cover from the rear of the headlight **(see illustrations)**.
4 Pull the wiring plug from the bulb, then release the retaining clip and remove the bulb **(see illustrations)**. If the bulb is to be refitted, do not touch the glass with the fingers. If the glass is accidentally touched, clean it with methylated spirit.
5 Fit the new bulb using a reversal of the removal procedure.

Models from 12/2007

6 Peel away the plastic cap from the rear of the unit.
7 Pull the wiring plug from the bulb **(see illustration)**. Unhook and lower the bulb retaining wire catch.
8 Remove the bulb from the reflector **(see illustration)**. If the bulb is to be refitted, do not

touch the glass with the fingers. If the glass is accidentally touched, clean it with methylated spirit.
9 Fit the new bulb using a reversal of the removal procedure.

Halogen dipped beam

10 Remove the headlight as described in Section 8.

Models up to 12/2007

11 Push the retaining clips inwards and remove the plastic cover from the rear of the headlight **(see illustrations 6.3a and 6.3b)**.
12 Disconnect the wiring plug from the rear of the bulb, then release the retaining clip and remove the bulb from the headlight, noting which way around it's fitted **(see illustrations)**. If the bulb is to be refitted, do not touch the glass with the fingers. If the glass is accidentally touched, clean it with methylated spirit.

6.4a Disconnect the wiring plug and unhook the clip (arrowed) . . .

6.4b . . . then pull the bulb from the reflector

6.7 Pull the wiring plug from the bulb

6.8 Pull the bulb from the reflector

6.12a Pull the wiring plug from the bulb . . .

6.12b . . . then unhook the bulb retaining clip

6.14 Remove the cover

6.16 Pull the bulb from the holder

6.19 Squeeze together the clips (arrowed)

6.23 The sidelight bulb location (arrowed)

6.24 Pull the wedge-type bulb from the holder

13 Fit the new bulb using a reversal of the removal procedure.

Models from 12/2007

14 Peel away the plastic cap from the rear of the unit **(see illustration)**.
15 Rotate the wiring plug and remove it complete with the bulb.
16 Remove the bulb from the bulbholder **(see illustration)**. If the bulb is to be refitted, do not touch the glass with the fingers. If the glass is accidentally touched, clean it with methylated spirit.
17 Fit the new bulb using a reversal of the removal procedure.

Sidelight

Models up to 12/2007

18 Remove the headlight unit as described in Section 8, then remove the cover from the rear of the headlight **(see illustrations 6.3a and 6.3b)**.

19 Squeeze together the clips and pull the bulbholder from the headlight unit **(see illustration)**. Pull only on the bulbholder – not the cable.
20 Pull the wedge-type bulb directly from the bulbholder.
21 Fit the new bulb using a reversal of the removal procedure.

Models from 12/2007

22 Remove the headlight as described in Section 8, then pull the rubber cover from the rear of the sidelight location.
23 Squeeze together the clips and pull the bulbholder from the headlight unit **(see illustration)**. Pull only on the bulbholder – not the cable.
24 Pull the wedge-type bulb from the holder **(see illustration)**.
25 Fit the new bulb using a reversal of the removal procedure.

Front foglight

26 Remove the foglight as described in Section 8.
27 Disconnect the wiring from the bulb-holder.
28 Rotate the bulbholder anti-clockwise and pull it from the foglight **(see illustration)**. Note that the bulb is integral with the bulbholder.
29 Fit the new bulb using a reversal of the removal procedure.

Front indicator

30 Remove the headlight as described in Section 8.
31 Rotate the bulbholder anti-clockwise and pull it from the headlight **(see illustration)**.
32 Depress and twist the bulb to remove it from the bulbholder **(see illustration)**.
33 Fit the new bulb using a reversal of the removal procedure.

6.28 Rotate the foglight bulbholder anti-clockwise

6.31 Rotate the bulbholder anti-clockwise

6.32 Depress and twist the bulb

6.34 Release the repeater at the rear

6.35 Release the bulbholder

6.36 Pull the wedge-type bulb free

6.50a Remove the screws . . .

6.50b . . . and release the bulbholder

6.50c If required unplug the electrical supply to the LED cluster in the light

Front indicator side repeater

In wing

34 Use a plastic type trim tool to release the repeater from the wing **(see illustration)**.
35 Holding the bulbholder, twist the lens anti-clockwise and remove the bulb and holder **(see illustration)**.
36 Pull the wedge-type bulb from the holder **(see illustration)**.
37 Refitting is a reversal of removal.

In mirror

38 Remove the mirror cover by levering the lower edge free. Take care as the retaining tabs are very fragile.
39 Use a small screwdriver in the exposed hole to release the repeater.
40 Twist the bulbholder to release it from the light.
41 Pull the wedge-type bulb from the holder.

42 Refitting is a reversal of removal, but engage the top edge of the wing cover first to avoid any damage to the retaining tabs.

Approach light

43 Use a small screwdriver on the outer edge of the light to remove it.
44 Twist the bulbholder to release it from the light.
45 Pull the wedge-type bulb from the bulbholder.
46 Fit the new bulb using a reversal of the removal procedure.

Rear combination light

47 The rear combination light houses the following bulbs:
a) Brake light.
b) Direction indicator.
c) Reverse light.
d) Combined fog and tail light.

48 Note that some models have an LED (light emitting diode) board instead of the standard tail light. If a fault develops with the LEDs the tail light must be renewed.
49 Remove the rear light unit as described in Section 8.
50 Remove the screws to access the bulb-holders **(see illustrations)**.
51 Rotate the relevant bulb anti-clockwise and pull it from the light.
52 Push and twist the bulb anti-clockwise, and pull it from the bulbholder.
53 Refitting is a reversal of removal.

Number plate light

54 Remove the screws and release the light **(see illustrations)**.
55 Pull the festoon-type type bulb from the contacts **(see illustration)**.
56 Fit the new bulb using a reversal of the removal procedure.

6.54a Remove the screws . . .

6.54b . . . and release the light

6.55 Remove the bulb

6.57a Remove the screws . . .

6.57b . . . and unplug the light

6.58 Bulbholder retaining clips (arrowed)

High-level brake light

57 Undo the bolts and remove the light unit **(see illustrations)**.

58 Unclip the bulbholder, and pull the wedge-type bulb from place **(see illustration)**.

59 Fit a new bulb using a reversal of the removal procedure.

7 Interior light bulbs – renewal

1 Whenever a bulb is renewed, note the following points:

a) *Remember that if the light has just been in use, the bulb may be extremely hot.*

b) *Always check the bulb contacts and* holder, ensuring that there is clean metal-to-metal contact between the bulb and its live and earth. Clean off any corrosion or dirt before fitting a new bulb.

c) *Wherever bayonet-type bulbs are fitted, ensure that the live contact(s) bear firmly against the bulb contact.*

d) *Always ensure that the new bulb is of the correct rating and that it is completely clean before fitting it.*

Reading lights

2 Inset a small flat-bladed screwdriver into the slot in the front face, depress the clip, and carefully prise the light unit from place **(see illustration)**.

3 Twist the reading light bulbholder anti-clockwise and remove it **(see illustration)**. Pull the wedge-type bulb from the holder.

4 Fit a new bulb using a reversal of the removal procedure.

Interior lights

5 Unclip the light and twist the bulbholder anti-clockwise. Pull the bulb free **(see illustrations)**. Note that some models have a festoon-type bulb fitted.

6 Fit a new bulb using a reversal of the removal procedure.

Glovebox light

7 Remove the glovebox and unplug the wiring connector **(see illustration)**. Press the tabs to release the light and then remove the light.

8 Pull the wedge-type bulb from its holder **(see illustration)**.

9 Fit the new bulb using a reversal of the removal procedure.

7.2 Depress the clip at the front of the interior light

7.3 Twist the reading light bulbholder anti-clockwise and remove it

7.5a Prise the light from place . . .

7.5b . . . then twist the bulbholder free . . .

7.5c . . . and pull the wedge-type bulb free

7.7 Unplug the electrical connector

7.8 A small screwdriver aids removal of the wedge-type bulb

7.10 Pull the footwell light bulb (arrowed) from the holder

7.12 Carefully prise the vanity light lens from place

7.13 Pull the bulb (arrowed) from the holder

7.15 Prise the light free

7.16 Pull the bulb from the bulbholder

Footwell lights

10 Reach under the facia, and pull the wedge-type capless bulb from the holder **(see illustration)**.

11 Fit the new bulb using a reversal of the removal procedure.

Sunvisor/vanity mirror light

12 Carefully prise the light unit from place **(see illustration)**.

13 Pull the wedge-type bulb from the bulbholder **(see illustration)**.

14 Fit the new bulb using a reversal of the removal procedure.

Luggage area light

15 Use a small screwdriver and prise the light free **(see illustration)**.

16 Pull the wedge-type bulb free from the light **(see illustration)**.

17 Fit the new bulb using a reversal of the removal procedure.

Instrument panel bulbs

18 On all models covered by this Manual, it is not possible to renew the instrument panel bulbs individually as they are of LED design and soldered to a printed circuit board. Where an LED is not functioning, the complete instrument panel must be renewed.

Switch illumination

19 The switches are illuminated by LEDs, and cannot be renewed separately. Refer to Section 5 and remove the switch.

Heater/air conditioning control panel illumination

20 The control panel is illuminated by non-renewable LEDs. If defective, the control panel may need to be renewed.

8 Exterior light units – removal, refitting and beam adjustment

Headlight unit

Caution: On models equipped with gas discharge headlights, disconnect the battery negative lead, as described in Chapter 5, prior to working on the headlights.

1 Open the bonnet, and undo the headlight upper retaining bolt **(see illustration)**.

2 Depress the retaining clips on the rear of the headlight, and pull the unit from place **(see illustration)**.

3 Disconnect the wiring plugs from the rear of the headlight as it's withdrawn **(see illustration)**.

4 If required, the headlight levelling motor can be renewed after the headlight has been

8.1 Remove the headlight retaining bolt

8.2 Use a long screwdriver to depress the retaining clips and pull the headlight forwards

8.3 Use a screwdriver to disconnect the headlight wiring plug

8.6a Disconnect the levelling motor wiring plug . . .

8.6b . . . then rotate the motor (see text) and disengage the ball-head from the guide on the reflector

8.8a On early models prise out the trim above the foglight . . .

8.8b . . . and then the trim around the foglight

8.8c Prise the trim free on later models

removed, as follows. **Note:** *On models after 12/2007, it is not possible to renew the motor separately. If defective, it would appear that the complete headlight assembly must be renewed – check with your local dealer or parts specialist.*

5 Release the clips and remove the plastic cover from the rear of the headlight.

6 Disconnect the motor wiring plug, then rotate the motor clockwise (left-hand headlight) or anti-clockwise (right-hand headlight), manoeuvre the motor ball-head

from the guide on the reflector and pull it from the headlight (see illustrations).
7 Refitting is a reversal of the removal procedure. On completion check for satisfactory operation, and have the headlight beam adjustment checked as soon as possible (see below).

Front foglight

8 Carefully prise out the trim above the foglight, and the foglight surround trim (see illustrations).
9 Undo the 2 mounting bolts or single bolt on later models (see illustrations). Withdraw the foglight from the front bumper, and disconnect the wiring.
10 On later models use a suitable tool to release the locking tabs (see illustration).
11 Refitting is a reversal of removal, but have the foglight beam setting checked at the earliest opportunity. An approximate adjustment can be made by positioning the car 10 metres in front of a wall marked with the centre point of the foglight lens. Turn the adjustment screw as required (see illustration). Note that only height adjustment is possible – there is no lateral adjustment.

Front indicator side repeater

12 The procedure is as described for bulb renewal in Section 6.

Rear combination light

13 Open the tailgate and remove the parcel shelf.
14 Remove the upper quarter trim panel (see illustration).

8.9a Foglight mounting bolts (arrowed) on early models . . .

8.9b . . . and on later models

8.10 Release the locking tabs (arrowed)

8.11 Foglight adjustment screw (arrowed) – pre 12/2007 models

8.14 Remove the trim panel

8.15a Remove the upper fixing . . .

8.15b . . . and the lower

8.16 Disconnect the wiring plug

15 Remove the upper and lower fixings **(see illustrations)**. Note the poor access to the lower fixing.
16 Pull the light unit rearwards, and disconnect the wiring plug **(see illustration)**.
17 Refitting is a reversal of removal, but locate the pegs correctly into the D-pillar **(see illustration)**.

Number plate light

18 The procedure is as described for bulb renewal in Section 6.

High-level brake light

19 The procedure is as described for bulb renewal in Section 6.

Rear foglight/reversing lights

20 The foglight and reversing lights are part of the rear combination light – see above for removal details.

Beam adjustment

Halogen headlights

21 Accurate adjustment of the headlight beam is only possible using optical beam setting equipment, and this work should therefore be carried out by a Ford dealer or suitably-equipped workshop. All MOT testing stations have suitable equipment.
22 For reference, the headlights can be adjusted using the adjuster screws, accessible via the top of each light unit **(see illustration)**.
23 On vehicles with adaptive front headlights (the headlight reflectors turn in the direction of the steering) it is possible to adjust the headlight beams for driving on the right-hand or left-hand side of the road. Remove the headlight as described in this Section.
24 Locate the adjustment screw and rotate it two and a half times in a clockwise direction.

> **9 Xenon gas discharge headlight system** – component removal, refitting and adjustment

General information

1 Xenon gas discharge headlights were available as an optional extra on all models

8.17 Locate the peg correctly (arrowed)

covered in this manual. The headlight dipped beam bulbs produce light by means of an electric arc, rather than by heating a metal filament as in conventional halogen bulbs. An electronically-operated shutter is fitted in front of the bulb which angles the light for dipped beam, then re-angles the light for main beam. A conventional halogen bulb is also fitted to augment the main beam light output. The arc is generated by a control circuit which operates at voltages of above 28 000 volts. The intensity of the emitted light means that the headlight beam has to be controlled dynamically to avoid dazzling other road users. An electronic control unit monitors the vehicle's pitch and overall ride height by sensors mounted on the front and rear suspension and adjusts the beam range accordingly, using the range control motors built into the headlight units.

⚠ **Warning: The discharge bulb starter circuitry operates at extremely high voltages. To avoid the risk of electric shock, ensure that the battery negative cable is disconnected before working on the headlight units (see Chapter 5), then additionally switch the dipped beam on and off to discharge any residual voltage.**

Headlight main beam

2 Remove the headlight as described in Section 8.
3 Push the retaining clips outwards, and remove the plastic cover from the rear of the headlight **(see illustrations 6.3a and 6.3b)**.
4 Disconnect the wiring plug from the rear

8.22 Headlight beam adjustment screws (arrowed)

of the bulb, then release the retaining clip and pull the bulb from the reflector **(see illustrations 6.4a and 6.4b)**. Note how the lugs on the bulb engage with the slots in the reflector. If the bulb is to be refitted, do not touch the glass with the fingers. If the glass is accidentally touched, clean it with methylated spirit.
5 Fit the new bulb using a reversal of the removal procedure.

Headlight dipped beam

Caution: The dipped beam bulb is under gas pressure of at least 10 bars, therefore it is recommended that protective glasses are worn during this procedure.

6 Remove the headlight as described in Section 8 and then detach the cover from the rear of the light unit **(see illustrations 6.3a and 6.3b)**.
7 Disconnect the wiring plug, then rotate and remove the ignitor assembly.
8 Unhook the U-shaped clip and remove the bulb. If the glass is accidentally touched, clean it with methylated spirit.
9 Fit the new bulb using a reversal of the removal procedure.

Sidelight

10 Remove the headlight unit as described in Section 8.
11 Pull the bulbholder from the headlight unit. Pull only on the bulbholder – not the cable.
12 Pull the wedge-type bulb directly from the bulbholder.
13 Fit the new bulb using a reversal of removal procedure.

10.3 Unclip the gaiter from the column upper shroud

10.4a Remove the bolts at the lower edge (arrowed) . . .

10.4b . . . and lever the top of the instrument panel down

Lighting control module

Note: *If a new module is to be fitted, it must be configured using Ford dedicated diagnostic equipment (IDS). Entrust this task to a Ford dealer or suitably-equipped specialist.*

14 The lighting control module is fitted to vehicles with Xenon high-intensity gas discharge lights, or models with adaptive front lighting system. The module is located behind the driver's side lower facia.

15 Undo the single bolt, and remove the facia panel beneath the main light control switch. Unclip the diagnostic plug connector as the panel is withdrawn.

16 Disconnect the wiring plug, then release the clip each side and remove the module.

17 Refitting is a reversal of removal.

Front ride height sensor

18 The sensor is mounted on the lower control arm of the right-hand wheel. Apply the handbrake, then jack up the front of the vehicle and support it on axle stands (see *Jacking and vehicle support*). Remove the wheel.

19 Undo the bolt securing the sensor arm bracket to the control arm.

20 Drill out the 2 rivets securing the sensor bracket to the vehicle body.

21 Disconnect the wiring plug as the sensor is withdrawn.

22 Refitting is a reversal of removal. Note that if a new sensor has been fitted, then a calibration procedure must be carrier out. This requires access to Ford diagnostic equipment – entrust this task to a Ford dealer or suitably-equipped specialist.

Rear ride height sensor

23 The sensor is secured to the left-hand lower control arm and the rear subframe. Chock the front wheels, then jack up the rear of the vehicle and support it on axle stands (*see Jacking and vehicle support*).

24 Disconnect the sensor wiring plug, then undo the bolts and remove the sensor, bracket and lever arm assembly.

25 Refitting is a reversal of removal. Note that if a new sensor has been fitted, then a calibration procedure must be carried out. This requires access to Ford diagnostic equipment – entrust this task to a Ford dealer or suitably-equipped specialist.

Driving on the right or left

Note: *This feature is also available on some halogen headlights (see Section 8, paragraphs 23 and 24).*

26 On models equipped with gas discharge headlights, the 'dipping' characteristics of the unit can be set-up for countries who drive on the left or right. Remove the headlight as described in Section 9.

27 Release the clips and remove the plastic cover from the rear of the headlight behind the dipped beam location.

28 Press the lever on the side of the reflector upwards for driving on the right, and down for driving on the left.

Beam adjustment

29 The basic alignment procedure of the headlights is the same as normal halogen headlights (see Section 8). However, before the procedure is attempted, the ride height sensors must be calibrated using dedicated Ford test equipment. Therefore this task should be entrusted to a Ford dealer or suitably-equipped specialist.

Range control positioning motor

30 Remove the headlight as described in Section 8.

31 Remove the cover from the rear of the headlight.

32 Disconnect the motor wiring plug, then undo the 2 retaining bolts.

33 Disengage the motor ball-head from the guide in the reflector and remove the motor.

34 Refitting is a reversal of removal.

---

10 Instrument panel –
removal and refitting

Note: *The instrument panel and its function is included in the vehicle's self-diagnosis program. If the instrument panel has a fault, it would be prudent to have the vehicle's fault code memory interrogated by a Ford dealer or specialist, prior to removing the panel.*

Note: *If the instrument panel is being substituted with a new or exchange unit, the assistance of a Ford dealer or specialist is*

required to download necessary software, and initialise/adapt the various instrument panel functions.

Removal

1 Disconnect the battery negative lead as described in Chapter 5.

2 Fully extend the steering column, and move it to its lowest position.

3 Unclip the rubber gaiter from the steering column upper shroud, then pull the bezel attached to the lower part of the instrument panel rearwards and remove it **(see illustration)**.

4 Undo the 2 retaining bolts on the lower edge of the instrument panel, then carefully pull the top edge of the panel down and manoeuvre it from place **(see illustrations)**.

5 Disconnect the wiring plug(s) as the panel is withdrawn.

Refitting

6 Refitting is a reversal of removal, but see the note at the beginning of this section.

---

11 Windscreen wiper components –
removal and refitting

Wiper blades

1 Refer to *Weekly checks*.

Wiper arms

Removal

2 If the wipers are not in their parked position, switch on the ignition, and allow the motor to automatically park.

3 Before removing an arm, mark its parked position on the glass with a strip of adhesive tape. Prise off the cover and unscrew the spindle nut. Ease the arm from the spindle by rocking it slowly from side-to-side. If the arm is difficult to remove specialist tools are available **(see illustrations)**.

Refitting

4 Refitting is a reversal of removal, but before tightening the spindle nuts, position the wiper blades as marked before removal.

11.3a Some screens have an index mark to aid the correct positioning of the wiper blades (arrowed)

11.3b Pull off the rubber cap, undo the nut . . .

11.3c . . . and remove the wiper arm

11.3d Lift the cover to expose the wiper spindle nut – rear wiper

11.3e If the arm is difficult to remove specialist tools are available to pull the arm off the tapered spindle

11.6a Remove the extension panel

Wiper motor

Removal

5 Remove the wiper arms as described in the previous sub-Section.
6 On later models, remove the extension

panel and then remove the clips from the front edge of the cowl. Pull the scuttle cowling panel upwards to release it from the base of the windscreen (**see illustrations**). Lift the panel from place.
7 Undo the bolt at each end, release the 4

clips and remove the bulkhead extension panel (**see illustration**).
8 Undo the bolts securing the motor linkage (**see illustrations**).
9 Disconnect the wiper motor wiring plug as the assembly is withdrawn (**see illustration**).

11.6b Prise off the clips . . .

11.6c . . . then pull the scuttle cowling panel upwards from the base of the windscreen

11.7 Undo the bolt at each end (right-hand one shown) and pull the bulkhead extension panel forwards

11.8a Undo the central bolt . . .

11.8b . . . and the right-hand bolt

11.9 Disconnect the wiring plug

12.5a The washer fluid reservoir is retained by 2 bolts (arrowed) – viewed from under the wheel arch

10 Using a screwdriver, carefully prise the linkage arm from the balljoint stud.
11 Undo the 3 bolts and remove the motor.

Refitting

12 When refitting, with the motor/linkage back in place, reconnect the wiring plug then operate the touch-wipe button to set the motor in the rest position. The remainder of refitting is a reversal of removal.

12 Washer system – general

1 All models are fitted with a windscreen and tailgate washer system, and some models are fitted with headlight washers.
2 The fluid reservoir for the washers is located behind the right-hand side inner wing, behind the wheel arch liner. The windscreen washer

12.5b Pull the pump from the grommet in the reservoir

fluid pump is attached to the side of the reservoir body and, where headlight washers are fitted, a lift cylinder/accumulator is located in the supply tube, behind the front bumper. Access to the reservoir, pump and lift cylinder is achieved by removing either the right-hand front wheel arch liner or front bumper, and the plastic panel at the right-hand side of the engine compartment.
3 Working under the bonnet remove the trim panel. Remove the bolt and then remove the filler neck extension.
4 Jack up and support the front of the vehicle and remove the right-hand front roadwheel. Remove the wheel arch liner as described In Chapter 11.
5 Remove the bolts and lower the washer reservoir. Disconnect the wiring plug and outlet pipes from the washer pump. Alternatively pull the pump from the reservoir (have a container ready to catch the washer fluid) and remove the reservoir **(see illustrations)**.

12.6a Pull the grommet from the reservoir . . .

6 Pull the sealing grommet free from the reservoir and check the filter for debris **(see illustration)**.
7 The tailgate washer is fed by the same reservoir, with a dual output pump.
8 The reservoir fluid level must be regularly topped-up with windscreen washer fluid containing an antifreeze agent, but not cooling system antifreeze – see *Weekly checks*.
9 The supply hoses are attached by rubber couplings to their various connections, and if required, can be detached by simply pulling them free from the appropriate connector.
10 The windscreen washer jets can be adjusted by inserting a pin into the jet and altering the aim as required. To remove a washer jet, open the bonnet, and disconnect the hose from the jet **(see illustrations)**. Note that on some models, the bonnet insulation panel must be unclipped and removed.
11 Use a small screwdriver to release the jet

12.6b . . . and inspect the filter

12.10a Pull the washer hose free . . .

12.10b . . . and unplug the electrical connector

12.11a Release the washer jet . . .

12.11b . . . and remove it

12.13 Use a small screwdriver to release the rear screen washer jet

13.4a Tailgate wiper motor bolts (arrowed)

13.4b Recover the sleeve . . .

13.4c . . . and the sealing grommet

and then manoeuvre the jet from the bonnet (see illustrations).

12 The headlight washer jets are best adjusted using the Ford tool, and should therefore be entrusted to a Ford dealer or specialist to set.

13 To remove the rear washer jet, carefully prise it from the rear spoiler (see illustration). Disconnect the hose as the jet is withdrawn.

13 Tailgate wiper motor – removal and refitting

Removal

1 Make sure the tailgate wiper is switched off and in its rest position, then remove the tailgate trim panel.

2 Remove the wiper arm and blade as described in Section 11.

3 Detach the wiring connector from the wiper motor.

4 Undo the 3 wiper motor mounting bolts and remove the wiper motor from the tailgate (see illustrations). Check the condition of the spindle rubber grommet in the tailgate, and if necessary, renew it.

Refitting

5 Refit in the reverse order of removal. Refit the wiper arm and blade so that the arm is parked correctly.

14 Horns – removal and refitting

Removal

1 The horns are located at the front end of the vehicle. Raise the front of the vehicle and support it securely on axle stands (see *Jacking and vehicle support*).

2 Release the fasteners and remove the splash shield under the radiator.

3 Disconnect the horn wiring plug, undo the mounting bolt and remove the horn from the vehicle (see illustration).

Refitting

4 Refit in the reverse order of removal. Check for satisfactory operation on completion.

15 Sunroof motor – removal and refitting

Removal of the sunroof motor requires the headlining to be removed. This is an involved task, requiring patience and dexterity. Consequently, we recommend you entrust this task to a Ford dealer or upholstery specialist.

16 Central locking system – general information

1 All models are equipped with a central door locking system, which automatically locks all doors and the tailgate in unison with the manual locking of the driver's front door. The system is operated electronically with motors/switches incorporated into the door lock assemblies. The system is controlled by the Generic Electronic Module (GEM) and the Keyless Vehicle Module (KVM) – where fitted. The GEM and the KVM communicate with the vehicle's other control modules via an information network often known as a 'Canbus'. Control modules integral with electric window motors receive signals from the GEM via the canbus, and directly control the operation of the door locks. The tailgate has its own control module, integral with the lock assembly. If any module is renewed, new software for the unit must be downloaded from Ford. Entrust this task to a Ford dealer or suitably-equipped specialist.

2 The control module is equipped with a self-

14.3 Horn retaining bolt (arrowed) – viewed from above

diagnosis capability. Should the system develop a fault, have the module interrogated by a Ford dealer or suitably-equipped specialist. Once the fault has been established, refer to the relevant Section of Chapter 11 to renew a door module or tailgate lock as applicable.

17 Parking aid components – general, removal and refitting

General information

1 The parking aid system is available on all models. Four ultrasound sensors located in the bumpers measure the distance to the closest object behind or in front the car, and inform the driver using acoustic signals from a buzzer located under the rear luggage compartment trim. The nearer the object, the more frequent the acoustic signals.

2 The system includes a control module and self-diagnosis program, and therefore, in the event of a fault, the vehicle should be taken to a Ford dealer or suitably-equipped specialist who will be able to interrogate the system.

Parking Aid Module (PAM)
Removal

3 The control unit is located behind the right-hand luggage compartment side trim panel. Remove the luggage compartment side panel trim as described in Chapter 11, and remove the foam padding behind the panel.

4 Undo the 2 retaining bolts, and remove the PAM (see illustration). As the unit is removed, disconnect the wiring plugs.

17.4 The parking aid module and warning buzzer

17.7a Disconnect the wiring plug . . .

17.7b . . . and prise apart the clips (arrowed). Pull the sensor from place

Refitting

5 Refitting is a reversal of removal.

Range/distance sensor

Removal

6 Remove the relevant bumper as described in Chapter 11.

7 Disconnect the sensor wiring plug, then push the retaining clips apart, and pull the sensor from position **(see illustrations)**.

Refitting

8 Refitting is a reversal of removal. Press the sensor firmly into position until the retaining clips engage.

Speaker

9 The parking aid warning speaker is located adjacent to the right-hand side rear seat belt inertia reel units. To access the speakers, remove the luggage compartment side panels as described in Chapter 11.

10 Undo the 2 retaining bolts, and remove the speaker. Disconnect the wiring plug as the speaker is removed.

---

18 Audio/DVD units –
removal and refitting

Note: *This Section applies only to standard-fit audio equipment.*

1 Various audio units are fitted to the C-MAX. Higher specification models have a DVD-based navigation system and some vehicles may have a roof console-mounted DVD player fitted. The principle of removal remains the same in all cases.

Removal

Audio units

Note: *If a new audio unit is to be fitted, it must be configured using Ford diagnostic equipment (WDS). Entrust this task to a Ford dealer or suitably-equipped specialist.*

2 Disconnect the battery negative lead as described in Chapter 5.

3 Removal of the facia unit requires the use of Ford special tools No GV3301. Equivalent tools may be available from car audio specialist.

4 Insert the 4 tools into the slots in each corner of the audio control panel **(see illustrations)**. Note that the tools must be inserted with the straight-edges to the outside. Pull the audio unit from the facia.

5 Release the locking catches and disconnect the wiring plug(s) as the unit is withdrawn **(see illustrations)**.

CD auto-changer

Note: *If a new auto-changer is to be fitted, the new unit must be configured using Ford diagnostic equipment (IDS). Entrust this task to a Ford dealer or suitably-equipped specialist.*

6 Remove the passenger side front seat as described in Chapter 11.

7 Undo the 5 retaining bolts and pull the auto-changer from place. Disconnect the wiring plug as the unit is withdrawn.

Headlining-mounted DVD player

8 Fold down the DVD screen, and remove the 2 Torx security bolts **(see illustrations)**.

9 Slide the assembly rearwards and lower it

18.4a Insert the tools into the slots in the corners of the unit . . .

18.4b . . . and release it

18.4c Some units require the removal of blanking plugs to access the slots

18.5a Disconnect the wiring plug . . .

18.5b . . . and the aerial connector

18.8a Fold down the screen and undo the security bolts (arrowed)

from place **(see illustration)**. Disconnect the wiring plug as the assembly is withdrawn. **Note:** *Handle the DVD assembly with care – it's very delicate.*

10 No further dismantling is recommended. When refitting the assembly, position it in line with the front mounting bolt holes, and push it upwards to engage the rear clips.

Refitting

11 Refitting is a reversal of removal, but if a new unit has been fitted, suitable software must be downloaded from Ford. Entrust this task to a Ford dealer or suitably-equipped specialist.

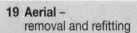

19 Aerial – removal and refitting

Removal and refitting of the aerial requires the headlining to be removed. This is an involved task, requiring patience and dexterity. Consequently, we recommend you entrust this task to a Ford dealer or upholstery specialist.

20 Speakers – removal and refitting

Door speakers

1 To remove a door-mounted speaker, remove the appropriate door trim as described in Chapter 11.

2 Drill out the rivets securing the speaker to the door **(see illustration)**.

3 Disconnect the wiring plugs as the speaker is withdrawn.

4 Refit in the reverse order of removal.

Tweeter speaker

5 Pull the trim panel over the door mirror mounting from place **(see illustration)**.

6 Unclip the speaker cover from the trim panel **(see illustration)**.

7 Release the retaining clips and remove the speaker. Disconnect the speaker wiring plug as it's withdrawn.

8 Refitting is a reversal of removal.

18.8b Note the pin in the centre of the security bolts

21 Airbag system – general information and precautions

⚠️ *Warning: Before carrying out any operations on the airbag system, disconnect the battery negative terminal (see Chapter 5). When operations are complete, make sure no one is inside the vehicle when the battery is reconnected.*

• *Note that the airbag(s) must not be subjected to temperatures in excess of 90°C. When the airbag is removed, ensure that it is stored the correct way up (pad upwards) to prevent possible inflation.*

• *Do not allow any solvents or cleaning agents to contact the airbag assemblies. They must be cleaned using only a damp cloth.*

• *The airbags and control unit are both sensitive to impact. If either is dropped or damaged they should be renewed.*

• *Disconnect the airbag control unit wiring plug prior to using arc-welding equipment on the vehicle.*

A driver's and passenger's airbag, side airbags (seat mounted) and overhead curtain airbags are fitted as standard equipment to models in the C-MAX range. The driver's airbag is fitted to the centre of the steering wheel. The passenger's airbag is fitted to the upper surface of the facia, above the glovebox. The airbag system comprises the airbag unit(s) (complete with gas generators), impact sensors, the control module and a warning light in the instrument panel.

The airbag system is triggered in the event

18.9 Slide the DVD assembly rearwards

of a direct or offset frontal impact above a predetermined force. The airbag is inflated within milliseconds, and forms a safety cushion between the driver and the steering wheel or (where applicable) the passenger and the facia. This prevents contact between the upper body and the steering wheel, column and facia, and therefore greatly reduces the risk of injury. The airbag then deflates almost immediately through vents in the side of the airbag. The side airbags and overhead curtain airbags are triggered by side impacts, registered by the sensors fitted to the base of the B-pillars on each side.

Every time the ignition is switched on, the airbag control unit performs a self-test. The self-test takes approximately 7 seconds, and during this time the airbag warning light on the facia is illuminated. After the self-test has been completed, the warning light should go out. If the warning light fails to come on or remains illuminated after the initial 7 second period, or comes on at any time when the vehicle is being driven, there is a fault in the airbag system. The vehicle should then be taken to a Ford dealer or specialist for examination at the earliest possible opportunity.

22 Airbag system components – removal and refitting

Note: *Refer to the warnings in Section 21 before carrying out the following operations.*

1 Disconnect the battery negative terminal (see Chapter 5). Wait at least 5 minutes for

20.2 Drill out the rivets (arrowed) and remove the speaker

20.5 Pull the mirror mounting trim panel from place

20.6 Unclip the cover from the panel

22.4a Insert a flat-bladed screwdriver and push the handle down to release the airbag clip

22.4b The airbag clips (arrowed) must be pushed outwards

22.4c There are 3 airbag retaining clips (arrowed)

any residual electrical energy to dissipate before commencing work. **Note:** *If removing the driver's airbag, turn the steering wheel 90° from straight-ahead before disconnecting the battery, otherwise the steering lock will engage.*

Driver's airbag

2 Set the steering wheel and front wheels in the 'straight-ahead' position.

3 Rotate the steering wheel 90° in each direction to access the steering column upper shroud retaining clips. Release the clips and remove the shroud (**see illustrations 4.2, 4.3 and 4.4**).

4 Locate the access hole in the reverse side of the steering wheel, and insert a flat-bladed screwdriver into the hole, then push the handle downwards to release the retaining clip (**see illustrations**). Turn the steering wheel 180°

and release the clip on the other side, followed by the clip at the base of the unit.

5 Temporarily touch the striker plate of the front door to discharge any electrostatic electricity. Return the steering wheel to the straight-ahead position, then carefully lift the airbag assembly away from the steering wheel and disconnect the wiring connectors from the rear of the unit (**see illustration**). Note that the airbag must not be knocked or dropped, and should be stored the correct way up with its padded surface uppermost.

6 On refitting, reconnect the wiring connectors and locate the airbag unit in the steering wheel, making sure the wire does not become trapped, and push the airbag into place to engage the retaining clips. Reconnect the battery negative lead (see Chapter 5). Ensure no-one is in the vehicle when the battery is reconnected.

Passenger airbag

Models up to 10/2005

7 Remove the passenger's glovebox as described in Chapter 11.

8 Using a small screwdriver, release the upper retaining clips from the passenger's side central facia air vent, then pull the top edge forwards, release the lower clips and remove the vent (**see illustration**).

9 Disconnect the airbag wiring plug.

10 Undo the airbag module inner retaining bolts.

11 Working underneath the facia, undo the 4 remaining airbag mounting bolts (**see illustration**). Manoeuvre the airbag from place.

12 Refitting is a reversal of removal. Ensure that the wiring connector is securely reconnected. Ensure that no-one is inside the vehicle. Reconnect the battery negative lead as described in Chapter 5.

Models from 10/2005

13 Remove the facia as described in Chapter 11.

14 Undo the 6 nuts and remove the airbag from the facia (**see illustration**).

15 Refitting is a reversal of removal. Ensure that the wiring connector is securely reconnected. Ensure that no-one is inside the vehicle. Reconnect the battery negative lead as described in Chapter 5.

Airbag wiring contact unit

16 Remove the steering wheel as described in Chapter 10.

17 Fully extend the steering column, then on models with an audio control switch fitted to the column shroud, release the locking tang, pull the switch from place and disconnect the wiring plug (**see illustration 4.2**).

18 Undo the fasteners and remove the lower facia panel on the driver's side.

19 Release the retaining clips and remove the steering column upper shroud (**see illustration 4.3**).

20 Undo the retaining bolts, and remove the steering column lower shroud (**see illustration 4.4**). Release the steering column locking lever to remove the shroud completely.

21 Disconnect the wiring plug from the contact unit and the steering angle sensor (where fitted).

22.5 Squeeze together the clips (arrowed) and pull the connector from the airbag

22.8 Remove the passenger's side air vent

22.11 Undo the remaining airbag bolts (arrowed)

22.14 Passenger's airbag nuts (arrowed)

22 If the contact unit is to be refitted, apply tape to lock the unit in position (see illustration). Do not attempt to rotate the unit.

23 Undo the 4 bolts and remove the contact unit (see illustration).

24 If required, release the clips and detach the steering angle sensor from the contact unit.

25 Begin refitting by attaching the steering angle sensor to the contact unit. Ensure the retaining clips fully engage and the sensor locating tangs align with the ones on the contact unit. **Note:** *If a new sensor is being fitted, it must be configured and calibrated using Ford diagnostic equipment. Entrust this task to a Ford dealer or suitably-equipped specialist.*

26 Ensure the front wheels are still in the 'straight-ahead' position, and the directional indicator stalk is in the 'Off' position, then fit the contact unit into position. Tighten the retaining bolts.

27 If there is any doubt as to the position of the contact unit (eg, securing tape missing or disturbed), the unit must be centralised as follows:

a) *Rotate the contact unit rotor anti-clockwise until a resistance is felt.*

b) *Rotate the rotor clockwise until the arrow marked on the rotor aligns with the raised V section on the outer cover, at approximately the 7 o'clock position (see illustration).*

c) *Rotate the rotor 3 turns in a clockwise direction.*

28 The remainder of refitting is a reversal of removal.

Restraint Control Module (RCM)

29 Refer to Chapter 11 and remove the centre console.

30 Release the locking devices and disconnect the wiring plugs for the control module.

31 Undo the retaining bolts and remove the control module (see illustration).

32 Refitting is a reversal of removal, ensuring the module is refitted with the arrow mark on the top pointing forwards. Note that if a new module has been fitted, software for it will need to be downloaded from Ford. Entrust this task to a Ford dealer or suitably-equipped specialist.

22.22 Apply tape (arrowed) to secure the rotary contact unit

22.27 Align the marks (arrowed) on the contact unit rotor and cover

Side airbags

33 The side airbags are incorporated into the side of the front and rear seats. Removal of the units requires the seat upholstery to be removed. This is a specialist task, which we recommend should be entrusted to a Ford dealer or specialist.

Head/overhead curtain airbags

34 Renewal of the head airbags/inflatable curtain requires removal of the headlining. This is a specialist task, and should be entrusted to a Ford dealer or specialist.

Crash/lateral acceleration sensors

Front sensor (vehicles up to 05/2005)

35 Open the bonnet, undo the 4 scrivets and remove the air deflector panel (see illustrations). If required remove the front grille.

22.23 Contact unit retaining bolts (arrowed)

22.31 Note the arrow (arrowed) on the top of the RCM must point forwards

36 Undo the retaining bolt and remove the sensor.

37 Refitting is a reversal of removal.

Side sensors

38 The side sensors are located in the vehicle's B-pillars each side.

39 Remove the B-pillar (see Chapter 11).

40 Disconnect the sensor wiring pug, then undo the bolt and remove the sensor (see illustration). Take great care not to damage the sensor wiring harness. Note that the sensor must be handled carefully. Do not refit a sensor that has been dropped or knocked.

41 Refitting is a reversal of removal.

23 Anti-theft alarm system – general information

An anti-theft alarm and immobiliser system

22.35a Undo the bolt and prise out the scrivets . . .

22.35b . . . along the front edge (arrowed) of the air deflector panel

22.40 Side crash sensor (arrowed)

is fitted as standard equipment. Should the system become faulty, the vehicle should be taken to a Ford dealer or specialist for examination. They will have access to a special diagnostic tester which will quickly trace any fault present in the system.

24 Electronic control modules – removal and refitting

Note: *All of these modules are included in the vehicle's sophisticated self-diagnosis system. Should a fault occur, have the system interrogated using a fault code reader/Ford test equipment, via the diagnostic plug located under the driver's side of the facia, above the pedals* **(see illustration).**

Removal

1 Disconnect the battery negative lead as described in Chapter 5.

Generic Electronic Module (GEM)

2 The GEM is integral with the passenger compartment fusebox/central junction box. This module is responsible for the management of the following functions:

Current distribution.
Headlights.
Headlight range adjustment.
Foglights.
Sidelights.
Reversing lights.
High-level brake light.
Interior lights.

24.0 The diagnostic plug (arrowed) is located under the driver's side of the facia

Wipers.
Heated windscreen.
Cruise control.
Central locking.
Anti-theft system.
Handbrake switch.
Brake fluid level monitoring.
Fuel pump.
Battery charging.
Databus communications.

3 Remove the trim panel above the passenger's side footwell **(see illustration 3.2a).**
4 Undo the 2 fasteners and lift the GEM/junction/fusebox from the mounting bracket **(see illustration 3.2b and 3.2c).**
5 Note their fitted positions, and disconnect the wiring plugs as the GEM is withdrawn.
6 If a new GEM is to be fitted, the unit must be configured and initialised using Ford diagnostic equipment (IDS). Entrust this task to a Ford dealer or suitably-equipped specialist.

Lighting control module (LCM)

7 This module is only fitted to vehicles equipped with adaptive front lights (AFS), or Xenon high-intensity gas discharge headlights (HID). On models with AFS it controls the movement of the reflectors as the steering is operated, and on models with HID, it controls the range control as the suspension compresses or extends.
8 Renewal of the module is described in Section 9.

Keyless vehicle module (KVM)

9 Renewal of the KVM is described in Chapter 11, Section 20.

Climate control module (CCM)

10 Removal of the CCM is described in Chapter 3, Section 10.

Refitting

11 Refitting is a reversal of removal. If a new module has been fitted, software will need to be downloaded from Ford. Entrust this task to a Ford dealer or suitably-equipped specialist.

25 Fuel filler flap motor – removal and refitting

1 Slacken the right-hand rear roadwheel nuts, then raise the rear of the vehicle and support it securely on axle stands (see *Jacking and vehicle support*). Remove the roadwheel.
2 Undo the fasteners and remove the right-hand rear wheel arch liner **(see illustration).**
3 Undo the bolts securing the filler pipe assembly to the inner wing and chassis member **(see illustration).**
4 Reach up behind the wheel arch, depress the 2 retaining clips, and manoeuvre the filler flap assembly from place **(see illustration).** Disconnect the wiring plug and unclip with harness as the assembly is withdrawn.
5 Release the clip each side and slide the cover and motor from the filler funnel **(see illustration).**
6 Slide the motor from the cover **(see illustration).**
7 Refitting is a reversal of removal.

25.2 Remove the wheel arch liner

25.3 Undo the bolts (arrowed) securing the filler/breather pipe assembly

25.4 Reach up and depress the clips (arrowed)

25.5 Depress the clip each side (arrowed) then slide the cover and motor from the flap assembly

25.6 Slide the motor from the cover

Early Ford C-Max wiring diagrams

Diagram 1

WARNING: *This vehicle is fitted with a supplemental restraint system (SRS) consisting of a combination of driver (and passenger) airbag(s), side impact protection airbags and seatbelt pre-tensioners. The use of electrical test equipment on any SRS wiring systems may cause the seatbelt pre-tensioners to abruptly retract and airbags to explosively deploy, resulting in potentially severe personal injury. Extreme care should be taken to correctly identify any circuits to be tested to avoid choosing any of the SRS wiring in error.*

For further information see airbag system precautions in body electrical systems chapter.

Note: The SRS wiring harness can normally be identified by yellow and/or orange harness or harness connectors.

Key to symbols

Symbol	Symbol
Solenoid actuator	Bulb
Earth point and location	Switch
Wire colour (blue with white tracer) — Bu/Wh	Fuse/Fusible link F26
	Resistor
Dashed outline denotes part of a larger item, containing in this case an electronic or solid state device (pins 1 and 3 of a single connector).	Variable resistor
	Variable resistor

Wire splice, soldered joint, or unspecified connector	
Connecting wires	
Diode	
Light-emitting diode	
Item number **12**	
Motor/pump (M)	
Heating element	

Engine fusebox ④

Fuse	Rating	Circuit	Fuse	Rating	Circuit
F1	50A	Engine cooling fan	F20	15A	Horn
F2	80A	Power steering	F21	20A	Auxiliary heater
F3	60A	Passenger fusebox supply	F22	10A	Power steering control unit
F4	60A	Passenger fusebox supply	F23	30A	Headlight washer
F5	80A	Auxiliary heater	F24	15A	Diesel auxiliary heater
F6	60A	Glow plug (Diesel only)	F25	15A	Ignition relays
F7	30A	ABS, stability control pump	F26	15A	Automatic transmission
F8	20A	ABS, stability control valves	F27	10A	Air conditioning clutch
F9	20A	Engine management	F28	10A	Diesel glow plug monitoring
F10	30A	Heater blower	F29	10A	Climate control
F11	20A	Ignition switch	F30	3A	Engine management, auto. transmission
F12	40A	Ignition relay			
F13	20A	Starter solenoid	F31	10A	Battery smart charging
F14	40A	Heated front screen RH	F32	10A	Automatic transmission
F15	30A	Engine cooling fan relay	F33	10A	Heated oxygen sensor
F16	40A	Heated front screen LH		10A	Intercooler bypass valve
F17	30A	Convertible roof	F34	10A	Engine management
F18	30A	Power inverter	F35	10A	Engine management
F19	10A	ABS	F36	10A	Engine management

Passenger fusebox ⑱

Fuse	Rating	Circuit	Fuse	Rating	Circuit
F37	10A	Exterior lighting	F70	10A	Heated seats, sunroof, exterior lighting, SRS, wash/wipe, electric windows, air conditioning, instrument cluster/lighting, aut. transmission, parking aid
F38	10A	Exterior lighting			
F39	20A	Instrument cluster			
F40	20A	Sunroof			
F41	20A	Instrument cluster, instrument lighting, exterior lighting, interior lighting, mirrors, central locking	F71	10A	Exterior lighting
			F72	25A	Multifunction control unit, sunroof, central locking, electric windows, heating/ventilation, air conditioning, instrument cluster, exterior lighting, interior lighting, mirrors
F42	7.5A	Mirrors, electric windows			
F43	10A	Air conditioning			
F44	10A	Telephone	F73	7.5A	Exterior lighting
F45	10A	Exterior lighting	F74	15A	Exterior lighting
F46	10A	Speed control unit, heating/ventilation, air conditioning, instrument cluster, alarm, multifunction control unit, sunroof	F75	10A	Auto. transmission
			F76	7.5A	Hand brake
			F77	25A	Central locking
F47	15A	Wash/wipe	F78	15A	Wash/Wipe
F48	20A	Exterior lighting	F79	15A	Instrument cluster
F49	15A	Exterior lighting, instrument cluster/lighting	F80	10A	Interior lights, mirrors
F50	20A	Wash/wipe	F81	20A	Central locking, electric windows, instrument cluster/lighting
F51	-	Spare			
F52	25A	Electric windows	F82	20A	Central locking, electric windows, instrument cluster/lighting
F53	7.5A	Exterior lighting			
F54	7.5A	Exterior lighting	F83	10A	Navigation, audio
F55	20A	Air conditioning, exterior lighting, interior lighting, mirrors, central locking, electric windows	F84	10A	Exterior lighting
			F85	-	Spare
			F86	20A	Heated seats
F56	-	Spare			
F57	10A	Mirrors, alarm			
F58	15A	Audio, clock			
F59	20A	Exterior lighting			
F60	15A	Exterior lighting			
F61	15A	Exterior lighting			
F62	20A	Heated seats			
F63	25A	Electric windows, air conditioning			
F64	-	Spare			
F65	10A	SRS			
F66	7.5A	Exterior lighting, air conditioning, wash/wipe			
F67	10A	Instrument cluster, exterior lighting, SRS			
F68	7.5A	Navigation, audio, clock, instrument cluster, alarm, air conditioning			
F69	20A	Exterior lighting			

Earth locations

E1	On engine		E10	In engine bay, by LH strut tower
E2	On engine		E11	In passenger compartment, front of RH inner sill
E3	In engine bay, behind LH headlight		E12	In passenger compartment, front of RH inner sill
E4	'A' pillar driver's side		E13	In passenger compartment, front of RH inner sill
E5	In luggage compartment		E14	Roof opening panel
E6	LH side of luggage compartment		E15	Behind centre of dash
E7	In engine bay, behind RH headlight		E16	In passenger compartment, LH inner sill, below 'B' post
E8	In passenger compartment, front of LH inner sill			
E9	In passenger compartment, front of LH inner sill			

H47141

Colour codes

Wh	White	**Og**	Orange
Bu	Blue	**Rd**	Red
Gy	Grey	**Pk**	Pink
Ye	Yellow	**Gn**	Green
Bn	Brown	**Vt**	Violet
Bk	Black	**Sr**	Silver
Na	Natural	**Lg**	Light green

Key to items

1 Battery
2 Starter motor
3 Alternator
4 Engine fusebox
  R13 = power hold relay
  R22 = starter relay
  R33 = horn relay
  R212 = glow plug relay
5 Ignition switch
6 Engine cooling fan
7 Air conditioning pressure switch
8 Engine coolant temp. sensor
9 Horn (low tone)
10 Horn (high tone)
11 Steering wheel clock springs
12 Horn switch
13 Glow plug no. 1
14 Glow plug no. 2
15 Glow plug no. 3
16 Glow plug no. 4

Diagram 2

H47142

Typical starting & charging

Typical engine cooling fan

Typical pre-heating system

Typical horn

Colour codes

Wh	White	**Og**	Orange
Bu	Blue	**Rd**	Red
Gy	Grey	**Pk**	Pink
Ye	Yellow	**Gn**	Green
Bn	Brown	**Vt**	Violet
Bk	Black	**Sr**	Silver
Na	Natural	**Lg**	Light green

Key to items

1 Battery
4 Engine fusebox
  R41 = ignition relay
5 Ignition switch
18 Passenger fusebox
  a = GEM control unit
  b = autolighting relay
  c = dip beam relay
  d = main beam relay
19 LH rear light
  a = stop light
  b = reversing light
  c = fog/tail light
20 RH rear light
  (as above)
21 Stop light switch
22 Reversing light switch
24 High level stop light
25 Number plate light
26 Light switch
  a = park/off/side/head/auto
27 LH headlight
  a = side light
  b = dip beam
  c = main beam
  d = light shade
28 RH headlight
  (as above)
29 Autolighting/rain sensor
30 Multifunction switch
  a = main beam/flasher

Diagram 3

H47143

Typical stop & reversing lights

Typical side, tail & number plate lights

Typical headlights

Colour codes

Wh	White	Og	Orange
Bu	Blue	Rd	Red
Gy	Grey	Pk	Pink
Ye	Yellow	Gn	Green
Bn	Brown	Vt	Violet
Bk	Black	Sr	Silver
Na	Natural	Lg	Light green

Key to items

1 Battery
4 Engine fusebox
  R41 = ignition relay
5 Ignition switch
18 Passenger fusebox
  a = GEM control unit
19 LH rear light
  c = fog/tail light
  d = direction indicator
20 RH rear light (as above)

26 Light switch
  b = front/rear foglight
27 LH headlight
  e = direction indicator
28 RH headlight
  (as above)
30 Multifunction switch
  b = direction indicator
33 LH front side repeater
34 RH front side repeater

35 Hazard warning switch
36 LH exterior mirror
  a = indicator side repeater
37 RH exterior mirror
  a = indicator side repeater
38 LH front foglight
39 RH front foglight
95 Driver's door control unit
96 Passenger's door control unit

Diagram 4

H47144

Typical direction indicators & hazard warning lights

Typical foglights

See diagram 7
Interior lighting

Middle
CAN bus

See diagram 7
Instrument cluster
(rear foglight warning light)

See diagram 7
Instrument cluster
(front foglight warning light)

Colour codes

Wh	White	**Og**	Orange
Bu	Blue	**Rd**	Red
Gy	Grey	**Pk**	Pink
Ye	Yellow	**Gn**	Green
Bn	Brown	**Vt**	Violet
Bk	Black	**Sr**	Silver
Na	Natural	**Lg**	Light green

Key to items

1   Battery
4   Engine fusebox
    R14 = heater blower relay
5   Ignition switch
18   Passenger fusebox
    a = GEM control unit
44   Trailer control unit
45   Rear foglight cut-off relay

46   7 pin socket
47   Heater blower motor
48   Heater panel
    a = recirculation switch
    b = air cond. switch
    c = heater blower switch
    d = switch illumination
49   Recirculation flap motor

50   Heater blower resistors

Diagram 5

H47145

Typical trailer socket

Typical air conditioning

Colour codes

Wh	White	Og	Orange
Bu	Blue	Rd	Red
Gy	Grey	Pk	Pink
Ye	Yellow	Gn	Green
Bn	Brown	Vt	Violet
Bk	Black	Sr	Silver
Na	Natural	Lg	Light green

Key to items

1 Battery
4 Engine fusebox
   R34 = headlight cleaning relay
   R41 = ignition relay
5 Ignition switch
18 Passenger fusebox
   a = GEM control unit
   e = rear wiper relay
   f = low speed wiper relay
   g = high speed wiper relay

26 Light switch
   a = park/off/side/head/auto
29 Autolighting/rain sensor
53 Wash/wipe switch
   a = variable wiper control
   b = front wiper switch
   c = rear wash/wipe switch
   d = front washer switch
54 Front wiper motor
55 Rear wiper motor

56 Headlight washer pump
57 LH washer jet heater
58 RH washer jet heater
59 Front/rear washer pump

Diagram 6

H47146

Typical wash/wipe

Colour codes

Wh	White	**Og**	Orange
Bu	Blue	**Rd**	Red
Gy	Grey	**Pk**	Pink
Ye	Yellow	**Gn**	Green
Bn	Brown	**Vt**	Violet
Bk	Black	**Sr**	Silver
Na	Natural	**Lg**	Light green

Key to items

1 Battery
4 Engine fusebox
5 Ignition switch
18 Passenger fusebox
  a = GEM control unit
  h = battery saver relay
26 Light switch
  a = park/off/side/head/auto
  c = interior lighting dimmer
30 Multifunction switch
  c = display mode
  d = set/reset
60 Instrument cluster
  a = tachometer
  b = coolant temp. gauge
  c = speedometer
  d = alternator warning light

e = low oil pressure warning light
f = shift up warning light
g = MIL warning light
h = speed control warning light
i = check engine warning light
j = preheater warning light
k = ice warning light
l = low brake fluid/handbrake warning light
m = electric power stering warning light
n = seatbelt warning light
o = airbag warning light
p = instrument illumination
q = lights on warning light
r = door ajar warning light
s = LCD display
61 Handbrake switch
62 Outside air temp. sensor

Diagram 7

63 Brake fluid level switch
64 Low washer fluid level switch
65 Fuel gauge sender unit
66 Driver's door lock assy
67 Passenger's door lock assy
68 LH rear door lock assy
69 RH rear door lock assy
70 Glovebox light/switch
71 LH footwell light
72 RH footwell light
73 LH vanity mirror light
74 RH vanity mirror light
75 Front interior light
76 Rear interior light
77 Luggae compartment light (not estate)
78 Luggage compartment light (estate)
79 Tailgate lock unit

H47147

Typical instrument cluster

Typical interior lighting

See diagrams
4, 5, 7 & 10
Interior lighting
feed

Colour codes

Wh	White	**Og**	Orange
Bu	Blue	**Rd**	Red
Gy	Grey	**Pk**	Pink
Ye	Yellow	**Gn**	Green
Bn	Brown	**Vt**	Violet
Bk	Black	**Sr**	Silver
Na	Natural	**Lg**	Light green

Key to items

1 Battery
4 Engine fusebox
5 Ignition switch
18 Passenger fusebox
  a = GEM control unit
  h = door lock relay
  i = double locking relay
  j = driver's door lock relay
  k = door unlock relay

64 Driver's door lock unit
65 Passenger's door lock unit
66 LH rear door lock unit
67 RH rear door lock unit
79 Tailgate lock unit
83 Remote control unit
88 Tailgate lock switch
89 Fuel filler lock motor

Diagram 8

H47148

Typical central locking

Colour codes

Wh	White	Og	Orange
Bu	Blue	Rd	Red
Gy	Grey	Pk	Pink
Ye	Yellow	Gn	Green
Bn	Brown	Vt	Violet
Bk	Black	Sr	Silver
Na	Natural	Lg	Light green

Key to items

1 Battery
4 Engine fusebox
18 Passenger fusebox
36 LH exterior mirror
  b = fold motor
  c = up/down motor
  d = left/right motor
  e = heater element
  f = puddle light
37 RH exterior mirror
  b = fold motor
  c = up/down motor
  d = left/right motor
  e = heater element
  f = puddle light
92 Driver's window/mirror control switch
93 Electric mirror fold control unit
95 Driver's door control unit
96 Passenger's door control unit

Diagram 9

H47149

Typical electric mirrors

Colour codes

Wh	White	**Og**	Orange
Bu	Blue	**Rd**	Red
Gy	Grey	**Pk**	Pink
Ye	Yellow	**Gn**	Green
Bn	Brown	**Vt**	Violet
Bk	Black	**Sr**	Silver
Na	Natural	**Lg**	Light green

Key to items

1 Battery
4 Engine fusebox
  R41 = ignition relay
5 Ignition switch
18 Passenger fusebox
  a = GEM control unit
92 Driver's window/mirror control switch
98 Passenger's window switch

99 Driver's window motor
100 Passenger's window motor
101 Audio unit
102 CD changer
103 Steering wheel remote control
104 LH front speaker 1
105 LH front speaker 2
106 RH front speaker 1

107 RH front speaker 2
108 LH rear door speaker 1
109 LH rear door speaker 2
110 RH rear door speaker 1
111 RH rear door speaker 2

Diagram 10

H47150

Typical electric windows

Typical audio system

Later Ford C-Max wiring diagrams

Diagram 1

WARNING: This vehicle is fitted with a supplemental restraint system (SRS) consisting of a combination of driver (and passenger) airbag(s), side impact protection airbags and seatbelt pre-tensioners. The use of electrical test equipment on any SRS wiring systems may cause the seatbelt pre-tensioners to abruptly retract and airbags to explosively deploy, resulting in potentially severe personal injury. Extreme care should be taken to correctly identify any circuits to be tested to avoid choosing any of the SRS wiring in error.
For further information see airbag system precautions in body electrical systems chapter.
Note: The SRS wiring harness can normally be identified by yellow and/or orange harness or harness connectors.

Key to symbols

Symbol		Symbol		Symbol	
Solenoid actuator		Bulb		Wire splice, soldered joint, or unspecified connector	
Earth point and location	E7	Switch		Connecting wires	
Wire colour (blue with white tracer)	Bu/Wh	Fuse/Fusible link	F26	Diode	
Dashed outline denotes part of a larger item, containing in this case an electronic or solid state device (pins 1 and 3 of a single connector).		Resistor		Light-emitting diode	
		Variable resistor		Item number	12
		Variable resistor		Motor/pump	M
				Heating element	

Engine fusebox ④

F1	50A	Engine cooling fan	F20	15A	Horn	
F2	80A	Power steering	F21	20A	Auxiliary heater	
F3	60A	Passenger fusebox supply	F22	10A	Power steering control unit	
F4	60A	Passenger fusebox supply	F23	30A	Headlight washer	
F5	80A	Auxiliary heater	F24	15A	Diesel auxiliary heater	
F6	60A	Glow plug (Diesel only)	F25	10A	Ignition relays	
F7	40A	ABS, stability control pump	F26	15A	Automatic transmission	
F8	20A	ABS, stability control valves	F27	10A	Air conditioning clutch	
F9	20A	Engine management	F28	10A	Diesel glow plug monitoring	
F10	30A	Heater blower	F29	10A	Climate control	
F11	20A	Ignition switch	F30	3A	Engine management, auto. transmission	
F12	40A	Ignition relay	F31	10A	Battery smart charging	
F13	20A	Starter solenoid	F32	10A	Automatic transmission	
F14	40A	Heated front screen RH	F33	10A	Heated oxygen sensor	
F15	30A	Engine cooling fan relay		10A	Intercooler bypass valve	
F16	40A	Heated front screen LH	F34	10A	Engine management	
F17	30A	Convertible roof	F35	10A	Engine management	
F18	30A	Power inverter	F36	10A	Engine management	
F19	10A	ABS				

Passenger fusebox ⑱

F100	10A	Electronic control units ignition supply	F115	7.5A	Lighting control	F130	–	Not used		
F101	20A	Sunroof, driver's electric seat, convertible roof	F116	20A	Foglights	F131	15A	Rear window wiper		
F102	10A	Heater control, steering column, Diesel particulate filter, remote control receiver	F117	7.5A	Number plate lights	F132	15A	Stop lights		
			F118	20A	LH rear door control unit	F133	25A	Central locking, passenger door control unit		
F103	10A	Lighting	F119	15A	Luggage compartment auxiliary power socket	F134	20A	Central locking, driver's door control unit		
F104	10A	Battery saver, interior lights				F135	20A	Daytime running lights		
F105	25A	Heated rear window	F120	20A	RH rear door control unit	F136	10A	Washer pump, heated washer jets		
F106	20A	Keyless entry system	F121	20A	Heated front seats	F137	10A	Battery backup sounder		
F107	10A	Instrument cluster, diagnostics	F122	10A	Airbag	F138	10A	Engine management, automatic transmission		
F108	7.5A	Instrument cluster (audio and navigation unit)	F123	7.5A	Heated mirrors	F139	10A	RH main beam		
F109	20A	Cigar lighter, rear auxiliary power socket	F124	7.5A	Parking lights, side & tail lights LHS	F140	10A	LH main beam		
F110	10A	Daytime running lights, lighting control switch	F125	7.5A	Parking lights, side & tail lights RHS	F141	10A	Reversing light, electric mirrors		
F111	15A	Fuel pump (petrol)	F126	20A	Keyless entry system	F142	15A	RH dip beam		
F112	15A	Audio supply	F127	25A	Electric windows	F143	15A	LH dip beam		
F113	10A	Daytime running lights (parking lights)	F128	–	Not used					
F114	10A	Instrument cluster, engine immobiliser	F129	20A	Windscreen wiper					

Earth locations

E1	On engine
E2	On engine
E3	In engine bay, behind LH headlight
E4	'A' pillar driver's side
E5	In luggage compartment
E6	LH side of luggage compartment
E7	In engine bay, behind RH headlight
E8	In passenger compartment, front of LH inner sill
E9	In passenger compartment, front of LH inner sill
E10	In engine bay, by LH strut tower
E11	In passenger compartment, front of RH inner sill
E12	In passenger compartment, front of RH inner sill
E13	In passenger compartment, front of RH inner sill
E14	Roof opening panel
E15	Behind centre of dash
E16	In passenger compartment, LH inner sill, below 'B' post

H33944

Colour codes

Wh	White	**Og**	Orange
Bu	Blue	**Rd**	Red
Gy	Grey	**Pk**	Pink
Ye	Yellow	**Gn**	Green
Bn	Brown	**Vt**	Violet
Bk	Black	**Sr**	Silver
Na	Natural	**Lg**	Light green

Key to items

1 Battery
2 Starter motor
3 Alternator
4 Engine fusebox
   R13 = power hold relay
   R22 = starter relay
   R33 = horn relay
   R212 = glow plug relay

5 Ignition switch
6 Engine cooling fan
7 Air conditioning pressure switch
8 Engine coolant temp. sensor
9 Horn (low tone)
10 Horn (high tone)
11 Steering wheel clock springs
12 Horn switch

13 Glow plug no. 1
14 Glow plug no. 2
15 Glow plug no. 3
16 Glow plug no. 4

Diagram 2

H33945

Typical starting & charging

Typical engine cooling fan

Typical horn

Typical pre-heating system

Colour codes

Wh	White	**Og**	Orange
Bu	Blue	**Rd**	Red
Gy	Grey	**Pk**	Pink
Ye	Yellow	**Gn**	Green
Bn	Brown	**Vt**	Violet
Bk	Black	**Sr**	Silver
Na	Natural	**Lg**	Light green

Key to items

1 Battery
4 Engine fusebox
  R41 = ignition relay
5 Ignition switch
18 Passenger fusebox
  a = GEM control unit
  b = autolighting relay
  c = dip beam relay
  d = main beam relay
19 LH rear light
  a = stop/tail light
20 RH rear light
  (as above)
21 Stop light switch
22 Reversing light switch
23 Reversing light
24 High level stop light
25 Number plate light
26 Light switch
  a = park/off/side/head/auto
27 LH headlight
  a = side light
  b = dip beam
  c = main beam
  d = light shade
28 RH headlight
  (as above)
29 Autolighting/rain sensor
30 Multifunction switch
  a = main beam/flasher

Diagram 3

H33946

Typical stop & reversing lights

Typical headlights

Typical side, tail & number plate lights

Colour codes

Wh	White	**Og**	Orange
Bu	Blue	**Rd**	Red
Gy	Grey	**Pk**	Pink
Ye	Yellow	**Gn**	Green
Bn	Brown	**Vt**	Violet
Bk	Black	**Sr**	Silver
Na	Natural	**Lg**	Light green

Key to items

1   Battery
4   Engine fusebox
    R41 = ignition relay
5   Ignition switch
18 Passenger fusebox
    a = GEM control unit
19 LH rear light
    b = direction indicator
20 RH rear light
    (as above)

26 Light switch
    b = front/rear foglight
27 LH headlight
    e = direction indicator
28 RH headlight
    (as above)
30 Multifunction switch
    b = direction indicator
33 LH front side repeater
34 RH front side repeater

35 Hazard warning switch
36 LH exterior mirror
    a = indicator side repeater
37 RH exterior mirror
    a = indicator side repeater
38 LH front foglight
39 RH front foglight
40 Rear foglight

Diagram 4

H33947

*Typical direction indicators
& hazard warning lights*

Typical foglights

Colour codes

Wh	White	**Og**	Orange
Bu	Blue	**Rd**	Red
Gy	Grey	**Pk**	Pink
Ye	Yellow	**Gn**	Green
Bn	Brown	**Vt**	Violet
Bk	Black	**Sr**	Silver
Na	Natural	**Lg**	Light green

Key to items

1   Battery
4   Engine fusebox
    R14 = heater blower relay
5   Ignition switch
18 Passenger fusebox
    a = GEM control unit
44 Trailer control unit
45 Rear foglight cut-off relay

46 7 pin socket
47 Heater blower motor
48 Heater panel
    a = recirculation switch
    b = air cond. switch
    c = heater blower switch
    d = switch illumination
49 Recirculation flap motor

50 Heater blower resistors

Diagram 5

H33948

Typical trailer socket

Typical air conditioning

Colour codes

Wh	White	**Og**	Orange
Bu	Blue	**Rd**	Red
Gy	Grey	**Pk**	Pink
Ye	Yellow	**Gn**	Green
Bn	Brown	**Vt**	Violet
Bk	Black	**Sr**	Silver
Na	Natural	**Lg**	Light green

Key to items

1 Battery
4 Engine fusebox
  R34 = headlight cleaning relay
  R41 = ignition relay
5 Ignition switch
18 Passenger fusebox
  a = GEM control unit
  e = rear wiper relay
  f = low speed wiper relay
  g = high speed wiper relay

26 Light switch
  a = park/off/side/head/auto
29 Autolighting/rain sensor
53 Wash/wipe switch
  a = variable wiper control
  b = front wiper switch
  c = rear wash/wipe switch
  d = front washer switch
54 Front wiper motor
55 Rear wiper motor

56 Headlight washer pump
57 LH washer jet heater
58 RH washer jet heater
59 Front/rear washer pump

Diagram 6

H33949

Typical wash/wipe

Colour codes

Wh	White	Og	Orange
Bu	Blue	Rd	Red
Gy	Grey	Pk	Pink
Ye	Yellow	Gn	Green
Bn	Brown	Vt	Violet
Bk	Black	Sr	Silver
Na	Natural	Lg	Light green

Key to items

1 Battery
4 Engine fusebox
5 Ignition switch
18 Passenger fusebox
  a = GEM control unit
  b = battery saver relay
26 Light switch
  a = park/off/side/head/auto
  c = interior lighting dimmer
30 Multifunction switch
  c = display mode
  d = set/reset
60 Instrument cluster
  a = tachometer
  b = coolant temp. gauge
  c = speedometer
  d = alternator warning light

e = low oil pressure warning light
f = shift up warning light
g = MIL warning light
h = speed control warning light
i = check engine warning light
j = preheater warning light
k = ice warning light
l = low brake fluid/handbrake warning light
m = electric power stering warning light
n = seatbelt warning light
o = airbag warning light
p = instrument illumination
q = lights on warning light
r = door ajar warning light
s = LCD display
61 Handbrake switch
62 Outside air temp. sensor

63 Brake fluid level switch
64 Low washer fluid level switch
65 Fuel gauge sender unit
66 Driver's door lock assy
67 Passenger's door lock assy
68 LH rear door lock assy
69 RH rear door lock assy
70 Glovebox light/switch
71 LH footwell light
72 RH footwell light
73 LH vanity mirror light
74 RH vanity mirror light
75 Front interior light
76 Rear interior light
77 Luggage compartment light (not estate)
78 Luggage compartment light (estate)
79 Tailgate lock unit

Diagram 7

H33950

Typical instrument cluster

Typical interior lighting

Colour codes

Wh	White	Og	Orange
Bu	Blue	Rd	Red
Gy	Grey	Pk	Pink
Ye	Yellow	Gn	Green
Bn	Brown	Vt	Violet
Bk	Black	Sr	Silver
Na	Natural	Lg	Light green

Key to items

1 Battery
4 Engine fusebox
5 Ignition switch
18 Passenger fusebox
  a = GEM control unit
  h = door lock relay
  i = double locking relay
  j = driver's door lock relay
  k = door unlock relay

64 Driver's door lock unit
65 Passenger's door lock unit
66 LH rear door lock unit
67 RH rear door lock unit
79 Tailgate lock unit
83 Remote control unit
88 Tailgate lock switch
89 Fuel filler lock motor

Diagram 8

H33951

Typical central locking

Colour codes

Wh	White	Og	Orange
Bu	Blue	Rd	Red
Gy	Grey	Pk	Pink
Ye	Yellow	Gn	Green
Bn	Brown	Vt	Violet
Bk	Black	Sr	Silver
Na	Natural	Lg	Light green

Key to items

1 Battery
4 Engine fusebox
18 Passenger fusebox
36 LH exterior mirror
  b = fold motor
  c = up/down motor
  d = left/right motor
  e = heater element
  f = puddle light

37 RH exterior mirror
  b = fold motor
  c = up/down motor
  d = left/right motor
  e = heater element
  f = puddle light
92 Driver's window/mirror control switch
93 Electric mirror fold control unit
94 Electric mirror fold switch

95 Driver's door control unit
96 Passenger's door control unit

Diagram 9

H33952

Typical central locking

Colour codes

Wh	White	**Og**	Orange
Bu	Blue	**Rd**	Red
Gy	Grey	**Pk**	Pink
Ye	Yellow	**Gn**	Green
Bn	Brown	**Vt**	Violet
Bk	Black	**Sr**	Silver
Na	Natural	**Lg**	Light green

Key to items

1 Battery
4 Engine fusebox
    R41 = ignition relay
5 Ignition switch
18 Passenger fusebox
    a = GEM control unit
92 Driver's window/mirror control switch
98 Passenger's window switch

99 Driver's window motor
100 Passenger's window motor
101 Audio unit
102 CD changer
103 Steering wheel remote control
104 LH front speaker 1
105 LH front speaker 2
106 RH front speaker 1

107 RH front speaker 2
108 LH rear door speaker 1
109 LH rear door speaker 2
110 RH rear door speaker 1
111 RH rear door speaker 2

Diagram 10

H33953

Typical electric windows

Typical audio system

Dimensions and weights . . . . **REF•1**
Fuel economy. . . . . **REF•2**
Conversion factors. . . . . **REF•6**
Buying spare parts . . . . **REF•7**
Vehicle identification numbers . . . . **REF•7**
General repair procedures . . . . **REF•8**

Jacking and vehicle support . . . . **REF•9**
Tools and working facilities . . . . **REF•10**
MOT test checks . . . . **REF•12**
Fault finding . . . . **REF•16**
Index. . . . . **REF•24**

Dimensions and weights

Note: *All figures are approximate, and may vary according to model. Refer to manufacturer's data for exact figures.*

Dimensions

Overall length	4372 to 4391 mm
Overall width (including mirrors).	2022 to 2023 mm
Wheelbase	2640 mm
Height (without roof bars).	1564 mm

Weights

Gross vehicle weight	See Vehicle Identification Plate
Maximum towing weight	See Vehicle Identification Plate

Fuel economy

Although depreciation is still the biggest part of the cost of motoring for most car owners, the cost of fuel is more immediately noticeable. These pages give some tips on how to get the best fuel economy.

Working it out

Manufacturer's figures

Car manufacturers are required by law to provide fuel consumption information on all new vehicles sold. These 'official' figures are obtained by simulating various driving conditions on a rolling road or a test track. Real life conditions are different, so the fuel consumption actually achieved may not bear much resemblance to the quoted figures.

How to calculate it

Many cars now have trip computers which will

display fuel consumption, both instantaneous and average. Refer to the owner's handbook for details of how to use these.

To calculate consumption yourself (and maybe to check that the trip computer is accurate), proceed as follows.

1. Fill up with fuel and note the mileage, or zero the trip recorder.
2. Drive as usual until you need to fill up again.
3. Note the amount of fuel required to refill the tank, and the mileage covered since the previous fill-up.
4. Divide the mileage by the amount of fuel used to obtain the consumption figure.

For example:

Mileage at first fill-up (a) = 27,903
Mileage at second fill-up (b) = 28,346
Mileage covered (b - a) = 443
Fuel required at second fill-up = 48.6 litres

The half-completed changeover to metric units in the UK means that we buy our fuel in litres, measure distances in miles and talk about fuel consumption in miles per gallon. There are two ways round this: the first is to convert the litres to gallons before doing the calculation (by dividing by 4.546, or see Table 1). So in the example:

48.6 litres ÷ 4.546 = 10.69 gallons
443 miles ÷ 10.69 gallons = 41.4 mpg

The second way is to calculate the consumption in miles per litre, then multiply that figure by 4.546 (or see Table 2).

So in the example, fuel consumption is:

443 miles ÷ 48.6 litres = 9.1 mpl
9.1 mpl x 4.546 = 41.4 mpg

The rest of Europe expresses fuel consumption in litres of fuel required to travel 100 km (l/100 km). For interest, the conversions are given in Table 3. In practice it doesn't matter what units you use, provided you know what your normal consumption is and can spot if it's getting better or worse.

Table 1: conversion of litres to Imperial gallons

litres	1	2	3	4	5	10	20	30	40	50	60	70
gallons	0.22	0.44	0.66	0.88	1.10	2.24	4.49	6.73	8.98	11.22	13.47	15.71

Table 2: conversion of miles per litre to miles per gallon

miles per litre	5	6	7	8	9	10	11	12	13	14
miles per gallon	23	27	32	36	41	46	50	55	59	64

Table 3: conversion of litres per 100 km to miles per gallon

litres per 100 km	4	4.5	5	5.5	6	6.5	7	8	9	10
miles per gallon	71	63	56	51	47	43	40	35	31	28

Maintenance

A well-maintained car uses less fuel and creates less pollution. In particular:

Filters

Change air and fuel filters at the specified intervals.

Oil

Use a good quality oil of the lowest viscosity specified by the vehicle manufacturer (see *Lubricants and fluids*). Check the level often and be careful not to overfill.

Spark plugs

When applicable, renew at the specified intervals.

Tyres

Check tyre pressures regularly. Under-inflated tyres have an increased rolling resistance. It is generally safe to use the higher pressures specified for full load conditions even when not fully laden, but keep an eye on the centre band of tread for signs of wear due to over-inflation.

When buying new tyres, consider the 'fuel saving' models which most manufacturers include in their ranges.

Driving style

Acceleration

Acceleration uses more fuel than driving at a steady speed. The best technique with modern cars is to accelerate reasonably briskly to the desired speed, changing up through the gears as soon as possible without making the engine labour.

Air conditioning

Air conditioning absorbs quite a bit of energy from the engine – typically 3 kW (4 hp) or so. The effect on fuel consumption is at its worst in slow traffic. Switch it off when not required.

Anticipation

Drive smoothly and try to read the traffic flow so as to avoid unnecessary acceleration and braking.

Automatic transmission

When accelerating in an automatic, avoid depressing the throttle so far as to make the transmission hold onto lower gears at higher speeds. Don't use the 'Sport' setting, if applicable.

When stationary with the engine running, select 'N' or 'P'. When moving, keep your left foot away from the brake.

Braking

Braking converts the car's energy of motion into heat – essentially, it is wasted. Obviously some braking is always going to be necessary, but with good anticipation it is surprising how much can be avoided, especially on routes that you know well.

Carshare

Consider sharing lifts to work or to the shops. Even once a week will make a difference.

Electrical loads

Electricity is 'fuel' too; the alternator which charges the battery does so by converting some of the engine's energy of motion into electrical energy. The more electrical accessories are in use, the greater the load on the alternator. Switch off big consumers like the heated rear window when not required.

Freewheeling

Freewheeling (coasting) in neutral with the engine switched off is dangerous. The effort required to operate power-assisted brakes and steering increases when the engine is not running, with a potential lack of control in emergency situations.

In any case, modern fuel injection systems automatically cut off the engine's fuel supply on the overrun (moving and in gear, but with the accelerator pedal released).

Gadgets

Bolt-on devices claiming to save fuel have been around for nearly as long as the motor car itself. Those which worked were rapidly adopted as standard equipment by the vehicle manufacturers. Others worked only in certain situations, or saved fuel only at the expense of unacceptable effects on performance, driveability or the life of engine components.

The most effective fuel saving gadget is the driver's right foot.

Journey planning

Combine (eg) a trip to the supermarket with a visit to the recycling centre and the DIY store, rather than making separate journeys.

When possible choose a travelling time outside rush hours.

Load

The more heavily a car is laden, the greater the energy required to accelerate it to a given speed. Remove heavy items which you don't need to carry.

One load which is often overlooked is the contents of the fuel tank. A tankful of fuel (55 litres / 12 gallons) weighs 45 kg (100 lb) or so. Just half filling it may be worthwhile.

Lost?

At the risk of stating the obvious, if you're going somewhere new, have details of the route to hand. There's not much point in achieving record mpg if you also go miles out of your way.

Parking

If possible, carry out any reversing or turning manoeuvres when you arrive at a parking space so that you can drive straight out when you leave. Manoeuvering when the engine is cold uses a lot more fuel.

Driving around looking for free on-street parking may cost more in fuel than buying a car park ticket.

Premium fuel

Most major oil companies (and some supermarkets) have premium grades of fuel which are several pence a litre dearer than the standard grades. Reports vary, but the consensus seems to be that if these fuels improve economy at all, they do not do so by enough to justify their extra cost.

Roof rack

When loading a roof rack, try to produce a wedge shape with the narrow end at the front. Any cover should be securely fastened – if it flaps it's creating turbulence and absorbing energy.

Remove roof racks and boxes when not in use – they increase air resistance and can create a surprising amount of noise.

Short journeys

The engine is at its least efficient, and wear is highest, during the first few miles after a cold start. Consider walking, cycling or using public transport.

Speed

The engine is at its most efficient when running at a steady speed and load at the rpm where it develops maximum torque. (You can find this figure in the car's handbook.) For most cars this corresponds to between 55 and 65 mph in top gear.

Above the optimum cruising speed, fuel consumption starts to rise quite sharply. A car travelling at 80 mph will typically be using 30% more fuel than at 60 mph.

Supermarket fuel

It may be cheap but is it any good? In the UK all supermarket fuel must meet the relevant British Standard. The major oil companies will say that their branded fuels have better additive packages which may stop carbon and other deposits building up. A reasonable compromise might be to use one tank of branded fuel to three or four from the supermarket.

Switch off when stationary

Switch off the engine if you look like being stationary for more than 30 seconds or so. This is good for the environment as well as for your pocket. Be aware though that frequent restarts are hard on the battery and the starter motor.

Windows

Driving with the windows open increases air turbulence around the vehicle. Closing the windows promotes smooth airflow and

reduced resistance. The faster you go, the more significant this is.

And finally . . .

Driving techniques associated with good fuel economy tend to involve moderate acceleration and low top speeds. Be considerate to the needs of other road users who may need to make brisker progress; even if you do not agree with them this is not an excuse to be obstructive.

Safety must always take precedence over economy, whether it is a question of accelerating hard to complete an overtaking manoeuvre, killing your speed when confronted with a potential hazard or switching the lights on when it starts to get dark.

Conversion factors

Length (distance)

Inches (in)	x 25.4	= Millimetres (mm)	x 0.0394	=	Inches (in)
Feet (ft)	x 0.305	= Metres (m)	x 3.281	=	Feet (ft)
Miles	x 1.609	= Kilometres (km)	x 0.621	=	Miles

Volume (capacity)

Cubic inches (cu in; in³)	x 16.387	= Cubic centimetres (cc; cm³)	x 0.061	=	Cubic inches (cu in; in³)
Imperial pints (Imp pt)	x 0.568	= Litres (l)	x 1.76	=	Imperial pints (Imp pt)
Imperial quarts (Imp qt)	x 1.137	= Litres (l)	x 0.88	=	Imperial quarts (Imp qt)
Imperial quarts (Imp qt)	x 1.201	= US quarts (US qt)	x 0.833	=	Imperial quarts (Imp qt)
US quarts (US qt)	x 0.946	= Litres (l)	x 1.057	=	US quarts (US qt)
Imperial gallons (Imp gal)	x 4.546	= Litres (l)	x 0.22	=	Imperial gallons (Imp gal)
Imperial gallons (Imp gal)	x 1.201	= US gallons (US gal)	x 0.833	=	Imperial gallons (Imp gal)
US gallons (US gal)	x 3.785	= Litres (l)	x 0.264	=	US gallons (US gal)

Mass (weight)

Ounces (oz)	x 28.35	= Grams (g)	x 0.035	=	Ounces (oz)
Pounds (lb)	x 0.454	= Kilograms (kg)	x 2.205	=	Pounds (lb)

Force

Ounces-force (ozf; oz)	x 0.278	= Newtons (N)	x 3.6	=	Ounces-force (ozf; oz)
Pounds-force (lbf; lb)	x 4.448	= Newtons (N)	x 0.225	=	Pounds-force (lbf; lb)
Newtons (N)	x 0.1	= Kilograms-force (kgf; kg)	x 9.81	=	Newtons (N)

Pressure

Pounds-force per square inch (psi; lbf/in²; lb/in²)	x 0.070	= Kilograms-force per square centimetre (kgf/cm²; kg/cm²)	x 14.223	=	Pounds-force per square inch (psi; lbf/in²; lb/in²)
Pounds-force per square inch (psi; lbf/in²; lb/in²)	x 0.068	= Atmospheres (atm)	x 14.696	=	Pounds-force per square inch (psi; lbf/in²; lb/in²)
Pounds-force per square inch (psi; lbf/in²; lb/in²)	x 0.069	= Bars	x 14.5	=	Pounds-force per square inch (psi; lbf/in²; lb/in²)
Pounds-force per square inch (psi; lbf/in²; lb/in²)	x 6.895	= Kilopascals (kPa)	x 0.145	=	Pounds-force per square inch (psi; lbf/in²; lb/in²)
Kilopascals (kPa)	x 0.01	= Kilograms-force per square centimetre (kgf/cm²; kg/cm²)	x 98.1	=	Kilopascals (kPa)
Millibar (mbar)	x 100	= Pascals (Pa)	x 0.01	=	Millibar (mbar)
Millibar (mbar)	x 0.0145	= Pounds-force per square inch (psi; lbf/in²; lb/in²)	x 68.947	=	Millibar (mbar)
Millibar (mbar)	x 0.75	= Millimetres of mercury (mmHg)	x 1.333	=	Millibar (mbar)
Millibar (mbar)	x 0.401	= Inches of water (inH₂O)	x 2.491	=	Millibar (mbar)
Millimetres of mercury (mmHg)	x 0.535	= Inches of water (inH₂O)	x 1.868	=	Millimetres of mercury (mmHg)
Inches of water (inH₂O)	x 0.036	= Pounds-force per square inch (psi; lbf/in²; lb/in²)	x 27.68	=	Inches of water (inH₂O)

Torque (moment of force)

Pounds-force inches (lbf in; lb in)	x 1.152	= Kilograms-force centimetre (kgf cm; kg cm)	x 0.868	=	Pounds-force inches (lbf in; lb in)
Pounds-force inches (lbf in; lb in)	x 0.113	= Newton metres (Nm)	x 8.85	=	Pounds-force inches (lbf in; lb in)
Pounds-force inches (lbf in; lb in)	x 0.083	= Pounds-force feet (lbf ft; lb ft)	x 12	=	Pounds-force inches (lbf in; lb in)
Pounds-force feet (lbf ft; lb ft)	x 0.138	= Kilograms-force metres (kgf m; kg m)	x 7.233	=	Pounds-force feet (lbf ft; lb ft)
Pounds-force feet (lbf ft; lb ft)	x 1.356	= Newton metres (Nm)	x 0.738	=	Pounds-force feet (lbf ft; lb ft)
Newton metres (Nm)	x 0.102	= Kilograms-force metres (kgf m; kg m)	x 9.804	=	Newton metres (Nm)

Power

Horsepower (hp)	x 745.7	= Watts (W)	x 0.0013	=	Horsepower (hp)

Velocity (speed)

Miles per hour (miles/hr; mph)	x 1.609	= Kilometres per hour (km/hr; kph)	x 0.621	=	Miles per hour (miles/hr; mph)

Fuel consumption*

Miles per gallon, Imperial (mpg)	x 0.354	= Kilometres per litre (km/l)	x 2.825	=	Miles per gallon, Imperial (mpg)
Miles per gallon, US (mpg)	x 0.425	= Kilometres per litre (km/l)	x 2.352	=	Miles per gallon, US (mpg)

Temperature

Degrees Fahrenheit = (°C x 1.8) + 32   Degrees Celsius (Degrees Centigrade; °C) = (°F - 32) x 0.56

It is common practice to convert from miles per gallon (mpg) to litres/100 kilometres (l/100km), where mpg x l/100 km = 282

Spare parts are available from many sources, including maker's appointed garages, accessory shops, and motor factors. To be sure of obtaining the correct parts, it will sometimes be necessary to quote the vehicle identification number. If possible, it can also be useful to take the old parts along for positive identification. Items such as starter motors and alternators may be available under a service exchange scheme – any parts returned should be clean.

Our advice regarding spare parts is as follows.

Officially appointed garages

This is the best source of parts which are peculiar to your car, and which are not otherwise generally available (eg, badges, interior trim, certain body panels, etc). It is also the only place at which you should buy parts if the car is still under warranty.

Accessory shops

These are very good places to buy materials and components needed for the maintenance of your car (oil, air and fuel filters, light bulbs, drivebelts, greases, brake pads, touch-up paint, etc). Components of this nature sold by a reputable shop are usually of the same standard as those used by the car manufacturer.

Besides components, these shops also sell tools and general accessories, usually have convenient opening hours, charge lower prices, and can often be found close to home. Some accessory shops have parts counters where components needed for almost any repair job can be purchased or ordered.

Motor factors

Good factors will stock all the more important components which wear out comparatively quickly, and can sometimes supply individual components needed for the overhaul of a larger assembly (eg, brake seals and hydraulic parts, bearing shells, pistons, valves). They may also handle work such as cylinder block reboring, crankshaft regrinding, etc.

Engine reconditioners

These specialise in engine overhaul and can also supply components. It is recommended that the establishment is a member of the Federation of Engine Re-Manufacturers, or a similar society.

Tyre and exhaust specialists

These outlets may be independent, or members of a local or national chain. They frequently offer competitive prices when compared with a main dealer or local garage, but it will pay to obtain several quotes before making a decision. When researching prices, also ask what extras may be added – for instance fitting a new valve, balancing the wheel and tyre disposal all both commonly charged on top of the price of a new tyre.

Other sources

Beware of parts or materials obtained from market stalls, car boot sales, on-line auctions or similar outlets. Such items are not invariably sub-standard, but there is little chance of compensation if they do prove unsatisfactory. In the case of safety-critical components such as brake pads, there is the risk not only of financial loss, but also of an accident causing injury or death.

Second-hand components or assemblies obtained from a car breaker can be a good buy in some circumstances, but this sort of purchase is best made by the experienced DIY mechanic.

Vehicle identification numbers

Modifications are a continuing and unpublicised process in vehicle manufacture, quite apart from major model changes. Spare parts manuals and lists are compiled upon a numerical basis, the individual vehicle identification numbers being essential to correct identification of the component concerned.

When ordering spare parts, always give as much information as possible. Quote the car model, year of manufacture, body and engine numbers as appropriate.

The *vehicle identification plate* is situated on the driver's side B-pillar **(see illustration)**. The *vehicle identification number* is also repeated in the form of plate visible through the windscreen on the passenger's side **(see illustration)**.

The engine identification numbers are stamped in various locations depending on the engine type:

Petrol engines

1.6 litre engine – on the front of the block at the left-hand end.
1.8 and 2.0 litre engines – on the rear of the block on the left-hand end.

Diesel engines

1.6 and 2.0 litre engines – next to the oil filter.
1.8 litre engine – on the intake manifold.

Other identification numbers or codes are stamped on major items such as the gearbox, etc.

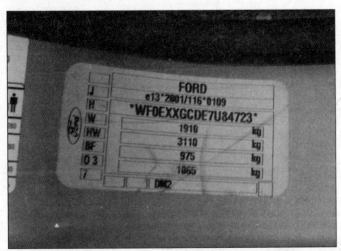

The VIN plate is mounted on the right-hand door pillar . . .

. . . and on a plate on the facia (visible through the windcreen)

Whenever servicing, repair or overhaul work is carried out on the car or its components, observe the following procedures and instructions. This will assist in carrying out the operation efficiently and to a professional standard of workmanship.

Joint mating faces and gaskets

When separating components at their mating faces, never insert screwdrivers or similar implements into the joint between the faces in order to prise them apart. This can cause severe damage which results in oil leaks, coolant leaks, etc upon reassembly. Separation is usually achieved by tapping along the joint with a soft-faced hammer in order to break the seal. However, note that this method may not be suitable where dowels are used for component location.

Where a gasket is used between the mating faces of two components, a new one must be fitted on reassembly; fit it dry unless otherwise stated in the repair procedure. Make sure that the mating faces are clean and dry, with all traces of old gasket removed. When cleaning a joint face, use a tool which is unlikely to score or damage the face, and remove any burrs or nicks with an oilstone or fine file.

Make sure that tapped holes are cleaned with a pipe cleaner, and keep them free of jointing compound, if this is being used, unless specifically instructed otherwise.

Ensure that all orifices, channels or pipes are clear, and blow through them, preferably using compressed air.

Oil seals

Oil seals can be removed by levering them out with a wide flat-bladed screwdriver or similar implement. Alternatively, a number of self-tapping screws may be screwed into the seal, and these used as a purchase for pliers or some similar device in order to pull the seal free.

Whenever an oil seal is removed from its working location, either individually or as part of an assembly, it should be renewed.

The very fine sealing lip of the seal is easily damaged, and will not seal if the surface it contacts is not completely clean and free from scratches, nicks or grooves. If the original sealing surface of the component cannot be restored, and the manufacturer has not made provision for slight relocation of the seal relative to the sealing surface, the component should be renewed.

Protect the lips of the seal from any surface which may damage them in the course of fitting. Use tape or a conical sleeve where possible. Where indicated, lubricate the seal lips with oil before fitting and, on dual-lipped seals, fill the space between the lips with grease.

Unless otherwise stated, oil seals must be fitted with their sealing lips toward the lubricant to be sealed.

Use a tubular drift or block of wood of the appropriate size to install the seal and, if the seal housing is shouldered, drive the seal down to the shoulder. If the seal housing is unshouldered, the seal should be fitted with its face flush with the housing top face (unless otherwise instructed).

Screw threads and fastenings

Seized nuts, bolts and screws are quite a common occurrence where corrosion has set in, and the use of penetrating oil or releasing fluid will often overcome this problem if the offending item is soaked for a while before attempting to release it. The use of an impact driver may also provide a means of releasing such stubborn fastening devices, when used in conjunction with the appropriate screwdriver bit or socket. If none of these methods works, it may be necessary to resort to the careful application of heat, or the use of a hacksaw or nut splitter device. Before resorting to extreme methods, check that you are not dealing with a left-hand thread!

Studs are usually removed by locking two nuts together on the threaded part, and then using a spanner on the lower nut to unscrew the stud. Studs or bolts which have broken off below the surface of the component in which they are mounted can sometimes be removed using a stud extractor.

Always ensure that a blind tapped hole is completely free from oil, grease, water or other fluid before installing the bolt or stud. Failure to do this could cause the housing to crack due to the hydraulic action of the bolt or stud as it is screwed in.

For some screw fastenings, notably cylinder head bolts or nuts, torque wrench settings are no longer specified for the latter stages of tightening, "angle-tightening" being called up instead. Typically, a fairly low torque wrench setting will be applied to the bolts/nuts in the correct sequence, followed by one or more stages of tightening through specified angles.

When checking or retightening a nut or bolt to a specified torque setting, slacken the nut or bolt by a quarter of a turn, and then retighten to the specified setting. However, this should not be attempted where angular tightening has been used.

Locknuts, locktabs and washers

Any fastening which will rotate against a component or housing during tightening should always have a washer between it and the relevant component or housing.

Spring or split washers should always be renewed when they are used to lock a critical component such as a big-end bearing retaining bolt or nut. Locktabs which are folded over to retain a nut or bolt should always be renewed.

Self-locking nuts can be re-used in non-critical areas, providing resistance can be felt when the locking portion passes over the bolt or stud thread. However, it should be noted that self-locking stiffnuts tend to lose their effectiveness after long periods of use, and should then be renewed as a matter of course.

Split pins must always be replaced with new ones of the correct size for the hole.

When thread-locking compound is found on the threads of a fastener which is to be re-used, it should be cleaned off with a wire brush and solvent, and fresh compound applied on reassembly.

Special tools

Some repair procedures in this manual entail the use of special tools such as a press, two or three-legged pullers, spring compressors, etc. Wherever possible, suitable readily-available alternatives to the manufacturer's special tools are described, and are shown in use. In some instances, where no alternative is possible, it has been necessary to resort to the use of a manufacturer's tool, and this has been done for reasons of safety as well as the efficient completion of the repair operation. Unless you are highly-skilled and have a thorough understanding of the procedures described, never attempt to bypass the use of any special tool when the procedure described specifies its use. Not only is there a very great risk of personal injury, but expensive damage could be caused to the components involved.

Environmental considerations

When disposing of used engine oil, brake fluid, antifreeze, etc, give due consideration to any detrimental environmental effects. Do not, for instance, pour any of the above liquids down drains into the general sewage system, or onto the ground to soak away. Many local council refuse tips provide a facility for waste oil disposal, as do some garages. You can find your nearest disposal point by calling the Environment Agency on 08708 506 506 or by visiting www.oilbankline.org.uk.

Note: It is illegal and anti-social to dump oil down the drain. To find the location of your local oil recycling bank, call 08708 506 506 or visit www.oilbankline.org.uk.

The jack supplied with the vehicle tool kit should only be used for changing the roadwheels – see *Wheel changing* at the front of this manual. When carrying out any other kind of work, raise the vehicle using a hydraulic trolley jack, and always supplement the jack with axle stands positioned under the vehicle jacking points.

When using a trolley jack or axle stands, position the jack head or axle stand head adjacent to one of the relevant wheel changing jacking points under the sills **(see illustration)**. Use a block of wood between the jack or axle stand and the sill.

Do not attempt to jack the vehicle under the sump, or any of the suspension components.

The jack supplied with the vehicle locates in the jacking points on the underside of the sills – see *Wheel changing* at the front of this manual. Ensure that the jack head is correctly engaged before attempting to raise the vehicle.

Never work under, around, or near a raised vehicle, unless it is adequately supported in at least two places.

J46808

Use a workshop trolley jack at the points indicated

Introduction

A selection of good tools is a fundamental requirement for anyone contemplating the maintenance and repair of a motor vehicle. For the owner who does not possess any, their purchase will prove a considerable expense, offsetting some of the savings made by doing-it-yourself. However, provided that the tools purchased meet the relevant national safety standards and are of good quality, they will last for many years and prove an extremely worthwhile investment.

To help the average owner to decide which tools are needed to carry out the various tasks detailed in this manual, we have compiled three lists of tools under the following headings: *Maintenance and minor repair, Repair and overhaul*, and *Special*. Newcomers to practical mechanics should start off with the *Maintenance and minor repair* tool kit, and confine themselves to the simpler jobs around the vehicle. Then, as confidence and experience grow, more difficult tasks can be undertaken, with extra tools being purchased as, and when, they are needed. In this way, a *Maintenance and minor repair* tool kit can be built up into a *Repair and overhaul* tool kit over a considerable period of time, without any major cash outlays. The experienced do-it-yourselfer will have a tool kit good enough for most repair and overhaul procedures, and will add tools from the *Special* category when it is felt that the expense is justified by the amount of use to which these tools will be put.

Maintenance and minor repair tool kit

The tools given in this list should be considered as a minimum requirement if routine maintenance, servicing and minor repair operations are to be undertaken. We recommend the purchase of combination spanners (ring one end, open-ended the other); although more expensive than open-ended ones, they do give the advantages of both types of spanner.

- [ ] *Combination spanners:*
  Metric - 8 to 19 mm inclusive
- [ ] *Adjustable spanner - 35 mm jaw (approx.)*
- [ ] *Spark plug spanner (with rubber insert) - petrol models*
- [ ] *Spark plug gap adjustment tool - petrol models*
- [ ] *Set of feeler gauges*
- [ ] *Brake bleed nipple spanner*
- [ ] *Screwdrivers:*
  Flat blade - 100 mm long x 6 mm dia
  Cross blade - 100 mm long x 6 mm dia
  Torx - various sizes (not all vehicles)
- [ ] *Combination pliers*
- [ ] *Hacksaw (junior)*
- [ ] *Tyre pump*
- [ ] *Tyre pressure gauge*
- [ ] *Oil can*
- [ ] *Oil filter removal tool (if applicable)*
- [ ] *Fine emery cloth*
- [ ] *Wire brush (small)*
- [ ] *Funnel (medium size)*
- [ ] *Sump drain plug key (not all vehicles)*

Repair and overhaul tool kit

These tools are virtually essential for anyone undertaking any major repairs to a motor vehicle, and are additional to those given in the *Maintenance and minor repair* list. Included in this list is a comprehensive set of sockets. Although these are expensive, they will be found invaluable as they are so versatile - particularly if various drives are included in the set. We recommend the half-inch square-drive type, as this can be used with most proprietary torque wrenches.

The tools in this list will sometimes need to be supplemented by tools from the *Special* list:

- [ ] *Sockets to cover range in previous list (including Torx sockets)*
- [ ] *Reversible ratchet drive (for use with sockets)*
- [ ] *Extension piece, 250 mm (for use with sockets)*
- [ ] *Universal joint (for use with sockets)*
- [ ] *Flexible handle or sliding T "breaker bar" (for use with sockets)*
- [ ] *Torque wrench (for use with sockets)*
- [ ] *Self-locking grips*
- [ ] *Ball pein hammer*
- [ ] *Soft-faced mallet (plastic or rubber)*
- [ ] *Screwdrivers:*
  Flat blade - long & sturdy, short (chubby), and narrow (electrician's) types
  Cross blade – long & sturdy, and short (chubby) types
- [ ] *Pliers:*
  Long-nosed
  Side cutters (electrician's)
  Circlip (internal and external)
- [ ] *Cold chisel - 25 mm*
- [ ] *Scriber*
- [ ] *Scraper*
- [ ] *Centre-punch*
- [ ] *Pin punch*
- [ ] *Hacksaw*
- [ ] *Brake hose clamp*
- [ ] *Brake/clutch bleeding kit*
- [ ] *Selection of twist drills*
- [ ] *Steel rule/straight-edge*
- [ ] *Allen keys (inc. splined/Torx type)*
- [ ] *Selection of files*
- [ ] *Wire brush*
- [ ] *Axle stands*
- [ ] *Jack (strong trolley or hydraulic type)*
- [ ] *Light with extension lead*
- [ ] *Universal electrical multi-meter*

Sockets and reversible ratchet drive

Brake bleeding kit

Hose clamp

Angular-tightening gauge

Special tools

The tools in this list are those which are not used regularly, are expensive to buy, or which need to be used in accordance with their manufacturers' instructions. Unless relatively difficult mechanical jobs are undertaken frequently, it will not be economic to buy many of these tools. Where this is the case, you could consider clubbing together with friends (or joining a motorists' club) to make a joint purchase, or borrowing the tools against a deposit from a local garage or tool hire specialist.

The following list contains only those tools and instruments freely available to the public, and not those special tools produced by the vehicle manufacturer specifically for its dealer network. You will find occasional references to these manufacturers' special tools in the text of this manual. Generally, an alternative method of doing the job without the vehicle manufacturers' special tool is given. However, sometimes there is no alternative to using them. Where this is the case and the relevant tool cannot be bought or borrowed, you will have to entrust the work to a dealer.

- ☐ Angular-tightening gauge
- ☐ Valve spring compressor
- ☐ Valve grinding tool
- ☐ Piston ring compressor
- ☐ Piston ring removal/installation tool
- ☐ Cylinder bore hone
- ☐ Balljoint separator
- ☐ Coil spring compressors (where applicable)
- ☐ Two/three-legged hub and bearing puller
- ☐ Impact screwdriver
- ☐ Micrometer and/or vernier calipers
- ☐ Dial gauge
- ☐ Tachometer
- ☐ Fault code reader
- ☐ Cylinder compression gauge
- ☐ Hand-operated vacuum pump and gauge
- ☐ Clutch plate alignment set
- ☐ Brake shoe steady spring cup removal tool
- ☐ Bush and bearing removal/installation set
- ☐ Stud extractors
- ☐ Tap and die set
- ☐ Lifting tackle

Buying tools

Reputable motor accessory shops and superstores often offer excellent quality tools at discount prices, so it pays to shop around.

Remember, you don't have to buy the most expensive items on the shelf, but it is always advisable to steer clear of the very cheap tools. Beware of 'bargains' offered on market stalls, on-line or at car boot sales. There are plenty of good tools around at reasonable prices, but always aim to purchase items which meet the relevant national safety standards. If in doubt, ask the proprietor or manager of the shop for advice before making a purchase.

Care and maintenance of tools

Having purchased a reasonable tool kit, it is necessary to keep the tools in a clean and serviceable condition. After use, always wipe off any dirt, grease and metal particles using a clean, dry cloth, before putting the tools away. Never leave them lying around after they have been used. A simple tool rack on the garage or workshop wall for items such as screwdrivers and pliers is a good idea. Store all normal spanners and sockets in a metal box. Any measuring instruments, gauges, meters, etc, must be carefully stored where they cannot be damaged or become rusty.

Take a little care when tools are used. Hammer heads inevitably become marked, and screwdrivers lose the keen edge on their blades from time to time. A little timely attention with emery cloth or a file will soon restore items like this to a good finish.

Working facilities

Not to be forgotten when discussing tools is the workshop itself. If anything more than routine maintenance is to be carried out, a suitable working area becomes essential.

It is appreciated that many an owner-mechanic is forced by circumstances to remove an engine or similar item without the benefit of a garage or workshop. Having done this, any repairs should always be done under the cover of a roof.

Wherever possible, any dismantling should be done on a clean, flat workbench or table at a suitable working height.

Any workbench needs a vice; one with a jaw opening of 100 mm is suitable for most jobs. As mentioned previously, some clean dry storage space is also required for tools, as well as for any lubricants, cleaning fluids, touch-up paints etc, which become necessary.

Another item which may be required, and which has a much more general usage, is an electric drill with a chuck capacity of at least 8 mm. This, together with a good range of twist drills, is virtually essential for fitting accessories.

Last, but not least, always keep a supply of old newspapers and clean, lint-free rags available, and try to keep any working area as clean as possible.

Micrometers

Dial test indicator ("dial gauge")

Oil filter removal tool (strap wrench type)

Compression tester

Fault code reader

This is a guide to getting your vehicle through the MOT test. Obviously it will not be possible to examine the vehicle to the same standard as the professional MOT tester. However, working through the following checks will enable you to identify any problem areas before submitting the vehicle for the test.

It has only been possible to summarise the test requirements here, based on the regulations in force at the time of printing. Test standards are becoming increasingly stringent, although there are some exemptions for older vehicles.

An assistant will be needed to help carry out some of these checks.

The checks have been sub-divided into four categories, as follows:

1 Checks carried out **FROM THE DRIVER'S SEAT**

2 Checks carried out **WITH THE VEHICLE ON THE GROUND**

3 Checks carried out **WITH THE VEHICLE RAISED AND THE WHEELS FREE TO TURN**

4 Checks carried out on **YOUR VEHICLE'S EXHAUST EMISSION SYSTEM**

---

1 Checks carried out **FROM THE DRIVER'S SEAT**

Handbrake

☐ Test the operation of the handbrake. Excessive travel (too many clicks) indicates incorrect brake or cable adjustment.
☐ Check that the handbrake cannot be released by tapping the lever sideways. Check the security of the lever mountings.

Footbrake

☐ Depress the brake pedal and check that it does not creep down to the floor, indicating a master cylinder fault. Release the pedal, wait a few seconds, then depress it again. If the pedal travels nearly to the floor before firm resistance is felt, brake adjustment or repair is necessary. If the pedal feels spongy, there is air in the hydraulic system which must be removed by bleeding.

☐ Check that the brake pedal is secure and in good condition. Check also for signs of fluid leaks on the pedal, floor or carpets, which would indicate failed seals in the brake master cylinder.
☐ Check the servo unit (when applicable) by operating the brake pedal several times, then keeping the pedal depressed and starting the engine. As the engine starts, the pedal will move down slightly. If not, the vacuum hose or the servo itself may be faulty.

Steering wheel and column

☐ Examine the steering wheel for fractures or looseness of the hub, spokes or rim.
☐ Move the steering wheel from side to side and then up and down. Check that the steering wheel is not loose on the column, indicating wear or a loose retaining nut. Continue moving the steering wheel as before, but also turn it slightly from left to right.
☐ Check that the steering wheel is not loose on the column, and that there is no abnormal movement of the steering wheel, indicating

wear in the column support bearings or couplings.

Windscreen, mirrors and sunvisor

☐ The windscreen must be free of cracks or other significant damage within the driver's field of view. (Small stone chips are acceptable.) Rear view mirrors must be secure, intact, and capable of being adjusted.

☐ The driver's sunvisor must be capable of being stored in the "up" position.

Seat belts and seats

Note: *The following checks are applicable to all seat belts, front and rear.*

☐ Examine the webbing of all the belts (including rear belts if fitted) for cuts, serious fraying or deterioration. Fasten and unfasten each belt to check the buckles. If applicable, check the retracting mechanism. Check the security of all seat belt mountings accessible from inside the vehicle.

☐ Seat belts with pre-tensioners, once activated, have a "flag" or similar showing on the seat belt stalk. This, in itself, is not a reason for test failure.

☐ The front seats themselves must be securely attached and the backrests must lock in the upright position.

Doors

☐ Both front doors must be able to be opened and closed from outside and inside, and must latch securely when closed.

2 Checks carried out WITH THE VEHICLE ON THE GROUND

Vehicle identification

☐ Number plates must be in good condition, secure and legible, with letters and numbers correctly spaced – spacing at (A) should be 33 mm and at (B) 11 mm.

☐ The VIN plate and/or homologation plate must be legible.

Electrical equipment

☐ Switch on the ignition and check the operation of the horn.

☐ Check the windscreen washers and wipers, examining the wiper blades; renew damaged or perished blades. Also check the operation of the stop-lights.

☐ Check the operation of the sidelights and number plate lights. The lenses and reflectors must be secure, clean and undamaged.

☐ Check the operation and alignment of the headlights. The headlight reflectors must not be tarnished and the lenses must be undamaged.

☐ Switch on the ignition and check the operation of the direction indicators (including the instrument panel tell-tale) and the hazard warning lights. Operation of the sidelights and stop-lights must not affect the indicators - if it does, the cause is usually a bad earth at the rear light cluster.

☐ Check the operation of the rear foglight(s), including the warning light on the instrument panel or in the switch.

☐ The ABS warning light must illuminate in accordance with the manufacturers' design. For most vehicles, the ABS warning light should illuminate when the ignition is switched on, and (if the system is operating properly) extinguish after a few seconds. Refer to the owner's handbook.

Footbrake

☐ Examine the master cylinder, brake pipes and servo unit for leaks, loose mountings, corrosion or other damage.

☐ The fluid reservoir must be secure and the fluid level must be between the upper (**A**) and lower (**B**) markings.

☐ Inspect both front brake flexible hoses for cracks or deterioration of the rubber. Turn the steering from lock to lock, and ensure that the hoses do not contact the wheel, tyre, or any part of the steering or suspension mechanism. With the brake pedal firmly depressed, check the hoses for bulges or leaks under pressure.

Steering and suspension

☐ Have your assistant turn the steering wheel from side to side slightly, up to the point where the steering gear just begins to transmit this movement to the roadwheels. Check for excessive free play between the steering wheel and the steering gear, indicating wear or insecurity of the steering column joints, the column-to-steering gear coupling, or the steering gear itself.

☐ Have your assistant turn the steering wheel more vigorously in each direction, so that the roadwheels just begin to turn. As this is done, examine all the steering joints, linkages, fittings and attachments. Renew any component that shows signs of wear or damage. On vehicles with power steering, check the security and condition of the steering pump, drivebelt and hoses.

☐ Check that the vehicle is standing level, and at approximately the correct ride height.

Shock absorbers

☐ Depress each corner of the vehicle in turn, then release it. The vehicle should rise and then settle in its normal position. If the vehicle continues to rise and fall, the shock absorber is defective. A shock absorber which has seized will also cause the vehicle to fail.

Exhaust system

☐ Start the engine. With your assistant holding a rag over the tailpipe, check the entire system for leaks. Repair or renew leaking sections.

3 Checks carried out **WITH THE VEHICLE RAISED AND THE WHEELS FREE TO TURN**

Jack up the front and rear of the vehicle, and securely support it on axle stands. Position the stands clear of the suspension assemblies. Ensure that the wheels are clear of the ground and that the steering can be turned from lock to lock.

Steering mechanism

☐ Have your assistant turn the steering from lock to lock. Check that the steering turns smoothly, and that no part of the steering mechanism, including a wheel or tyre, fouls any brake hose or pipe or any part of the body structure.

☐ Examine the steering rack rubber gaiters for damage or insecurity of the retaining clips. If power steering is fitted, check for signs of damage or leakage of the fluid hoses, pipes or connections. Also check for excessive stiffness or binding of the steering, a missing split pin or locking device, or severe corrosion of the body structure within 30 cm of any steering component attachment point.

Front and rear suspension and wheel bearings

☐ Starting at the front right-hand side, grasp the roadwheel at the 3 o'clock and 9 o'clock positions and rock gently but firmly. Check for free play or insecurity at the wheel bearings, suspension balljoints, or suspension mount-ings, pivots and attachments.

☐ Now grasp the wheel at the 12 o'clock and 6 o'clock positions and repeat the previous inspection. Spin the wheel, and check for roughness or tightness of the front wheel bearing.

☐ If excess free play is suspected at a component pivot point, this can be confirmed by using a large screwdriver or similar tool and levering between the mounting and the component attachment. This will confirm whether the wear is in the pivot bush, its retaining bolt, or in the mounting itself (the bolt holes can often become elongated).

☐ Carry out all the above checks at the other front wheel, and then at both rear wheels.

Springs and shock absorbers

☐ Examine the suspension struts (when applicable) for serious fluid leakage, corrosion, or damage to the casing. Also check the security of the mounting points.

☐ If coil springs are fitted, check that the spring ends locate in their seats, and that the spring is not corroded, cracked or broken.

☐ If leaf springs are fitted, check that all leaves are intact, that the axle is securely attached to each spring, and that there is no deterioration of the spring eye mountings, bushes, and shackles.

☐ The same general checks apply to vehicles fitted with other suspension types, such as torsion bars, hydraulic displacer units, etc. Ensure that all mountings and attachments are secure, that there are no signs of excessive wear, corrosion or damage, and (on hydraulic types) that there are no fluid leaks or damaged pipes.

☐ Inspect the shock absorbers for signs of serious fluid leakage. Check for wear of the mounting bushes or attachments, or damage to the body of the unit.

Driveshafts (fwd vehicles only)

☐ Rotate each front wheel in turn and inspect the constant velocity joint gaiters for splits or damage. Also check that each driveshaft is straight and undamaged.

Braking system

☐ If possible without dismantling, check brake pad wear and disc condition. Ensure that the friction lining material has not worn excessively, (A) and that the discs are not fractured, pitted, scored or badly worn (B).

☐ Examine all the rigid brake pipes underneath the vehicle, and the flexible hose(s) at the rear. Look for corrosion, chafing or insecurity of the pipes, and for signs of bulging under pressure, chafing, splits or deterioration of the flexible hoses.

☐ Look for signs of fluid leaks at the brake calipers or on the brake backplates. Repair or renew leaking components.

☐ Slowly spin each wheel, while your assistant depresses and releases the footbrake. Ensure that each brake is operating and does not bind when the pedal is released.

☐ Examine the handbrake mechanism, checking for frayed or broken cables, excessive corrosion, or wear or insecurity of the linkage. Check that the mechanism works on each relevant wheel, and releases fully, without binding.

☐ It is not possible to test brake efficiency without special equipment, but a road test can be carried out later to check that the vehicle pulls up in a straight line.

Fuel and exhaust systems

☐ Inspect the fuel tank (including the filler cap), fuel pipes, hoses and unions. All components must be secure and free from leaks.

☐ Examine the exhaust system over its entire length, checking for any damaged, broken or missing mountings, security of the retaining clamps and rust or corrosion.

Wheels and tyres

☐ Examine the sidewalls and tread area of each tyre in turn. Check for cuts, tears, lumps, bulges, separation of the tread, and exposure of the ply or cord due to wear or damage. Check that the tyre bead is correctly seated on the wheel rim, that the valve is sound and properly seated, and that the wheel is not distorted or damaged.

☐ Check that the tyres are of the correct size for the vehicle, that they are of the same size

and type on each axle, and that the pressures are correct.

☐ Check the tyre tread depth. The legal minimum at the time of writing is 1.6 mm over at least three-quarters of the tread width. Abnormal tread wear may indicate incorrect front wheel alignment.

Body corrosion

☐ Check the condition of the entire vehicle structure for signs of corrosion in load-bearing areas. (These include chassis box sections, side sills, cross-members, pillars, and all suspension, steering, braking system and seat belt mountings and anchorages.) Any corrosion which has seriously reduced the thickness of a load-bearing area is likely to cause the vehicle to fail. In this case professional repairs are likely to be needed.

☐ Damage or corrosion which causes sharp or otherwise dangerous edges to be exposed will also cause the vehicle to fail.

4 Checks carried out on YOUR VEHICLE'S EXHAUST EMISSION SYSTEM

Petrol models

☐ The engine should be warmed up, and running well (ignition system in good order, air filter element clean, etc).

☐ Before testing, run the engine at around 2500 rpm for 20 seconds. Let the engine drop to idle, and watch for smoke from the exhaust. If the idle speed is too high, or if dense blue or black smoke emerges for more than 5 seconds, the vehicle will fail. Typically, blue smoke signifies oil burning (engine wear); black smoke means unburnt fuel (dirty air cleaner element, or other fuel system fault).

☐ An exhaust gas analyser for measuring carbon monoxide (CO) and hydrocarbons (HC) is now needed. If one cannot be hired or borrowed, have a local garage perform the check.

CO emissions (mixture)

☐ The MOT tester has access to the CO limits for all vehicles. The CO level is measured at idle speed, and at 'fast idle' (2500 to 3000 rpm). The following limits are given as a general guide:

At idle speed – Less than 0.5% CO
At 'fast idle' – Less than 0.3% CO
Lambda reading – 0.97 to 1.03

☐ If the CO level is too high, this may point to poor maintenance, a fuel injection system problem, faulty lambda (oxygen) sensor or catalytic converter. Try an injector cleaning treatment, and check the vehicle's ECU for fault codes.

HC emissions

☐ The MOT tester has access to HC limits for all vehicles. The HC level is measured at 'fast idle' (2500 to 3000 rpm). The following limits are given as a general guide:

At 'fast idle' – Less then 200 ppm

☐ Excessive HC emissions are typically caused by oil being burnt (worn engine), or by a blocked crankcase ventilation system ('breather'). If the engine oil is old and thin, an oil change may help. If the engine is running badly, check the vehicle's ECU for fault codes.

Diesel models

☐ The only emission test for diesel engines is measuring exhaust smoke density, using a calibrated smoke meter. The test involves accelerating the engine at least 3 times to its maximum unloaded speed.

Note: *On engines with a timing belt, it is VITAL that the belt is in good condition before the test is carried out.*

☐ With the engine warmed up, it is first purged by running at around 2500 rpm for 20 seconds. A governor check is then carried out, by slowly accelerating the engine to its maximum speed. After this, the smoke meter is connected, and the engine is accelerated quickly to maximum speed three times. If the smoke density is less than the limits given below, the vehicle will pass:

Non-turbo vehicles: 2.5m-1
Turbocharged vehicles: 3.0m-1

☐ If excess smoke is produced, try fitting a new air cleaner element, or using an injector cleaning treatment. If the engine is running badly, where applicable, check the vehicle's ECU for fault codes. Also check the vehicle's EGR system, where applicable. At high mileages, the injectors may require professional attention.

Engine

- ☐ Engine fails to rotate when attempting to start
- ☐ Engine rotates, but will not start
- ☐ Engine difficult to start when cold
- ☐ Engine difficult to start when hot
- ☐ Starter motor noisy or excessively-rough in engagement
- ☐ Engine starts, but stops immediately
- ☐ Engine idles erratically
- ☐ Engine misfires at idle speed
- ☐ Engine misfires throughout the driving speed range
- ☐ Engine hesitates on acceleration
- ☐ Engine stalls
- ☐ Engine lacks power
- ☐ Engine backfires
- ☐ Oil pressure warning light illuminated with engine running
- ☐ Engine runs-on after switching off
- ☐ Engine noises

Cooling system

- ☐ Overheating
- ☐ Overcooling
- ☐ External coolant leakage
- ☐ Internal coolant leakage
- ☐ Corrosion

Fuel and exhaust systems

- ☐ Excessive fuel consumption
- ☐ Fuel leakage and/or fuel odour
- ☐ Excessive noise or fumes from exhaust system

Clutch

- ☐ Pedal travels to floor – no pressure or very little resistance
- ☐ Clutch fails to disengage (unable to select gears)
- ☐ Clutch slips (engine speed increases, with no increase in vehicle speed)
- ☐ Judder as clutch is engaged
- ☐ Noise when depressing or releasing clutch pedal

Manual transmission

- ☐ Noisy in neutral with engine running
- ☐ Noisy in one particular gear
- ☐ Difficulty engaging gears
- ☐ Jumps out of gear
- ☐ Vibration
- ☐ Lubricant leaks

Automatic transmission

- ☐ Fluid leakage
- ☐ General gear selection problems
- ☐ Transmission will not downshift (kickdown) with accelerator pedal fully depressed
- ☐ Engine will not start in any gear, or starts in gears other than Park or Neutral
- ☐ Transmission slips, shifts roughly, is noisy, or has no drive in forward or reverse gears

Driveshafts

- ☐ Vibration when accelerating or decelerating
- ☐ Clicking or knocking noise on turns (at slow speed on full-lock)

Braking system

- ☐ Vehicle pulls to one side under braking
- ☐ Noise (grinding or high-pitched squeal) when brakes applied
- ☐ Excessive brake pedal travel
- ☐ Brake pedal feels spongy when depressed
- ☐ Excessive brake pedal effort required to stop vehicle
- ☐ Judder felt through brake pedal or steering wheel when braking
- ☐ Pedal pulsates when braking hard
- ☐ Brakes binding
- ☐ Rear wheels locking under normal braking

Steering and suspension

- ☐ Vehicle pulls to one side
- ☐ Wheel wobble and vibration
- ☐ Excessive pitching and/or rolling around corners, or during braking
- ☐ Wandering or general instability
- ☐ Excessively-stiff steering
- ☐ Excessive play in steering
- ☐ Lack of power assistance
- ☐ Tyre wear excessive

Electrical system

- ☐ Battery will not hold a charge for more than a few days
- ☐ Ignition/no-charge warning light remains illuminated with engine running
- ☐ Ignition/no-charge warning light fails to come on
- ☐ Lights inoperative
- ☐ Instrument readings inaccurate or erratic
- ☐ Horn inoperative, or unsatisfactory in operation
- ☐ Windscreen/tailgate wipers inoperative, or unsatisfactory in operation
- ☐ Windscreen washers inoperative, or unsatisfactory in operation
- ☐ Electric windows inoperative, or unsatisfactory in operation

Introduction

The vehicle owner who does his or her own maintenance according to the recommended service schedules should not have to use this section of the manual very often. Modern component reliability is such that, provided those items subject to wear or deterioration are inspected or renewed at the specified intervals, sudden failure is comparatively rare. Faults do not usually just happen as a result of sudden failure, but develop over a period of time. Major mechanical failures in particular are usually preceded by characteristic symptoms over hundreds or even thousands of miles. Those components which do occasionally fail without warning are often small and easily carried in the vehicle.

With any fault-finding, the first step is to decide where to begin investigations. Sometimes this is obvious, but on other occasions, a little detective work will be necessary. The owner who makes half a dozen haphazard adjustments or replacements may be successful in curing a fault (or its symptoms), but will be none the wiser if the fault recurs, and ultimately may have spent more time and money than was necessary. A calm and logical approach will be found to be more satisfactory in the long run. Always take into account any warning signs or abnormalities that may have been noticed in the period preceding the fault – power loss, high or low gauge readings, unusual smells,

etc – and remember that failure of components such as fuses or spark plugs may only be pointers to some underlying fault.

The pages which follow provide an easy-reference guide to the more common problems which may occur during the operation of the vehicle. These problems and their possible causes are grouped under headings denoting various components or systems, such as Engine, Cooling system, etc. The general Chapter which deals with the problem is also shown in brackets; refer to the relevant part of that Chapter for system-specific information. Whatever the fault, certain basic principles apply. These are as follows:

Verify the fault. This is simply a matter of

being sure that you know what the symptoms are before starting work. This is particularly important if you are investigating a fault for someone else, who may not have described it very accurately.

Don't overlook the obvious. For example, if the vehicle won't start, is there fuel in the tank? (Don't take anyone else's word on this particular point, and don't trust the fuel gauge either!) If an electrical fault is indicated, look for loose or broken wires before digging out the test gear.

Cure the disease, not the symptom. Substituting a flat battery with a fully-charged one will get you off the hard shoulder, but if the underlying cause is not attended to, the new battery will go the same way.

Don't take anything for granted. Particularly, don't forget that a new component may itself be defective (especially if its been rattling around in the boot for months), and don't leave components out of a fault diagnosis sequence just because they are new or recently-fitted. When you do finally diagnose a difficult fault, you'll probably realise that all the evidence was there from the start.

Diesel fault diagnosis

The majority of starting problems on small diesel engines are electrical in origin. The mechanic who is familiar with petrol engines but less so with diesel may be inclined to view the diesel's injectors and pump in the same light as the spark plugs and distributor, but this is generally a mistake.

When investigating complaints of difficult starting for someone else, make sure that the correct starting procedure is understood and is being followed. Some drivers are unaware of the significance of the preheating warning light – many modern engines are sufficiently forgiving for this not to matter in mild weather, but with the onset of winter, problems begin. Glow plugs in particular are often neglected – just one faulty plug will make cold-weather starting very difficult.

As a rule of thumb, if the engine is difficult to start but runs well when it has finally got going, the problem is electrical (battery, starter motor or preheating system). If poor performance is combined with difficult starting, the problem is likely to be in the fuel system. The low-pressure (supply) side of the fuel system should be checked before suspecting the injectors and high-pressure pump. The most common fuel supply problem is air getting into the system, and any pipe from the fuel tank forwards must be scrutinised if air leakage is suspected.

Engine

Engine fails to rotate when attempting to start

☐ Battery terminal connections loose or corroded (see *Weekly checks*).
☐ Battery discharged or faulty (Chapter 5).
☐ Broken, loose or disconnected wiring in the starting circuit (Chapter 5).
☐ Defective starter solenoid or switch (Chapter 5).
☐ Defective starter motor (Chapter 5).
☐ Starter pinion or flywheel/driveplate ring gear teeth loose or broken (Chapter 2 and 5).
☐ Engine earth strap broken or disconnected (Chapter 5 or 12).

Engine rotates, but will not start

☐ Fuel tank empty.
☐ Battery discharged (engine rotates slowly) (Chapter 5).
☐ Battery terminal connections loose or corroded (see *Weekly checks*).
☐ Preheating system faulty (Chapter 5).
☐ Air in fuel system (Chapter 4).
☐ Major mechanical failure (e.g., timing belt) (Chapter 2).

Engine difficult to start when cold

☐ Battery discharged (Chapter 5).
☐ Battery terminal connections loose or corroded (see *Weekly checks*).
☐ Preheating system faulty (Chapter 5).
☐ Low cylinder compressions (Chapter 2).

Engine difficult to start when hot

☐ Air filter element dirty or clogged (Chapter 1).
☐ Low cylinder compressions (Chapter 2).

Starter motor noisy or excessively-rough in engagement

☐ Starter pinion or flywheel ring gear teeth loose or broken (Chapter 2 and 5).
☐ Starter motor mounting bolts loose or missing (Chapter 5).
☐ Starter motor internal components worn or damaged (Chapter 5).

Engine idles erratically

☐ Air filter element clogged (Chapter 1).
☐ Uneven or low cylinder compressions (Chapter 2).
☐ Camshaft lobes worn (Chapter 2).
☐ Timing belt incorrectly fitted (Chapter 2).
☐ Faulty injector(s) (Chapter 4).

Engine misfires at idle speed

☐ Faulty injector(s) (Chapter 4).
☐ Uneven or low cylinder compressions (Chapter 2).
☐ Disconnected, leaking, or perished crankcase ventilation hoses (Chapter 4).

Engine misfires throughout the driving speed range

☐ Fuel filter choked (Chapter 1).
☐ Fuel tank vent blocked, or fuel pipes restricted (Chapter 4).
☐ Faulty injector(s) (Chapter 4).
☐ Uneven or low cylinder compressions (Chapter 2).

Engine hesitates on acceleration

☐ Faulty injector(s) (Chapter 4).

Engine stalls

☐ Fuel filter choked (Chapter 1).
☐ Fuel tank vent blocked, or fuel pipes restricted (Chapter 4).
☐ Faulty injector(s) (Chapter 4).

Engine lacks power

☐ Timing belt incorrectly fitted or tensioned (Chapter 2).
☐ Fuel filter choked (Chapter 1).
☐ Uneven or low cylinder compressions (Chapter 2).
☐ Faulty injector(s) (Chapter 4).
☐ Brakes binding (Chapter 9).
☐ Clutch slipping (Chapter 6).
☐ Air filter element clogged (Chapter 1).

Engine (continued)

Engine backfires

☐ Timing belt incorrectly fitted or tensioned (Chapter 2).

Oil pressure warning light illuminated with engine running

☐ Low oil level, or incorrect oil grade (Weekly checks).
☐ Faulty oil pressure switch (Chapter 2).
☐ Worn engine bearings and/or oil pump (Chapter 2).
☐ High engine operating temperature (Chapter 3).
☐ Oil pressure relief valve defective (Chapter 2).
☐ Oil pick-up strainer clogged (Chapter 2).

Engine runs-on after switching off

☐ Excessive carbon build-up in engine (Chapter 2).
☐ High engine operating temperature (Chapter 3).

Engine noises

Pre-ignition (pinking) or knocking during acceleration or under load

☐ Excessive carbon build-up in engine (Chapter 2).

Whistling or wheezing noises

☐ Leaking exhaust manifold gasket or pipe-to-manifold joint (Chapter 4).
☐ Leaking vacuum hose (Chapters 4 and 9).
☐ Blowing cylinder head gasket (Chapter 2).

Tapping or rattling noises

☐ Worn valve gear or camshaft (Chapter 2).
☐ Ancillary component fault (coolant pump, alternator, etc) (Chapters 3, 5, etc).

Knocking or thumping noises

☐ Worn big-end bearings (regular heavy knocking, perhaps less under load) (Chapter 2).
☐ Worn main bearings (rumbling and knocking, perhaps worsening under load) (Chapter 2).
☐ Piston slap (most noticeable when cold) (Chapter 2).
☐ Ancillary component fault (coolant pump, alternator, etc) (Chapters 3, 5, etc).

Cooling system

Overheating

☐ Insufficient coolant in system (Weekly checks).
☐ Thermostat faulty (Chapter 3).
☐ Radiator core blocked, or grille restricted (Chapter 3).
☐ Electric cooling fan or thermostatic switch faulty (Chapter 3).
☐ Inaccurate temperature gauge sender unit (Chapter 3).
☐ Airlock in cooling system (Chapter 1).
☐ Expansion tank pressure cap faulty (Chapter 3).

Overcooling

☐ Thermostat faulty (Chapter 3).
☐ Inaccurate temperature gauge sender unit (Chapter 3).

External coolant leakage

☐ Deteriorated or damaged hoses or hose clips (Chapter 1).

☐ Radiator core or heater matrix leaking (Chapter 3).
☐ Pressure cap faulty (Chapter 1).
☐ Coolant pump internal seal leaking (Chapter 3).
☐ Coolant pump-to-housing seal leaking (Chapter 3).
☐ Boiling due to overheating (Chapter 3).
☐ Core plug leaking (Chapter 2).

Internal coolant leakage

☐ Leaking cylinder head gasket (Chapter 2).
☐ Cracked cylinder head or cylinder block (Chapter 2).

Corrosion

☐ Infrequent draining and flushing (Chapter 1).
☐ Incorrect coolant mixture or inappropriate coolant type (see Weekly checks).

Fuel and exhaust systems

Excessive fuel consumption

☐ Air filter element dirty or clogged (Chapter 1).
☐ Faulty injector(s) (Chapter 4).
☐ Tyres under-inflated (see Weekly checks).

Fuel leakage and/or fuel odour

☐ Damaged fuel tank, pipes or connections (Chapter 4).

Excessive noise or fumes from exhaust system

☐ Leaking exhaust system or manifold joints (Chapters 1 and 4).
☐ Leaking, corroded or damaged silencers or pipe (Chapters 1 and 4).
☐ Broken mountings causing body or suspension contact (Chapter 1).

Clutch

Pedal travels to floor – no pressure or very little resistance

- [ ] Faulty master or slave cylinder (Chapter 6).
- [ ] Faulty hydraulic release system (Chapter 6).
- [ ] Broken clutch release bearing or arm (Chapter 6).
- [ ] Broken diaphragm spring in clutch pressure plate (Chapter 6).

Clutch fails to disengage (unable to select gears)

- [ ] Faulty master or slave cylinder (Chapter 6).
- [ ] Faulty hydraulic release system (Chapter 6).
- [ ] Clutch driven plate sticking on gearbox input shaft splines (Chapter 6).
- [ ] Clutch driven plate sticking to flywheel or pressure plate (Chapter 6).
- [ ] Faulty pressure plate assembly (Chapter 6).
- [ ] Clutch release mechanism worn or incorrectly assembled (Chapter 6).

Clutch slips (engine speed increases, with no increase in vehicle speed)

- [ ] Faulty hydraulic release system (Chapter 6).

- [ ] Clutch driven plate linings excessively worn (Chapter 6).
- [ ] Clutch driven plate linings contaminated with oil or grease (Chapter 6).
- [ ] Faulty pressure plate or weak diaphragm spring (Chapter 6).

Judder as clutch is engaged

- [ ] Clutch driven plate linings contaminated with oil or grease (Chapter 6).
- [ ] Clutch driven plate linings excessively worn (Chapter 6).
- [ ] Faulty or distorted pressure plate or diaphragm spring (Chapter 6).
- [ ] Worn or loose engine or gearbox mountings (Chapter 2).
- [ ] Clutch driven plate hub or gearbox input shaft splines worn (Chapter 6).

Noise when depressing or releasing clutch pedal

- [ ] Worn clutch release bearing (Chapter 6).
- [ ] Worn or dry clutch pedal pivot (Chapter 6).
- [ ] Faulty pressure plate assembly (Chapter 6).
- [ ] Pressure plate diaphragm spring broken (Chapter 6).
- [ ] Broken clutch friction plate cushioning springs (Chapter 6).

Manual transmission

Noisy in neutral with engine running

- [ ] Input shaft bearings worn (noise apparent with clutch pedal released, but not when depressed) (Chapter 7).*
- [ ] Clutch release bearing worn (noise apparent with clutch pedal depressed, possibly less when released) (Chapter 6).

Noisy in one particular gear

- [ ] Worn, damaged or chipped gear teeth (Chapter 7).*

Difficulty engaging gears

- [ ] Clutch fault (Chapter 6).
- [ ] Worn or damaged gear linkage (Chapter 7).
- [ ] Worn synchroniser units (Chapter 7).*

Jumps out of gear

- [ ] Worn or damaged gear linkage (Chapter 7).

- [ ] Worn synchroniser units (Chapter 7).*
- [ ] Worn selector forks (Chapter 7).*

Vibration

- [ ] Lack of oil (Chapter 1).
- [ ] Worn bearings (Chapter 7).*

Lubricant leaks

- [ ] Leaking oil seal (Chapter 7).
- [ ] Leaking housing joint (Chapter 7).*
- [ ] Leaking input shaft oil seal (Chapter 7).

Although the corrective action necessary to remedy the symptoms described is beyond the scope of the home mechanic, the above information should be helpful in isolating the cause of the condition, so that the owner can communicate clearly with a professional mechanic.

Automatic transmission

Note: *Due to the complexity of the automatic transmission, it is difficult for the home mechanic to properly diagnose and service this unit. For problems other than the following, the vehicle should be taken to a dealer service department or automatic transmission specialist. Do not be too hasty in removing the transmission if a fault is suspected, as most of the testing is carried out with the unit still fitted.*

Fluid leakage

- [ ] Automatic transmission fluid is usually dark in colour. Fluid leaks should not be confused with engine oil, which can easily be blown onto the transmission by airflow.
- [ ] To determine the source of a leak, first remove all built-up dirt and grime from the transmission housing and surrounding areas using a degreasing agent, or by steam-cleaning. Drive the vehicle at low speed, so airflow will not blow the leak far from its source. Raise and support the vehicle, and determine where the leak is coming from.

General gear selection problems

- [ ] Chapter 7 deals with checking and adjusting the selector mechanism on automatic transmissions. The following are common problems which may be caused by a poorly-adjusted mechanism:
  - a) Engine starting in gears other than Park or Neutral.

  - b) Indicator panel indicating a gear other than the one actually being used.
  - c) Vehicle moves when in Park or Neutral.
  - d) Poor gear shift quality or erratic gear changes.
- [ ] Refer to Chapter 7B for the selector mechanism adjustment procedure.

Transmission will not downshift (kickdown) with accelerator pedal fully depressed

- [ ] Low transmission fluid level (Chapter 1).
- [ ] Incorrect selector mechanism adjustment (Chapter 7B).

Engine will not start in any gear, or starts in gears other than Park or Neutral

- [ ] Incorrect selector mechanism adjustment (Chapter 7B).

Transmission slips, shifts roughly, is noisy, or has no drive in forward or reverse gears

- [ ] There are many probable causes for the above problems, but unless there is a very obvious reason (such as a loose or corroded wiring plug connection on or near the transmission), the car should be taken to a franchise dealer or specialist for the fault to be diagnosed. The transmission control unit incorporates a self-diagnosis facility, and any fault codes can quickly be read and interpreted by a dealer with the proper diagnostic equipment.

Driveshafts

Vibration when accelerating or decelerating

☐ Worn inner constant velocity joint (Chapter 8).
☐ Bent or distorted driveshaft (Chapter 8).

Clicking or knocking noise on turns (at slow speed on full-lock)

☐ Worn outer constant velocity joint (Chapter 8).
☐ Lack of constant velocity joint lubricant, possibly due to damaged gaiter (Chapter 8).

Braking system

Note: *Before assuming that a brake problem exists, make sure that the tyres are in good condition and correctly inflated, that the front wheel alignment is correct, and that the vehicle is not loaded with weight in an unequal manner. Apart from checking the condition of all pipe and hose connections, any faults occurring on the anti-lock braking system should be referred to a Audi dealer for diagnosis.*

Vehicle pulls to one side under braking

☐ Worn, defective, damaged or contaminated front or rear brake pads on one side (Chapters 1 and 9).
☐ Seized or partially-seized front or rear brake caliper (Chapter 9).
☐ A mixture of brake pad lining materials fitted between sides (Chapter 9).
☐ Brake caliper mounting bolts loose (Chapter 9).
☐ Worn or damaged steering or suspension components (Chapters 1 and 10).

Noise (grinding or high-pitched squeal) when brakes applied

☐ Brake pad friction lining material worn down to metal backing (Chapters 1 and 9).
☐ Excessive corrosion of brake disc – may be apparent after the vehicle has been standing for some time (Chapters 1 and 9).
☐ Foreign object (stone chipping, etc) trapped between brake disc and shield (Chapters 1 and 9).

Excessive brake pedal travel

☐ Faulty master cylinder (Chapter 9).
☐ Air in hydraulic system (Chapter 9).
☐ Faulty vacuum servo unit (Chapter 9).
☐ Faulty vacuum pump (Chapter 9).

Brake pedal feels spongy when depressed

☐ Air in hydraulic system (Chapter 9).
☐ Deteriorated flexible rubber brake hoses (Chapters 1 and 9).

☐ Master cylinder mountings loose (Chapter 9).
☐ Faulty master cylinder (Chapter 9).

Excessive brake pedal effort required to stop vehicle

☐ Faulty vacuum servo unit (Chapter 9).
☐ Disconnected, damaged or insecure brake servo vacuum hose (Chapters 1 and 9).
☐ Faulty vacuum pump (Chapter 9).
☐ Primary or secondary hydraulic circuit failure (Chapter 9).
☐ Seized brake caliper (Chapter 9).
☐ Brake pads incorrectly fitted (Chapter 9).
☐ Incorrect grade of brake pads fitted (Chapter 9).
☐ Brake pads contaminated (Chapter 9).

Judder felt through brake pedal or steering wheel when braking

☐ Excessive run-out or distortion of brake disc(s) (Chapter 9).
☐ Brake pad linings worn (Chapters 1 and 9).
☐ Brake caliper mounting bolts loose (Chapter 9).
☐ Wear in suspension or steering components or mountings (Chapters 1 and 10).

Pedal pulsates when braking hard

☐ Normal feature of ABS – no fault.

Brakes binding

☐ Seized brake caliper piston(s) (Chapter 9).
☐ Incorrectly-adjusted handbrake mechanism (Chapter 9).
☐ Faulty master cylinder (Chapter 9).

Rear wheels locking under normal braking

☐ Rear brake pad linings contaminated (Chapters 1 and 9).
☐ Rear brake discs warped (Chapters 1 and 9).

Steering and suspension

Note: *Before diagnosing suspension or steering faults, be sure that the trouble is not due to incorrect tyre pressures, mixtures of tyre types, or binding brakes.*

Vehicle pulls to one side

- ☐ Defective tyre (see *Weekly checks*).
- ☐ Excessive wear in suspension or steering components (Chapters 1 and 10).
- ☐ Incorrect front wheel alignment (Chapter 10).
- ☐ Accident damage to steering or suspension components (Chapters 1 and 10).

Wheel wobble and vibration

- ☐ Front roadwheels out of balance (vibration felt mainly through the steering wheel) (Chapter 10).
- ☐ Rear roadwheels out of balance (vibration felt throughout the vehicle) (Chapter 10).
- ☐ Roadwheels damaged or distorted (Chapter 10).
- ☐ Faulty or damaged tyre (*Weekly checks*).
- ☐ Worn steering or suspension joints, bushes or components (Chapters 1 and 10).
- ☐ Wheel nuts loose (Chapter 1 and 10).

Excessive pitching and/or rolling around corners, or during braking

- ☐ Defective shock absorbers (Chapters 1 and 10).
- ☐ Broken or weak coil spring and/or suspension component (Chapters 1 and 10).
- ☐ Worn or damaged anti-roll bar or mountings (Chapter 10).

Wandering or general instability

- ☐ Incorrect front wheel alignment (Chapter 10).
- ☐ Worn steering or suspension joints, bushes or components (Chapters 1 and 10).
- ☐ Roadwheels out of balance (Chapter 10).
- ☐ Faulty or damaged tyre (*Weekly checks*).
- ☐ Wheel nuts loose (Chapter 10).
- ☐ Defective shock absorbers (Chapters 1 and 10).

Excessively-stiff steering

- ☐ Seized track rod end balljoint or suspension balljoint (Chapters 1 and 10).

- ☐ Broken or incorrectly adjusted auxiliary drivebelt (Chapter 1).
- ☐ Incorrect front wheel alignment (Chapter 10).
- ☐ Steering gear damaged (Chapter 10).

Excessive play in steering

- ☐ Worn steering column universal joint(s) (Chapter 10).
- ☐ Worn steering track rod end balljoints (Chapters 1 and 10).
- ☐ Worn steering gear (Chapter 10).
- ☐ Worn steering or suspension joints, bushes or components (Chapters 1 and 10).

Lack of power assistance

- ☐ Broken or incorrectly-adjusted auxiliary drivebelt (Chapter 1).
- ☐ Incorrect power steering fluid level (*Weekly checks*).
- ☐ Restriction in power steering fluid hoses (Chapter 10).
- ☐ Faulty power steering pump (Chapter 10).
- ☐ Faulty steering gear (Chapter 10).

Tyre wear excessive

Tyres worn on inside or outside edges

- ☐ Incorrect camber or castor angles (Chapter 10).
- ☐ Worn steering or suspension joints, bushes or components (Chapters 1 and 10).
- ☐ Excessively-hard cornering.
- ☐ Accident damage.

Tyre treads exhibit feathered edges

- ☐ Incorrect toe setting (Chapter 10).

Tyres worn in centre of tread

- ☐ Tyres over-inflated (*Weekly checks*).

Tyres worn on inside and outside edges

- ☐ Tyres under-inflated (*Weekly checks*).
- ☐ Worn shock absorbers (Chapter 10).

Tyres worn unevenly

- ☐ Tyres/wheels out of balance (*Weekly checks*).
- ☐ Excessive wheel or tyre run-out (Chapter 10).
- ☐ Worn shock absorbers (Chapters 1 and 10).
- ☐ Faulty tyre (*Weekly checks*).

Electrical system

Note: *For problems associated with the starting system, refer to the faults listed under Engine earlier in this Section.*

Battery will not hold a charge more than a few days

- ☐ Battery defective internally (Chapter 5).
- ☐ Battery terminal connections loose or corroded (*Weekly checks*).
- ☐ Auxiliary drivebelt worn – or incorrectly adjusted, where applicable (Chapter 1).
- ☐ Alternator not charging at correct output (Chapter 5).
- ☐ Alternator or voltage regulator faulty (Chapter 5).
- ☐ Short-circuit causing continual battery drain (Chapters 5 and 12).

Ignition/no-charge warning light remains illuminated with engine running

- ☐ Auxiliary drivebelt broken, worn, or incorrectly adjusted (Chapter 1).
- ☐ Internal fault in alternator or voltage regulator (Chapter 5).
- ☐ Broken, disconnected, or loose wiring in charging circuit (Chapter 5).

Ignition/no-charge warning light fails to come on

- ☐ Broken, disconnected, or loose wiring in warning light circuit (Chapter 12).
- ☐ Alternator faulty (Chapter 5).

Electrical system (continued)

Lights inoperative

- ☐ Bulb blown (Chapter 12).
- ☐ Corrosion of bulb or bulbholder contacts (Chapter 12).
- ☐ Blown fuse (Chapter 12).
- ☐ Faulty relay (Chapter 12).
- ☐ Broken, loose, or disconnected wiring (Chapter 12).
- ☐ Faulty switch (Chapter 12).

Instrument readings inaccurate or erratic

Fuel or temperature gauges give no reading

- ☐ Faulty coolant temperature sensor (Chapter 3).
- ☐ Wiring open-circuit (Chapter 12).
- ☐ Faulty gauge (Chapter 12).

Fuel or temperature gauges give continuous maximum reading

- ☐ Faulty coolant temperature sensor (Chapters 3).
- ☐ Wiring short-circuit (Chapter 12).
- ☐ Faulty gauge (Chapter 12).

Horn inoperative, or unsatisfactory in operation

Horn operates all the time

- ☐ Horn contacts permanently bridged or horn push stuck down (Chapter 12).

Horn fails to operate

- ☐ Blown fuse (Chapter 12).
- ☐ Cable or cable connections loose, broken or disconnected (Chapter 12).
- ☐ Faulty horn (Chapter 12).

Horn emits intermittent or unsatisfactory sound

- ☐ Cable connections loose (Chapter 12).
- ☐ Horn mountings loose (Chapter 12).
- ☐ Faulty horn (Chapter 12).

Windscreen/tailgate wipers inoperative, or unsatisfactory in operation

Wipers fail to operate, or operate very slowly

- ☐ Wiper blades stuck to screen, or linkage seized or binding (*Weekly checks* and Chapter 12).
- ☐ Blown fuse (Chapter 12).
- ☐ Cable or cable connections loose, broken or disconnected (Chapter 12).
- ☐ Faulty relay (Chapter 12).
- ☐ Faulty wiper motor (Chapter 12).

Wiper blades sweep over too large or too small an area of the glass

- ☐ Wiper arms incorrectly positioned on spindles (Chapter 12).
- ☐ Excessive wear of wiper linkage (Chapter 12).
- ☐ Wiper motor or linkage mountings loose or insecure (Chapter 12).

Wiper blades fail to clean the glass effectively

- ☐ Wiper blade rubbers worn or perished (*Weekly checks*).
- ☐ Wiper arm tension springs broken, or arm pivots seized (Chapter 12).
- ☐ Insufficient windscreen washer additive to adequately remove road film (*Weekly checks*).

Windscreen washers inoperative, or unsatisfactory in operation

One or more washer jets inoperative

- ☐ Blocked washer jet (Chapter 12).
- ☐ Disconnected, kinked or restricted fluid hose (Chapter 12).
- ☐ Insufficient fluid in washer reservoir (*Weekly checks*).

Washer pump fails to operate

- ☐ Broken or disconnected wiring or connections (Chapter 12).
- ☐ Blown fuse (Chapter 12).
- ☐ Faulty washer switch (Chapter 12).
- ☐ Faulty washer pump (Chapter 12).

Electric windows inoperative, or unsatisfactory in operation

Window glass will only move in one direction

- ☐ Faulty switch (Chapter 12).

Window glass slow to move

- ☐ Regulator seized or damaged, or in need of lubrication (Chapter 11).
- ☐ Door internal components or trim fouling regulator (Chapter 11).
- ☐ Faulty motor (Chapter 11).

Window glass fails to move

- ☐ Blown fuse (Chapter 12).
- ☐ Broken or disconnected wiring or connections (Chapter 12).
- ☐ Faulty motor (Chapter 12).

Central locking system inoperative, or unsatisfactory in operation

Complete system failure

- ☐ Blown fuse (Chapter 12).
- ☐ Faulty ECM (Chapter 12).
- ☐ Broken or disconnected wiring or connections (Chapter 12).

Latch locks but will not unlock, or unlocks but will not lock

- ☐ Faulty switch (Chapter 12).
- ☐ Broken or disconnected latch operating rods or levers (Chapter 11).
- ☐ Faulty ECM (Chapter 12).

One lock fails to operate

- ☐ Broken or disconnected wiring or connections (Chapter 12).
- ☐ Faulty motor (Chapter 11).
- ☐ Broken, binding or disconnected lock operating rods or levers (Chapter 11).
- ☐ Fault in door lock (Chapter 11).

Note: *References throughout this index are in the form "Chapter number" • "Page number". So, for example, 2C•15 refers to page 15 of Chapter 2C.*

A

A-pillar trim – 11•18
ABS hydraulic unit – 9•14
Abs wheel sensor – 9•14
Accelerator pedal – 4A•4, 4B•5
  position sensor – 4B•14
Accelerometer sensor – 9•15
Accessory shops – REF•7
Accumulator/dehydrator – 3•16
Acknowledgements – 0•4
Aerial – 12•19
Air conditioning system – 3•13, 3•14
  control panel illumination – 12•11
  controls – 3•13
Air filter – 1A•13, 1B•11, 4A•3, 4B•3
Air temperature sensor – 4B•15
Airbag system – 0•5, 12•19 et seq
Airflow sensor – 4A•10, 4B•14
Airlocks – 1A•21, 1B•16
Alarm system – 12•21
Alternator – 5A•4
Antifreeze – 0•11, 0•16, 1A•21, 1B•15, 3•3
  check – 1A•13, 1B•8
Anti-roll bar – 10•7, 10•10
Anti-shudder control valve – 4B•17
Anti-theft alarm system – 12•21
Approach light – 12•9
Asbestos – 0•5
Audio units – 12•18
Auto-dimming mirror – 11•13
Automatic temperature control – 3•13
Automatic transmission – 7B•1 et seq
  fault finding – 7B•2, REF•19
  fluid – 0•16
  fluid level check – 1A•18
Auxiliary drivebelt – 1A•15, 1B•12
  check – 1A•7, 1B•8

B

B-pillar trim – 11•18
Balljoint – 10•6
Battery – 0•5, 0•15, 5A•2
  remote control – 1A•19, 1B•14
Beam adjustment – 12•13
  xenon headlight – 12•14
Big-end bearings – 2F•13
Bleeding
  brakes – 9•12
  clutch – 6•3
  fuel system – 4B•6
  power steering – 10•13
Blower motor – 3•10, 3•11
  switch – 3•13
Body corrosion – REF•15
Body electrical system – 12•1 et seq
Bodywork and fittings – 11•1 et seq
Bonnet – 11•6
Boost pressure regulator valve – 4B•17
Booster heater (diesel engines) – 3•17
Braking system – 9•1 et seq, REF•12,
  REF•13, REF•14
  discs – 1A•8, 1B•8, 9•5, 9•10
  drums – 1A•8, 1B•8, 9•5

fault finding – REF•20
  fluid – 0•11, 0•16, 1A•19, 1B•14
  fluid reservoir – 9•11
  light – 12•10, 12•13
  light switch – 9•15
  pads – 1A•8, 1B•8, 9•2, 9•8
  pedal – 9•11
  pedal position switch – 7B•4, 9•15
  pedal shift interlock actuator – 7B•4
  shoes – 1A•8, 1B•8, 9•6
Bulbs – 0•16, 12•7 et seq
Bumpers – 11•4
Burning – 0•5
Buying spare parts – REF•7

C

C-pillar trim – 11•19
Cables
  gearchange – 7A•2, 7A•3
  handbrake – 9•16
  selector – 7B•2
Calipers – 9•4, 9•10
Cam followers – 2A•12, 2B•9, 2C•10,
  2D•10, 2E•8
Camshafts – 2A•12, 2B•9, 2C•10, 2D•10,
  2E•8
  oil seals – 2A•12, 2C•18, 2D•11, 2E•11
  position sensor – 4A•11, 4B•17
  sprockets – 2A•10, 2C•9, 2D•10
  timing oil control solenoids – 4A•12
Canister purge valve (EVAP) – 4C•3
Carbon canister – 4C•2
Carpets – 11•2
Catalytic converter – 4B•22, 4B•23, 4C•2,
  4C•3, 4D•1, 4D•2
CD auto-changer – 12•18
Central locking system – 11•15, 12•17
Centre console – 11•20
Charging – 5A•2, 5A•3
Climate control module (CCM) – 3•13,
  12•22
Clutch – 1A•12, 6•1 et seq
  fault finding – REF•19
  fluid – 0•11, 0•16
  pedal – 6•1
  pedal position switch – 4A•12
Coil spring – 10•9
Coil(s) – 5B•2
Common rail – 4B•15
Compression test – 2A•3, 2B•3, 2C•3,
  2D•4, 2E•3
Compressor – 3•16
Condenser – 3•14
Connecting rods – 2F•9, 2F•12, 2F•17
Console – 11•20
Control arm – 10•7, 10•10
Control module
  climate control (CCM) – 3•13, 12•22
  door lock – 11•11, 11•12
  generic (GEM) – 11•15, 12•22
  keyless entry system (KVM) – 11•15, 12•22
  lighting (LCM) – 12•22
  lighting (xenon headlight) – 12•14
  parking aid (PAM) – 12•17

particulate filter additive system – 4D•4
  Powertrain control (PCM) – 4A•10, 4B•14
  restraint control (RCM) – 12•21
  transmission control (TCM) – 7B•4
Conversion factors – REF•6
Coolant – 0•11, 0•16, 1A•20, 1B•14, 3•3
  by-pass valve – 3•7
  degas shut-off valve – 3•7
  pump – 3•9
  pump sprocket – 2C•10
  shut-off valve – 3•7
  strength check – 1A•13, 1B•8
  temperature sensor – 3•6
Cooling, heating and air conditioning
  systems – 3•1 et seq
  system checks – 1A•21, 1B•15
  fault finding – REF•18
Courtesy lights – 12•10
  light switches – 12•6
Crankcase – 2F•11
Crankcase emission control – 4C•1, 4C•2,
  4D•1, 4D•2
Crankshaft – 2F•9, 2F•13, 2F•15
  oil seals – 2A•17, 2B•12, 2C•17, 2D•19,
  2E•15
  position sensor – 4A•11, 4B•13
  pulley – 2A•6, 2B•6, 2C•6, 2D•7, 2E•5
  sprocket – 2A•11, 2C•9
  vibration damper – 2A•6
Crash/lateral acceleration sensors – 12•21
Crushing – 0•5
Curtain airbags – 12•21
Cylinder block – 2F•11
Cylinder head – 2A•14, 2B•12, 2C•13,
  2D•12, 2E•11, 2F•6
  cover – 2A•5, 2B•5, 2C•4, 2D•5, 2E•4
  temperature sensor – 3•7

D

D-pillar trim – 11•19
Degas shut-off valve – 3•7
Dents – 11•3
Depressurisation fuel system – 4A•2
Diesel engine fault diagnosis – REF•17
Diesel engine in-car repair procedures
  1.6 litre – 2C•1 et seq
  1.8 litre – 2D•1 et seq
  2.0 litre – 2E•1 et seq
Diesel injection equipment – 0•5
Dimensions – REF•1
Dipped beam
  halogen – 12•7
  xenon headlight – 12•13
Direction indicator – 12•8, 12•9, 12•12
Discs – 9•5, 9•10
  check – 1A•8, 1B•8
Distance sensor (parking aid) – 12•18
Doors – 11•12, REF•13
  handles – 11•10
  inner trim panel – 11•6
  lock components – 11•10, 11•15
  mirror – 11•13
  mirror adjuster switch – 12•5
  window glass – 11•7
  window regulator – 11•8

Note: *References throughout this index are in the form* **"Chapter number"** • **"Page number".** *So, for example, 2C•15 refers to page 15 of Chapter 2C.*

Drain tubes – 11•16
Drivebelt – 1A•15, 1B•12
    check – 1A•7, 1B•8
Driveplate – 2A•18, 2B•16
Driveshafts – 8•1 *et seq,* REF•14
    fault finding – REF•20
    gaiters – 8•3
    gaiter check – 1A•10, 1B•8
    joint check – 1A•10, 1B•8
    oil seals – 7A•4
Drivetrain – 1A•12
Driving on the right or left – 12•14
Drums – 9•5
    check – 1A•8
DVD units – 12•18

E

Earth fault – 12•3
Electric parking brake – 9•16
Electric shock – 0•5
Electrical equipment – 1A•12, REF•13
    fault finding – 12•2, REF•21, REF•22
Electro-hydraulic power steering – 10•13
Electronic control modules – 12•22
Electronic stability control – 9•14
Emblems – 11•15
Emission control systems – diesel
    engines – 4D•1 *et seq*
Emission control systems – petrol
    engines – 4C•1 *et seq*
Emission system – REF•15
Engine compartment wiring check – 1A•7,
    1B•8
Engine fault finding – 5B•2, REF•17, REF•18
Engine management system – 4B•13
Engine oil – 0•11, 0•16, 1A•6, 1B•6
Engine reconditioners – REF•7
Engine removal and overhaul procedures –
    2F•1 *et seq*
Environmental considerations – REF•8
Evaporative emission control – 4C•1, 4C•2
Evaporator – 3•14
Exhaust emission control – 4C•1, 4C•3,
    4D•1, 4D•2
Exhaust gas recirculation (EGR) – 4C•2,
    4D•1
    cooler – 4D•3
    solenoid/valve – 004C•3, 4D•2
Exhaust manifold – 4A•13, 4B•21
Exhaust particulate filter – 1B•12
    additive tank refilling – 1B•11
Exhaust specialists – REF•7
Exhaust system – 4A•14, 4B•22, REF•14,
    REF•15
    check – 1A•9, 1B•8
Expansion tank – 3•8
    pressure cap check – 1A•21, 1B•16

F

Facia – 11•21
    centre panel switches – 12•6
Factors – REF•7
Fan(s) – 3•5

Fault finding – REF•16 *et seq*
    automatic transmission – 7B•2, REF•19
    braking system – REF•20
    clutch – REF•19
    cooling system – REF•18
    diesel engine – REF•17
    driveshafts – REF•20
    electrical system – 12•2, REF•21, REF•22
    engine – 5B•2, REF•17, REF•18
    fuel and exhaust systems – REF•18
    manual transmission – REF•19
    steering and suspension – REF•20, REF•21
Filling – 11•3
Filter
    air – 1A•13, 1B•11, 4A•3, 4B•3
    exhaust particulate – 1B•11, 1B•12
    fuel – 1B•9
    oil – 1A•6, 1B•6
    particulate – 4B•22, 4B•23, 4D•1, 4D•4
    pollen – 1A•12, 1B•8
Fire – 0•5
Fixed windows – 11•15
Flap motor – 12•22
Fluids – 0•16
Flywheel – 2A•18, 2B•16, 2C•18, 2D•20,
    2E•16
Foglight – 12•8, 12•12, 12•13
    switch – 12•6
Footwell lights – 12•11
Ford C-MAX manual – 0•4
Fuel (common) rail – 4B•15
Fuel and exhaust systems – diesel
    engines – 4B•1 *et seq*
Fuel and exhaust systems – petrol
    models – 4A•1 *et seq*
    fault finding – REF•18
Fuel economy – REF•2 *et seq*
Fuel filler flap motor – 12•22
Fuel filter – 1B•9
Fuel gauge sender unit – 4A•6, 4B•7
Fuel hoses check – 1A•11
Fuel injection pump – 4B•7
    drive chain – 2F•8
    sprockets – 2D•10
Fuel injection system – 4A•7, 4B•5, 4B•7,
    REF•15
    shut-off (inertia) switch – 4A•7
Fuel injectors – 4A•8, 4B•10
Fuel lines and fittings – 4A•3
Fuel pressure control valve – 4B•17
Fuel pressure sensor – 4B•15
Fuel pump – 4A•6, 4B•7
    drive chain – 2F•8
    sprocket – 2C•9
Fuel rail – 4A•8
Fuel tank – 4A•4, 4B•4
    roll-over valve – 4A•6
Fuel volume control valve – 4B•17
Fume or gas intoxication – 0•5
Fuses – 0•16, 12•3

G

Gaiters
    driveshaft – 1A•10, 1B•8, 8•3
    steering rack – 10•13

Garages – REF•7
Gas discharge headlight system –
    12•13 *et seq*
Gashes – 11•3
Gaskets – REF•8
Gear lever – 7A•3
Gearchange cables – 7A•2, 7A•3
General repair procedures – REF•8
Generic electronic module (GEM) – 11•15,
    12•22
Glass
    doors– 11•7
    mirror – 11•13
    windscreen and fixed windows – 11•15
Glovebox – 11•21
    light – 12•10
    light switch – 12•5
Glow plugs – 5C•1
Grab handle – 11•18
Grille – 11•5

H

Halogen headlight
    dipped beam – 12•7
    main beam – 12•7
Handbrake – 9•15, 9•16, REF•12
    warning switch – 12•6
Handles
    doors – 11•10
    grab handle – 11•18
Hazard warning switch – 12•6
Head airbags – 12•21
Headlight unit – 12•11
    control switch – 12•6
Heat shields – 4A•14
Heating/ventilation system – 3•3, •10
    blower motor – 3•10, 3•11
    control panel – 3•13
    control panel illumination – 12•11
    heater booster (diesel engines only) – 3•17
    matrix – 3•11
    seat heating – 12•7
Height sensor (xenon headlight) – 12•14
High-level brake light – 12•10, 12•13
High-pressure cut-off switch (air
    conditioning) – 3•17
Hinges lubrication – 1A•11, 1B•8
Horns – 12•17
    check – 1A•7, 1B•8
Hoses – 3•3, 4A•3, 9•12
    check – 1A•10, 1B•8
HT coil(s) – 5B•2
Hub
    bearing – 10•3, 10•8
    carrier – 10•3, 10•8
Hydraulic unit ABS – 9•14
Hydrofluoric acid – 0•5

I

Identifying leaks – 0•9
Idler pulley – 2C•10
Ignition switch – 12•4
Ignition system – petrol engines –
    5B•1 *et seq*

Note: *References throughout this index are in the form* **"Chapter number"** • **"Page number".** *So, for example, 2C•15 refers to page 15 of Chapter 2C.*

Indicator – 12•8, 12•9, 12•12
Inertia switch – 4A•7
Injection pump – 4B•7
  drive chain – 2F•8
Injection system – 4A•7
Injectors – 4A•8, 4B•10
Input shaft
  oil seals – 7A•5
  speed sensor – 7B•4
Instruments – 1A•12, 12•14
  bulbs – 12•11
  illumination switch – 12•6
Intake air temperature sensor – 4B•15
Intake manifold – 2C•4, 4A•12, 4B•21
Intercooler – 4B•21
Interior lights – 12•10
  switches – 12•6
Interior mirror – 11•13
Introduction – 0•4

J

Jacking and vehicle support – REF•9
Joint mating faces – REF•8
Jump starting – 0•7

K

Keyless vehicle module (KVM) – 11•15,
  12•22
Knock sensor – 5B•3

L

Lambda sensors – 4C•1, 4C•3
Lateral acceleration sensors – 12•21
Lateral link – 10•8
Leakdown test – 2C•4, 2D•4, 2E•3
Leaks – 0•9
  check – 1A•10, 1B•8
  cooling system – 1A•21, 1B•15
Light units – 12•11
  check – 1A•7, 1B•8
  switch – 12•5
Lighting control module (LCM) – 12•22
  xenon headlight – 12•14
Limited Operation Strategy – 4A•7
Link arms – 10•10
Locknuts, locktabs and washers – REF•8
Locks
  bonnet – 11•6
  central locking system – 11•15
  doors – 11•10, 11•15
  lubrication – 1A•11, 1B•8
  tailgate – 11•15, 11•15
**Low-pressure cut-off switch (air
  conditioning)** – 3•17
Lubricants and fluids – 0•16
Luggage area
  light – 12•11
  side panel – 11•19

M

Main beam
  halogen – 12•7
  xenon headlight – 12•13

Main bearings – 2F•13, 2F•15
Manifold absolute pressure (MAP) sensor –
  4B•14
Manifolds
  exhaust – 4A•12, 4B•21
  intake – 2C•4, 4A•12, 4B•21
Manual transmission – 7A•1 et seq
  fault finding – REF•19
  oil – 0•16, 1A•18, 1B•16, 7A•5
Mass airflow sensor – 4A•10, •14
Master cylinder
  brake – 9•10
  clutch – 6•3
Matrix – 3•11
Mirror – 11•13, REF•12
  adjuster switch – 12•5
  light – 12•11
Misfire – 5B•2
MOT test checks – REF•12 et seq
Motor factors – REF•7
Mountings – 2A•18, 2B•17, 2C•19, 2D•20,
  2E•17
Movement limiter link – 2C•19

N

Number plate light – 12•9, 12•13

O

Oil
  engine – 0•11, 0•16, 1A•6, 1B•6
  manual transmission – 0•16, 1A•18,
  1B•16, 7A•5
Oil cooler – 2C•17, 2D•18, 2E•15
Oil filter – 1A•6, 1B•6
Oil level sensor – 2C•18
Oil pressure switch – 2A•17, 002B•15,
  2C•18, 2D•18, 2E•15
Oil pump – 2A•16, 2B•14, 2C•15, 2D•17,
  2E•14
Oil seals – REF•8
  camshafts – 2A•12, 2C•18, 2D•11, 2E•11
  crankshaft – 2A•17, 2B•12, 2C-17, 2D•19,
  2E•15
  driveshaft – 7A•4
  input shaft – 7A•5
  output shaft speed sensor – 7B•5
  selector shaft – 7A•5
Oil separator – 4C•2, 4D•2
Open-circuit – 12•2
Output shaft speed sensor – 7B•4
  seal – 7B•5
Overhead console – 11•20
Oxygen (lambda) sensors – 4C•1, 4C•3

P

Pads – 9•2, 9•8
  check – 1A•8, 1B•8
Parking aid module (PAM) – 12•17
Parking brake – 9•16
Particulate filter – 4B•22, 4B•23, 4D•1
  additive system module (ASM) – 4D•4
Parts – REF•7
Passenger grab handle – 11•18

Pedals
  accelerator – 4A•4, 4B•5
  accelerator position sensor – 4B•14
  brake – 9•11
  brake position switch – 7B•4
  clutch – 6•1
  clutch position switch – 4A•12
Petrol engine in-car repair procedures
  1.6 litre – 2A•1 et seq
  1.8 & 2.0 litre – 2B•1 et seq
Pipes – 4A•3, 9•12
  check – 1A•10, 1B•8
Piston rings – 2F•14
Pistons – 2F•9, 2F•12, 2F•17
Plastic components – 11•4
Poisonous or irritant substances – 0•5
Pollen filter – 1A•12, 1B•8
Power steering
  fluid – 0•12, 0•16
  pump – 10•13
Powertrain Control Module (PCM) – 4A•10,
  4B•14
Pre/post-heating system – diesel engines –
  5C•1 et seq
Pressure cap check – 1A•21, 1B•16
Priming and bleeding fuel system – 4B•6
Puncture repair – 0•8

R

Radiator – 3•8
  fan(s) – 3•5
  grille – 11•5
**Range control positioning motor (xenon
  headlight)** – 12•14
Range sensor
  automatic transmission – 7B•3
  parking aid – 12•18
Reading lights – 12•10
Rear combination light – 12•9, 12•12
Regulator (door window) – 11•8
Relays – 12•4
Release bearing – 6•5
Remote control battery – 1A•19, 1B•14
Repair procedures – REF•8
Respraying – 11•3
Restraint control module (RCM) – 12•21
Reversing lights – 12•13
  switch – 7A•4
Ride height sensor (xenon headlight) –
  12•14
Road test – 1A•12, 1B•8
Roadside repairs – 0•6 et seq
Roadwheel
  check and balancing – 1A•10, 1B•8
  nut tightness check – 1A•11, 1B•8
Rocker arms – 2C•10, 2E•8
Roll restrictor – 2A•19, 2B•17
Roll-over valve – 4A•6
Routine maintenance –
  bodywork and underframe – 11•2
  upholstery and carpets – 11•2
Routine maintenance & servicing –
  diesel models – 1B•1 et seq
  petrol models – 1A•1 et seq
Rust holes – 11•3

Note: *References throughout this index are in the form* "**Chapter number**" • "**Page number**". *So, for example, 2C•15 refers to page 15 of Chapter 2C.*

S

Safety first! – 0•5, 0•11, 0•12
Scalding – 0•5
Scratches – 11•2
Screw threads and fastenings – REF•8
Seat belts – 11•17
   check – 1A•13, 1B•8
Seats – 11•16
   heating switches – 12•7
Selector – 7B•3
   cable – 7B•2
   lever – 7B•3
   lever shift interlock solenoid – 7B•4
   shaft oil seals – 7A•5
Shift interlock – 7B•4
Shock absorbers – 10•9, REF•13, REF•14
Shoes – 9•6
   check – 1A•8, 1B•8
Short-circuit – 12•2
Shut-off (inertia) switch – 4A•7
Side airbags – 12•21
Sidelight – 12•8
   xenon headlight – 12•13
Side-trim mouldings – 11•15
Silencer – 4A•14, 4B•23
Slave cylinder (clutch) – 6•3
Spare parts – REF•7
Spark plugs – 1A•14
Speakers – 12•19
   parking aid – 12•18
Springs – 10•9, REF•14
Sprockets
   camshafts – 2A•10, 2C•9, 2D•10
   coolant pump – 2C•10
   crankshaft – 2A•11, 2C•9
   fuel pump – 2C•9, 2D•10
Stability control – 9•14
Starting and charging systems – 5A•1 *et seq*
Start-up after overhaul – 2F•18
Steering – 1A•12, REF•13, REF•14
   angles – 10•14
   check – 1A•9, 1B•8
   column – 10•11, REF•12
   column shrouds – 11•19
   column switches – 12•5
   rack – 10•12
   rack gaiters – 10•13
   wheel – 10•11, REF•12
   wheel rotation sensor – 9•15
   wheel switches – 12•6
Stop-light switch – 4B•14
Struts
   suspension – 10•5
   tailgate – 11•15
Subframe – 10•15
Sump – 2A•15, 2B•14, 2C•15, 2D•16, 2E•13
Sun blind – 11•16
Sunroof – 11•16
   control switch – 12•6
   motor – 12•17
Sunvisor – 11•18
   light – 12•11

Suspension and steering – 1A•12, 10•1 *et seq*, REF•13, REF•14
   check – 1A•9, 1A•10, 1B•8
   fault finding – REF•21
Switches – 12•5 *et seq*
   air conditioning high- and low-pressure cut-off – 3•17
   blower motor – 3•13
   brake light – 9•15
   brake pedal position – 9•15
   ignition – 12•4
   illumination – 12•11
   oil pressure – 2A•17, 2B•15, 2C•18, 2D•18, 2E•15
   reversing light – 7A•4
   stop-light – 4B•14

T

Tailgate – 11•14
   lock – 11•15
   lock components – 11•15
   struts – 11•15
   wiper – 12•17
Tappets – 2A•12, 2B•9, 2C•10, 2D•10, 2E•8
Temperature sensor – 3•6, 3•7, 4B•15, 7B•4
Tensioner – 2A•10, 2B•8, 2C•10, 2D•10, 2E•5, 2E•8
Thermostat – 3•3
Throttle body – 4A•7
Tie-rod – 10•10
Timing belt – 2A•8, 2C•8, 2D•7, 2E•5
   covers – 2A•8, 2C•7
   tensioner and sprockets – 2A•10, 2C•9, 2D•10
Timing chain – 2E•8
   cover – 2B•6
   tensioner and guides – 2B•8
Timing holes – 2C•4
Timing (ignition) – 5B•2
TMAP sensor – 4A•9
Tools and working facilities – REF•8, REF•10 *et seq*
Top Dead Centre (TDC) for No 1 piston location – 2A•4, 2B•4, 2D•4
Torque rod/movement limiter link – 2C•19
Towing – 0•9
Track rod end – 10•14
Traction control system – 9•15
Transmission control module – 7B•4
Transmission fluid
   cooler – 7B•5
   pan – 7B•5
   temperature sensor – 7B•4
Transmission sensors – 7B•3
Trim panels – 11•15, 11•18
   doors – 11•6
Turbine (input) shaft speed sensor – 7B•4
Turbocharger – 4B•17, 4B•18, 4B•21
   boost pressure regulator valve – 4B•17
Tyres – REF•15
   condition – 0•13
   pressures – 0•16
   sealant – 0•8
   specialists – REF•7

U

Underbody check – 1A•11, 1B•8
Underframe – 11•2
Unleaded petrol – 4A•3
Upholstery – 11•2

V

Vacuum hoses check – 1A•11
Vacuum pump – 9•17
Vacuum servo unit – 9•13, 9•14
Valves – 2F•8
   clearances – 2A•6, 2B•5, 2D•6
   timing holes – 2C•4
Vanity mirror light – 12•11
Variable camshafts timing oil control solenoids – 4A•12
Vehicle identification numbers – REF•7, REF•13
Vehicle support – REF•9
Ventilation system – 3•3, 3•10
Vibration damper – 2A•6

W

Washer system – 12•16
   fluid – 0•14
Weekly checks – 0•10 *et seq*
Weights – REF•1
Wheels – REF•15
   alignment – 10•14
   bearings – 10•3, 10•8, REF•14
   changing – 0•8
Wheel arch liner – 11•22
Wheel cylinders – 9•7
Wheel sensor – 9•14
Windows
   doors – 11•7
   fixed – 11•15
   regulator – 11•8
   switches – 12•6
Windscreen – 11•15, REF•12
   wiper – 12•14
Wipers
   arms – 12•14
   blades – 0•14
   motor – 12•15
   tailgate – 12•17
   windscreen – 12•14
Wiring diagrams – 12•23 *et seq*
   wiring check – 1A•7, 1B•8
Working facilities – REF•11

X

Xenon gas discharge headlight system – 12•13 *et seq*

Y

Yaw rate sensor – 9•15

Haynes Manuals – The Complete **UK Car** List

Title	Book No.
ALFA ROMEO Alfasud/Sprint (74 - 88) up to F *	0292
Alfa Romeo Alfetta (73 - 87) up to E *	0531
AUDI 80, 90 & Coupe Petrol (79 - Nov 88) up to F	0605
Audi 80, 90 & Coupe Petrol (Oct 86 - 90) D to H	1491
Audi 100 & 200 Petrol (Oct 82 - 90) up to H	0907
Audi 100 & A6 Petrol & Diesel (May 91 - May 97) H to P	3504
Audi A3 Petrol & Diesel (96 - May 03) P to 03	4253
Audi A4 Petrol & Diesel (95 - 00) M to X	3575
Audi A4 Petrol & Diesel (01 - 04) X to 54	4609
AUSTIN A35 & A40 (56 - 67) up to F *	0118
Austin/MG/Rover Maestro 1.3 & 1.6 Petrol (83 - 95) up to M	0922
Austin/MG Metro (80 - May 90) up to G	0718
Austin/Rover Montego 1.3 & 1.6 Petrol (84 - 94) A to L	1066
Austin/MG/Rover Montego 2.0 Petrol (84 - 95) A to M	1067
Mini (59 - 69) up to H *	0527
Mini (69 - 01) up to X	0646
Austin/Rover 2.0 litre Diesel Engine (86 - 93) C to L	1857
Austin Healey 100/6 & 3000 (56 - 68) up to G *	0049
BEDFORD CF Petrol (69 - 87) up to E	0163
Bedford/Vauxhall Rascal & Suzuki Supercarry (86 - Oct 94) C to M	3015
BMW 316, 320 & 320i (4-cyl) (75 - Feb 83) up to Y *	0276
BMW 320, 320i, 323i & 325i (6-cyl) (Oct 77 - Sept 87) up to E	0815
BMW 3- & 5-Series Petrol (81 - 91) up to J	1948
BMW 3-Series Petrol (Apr 91 - 99) H to V	3210
BMW 3-Series Petrol (Sept 98 - 03) S to 53	4067
BMW 520i & 525e (Oct 81 - June 88) up to E	1560
BMW 525, 528 & 528i (73 - Sept 81) up to X *	0632
BMW 5-Series 6-cyl Petrol (April 96 - Aug 03) N to 03	4151
BMW 1500, 1502, 1600, 1602, 2000 & 2002 (59 - 77) up to S *	0240
CHRYSLER PT Cruiser Petrol (00 - 03) W to 53	4058
CITROËN 2CV, Ami & Dyane (67 - 90) up to H	0196
Citroën AX Petrol & Diesel (87 - 97) D to P	3014
Citroën Berlingo & Peugeot Partner Petrol & Diesel (96 - 05) P to 55	4281
Citroën BX Petrol (83 - 94) A to L	0908
Citroën C15 Van Petrol & Diesel (89 - Oct 98) F to S	3509
Citroën C3 Petrol & Diesel (02 - 05) 51 to 05	4197
Citroen C5 Petrol & Diesel (01-08) Y to 08	4745
Citroën CX Petrol (75 - 88) up to F	0528
Citroën Saxo Petrol & Diesel (96 - 04) N to 54	3506
Citroën Visa Petrol (79 - 88) up to F	0620
Citroën Xantia Petrol & Diesel (93 - 01) K to Y	3082
Citroën XM Petrol & Diesel (89 - 00) G to X	3451
Citroën Xsara Petrol & Diesel (97 - Sept 00) R to W	3751
Citroën Xsara Picasso Petrol & Diesel (00 - 02) W to 52	3944
Citroen Xsara Picasso (03-08)	4784
Citroën ZX Diesel (91 - 98) J to S	1922
Citroën ZX Petrol (91 - 98) H to S	1881
Citroën 1.7 & 1.9 litre Diesel Engine (84 - 96) A to N	1379
FIAT 126 (73 - 87) up to E *	0305
Fiat 500 (57 - 73) up to M *	0090
Fiat Bravo & Brava Petrol (95 - 00) N to W	3572
Fiat Cinquecento (93 - 98) K to R	3501
Fiat Panda (81 - 95) up to M	0793
Fiat Punto Petrol & Diesel (94 - Oct 99) L to V	3251
Fiat Punto Petrol (Oct 99 - July 03) V to 03	4066
Fiat Punto Petrol (03-07) 03 to 07	4746
Fiat Regata Petrol (84 - 88) A to F	1167
Fiat Tipo Petrol (88 - 91) E to J	1625
Fiat Uno Petrol (83 - 95) up to M	0923
Fiat X1/9 (74 - 89) up to G *	0273
FORD Anglia (59 - 68) up to G *	0001

Title	Book No.
Ford Capri II (& III) 1.6 & 2.0 (74 - 87) up to E *	0283
Ford Capri II (& III) 2.8 & 3.0 V6 (74 - 87) up to E	1309
Ford Cortina Mk I & Corsair 1500 ('62 - '66) up to D*	0214
Ford Cortina Mk III 1300 & 1600 (70 - 76) up to P *	0070
Ford Escort Mk I 1100 & 1300 (68 - 74) up to N *	0171
Ford Escort Mk I Mexico, RS 1600 & RS 2000 (70 - 74) up to N *	0139
Ford Escort Mk II Mexico, RS 1800 & RS 2000 (75 - 80) up to W *	0735
Ford Escort (75 - Aug 80) up to V *	0280
Ford Escort Petrol (Sept 80 - Sept 90) up to H	0686
Ford Escort & Orion Petrol (Sept 90 - 00) H to X	1737
Ford Escort & Orion Diesel (Sept 90 - 00) H to X	4081
Ford Fiesta (76 - Aug 83) up to Y	0334
Ford Fiesta Petrol (Aug 83 - Feb 89) A to F	1030
Ford Fiesta Petrol (Feb 89 - Oct 95) F to N	1595
Ford Fiesta Petrol & Diesel (Oct 95 - Mar 02) N to 02	3397
Ford Fiesta Petrol & Diesel (Apr 02 - 07) 02 to 57	4170
Ford Focus Petrol & Diesel (98 - 01) S to Y	3759
Ford Focus Petrol & Diesel (Oct 01 - 05) 51 to 05	4167
Ford Galaxy Petrol & Diesel (95 - Aug 00) M to W	3984
Ford Granada Petrol (Sept 77 - Feb 85) up to B *	0481
Ford Granada & Scorpio Petrol (Mar 85 - 94) B to M	1245
Ford Ka (96 - 02) P to 52	3570
Ford Mondeo Petrol (93 - Sept 00) K to X	1923
Ford Mondeo Petrol & Diesel (Oct 00 - Jul 03) X to 03	3990
Ford Mondeo Petrol & Diesel (July 03 - 07) 03 to 56	4619
Ford Mondeo Diesel (93 - 96) L to N	3465
Ford Orion Petrol (83 - Sept 90) up to H	1009
Ford Sierra 4-cyl Petrol (82 - 93) up to K	0903
Ford Sierra V6 Petrol (82 - 91) up to J	0904
Ford Transit Petrol (Mk 2) (78 - Jan 86) up to C	0719
Ford Transit Petrol (Mk 3) (Feb 86 - 89) C to G	1468
Ford Transit Diesel (Feb 86 - 99) C to T	3019
Ford Transit Diesel (00-06)	4775
Ford 1.6 & 1.8 litre Diesel Engine (84 - 96) A to N	1172
Ford 2.1, 2.3 & 2.5 litre Diesel Engine (77 - 90) up to H	1606
FREIGHT ROVER Sherpa Petrol (74 - 87) up to E	0463
HILLMAN Avenger (70 - 82) up to Y	0037
Hillman Imp (63 - 76) up to R *	0022
HONDA Civic (Feb 84 - Oct 87) A to E	1226
Honda Civic (Nov 91 - 96) J to N	3199
Honda Civic Petrol (Mar 95 - 00) M to X	4050
Honda Civic Petrol & Diesel (01 - 05) X to 55	4611
Honda CR-V Petrol & Diesel (01-06)	4747
Honda Jazz (01 - Feb 08) 51 - 57	4735
HYUNDAI Pony (85 - 94) C to M	3398
JAGUAR E Type (61 - 72) up to L *	0140
Jaguar MkI & II, 240 & 340 (55 - 69) up to H *	0098
Jaguar XJ6, XJ & Sovereign; Daimler Sovereign (68 - Oct 86) up to D	0242
Jaguar XJ6 & Sovereign (Oct 86 - Sept 94) D to M	3261
Jaguar XJ12, XJS & Sovereign; Daimler Double Six (72 - 88) up to F	0478
JEEP Cherokee Petrol (93 - 96) K to N	1943
LADA 1200, 1300, 1500 & 1600 (74 - 91) up to J	0413
Lada Samara (87 - 91) D to J	1610
LAND ROVER 90, 110 & Defender Diesel (83 - 07) up to 56	3017
Land Rover Discovery Petrol & Diesel (89 - 98) G to S	3016
Land Rover Discovery Diesel (Nov 98 - Jul 04) S to 04	4606
Land Rover Freelander Petrol & Diesel (97 - Sept 03) R to 53	3929
Land Rover Freelander Petrol & Diesel (Oct 03 - Oct 06) 53 to 56	4623

Title	Book No.
Land Rover Series IIA & III Diesel (58 - 85) up to C	0529
Land Rover Series II, IIA & III 4-cyl Petrol (58 - 85) up to C	0314
MAZDA 323 (Mar 81 - Oct 89) up to G	1608
Mazda 323 (Oct 89 - 98) G to R	3455
Mazda 626 (May 83 - Sept 87) up to E	0929
Mazda B1600, B1800 & B2000 Pick-up Petrol (72 - 88) up to F	0267
Mazda RX-7 (79 - 85) up to C *	0460
MERCEDES-BENZ 190, 190E & 190D Petrol & Diesel (83 - 93) A to L	3450
Mercedes-Benz 200D, 240D, 240TD, 300D & 300TD 123 Series Diesel (Oct 76 - 85)	1114
Mercedes-Benz 250 & 280 (68 - 72) up to L *	0346
Mercedes-Benz 250 & 280 123 Series Petrol (Oct 76 - 84) up to B *	0677
Mercedes-Benz 124 Series Petrol & Diesel (85 - Aug 93) C to K	3253
Mercedes-Benz A-Class Petrol & Diesel (98-04) S to 54	4748
Mercedes-Benz C-Class Petrol & Diesel (93 - Aug 00) L to W	3511
Mercedes-Benz C-Class (00-06)	4780
MGA (55 - 62) *	0475
MGB (62 - 80) up to W	0111
MG Midget & Austin-Healey Sprite (58 - 80) up to W *	0265
MINI Petrol (July 01 - 05) Y to 05	4273
MITSUBISHI Shogun & L200 Pick-Ups Petrol (83 - 94) up to M	1944
MORRIS Ital 1.3 (80 - 84) up to B	0705
Morris Minor 1000 (56 - 71) up to K	0024
NISSAN Almera Petrol (95 - Feb 00) N to V	4053
Nissan Almera & Tino Petrol (Feb 00 - 07) V to 56	4612
Nissan Bluebird (May 84 - Mar 86) A to C	1223
Nissan Bluebird Petrol (Mar 86 - 90) C to H	1473
Nissan Cherry (Sept 82 - 86) up to D	1031
Nissan Micra (83 - Jan 93) up to K	0931
Nissan Micra (93 - 02) K to 52	3254
Nissan Micra Petrol (03-07) 52 to 57	4734
Nissan Primera Petrol (90 - Aug 99) H to T	1851
Nissan Stanza (82 - 86) up to D	0824
Nissan Sunny Petrol (May 82 - Oct 86) up to D	0895
Nissan Sunny Petrol (Oct 86 - Mar 91) D to H	1378
Nissan Sunny Petrol (Apr 91 - 95) H to N	3219
OPEL Ascona & Manta (B Series) (Sept 75 - 88) up to F *	0316
Opel Ascona Petrol (81 - 88)	3215
Opel Astra Petrol (Oct 91 - Feb 98)	3156
Opel Corsa Petrol (83 - Mar 93)	3160
Opel Corsa Petrol (Mar 93 - 97)	3159
Opel Kadett Petrol (Nov 79 - Oct 84) up to B	0634
Opel Kadett Petrol (Oct 84 - Oct 91)	3196
Opel Omega & Senator Petrol (Nov 86 - 94)	3157
Opel Rekord Petrol (Feb 78 - Oct 86) up to D	0543
Opel Vectra Petrol (Oct 88 - Oct 95)	3158
PEUGEOT 106 Petrol & Diesel (91 - 04) J to 53	1882
Peugeot 205 Petrol (83 - 97) A to P	0932
Peugeot 206 Petrol & Diesel (98 - 01) S to X	3757
Peugeot 206 Petrol & Diesel (02 - 06) 51 to 06	4613
Peugeot 306 Petrol & Diesel (93 - 02) K to 02	3073
Peugeot 307 Petrol & Diesel (01 - 04) Y to 54	4147
Peugeot 309 Petrol (86 - 93) C to K	1266
Peugeot 405 Petrol (88 - 97) E to P	1559
Peugeot 405 Diesel (88 - 97) E to P	3198
Peugeot 406 Petrol & Diesel (96 - Mar 99) N to T	3394
Peugeot 406 Petrol & Diesel (Mar 99 - 02) T to 52	3982

* Classic reprint

Title	Book No.
Peugeot 505 Petrol (79 - 89) up to G	0762
Peugeot 1.7/1.8 & 1.9 litre Diesel Engine (82 - 96) up to N	0950
Peugeot 2.0, 2.1, 2.3 & 2.5 litre Diesel Engines (74 - 90) up to H	1607
PORSCHE 911 (65 - 85) up to C	0264
Porsche 924 & 924 Turbo (76 - 85) up to C	0397
PROTON (89 - 97) F to P	3255
RANGE ROVER V8 Petrol (70 - Oct 92) up to K	0606
RELIANT Robin & Kitten (73 - 83) up to A *	0436
RENAULT 4 (61 - 86) up to D *	0072
Renault 5 Petrol (Feb 85 - 96) B to N	1219
Renault 9 & 11 Petrol (82 - 89) up to F	0822
Renault 18 Petrol (79 - 86) up to D	0598
Renault 19 Petrol (89 - 96) F to N	1646
Renault 19 Diesel (89 - 96) F to N	1946
Renault 21 Petrol (86 - 94) C to M	1397
Renault 25 Petrol & Diesel (84 - 92) B to K	1228
Renault Clio Petrol (91 - May 98) H to R	1853
Renault Clio Diesel (91 - June 96) H to N	3031
Renault Clio Petrol & Diesel (May 98 - May 01) R to Y	3906
Renault Clio Petrol & Diesel (June '01 - '05) Y to 55	4168
Renault Espace Petrol & Diesel (85 - 96) C to N	3197
Renault Laguna Petrol & Diesel (94 - 00) L to W	3252
Renault Laguna Petrol & Diesel (Feb 01 - Feb 05) X to 54	4283
Renault Mégane & Scénic Petrol & Diesel (96 - 99) N to T	3395
Renault Mégane & Scénic Petrol & Diesel (Apr 99 - 02) T to 52	3916
Renault Megane Petrol & Diesel (Oct 02 - 05) 52 to 55	4284
Renault Scenic Petrol & Diesel (Sept 03 - 06) 53 to 06	4297
ROVER 213 & 216 (84 - 89) A to G	1116
Rover 214 & 414 Petrol (89 - 96) G to N	1689
Rover 216 & 416 Petrol (89 - 96) G to N	1830
Rover 211, 214, 216, 218 & 220 Petrol & Diesel (Dec 95 - 99) N to V	3399
Rover 25 & MG ZR Petrol & Diesel (Oct 99 - 04) V to 54	4145
Rover 414, 416 & 420 Petrol & Diesel (May 95 - 98) M to R	3453
Rover 45 / MG ZS Petrol & Diesel (99 - 05) V to 55	4384
Rover 618, 620 & 623 Petrol (93 - 97) K to P	3257
Rover 75, MG ZT Petrol & Diesel (99 - 06) S to 06	4292
Rover 820, 825 & 827 Petrol (86 - 95) D to N	1380
Rover 3500 (76 - 87) up to E *	0365
Rover Metro, 111 & 114 Petrol (May 90 - 98) G to S	1711
SAAB 95 & 96 (66 - 76) up to R *	0198
Saab 90, 99 & 900 (79 - Oct 93) up to L	0765
Saab 900 (Oct 93 - 98) L to R	3512
Saab 9000 (4-cyl) (85 - 98) C to S	1686
Saab 9-3 Petrol & Diesel (98 - Aug 02) R to 02	4614
Saab 9-3 Petrol & Diesel (02-07) 52 to 57	4749
Saab 9-5 4-cyl Petrol (97 - 04) R to 54	4156
SEAT Ibiza & Cordoba Petrol & Diesel (Oct 93 - Oct 99) L to V	3571
Seat Ibiza & Malaga Petrol (85 - 92) B to K	1609
SKODA Estelle (77 - 89) up to G	0604
Skoda Fabia Petrol & Diesel (00 - 06) W to 06	4376
Skoda Favorit (89 - 96) F to N	1801
Skoda Felicia Petrol & Diesel (95 - 01) M to X	3505
Skoda Octavia Petrol & Diesel (98 - Apr 04) R to 04	4285
SUBARU 1600 & 1800 (Nov 79 - 90) up to H *	0995

Title	Book No.
SUNBEAM Alpine, Rapier & H120 (67 - 74) up to N *	0051
SUZUKI SJ Series, Samurai & Vitara (4-cyl) Petrol (82 - 97) up to P	1942
Suzuki Supercarry & Bedford/Vauxhall Rascal (86 - Oct 94) C to M	3015
TALBOT Alpine, Solara, Minx & Rapier (75 - 86) up to D	0337
Talbot Horizon Petrol (78 - 86) up to D	0473
Talbot Samba (82 - 86) up to D	0823
TOYOTA Avensis Petrol (98 - Jan 03) R to 52	4264
Toyota Carina E Petrol (May 92 - 97) J to P	3256
Toyota Corolla (80 - 85) up to C	0683
Toyota Corolla (Sept 83 - Sept 87) A to E	1024
Toyota Corolla (Sept 87 - Aug 92) E to K	1683
Toyota Corolla Petrol (Aug 92 - 97) K to P	3259
Toyota Corolla Petrol (July 97 - Feb 02) P to 51	4286
Toyota Hi-Ace & Hi-Lux Petrol (69 - Oct 83) up to A	0304
Toyota RAV4 Petrol & Diesel (94-06) L to 55	4750
Toyota Yaris Petrol (99 - 05) T to 05	4265
TRIUMPH GT6 & Vitesse (62 - 74) up to N *	0112
Triumph Herald (59 - 71) up to K *	0010
Triumph Spitfire (62 - 81) up to X	0113
Triumph Stag (70 - 78) up to T *	0441
Triumph TR2, TR3, TR3A, TR4 & TR4A (52 - 67) up to F *	0028
Triumph TR5 & 6 (67 - 75) up to P *	0031
Triumph TR7 (75 - 82) up to Y *	0322
VAUXHALL Astra Petrol (80 - Oct 84) up to B	0635
Vauxhall Astra & Belmont Petrol (Oct 84 - Oct 91) B to J	1136
Vauxhall Astra Petrol (Oct 91 - Feb 98) J to R	1832
Vauxhall/Opel Astra & Zafira Petrol (Feb 98 - Apr 04) R to 04	3758
Vauxhall/Opel Astra & Zafira Diesel (Feb 98 - Apr 04) R to 04	3797
Vauxhall/Opel Astra Petrol (04 - 08)	4732
Vauxhall/Opel Astra Diesel (04 - 08)	4733
Vauxhall/Opel Calibra (90 - 98) G to S	3502
Vauxhall Carlton Petrol (Oct 78 - Oct 86) up to D	0480
Vauxhall Carlton & Senator Petrol (Nov 86 - 94) D to L	1469
Vauxhall Cavalier Petrol (81 - Oct 88) up to F	0812
Vauxhall Cavalier Petrol (Oct 88 - 95) F to N	1570
Vauxhall Chevette (75 - 84) up to B	0285
Vauxhall/Opel Corsa Diesel (Mar 93 - Oct 00) K to X	4087
Vauxhall Corsa Petrol (Mar 93 - 97) K to R	1985
Vauxhall/Opel Corsa Petrol (Apr 97 - Oct 00) P to X	3921
Vauxhall/Opel Corsa Petrol & Diesel (Oct 00 - Sept 03) X to 53	4079
Vauxhall/Opel Corsa Petrol & Diesel (Oct 03 - Aug 06) 53 to 06	4617
Vauxhall/Opel Frontera Petrol & Diesel (91 - Sept 98) J to S	3454
Vauxhall Nova Petrol (83 - 93) up to K	0909
Vauxhall/Opel Omega Petrol (94 - 99) L to T	3510
Vauxhall/Opel Vectra Petrol & Diesel (95 - Feb 99) N to S	3396
Vauxhall/Opel Vectra Petrol & Diesel (Mar 99 - May 02) T to 02	3930
Vauxhall/Opel Vectra Petrol & Diesel (June 02 - Sept 05) 02 to 55	4618
Vauxhall/Opel 1.5, 1.6 & 1.7 litre Diesel Engine (82 - 96) up to N	1222
VW 411 & 412 (68 - 75) up to P *	0091
VW Beetle 1200 (54 - 77) up to S	0036
VW Beetle 1300 & 1500 (65 - 75) up to P	0039

Title	Book No.
VW 1302 & 1302S (70 - 72) up to L *	0110
VW Beetle 1303, 1303S & GT (72 - 75) up to P	0159
VW Beetle Petrol & Diesel (Apr 99 - 07) T to 57	3798
VW Golf & Jetta Mk 1 Petrol 1.1 & 1.3 (74 - 84) up to A	0716
VW Golf, Jetta & Scirocco Mk 1 Petrol 1.5, 1.6 & 1.8 (74 - 84) up to A	0726
VW Golf & Jetta Mk 1 Diesel (78 - 84) up to A	0451
VW Golf & Jetta Mk 2 Petrol (Mar 84 - Feb 92) A to J	1081
VW Golf & Vento Petrol & Diesel (Feb 92 - Mar 98) J to R	3097
VW Golf & Bora Petrol & Diesel (April 98 - 00) R to X	3727
VW Golf & Bora 4-cyl Petrol & Diesel (01 - 03) X to 53	4169
VW Golf & Jetta Petrol & Diesel (04 - 07) 53 to 07	4610
VW LT Petrol Vans & Light Trucks (76 - 87) up to E	0637
VW Passat & Santana Petrol (Sept 81 - May 88) up to E	0814
VW Passat 4-cyl Petrol & Diesel (May 88 - 96) E to P	3498
VW Passat 4-cyl Petrol & Diesel (Dec 96 - Nov 00) P to X	3917
VW Passat Petrol & Diesel (Dec 00 - May 05) X to 05	4279
VW Polo & Derby (76 - Jan 82) up to X	0335
VW Polo (82 - Oct 90) up to H	0813
VW Polo Petrol (Nov 90 - Aug 94) H to L	3245
VW Polo Hatchback Petrol & Diesel (94 - 99) M to S	3500
VW Polo Hatchback Petrol (00 - Jan 02) V to 51	4150
VW Polo Petrol & Diesel (02 - May 05) 51 to 05	4608
VW Scirocco (82 - 90) up to H *	1224
VW Transporter 1600 (68 - 79) up to V	0082
VW Transporter 1700, 1800 & 2000 (72 - 79) up to V *	0226
VW Transporter (air-cooled) Petrol (79 - 82) up to Y *	0638
VW Transporter (water-cooled) Petrol (82 - 90) up to H	3452
VW Type 3 (63 - 73) up to M *	0084
VOLVO 120 & 130 Series (& P1800) (61 - 73) up to M *	0203
Volvo 142, 144 & 145 (66 - 74) up to N *	0129
Volvo 240 Series Petrol (74 - 93) up to K	0270
Volvo 262, 264 & 260/265 (75 - 85) up to C *	0400
Volvo 340, 343, 345 & 360 (76 - 91) up to J	0715
Volvo 440, 460 & 480 Petrol (87 - 97) D to P	1691
Volvo 740 & 760 Petrol (82 - 91) up to J	1258
Volvo 850 Petrol (92 - 96) J to P	3260
Volvo 940 petrol (90 - 98) H to R	3249
Volvo S40 & V40 Petrol (96 - Mar 04) N to 04	3569
Volvo S40 & V50 Petrol & Diesel (Mar 04 - Jun 07) 04 to 07	4731
Volvo S60 Petrol & Diesel (01-08)	4793
Volvo S70, V70 & C70 Petrol (96 - 99) P to V	3573
Volvo V70 / S80 Petrol & Diesel (98 - 05) S to 55	4263

DIY MANUAL SERIES

Title	Book No.
The Haynes Air Conditioning Manual	4192
The Haynes Car Electrical Systems Manual	4251
The Haynes Manual on Bodywork	4198
The Haynes Manual on Brakes	4178
The Haynes Manual on Carburettors	4177
The Haynes Manual on Diesel Engines	4174
The Haynes Manual on Engine Management	4199
The Haynes Manual on Fault Codes	4175
The Haynes Manual on Practical Electrical Systems	4267
The Haynes Manual on Small Engines	4250
The Haynes Manual on Welding	4176

* Classic reprint

CL24.08/09

Preserving Our Motoring Heritage

< *The Model J Duesenberg Derham Tourster. Only eight of these magnificent cars were ever built – this is the only example to be found outside the United States of America*

Almost every car you've ever loved, loathed or desired is gathered under one roof at the Haynes Motor Museum. Over 300 immaculately presented cars and motorbikes represent every aspect of our motoring heritage, from elegant reminders of bygone days, such as the superb Model J Duesenberg to curiosities like the bug-eyed BMW Isetta. There are also many old friends and flames. Perhaps you remember the 1959 Ford Popular that you did your courting in? The magnificent 'Red Collection' is a spectacle of classic sports cars including AC, Alfa Romeo, Austin Healey, Ferrari, Lamborghini, Maserati, MG, Riley, Porsche and Triumph.

A Perfect Day Out

Each and every vehicle at the Haynes Motor Museum has played its part in the history and culture of Motoring. Today, they make a wonderful spectacle and a great day out for all the family. Bring the kids, bring Mum and Dad, but above all bring your camera to capture those golden memories for ever. You will also find an impressive array of motoring memorabilia, a comfortable 70 seat video cinema and one of the most extensive transport book shops in Britain. The Pit Stop Cafe serves everything from a cup of tea to wholesome, home-made meals or, if you prefer, you can enjoy the large picnic area nestled in the beautiful rural surroundings of Somerset.

> *John Haynes O.B.E., Founder and Chairman of the museum at the wheel of a Haynes Light 12.*

< *Graham Hill's Lola Cosworth Formula 1 car next to a 1934 Riley Sports.*

The Museum is situated on the A359 Yeovil to Frome road at Sparkford, just off the A303 in Somerset. It is about 40 miles south of Bristol, and 25 minutes drive from the M5 intersection at Taunton.
Open 9.30am - 5.30pm (10.00am - 4.00pm Winter) 7 days a week, *except Christmas Day, Boxing Day and New Years Day*
Special rates available for schools, coach parties and outings Charitable Trust No. 292048